THE LAW OF SEX
DISCRIMINATION

THE LAW OF SEX DISCRIMINATION

FOURTH EDITION

J. RALPH LINDGREN
Lehigh University, Clara H. Stewardson Professor Emeritus of Philosophy

NADINE TAUB
Rutgers University, S.I. Newhouse Professor of Law Emerita

BETH ANNE WOLFSON
Law, Taxation and Financial Planning Department, Bentley University

CARLA M. PALUMBO
Legal Aid Society of Rochester, New York

WADSWORTH
CENGAGE Learning

Australia • Brazil • Japan • Korea • Mexico • Singapore • Spain • United Kingdom • United States

WADSWORTH
CENGAGE Learning™

**The Law of Sex Discrimination,
Fourth Edition**

J. Ralph Lindgren, Nadine Taub, Beth Anne
Wolfson, Carla M. Palumbo

Senior Publisher: Suzanne Jeans

Executive Editor: Carolyn Merrill

Assistant Editor: Katherine Hayes

Editorial Assistant: Angela Hodge

Senior Marketing Manager: Amy Whitaker

Marketing Coordinator: Josh Hendrick

Marketing Communications Manager:
Heather Baxley

Art Director: Linda Helcher

Front list Manufacturing Buyer: Linda Hsu

Senior Rights Acquisition Account Manager:
Katie Huha

Content Project Management: Pre-PressPMG

Production Service: Pre-PressPMG

Cover Designer: Grannan Graphic
Design, Ltd.

Compositor: Pre-PressPMG

For product information and technology assistance, contact us at
Cengage Learning Customer & Sales Support, 1-800-354-9706

For permission to use material from this text or product,
submit all requests online at **www.cengage.com/permissions**
Further permissions questions can be emailed to
permissionrequest@cengage.com

Library of Congress Control Number: 2009936594

ISBN-13: 978-0-495-79322-9

ISBN-10: 0-495-79322-1

Wadsworth
20 Channel Center Street
Boston, MA 02210
USA

Cengage Learning is a leading provider of customized learning solutions
with office locations around the globe, including Singapore, the United
Kingdom, Australia, Mexico, Brazil, and Japan. Locate your local office at
international.cengage.com/region

Cengage Learning products are represented in Canada by
Nelson Education, Ltd.

For your course and learning solutions, visit **www.cengage.com**

Purchase any of our products at your local college store or at our
preferred online store **www.ichapters.com**

Printed in Canada
1 2 3 4 5 6 7 13 12 11 10 09

Brief Contents

CONTENTS

CASES

PREFACE

THIS BOOK is designed for use as an undergraduate textbook for courses on women and the law, gender and the law, and sex discrimination law in the United States. When we published the third edition, it was in response to both our and others' concerns that a college course concerning such contemporary issues had to keep current with events in society as well as developments in the law. The fourth edition reflects our continuing goal to provide students and professors with a textbook that presents the historical background for understanding the development of sex discrimination law and discusses changes in the law that mirror the ever-changing mores of our society and the manner in which it treats women and gender issues.

The study of women, sex discrimination, and gender issues fosters debate and discussion on contemporary policy and the future direction of society, as well as the historical development of the feminist movement. This book looks at how the law has responded to women's status, to gender issues, and to discrimination on the basis of sex. It also considers how the feminist movement has been used as a means of raising feminist consciousness.

Since the publication of the third edition there has been major social movement in the area of gender, gender equality, and discrimination. This new edition addresses the legal issues and discussions that flow from some of our most cutting-edge societal events involving gender and sex discrimination. As you will see from the chapter outline, the fourth edition focuses not only on the historical perspective but also on the debates emanating from today's current events. Modern legal issues involving abortion and reproduction, rights of same-sex couples, domestic violence, single-sex education, and issues of workplace discrimination, which are the focus of current societal debate, are featured prominently in this book.

The legal materials are presented in formats that are accessible and understandable for college students who have had no formal legal training or who have little experience in working with court opinions. Cases are abridged to retain the human drama, focus attention on key rulings, and emphasize crucial factors motivating the decisions. Law review articles, essays, and topical book chapters have been excerpted to provide background information, as well as insight into key points of view and the larger significance of legal events. The narrative highlights the relationships between cases and identifies central themes. Each article or case is followed by study questions to help students better understand the material and to foster discussion. Each chapter contains suggested on-line resources. Other study aids found at the end of the book include a review of the court system, selected amendments to the U.S. Constitution, directions on how to outline cases, a glossary of legal and technical terms, a table of abbreviations, and an index.

CHANGES TO THE FOURTH EDITION

This edition expands on the work of the original authors, Nadine Taub and Ralph Lindgren, as well as on newer material introduced in the third edition by authors Beth Anne Wolfson and Carla M. Palumbo. In the fourth edition, chapters are updated, infused with new material, and revised based on comments from instructors and students, as well as developments in the field.

Principal changes include the following:

- Cases and other excerpted materials are updated to reflect the current state of the law and of legal issues.
- The connective narrative has been expanded in most chapters to help students better understand the issues addressed in these cases and materials, as well as appreciate their relationship to the legal developments being discussed.
- Chapter 2 updates the discussion of statutory rapes laws by examining recent state case law concerning the application and enforcement of gender-neutral rape laws. This chapter also includes a discussion of recent Federal ERA activity.
- Chapter 3 considers recent developments vis-a-vis Title VII, including the impact of the Lilly Ledbetter Act, the Supreme Court's pronouncement on the standard applicable to causes of action for retaliation, and gender discrimination class actions. It also updates the discussion of federal court cases considering the meaning of "because of sex" in discrimination cases.
- Chapter 4 includes new material on, and expands discussion of, how the public assesses conduct of purported male harassers and female victims in sexual harassment cases. It also discusses the Supreme Court's pronouncement on employer liability for a supervisor's harassment in constructive discharge cases, as well as recent federal court consideration of the issue of sexual orientation as motivation for discrimination based on sex under Title VII. The Pay Equity section has been revised to include material on and discussion of the "Mommy Track." A new "Benefits" section has been added that includes the FMLA (moved from Chapter 6 and expanded), the PDA, and benefits for same-sex partners.
- Chapter 5 addresses such recent developments as retaliation claims under Title IX and the Department of Education's Additional Clarification of Intercollegiate Athletics Policy. It also expands discussion of current perspectives on single-sex education.
- Chapter 6 has been updated to include the latest cases and articles on the law as it relates to the family. In particular, the section previously entitled "Beyond the Nuclear Family" has been expanded and revised to include the latest cases regarding the "New Definition of Family." This section looks beyond the traditional family and considers issues germane to same-sex marriage, same-sex adoption, same-sex divorce, and the break-up of same-sex partnerships.
- Chapter 7 includes a discussion of the status of abortion since *Roe v. Wade*, with a particular focus on case law surrounding "partial birth abortion". The chapter looks at some current issues including "the pregnant man," increased violence at abortion clinics and insurance coverage for contraception by religious employers. In addition, this chapter analyzes the most recent state court decisions addressing the issues of parental and property rights in donor and in vitro insemination and expands on the subject of contract parenthood with a discussion of international surrogacy issues.
- Chapter 9 has been revised and expanded as it addresses issues relevant to twenty-first century feminism. The section entitled "Feminization of Poverty" from Chapter 6 has been moved to this chapter and expanded to address the issue of women and poverty in a more global way. The chapter continues its focus on international women's issues and the relation between second wave and third wave feminists. It includes a new discussion of the issue of intersectionality, the discussion of the intersection between race and gender issues.

ACKNOWLEDGMENTS

This fourth edition marks the continued collaboration of authors, Professor Beth Anne Wolfson and Attorney Carla M. Palumbo. Both would like to thank the original authors, Nadine Taub and Ralph Lindgren, for their solid development of the materials on which subsequent editions have been built. Both deeply appreciate the support and assistance of their colleagues at Bentley University and the Legal Aid Society of Rochester. They particularly wish to thank Joseph Levens and Patty Harris, who provided invaluable technical assistance; and the following reviewers for their comments and suggestions: Susan Patnode, Esq., Director, Rural Law Center of New York, Inc. and Adjunct Faculty, SUNY Plattsburgh; Ann Lucas, San Jose State University, Justice Studies Department; and Patricia Boling, Purdue University, Political Science Department and Women's Studies Program.

THE LAW OF SEX DISCRIMINATION

CHAPTER 1

THE HISTORICAL CONTEXT

THE CHOICE OF a characteristic such as gender, race, or age as the basis of laws and doctrines has long been the determining factor of rights afforded to segments of our society. The use of gender as the basis for determining policy, law, and custom, as well as its application to women, is the focus of this book. This book will help sort out the evolution of laws affecting women—what the laws were and how they have changed. In so doing we also examine where women are today and where issues of women's rights are going or should go. Are we on the right track? Is society best served by a legal system that attempts to treat women and men as individuals, or by one that acknowledges differences while seeking to eliminate hierarchical distinctions based upon them? Is it possible to construct a system whereby the needs of both sexes are met equally?

From the first women's movement in the United States, led by several notable women of colonial times, to the women's movement of the 1960s, and to what is being called the "third wave of feminism" of the twenty-first century, women have struggled for equality in all aspects of their lives. This book will look at the changing laws that affect women—the changing perception of gender as a basis for including or excluding a person from a right or obligation.

This first chapter provides the backdrop for the legal changes that occur as we journey through 200 years of legal decisions from the 1800s to the 2000s. The selected court decisions reflect the relevant moments that bring to light the thinking and analysis used in early colonial times and provide an historical context for more recent legal developments. The decisions highlighted in this chapter show how societal norms and the legal status of women have changed through history, and also set the stage for the legal challenges to come.

I. THE PATRIARCHAL TRADITION

Social systems that treat people differently because of their sex are of ancient origin. Although evidence exists of even earlier matriarchal practices, patriarchal patterns have dominated Western cultures for several millennia. Historian Gerda Lerner dates the rise of patriarchy as the period between 3100 and 600 b.c.e. She identifies the central features of this tradition as follows:

> Patriarchy . . . means the manifestation and institutionalization of male dominance over women and children in the family and the extension of male dominance over women in

1

society in general. It implies that men hold power in all the important institutions of society and that women are deprived of access to such power. It does *not* imply that women are either totally powerless or totally deprived of rights, influence, and resources.

Gerda Lerner, The Creation of Patriarchy. New York: Oxford University Press, 1986, p. 239.

Patriarchal patterns have been expressed, enforced, legitimated, and perpetuated in a variety of ways over the ages. One of the ways has been through religion; another way has been through the law.

The law is an important cultural vehicle for sex-based customs. Just before the American Revolution, William Blackstone produced a recapitulation of the common law of England. This proved to be an especially influential treatise among American jurists of the day because of its portability. Because it could be transported easily, Blackstone's *Commentaries* was relied upon even longer in America than in Blackstone's native England.

The legal arrangements that the colonists brought to the New World both reflected and reinforced the division of labor in society along gender lines and the subordination of women found in Europe. Life in colonial America was organized around a preindustrial, agricultural, and family-based economy. Women made crucial economic contributions, usually through the household production necessary to meet their family needs. Yet these contributions rarely allowed women to participate significantly in economic decision making, religious matters, or community affairs.

Although legal practices varied somewhat from colony to colony and were probably less rigid than their British counterparts, the principles and doctrines followed by the English courts of the day constituted the common point of departure. To the extent that the colonists followed the English law, they greatly restricted opportunities open to married women. Under the doctrine of coverture, developed in the English common law during the late Middle Ages, the husband was considered the lord of the manor. The husband and the wife were viewed legally as one person, and that "one person," as Justice Black pointed out in the 1960s, was the husband. William Blackstone summarized the principal features of the doctrine of coverture as it survived into the mid-eighteenth century.

BLACKSTONE ON COVERTURE
William Blackstone
1765–69. Commentaries on the Laws of England.
4 vols. Book I, Chapter 15.

By marriage, the husband and wife are one person in law: that is, the very being or legal existence of the woman is suspended during the marriage, or at least is incorporated and consolidated into that of the husband: under whose wing, protection, and *cover,* she performs every thing; and is therefore called in our law-french a *feme-covert;* is said to be *covert-baron,* or under the protection and influence of her husband, her *baron,* or lord; and her condition during her marriage is called her *coverture.* Upon this principle, of an union of person in husband and wife, depend almost all the legal rights, duties, and disabilities, that either of them acquire by the marriage. I speak not at present of the rights of property, but of such as are merely *personal.* For this reason, a man cannot grant any thing to his wife, or enter into covenant with her: for the grant would be to suppose her separate existence; and to covenant with her, would be only to covenant with himself: and therefore it is also generally true, that all compacts made between husband and wife, when single, are voided by the intermarriage. A woman indeed may be attorney for her husband; for that implies no separation from, but is rather a representation of, her lord. And a husband may also bequeath any thing to his wife by will; for that cannot take effect till the coverture is determined by his death. The husband is bound to provide his wife with necessaries by law, as much as himself; and if she contracts debts for them, he is obliged to pay them: but for any thing besides necessaries, he is not chargeable. Also if a wife elopes, and lives with another man, the husband is not chargeable even for necessaries; at least if the person, who furnishes them, is sufficiently apprized of her elopement. If the wife be indebted before marriage, the husband is bound afterwards to pay the debt; for he has adopted her and her circumstances together. If the wife be injured in her person or her property, she can bring no action for redress without her husband's concurrence, and in his name, as well as her own: neither can she be sued, without making the husband a defendant. There is indeed one case where the wife shall sue and be sued as a feme sole, viz. where the husband has abjured the realm, or is banished: for then he is dead in law; and, the husband being thus disabled to sue for or defend the wife, it would be most unreasonable if she had no remedy, or could make no defence at all. In criminal prosecutions, it is true, the wife may be indicted and punished separately; for the union is only a civil union. But, in trials of any sort, they are not allowed to be evidence for, or against, each other: partly because it is impossible their testimony should be indifferent; but principally because of the union of person: and therefore, if they were admitted to be witnesses *for* each other, they would contradict one maxim of law, "*nemo in propria causa testis esse debet*" [one ought not be a witness in his own cause]; and if *against* each other, they would contradict another maxim, "*nemo tenetur seipsum accusare*" [no one is bound to accuse himself]. But where the offence is directly against the person of the wife, this rule has been usually dispensed with: and therefore, by statute 3 Hen. VII. c. 2.

in case a woman be forcibly taken away, and married, she may be a witness against such her husband, in order to convict him of felony. For in this case she can with no propriety be reckoned his wife; because a main ingredient, her consent, was wanting to the contract: and also there is another maxim of law, that no man shall take advantage of his own wrong; which the ravisher here would do, if by forcibly marrying a woman, he could prevent her from being a witness, who is perhaps the only witness, to that very fact. . . .

But, though our law in general considers man and wife as one person, yet there are some instances in which she is separately considered; as inferior to him, and acting by his compulsion. And therefore all deeds executed, and acts done, by her, during her coverture, are void, or at least voidable; except it be a fine, or the like matter of record, in which case she must be solely and secretly examined, to learn if her act be voluntary. She cannot by will devise lands to her husband, unless under special circumstances; for at the time of making it she is supposed to be under his coercion. And in some felonies, and other inferior crimes, committed by her, through constraint of her husband, the law excuses her: but this extends not to treason or murder.

The husband also (by the old law) might give his wife moderate correction. For, as he is to answer for her misbehaviour, the law thought it reasonable to intrust him with this power of restraining her, by domestic chastisement, in the same moderation that a man is allowed to correct his servants or children; for whom the master or parent is also liable in some cases to answer. But this power of correction was confined within reasonable bounds; and the husband was prohibited to use any violence to his wife, *aliter quam ad virum, excausa regiminis et castigationis uxoris suae, licite et rationabiliter pertinet* [other than what is reasonably necessary to the discipline and correction of the wife]. The civil law gave the husband the same, or a larger, authority over his wife; allowing him, for some misdemesnors, *flagellis et fustibus acriter verberare uxorem* [to wound his wife severely with whips and fists]; for others, only *modicam castigationem adhibere* [to apply modest corrective punishment]. But, with us, in the politer reign of Charles the second; this power of correction began to be doubted: and a wife may now have security of the peace against her husband; or, in return, a husband against his wife. Yet the lower rank of people, who were always fond of the old common law, still claim and exert their antient privilege and the courts of law will still permit a husband to restrain a wife of her liberty, in case of any gross misbehaviour.

These are the chief legal effects of marriage during the coverture; upon which we may observe, that even the disabilities, which the wife lies under, are for the most part intended for her protection and benefit. So great a favourite is the female sex of the laws of England.

STUDY QUESTIONS

1. What were the legal consequences of marriage for the woman? For the man? Does that arrangement seem fair to the woman? To the man?
2. What are your reactions to Blackstone's discussion of "domestic chastisement"?
3. Were women legally better off if they did not marry? Why do you suppose they continued to marry?
4. Do any of these maxims hold true today?

The legal and cultural norms brought by the settlers, including the gender-based division of labor and the subordinate position of women, formed the dominant tradition shaping this country's legal, political, economic, and social institutions. This tradition, however, reflects only part of this country's cultural heritage. Compare the traditions of the early settlers to the traditions of Native American peoples. The Navajo legend of creation puts women and men at a much more equal footing as ". . . a solid harmony of kinship."

The Iroquois people afforded women much more influence in the affairs of their community:

> . . . [T]he gender system of the Iroquois, as described by French missionaries in the eighteenth century, seemed to have been remarkably generous to women. Although by no means a matriarchy, the Iroquois social system came perhaps as close as any known civilization to the standard of sexual equality. Iroquois matrons chose the chieftains and delegates to tribal councils, where they also had a vote on issues of war and peace.
>
> *Mary Ryan.* Womenhood in America. *2d ed. New York: New Viewpoints, 1979, pp. xii–xiii.*

Yet within the culture and customs of the early settlers, the inequality of women was pervasive. The legal status of married women continued to be governed by the law of coverture following the Revolutionary War. One direct result of strict adherence to the principles of coverture was that when women married, control of their property and their earnings passed to their husbands. A secondary consequence of this restriction was to reinforce the restriction on women's participation in political affairs. During the Revolutionary period, fundamental questions were being asked about citizens' right to participate in their own governance. Yet these rights pertained only to men. Abigail Adams asked that the interests of women be considered in these deliberations, but her husband, who was busy with the Second Continental Congress charting the course of the colonies after the British occupation of Boston, found that proposal amusing.

REMEMBER THE LADIES

Letters between Abigail and John Adams. Charles Francis Adams
Familiar Letters of John Adams and His Wife Abigail Adams,
During the Revolution.
New York: Hurd and Houghton, 1876, pp. 149–150, 155, 169.

Abigail Adams to John Adams

Braintree, 31 March, 1776.

. . . I long to hear that you have declared an independency. And, by the way, in the new code of laws which I suppose it will be necessary for you to make, I desire you would remember the ladies and be more generous and favorable to them than your ancestors. Do not put such unlimited power into the hands of the husbands. Remember, all men would be tyrants if they could. If particular care and attention is not paid to the ladies, we are determined to foment a rebellion, and will not hold ourselves bound by any laws in which we have no voice or representation.

That your sex are naturally tyrannical is a truth so thoroughly established as to admit of no dispute; but such of you as wish to be happy willingly give up the harsh title of master for the more tender and endearing one of friend. Why, then, not put it out of the power of the vicious and the lawless to use us with cruelty and indignity with impunity? Men of sense in all ages abhor those customs which treat us only as the vassals of your sex; regard us then as beings placed by Providence under your protection, and in imitation of the Supreme Being make use of that power only for our happiness.

John Adams to Abigail Adams

14 April (1776)

. . . As to declarations of independency, be patient. Read our privateering laws, and our commercial laws? What signifies a Word?

As to your extraordinary code of laws, I cannot but laugh. We have been told that our struggle has loosened the bonds of government everywhere; that children and apprentices were disobedient; that schools and colleges were grown turbulent; that Indians slighted their guardians, and negroes grew insolent to their masters. But your letter was the first intimation that another tribe, more numerous and powerfull than all the rest, were grown discontented. This is rather too coarse a compliment, but you are so saucy, I won't blot it out. Depend upon it, we know better than to repeal our masculine systems. Although they are in full force, you know they are little more than theory. We dare not exert our power in its full latitude. We are obliged to go fair and softly, and, in practice, you know we are the subjects. We have only the name of masters, and rather than give up this, which would completely subject us to the despotism of the petticoat, I hope General Washington and all our brave heroes would fight; I am sure every good politician would plot, as long as he would against despotism, empire, monarchy, aristocracy, oligarchy, or ochlocracy . . .

Abigail Adams to John Adams

Braintree, 7 May, 1776

. . . I cannot say that I think you are very generous to the ladies; for, whilst you are proclaiming peace and good-will to men, emancipating all nations, you insist upon retaining an absolute power over wives. But you must remember that arbitrary power is like most other things which are very hard, very liable to be broken; and, notwithstanding all your wise laws and maxims, we have it in our power, not only to free ourselves, but to subdue our masters, and, without violence, throw both your natural and legal authority at our feet;—

"Charm by accepting, by submitting sway,
Yet have our humor most when we obey.". . .

STUDY QUESTIONS *Rachel*

1. Abigail argued that legal enforcement of subservience makes women vulnerable to "the power of the vicious and lawless to use us with cruelty and indignity with impunity." To what abuses do you think she was alluding?
2. What seemed laughable about that argument for John? What considerations did he suggest temper the fear of abuse by one's spouse?
3. In her response, Abigail spoke of a power that, even in their subordinate position, women had to free themselves and subdue their masters. What is your interpretation of that passage?

As the Adams' correspondence suggests, the ways that women are treated depend on the way they are perceived. Perceptions of appropriate sex roles, however, change with changing circumstances. During the years that intervened between the Revolutionary and Civil Wars, the sexual division of labor in most American families further intensified. With the advent of industrialization, production increasingly moved out of the home. As Americans adapted to this trend, the population experienced a heightening of sex segregation. Increasingly, men went out of the home to work and women shouldered the responsibilities for managing the household and raising the children. Advice about how women should adjust to these new realities was forthcoming from the media as well as the pulpit: Both endorsed a set of values and relationships that were variously referred to at the time and since as "the cult of domesticity" and "the cult of true womanhood." The attributes of true womanhood, by which a woman judged herself and was judged by her husband, her neighbors and society, could be divided into four cardinal virtues—piety, purity, submissiveness, and domesticity. The "true" woman's place was in her home—as daughter, sister, but most of all as wife and mother.[1]

In the nineteenth century, ideology assumed even greater importance in shaping opportunities for women and men. During that period, the view that women and men had very different natures and occupied entirely different worlds became dominant. The "separate spheres" ideology was used in legal decisions to justify limiting the rights of women. Remnants of this view are with us today.

SEPARATE SPHERES
Nadine Taub and Elizabeth M. Schneider
"Perspectives on Women's Subordination and the Law."
In *The Politics of Law*, edited by D. Kairys.
New York: Basic Books, Inc., 1998, pp. 339–340.

. . . Although women were in no way the equals of men during the colonial and Revolutionary periods, the nature of their subordination, particularly in the middle classes, changed dramatically between the end of the eighteenth century and the middle of the nineteenth century. The early stages of industrial capitalism involved

[1] The Cult of True Womanhood: 1820–1860 Barbara Welter *18 American Quarterly 151–74 (1966)*.

increasing specialization and the movement of production out of the home, which resulted in heightened sex segregation. Men went out of the house to work; and women's work, influence, and consciousness remained focused at home. Although women continued to be dependent on and subservient to men, women were no longer placed at the bottom of a hierarchy dominated by men. Rather, they came to occupy women's "separate sphere," a qualitatively different world centered on home and family. Women's role was by definition incompatible with full participation in society.

"Separate-sphere" ideology clearly delineated the activities open to women. Women's role within the home was glorified, and women's limited participation in paid labor outside the home was most often in work that could be considered an extension of their work within the home. For example, native-born mill girls in the 1820s and 1830s, and immigrant women in the 1840s and 1850s, worked in largely sex-segregated factories manufacturing textiles, clothing, and shoes. Likewise, after a period of time, teaching became a woman's occupation. Unpaid charitable and welfare activities, however, were encouraged as consistent with women's domestic responsibilities.

Although ultimately quite constraining, the development of women's separate sphere had some important benefits. While the emphasis on women's moral purity and the cult of domesticity tended to mask women's inferior position, it also allowed women a certain degree of autonomy. It gave them the opportunity to organize extensively into religious and secular welfare associations, afforded access to education, and provided them with a basis for uniting with other women. Evaluations of the cult of domesticity and women's separate sphere by feminist historians have consequently ranged from the view that women were victims of this ideology to the recognition that women found a source of strength and identity in their separate world.

The development of separate-sphere ideology appears in large measure to have been a consequence of changes in the conditions of production. Behavior was then further channeled by a vast cultural transformation promoted through books and magazines. The law does not seem to have played an overt role in the initial articulation of the separate-sphere ideology; but to the extent that the ideological transformation that occurred in the early part of the nineteenth century was a reaction to a strict hierarchy imposed by the previous legal order, the legal system may well have played an important part at the outset.

In any event, the law appears to have contributed significantly to the perpetuation of this ideology.

STUDY QUESTIONS

1. Describe the ways that sex roles and attitudes appear to have changed between colonial times and the nineteenth century.

2. How important do rules governing legal status appear to be in determining sex roles? How important do prevailing sex roles appear to be in determining the rules governing legal status?

3. To what extent was the differentiation of sex roles due to the way goods and services were produced? To what extent did it seem to work the other way around?

4. In what ways are the ideologies described in this and earlier readings relevant today?

The features described by Taub and Schneider were not widely contested during the early decades of the nineteenth century. Indeed, reform-minded women of the day often appealed to the cult of true womanhood and the ideology of separate spheres to justify projects designed to enhance opportunities available to women.

II. THE EARLY FEMINIST CHALLENGE

Among the earliest American writers to call for sexual equality were the Grimké sisters. Sarah and Angelina Grimké were daughters of a well-established, upper-class, slave-holding family in Charleston, South Carolina. During the late 1830s, while still in their twenties, they joined the Society of Friends, colloquially known as the Quaker religion; moved to Philadelphia; and took active parts in the abolitionist movement. It was their work in that movement that helped them recognize that women, too, were oppressed by existing social arrangements. The following selection illustrates the themes that Angelina Grimké stressed in her public addresses and writings.

HUMAN RIGHTS NOT FOUNDED ON SEX
Angelina E. Grimké
Letters to Catharine E. Beecher.
Boston: Isaac Knapp, 1838, pp. 114–21.

East Boylston, Mass. *10th mo. 2d*, 1837.
Dear Friend:

The investigation of the rights of the slave has led me to a better understanding of my own. I have found the Anti-Slavery cause to be the high school of morals in our land—the school in which *human rights* are more fully investigated, and better understood and taught, than in any other. Here a great fundamental principle is uplifted and illuminated, and from this central light, rays innumerable stream all around. Human beings have *rights*, because they are *moral* beings: the rights of *all* men grow out of their moral nature; and as all men have the same moral nature, they have essentially the same rights. These rights may be wrested from the slave, but they cannot be alienated: his title to himself is as perfect *now*, as is that of Lyman Beecher: it is stamped on his moral being, and is, like it, imperishable. Now if rights are founded in the nature of our moral being, then the *mere circumstance of sex* does not give to man higher rights and responsibilities, than to woman. To suppose that

it does, would be to deny the self-evident truth, that the physical constitution is the mere instrument of the moral nature.' To suppose that it does, would be to break up utterly the relations, of the two natures, and to reverse their functions, exalting the animal nature into a monarch, and humbling the moral into a slave; making the former a proprietor, and the latter its property. When human beings are regarded as *moral* beings, *sex*, instead of being enthroned upon the summit, administering upon rights and responsibilities, sinks into insignificance and nothingness. My doctrine then is, that whatever it is morally right for man to do, it is morally right for woman to do. Our duties originate, not from difference of sex, but from the diversity of our relations in life, the various gifts and talents committed to our care, and the different eras in which we live.

This regulation of duty by the mere circumstance of sex, rather than by the fundamental principle of moral being, has led to all that multifarious train of evils flowing out of the anti-christian doctrine of masculine and feminine virtues. By this doctrine, man has been converted into the warrior, and clothed with sternness, and those other kindred qualities, which in common estimation belong to his character as a *man*; whilst woman has been taught to lean upon an arm of flesh, to sit as a doll arrayed in 'gold, and pearls, and costly array,' to be admired for her personal charms, and caressed and humored like a spoiled child, or converted into a mere drudge to suit the convenience of her lord and master. Thus have all the diversified relations of life been filled with 'confusion and every evil work.' This principle has given to man a charter for the exercise of tyranny and selfishness, pride and arrogance, lust and brutal violence. It has robbed woman of essential rights, the right to think and speak and act on all great moral questions, just as men think and speak and act; the right to share their responsibilities, perils and toils; the right to fulfil the great end of her being, as a moral, intellectual and immortal creature, and of glorifying God in her body and her spirit which are His. Hitherto, instead of being a help mate to man, in the highest, noblest sense of the term, as a companion, a co-worker, an equal; she has been a mere appendage of his being, an instrument of his convenience and pleasure, the pretty toy with which he wiled away his leisure moments, or the pet animal whom he humored into playfulness and submission. Woman, instead of being regarded as the equal of man, has uniformly been looked down upon as his inferior, a mere gift to fill up the measure of his happiness. In 'the poetry of romantic gallantry,' it is true, she has been called 'the last *best* gift of God to man;' but I believe I speak forth the words of truth and soberness when I affirm, that woman never was given to man . . .

Dost thou ask me, if I would wish to see woman engaged in the contention and strife of sectarian controversy, or in the intrigues of political partizans? I say no! never—never. I rejoice that she does not stand on the same platform which man now occupies in these respects; but I mourn, also, that he should thus prostitute his higher nature, and vilely cast away his birthright. I prize the purity of *his* character as highly as I do that of hers. As a moral being, *whatever it is morally wrong for her to do, it is morally wrong for him to do.* The fallacious doctrine of male and female virtues has well nigh ruined all that is morally great and lovely in his character: he has been quite as deep a sufferer by it as woman, though mostly in different respects and by other processes . . .

That thou and all my country-women may better understand the true dignity of woman, is the sincere desire of

Thy Friend,

A. E. GRIMKÉ.

STUDY QUESTIONS

1. What grounds were advanced to support the claim that women and men have equal rights? Is this a claim that advocates of the cult of true womanhood and the separate spheres ideology would accept?

2. What are some of the evils Grimké saw as flowing from the view that masculine and feminine virtues are distinct? In her view, how are women diminished by that doctrine? How are men? Do you agree?

What is distinctive about the contribution of the Grimké sisters is that they confronted the system of subordination directly. Whereas others had been willing to work within the confines of second-class citizenship and the domestic sphere, they were not. In their view, one's moral status or standing is a matter of yes or no, not a matter of more or less. Those who have moral standing and are treated in abusive ways have been denied what they have a right to demand. As African slaves have moral standing, treating them as though they were but domestic animals is morally outrageous. It was this step that enabled the Grimké sisters to recognize that the systematic subordination of women is also morally outrageous and for the same reason. Women have moral standing, just as do men, and so they should have the same political and legal rights as men.

Only a decade later, this same argument prevailed at the first women's rights convention, although on the basis of a different analogy. Organized by Elizabeth Cady Stanton and Lucretia Mott and attended by approximately three hundred women and men, including Frederick Douglass, the convention endorsed an argument based on a parallel with the Declaration of Independence in which American men asserted their legal rights on the basis of their moral standing. The convention produced what is widely regarded as the most famous document in the history of feminism.

DECLARATION OF SENTIMENTS

Seneca Falls, New York.
July 19–20, 1848.
In *The Concise History of Woman Suffrage*, edited by Mari Jo and Paul Buhle.
Urbana, Ill.: University of Illinois Press, 1978, pp. 94–95.

When, in the course of human events, it becomes necessary for one portion of the family of man to assume among the people of the earth a position different from that which they have hitherto occupied, but one to which the laws of nature and of nature's God entitle them, a decent respect to the opinions of mankind requires that they should declare the causes that impel them to such a course.

We hold these truths to be self-evident: that all men and women are created equal; that they are endowed by their Creator with certain inalienable rights, that among these are life, liberty, and the pursuit of happiness; that to secure these rights governments are instituted, deriving their just powers from the consent of the governed. Whenever any form of government becomes destructive of these ends, it is the right of those who suffer from it to refuse allegiance to it, and to insist upon the institution of a new government, laying its foundation on such principles, and organizing its powers in such form as to them shall seem most likely to effect their safety and happiness. Prudence, indeed, will dictate that governments long established should not be changed for light and transient causes; and accordingly, all experience hath shown that mankind are more disposed to suffer, while evils are sufferable, than to right themselves by abolishing the forms to which they were accustomed. But when a long train of abuses and usurpations, pursuing invariably the same object evinces a design to reduce them under absolute despotism, it is their duty to throw off such government, and to provide new guards for their future security. Such has been the patient sufferance of the women under this government, and such is now the necessity which constrains them to demand the equal station to which they are entitled.

The history of mankind is a history of repeated injuries and usurpations on the part of man toward woman, having in direct object the establishment of an absolute tyranny over her. To prove this, let facts be submitted to a candid world.

He has never permitted her to exercise her inalienable right to the elective franchise.

He has compelled her to submit to laws, in the formation of which she had no voice.

He has withheld from her rights which are given to the most ignorant and degraded men—both natives and foreigners.

Having deprived her of this first right of a citizen, the elective franchise, thereby leaving her without representation in the halls of legislation, he has oppressed her on all sides.

He has made her, if married, in the eye of the law, civilly dead.

He has taken from her all right in property, even to the wages she earns.

He has made her, morally, an irresponsible being, as she can commit many crimes with impunity, provided they be done in the presence of her husband. In the covenant of marriage, she is compelled to promise obedience to her husband, he becoming, to all intents and purposes, her master—the law giving him power to deprive her of her liberty, and to administer chastisement.

He has so framed the laws of divorce, as to what shall be the proper causes of divorce; in case of separation, to whom the guardianship of the children shall be given; as to be wholly regardless of the happiness of women—the law, in all cases, going upon a false supposition of the supremacy of man, and giving all power into his hands.

After depriving her of all rights as a married woman, if single and the owner of property, he has taxed her to support a government which recognizes her only when her property can be made profitable to it.

He has monopolized nearly all the profitable employments, and from those she is permitted to follow, she receives but a scanty remuneration.

He closes against her all the avenues to wealth and distinction, which he considers most honorable to himself. As a teacher of theology, medicine, or law, she is not known.

He has denied her the facilities for obtaining a thorough education—all colleges being closed against her.

He allows her in Church, as well as State, but a subordinate position, claiming Apostolic authority for her exclusion from the ministry, and, with some exceptions, from any public participation in the affairs of the Church.

He has created a false public sentiment, by giving to the world a different code of morals for men and women, by which moral delinquencies which exclude women from society, are not only tolerated but deemed of little account in man.

He has usurped the prerogative of Jehovah himself, claiming it as his right to assign for her a sphere of action, when that belongs to her conscience and to her God.

He has endeavored, in every way that he could, to destroy her confidence in her own powers, to lessen her self-respect, and to make her willing to lead a dependent and abject life.

Now, in view of this entire disfranchisement of one-half the people of this country, their social and religious degradation,—in view of the unjust laws above mentioned, and because women do feel themselves aggrieved, oppressed, and fraudulently deprived of their most sacred rights, we insist that they have immediate admission to all the rights and privileges which belong to them as citizens of the United States.

In entering upon the great work before us, we anticipate no small amount of misconception, misrepresentation, and ridicule; but we shall use every instrumentality within our power to effect our object. We shall employ agents, circulate tracts, petition the state and national legislatures, and endeavor to enlist the pulpit and the press in our behalf. We hope this Convention will be followed by a series of Conventions, embracing every part of the country.

STUDY QUESTIONS

1. Upon what document was the Declaration modeled?
2. What complaints against current legal arrangements were listed?
3. To what program of reform did the convention commit itself? Did nineteenth-century feminists call for a radical redistribution of roles within the family?
4. Seen in the context of that program, was the aspiration of suffrage likely to provoke ridicule?

During the Civil War and post–Civil War era, women's rights activists focused on three campaigns to champion their cause: the right to own property in their own names, the right to work in their chosen professions, and the right to vote. The next series of readings explores these three campaigns, including the issues and conflicts that arose during those time periods.

During the Civil War period, feminists threw their support to the abolitionist movement, for a time suspending their own push for equality of the sexes. The emergence of black suffrage as a central issue following the Civil War helped focus feminist demands on the vote. While the hope was that both race and sex discrimination would be addressed in the passage of the Fourteenth and Fifteenth Amendments, they were not. The Fifteenth Amendment deliberately excluded women from the language by refusing to add "sex" to the list of prohibited bases for denying the right to vote. It also provided that only "male" citizens would count in the calculation of congressional representation. In so doing, Congress drove a wedge between the feminists and the abolitionists. These defeats caused some feminists to collaborate with racists in opposing the adoption of the two amendments, causing a deep and long-lasting division within the feminist movement and among some feminists and abolitionists. Stanton and others were deeply disheartened by this. As they saw it, feminists had sacrificed for the benefit of the abolitionist cause only to be abandoned in the moment of triumph.

Though the setback in the Women's Suffrage Movement was serious, the feminist movement persevered and, true to the resolve at Seneca Falls, launched a campaign to abolish the common law rules of coverture that limited a married women's ability to own property and to sue and be sued. It was this campaign, in part, that led several states, during the nineteenth century, to adopt legislation known collectively as Married Women's Property Acts.

THE MARRIED WOMEN'S PROPERTY ACTS, 1839–1865
Reform, Reaction, or Revolution?
Linda E. Speth

In *Women and the Law: A Social Historical Perspective*, edited by D. Kelly Weisberg. Vol. 2. Cambridge, Mass.: Schenkman, 1982, pp. 69–85.

Prior to the enactment of the married women's property legislation, marriage for all practical purposes ensured a woman's "civil death." A wife could neither sue nor be sued. She could not execute a will or enter into a contract. The wife's civil disabilities and limitations were mirrored by a loss of economic autonomy. Her personal property became her husband's at the moment of marriage. He owned her jewels, furniture, or goods, whether she brought them with her to the marriage or thereafter acquired them, and he could sell or give away even the clothes on her back. In addition, any wages she received for work performed outside the home belonged to her husband. Though he could not sell her real estate without her permission, he acquired rights to control and manage her land. Any proceeds derived from improving the property, harvesting and selling crops, or leasing her land belonged to the husband alone. The common law also recognized the husband's total authority within the confines of the family. He could legally chastise his wife and had the sole right to appoint guardians of the children even while the mother was alive . . .

During the second quarter of the nineteenth century, state legislatures and constitutional conventions began to make inroads on the common-law fiction of marital unity by enacting married women's property acts. Mississippi became the first state to enact such legislation in 1839, followed by Maryland in 1843. Later, states as geographically and economically diverse as Maine, Massachusetts, Iowa, and New York followed suit. By the end of the Civil War, a total of twenty-nine states had passed married women's property acts that seemed, at first glance, to herald a revolution in the legal and economic relationship between husband and wife. . . .

Despite these early objections to common-law inequities associated with coverture, the first married women's property acts in the nation had little to do with either feminist agitation or concern for female equality. Instead, initial legislative inroads on the common-law fiction of marital unity stemmed from many factors and were often supported by conservative groups.

In the winter of 1839, Mississippi led the way by enacting the nation's first married women's property act. The legislation was limited, however, and referred mainly to the wife's property rights in slaves. In fact, the act was passed not so much to improve women's rights but rather to protect family property, particularly slaves, from attachment by creditors. . . .

. . . Although the Mississippi act altered the traditional, common-law relationship between husband and wife by creating a wife's separate estate, it accomplished little else. The husband still retained the sole right to manage and control the slaves and to enjoy any profits from their labor.

On March 10, 1843, another southern state whose planters were burdened by debts and economic difficulties passed a married women's property act. Maryland's legislation was similar to that of Mississippi in dealing primarily with the wife's property in slaves, and appears to have been passed for much the same reason. Overall, both the Mississippi and the Maryland acts, and later the Arkansas act of 1846, were limited in scope and represented a conservative effort to safeguard family property rather than an attempt to expand women's right. . . .

The conservative efforts to protect family property and safeguard the wife's original economic assets from the husband's creditors were apparent in other jurisdictions as well. In 1844 Michigan passed an act stipulating that any personal or real property a woman received either before or after her marriage remained her separate estate. Within the next two years, Ohio, Indiana, and Iowa passed more limited legislation declaring that a wife's real estate could not be seized for her husband's debts. . . .

States along the eastern seaboard began altering the common-law fiction of marital unity during the same period. New England legislatures moved hesitantly to give law courts the power to enforce equity principles. As in the South, much of this legislation attempted to mitigate indebtedness. . .

In the North, however, other factors along with creditor-debtor relations were at work in securing the passage of the married women's property acts, the codification movement and growing demands for female equality chief among them. . . .

The complex interplay of factors which led to the implementation of the nation's first married women's property acts can best be illustrated by examining one jurisdiction in some detail. . . .

In New York the codification movement led "inexorably" to the early married women's property act. Following the Revolution, many citizens of the new republic began to object to the legal heritage derived from England. The English common law was regarded as a feudal, anachronistic system that had little applicability to an egalitarian society. Both the common law and, at times, equity were perceived as judge-made rules that subverted the will of the people. It was argued that law should be known and rational, approved by the people via state legislatures and available to all by codification. During the 1820s proponents of codification turned to the works of Jeremy Bentham, the English utilitarian philosopher, who argued that codified law would ensure the greatest good of the greatest number. Besides attacking the common law, other codifiers also objected to trusts and uses as the trappings of and for an aristocratic elite. During the 1820s and 1830s New York began a conscious effort to "defeudalize" its law of real property and weaken equity as a separate system of law, available primarily to the wealthy. . . .

Ernestine Rose, a twenty-six-year-old Polish immigrant who had been involved in at least two legal cases in Europe that centered on a woman's property rights, believed that the economic dominance afforded the husband by law was nothing short of criminal. In 1836 she began a long battle to educate the public and convince the New York State Legislature to remedy the proprietary disabilities of the married woman. She lectured and traveled throughout the state in an effort to stir public consciousness but was able to obtain only six women's signatures (including her own) for a petition she drafted demanding equal property rights for wives. Initially, Rose's effort met with indifference or ridicule from both men and women; but she stubbornly persisted in attacking the legal disabilities of wives. By 1840 she was joined by other feminists such as Paulina Wright Davis and Elizabeth Cady Stanton. At this time, however, Rose's work probably constituted the most important feminist agitation for the legislation. Between 1837 and 1848 when New York passed its married women's property act, Rose drafted several more petitions and helped keep the issue of equal property rights before the politicians. . . .

Despite the intent or impact of the legislation, women did have some effect. Liberal feminist reform impulses became increasingly important in the twelve years before the Civil War. The limitations in the early legislation as well as the overall disabilities suffered by married women in other jurisdictions came under increasing

attack by the fledgling women's rights movement. . . .

During the 1850s New York feminists mounted intensive lobbying and organizational drives to obtain a wife's rights to her own wages, a right that Rose had indicted the American legal system for systematically denying her. Two other women played critical roles as well in achieving some redress for married women in New York—Susan B. Anthony and Elizabeth Cady Stanton. . . .

By 1860, the groundwork laid by Anthony, Rose, and Stanton began to show results . . . . In March 1860 Stanton addressed a joint session of the legislature, and the following day the Married Women's Earning Act became law. In addition, New York wives gained greater rights and received equal power and authority with their husbands in guardianship matters.

Limitations in the first married women's property acts spurred feminists to action in other states as well. . . .

By the outbreak of the Civil War, the American woman's legal status and her corresponding proprietary disabilities differed in each jurisdiction. While generalizations need to be tested by systematic studies of each state, overall, northern wives had obtained more redress in their traditional legal disabilities than had southern wives. This rough geographical breakdown reinforces the supposition that the early women's rights movement had some connection with the most liberal legislation. At this time, the women's rights movement was primarily a northern phenomenon. Certainly feminist efforts were important in changing the original and tentative acts in the North. . . .

After the Civil War, feminists continued to fight for additional legislation for equality, although as in the earlier period, legislation was not passed solely in response to feminism. . . .

Despite such efforts; the battle for female legal and economic equality was far from won and seemed in abeyance, especially after the 1870s as the women's rights movement increasingly emphasized suffrage as the panacea for sex-based inequality. Ironically, the married women's property acts helped fuel and intensify the drive for the vote, often at the cost of obtaining other reforms for women. . . .

STUDY QUESTIONS *Purse*

1. What aspects of the doctrine of coverture were modified by the different statutes? What aspects were not modified?
2. What motivated the states to adopt these changes? What role did feminists play?

The second initiative that feminists pressed after the Civil War was the elimination of restrictions on women's access to the professions. Myra Bradwell pressed this point in the form of a constitutional challenge before the U.S. Supreme Court. Bradwell, a feminist active in women's suffrage organizations, was the founder and editor of an important legal publication, the *Chicago Legal News*. Herself the beneficiary of special legislation chartering the paper and permitting her to contract, she was instrumental in obtaining legislation eliminating women's disabilities. She passed the Illinois bar exam in 1869 only to be denied admission to the practice of law by the Supreme Court of Illinois on the grounds that, under the law of that state, females were not eligible to practice law. Bradwell appealed that decision to the U.S. Supreme Court, arguing that the state of Illinois had violated her rights under the Fourteenth Amendment by denying one of her privileges of citizenship, viz., the privilege of practicing law. Writing for the Court, Justice Miller rejected her claim and held that the practice of law is not a privilege of citizenship protected by the Fourteenth Amendment. Justice Bradley concurred in the result but for different reasons. Justice Bradley's concurring opinion in *Bradwell* is a classic statement of the separate spheres ideology that had long been used to legitimate the exclusion of women from opportunities outside the home.

BRADWELL V. ILLINOIS
Supreme Court of the United States, 1873.
83 U.S. 130, 21 L.Ed. 442.

Mr. Justice MILLER delivered the opinion of the court.

The fourteenth amendment declares that citizens of the United States are citizens of the state within which they reside; therefore the plaintiff was, at the time of making her application, a citizen of the United States and a citizen of the State of Illinois.

In regard to that amendment counsel for the plaintiff in this court truly says that there are certain privileges and immunities which belong to a citizen of the United States as such; otherwise it would be nonsense for the fourteenth amendment to prohibit a State from abridging them, and he proceeds to argue that admission to the bar of a State of a person who possesses the requisite learning and character is one of those which a State may not deny.

In this latter proposition we are not able to concur with counsel. We agree with him that there are privileges and immunities belonging to citizens of the United States, in that relation and character, and that it is these and these alone which a State is forbidden to abridge. But the right to admission to practice in the courts of a State is not one of them. This right in no sense depends on citizenship of the United States. It has not, as far as we know, ever been made in any State, or in any case, to depend on citizenship at all. Certainly many prominent and distinguished lawyers have been admitted to practice, both in the State and Federal courts, who were not citizens of the United States or of any State. But, on whatever basis this right may be placed, so far as it can have any relation to citizenship at all, it would seem that, as to the courts of a State, it would relate to citizenship of the State, and as to Federal courts, it would relate to citizenship of the United States.

The opinion just delivered in the *Slaughter-House Cases* renders elaborate argument in the present case unnecessary; for, unless we are wholly and radically mistaken in the principles on which those cases are decided, the right to control and regulate the granting of license to practice law in the courts of a State is one of those powers which are not transferred for its protection to the Federal government, and its exercise is in no manner governed or controlled by citizenship of the United States in the party seeking such license.

Judgment Affirmed.

Mr. Justice BRADLEY:

I concur in the judgment of the court in this case, by which the judgment of the Supreme Court of Illinois is affirmed, but not for the reasons specified in the opinion just read. . . .

The claim that, under the fourteenth amendment of the Constitution, which declares that no State shall make or enforce any law which shall abridge the privileges and immunities of citizens of the United States, the statute law of Illinois, or the common law prevailing in that State, can no longer be set up as a barrier against the right of females to pursue any lawful employment for a livelihood (the practice of law included), assumes that it is one of the privileges and immunities of women as citizens to engage in any and every profession, occupation, or employment in civil life.

It certainly cannot be affirmed, as an historical fact, that this has ever been established as one of the fundamental privileges and immunities of the sex. On the contrary, the civil law, as well as nature herself, has always recognized a wide difference in the respective spheres and destinies of man and woman. Man is, or should be, woman's protector and defender. The natural and proper timidity and delicacy which belongs to the female sex evidently unfits it for many of the occupations of civil life. The constitution of the family organization, which is founded in the divine ordinance, as well as in the nature of things, indicates the domestic sphere as that which properly belongs to the domain and functions of womanhood. The harmony, not to say identity, of interests and views which belong, or should belong, to the family institution is repugnant to the idea of a woman adopting a distinct and independent career from that of her husband. So firmly fixed was this sentiment in the founders of the common law that it became a maxim of that system of jurisprudence that a woman had no legal existence separate from her husband, who was regarded as her head and representative in the social state; and, notwithstanding some recent modifications of this civil status, many of the special rules of law flowing from and dependent upon this cardinal principle still exist in full force in most States. One of these is, that a married woman is incapable, without her husband's consent, of making contracts which shall be binding on her or him. This very incapacity was one circumstance which the Supreme Court of Illinois deemed important in rendering a married woman incompetent fully to perform the duties and trusts that belong to the office of an attorney and counsellor.

It is true that many women are unmarried and not affected by any of the duties, complications, and incapacities arising out of the married state, but these are exceptions to the general rule. The paramount destiny and mission of woman are to fulfil the noble and benign offices of wife and mother. This is the law of the Creator. And the rules of civil society must be adapted to the general constitution of things, and cannot be based upon exceptional cases.

The humane movements of modern society, which have for their object the multiplication of avenues for woman's advancement, and of occupations adapted to her condition and sex, have my heartiest concurrence. But I am not prepared to say that it is one of her fundamental rights and privileges to be admitted into every office and position, including those which require highly special qualifications and demanding special responsibilities. In the nature of things it is not every citizen of every age, sex, and condition that is qualified for every calling and position. It is the prerogative of the legislator to prescribe regulations founded on nature, reason, and experience for the due admission of qualified persons to professions and callings demanding special skill and confidence. This fairly belongs to the police power of the State; and, in my opinion, in view of the peculiar characteristics, destiny, and mission of woman, it is within the province of the legislature to ordain what offices, positions, and callings shall be filled and discharged by men, and shall receive the benefit of those energies and responsibilities, and that decision and firmness which are presumed to predominate in the sterner sex.

For these reasons I think that the laws of Illinois now complained of are not obnoxious to the charge of abridging any of the privileges and immunities of citizens of the United States.

STUDY QUESTIONS

1. What assumption did Justice Bradley detect behind Bradwell's Fourteenth Amendment claim? Why might that have seemed preposterous at the time?
2. What reasons were given by Justice Bradley for rejecting that assumption? What kinds of differences did he identify between the sexes? Were they physical, social, or legal? Why did he consider these differences relevant in evaluating the assumption in question? Why did he accept the view that men and women belong to different spheres and have different destinies?
3. Which of these lines of reasoning seem most appropriate for a court to rely upon? Least appropriate? Which, if any, actually applied to Myra Bradwell?

A third feminist campaign was for suffrage. This objective eventually was achieved but at great cost. Having failed to gain explicit protections for women in the Fourteenth and Fifteenth Amendments, the more militant National Women's Suffrage Association (NWSA) pursued the legal argument that women were nevertheless enfranchised by those amendments. The argument's dramatic introduction by feminist and radical Victoria Woodhull at a congressional hearing in 1871 sparked a NWSA campaign for its recognition by congressional act or judicial decision. As part of that campaign, Susan B. Anthony and thirteen other women voted in Rochester, New York, on November 5, 1872. They were arrested and charged with the violation of a federal statute making it a crime for anyone to vote "without the lawful right to vote." At her trial, Anthony argued that by restricting the right to vote to male citizens, the state of New York had violated her rights as guaranteed by the Fourteenth Amendment. The court found her guilty on the ground that "[t]he Fourteenth Amendment gives no right to a woman to vote. . . ." *U.S. v. Anthony,* 24 Fed. Cas. 829, 831 (1873). The verdict could not be appealed because the judge declined to enforce his order that Anthony pay a fine of one hundred dollars.

Virginia Minor, who ironically had sought to interest the NWSA in the constitutional argument in 1869, carried the issue to the U.S. Supreme Court after she was barred from voting in the fall election of 1872. She argued that the state of Missouri had violated her rights under the Fourteenth Amendment as a person born or naturalized in the United States and therefore entitled to the privileges and immunities of national citizenship. The right to vote, she argued, is a privilege of citizenship. The Court, in rejecting her claim, admitted that women are citizens but insisted that not all citizens have the right to vote. In doing so, the Court asserted in effect that women enjoy a special class of citizenship—a second class.

MINOR V. HAPPERSETT
Supreme Court of the United States, 1875.
88 U.S. 162, 22 L.Ed. 627.

The Chief Justice delivered the opinion of the court.

The question is presented in this case, whether, since the adoption of the fourteenth amendment, a woman, who is a citizen of the United States and of the State of Missouri, is a voter in that State, notwithstanding the provision of the constitution and laws of the State, which confine the right of suffrage to men alone.

It is contended that the provisions of the constitution and laws of the State of Missouri which confine the right of suffrage and registration therefore to men, are in violation of the Constitution of the United States, and therefore void. The argument is, that as a woman, born or naturalized in the United States and subject to the jurisdiction thereof, is a citizen of the United States and of the State in which she resides, she has the right of suffrage as one of the privileges and immunities of her citizenship, which the State cannot by its laws or constitution abridge.

There is no doubt that women may be citizens. They are persons, and by the fourteenth amendment "all persons born or naturalized in the United States and subject to the jurisdiction thereof" are expressly declared to be "citizens of the United States and of the State wherein they reside." But, in our opinion, it did not need this amendment to give them that position.

If the right of suffrage is one of the necessary privileges of a citizen of the United States, then the constitution and laws of Missouri confining it to men are in violation of the Constitution of the United States, as

amended, and consequently void. The direct question is, therefore, presented whether all citizens are necessarily voters.

The Constitution does not define the privileges and immunities of citizens. For that definition we must look elsewhere. In this case we need not determine what they are, but only whether suffrage is necessarily one of them.

It certainly is nowhere made so in express terms. [The Court then outlined the voting restrictions in effect at the time that the Fourteenth Amendment was adopted.]. . .

The amendment did not add to the privileges and immunities of a citizen. It simply furnished an additional guaranty for the protection of such as he already had. No new voters were necessarily made by it. . . .

In this condition of the law in respect to suffrage in the several States it cannot for a moment be doubted that if it had been intended to make all citizens of the United States voters, the framers of the Constitution would not have left it to implication. So important a change in the condition of citizenship as it actually existed, if intended, would have been expressly declared. . . .

But we have already sufficiently considered the proof found upon the inside of the Constitution. That upon the outside is equally effective.

The Constitution was submitted to the States for adoption in 1787, and was ratified by nine States in 1788, and finally by the thirteen original States in 1790. Vermont was the first new State admitted to the Union, and it came in under a constitution which conferred the right of suffrage only upon men of the full age of twenty-one years, having resided in the State for the space of one whole year next before the election, and who were of quiet and peaceable behavior. This was in 1791. The next year, 1792, Kentucky followed with a constitution confining the right of suffrage to free male citizens of the age of twenty-one years who had resided in the State two years or in the county in which they offered to vote one year next before the election. Then followed Tennessee, in 1796, with voters of freemen of the age of twenty-one years and upwards, possessing a freehold in the county wherein they may vote, and being inhabitants of the State or freemen being inhabitants of any one county in the State six months immediately preceding the day of election. But we need not particularize further. No new State has ever been admitted to the Union which has conferred the right of suffrage upon women, and this has never been considered a valid objection to her admission. On the contrary, as is claimed in the argument, the right of suffrage was withdrawn from women as early as 1807 in the State of New Jersey, without any attempt to obtain the interference of the United States to prevent it. Since then the governments of the insurgent States have been reorganized under a requirement that before their representatives could be admitted to seats in Congress they must have adopted new constitutions, republican in form. In no one of these constitutions was suffrage conferred upon women, and yet the States have all been restored to their original position as States in the Union. . . .

Certainly, if the courts can consider any question settled, this is one. For nearly ninety years the people have acted upon the idea that the Constitution, when it conferred citizenship, did not necessarily confer the right of suffrage. If uniform practice long continued can settle the construction of so important an instrument as the Constitution of the United States confessedly is, most certainly it has been done

here. Our province is to decide what the law is, not to declare what it should be.

We have given this case the careful consideration its importance demands. If the law is wrong, it ought to be changed; but the power for that is not with us. The arguments addressed to us bearing upon such a view of the subject may perhaps be sufficient to induce those having the power, to make the alteration, but they ought not to be permitted to influence our judgment in determining the present rights of the parties now litigating before us. No argument as to woman's need of suffrage can be considered. We can only act upon her rights as they exist. It is not for us to look at the hardship of withholding. Our duty is at an end if we find it is within the power of a State to withhold.

Being unanimously of the opinion that the Constitution of the United States does not confer the right of suffrage upon any one, and that the constitutions and laws of the several States which commit that important trust to men alone are not necessarily void, we . . .

Affirm the Judgment.

STUDY QUESTIONS

1. What reasons did the Court cite in support of its ruling that the right to vote is not a right of citizenship? That women do not have a right to vote? Do these reasons appear sufficient to justify the Court's decision?

2. Was the Chief Justice correct in saying that the duty of the Court is at an end when it finds what the law is? What are the alternatives, particularly where it seems clear that the provision in question was not originally intended to give the relief sought?

3. The Court handed down its decision in *Bradwell* two years before *Minor*. What effect do you suppose the feminists' failure to have specific guarantees for women included in the Civil War Amendments had on the justices' decision-making process in these cases?

The Court's emphasis in *Minor* on the parallel between state and federal constitutional experience may have been overdrawn. While it was true in 1875 that no "new" states had ever extended the franchise to women, the same was not true of the original states. In the colonial period, unmarried women with enough property had the legal right to vote on local issues. All of the original states, except New Jersey, disenfranchised women when they drafted their first state constitutions. New Jersey did so, as the Court noted, in 1807. It is also worth noting that two new states admitted after the decision in *Minor* but before the adoption of the Nineteenth Amendment extended the franchise to women from their inception—Wyoming (1890) and Utah (1896).

The women's rights movement in the late nineteenth century was split into two camps. The more militant NWSA, led by Elizabeth Cady Stanton, predominated until the turn of the century. It was convinced that a complete transformation of the patriarchy that placed women in a separate sphere subordinate to men, indeed incorporated them into their husbands, had to take place if women were ever to be emancipated. To this end, it argued that women are the same as men in all relevant respects, and therefore no basis exists for treating women as separate and inferior. To the NWSA, the franchise was an incidental ingredient in the larger revolutionary package. The strategy and rhetoric of the NWSA so provoked the political mainstream that the women's rights program was perceived as radical. As such, it became political suicide for a public figure to be associated with the movement.

The feminist agenda began to unravel in the final decades of the century. The union, in 1890, of the NWSA with the more conservative American Women's Suffrage Association to form the National American Women's Suffrage Association (NAWSA) was a key moment for two developments within the movement. Unable to achieve consensus among themselves on the broader agenda of reform, feminists increasingly narrowed their objectives to the one thing that all agreed upon, viz., the vote. They came increasingly to substitute considerations of expediency for the appeal for equal treatment that had informed feminist aspirations since the Grimké sisters and the Declaration of Sentiments in mid-nineteenth century.[2]

By the turn of the century, after most members of the earlier feminist generation had died or become less active, the NAWSA focused on suffrage as the key to achieving complete emancipation and was committed to a strategy of reform rather than confrontation. Under the leadership of Carrie Chapman Catt and Jane Addams, the NAWSA argued for the extension of the franchise to women not because women are essentially the same but because women are essentially different from men. The special influence of sensitive, nurturing, spiritual creatures is needed in governmental matters just as it is needed in the home. They showed that the vote was compatible with, indeed a natural extension of, the role of women in the home. The strategy and rhetoric of the women's rights movement under the leadership of Catt and Addams persuaded the public that the suffrage movement was middle-of-the-road and, therefore, politically congenial.

Catt designed a grassroots campaign for achieving the franchise. The campaign was well organized, timed, and executed. Beginning with Washington in 1910, six states amended their constitutions to extend the franchise to women. By 1919, twenty-six states had petitioned Congress to enact a similar amendment to the federal constitution. Congress passed the Nineteenth Amendment that same year by a wide margin. It was ratified within fourteen months with a minimum of controversy.

From the turn of the century, the movement concentrated its efforts on obtaining the vote as the key to making progress on the remaining issues identified in the Seneca Falls Declaration. It soon became apparent that this was not to be. By the mid-1920s, it was

---

[2] **The Rising Influence of Racism** Angela Y. Davis *Women, Race & Class.* New York: Random House, 1983, pp. 111–19.

clear that women were not voting in a block. Indeed, there was little or no difference between the voting patterns of women and men.

It was also clear by the mid-1920s that after suffrage was obtained, the coalition that had fought so long and hard to achieve it had collapsed. The demise of the first feminist movement is still the subject of scholarly debate. Some argue that it expired because of the absence of an overarching agenda on which feminists could agree. Florence Kelley continued to emphasize the need for protective legislation; the National Women's Party espoused the Equal Rights Amendment, and African American feminists emphasized the struggle against racial discrimination. Others argue that the first feminist movement collapsed long before the mid-1920s. In this view, it had passed from the scene when a disheartened leadership stopped arguing for a single moral standing for men and women and settled for arguments from expediency. This abandoned both the principles articulated by the Grimkés and the Seneca Falls Convention and solidarity with working-class women, women of color, and men who shared their convictions.

III. JUSTIFYING DIFFERENTIAL TREATMENT

During the late nineteenth century, in the *Bradwell* and *Minor* decisions, the Supreme Court approved limitations on women's employment opportunities and on their full participation in the responsibilities of citizenship. During the first six decades of the twentieth century, the federal courts continued along these same lines, although they tended to state more specific reasons. Two types of argument were generally used to justify sex-based laws during that period. First, restrictions on employment opportunities were frequently approved because they were thought necessary to protect women from workplace hazards that only men were believed capable of managing safely. Second, limitations on women's responsibilities as citizens were often approved as compensating for the fact that women bear special burdens not shared by men. Both rationales had been used over the ages to justify confining women to subordinate and dependent positions.

The protectionist rationale was developed first. At the turn of the nineteenth century, the working conditions of most American workers were widely regarded as wretched. The grueling hours spent in filthy and dangerous workplaces by men, women, and children had sparked a drive for legislation at the state level that would shield workers from such gross exploitation by their employers. This drive was blocked by a Supreme Court decision that declared that states may not regulate working conditions in the interest of the general welfare, for that would be "an illegal interference with the rights of individuals to make contracts." This 1905 decision, *Lochner v. New York*, 198 U.S. 45, struck down a New York law limiting the hours of bakers to sixty per week or ten per day. The Court reasoned that the state's limitation of the hours of work denied workers the opportunity to contract for more hours if it suited their needs and therefore denied them of liberty without due process of law in violation of the Fourteenth Amendment.

The decision in *Lochner* did not stop the drive for state regulation of working conditions but only caused it to veer from its more extensive objective of securing safer working conditions for workers generally. It turned to gaining protection, if not for all workers, then at least for the women workers. Within three years of the *Lochner* decision, nineteen states had enacted laws setting maximum hours and/or prohibiting night work for women. The challenge to these laws came before the Supreme Court in the case of *Muller v. Oregon*. Carl Muller, the operator of a laundry that required a female employee to work more than the state-mandated maximum of ten hours in any one day, was tried, found guilty, and fined ten dollars by an Oregon court. He appealed, arguing that *Lochner* denied the state authority to interfere with his liberty of contract and that of his employee.

The state's argument in defense of the statute was supported by an *amicus curiae* (friend of the court) brief prepared by Louis Brandeis, Josephine and Pauline Goldmark, and Florence Kelley on behalf of the National Consumer League (NCL), a middle- and upper-class organization that actively fought for sex-based protective legislation. The brief argued that the Oregon statute was well within the state's legitimate police powers because there existed reasonable grounds to believe that women's health in particular was severely jeopardized by long work days. The evidence offered in support of this contention consisted of a 113-page collection of short quotations that stressed women's special vulnerabilities and the implications of these for the well-being of family life. Although described in the brief as "facts of common knowledge," the passages were mainly anecdotal reports interwoven with expert opinion. The following selections illustrate the flavor of this famous document.

THE BRANDEIS BRIEF

Louis D. Brandeis and Josephine Goldmark
Women in Industry. New York: Arno & *The New York Times*, 1969,
pp. 22–3, 45–6, 50–1.

HYGIENE OF OCCUPATION IN REFERENCE HANDBOOK OF THE MEDICAL SCIENCES. GEORGE M. PRICE, M.D., MEDICAL SANITARY INSPECTOR, HEALTH DEPARTMENT OF THE CITY OF NEW YORK. VOL. VI.

In many industries . . . female labor is very largely employed; and the effect of work on them is very detrimental to health. The injurious influences of female labor are due to the following factors: (1) The comparative physical weakness of the female organism; (2) The greater predisposition to harmful and poisonous elements in the trades; (3) The periodical semi-pathological state of health of women; (4) The effect of labor on the reproductive organs; and (5) The effects on the offspring. As the muscular organism of woman is less developed than that of man, it is evident that those industrial occupations which require intense, constant, and prolonged muscular efforts must become highly detrimental to their health. This is shown in the general debility, anaemia, chlorosis, and lack of tone in most women who are compelled to work in factories and in shops for long periods.

The increased susceptibility of women to industrial poisons and to diseases has been demonstrated by a great number of observers. The female organism, especially when young, offers very little resistance to the inroads of disease and to the various dangerous elements of certain trades. Hirt says, "It must be conceded that certain trades affect women a great deal more injuriously than men;" and he mentions, among others, the effects of lead, mercury, phosphorus, and other poisons. Even where there are no special noxious elements, work may produce, as already mentioned, harmful effects on the health of women; but when to the general effects of industrial occupation are added the dangers of dust, fumes, and gases, we find that the female organism succumbs very readily, as compared with that of the male. . . .

It has been estimated that out of every one hundred days women are in a semi-pathological state of health for from fourteen to sixteen days. The natural congestion of the pelvic organs during menstruation is augmented and favored by work on sewing-machines and other industrial occupations necessitating the constant use of the lower part of the body. Work during these periods tends to induce chronic congestion of the uterus and appendages, and dysmenorrhœa and flexion of the uterus are well known affections of working girls. (Page 321.)

THE CASE FOR THE FACTORY ACTS. EDITED BY MRS. SIDNEY WEBB. LONDON, 1901.
If working long and irregular hours, accepting a bare subsistence wage and enduring insanitary conditions tended to increase women's physical strength and industrial skill—if these conditions of unregulated industry even left unimpaired the woman's natural stock of strength and skill—we might regard factory legislation as irrelevant. But as a matter of fact a whole century of evidence proves exactly the contrary. To leave women's labor unregulated by law means inevitably to leave it exposed to terribly deteriorating influences. The woman's lack of skill and lack of strength is made worse by lack of regulation. And there is still a further deterioration. Any one who has read the evidence given in the various inquiries into the Sweating System will have been struck by the invariable coincidence of a low standard of regularity, sobriety, and morality, with the conditions to which women, under free competition, are exposed. (Page 209.)

LABOR LAWS FOR WOMEN IN GERMANY. DR. ALICE SALOMON. PUBLISHED BY THE WOMEN'S INDUSTRIAL COUNCIL LONDON, 1907.
A study of the laws relating to female labor reveals that it has been the special aim of the legislators to protect and preserve the health of the women in their character as wives and as the mothers of future generations. On the one hand, the regulations are intended to prevent injury to health through over-long hours, or the resumption of work too soon after confinement, often the cause of serious illness which may render the patient incapable of bearing healthy offspring. . . . But if work in the factory be a necessity for women—even for married ones—it is all the more desirable that protective legislation should be so extended and worked out in such detail as to ensure the fullest attainment of its object, viz.: protection for the health of the female working population, as well as for the family and the home. (Page 5.)

STUDY QUESTIONS

1. What reasons are given for believing that long, hard hours have a greater impact on women workers than upon men workers in the same circumstances? Do these statements appear to rely on well-researched, factual information about women?
2. What consequences, besides those on women's health, are of concern to these authorities?
3. In *Lochner,* the Court was content to allow workers to look after their own health and safety interests when bargaining for their labor. Does the demand for special protection of women workers imply less confidence in women's ability to look after their own well-being?

MULLER V. OREGON
Supreme Court of the United States, 1908.
208 U.S. 412, 28 S. Ct. 324, 52 L.Ed. 551.

Mr. Justice BREWER delivered the opinion of the court.

On February 19, 1903, the legislature of the state of Oregon passed an act (Session Laws 1903, p. 148) the first section of which is in these words:

"Sec. 1. That no female (shall) be employed in any mechanical establishment, or factory, or laundry in this state more than ten hours during any one day. The hours of work may be so arranged as to permit the employment of females at any time so that they shall not work more than ten hours during the twenty-four hours of any one day."

Sec. 3 made a violation of the provisions of the prior sections a misdemeanor subject to a fine of not less than $10 nor more than $25.

On September 18, 1905, an information was filed in the circuit court of the state for the county of Multnomah, charging that the defendant "on the 4th day of September, A.D. 1905, in the county of Multnomah and state of Oregon, then and there being the owner of a laundry, known as the Grand Laundry, in the city of Portland, and the employer of females therein, did then and there unlawfully permit and suffer one Joe Haselbock, he, the said Joe Haselbock, then and there being an overseer, superintendent, and agent of said Curt Muller, in the said Grand Laundry, to require a female, to wit, one Mrs. E. Gotcher, to work more than ten hours in said laundry on said 4th day of September, A.D. 1905, contrary to the statutes in such cases made and provided, and against the peace and dignity of the state of Oregon."

A trial resulted in a verdict against the defendant, who was sentenced to pay a fine of $10. The supreme court of the state affirmed the conviction, whereupon the case was brought here on writ of error.

The single question is the constitutionality of the statute under which the defendant was convicted, so far as it affects the work of a female in a laundry. . . .

We held in *Lochner v. New York* that a law providing that no laborer shall be required or permitted to work in bakeries more than sixty hours in a week or ten hours in a day was not as to mean a legitimate exercise of the police power of the state, but an unreasonable, unnecessary, and arbitrary interference with the right and liberty of the individual to contract in relation to his labor, and as such was in conflict with, and void under, the Federal Constitution. That decision is invoked by plaintiff in error as decisive of the question before us. But this assumes that the difference between the sexes does not justify a different rule respecting a restriction of the hours of labor.

In patent cases counsel are apt to open the argument with a discussion of the state of the art. It may not be amiss, in the present case, before examining the constitutional question, to notice the course of legislation, as well as expressions of opinion from other than judicial sources. In the brief filed by Mr. Louis D. Brandeis for the defendant in error is a very copious collection of all these matters. . . .

The legislation and opinions referred to in the margin . . . are significant of a widespread belief that woman's physical structure, and the functions she performs in consequence thereof, justify special legislation restricting or qualifying the conditions under which she should be permitted to toil. Constitutional questions, it is true, are not settled by even a consensus of present public opinion, for it is the peculiar value of a written constitution that it places in unchanging form limitations upon legislative action, and thus gives a permanence and stability to popular government which otherwise would be lacking. At the same time, when a question of fact is debated and debatable, and the extent to which a special constitutional limitation goes is affected by the truth in respect to that fact, a widespread and long-continued belief concerning it is worthy of consideration. We take judicial cognizance of all matters of general knowledge. . .

That woman's physical structure and the performance of maternal functions place her at a disadvantage in the struggle for subsistence is obvious. This is especially true when the burdens of motherhood are upon her. Even when they are not, by abundant testimony of the medical fraternity continuance for a long time on her feet at work, repeating this from day to day, tends to injurious effects upon the body, and, as healthy mothers are essential to vigorous offspring, the physical well-being of woman becomes an object of public interest and care in order to preserve the strength and vigor of the race.

Still again, history discloses the fact that woman has always been dependent upon man. He established his control at the outset by superior physical strength, and this control in various forms, with diminishing intensity, has continued to the present.

As minors, though not to the same extent, she has been looked upon in the courts as needing especial care that her rights may be preserved. Education was long denied her, and while now the doors of the school-room are opened and her opportunities for acquiring knowledge are great, yet even with that and the consequent increase of capacity for business affairs it is still true that in the struggle for subsistence she is not an equal competitor with her brother. Though limitations upon personal and contractual rights may be removed by legislation, there is that in her disposition and habits of life which will operate against a full assertion of those rights. She will still be where some legislation to protect her seems necessary to secure a real equality of right. Doubtless there are individual exceptions, and there are many respects in which she has an advantage over him; but looking at it from the viewpoint of the effort to maintain an independent position in life, she is not upon an equality. Differentiated by these matters from the other sex, she is properly placed in a class by herself, and legislation designed for her protection may be sustained, even when like legislation is not necessary for men, and could not be sustained. It is impossible to close one's eyes to the fact that she still looks to her brother and depends upon him. Even though all restrictions on political, personal, and contractual rights were taken away, and she stood, so far as statutes are concerned, upon an absolutely equal plane with him, it would still be true that she is so constituted that she will rest upon and look to him for protection: that her physical structure and a proper discharge of her maternal functions—having in view not merely her own health, but the well-being of the race—justify legislation to protect her from the greed as well as the passion of man. The limitations which this statute places upon her contractual powers, upon her right to agree with her employer as to the time she shall labor, are not imposed solely for her benefit, but also largely for the benefit of all. Many words cannot make this plainer. The two sexes differ in structure of body, in the functions to be performed by each, in the amount of physical strength, in the capacity for long continued labor, particularly when done standing, the influence of vigorous health upon the future well-being of the race, the self-reliance which enables one to assert full rights, and in the capacity to maintain the struggle for subsistence. This difference justifies a difference in legislation, and upholds that which is designed to compensate for some of the burdens which rest upon her. . . .

For these reasons, and without questioning in any respect the decision in *Lochner v. New York*, we are of the opinion that it cannot be adjudged that the act in question is in conflict with the Federal Constitution, so far as it respects the work of a female in a laundry, and the judgment of the Supreme Court of Oregon is affirmed.

STUDY QUESTIONS

1. What differences between the sexes did the Court indicate are relevant in deciding whether a state may interfere with a woman's, but not a man's, liberty of contract? Are they physical, social, or legal differences? Compare these differences with those identified by Justice Bradley in *Bradwell*.

2. To what extent did the Court recognize that not all women share the characteristics that it attributes to them?

3. What interest did the Court assert a state has in protecting women from the hazards of long hours of arduous labor in an employment setting? Would that same argument be relevant to the long and arduous hours of labor that women perform in the home?

4. Does the distinctive reproductive function of men warrant different treatment?

5. What effect besides "protection" did these restrictions have on women and on women's ability to work?

In the wake of the *Muller* decision, states enacted legislation that limited women's employment opportunities in a variety of ways. Within the next nine years, for example, nineteen states passed laws restricting women's working day. As historian Alice Kessler-Harris points out, these restrictions contain many an irony.

> Regulations differed not only from state to state but from industry to industry within each state. Manufacturing and mercantile enterprises were the first statutory targets, with laundries and telegraph and telephone companies running a close second. Hotels, restaurants, and cabarets often escaped regulation entirely. Domestic service and agriculture, still the two leading female occupations and the most arduous, remained untouched.
>
> Alice Kessler-Harris, Out to Work: A History of Wage-Earning Women in the United States. *New York: Oxford University Press, 1982, pp. 197–8.*

Another common technique for limiting the employment opportunities of women was to ban them from working nights in selected occupations. One such statute, a New York law prohibiting women from working in restaurants in cities between 10 P.M. and 6 A.M., was approved by the Supreme Court because "night work of the kind prohibited so injuriously affects the physical condition of women, and so threatens to impair their peculiar and natural functions, and so exposes them to the dangers and menaces incident to night life in large cities." *Radice v. New York*, 264 U.S. 292 (1924). This language is clearly reminiscent of *Muller's* discussion of women's "physical structure," her "maternal functions," and her vulnerability to the "greed as well as the passion of man."

As is well recognized today, these "protective" regulations had two distinctive effects. On the one hand, they resulted in an immediate decrease in the weekly income of women who worked full time outside the home. With fewer hours of work turned in at the same hourly wage rate, the result was less in the pay envelope. For women whose income was low to begin with, that decrease had to be offset by finding second jobs, such as doing the laundry for other families. On the other hand, women applicants for jobs became less attractive to prospective employers because the law permitted men to be worked for more hours than women. By limiting the workdays and workweeks of women but not men, men's privileged situation in the American workplace became even more pronounced.

The strategy adopted by the NCL, Florence Kelley, Jane Addams, and other feminists who advocated "protective" legislation may have seemed worthwhile for the first nine years after the *Muller* decision. But then, in 1917, the Court approved maximum-hour laws for men (*Bunting v. Oregon*, 243 U.S. 426). The Court reached that decision based on arguments listing the hazards of long, arduous working hours for men without mentioning *Lochner*. *Bunting*, unlike *Muller*, however, was not followed by a flood of maximum-hour laws for men. Labor unions preferred organization as a strategy to protect mainly their male members and therefore did not press for further protective legislation.

Limiting the hours a person may work results in low take-home pay unless a minimum wage is established. Soon after *Muller*, Congress and the states began to enact minimum wage laws. They were immediately confronted by a Supreme Court that saw minimum wage laws as overt attempts to fix the price of labor. In 1923, the Court struck down a statute affecting the District of Columbia that fixed minimum wages for women and children (*Adkins v. Children's Hospital*, 261 U.S. 525). In distinguishing *Muller* and finding that woman's liberty of contract was now as great as man's, the Court emphasized recent legal developments concerning women's status. "In view of the great—not to say revolutionary—changes which have taken place since [*Muller*] in the contractual, political and civil status of women, culminating in the Nineteenth Amendment, it is not unreasonable to say that these differences [of physical structure, especially in respect of the maternal functions] have now come almost, if not quite, to the vanishing point."

Reasoning that there was no direct relationship between women's physical frailty and low wages, the Court declared the statute challenged in *Adkins* unconstitutional. This insensitivity to the actual circumstances of women workers combined with the Court's general willingness to invalidate state statutes regulating economic and social relations suggest that it might be well to take the Court's feminism with several grains of salt. Consider, for example, whether the Court could have upheld the statute in *Adkins* and extended its protection to men.

Beginning in 1934, after President Franklin Roosevelt's threat to expand the Court and fill it with more liberal justices, the Supreme Court granted greater deference to the judgment of legislatures. This change of posture showed itself in 1937 when, by a 5–4 decision, the Court overruled *Adkins* and approved a Washington state statute establishing a minimum wage for women and children. The case, *West Coast Hotel v. Parrish*, 300 U.S. 379, revived a principle announced in 1898 that a state may act to equalize inequalities of bargaining power between workers and employers. The majority went on to find, citing *Muller*, "that this established principle is peculiarly applicable in relation to the employment of women in whose protection the State has a special interest."

Statutes that excluded women altogether from certain occupations were commonplace until such practices were made unlawful by the Civil Rights Act of 1964. The functions served by such restrictions were many: They reinforced the conventional view that a woman's place is in the home; they reduced the competition men faced in obtaining and holding jobs in affected professions; and they reduced the incidence of assaults on women by minimizing the occasions for women to work with men. The following decision, later disapproved in *Craig v. Boren* (see Chapter 2), illustrates these themes, as well as judicial attitudes at mid-twentieth century.

GOESAERT V. CLEARY
Supreme Court of the United States, 1948.
335 U.S. 464, 69 S. Ct. 198, 93 L.Ed. 163.

Mr. Justice FRANKFURTER delivered the opinion of the Court.

As part of the Michigan system for controlling the sale of liquor, bartenders are required to be licensed in all cities having a population of 50,000 or more, but no female may be so licensed unless she be "the wife or daughter of the male owner" of a licensed liquor establishment. The case is here on direct appeal from an order of the District Court of three judges . . . denying an injunction to restrain the enforcement of the Michigan law. The claim . . . is that Michigan cannot forbid females generally from being barmaids and at the same time make an exception in favor of the wives and daughters of the owners of liquor establishments. Beguiling as the

subject is, it need not detain us long. To ask whether or not the Equal Protection of the Laws Clause of the Fourteenth Amendment barred Michigan from making the classification the State has made between wives and daughters of owners of liquor places and wives and daughters of nonowners, is one of those rare instances where to state the question is in effect to answer it.

We are, to be sure, dealing with a historic calling. We meet the ale-wife, sprightly and ribald, in Shakespeare, but centuries before him she played a role in the social life of England. The Fourteenth Amendment did not tear history up by the roots, and the regulation of the liquor traffic is one of the oldest and most untrammeled of legislative powers.

Michigan could, beyond question, forbid all women from working behind a bar. This is so despite the vast changes in the social and legal position of women. The fact that women may now have achieved the virtues that men have long claimed as their prerogatives and now indulge in vices that men have long practiced does not preclude the States from drawing a sharp line between the sexes, certainly in such matters as the regulation of the liquor traffic. The Constitution does not require sociological insight, or shifting social standards, any more than it requires them to keep abreast of the latest scientific standards.

While Michigan may deny to all women opportunities for bartending, Michigan cannot play favorites among women without rhyme or reason. The Constitution in enjoining the equal protection of the laws upon States precludes irrational discrimination as between persons or groups of persons in the incidence of a law. But the Constitution does not require situations "which are different in fact or opinion to be treated in law as though they were the same." Since bartending by women may, in the allowable legislative judgment, give rise to moral and social problems against which it may devise preventive measures, the legislature need not go to the full length of prohibition if it believes that as to a defined group of females other factors are operating which either eliminate or reduce the moral and social problems otherwise calling for prohibition. Michigan evidently believes that the oversight assured through ownership of a bar by a barmaid's husband or father minimizes hazards that may confront a barmaid without such protecting oversight. This Court is certainly not in a position to gainsay such belief by the Michigan legislature. If it is entertainable, as we think it is, Michigan has not violated its duty to afford equal protection of its laws. We cannot cross-examine either actually or argumentatively the mind of Michigan legislators nor question their motives. Since the line they have drawn is not without a basis in reason, we cannot give ear to the suggestion that the real impulse behind this legislation was

an unchivalrous desire of male bartenders to try to monopolize the calling.

It would be an idle parade of familiar learning to review the multitudinous cases in which the constitutional assurance of the equal protection of the laws has been applied. The generalities on this subject are not in dispute; their application turns peculiarly on the particular circumstances of a case . . . Suffice it to say that "A statute is not invalid under the Constitution because it might have gone farther than it did, or because it may not succeed in bringing about the result that it tends to produce."

Nor is it unconstitutional for Michigan to withdraw from women the occupation of bartending because it allows women to serve as waitresses where liquor is dispensed. The District Court has sufficiently indicated the reasons that may have influenced the legislature in allowing women to be waitresses in a liquor establishment over which a man's ownership provides control. Nothing need be added to what was said below as to the other grounds on which the Michigan law was assailed.

Judgment Affirmed.

Mr. Justice RUTLEDGE, with whom Mr. Justice DOUGLAS and Mr. Justice MURPHY join, dissenting.

While the equal protection clause does not require a legislature to achieve "abstract symmetry" or to classify with "mathematical nicety," that clause does require lawmakers to refrain from invidious distinctions of the sort drawn by the statute challenged in this case.

The statute arbitrarily discriminates between male and female owners of liquor establishments. A male owner, although he himself is always absent from his bar, may employ his wife and daughter as barmaids. A female owner may neither work as a barmaid herself nor employ her daughter in that position, even if a man is always present in the establishment to keep order. This inevitable result of the classification belies the assumption that the statute was motivated by a legislative solicitude for the moral and physical well-being of women who, but for the law, would be employed as barmaids. Since there could be no other conceivable justification for such discrimination against women owners of liquor establishments, the statute should be held invalid as a denial of equal protection.

STUDY QUESTIONS

1. To what "moral and social problems" was the Court referring? Who pays the cost of reducing the incidence of those problems? Did the Michigan statute "punish the victims"?

2. The Court refused even to consider that the statute was motivated by the desire to establish a male monopoly over the trade of bartending. Does that interpretation of the statutory objective seem more plausible than the one the Court adopted? Why did the Court refuse to even consider the alternative interpretation?

The dominant theme running through justifications given for differential treatment of women and men during the first half of the twentieth century was that of protection. Women were denied employment opportunities because they were believed to be too vulnerable to handle themselves safely and their "maternal function" was seen as too important to the survival of the species to leave such matters to individual choice. The foregoing cases illustrate that theme. A secondary justifying theme was that of compensation. Women were relieved of certain burdens of citizenship in order to compensate for or offset the heavier burdens they carry because of their "maternal functions." Though the cases attempted to justify the unequal treatment of women as protectionist, the unintended, or *at least unspoken,* intent and affect was the unequal ability women had to compete in the workplace due to the restrictions placed on them. The "monopoly" that the Court in *Goesaert v. Cleary* refused to acknowledge was, in fact, perpetrated by these restrictions.

The first decision to explicitly rely on the compensatory rationale came in 1937 in a case challenging a Georgia statute that exempted women from the payment of a poll tax. This type of tax, made unconstitutional by the Twenty-fourth Amendment that was ratified in 1964, was a device that served to deter poor people from voting. In upholding the statute, the Court declared that states may discriminate in favor of women by granting them special considerations that they deserve because of the special burdens associated with their reproductive role.

> The tax being upon persons, women may be exempted on the basis of special considerations to which they are naturally entitled. In view of burdens necessarily borne by them for the preservation of the race, the state reasonably may exempt them from poll taxes. The laws of Georgia declare the husband to be the head of the family and the wife to be subject to him. To subject her to the levy would be to add to his burden.
> *Breedlove v. Suttles, 302 U.S. 277, 282 (1937).*

The outcome in *Breedlove* does not seem, at first glance at least, to be lamentable. Who wouldn't welcome being excused from having to pay a tax? However in *Breedlove,* as in *Minor,* the Court permitted a state to exclude women from one of the responsibilities of full citizenship. In the one case, the responsibility was paying a tax; in the other, voting. In this way, both decisions affirmed that women are second-class citizens. Seen in this light, *Breedlove* takes on a considerably more sinister coloration.

That interpretation is further bolstered when we notice the way that the Court, in *Breedlove,* saw the tax exemption as linked to the doctrine of coverture. According to that doctrine, the husband, as head of the family, is responsible in the eyes of the law for the obligations of the wife. By excusing women from this burden, the Court consciously acted to protect the doctrine of coverture. The decision that appeared to be a welcome courtesy to women in acknowledgment of their special needs turns out to be, on more thorough consideration, both one more nail in the coffin of second-class citizenship and part of the price that is paid for perpetuating the very system that creates the special needs that in turn warrant the special considerations.

Two decisions handed down during the 1960s, one by the Supreme Court, the other by a federal district court, illustrate both how attractive these special considerations can seem and how insidious they turn out to be. Both relate to excusing women from other burdens of full citizenship.

An area where "special considerations" greatly diluted a women's ability to full citizenship was in the area of jury duty. The right of a person charged in a criminal proceeding to a trial by an impartial jury is a cornerstone of American jurisprudence. Indeed, that right is guaranteed by the Sixth Amendment to the U.S. Constitution. Corresponding to that right is the duty of citizens to be available to serve on juries. Until the enactment of the Civil Rights Act of 1957, the inclusion or exclusion of women on federal juries depended upon whether they were eligible for jury service under the law of the state where the federal court sat. That act made women eligible for federal jury service even though ineligible under state law. States, however, were still permitted to exempt women from jury service. The following case, overturned in effect by *Taylor v. Louisiana*, 419 U.S. 522(1975), and *Duren v. Missouri*, 439 U.S. 357(1979), shows the rationale for this exemption.

HOYT V. FLORIDA
Supreme Court of the United States, 1961.
368 U.S. 57, 82 S. Ct. 159, 7 L.Ed.2d 118.

Mr. Justice HARLAN delivered the opinion of the Court.

Appellant, a woman, has been convicted in Hillsborough County, Florida, of second degree murder of her husband. On this appeal . . . from the Florida Supreme Court's affirmance of the judgment of conviction we noted probable jurisdiction to consider appellant's claim that her trial before an all-male jury violated rights assured by the Fourteenth Amendment. The claim is that such jury was the product of a state jury statute which works an unconstitutional exclusion of women from jury service.

The jury law primarily in question is Fla Stat, 1959, § 40.01(1). This Act, which requires that grand and petit jurors be taken from "male and female" citizens of the State possessed of certain qualifications, contains the following proviso: "provided, however, that the name of no female person shall be taken for jury service unless said person has registered with the clerk of the circuit court her desire to be placed on the jury list."

Showing that since the enactment of the statute only a minimal number of women have so registered, appellant challenges the constitutionality of the statute both on its face and as applied in this case. For reasons now to follow we decide that both contentions must be rejected.

At the core of appellant's argument is the claim that the nature of the crime of which she was convicted peculiarly demanded the inclusion of persons of her own sex on the jury. She was charged with killing her husband by assaulting him with a baseball bat. An information was filed against her under Fla Stat, 1959, § 782.04, which punishes as murder in the second degree "any act imminently dangerous to another, and evincing a depraved mind regardless of human life, although without any premeditated design to effect the death of any particular individual. . . ." As described by the Florida Supreme Court, the affair occurred in the context of a marital upheaval involving, among other things, the suspected infidelity of appellant's husband, and culminating in the husband's final rejection of his wife's efforts at reconciliation. It is claimed, in substance, that women jurors would have been more understanding or compassionate than men in assessing the quality of appellant's act and her defense of "temporary insanity."

Of course, these premises misconceive the scope of the right to an impartially selected jury assured by the Fourteenth Amendment. That right does not entitle one accused of crime to a jury tailored to the circumstances of the particular case, whether relating to the sex or other condition of the defendant, or to the nature of the charges to be tried. It requires only that the jury be indiscriminately drawn from among those eligible in the community for jury service, untrammeled by any arbitrary and systematic exclusions. The result of this appeal must therefore depend on whether such an exclusion of women from jury service has been shown.

In the selection of jurors Florida has differentiated between men and women in two respects. It has given women an absolute exemption from jury duty based solely on their sex, no similar exemption obtaining as to men. And it has provided for its effectuation in a manner less onerous than that governing exemptions exercisable by men: women are not to be put on the jury list unless they have voluntarily registered for such service; men, on the other hand, even if entitled to an exemption, are to be included on the list unless they have filed a written claim of exemption as provided by law.

In neither respect can we conclude that Florida's statute is not "based on some reasonable classification," and that it is thus infected with unconstitutionality. Despite the enlightened emancipation of women from the restrictions and protections of bygone years, and their entry into many parts of community life formerly considered to be reserved to men, woman is still regarded as the center of home and family life. We cannot say that it is constitutionally impermissible for a State, acting in pursuit of the general welfare, to conclude that a woman should be relieved from the civic duty of jury service unless she herself determines that such service is consistent with her own special responsibilities.

Likewise we cannot say that Florida could not reasonably conclude that full effectuation of this exemption made it desirable to relieve women of the necessity of affirmatively claiming it, while at the same time requiring of men an assertion of the exemptions available to them. Moreover, from the standpoint of its own administrative concerns the State might well consider that it was "impractical to compel large numbers of women, who have an absolute exemption, to come to the clerk's office for examination since they so generally assert their exemption."

Appellant argues that whatever may have been the design of this Florida enactment, the statute in practical operation results in an exclusion of women from jury service, because women, like men, can be expected to be available for jury service only under compulsion. In this connection she points out that by 1957, when this trial took place, only some 220 women out of approximately 46,000 registered female voters in Hillsborough County—constituting about 40 per cent of the total voting population of that county— had volunteered for jury duty since the limitation of jury service to males. . . .

We cannot hold this statute as written offensive to the Fourteenth Amendment.

Affirmed.

STUDY QUESTIONS

1. What "special responsibilities" do women bear that men do not? Are these the result of differences in their physical makeup, their social roles, or their legal status? Do all women have these responsibilities?

2. If being permitted, unlike men, to decide when they will serve on juries is another type of "special consideration to which they are naturally entitled," to use the language of *Breedlove*, should Florida women have a complaint of unjust treatment if this statute were overturned? Does this type of special consideration set that complaint to rest or only insulate the sexual division of labor from effective criticism?

J.E.B. v. ALABAMA
511 U.S. 127, 114 S. Ct. 1419, 128 L.Ed.2d 89 (1994)

Justice BLACKMUN delivered the opinion of the Court.

Although premised on equal protection principles that apply equally to gender discrimination, all our recent cases defining the scope of *Batson* involved alleged racial discrimination in the exercise of peremptory challenges. Today we are faced with the question whether the Equal Protection Clause forbids intentional discrimination on the basis of gender, just as it prohibits discrimination on the basis of race. We hold that gender, like race, is an unconstitutional proxy for juror competence and impartiality.

On behalf of relator T.B., the mother of a minor child, respondent State of Alabama filed a complaint for paternity and child support against petitioner J.E.B. in the District Court of Jackson County, Alabama. On October 21, 1991, the matter was called for trial and jury selection began. The trial court assembled a panel of 36 potential jurors, 12 males and 24 females. After the court excused three jurors for cause, only 10 of the remaining 33 jurors were male. The State then used 9 of its 10 peremptory strikes to remove male jurors; petitioner used all but one of his strikes to remove female jurors. As a result, all the selected jurors were female.

Before the jury was empaneled, petitioner objected to the State's peremptory challenges on the ground that they were exercised against male jurors solely on the basis of gender, in violation of the Equal Protection Clause of the Fourteenth Amendment. Petitioner argued that the logic and reasoning of *Batson v. Kentucky*, which prohibits peremptory strikes solely on the basis of race, similarly forbids intentional discrimination on the basis of gender. The court rejected petitioner's claim and empaneled the all-female jury. The jury found petitioner to be the father of the child

and the court entered an order directing him to pay child support. On post-judgment motion, the court reaffirmed its ruling that *Batson* does not extend to gender-based peremptory challenges. The Alabama Court of Civil Appeals affirmed. The Supreme Court of Alabama denied certiorari.

We granted certiorari to resolve a question that has created a conflict of authority— whether the Equal Protection Clause forbids peremptory challenges on the basis of gender as well as on the basis of race. Today we reaffirm what, by now, should be axiomatic: Intentional discrimination on the basis of gender by state actors violates the Equal Protection Clause, particularly where, as here, the discrimination serves to ratify and perpetuate invidious, archaic, and overbroad stereotypes about the relative abilities of men and women.

. . . Despite the heightened scrutiny afforded distinctions based on gender, respondent argues that gender discrimination in the selection of the petit jury should be permitted, though discrimination on the basis of race is not. Respondent suggests that "gender discrimination in this country . . . has never reached the level of discrimination" against African-Americans, and therefore gender discrimination, unlike racial discrimination, is tolerable in the courtroom. . . .

We need not determine, however, whether women or racial minorities have suffered more at the hands of discriminatory state actors during the decades of our Nation's history. It is necessary only to acknowledge that "our Nation has had a long and unfortunate history of sex discrimination," a history which warrants the heightened scrutiny we afford all gender-based classifications today. Under our equal protection jurisprudence, gender-based classifications require "an exceedingly persuasive justification" in order to survive constitutional scrutiny. See *Personnel Administrator of Mass. v. Feeney,* and *Mississippi University for Women v. Hogan*. Thus, the only question is whether discrimination on the basis of gender in jury selection substantially furthers the State's legitimate interest in achieving a fair and impartial trial. In making this assessment, we do not weigh the value of peremptory challenges as an institution against our asserted commitment to eradicate invidious discrimination from the courtroom. Instead, we consider whether peremptory challenges based on gender stereotypes provide substantial aid to a litigant's effort to secure a fair and impartial jury.

Far from proffering an exceptionally persuasive justification for its gender based peremptory challenges, respondent maintains that its decision to strike virtually all the males from the jury in this case "may reasonably have been based upon the perception, supported by history, that men otherwise totally qualified to serve upon a jury might be more sympathetic and receptive to the arguments of a man alleged in a paternity action to be the father of an out-of-wedlock child, while women equally qualified to serve upon a jury might be more sympathetic and receptive to the arguments of the complaining witness who bore the child."

We shall not accept as a defense to gender-based peremptory challenges "the very stereotype the law condemns." Respondent's rationale, not unlike those regularly expressed for gender-based strikes, is reminiscent of the arguments advanced to justify the total exclusion of women from juries. Respondent offers virtually no support for the conclusion that gender alone is an accurate predictor of juror's attitudes; yet it urges this Court to condone the same stereotypes that justified the wholesale exclusion of women from juries and the ballot box. Respondent seems to assume that gross generalizations that would be deemed impermissible if made on the basis of race are somehow permissible when made on the basis of gender. . . .

Equal opportunity to participate in the fair administration of justice is fundamental to our democratic system. It not only furthers the goals of the jury system. It reaffirms the promise of equality under the law—that all citizens, regardless of race, ethnicity, or gender, have the chance to take part directly in our democracy. When persons are excluded from participation in our democratic processes solely because of race or gender, this promise of equality dims, and the integrity of our judicial system is jeopardized.

In view of these concerns, the Equal Protection Clause prohibits discrimination in jury selection on the basis of gender, or on the assumption that an individual will be biased in a particular case for no reason other than the fact that the person happens to be a woman or happens to be a man. As with race, the "core guarantee of equal protection, ensuring citizens that their State will not discriminate . . ., would be meaningless were we to approve the exclusion of jurors on the basis of such assumptions, which arise solely from the jurors' [gender]."

The judgment of the Court of Civil Appeals of Alabama is reversed and the case is remanded to that court for further proceedings not inconsistent with this opinion.

STUDY QUESTIONS

1. What was the basis of the Court's decision?
2. Can gender ever be a factor in peremptory challenges?
3. Compare and contrast the Court's reasoning in *J.E.B.* with its reasoning in *Hoyt*.
4. Did the Court go too far in *J.E.B.*? Who does eliminating certain people from jury duty harm?

IV. THE TURN OF THE TIDE

From the earliest times, the choices afforded to women in society have been severely restricted for no reason other than their gender. Though many theories have been expounded for why the laws were applied as they were, the result has been that during the past century, courts have approved statutes diminishing the status of women as citizens. Courts found that women did not have the right to vote in federal elections (*Minor*) or sit on a jury (*Hoyt*). Courts approved statutes restricting women's rights to full participation in employment by barring them entirely from certain occupations, such as the practice of law (*Bradwell*); limiting their access to certain other work (*Goesaert*); or imposing severe restrictions on the hours and times women could work (*Muller and Radice*). The result of these restrictions was that women were less desirable as employees and often forced to take on a second job and additional work in order to earn a sufficient salary. The only acceptable realm was that of the family and the home.

The basic principle used to justify permitting these sex-based laws was most clearly expressed by Justice Holmes in *Quong Wing v. Kirkendall*: ". . . The 14th Amendment does not interfere [with state legislation] by erecting a fictitious equality where there is a real difference" (223 U.S. 59, 63 (1912)). During the nineteenth and early twentieth centuries, courts regularly found a variety of "real differences" between the sexes sufficient to make sex-based laws constitutionally acceptable. These ranged from physical differences, especially those associated with "maternal functions" (*Muller* and *Radice*) to social differences, especially those stereotypes representing woman as the center of family life and maintaining her vulnerability to harassment by men (*Goesaert* and *Hoyt*), to legal differences, especially those deriving from the medieval doctrine of coverture (*Bradwell* and *Breedlove*). By stressing these differences, the courts were able to deny constitutional remedies for legally enforced sex discrimination.

The ideological bases for considering these differences "real" have varied over the past century. The separate spheres ideology of the nineteenth century portrayed men and women as having different natures and different responsibilities (*Bradwell*). The justification of sex-based laws in the twentieth century retains many of the elements of the separate spheres ideology, but the coloration has changed. Court decisions in this century tend to highlight two justifying themes: viz., protection of women from the burdens perceived as more than they can safely or conveniently manage (*Muller, Radice,* and *Goesaert*) and compensation that, for one of several reasons, they are thought to be owed (*Breedlove* and *Hoyt*). Until the early 1960s, these notions constituted the prevailing ideology of the country.

By the 1960s, key aspects of the legal status of women had changed. Women could own property, vote, and practice law. Yet, the vestiges of colonial thinking remained. The cult of domesticity and separate spheres ideology continued to shape the culture and the lives of women. Out of that colonial thinking emerged what is referred to as the second feminist movement. Not as single-minded as the early suffragettes, the feminist movement of the 1960s was multifaceted and involved many significant challenges.

Of particular note were the writings of Betty Friedan in her 1963 best-seller *The Feminine Mystique*. A central thesis of her book struck a responsive chord with thousands of white, educated, middle-class housewives. Friedan called it "The Problem That Has No Name."

> The problem lay buried, unspoken, for many years in the minds of American women. It was a strange stirring, a sense of dissatisfaction, a yearning that women suffered in the middle of the twentieth century in the United States. Each suburban wife struggled with it alone. As she made the beds, shopped for groceries, matched slipcover material, ate peanut butter sandwiches with her children, chauffeured Cub Scouts and Brownies, lay beside her husband at night—she was afraid to ask even of herself the silent question—"Is this all?"
>
> Betty Friedan, The Feminine Mystique. *New York: Norton & Co., 1963, p. 11.*

Middle-class women had long been taught—propagandized—to believe that achieving a certain status—that of a successful suburban housewife—would bring them all the satisfaction and happiness they needed in their lives. Friedan's words, "Is *this all?*," touched a chord of discontent that echoed back to the discontent of the Grimké sisters and early feminists: a discontent born of the knowledge that gender-based stratification deprived women of dignity as human beings.

Another important step forward occurred when Catharine East, senior staff aide to the various presidential commissions on the status of women between 1962 and 1967, persuaded Friedan to start an organization to lobby for the enforcement of the Civil Rights Act of 1964. When East arranged for Friedan to attend a 1966 conference of state commissions on the status of women, the National Organization for Women (NOW) was born. Within a few years, women and men by the thousands, sharing that perspective, joined NOW. The founding statement declared the purpose of NOW to be "to take action to bring women into full participation in the mainstream of American society now, exercising all the privileges and responsibilities thereof in truly equal partnership with men." In that statement, NOW acknowledged that "human rights are indivisible" and so pledged to work rather than compete with others who suffer discrimination. It rejected the tactics of both "pleas for special privilege [and] enmity toward men, who are also victims of the current, half-equality between the sexes," instead affirming the aspiration of an "active, self-respecting partnership with men." It pledged, finally, "to break through the silken curtains of prejudice and discrimination" that prevent women from taking full part in American life. With the dawning of the second feminist movement, hopes ran high that the mistakes of the first would not be repeated.

Complementing this relatively mainstream liberal effort was a more radical feminist movement. With roots in the Civil Rights Movement of the 1960s, this movement congealed in the late 1960s. Terming its goal as "genuine self-determination" and not merely formal equality, the movement sought to reach beyond equal opportunity and to achieve basic changes in personal consciousness and in the distribution of power. The movement's prime organizing tool was its militant campaign for the repeal of the criminal abortion laws, both through legislation and through litigation. Though short lived, the movement made lasting contributions, not the least of which was the term "sexist" and its insights into the interrelations between sex and the family.

Between the late 1950s and the early 1970s, all three branches of the federal government endorsed basic departures from the traditional patriarchal approach to sex-based laws. Congress was the first to break ranks with the passages of the Civil Rights Act of 1957, the Equal Pay Act of 1963, and Title VII of the Civil Rights Act of 1964. The first permitted women to serve on federal juries, the second required that all workers—women as well as men—be paid on an "equal pay for equal work" basis (see Chapter 4), and the third became the bulwark of the fight against sex discrimination in employment (see Chapters 3 and 4). Congress also enacted Title IX of the Educational Amendments Act of 1972 prohibiting sex discrimination in education (see Chapter 5), amended Title VII to include governmental employers, and passed the Equal Rights Amendment (see Chapter 2).

The executive branch was the next to follow. In 1967, President Lyndon Johnson amended Executive Order 11246, thereby requiring federal contractors to accept a contractual obligation to avoid sex discrimination in their employment practices and to undertake affirmative action to ensure equal employment opportunities for men and women. The Supreme Court broke new constitutional ground in 1971 when it unanimously struck down an Idaho statute that discriminated on the basis of sex (see Chapter 2).

Toward the end of the 1960s and the beginning of the 1970s, state supreme courts began to rethink the legal principles underlying the place of gender in the law. These courts pointed the way later followed by the U.S. Supreme Court. The Supreme Court of California, in an influential decision handed down in 1971, struck down a provision of that state's Business and Professional Code that prohibited the hiring of women as bartenders. The court found the provision to be in violation of the California Constitution and of the Equal Protection Clause of the Fourteenth Amendment to the federal constitution. When discussing the equal protection grounds for its decision, the court declared sex and race discrimination to be analogous and helped disseminate a central image of the second wave of feminism—the pedestal as cage.

> Laws which disable women from full participation in the political, business and economic arenas are often characterized as "protective" and beneficial. Those same laws applied to racial or ethnic minorities would readily be recognized as invidious and impermissible. The pedestal upon which women have been placed has all too often, upon closer inspection, been revealed as a cage.
> Sail'er Inn, Inc. v. Kirby, 485 P.2d 529, 541 (Supreme Court of California, 1971).

As we step over the threshold to the twenty-first century, the struggle for equality of women's rights continues. The 1980s and 1990s have brought a rapid change in many of the ideologies affecting life issues for women. Legislation addressing issues such as reproductive rights, violence against women, and equality in the workplace have taken giant steps toward resolving the issues of our early foremothers, but still fall short on many fronts. Organizations such as NOW continue to struggle with issues of equality both in the United States and abroad. A lack of equal rights for many international women may translate to death. Though the latter part of the twentieth century has brought change and growth, there is still an uphill road to travel. Patricia Ireland, president of NOW, said it best in her 1997 article "Women's Less Than Full Equality Under the U.S. Constitution."

> At a time when women are astronauts and truck drivers, it is hard to believe that the U.S. Constitution does not guarantee women the same rights as men. For most women, equality is a bread-and-butter issue. Women are still paid less on the job and charged more for everything from dry cleaning to insurance. The value of a woman's unpaid work in the home is often not taken into account in determining divorce settlements and pension benefits. When women turn to the courts to right these wrongs, they are at a distinct disadvantage because of what has and hasn't happened to the Constitution.

And in 2007 one of the women still dealing with these challenges is Lilly Ledbetter whose wage discrimination case will be discussed in later chapters of this book *Ledbetter v. Goodyear Tire & Rubber Co.*, 550 U.S. 618 (2007). On January 20, 2009, the United States elected Barack Obama the first African-American to serve as President of the United States. On January 29, 2009, President Obama signed into law the Lilly Ledbetter Fair Pay Act—legislation to fight pay discrimination and ensure fundamental fairness to American workers. This legislation is in response to a finding that the *Ledbetter* decision undermines the statutory protections contrary to the intent of Congress.

The next chapters of this book will examine the changes in the laws governing how women are treated in the workplace, and in the military, as equal members of society. It will also explore some of the emerging theories and challenges facing modern day feminists. As Betty Friedan first said, "Is this all?"

ON-LINE RESOURCES

Legacy '98 Detailed Timeline
www.legacy98.org/timeline.html

Women in the United States
www.census.gov/population/www/socdemo/pp1-121.html

Women's History on the Web
search.eb.com/women/ind womenweb.html

CHAPTER 2

CONSTITUTIONAL PROTECTION FOR EQUALITY

THE SEX OF INDIVIDUALS has determined their legal status since colonial times. The last chapter sketched the nature and justifications of gender constraints through the 1960s. Constitutional challenges decided during that period provide the immediate context for the recent changes in constitutional doctrine relating to sex-based laws discussed in this chapter.

Since 1971, the U.S. Supreme Court has reexamined and reconsidered the ideologies used to justify sex-based laws. This chapter reviews the key moments in that reconsideration. The Court continues to grapple with these vexing questions and has yet to develop a fully coherent constitutional doctrine for equal protection challenges to laws that treat people differently on the basis of their sex.

I. AN INTRODUCTION TO EQUAL PROTECTION ANALYSIS

The equal protection doctrine was developed primarily under the Fourteenth Amendment to the federal constitution. Similar analysis is now used when interpreting the Fifth Amendment and various state constitutional provisions. The Equal Protection Clause of the Fourteenth Amendment reads as follows: " . . . [N]or shall any state . . . deny to any person within its jurisdiction the equal protection of the laws."

That guarantee was part of a package of post–Civil War provisions designed to eliminate the badges of slavery and to ensure full rights for blacks. From 1868, when the Fourteenth Amendment was ratified, to 1954, when it was used in *Brown v. Board of Education*, 347 U.S. 483, to bar racial segregation in the public schools, equal protection analysis played a relatively modest role in Supreme Court decision making. Since the *Brown* decision, however, the doctrine has become extremely important. During the 1960s, a number of conceptual tools were developed by the Court under Chief Justice Earl Warren. Beginning in 1971, while Warren Burger was chief justice, these tools were applied in Supreme Court challenges to sex-based laws and government practices. This section reviews those key conceptual tools.

State Action and Formal Justice

Two general points are crucial to an understanding of equal protection guarantees. The first involves what is called *state action*. The Equal Protection Clause, like most provisions of the federal constitution, addresses government conduct. Private parties, be they individuals, groups, or corporations, cannot violate the Equal Protection Clause. Only governments can violate the command of that clause.

The state action requirement, however, has been construed rather broadly. It includes the actions of state, county, and local governments, as well as such state-operated entities as public schools and state universities. The federal government and its instrumentalities are also required to comply with the equal protection guarantee as a result of the Court's decision in *Bolling v. Sharpe*, 347 U.S. 497 (1954). That decision interprets the Due Process Clause of the Fifth Amendment to include the equal protection analysis developed under the Fourteenth Amendment. You will notice in this chapter that the equal protection challenges directed against the federal government are brought under the Due Process Clause of the Fifth Amendment. The first example of this is *Frontiero v. Richardson*.

The second general point is the meaning of *equality* under the Equal Protection Clause. The Equal Protection Clause does not require that people who are in fact different be treated in the same way by the law. What it actually requires is the subject of controversy among legal scholars. At times, the Court has appeared to be concerned with ensuring that people be placed in more equal positions. Since the early 1970s, a different and much less ambitious interpretation of the equal protection guarantee has been in evidence. The interpretation currently favored by the Court can be stated with deceptive simplicity by a term borrowed from the vocabulary of philosophy. It requires *formal justice* (i.e., that like cases be treated alike).

We noted that the definition of formal justice is deceptive in its simplicity. It is clear what the concept means, but it is not clear how to use it. If there were any cases that are exactly alike, we could easily arrange to treat them in identical ways. Since no two cases are ever exactly alike, equal protection analysis must be enriched beyond the mere definition of formal justice. Otherwise, the guarantee extended to citizens would be empty.

Statutory Objective and Statutory Classification

In everyday life, we tend to classify people and situations on the basis of similarities, even though each is unique. This is done by means of the criteria of relevance that enable us to decide which similarities are important or relevant for a given decision. Thus, agility is relevant when choosing members of a basketball team; race is not.

In law generally, and equal protection analysis in particular, the criterion of relevance used to identify similarly situated people is the aim or objective of the law in question. (For the sake of simplicity, such laws will be referred to as *statutes*. The same points apply, however, to ordinances, regulations, and government practices.) This is called the legislative or statutory objective of that law. A *statutory objective* can be defined as the result that courts understand the statute to be aimed at promoting. Of course, not every statutory objective is permitted under equal protection analysis (e.g., racially segregated schools).

Once the statutory objective is specified, the next steps are to identify the characteristics of people relevant to the advancement of that objective and to classify those possessing these characteristics. For the sake of clarity, the class of people and/or objects that possess *any* characteristic relevant to the advancement of the statutory objective can be called the *relevant population*.

Imagine that a town council wishes to improve pedestrian safety in the town's public park. Its first task is to identify factors that might pose a hazard for pedestrians in its park. If the council decides to act on that statutory objective, it must decide which hazards it will try to lessen and how to go about doing that. Suppose that it resolves to do so by means of an ordinance that provides for the imposition of a fine of fifteen dollars on anyone who operates a vehicle in the public park. In doing so, the council has used a statutory classification. A *statutory classification* may be defined as those characteristics used to identify people who will be treated alike under the statute. Here the statutory classification is "anyone who operates a vehicle in the public park," and the like treatment is the fine of fifteen dollars. Again, for the sake of clarity, call the class of people who possess the characteristics mentioned in the statutory classification the *targeted population*. Neither *relevant population* nor *targeted population* is a legal concept, but they will help clarify the legal concepts that follow.

The Rational Basis and Strict Scrutiny Standards

If the elegance of law were the same as the elegance of logic or mathematics, equal protection analysis would require no further development. In that case, all that would be needed to ensure compliance with the equal protection guarantee would be to see to it that for every governmental action, the targeted population is coextensive with the relevant population. The requirement does not seem, on the face of it, to be an especially difficult one to understand. The fact is, however, that it is not just a tall order; it's an impossible one! Scarce resources, such as funds, personnel, time, organization, reliable information, and political will, always prevent governments from tackling all dimensions of any problem. Like all of us, governments, too, must attack problems piecemeal.

The Equal Protection Clause does not require that our laws fully satisfy the requirements of formal justice. It does, however, require that they be approximated. During the last half of the twentieth century, the courts developed a set of standards that are used in deciding whether particular statutes approximate the requirements of formal justice well enough to satisfy the equal protection guarantee. By the early 1970s, the Supreme Court had developed two contrasting equal protection standards. These can be understood as lying along a continuum ranging from lenient to stern. At the lenient end is the rational basis standard that is used when reviewing the great majority of laws and regulations. At the stern end is the strict scrutiny standard that is used when the statute is suspected of being used as an instrument for discrimination against a traditionally disadvantaged group.

These standards differ in three ways. The rational basis standard (1) places the burden of proof on those who challenge a law to show that either (2) the statutory objective is not legitimate or (3) the statutory classification is not rationally related to the advancement of its objective. Suppose that someone were to challenge the ordinance in our park example on equal protection grounds. To prevail under the rational basis standard, she would need to show that either the town council lacks the authority to attempt improving pedestrian safety in the public park or the ban on vehicular traffic from the park has no reasonable chance of making the park safer for pedestrians. Until 1971, sex-based laws were reviewed under this lenient standard. As the cases discussed in Chapter 1 show, challengers seldom prevail when the courts invoke that equal protection standard.

When the courts believe that a law or government practice is being used invidiously to discriminate against traditionally disadvantaged groups, matters are quite different. Then the courts (1) place the burden of proof on the government to show that (2) the statutory objective is of compelling importance *and* (3) the use of the statutory classification is necessary to the advancement of that objective. For example, in *McLaughlin v. Florida*, 379 U.S. 184 (1964), the Supreme Court struck down laws that prohibited interracial cohabitation because these were seen as designed to maintain white supremacy. Although race is the clearest case of a suspect classification, the Court also regards national origin and alien status as suspect classifications

TABLE 2-1 Pre-1971 Equal Protection Standards

CONSTITUTIONAL STANDARD	BURDEN OF PROOF	OBJECTIVE MUST BE:	CLASSIFICATION MUST BE:
Rational Basis	Challenger	Legitimate	Rationally Related
Strict Scrutiny	Government	Compelling	Necessary

because these too involve a long history of unfair treatment. Ironically, the first case in which the Court declared that "legal restrictions which curtail the civil rights of a single racial group are immediately suspect" (*Korematsu v. U.S.*, 323 U.S. 214, 216 (1944)) was the infamous decision that approved the internment of Japanese-Americans living on the West Coast following Japan's attack on Pearl Harbor at the beginning of the United States' involvement in World War II. For practical purposes, however, the strict scrutiny standard is barely distinguishable from an absolute bar, so rarely do statutes survive review under this standard.

Table 2-1 summarizes the contrast between the two equal protection standards that had been developed prior to 1971.

II. A New Beginning

During the 1960s and the early 1970s, feminists argued that government-sanctioned discrimination against people on the basis of sex is analogous to race discrimination. Sex discrimination also relegates an entire group of people, viz., women, to an inferior status on the basis of a highly visible, immutable characteristic. For that reason, it, too, should be recognized as a suspect classification that requires strict judicial scrutiny.

In November 1971, for the first time in its history, the Supreme Court overturned a state statute on the grounds of sex discrimination. The statute was quite ordinary by mid-twentieth century standards. Under the Idaho law before the Court, men were to be preferred to equally qualified women as administrators of estates. The statutory objective undoubtedly had been based on familiar assumptions. One constitutional scholar speculated that two were involved: "wives are more likely than husbands to be dependent, and men are more apt than women to be more experienced in managing money" (Harry Wellington, *Interpreting the Constitution* (New Haven: Yale University Press 1990), p. 17). As we saw in Chapter 1, statutes such as these had been routinely approved without a second glance throughout the Court's history. On this day, however, a unanimous court asserted that the equal protection guarantee requires that sex-based laws meet a somewhat more demanding standard. In doing so, the Court signaled the beginning of a new judicial era. Governmental bodies can no longer confidently assume that sex-based laws will be routinely approved by the courts. The case that set the courts on this new heading, however, raised more questions than it answered.

REED V. REED

Supreme Court of the United States, 1971.
404 U.S. 71, 92 S.Ct. 251, 30 L.Ed.2d 225.

Mr. Chief Justice BURGER delivered the opinion of the Court.

Richard Lynn Reed, a minor, died intestate in Ada County, Idaho, on March 29, 1967.

His adoptive parents, who had separated sometime prior to his death, are the parties to this appeal. Approximately seven months after Richard's death, his mother, appellant

Sally Reed, filed a petition in the Probate Court of Ada County, seeking appointment as administratrix of her son's estate. Prior to the date set for a hearing on the mother's petition, appellee Cecil Reed, the father of the decedent, filed a competing petition seeking to have himself appointed administrator of the son's estate. The probate court held a joint hearing on the two petitions and thereafter ordered that letters of administration be issued to appellee Cecil Reed upon his taking the oath and filing the bond required by law. The court treated §§ 15–312 and 15–314 of the Idaho Code as the controlling statutes and read those sections as compelling a preference for Cecil Reed because he was a male.

Section 15–312 designates the persons who are entitled to administer the estate of one who dies intestate. In making these designations, that section lists 11 classes of persons who are so entitled and provides, in substance, that the order in which those classes are listed in the section shall be determinative of the relative rights of competing applicants for letters of administration. One of the 11 classes so enumerated is "[t]he father or mother" of the person dying intestate. Under this section, then, appellant and appellee, being members of the same entitlement class, would seem to have been equally entitled to administer their son's estate. Section 15–314 provides, however, that "[o]f several persons claiming and equally entitled [under § 15–312] to administer, males must be preferred to females, and relatives of the whole to those of the half blood."

In issuing its order, the probate court implicitly recognized the equality of entitlement of the two applicants under § 15–312 and noted that neither of the applicants was under any legal disability; the court ruled, however, that appellee, being a male, was to be preferred to the female appellant "by reason of Section 15–314 of the Idaho Code." In stating this conclusion, the probate judge gave no indication that he had attempted to determine the relative capabilities of the competing applicants to perform the functions incident to the administration of an estate.

It seems clear the probate judge considered himself bound by statute to give preference to the male candidate over the female, each being otherwise "equally entitled."

Sally Reed appealed from the probate court order, and her appeal was treated by the District Court of the Fourth Judicial District of Idaho as a constitutional attack on § 15–314. In dealing with the attack, that court held that the challenged section violated the Equal Protection Clause of the Fourteenth Amendment and was, therefore, void; the matter was ordered "returned to the Probate Court for its determination of which of the two parties" was better qualified to administer the estate.

This order was never carried out, however, for Cecil Reed took a further appeal to the Idaho Supreme Court, which reversed the District Court and reinstated the original order naming the father administrator of the estate. In reaching this result, the Idaho Supreme Court first dealt with the governing statutory law and held that under § 15–312 "a father and mother are 'equally entitled' to letters of administration," but the preference given to males by § 15–314 is "mandatory" and leaves no room for the exercise of a probate court's discretion in the appointment of administrators. . . .

Sally Reed thereupon appealed for review by this Court. . . . Idaho does not, of course, deny letters of administration to women altogether. . . . Section 15–314 is restricted in its operation to those situations where competing applications for letters of administration have been filed by both male and female members of the same entitlement class established by § 15–312. In such situations, § 15–314 provides that different treatment be accorded to the applicants on the basis of their sex; it thus establishes a classification subject to scrutiny under the Equal Protection Clause.

In applying that clause, this Court has consistently recognized that the Fourteenth Amendment does not deny to States the power to treat different classes of persons in different ways. The Equal Protection Clause of that amendment does, however, deny to

States the power to legislate that different treatment be accorded to persons placed by a statute into different classes on the basis of criteria wholly unrelated to the objective of that statute. A classification "must be reasonable, not arbitrary, and must rest upon some ground of difference having a fair and substantial relation to the object of the legislation, so that all persons similarly circumstanced shall be treated alike." *Royster Guano Co. v. Virginia*, 253 U.S. 412, 415 (1920). The question presented by this case, then, is whether a difference in the sex of competing applicants for letters of administration bears a rational relationship to a state objective that is sought to be advanced by the operation of §§ 15–312 and 15–314.

In upholding the latter section, the Idaho Supreme Court concluded that its objective was to eliminate one area of controversy when two or more persons, equally entitled under § 15–312, seek letters of administration and thereby present the probate court "with the issue of which one should be named." The court also concluded that where such persons are not of the same sex, the elimination of females from consideration "is neither an illogical nor arbitrary method devised by the legislature to resolve an issue that would otherwise require a hearing as to the relative merits . . . of the two or more petitioning relatives. . . ."

Clearly the objective of reducing the workload on probate courts by eliminating one class of contests is not without some legitimacy. The crucial question, however, is whether § 15–314 advances that objective in a manner consistent with the command

of the Equal Protection Clause. We hold that it does not. To give a mandatory preference to members of either sex over members of the other, merely to accomplish the elimination of hearings on the merits, is to make the very kind of arbitrary legislative choice forbidden by the Equal Protection Clause of the Fourteenth Amendment; and whatever may be said as to the positive values of avoiding intrafamily controversy, the choice in this context may not lawfully be mandated solely on the basis of sex.

The judgment of the Idaho Supreme Court is reversed and the case remanded for further proceedings not inconsistent with this opinion.

Reversed and Remanded.

STUDY QUESTIONS

1. What was the statutory classification here? The statutory objective? The relevant population? The targeted population?
2. The Court spoke of the need to show that sex bears a "rational relationship" to the objective of the legislation. Did the Court actually employ the rational basis test here? What language in the opinion sets forth the test the Court used? Who had the burden of proof?
3. Might an opposite decision have been justified by reference to protective and compensatory themes in much the same way as had been done, for example, in *Goesaert* and *Hoyt*? Does this case indicate that the Court no longer sees these as valid justifications of differential treatment?

Although *Reed* was not the legal equivalent of the "shot heard 'round the world," it did get the attention of the government community. Prior to that decision, governments drafting statutes and regulations regularly relied upon such stereotyped beliefs as "girls are poor at mathematics," "men think with their heads, women with their hearts," and "women are baffled by financial matters." After *Reed*, they could no longer be confident that this casual reliance on such stereotypes would survive judicial scrutiny.

The decision in *Reed* is clearer than the reasons supporting it. When the Court announced that sex is a classification "subject to scrutiny under the Equal Protection Clause," it meant subject to *special* scrutiny. The standard of review used here was clearly not the rational basis standard. Although the Court acknowledged that the statutory objective was legitimate and that the sex-based classification did advance that objective, it nevertheless declared that the arrangement violated the Equal Protection Clause.

If sex-based classifications were not to be reviewed under the rational basis standard, what standard would be used? The only alternative identified at the time was the strict scrutiny standard used in race, alienage, and national origin cases. Did *Reed* signal that sex is a suspect classification and, like race, triggers strict judicial scrutiny? Feminists had argued since the mid-1960s that sex and race discrimination are analogous. The Court's response came two years later in *Frontiero v. Richardson*.

The Court's answer was that it does not. The justices were badly split in this case. Four voted to recognize sex as a suspect classification, requiring strict judicial scrutiny, and to overturn the statute. These were justices Brennan, Douglas, Marshall, and White. Four also voted to overturn the statute but not to recognize sex as a suspect classification. These were Chief Justice Burger and Justices Stewart, Powell, and Blackmun. Justice Rehnquist, who had joined the Court in January 1972, replacing Justice Harlan, and who had not taken part in the *Reed* decision, voted to uphold the statute. Thus, although the statute was invalidated by a vote of 8–1, only the Brennan minority endorsed the use of strict scrutiny for sex-based laws. Had one more justice joined the Brennan opinion, thereby making it a majority rather than a plurality opinion, the views announced in it would have had precedential value, binding on the Court in future decisions.

FRONTIERO V. RICHARDSON

Supreme Court of the United States, 1973.
411 U.S. 677, 39 S.Ct. 1764, 36 L.Ed.2d 583.

Mr. Justice BRENNAN announced the judgment of the Court and an opinion in which Mr. Justice DOUGLAS, Mr. Justice WHITE, and Mr. Justice MARSHALL join.

The question before us concerns the right of a female member of the uniformed services to claim her spouse as a "dependent" for the purposes of obtaining increased quarters allowances and medical and dental benefits . . . on an equal footing with male members. Under these statutes, a serviceman may claim his wife as a "dependent" without regard to whether she is in fact dependent upon him for any part of her support. A servicewoman, on the other hand, may not claim her husband as a "dependent" under these programs unless he is in fact dependent upon her for over one-half of his support. Thus, the question for decision is whether this difference in treatment constitutes an unconstitutional discrimination against servicewomen in violation of the Due Process Clause of the Fifth Amendment. A three-judge District Court for the Middle District of Alabama, one judge dissenting, rejected this contention and sustained the constitutionality of the provisions of the statutes making this distinction. . . .

In an effort to attract career personnel through re-enlistment, Congress established . . . a scheme for the provision of fringe benefits to members of the uniformed services on a competitive basis with business and industry. Thus, . . . a member of the uniformed services with dependents is entitled to an increased "basic allowance for quarters" and . . . a member's dependents are provided comprehensive medical and dental care.

Appellant Sharon Frontiero, a lieutenant in the United States Air Force, sought increased quarters allowances, and housing and medical benefits for her husband, appellant Joseph Frontiero, on the ground that he was her "dependent." Although such benefits would automatically have been granted with respect to the wife of a male member of the uniformed services, appellant's application was denied because she failed to demonstrate that her husband was dependent on her for more than one-half of his support.[4] Appellants then commenced this suit, contending that, by making this distinction, the statutes unreasonably discriminate on the basis of sex in violation of the Due Process Clause of the Fifth Amendment. In essence, appellants asserted that the discriminatory impact of the statutes is twofold: first, as a procedural matter, a female member is required to demonstrate her spouse's dependency, while no such burden is imposed upon male members; and, second, as a substantive matter, a male member who does not provide more than one-half of his wife's support receives benefits, while a similarly situated female member is denied such benefits. Appellants therefore sought a permanent injunction against the continued enforcement of these statutes and an order directing the appellees to provide Lieutenant Frontiero with the same housing and medical benefits that a similarly situated male member would receive.

Although the legislative history of these statutes sheds virtually no light on the purposes underlying the differential treatment accorded male and female members, a majority of the three-judge District Court surmised that Congress might reasonably have concluded that, since the husband in our society is generally the "breadwinner" in the family—and the wife typically the "dependent" partner—"it would be more economical to require married female members claiming husbands to prove actual dependency than to extend the presumption of dependency to such members." Indeed, given the fact that approximately 99% of all members of the uniformed services are male,

the District Court speculated that such differential treatment might conceivably lead to a "considerable saving of administrative expense and manpower."

At the outset, appellants contend that classifications based upon sex, like classifications based upon race, alienage, and national origin, are inherently suspect and must therefore be subjected to close judicial scrutiny. We agree and, indeed, find at least implicit support for such an approach in our unanimous decision only last Term in *Reed v. Reed.* . . .

There can be no doubt that our Nation has had a long and unfortunate history of sex discrimination. Traditionally, such discrimination was rationalized by an attitude of "romantic paternalism" which, in practical effect, put women, not on a pedestal, but in a cage. . . .

As a result of notions such as these, our statute books gradually became laden with gross, stereotyped distinctions between the sexes and, indeed, throughout much of the 19th century the position of women in our society was, in many respects, comparable to that of blacks under the pre-Civil War slave codes. Neither slaves nor women could hold office, serve on juries, or bring suit in their own names, and married women traditionally were denied the legal capacity to hold or convey property or to serve as legal guardians of their own children.

It is true, of course, that the position of women in America has improved markedly in recent decades. Nevertheless, it can hardly be doubted that, in part because of the high visibility of the sex characteristic, women still face pervasive, although at times more subtle, discrimination in our educational institutions, in the job market and, perhaps most conspicuously, in the political arena. . . .

Moreover, since sex, like race and national origin, is an immutable characteristic determined solely by the accident of birth,

[4]Appellant Joseph Frontiero is a full-time student at Huntingdon College in Montgomery, Alabama. According to the agreed stipulation of facts, his living expenses, including his share of the household expenses, total approximately $354 per month. Since he receives $205 per month in veterans' benefits, it is clear that he is not dependent upon appellant Sharon Frontiero for more than one-half of his support.

the imposition of special disabilities upon the members of a particular sex because of their sex would seem to violate "the basic concept of our system that legal burdens should bear some relationship to individual responsibility. . . ." And what differentiates sex from such nonsuspect statutes as intelligence or physical disability, and aligns it with the recognized suspect criteria, is that the sex characteristic frequently bears no relation to ability to perform or contribute to society. As a result, statutory distinctions between the sexes often have the effect of invidiously relegating the entire class of females to inferior legal status without regard to the actual capabilities of its individual members.

We might also note that, over the past decade, Congress has itself manifested an increasing sensitivity to sex-based classifications. In Title VII of the Civil Rights Act of 1964, for example, Congress expressly declared that no employer, labor union, or other organization subject to the provisions of the Act shall discriminate against any individual on the basis of "race, color, religion, *sex*, or national origin." Similarly, the Equal Pay Act of 1963 provides that no employer covered by the Act "shall discriminate . . . between employees on the basis of *sex*." And § 1 of the Equal Rights Amendment, passed by Congress on March 22, 1972, and submitted to the legislatures of the States for ratification, declares that "[e]quality of rights under the law shall not be denied or abridged by the United States or by any State on account of sex." Thus, Congress itself has concluded that classifications based upon sex are inherently invidious, and this conclusion of a coequal branch of Government is not without significance to the question presently under consideration.

With these considerations in mind, we can only conclude that classifications based upon sex, like classifications based upon race, alienage, or national origin, are inherently suspect, and must therefore be subjected to strict judicial scrutiny. Applying the analysis mandated by that stricter standard of review, it is clear that the statutory scheme now before us is constitutionally invalid.

The sole basis of the classification established in the challenged statutes is the sex of the individuals involved. . . .

Moreover, the Government concedes that the differential treatment accorded men and women under these statutes serves no purpose other than mere "administrative convenience." In essence, the Government maintains that, as an empirical matter, wives in our society frequently are dependent upon their husbands, while husbands rarely are dependent upon their wives. Thus, the Government argues that Congress might reasonably have concluded that it would be both cheaper and easier simply conclusively to presume that wives of male members are financially dependent upon their husbands, while burdening female members with the task of establishing dependency in fact. . . .

We therefore conclude that, by according differential treatment to male and female members of the uniformed services for the sole purpose of achieving administrative convenience, the challenged statutes violate the Due Process Clause of the Fifth Amendment insofar as they require a female member to prove the dependency of her husband.

Reversed.

Mr. Justice STEWART concurs in the judgment, agreeing that the statutes before us work an invidious discrimination in violation of the Constitution. *Reed v. Reed.*

Mr. Justice POWELL, with whom The Chief Justice and Mr. Justice BLACKMUN join, concurring in the judgment.

I agree that the challenged statutes constitute an unconstitutional discrimination against servicewomen in violation of the Due Process Clause of the Fifth Amendment, but I cannot join the opinion of Mr. Justice Brennan, which would hold that all classifications based upon sex, "like classifications based upon race, alienage, and national origin," are "inherently suspect and must therefore be subjected to close judicial scrutiny." It is unnecessary for the Court in this case to characterize sex as a suspect classification, with all of the far-reaching implications of such a holding. *Reed v. Reed,* which abundantly supports our decision today, did not add sex to the narrowly limited group of classifications which are inherently suspect. In my view, we can and should decide this case on the authority of *Reed* and reserve for the future any expansion of its rationale.

There is another, and I find compelling, reason for deferring a general categorizing of sex classifications as invoking the strictest test of judicial scrutiny. The Equal Rights Amendment, which if adopted will resolve the substance of this precise question, has been approved by the Congress and submitted for ratification by the States. If this Amendment is duly adopted, it will represent the will of the people accomplished in the manner prescribed by the Constitution. By acting prematurely and unnecessarily, as I view it, the Court has assumed a decisional responsibility at the very time when state legislatures, functioning within the traditional democratic process, are debating the proposed Amendment. It seems to me that this reaching out to pre-empt by judicial action a major political decision which is currently in process of resolution does not reflect appropriate respect for duly prescribed legislative processes.

There are times when this Court, under our system, cannot avoid a constitutional decision on issues which normally should be resolved by the elected representatives of the people. But democratic institutions are weakened, and confidence in the restraint of the Court is impaired, when we appear unnecessarily to decide sensitive issues of broad social and political importance at the very time they are under consideration within the prescribed constitutional processes.

Mr. Justice Rehnquist Dissents for the Reasons Stated by Judge Rives in his Opinion for the District Court, Frontiero v. Laird, *341 F Supp 201 (1972).*

STUDY QUESTIONS

1. What two burdens did the statute place upon women but not on men? What reasons did the Congress have for introducing this differential treatment into this statute?
2. The plurality opinion preferred a strict scrutiny standard of review for all sex-based statutes, at least those understood to hurt women. It saw an analogy between sex and race discrimination. Do you think that is a fair reading of the experiences of racial minorities and majority women? What about minority women? Are there important differences as well as similarities? What consequences should follow from those differences?
3. Were Justices Stewart and Powell right to believe that the standard adopted in *Reed* was sufficient to resolve this case?

Several aspects of the concurring opinions take on special significance as a result of subsequent developments. By declining to join Justice Brennan's opinion, Justices Powell and Blackmun and Chief Justice Burger made clear that they preferred to allow the shift to strict judicial scrutiny for sex-based classifications to come about with the ratification of the federal Equal Rights Amendment (ERA), which in 1973 seemed inevitable. How these justices would have voted had the ERA not been on the horizon, of course, is complete speculation.

Justice Rehnquist was appointed chief justice on September 17, 1986, replacing the retiring Chief Justice Burger. As a result, his views on all areas of the law are especially important. His dissent in *Frontiero* is the first intimation from the bench of his reluctance to acknowledge the law's role in perpetuating and eliminating sex discrimination. This dissent is difficult to interpret with certainty. In it, he endorsed the arguments of the lower court judge. Judge Rives had upheld the statute because the statutory scheme, as he saw it, was not based on sex but on the relationship between servicepeople and their dependents. As it did not discriminate invidiously against women in any event, he applied the rational basis standard and found for the government. By endorsing this line of reasoning, Justice Rehnquist hinted that he would not be prepared to submit a sex-based law to more than minimum scrutiny unless it was shown to be motivated by prejudice—unless it was invidious.

From *Reed* we learned that the standard of equal protection review applicable to gender classifications is not the rational basis standard. From *Frontiero* we learned that it is not the strict scrutiny standard either. Presumably the standard for sex-based classifications is somewhere in between these. Two questions remained open after *Frontiero*: What is the standard of review for laws that classify on the basis of sex, and why does the Court consider that standard more appropriate than either of the others?

III. SETTING THE STANDARD

In 1976, the Court finished fashioning a formula that captures the "intermediate" standard that it is prepared to use when reviewing laws it sees as sex based. As has so often been the case, the Court was considering complaints by men that sex discrimination had violated their equal protection rights. When reading this opinion, be careful not to overlook the significance of the standard used in deciding the validity of this relatively trivial statute.

CRAIG V. BOREN
Supreme Court of the United States, 1976.
429 U.S. 190, 97 S.Ct. 451, 50 L.Ed.2d 397.

Mr. Justice BRENNAN delivered the opinion of the Court.

The interaction of two sections of an Oklahoma statute Okla. Stat., Tit. 37, §§ 241 and 245 (1958 and Supp. 1976), prohibits the sale of "nonintoxicating" 3.2% beer to males under the age of 21 and to females under the age of 18. The question to be decided is whether such a gender-based differential constitutes a denial to males 18–20 years of age of the equal protection of the laws in violation of the Fourteenth Amendment. . . .

Before 1972, Oklahoma defined the commencement of civil majority at age 18 for females and age 21 for males. In contrast, females were held criminally responsible as adults at age 18 and males at age 16. After the Court of Appeals for the Tenth Circuit held in 1972, on the authority of *Reed v. Reed*, that the age distinction was unconstitutional for purposes of establishing criminal responsibility as adults, the Oklahoma Legislature fixed age 18 as applicable to both males and females. In 1972, 18 also was established as the age of majority for males and females in civil matters, except that §§ 241 and 245 of the 3.2% beer statute were simultaneously codified to create an exception to the gender-free rule.

Analysis may appropriately begin with the reminder that *Reed* emphasized that statutory classifications that distinguish between males and females are "subject to scrutiny under the Equal Protection Clause." To withstand constitutional challenge, previous cases establish that classifications by gender must serve important governmental objectives and must be substantially related to achievement of those objectives. . . .

We turn then to the question whether, under *Reed*, the difference between males and females with respect to the purchase of 3.2% beer warrants the differential in age drawn by the Oklahoma statute. We conclude that it does not. . . .

We accept for purposes of discussion the District Court's identification of the objective underlying §§ 241 and 245 as the enhancement of traffic safety. Clearly, the protection of public health and safety represents an important function of state and local governments. However, appellees' statistics in our view cannot support the conclusion that the gender-based distinction closely serves to achieve that objective and therefore the distinction cannot under *Reed* withstand equal protection challenge.

The appellees introduced a variety of statistical surveys. First, an analysis of arrest statistics for 1973 demonstrated that 18–20-year-old male arrests for "driving under the influence" and "drunkenness" substantially exceeded female arrests for that same age period. Similarly, youths aged 17–21 were found to be overrepresented among those killed or injured in traffic accidents, with males again numerically exceeding females in this regard. Third, a random roadside survey in Oklahoma City revealed that young males were more inclined to drive and drink beer than were their female counterparts. Fourth, Federal Bureau of Investigation nationwide statistics exhibited a notable increase in arrests for "driving under the influence." Finally, statistical evidence gathered in other jurisdictions, particularly Minnesota and Michigan, was offered to corroborate Oklahoma's experience by indicating the pervasiveness of youthful participation in motor vehicle accidents following the imbibing of alcohol. Conceding that "the case is not free from doubt," the District Court nonetheless concluded that this statistical showing substantiated "a rational basis for the legislative judgment underlying the challenged classification."

Even were this statistical evidence accepted as accurate, it nevertheless offers only a weak answer to the equal protection question presented here. The most focused and relevant of the statistical surveys, arrests of 18–20-year-olds for alcohol-related driving offenses, exemplifies the ultimate unpersuasiveness of this evidentiary record. Viewed in terms of the correlation between sex and the actual activity that Oklahoma seeks to regulate—driving while under the influence of alcohol—the statistics broadly establish that .18% of females and 2% of males in that age group were arrested for that offense. While such a disparity is not trivial in a statistical sense, it hardly can form the basis for employment of a gender line as a classifying device. Certainly if maleness is to serve as a proxy for drinking and driving, a correlation of 2% must be considered an unduly tenuous "fit.". . .

We conclude that the gender-based differential contained in Okla. Stat., Tit. 37, § 245 (1976 Supp.) constitutes a denial of the equal protection of the laws to males aged 18–20[23] and reverse the judgment of the District Court.

It Is So Ordered.

STUDY QUESTIONS

1. Why do you suppose the Oklahoma legislature kept this exception to the uniform rule of eighteen years as the age of majority? Could traditional stereotypes of women have played a role?
2. What is the standard of review announced here? Which of its two prongs did the Oklahoma statute fail to meet?
3. Compare the "Craig standard" with the rational basis and strict scrutiny standards. What is the difference between a legitimate, an important, and a compelling government interest? Between a rational, a substantial, and a necessary relationship? How do these standards differ in terms of burden of proof? What is it that triggers the use of each of these standards?

[23]Insofar as *Goesaert v. Cleary*, 335 U.S. 464 (1948), may be inconsistent, that decision is disapproved . . .

TABLE 2-2   Comparison of Equal Protection Standards

CONSTITUTIONAL STANDARD	BURDEN OF PROOF	OBJECTIVE MUST BE:	CLASSIFICATION MUST BE:
Rational Basis	Challenger	Legitimate	Rationally Related
Intermediate	Government	Important	Substantially Related
Strict Scrutiny	Government	Compelling	Necessary

The decision in *Craig* is the closest the Court has yet come to agreeing upon a formula for the standard used to review sex-based laws. In order to prevail under the intermediate standard announced here, the government has the burden to prove that the use of sex as a classifying tool is substantially related to the advancement of an important government objective. The element that is added by *Craig* to the standard sketched first in *Reed* is that the statutory objective must be an important one. Table 2-2 shows the ways in which this standard compares with the lenient and strict standards developed in previous years.

In formulating the intermediate standard more precisely than it had in previous decisions, the Court appeared to suggest that it had achieved firm agreement on its approach to sex-based laws. That appearance was reinforced by the following decision, which, in applying the intermediate standard, added to it in two ways. On the one hand, the Court in *Orr* required that the government show that a less discriminatory alternative is unavailable when it seeks to use sex-based laws. This is the import of "carefully tailored," a phrase that recurs in more recent decisions. On the other, it further diminished the prospects for the compensatory exception to the intermediate standard. Movement in that direction was signaled a few years earlier when, in *Weinberger v. Wiesenfeld,* 420 U.S. 636, 648 (1975), the Court indicated, in a departure from its previous practice, that "the mere recitation of a benign, compensatory purpose is not an automatic shield which protects against any inquiry into the actual purposes underlying a statutory scheme."

ORR V. ORR

Supreme Court of the United States, 1979.
440 U.S. 268, 99 S.Ct. 1102, 59 L.Ed.2d 306.

Mr. Justice BRENNAN delivered the opinion of the Court.

The question presented is the constitutionality of Alabama alimony statutes which provide that husbands, but not wives, may be required to pay alimony upon divorce.

On February 26, 1974, a final decree of divorce was entered, dissolving the marriage of William and Lillian Orr. That decree directed appellant, Mr. Orr, to pay appellee, Mrs. Orr, $1,240 per month in alimony. On July 28, 1976, Mrs. Orr initiated a contempt proceeding in the Circuit Court of Lee County, Ala., alleging that Mr. Orr was in arrears in his alimony payments. On August 19, 1976, at the hearing on Mrs. Orr's petition, Mr. Orr submitted in his defense a motion requesting that Alabama's alimony statutes be declared unconstitutional because they authorize courts to place an obligation of alimony upon husbands but never upon wives. The Circuit Court denied Mr. Orr's motion and entered judgment against him for $5,524; covering back alimony and attorney fees. Relying solely upon his federal constitutional claim,

Mr. Orr appealed the judgment. On March 16, 1977, the Court of Civil Appeals of Alabama sustained the constitutionality of the Alabama statutes. . . .

In authorizing the imposition of alimony obligations on husbands, but not on wives, the Alabama statutory scheme "provides that different treatment be accorded . . . on the basis of . . . sex; it thus establishes a classification subject to scrutiny under the Equal Protection Clause," *Reed v. Reed*. The fact that the classification expressly discriminates against men rather than women does not protect it from scrutiny. *Craig v. Boren*. "To withstand scrutiny" under the equal protection clause, "classifications by gender must serve important governmental objectives and must be substantially related to achievement of those objectives." We shall, therefore, examine the three governmental objectives that might arguably be served by Alabama's statutory scheme.

Appellant views the Alabama alimony statutes as effectively announcing the State's preference for an allocation of family responsibilities under which the wife plays a dependent role, and as seeking for their objective the reinforcement of that model among the State's citizens. We agree, as he urges, that prior cases settle that this purpose cannot sustain the statutes. *Stanton v. Stanton;* 421 U.S. 7 (1975). . . . If the statute is to survive constitutional attack, therefore, it must be validated on some other basis.

The opinion of the Alabama Court of Civil Appeals suggests other purposes that the statute may serve. Its opinion states that the Alabama statutes were "designed" for "the wife of a broken marriage who needs financial assistance." This may be read as asserting either of two legislative objectives. One is a legislative purpose to provide help for needy spouses, using sex as a proxy for need. The other is a goal of compensating women for past discrimination during marriage, which assertedly has left them unprepared to fend for themselves in the working world following divorce. We concede, of course, that assisting needy spouses is a legitimate and important governmental objective.

We have also recognized "[r]eduction of the disparity in economic condition between men and women caused by the long history of discrimination against women . . . as . . . an important governmental objective." It only remains, therefore, to determine whether the classification at issue here is "substantially related to achievement of those objectives."

Ordinarily, we would begin the analysis of the "needy spouse" objective by considering whether sex is a sufficiently "accurate proxy" for dependency to establish that the gender classification rests "upon some ground of difference having a fair and substantial relation to the object of the legislation."

Similarly, we would initially approach the "compensation" rationale by asking whether women had in fact been significantly discriminated against in the sphere to which the statute applied a sex-based classification, leaving the sexes "*not* similarly situated with respect to opportunities" in that sphere. . . .

But in this case, even if sex were a reliable proxy for need, and even if the institution of marriage did discriminate against women, these factors still would "not adequately justify the salient features of" Alabama's statutory scheme. Under the statute, individualized hearings at which the parties' relative financial circumstances are considered *already* occur. There is no reason, therefore, to use sex as a proxy for need. Needy males could be helped along with needy females with little if any additional burden on the State. In such circumstances, not even an administrative convenience rationale exists to justify operating by generalization or proxy. Similarly, since individualized hearings can determine which women were in fact discriminated against vis à vis their husbands, as well as which family units defied the stereotype and left the husband dependent on the wife, Alabama's alleged compensatory purpose may be effectuated without placing burdens solely on husbands. Progress toward fulfilling such a purpose would not be hampered, and it would cost the State nothing more, if it were to treat men and women equally by making alimony burdens independent of sex. "Thus, the gender-based distinction is gratuitous; without it the statutory scheme would only provide benefits to those men who are in fact similarly situated to the women the statute aids," *Wiesenfeld,* and the effort to help those women would not in any way be compromised. . . .

Legislative classifications which distribute benefits and burdens on the basis of gender carry the inherent risk of reinforcing stereotypes about the "proper place" of women and their need for special protection. Thus, even statutes purportedly designed to compensate for and ameliorate the effects of past discrimination must be carefully tailored. Where, as here, the State's compensatory and ameliorative purposes are as well served by a gender-neutral classification as

one that gender-classifies and therefore carries with it the baggage of sexual stereotypes, the State cannot be permitted to classify on the basis of sex. . . .

Reversed.

STUDY QUESTIONS

1. Identify the three possible governmental objectives served by Alabama's statutory scheme. What reasons did the Court give for rejecting each of these?
2. The Court announced that sex-based statutes, even those aimed at compensating women for past discrimination, must be "carefully tailored." What does that expression mean? Why was a "carefully tailored" sex-based alimony statute unnecessary here?

In many ways, *Orr* was an easy case. Like *Craig,* it dealt with an outmoded stereotype. It was easy enough to impose a more demanding standard of review where the stereotype was outmoded and to demand careful tailoring where alternative means of identifying who is needy and who deserves compensation were readily at hand. The Court later faced cases in which the stereotypes were not outmoded and the use of sex-based classifications appeared to be the most efficient means at hand.

Two close decisions in 1979 showed that the Court was still grappling with the concept of sex discrimination. Both dealt with the rights of unmarried fathers. Together, they reveal the difficulty the Court experiences in distinguishing between impermissible sex-role stereotypes and sex differences regarded as legitimate.

These cases presented more difficult problems than had *Craig* and *Orr* because they involved illegitimacy. The Court had been solicitous for some time to relieve children of the legal consequences of the stigma of illegitimacy. The Court had also been solicitous about the legal consequences of the stigma that attaches to fathers of out-of-wedlock children. In *Stanley v. Illinois,* 405 U.S. 645 (1972), the Court struck down, on Due Process grounds, a state statute that presumed such fathers to be unfit for custody of their children.

One of the two 1979 cases, *Caban v. Mohammed,* 441 U.S. 380, involved a New York law that permitted the adoption of out-of-wedlock children without their father's consent, although it required their mother's consent. The statute was invalidated in a 5–4 decision on equal protection grounds. As Justice Powell wrote for the majority:

. . . § 111 is another example of "overbroad generalizations" in gender-based classifications. The effect of New York's classification is to discriminate against unwed fathers even when their identity is known and they have manifested a significant paternal interest in the child. The facts of this case illustrate the harshness of classifying unwed fathers as being invariably less qualified and entitled than mothers to exercise a concerned judgment as to the fate of their children. Section 111 both excludes some loving fathers from full participation in the decision whether their children will be adopted and, at the same time, enables some alienated mothers arbitrarily to cut off the paternal rights of fathers. We conclude that this undifferentiated distinction between unwed mothers and unwed fathers, applicable in all circumstances where adoption of a child of theirs is at issue, does not bear a substantial relationship to the State's asserted interests. . . .

Justice Stewart's dissenting opinion, however, demonstrated a greater willingness to regard men and women as situated differently. Here, those differences derived mainly from role expectations then current in the culture.

> . . . Gender, like race, is a highly visible and immutable characteristic that has historically been the touchstone for pervasive but often subtle discrimination. Although the analogy to race is not perfect and the constitutional inquiry therefore somewhat different, gender-based statutory classifications deserve careful constitutional examination because they may reflect or operate to perpetuate mythical or stereotyped assumptions about the proper roles and the relative capabilities of men and women that are unrelated to any inherent differences between the sexes. Sex-based classifications are in many settings invidious because they relegate a person to the place set aside for the group on the basis of an attribute that the person cannot change. Such laws cannot be defended, as can the bulk of the classifications that fill the statute books, simply on the ground that the generalizations they reflect may be true of the majority of members of the class, for a gender-based classification need not ring false to work a discrimination that in the individual case might be invidious. Nonetheless, gender-based classifications are not invariably invalid. When men and women are not in fact similarly situated in the area covered by the legislation in question, the Equal Protection Clause is not violated.
>
> In my view, the gender-based distinction drawn by New York falls in this latter category. With respect to a large group of adoptions—those of newborn children and infants—unwed mothers and unwed fathers are simply not similarly situated. . . . Our law has given the unwed mother the custody of her illegitimate children precisely because it is she who bears the child and because the vast majority of unwed fathers have been unknown, unavailable, or simply uninterested. This custodial preference has carried with it a correlative power in the mother to place her child for adoption or not to do so.

In the second case, *Parham v. Hughes,* 441 U.S. 347 (1979), which also dealt with the rights of unmarried fathers as regards their children, the Court leaned in the other direction. In a 5–4 decision, with Justice Powell concurring in the judgment, the Court approved a Georgia statute that permitted mothers but not fathers of unlegitimated children to sue for the wrongful death of their children.

Stanley and *Craig* showed that the Court applies a more demanding standard of review to sex-based laws when it sees them as based on outmoded stereotypes. These decisions consolidate and develop the themes that first appeared in *Reed* and *Frontiero*. *Caban* and *Parham* show that the Court still finds merit in an approach followed in *Geduldig v. Aiello,* 417 U.S. 484 (1974); where the differences between the sexes are not rooted in myth and outmoded stereotype, a less demanding standard of review is used. There is, however, one important difference between the approach taken in *Geduldig* and the one in *Parham*. In the former, the difference was physical—only women can become pregnant; in the latter, the difference was legal—in Georgia, only fathers can legitimate a child born out-of-wedlock.

The Supreme Court has more recently held that gender-based statutory classifications differentiating between the status of mothers and fathers of out-of-wedlock children will withstand equal protection scrutiny if the classification serves important governmental objectives and the discriminatory means employed are substantially related to the achievement of those objectives. See *Nguyen v. Immigration and Naturalization Service,* 533 U.S. 53 (2001) (Title 8 U.S.C. §1409, which governs the citizenship of out-of-wedlock children born outside the United States to only one U.S. citizen parent, and provides that the citizen mother's child is automatically a U.S. citizen if the mother lived in the United States for at least one year at any time during her lifetime but imposes other requirements on the child of a citizen father—before the child's eighteenth birthday, the child must have been legitimated under the law of his residence, or the father must acknowledge paternity under oath, or paternity must be established by a court, and the father must agree to provide financial support for the child until age eighteen—met the intermediate scrutiny standard applied to sex-based classifications.)

Standing alone, *Parham* might have signaled either a deterioration in the Court's willingness to eliminate restrictions for both men and women or a willingness to accept the burdens imposed on fathers of illegitimate children in limited situations. Another decision that same year, however, lent more credence to the deterioration theory. It addressed a new question of far-reaching importance.

Most of the statutes and government programs challenged in the cases from *Reed* through *Craig* employed sex as an explicit statutory classification. These openly imposed special burdens upon or granted special privileges to people because of their sex. There is no difficulty in discerning that such statutes discriminate on the basis of sex. However, statutes can have the same effect even though they do not expressly use sex as a statutory classification. Suppose that 90 percent of women and only 10 percent of men are less than 5'6" tall. If a statute were to impose a special burden (e.g., a tax) on anyone under 5'6" tall, the weight of that burden would be felt disproportionately by women. Such statutes are said to be neutral on their face, even though they have a disparate impact on women. Do such statutes discriminate on the basis of sex? Should the equal protection guarantee permit such laws?

In 1971, the Court ruled in *Griggs v. Duke Power Co.*, 401 U.S. 424 (see Chapter 3), a landmark decision under the Civil Rights Act of 1964, facially neutral practices that have a disparate impact on African Americans do violate that statute, even though they do not flow from discriminatory intentions. Five years later, in *Washington v. Davis*, 426 U.S. 229 (1976), the Court ruled that a similar practice did not violate the equal protection guarantee. The practice challenged in *Davis*, like that challenged in *Griggs*, did not explicitly classify people on the basis of race, but did disproportionately exclude African Americans from jobs. Writing for the Court in *Davis*, Justice White announced that the equal protection guarantee, unlike the civil rights statute, is violated only if ". . . the invidious quality of the law . . . [is] ultimately traced to a . . . discriminatory purpose." That same rationale was followed and further developed in a later decision that addressed a challenge to a facially neutral state statute that disproportionately disadvantaged women.

Personnel Adm'r of Mass. v. Feeney

Supreme Court of the United States, 1979.
442 U.S. 256, 99 S.Ct. 2282, 60 L.Ed.2d 870.

Mr. Justice STEWART delivered the opinion of the Court.

This case presents a challenge to the constitutionality of the Massachusetts Veterans Preference Statute on the ground that it discriminates against women in violation of the Equal Protection Clause of the Fourteenth Amendment. Under ch. 31, § 23, all veterans who qualify for state civil service positions must be considered for appointment ahead of any qualifying nonveterans. The preference operates overwhelmingly to the advantage of males.

The appellee Helen B. Feeney is not a veteran. She brought this action pursuant to 42 U. S. C. § 1983 alleging that the absolute preference formula established in ch. 31, § 23 inevitably operates to exclude women from consideration for the best Massachusetts civil service jobs and thus unconstitutionally denies them the equal protection of the laws. The three-judge District Court agreed, one judge dissenting. . . .

The veterans' hiring preference in Massachusetts, as in other jurisdictions, has traditionally been justified as a measure designed to reward veterans for the sacrifice of military service, to ease the transition from military to civilian life, to encourage patriotic service, and to attract loyal and well disciplined people to civil service occupations. . . .

At the outset of this litigation the State conceded that for "many of the permanent positions for which males and females have competed" the veterans' preference has "resulted in a substantially greater proportion of female eligibles than male eligibles" not being certified for consideration. The impact of the veterans' preference law upon the public employment opportunities of women has thus been severe. This impact lies at the heart of the appellee's federal constitutional claim.

The sole question for decision on this appeal is whether Massachusetts, in granting an absolute lifetime preference to veterans, has discriminated against women in violation of the Equal Protection Clause of the Fourteenth Amendment. . . . [The Court next reviewed its decision in *Davis*.]

The dispositive question, then, is whether the appellee has shown that a gender-based discriminatory purpose has, at least in some measure, shaped the Massachusetts veterans' preference legislation. As did the District Court, she points to two basic factors which in her view distinguish ch. 31, § 23 from the neutral rules at issue in the *Washington v. Davis*. . . . The first is the nature of the preference, which is said to be demonstrably gender-biased in the sense that it favors a status reserved under federal military policy primarily to men. The second concerns the impact of the absolute lifetime preference upon the employment opportunities of women, an impact claimed to be

too inevitable to have been unintended. The appellee contends that these factors, coupled with the fact that the preference itself has little if any relevance to actual job performance, more than suffice to prove the discriminatory intent required to establish a constitutional violation. . . .

. . . The District Court's conclusion that the absolute veterans' preference was not originally enacted or subsequently reaffirmed for the purpose of giving an advantage to males as such necessarily compels the conclusion that the State intended nothing more than to prefer "veterans." Given this finding, simple logic suggests that an intent to exclude women from significant public jobs was not at work in this law. To reason that it was, by describing the preference as "inherently non-neutral" or "gender-biased," is merely to restate the fact of impact, not to answer the question of intent. . . .

The appellee's ultimate argument rests upon the presumption, common to the criminal and civil law, that a person intends the natural and foreseeable consequences of his voluntary actions. . . .

. . . The decision to grant a preference to veterans was of course "intentional." So, necessarily, did an adverse impact upon nonveterans follow from that decision. And it cannot seriously be argued that the legislature of Massachusetts could have been unaware that most veterans are men. It would thus be disingenuous to say that the adverse consequences of this legislation for women were unintended, in the sense that they were not volitional or in the sense that they were not foreseeable.

"Discriminatory purpose," however, implies more than intent as volition or intent as awareness of consequences. It implies that the decisionmaker, in this case a state legislature, selected or reaffirmed a particular course of action at least in part "because of," not merely "in spite of," its adverse effects upon an identifiable group. Yet nothing in the record demonstrates that this preference for veterans was originally devised or subsequently re-enacted because it would accomplish the collateral goal of keeping women in a stereotypic and predefined place in the Massachusetts Civil Service. . . .

. . . The substantial edge granted to veterans by ch. 31, § 23 may reflect unwise policy. The appellee, however, has simply failed to demonstrate that the law in any way reflects a purpose to discriminate on the basis of sex.

The judgment is reversed, and the case is remanded for further proceedings consistent with this opinion.

STUDY QUESTIONS

1. Did the Court give any weight to the fact that few women are veterans because of government restrictions on the number of women allowed in the armed forces?
2. What language did the Court use to explain what it meant by "discriminatory intent"? What sort of evidence would a challenger need to present in order to show intent in that sense? Is it enough that the consequences are foreseeable?
3. Given that legislatures seldom act single-mindedly, is it, as a practical matter, possible to mount a successful equal protection challenge to a statute on grounds of disparate impact?

The decision in *Feeney* applied the approach of *Washington v. Davis* to laws that, in fact, treat women and men differently. Unless a facially neutral statute that imposes a disproportionate disadvantage on members of one sex or race can be shown to have been adopted intentionally, it will be reviewed under the rational basis standard. One of the considerations that led the Court to adopt this restrictive approach to equal protection challenges of laws that are facially neutral but have disparate impact was expressed in *Davis* and other cases. The Court clearly was concerned about the enormous number and variety of laws that would be affected if a broader approach were taken. Sales taxes, for example, arguably impose a disproportionate burden on minorities and women because they are disproportionately poorer than whites and men.

Just as *Washington v. Davis* was a sore disappointment to those interested in promoting justice between the races, so, too, was *Feeney* a sore disappointment to those interested in promoting justice between the sexes. The equal protection guarantee can be used as a basis for challenging facially neutral laws that have a disparate impact on women or minorities only if discriminatory purpose as defined in *Feeney* can be proven. Such proof may be particularly difficult in the case of sex discrimination, where many laws and government practices are what Justice Stevens has called "the accidental by-product of a traditional way of thinking about females." Attitudes and predispositions rooted in such cultural stereotypes can be expressed both in overtly sex-based laws and in laws that are facially neutral but have a disparate impact on women. The latter, however, require only a minimal standard of equal protection review.

In retrospect, it appears that from *Reed* through *Craig*, sex-based classifications were generally reviewed under an intermediate standard. Two exceptions to this general practice were signaled in decisions handed down in the early 1970s. The first, invoked in *Kahn v. Shevin*, 416 U.S. 351 (1974) and *Schlesinger v. Ballard*, 419 U.S. 498 (1975), permits sex-based laws represented by a state as designed to compensate women for past and present discrimination to be reviewed under the rational relation standard. The second, followed in *Geduldig*, permits the use of the rational basis standard if the Court regards the classification to be based on real differences between the sexes. The differences regarded as real in *Geduldig* were physical. The decision in *Parham* expanded the second type of exception by including differences in the legal status of men and women within the category of "real differences."

By the end of the 1970s, the Court substantially narrowed the first type of exception. In *Kahn* and *Ballard*, the Court accepted without serious questioning the claim of the governments that the challenged statutes were designed to compensate women for discrimination and applied the rational relation standard of review. In *Orr*, the Court announced that even where it is satisfied that the purpose of the state was compensatory, a heightened standard of review must be applied. Following the decision in *Orr*, the viability of the compensatory rationale as an independent mode of analysis came into serious doubt. The decision in *Parham* suggested, however, that although the compensatory rationale was in jeopardy, the types of situations previously covered by it might be justified by the real difference exception. The decision expanded that exception to include differences in the legal status of men and women. While the utility of the compensatory exception appeared to be declining in the late 1970s, that of the real difference exception was secure.

IV. REFINING THE MODEL

By the time of the *Feeney* decision, the Court seemed to have consolidated the approach it would take toward laws that classify people on the basis of their sex. That approach involves a number of steps. The first question to be addressed when considering a challenge under the Equal Protection Clause, of course, is state action. If the state action requirement is satisfied, the next question is whether the classification is neutral on its face as regards sex. If it is, then the statute is reviewed under the rational basis standard, unless it is shown to have been adopted for the purpose of disadvantaging people on the basis of their sex. If the latter is shown or if the statute explicitly uses a sex-based classification, then it is reviewed under the intermediate standard formulated in *Craig*, and the state is required to show that the statute is carefully tailored to advance an important government interest. This model has one main exception. It does not apply where the Court perceives what it believes to be "real differences" between the sexes. In such situations, the rational basis standard is applied.

While the approach represented by this decision model went a long way toward systematizing the thinking of the Court on equal protection challenges to sex-based laws, it had yet to be applied to some of the most severely taxing questions. In 1981, two decisions addressing such questions were handed down. Both were authored by Justice Rehnquist, who had long opposed the use of any but the minimal standard of review for most laws that classify people on the basis of their sex. Both expand the real differences exception, relate to stereotypes that are not outmoded, and pose the question of whether men as well as women have equal protection rights against sex discrimination by governmental bodies.

MICHAEL M. V. SUPER. CT. OF SONOMA CTY.
Supreme Court of the United States, 1981.
450 U.S. 464, 101 S.Ct. 1200, 67 L.Ed.2d 437.

Justice REHNQUIST announced the judgment of the Court and delivered an opinion in which The Chief Justice, Justice STEWART, and Justice POWELL joined.

The question presented in this case is whether California's "statutory rape" law, § 261.5 of the California Penal Code, violates the Equal Protection Clause of the Fourteenth Amendment. Section 261.5 defines unlawful sexual intercourse as "an act of sexual intercourse accomplished with a female not the wife of the perpetrator, where the female is under the age of 18 years." The statute thus makes men alone criminally liable for the act of sexual intercourse.

In July 1978, a complaint was filed in the Municipal Court of Sonoma County, Cal., alleging that petitioner, then a 17½ year old male, had had unlawful sexual intercourse with a female under the age of 18, in violation of § 261.5. The evidence adduced at a preliminary hearing showed that at approximately midnight on June 3, 1978, petitioner and two friends approached Sharon, a 16½ year old female, and her sister as they waited at a bus stop. Petitioner and Sharon, who had already been drinking, moved away from the others and began to kiss. After being struck in the face for rebuffing petitioner's initial advances, Sharon submitted to sexual intercourse with petitioner. Prior to trial, petitioner sought to set aside the information on both state and federal constitutional grounds, asserting that § 261.5 unlawfully discriminated on the basis of gender. The trial court and the California Court of Appeal denied petitioner's request for relief and petitioner sought review in the Supreme Court of California.

The Supreme Court held that "Section 261.5 discriminates on the basis of sex because only females may be victims, and only males may violate the section." The court then subjected the classification to "strict scrutiny," stating that it must be justified by a compelling state interest. It found that the classification was "supported not by mere social convention but by the immutable physiological fact that it is the female exclusively who can become pregnant." Canvassing "the tragic human cost of illegitimate teenage pregnancies," including the large number of teenage abortions, the increased medical risk associated with teenage pregnancies, and the social consequences of teenage child bearing, the court concluded that the state has a compelling interest in preventing such pregnancies. Because males alone can "physiologically cause the result which the law properly seeks to avoid" the court further held that the gender classification was

readily justified as a means of identifying offender and victim. . . .

. . . Unlike the California Supreme Court, we have not held that gender-based classifications are "inherently suspect" and thus we do not apply so-called "strict scrutiny" to those classifications. Our cases have held, however, that the traditional minimum rationality test takes on a somewhat "sharper focus" when gender-based classifications are challenged.

In *Reed v. Reed*, for example, the Court stated that a gender-based classification will be upheld if it bears a "fair and substantial relationship" to legitimate state ends, while in *Craig v. Boren*, the Court restated the test to require the classification to bear a "substantial relationship" to "important governmental objectives."

Underlying these decisions is the principle that a legislature may not "make overbroad generalizations based on sex which are entirely unrelated to any differences between men and women or which demean the ability or social status of the affected class." *Parham v. Hughes*. But because the Equal Protection Clause does not "demand that a statute necessarily apply equally to all persons" or require "things which are different in fact . . . to be treated in law as though they were the same," this Court has consistently upheld statutes where the gender classification is not invidious, but rather realistically reflects the fact that the sexes are not similarly situated in certain circumstances. As the Court has stated, a legislature may "provide for the special problems of women." *Weinberger v. Wiesenfeld*.

Applying those principles to this case, the fact that the California Legislature criminalized the act of illicit sexual intercourse with a minor female is a sure indication of its intent or purpose to discourage that conduct. . . .

The justification for the statute offered by the State, and accepted by the Supreme Court of California, is that the legislature sought to prevent illegitimate teenage pregnancies. That finding, of course, is entitled to great deference. . . .

We are satisfied not only that the prevention of illegitimate pregnancy is at least one of the "purposes" of the statute, but that the State has a strong interest in preventing such pregnancy. At the risk of stating the obvious, teenage pregnancies, which have increased dramatically over the last two decades, have significant social, medical and economic consequences for both the mother and her child, and the State. Of particular concern to the State is that approximately half of all teenage pregnancies end in abortion. And of those children who are born, their illegitimacy makes them likely candidates to become wards of the State.

We need not be medical doctors to discern that young men and young women are not similarly situated with respect to the problems and the risks of sexual intercourse. Only women may become pregnant and they suffer disproportionately the profound physical, emotional, and psychological consequences of sexual activity. The statute at issue here protects women from sexual intercourse at an age when those consequences are particularly severe.

The question thus boils down to whether a State may attack the problem of sexual intercourse and teenage pregnancy directly by prohibiting a male from having sexual intercourse with a minor female. We hold that such a statute is sufficiently related to the State's objectives to pass constitutional muster.

Because virtually all of the significant harmful and inescapably identifiable consequences of teenage pregnancy fall on the young female, a legislature acts well within its authority when it elects to punish only the participant who, by nature, suffers few of the consequences of his conduct. It is hardly unreasonable for a legislature acting to protect minor females to exclude them from punishment. Moreover, the risk of pregnancy itself constitutes a substantial deterrence to young females. No similar natural sanctions deter males. A criminal sanction imposed solely on males thus serves to roughly "equalize" the deterrents on the sexes.

We are unable to accept petitioner's contention that the statute is impermissibly underinclusive and must, in order to pass judicial scrutiny, be *broadened* so as to hold the female as criminally liable as the male. It is argued that this statute is not *necessary* to deter teenage pregnancy because a gender-neutral statute, where both male and female would be subject to prosecution, would serve that goal equally well. The relevant inquiry, however, is not whether the statute is drawn as precisely as it might have been, but whether the line chosen by the California Legislature is within constitutional limitations.

In any event, we cannot say that a gender-neutral statute would be as effective as the statute California has chosen to enact. The State persuasively contends that a gender-neutral statute would frustrate its interest in effective enforcement. Its view is that a female is surely less likely to report violations of the statute if she herself would be subject to criminal prosecution. In an area already fraught with prosecutorial difficulties, we decline to hold that the Equal Protection Clause requires a legislature to enact a statute so broad that it may well be incapable of enforcement.

We similarly reject petitioner's argument that § 261.5 is impermissibly overbroad because it makes unlawful sexual intercourse with prepubescent females, who are, by definition, incapable of becoming pregnant. Quite apart from the fact that the statute could well be justified on the grounds that very young females are particularly susceptible to physical injury from sexual intercourse, it is ludicrous to suggest that the Constitution requires the California Legislature to limit the scope of its rape statute to older teenagers and exclude young girls.

There remains only petitioner's contention that the statute is unconstitutional as it is applied to him because he, like Sharon; was under 18 at the time of sexual intercourse. Petitioner argues that the statute is flawed because it presumes that as between two persons under 18, the male is the culpable aggressor. We find petitioner's contentions unpersuasive. Contrary to his assertions, the statute does not rest on the assumption that males are generally the aggressors. It is instead an attempt by a legislature to prevent illegitimate teenage pregnancy by providing an additional deterrent for men. The age of the man is irrelevant since young men are as capable as older men of inflicting the harm sought to be prevented. . . .

Accordingly, the judgment of the California Supreme Court is affirmed.

Affirmed.

Justice BRENNAN, with whom Justices WHITE and MARSHALL join, dissenting.

It is disturbing to find the Court so splintered on a case that presents such a straightforward issue: whether the admittedly gender-based classification in Cal. Penal Code § 261.5 bears a sufficient relationship to the State's asserted goal of preventing teenage pregnancies to survive the "mid-level" constitutional scrutiny mandated by *Craig v. Boren.* Applying the analytical framework provided by our precedents, I am convinced that there is only one proper resolution of this issue: the classification must be declared unconstitutional. I fear that the plurality and Justices Stewart and Blackmun reach the opposite result by placing too much emphasis on the desirability of achieving the State's asserted statutory goal—prevention of teenage pregnancy— and not enough emphasis on the fundamental question of whether the sex-based discrimination in the California statute is *substantially* related to the achievement of that goal. . . .

The plurality assumes that a gender-neutral statute would be less effective than § 261.5 in deterring sexual activity because a gender-neutral statute would create significant enforcement problems. The plurality thus accepts the State's assertion that

> "a female is surely less likely to report violations of the statute if she herself would be subject to criminal prosecution. In an area already fraught with prosecutorial difficulties, we decline to hold that the Equal

Protection Clause requires a legislature to enact a statute so broad that it may well be incapable of enforcement."

However, a State's bare assertion that its gender-based statutory classification substantially furthers an important governmental interest is not enough to meet its burden of proof under *Craig v. Boren.* Rather, the State must produce evidence that will persuade the Court that its assertion is true.

The State has not produced such evidence in this case. Moreover, there are at least two serious flaws in the State's assertion that law enforcement problems created by a gender-neutral statutory rape law would make such a statute less effective than a gender-based statute in deterring sexual activity.

First, the experience of other jurisdictions, and California itself, belies the plurality's conclusion that a gender-neutral statutory rape law "may well be incapable of enforcement." There are now at least 37 States that have enacted gender-neutral statutory rape laws. Although most of these laws protect young persons (of either sex) from the sexual exploitation of older individuals, the laws of Arizona, Florida, and Illinois permit prosecution of both minor females and minor males for engaging in mutual sexual conduct. California has introduced no evidence that those states have been handicapped by the enforcement problems the plurality finds so persuasive. Surely, if those States could provide such evidence, we might expect that California would have introduced it.

In addition, the California Legislature in recent years has revised other sections of the Penal Code to make them gender-neutral. For example, Cal. Penal Code §§ 286 (b)(1) and 288a (b)(1), prohibiting sodomy and oral copulation with a "person who is under 18 years of age," could cause two minor homosexuals to be subjected to criminal sanctions for engaging in mutually consensual conduct. Again, the State has introduced no evidence to explain why a gender-neutral statutory rape law would be any more difficult to enforce than those statutes.

The second flaw in the State's assertion is that even assuming that a gender-neutral statute would be more difficult to enforce, the State has still not shown that those enforcement problems would make such a statute less effective than a gender-based statute in deterring minor females from engaging in sexual intercourse. Common sense, however, suggests that a gender-neutral statutory rape law is potentially a *greater* deterrent of sexual activity than a gender-based law, for the simple reason that a gender-neutral law subjects both men and women to criminal sanctions and thus arguably has a deterrent effect on twice as many potential violators. Even if fewer persons were prosecuted under the gender-neutral law, as the State suggests, it would still be true that twice as many persons would be *subject* to arrest. The State's failure to prove that a gender-neutral law would be a less effective deterrent than a gender-based law, like the State's failure to prove that a gender-neutral law would be difficult to enforce, should have led this Court to invalidate § 261.5.

Until very recently, no California court or commentator had suggested that the purpose of California's statutory rape law was to protect young women from the risk of pregnancy. Indeed, the historical development of § 261.5 demonstrates that the law was initially enacted on the premise that young women, in contrast to young men, were to be deemed legally incapable of consenting to an act of sexual intercourse. Because their chastity was considered particularly precious, those young women were felt to be uniquely in need of the State's protection. In contrast, young men were assumed to be capable of making such decisions for themselves; the law therefore did not offer them any special protection.

It is perhaps because the gender classification in California's statutory rape law was initially designed to further these outmoded sexual stereotypes, rather than to reduce the incidence of teenage pregnancies, that the State has been unable to demonstrate a substantial relationship between the classification and its newly asserted goal. But whatever the reason, the State has not shown that Cal. Penal Code § 261.5 is any more effective than a gender-neutral law would be in deterring minor females from engaging in sexual intercourse. It has therefore not met its burden of proving that the statutory classification is substantially related to the achievement of its asserted goal.

I would hold that § 261.5 violates the Equal Protection Clause of the Fourteenth Amendment and I would reverse the judgment of the California Supreme Court.

Study Questions

1. In so readily accepting the California Supreme Court's assurances about the legislative objective and the ineffectiveness of alternatives, did the Court apply the rational basis or the intermediate standard? Who had the burden of proof here?
2. Did the plurality find that the classification involved here treated similarly situated people differently? Why or why not? Are the differences perceived between men and women physical, legal, or cultural?
3. Did the failure to recognize the function of cultural stereotypes relating to pregnancy and childbearing by the Court's plurality limit the equal protection rights of women? If so, how severely?

The message of the plurality in *Michael* M. seemed to be that governments ought to be permitted to enact sex-based statutes provided that they can colorably assert that the statutory objective is legitimate and that the classification reflects a physical difference between the sexes. In explaining why California was allowed to punish a male but not a female for engaging in sexual intercourse with another person, not a spouse, who is under the age of eighteen, Justice Rehnquist said that the differences reflected by the statute were only physical differences between the sexes—"Only women may become pregnant" and "males alone can 'physiologically cause [that] result'." The approach taken in the plurality opinion in *Michael M.* strained the commitment of the Court to using the intermediate standard announced in *Craig* and refined in *Orr*. Specifically, the Court failed to honor the requirement of "narrow tailoring" that was endorsed in *Orr*.

Even though the Supreme Court decision in *Michael M.* seemingly validated sex-based statutory rape laws, today almost all states have adopted gender-neutral statutory rape laws. The issue of gender-based discriminatory treatment still exists, however, with respect to the application and enforcement of these laws. A recent Massachusetts Supreme Judicial Court case, excerpted in the following text, considers this problem in the context of a discovery request concerning a potential claim of selective prosecution.

COMMONWEALTH V. BERNARDO B., A JUVENILE
Supreme Judicial Court, 2009
453 Mass. 158

MARSHALL, C.J. On September 30, 2008, the Commonwealth appealed from an order and judgment of a single justice denying its petition pursuant to G. L. c. 211, § 3, to vacate a juvenile court judge's pretrial discovery order. The order issued pursuant to Mass. R. Crim. P. 14 (a) (2), . . . at the request of the juvenile male (boy), charged with nine counts of sexual offenses, including rape of a child, G. L. c. 265, § 23 (statutory rape), which the boy allegedly perpetrated against three female children, who were his friends. At the time of the alleged offenses, between August 10 and October 15 of 2007, the boy was fourteen years old and entering the ninth grade, two of the girls were twelve years old and entering the seventh grade, and the third girl, who was born on October 15, 1995, was turning twelve years old and entering sixth grade. After his counsel unsuccessfully attempted to have the three girls charged with raping him in connection with the same alleged incidents, the boy sought discovery from the Commonwealth pursuant to rule 14 (a) (2), in order to investigate and, if possible, support his claim that he was being selectively prosecuted because of his gender. . . . The Juvenile Court judge granted the boy's discovery request

and denied the Commonwealth's two subsequent motions for reconsideration. The single justice upheld the judge's order. . . .

1. Facts. In early October, 2007, the boy's father, checked the "text messages" on his son's cellular telephone and discovered a text message from his son's friend, R.L., a girl, that stated: "I would have given you [a hand job] if [S.C.] wasn't there." The boy's father contacted S.C.'s mother to express his concerns. After questioning her daughter about her interactions with the boy and speaking with other parents, S.C.'s mother notified the police on October 13, 2007, that the boy had sexually assaulted S.C., R.L., and a third girl, A.L.

That same day, a police officer met jointly with the mothers of the three girls at S.C.'s mother's house and took statements from the mothers about what they had learned from their daughters concerning sexual contact with the boy. The girls were then questioned separately at a child advocacy center by a sexual assault intervention network (SAIN) interviewer employed by the district attorney, while the police officer, an assistant district attorney, and a victim witness advocate watched from a closed circuit television in a separate room. Each interview was recorded. Because the girls' interviews are the foundation of this case, we summarize them at some length.

a. Interview with A.L. A.L. described two incidents of sexual contact with the boy, whom she described as a friend. Both occurred in August or September, 2007, during "manhunt," a hide-and-seek game that the children played in the woods behind S.C.'s home. She reported that, on one occasion, in response to the boy's request, she gave the boy a "hand job" by reaching into his pants and touching his penis for about "two seconds."

The two then continued to play manhunt. During the second incident, she and the boy were kissing in the woods behind S.C.'s house when he began "pressuring me a little" for a "blow job" (fellatio). A.L. stated that she put her mouth on the boy's penis twice, each time for about "one second." Following these incidents, A.L. reported, she and the boy remained friends. At one point he told her that "he felt really bad for it [and] that he would never do that again to anyone."

b. Interview with R.L. R.L. reported that she performed oral or manual sex on the boy about four times in late summer or early fall of 2007. Three of these incidents occurred during the game of manhunt, when the boy "forc[ed]" her to have sexual contact with him by laying down, pulling off his pants, and telling her, "Just start doing it. I know you're gonna like it. Just, c'mon. Just please?" He also told R.L. that, if she did not perform the sex acts on him, he would tell a friend of R.L.'s that R.L. had said bad things about her. The other incident occurred in the basement of S.C.'s home, apparently during a game of "truth or dare." R.L. also told the interviewer that, on another occasion in S.C.'s basement, the boy showed her and S.C. a pornographic "video clip," using S.C.'s brother's computer, of a woman performing fellatio on a man.

c. Interview with S.C. S.C. reported a number of sexual contacts with the boy during the late summer and early fall of 2007. Most of these incidents occurred in S.C.'s

basement during games of "truth or dare," in which the boy told S.C. that if she wanted to "make out" with him, she had to give him a "hand job" because "[t]hose are my rules." She estimated that she performed manual sex on the boy approximately five times.

S.C. also reported one occasion in which the boy put his penis in her mouth. She told him that she did not want him to do this, and the boy replied, "Whatever." During another game of truth or dare, S.C. reported, the boy "dare[d]" S.C. and A.L. to grab his penis, and they both did and then kissed him. S.C. also stated that the boy showed her and R.L. a video clip on her brother's computer of a woman performing fellatio on a man. In response to a question from the SAIN interviewer, S.C. denied that the boy did or showed her anything else that made her uncomfortable. . . .

3. Discussion. . . . b. Selective prosecution.

(i) Burden of proof. The Commonwealth asserts that the boy is not entitled to the discovery he seeks because he has failed to "raise a reasonable inference, based on credible evidence that he is being selectively prosecuted in his own case." Our analysis begins with the premise that the district attorney has "wide discretion in determining whether to prosecute an individual.". . .

Prosecutorial discretion, however, is not unbounded. . . . The Federal and Massachusetts Constitutions guarantee individuals that the government will not proceed against them in a manner that is arbitrary or based on "an unjustifiable standard," such as membership in a protected class. . . . Notwithstanding the presumption of regularity that attaches to prosecutorial decisions, judicial scrutiny is necessary to protect individuals from prosecution based on arbitrary or otherwise impermissible classification. . . .

To bring a claim of selective prosecution successfully, the defendant bears the initial burden to "'present evidence which raises at least a reasonable inference of impermissible discrimination,' including evidence that 'a broader class of persons than those prosecuted violated the law, . . . that failure to prosecute was either consistent or deliberate, . . .

and that the decision not to prosecute was based on an impermissible classification such as race, religion, or sex.'" . . .

. . . What the boy seeks here is discovery, not dismissal. At the discovery stage, the question is whether the defendant has made a "threshold showing of relevance" under rule 14 (a) (2). . . . To adopt the higher burden suggested by the Commonwealth would place criminal defendants in the untenable position of having to produce evidence of selective enforcement in order to obtain evidence of selective enforcement.

We now turn to the question whether the boy had made a threshold showing that the material he seeks is relevant to the claim of selective enforcement, a point the Commonwealth also disputes.

(ii) The threshold showing. The boy sought material from the Commonwealth concerning the district attorney's policies and decisions to prosecute in cases alleging statutory rape where both a defendant and any complainants were minors, on the grounds that the information was relevant to his claim that the disparity in treatment between him and the complainant girl children was based on gender discrimination. The judge agreed, and in his order on the Commonwealth's first motion for reconsideration elaborated on the evidence supporting the boy's request, to wit: both the boy and the three complaining witnesses appeared to have engaged in "mutually consensual acts of oral sex," the district attorney did not dispute that the activity was consensual, all four children were under the age of consent, and the district attorney refused the request of the boy's counsel that the girls be charged with statutory rape of the boy. The Commonwealth argues that the judge impermissibly substituted his own characterization of the allegations for those of the Commonwealth. Further, it asserts that the charges are supported by the objective evidence, namely, the age and grade differences between the boy and the girls and the nature of the alleged sexual offenses. Because the central issues in this case all

arise in the context of the statutory rape charge, we briefly examine the statutory rape law before proceeding to the evidence of record.

Statutory rape is an offense of ancient origins. "First codified into English law in 1275, statutory rape criminalized sexual relations with females under the age of twelve." . . . The aim of this gender-specific statute was not the protection of young females but the protection of fathers' property interests in their young daughters, whose loss of virginity would severely depress the value of the dowry the father would receive on his daughter's marriage. . . . By the late Sixteenth Century, the aim of the law evolved to a statute designed to protect men from charges of illegal sex with young girls. The age of consent was lowered to ten years and so it stood when the American colonies, including Massachusetts, absorbed English common law and adopted the English law of statutory rape. . . . In the late Nineteenth Century, in response to the widespread sexual exploitation of young girls in factories and urban centers, temperance organizations and other reform groups launched a nationwide effort to raise the age of consent. In Massachusetts, between 1886 and 1898, the age of consent rose from ten to thirteen, then fourteen, then sixteen years of age. . . . As in Elizabethan times, however, only females could be the victims of statutory rape.

There have been more recent efforts to reform our American statutory rape law. Statute 1974, c. 474, § 3, struck the word "female" from G. L. c. 265, § 23. . . . As we noted in *Commonwealth v. Hackett*, 383 Mass. 888, 888 (1981): "In general, the 1974 amendment eliminated prior language which defined the victims of rape as female or female children. Instead, the victims are now defined as persons or children and the generic masculine pronoun is substituted throughout. Both males and females are protected from sexual assault by this same statute, which is neutral as to the gender of the victim. Nor does the statute define the various crimes with reference to the gender of the offender. The result is that the penalties for sexual intercourse and unnatural sexual intercourse are the same without regard to the gender of the victim."

Modern amendments leave no doubt about the Legislature's intent to protect all children under sixteen years old from sexual abuse. The statutory rape law, as well, makes clear that perpetrators of statutory rape may be either male or female. Statutory rape in Massachusetts is a strict liability felony. Only two elements are needed to support a conviction under G. L. c. 265, § 23: "(1) sexual intercourse or unnatural sexual intercourse with (2) a child under sixteen years of age." . . . Force is not a necessary element of the crime. Moreover, conviction of statutory rape has weighty consequence beyond incarceration. Those convicted enter the Commonwealth's sex offender registry and are required to abide by all of the obligations and restrictions contained therein. . . .

We turn now to the record before us, which principally consists of the videotaped and transcribed interviews of A.L., R.L., and S.C.

Both the judge's and the single justice's review of the videotaped evidence indicate that the incidents alleged involved no force. The judge described the incidents as mutually assented-to, and the single justice agreed with slight modification, stating: "[A]lthough there is some mention of the juvenile putting some 'pressure' on one or more of the complainants in his comments to them . . . [t]here is no indication . . . of any complainant refusing or saying 'no' to the proposed conduct, and the juvenile ignoring such a signal; indeed, the opposite is true." The boy apologized to A.L. for his behavior, and told S.C. "whatever" when she said she did not want him to put his penis in her mouth. When A.L. told him she did not want to give him a "blow job," she reported, the boy responded, "OK, it's fine. Whatever you want to do is fine." None of the complainants reported being afraid of the boy's behavior. Indeed, sexual behavior seemed to melt seamlessly into games of "manhunt,"

"truth or dare," and "making out." Some of it occurred with more than one complainant present. The judge was not correct, as the Commonwealth points out, to describe all of the children as teenagers. But the fact is that the complainants were on the cusp of their teenage years and the boy had just entered his teens. All of the children were too young to consent legally to the sexual activity in which they engaged. It is no slight to prosecutorial discretion but a sober view of the record that reveals that the facts fall far short of the Commonwealth's characterization of them.

This is not to say we are untroubled by the boy's alleged behavior. But the question here is whether his behavior was so dissimilar from that of the girls in nature, kind, and degree as to nullify the possibility that his discovery request might yield information relevant to a claim of selective prosecution. The boy was the only child charged with statutory rape, or any offense, as a result of the incidents alleged, and he was the only male among the four children. The district attorney affirmatively declined to bring charges against the female children where the facts described by the girls could be viewed as contravening those same laws by them. . . . In these circumstances, the single justice did not abuse her discretion in declining to vacate the ruling of the motion judge that the boy has made a threshold showing based on credible evidence that he is entitled to discovery for the purpose of investigating and, if warranted, raising a claim of selective prosecution.

(iii) Relevance and materiality. The Commonwealth next contends that the information the boy seeks would not be "material and relevant" to a claim of gender-based selective prosecution. See Mass. R. Crim. P. 14 (a) (2). The district attorney reasons that, because "there exists a link between violation of sexual assault laws and gender [and] [p]erpetrators of sexual assaults are overwhelmingly male, "the requested discovery" will say little or nothing about the selectivity of a decision to charge a male with rape versus a female." The short answer is that the district attorney's characterization of the requested information cannot speak to what the information will reveal when subjected to defense counsel's analysis.

We have recently enunciated standards governing the production of evidence concerning claims of selective prosecution. We held that "valid statistical evidence" demonstrating disparate treatment of a protected group "may be relevant and material to demonstrate" selective enforcement (emphasis added). . . .

The boy's discovery request falls squarely within the boundaries of these cases. The request seeks material only in the Commonwealth's possession, custody, or control. Having waived discovery requests numbers 4 and 5, . . . it is narrowly tailored to obtain data concerning the gender of complainants and accuseds under the age of sixteen in cases in Plymouth County concerning charges identical to certain charges brought against the boy. The material sought would, if it yielded evidence suggestive of selective prosecution, enable the boy to generate valid statistics or other objective data of the kind that has been found sufficient in other cases to present a prima facie case of discriminatory arrest and charging. . . . In addition, request number 6, asking for written policies regarding prosecution of statutory rape charges where both the accused and the complainant are under sixteen years old, goes to the heart of the boy's potential selective prosecution claim. Finally, as the motion judge noted, the district attorney's office appears to be the only source of the materials sought. The Commonwealth's claim that the discovery sought is irrelevant and immaterial to the boy's investigation and possible prosecution of a selective enforcement claim was rejected. . . .

4. Conclusion. For the foregoing reasons, on December 19, 2008, we ordered that the judgment of the single justice dated September 10, 2008, denying the Commonwealth's petition pursuant to G. L. C. 211, § 3, be affirmed. We further vacated the stay pending appeal ordered by the single justice on September 30, 2008. We ordered the

Commonwealth to respond to the juvenile's discovery request forthwith (except requests 4 and 5, which the boy had since waived). We ordered that the case proceed in the Juvenile Court on an expedited basis, with the judge ensuring that no nonemergency delays be tolerated.

SPINA, J. (dissenting, with whom Cowin, J., joins). . . . To be successful with such a claim (selective prosecution), a defendant must show "that a broader class of persons than those prosecuted has violated the law, . . . that failure to prosecute was either consistent or deliberate, . . . and that the decision not to prosecute was based on impermissible classification such as race, religion, or sex."

Although this case is only at the discovery stage, the juvenile has not come forward with any evidence of selective prosecution. First, the circumstances of his case, which is his entire support for the claim of selective prosecution, is not enough to show the two groups are similarly situated. The two-year difference in their ages and the differences in their school grades are not inconsequential. They are precisely the same differences used by the local school department to segregate children: age and grade. The local school system segregates children according to three familiar categories: elementary (kindergarten–5), middle school (6–8), and high school (9–12), corresponding roughly to stages in a child's development. Second, he has not shown the Commonwealth consistently has prosecuted only male juveniles in these cases, nor has he shown intentional or deliberate discrimination by the prosecutor. Third, he has not shown the decision to prosecute was based on an impermissible classification. The gender difference here is purely incidental. The age difference and grade difference were the basis for the decision.

Where the district attorney did nothing more than base his decision to prosecute the juvenile but not the three females on the two-year age difference between eleven year old and twelve year olds in middle school on the one hand, and a fourteen year old high school student, who also was on the football team, on the other hand, the juvenile has failed to support his claim of selective prosecution. . . . I respectfully dissent.

STUDY QUESTIONS

1. What assumptions underlie traditional, gender-specific statutory rape laws? Did these assumptions relate to physical differences between men and women or to cultural differences in our expectations about the behavior of women and men? Should these assumptions, even where they are widely believed and followed, be permitted to guide and justify decisions regarding who to prosecute under modern, gender-neutral laws?

2. The *Bernardo B.* case concerned a discovery motion precedent to arguing a motion to dismiss for selective prosecution based on gender. According to the majority, "the complainants [girls] were on the cusp of their teenage years and the boy had just entered his teens. All of the children were too young to consent legally to the sexual activity in which they engaged." The dissent, on the other hand, agreed with the prosecution that the boy and the three girls were not similarly situated because of "the two-year age difference between eleven year old and twelve year olds [females] in middle school on the one hand, and a fourteen year old [male] high school student, who also was on the football team . . . ." Can both characterizations be reconciled with the purpose of a gender-neutral statutory rape statute? Why or why not?

At the end of the 1980–81 term, Justice Stewart retired from active duty on the Court. He was replaced by the first woman ever to serve on that Court, Justice Sandra Day O'Connor. During her first term on the Court, Justice O'Connor's presence was felt in a sex discrimination case. The case involved the exclusion of one sex from a state-run school that prepared people for careers in a profession traditionally associated with the other sex. In this case, the profession was nursing, and those excluded were men. The challenge to this instance of single-sex public schools might have raised the more general issue of whether state-sponsored, sex-segregated schools are permitted by the equal protection guarantee. Just six years earlier, the Court faced that question in *Vorchheimer v. School District of Philadelphia.* It affirmed a lower court decision that held that they are, but did so by a 4–4 vote (Justice Rehnquist did not participate) and issued no opinion explaining the significance of that decision. In *Hogan,* as indicated in footnote 1, the Court steered clear of the more general issue and focused instead on the narrower question of whether the Equal Protection Clause bars states from excluding one sex from schools provided for the other.

MISS. UNIV. FOR WOMEN V. HOGAN
Supreme Court of the United States, 1982.
458 U.S. 718, 102 S.Ct. 3331, 73 L.Ed.2d 1090.

Justice O'CONNOR delivered the opinion of the Court.

This case presents the narrow issue of whether a state statute that excludes males from enrolling in a state-supported professional nursing school violates the Equal Protection Clause of the Fourteenth Amendment.

The facts are not in dispute. In 1884, the Mississippi legislature created the Mississippi

Industrial Institute and College for the Education of White Girls of the State of Mississippi, now the oldest state-supported all-female college in the United States. The school, known today as Mississippi University for Women (MUW), has from its inception limited its enrollment to women.[1]

In 1971, MUW established a School of Nursing, initially offering a two-year associate degree. Three years later, the school instituted a four-year baccalaureate program in nursing and today also offers a graduate program. The School of Nursing has its own faculty and administrative officers and establishes its own criteria for admission.

Respondent, Joe Hogan, is a registered nurse but does not hold a baccalaureate degree in nursing. Since 1974, he has worked as a nursing supervisor in a medical center in Columbus, the city in which MUW is located. In 1979, Hogan applied for admission to the MUW School of Nursing's baccalaureate program. Although he was otherwise qualified, he was denied admission to the School of Nursing solely because of his sex. School officials informed him that he could audit the courses in which he was interested, but could not enroll for credit.

Hogan filed an action in the United States District Court for the Northern District of Mississippi, claiming the single-sex admissions policy of MUW's School of Nursing violated the Equal Protection Clause of the Fourteenth Amendment. Hogan sought injunctive and declaratory relief, as well as compensatory damages.

Following a hearing, the District Court denied preliminary injunctive relief. The court concluded that maintenance of MUW as a single-sex school bears a rational relationship to the state's legitimate interest "of providing the greatest practical range of educational opportunities for its female student population." Furthermore, the court stated, the admissions policy is not arbitrary because providing single-sex schools

is consistent with a respected, though by no means universally accepted, educational theory that single-sex education affords unique benefits to students. Stating that the case presented no issue of fact, the court informed Hogan that it would enter summary judgment dismissing his claim unless he tendered a factual issue. When Hogan offered no further evidence, the District Court entered summary judgment in favor of the State.

The Court of Appeals for the Fifth Circuit reversed, holding that, because the admissions policy discriminates on the basis of gender, the District Court improperly used a "rational relationship" test to judge the constitutionality of the policy. Instead, the Court of Appeals stated, the proper test is whether the State has carried the heavier burden of showing that the gender-based classification is substantially related to an important governmental objective. Recognizing that the State has a significant interest in providing educational opportunities for all its citizens, the court then found that the State had failed to show that providing a unique educational opportunity for females, but not for males, bears a substantial relationship to that interest. . . .

We begin our analysis aided by several firmly established principles. Because the challenged policy expressly discriminates among applicants on the basis of gender, it is subject to scrutiny under the Equal Protection Clause of the Fourteenth Amendment. *Reed v. Reed*. That this statute discriminates against males rather than against females does not exempt it from scrutiny or reduce the standard of review, *Orr v. Orr*. Our decisions also establish that the party seeking to uphold a statute that classifies individuals on the basis of their gender must carry the burden of showing an "exceedingly persuasive justification" for the classification, *Feeney*. The burden is met only by showing at least that the classification serves "important

---

[1]Mississippi maintains no other single-sex public university or college. Thus, we are not faced with the question of whether States can provide "separate but equal" undergraduate institutions for males and females. *Cf. Vorchheimer v. School District of Philadelphia*.

governmental objectives and that the discriminatory means employed" are "substantially related to the achievement of those objectives." *Wengler v. Druggists Mutual Ins. Co.*, 446 U.S. 142 (1980). . . .

The State's primary justification for maintaining the single-sex admissions policy of MUW's School of Nursing is that it compensates for discrimination against women and, therefore, constitutes educational affirmative action. As applied to the School of Nursing, we find the State's argument unpersuasive.

In limited circumstances, a gender-based classification favoring one sex can be justified if it intentionally and directly assists members of the sex that is disproportionately burdened. See *Schlesinger v. Ballard*. However, we consistently have emphasized that "the mere recitation of a benign, compensatory purpose is not an automatic shield which protects against any inquiry into the actual purposes underlying a statutory scheme." *Weinberger v. Wiesenfeld*. The same searching analysis must be made, regardless of whether the State's objective is to eliminate family controversy, *Reed*, to achieve administrative efficiency, *Frontiero*, or to balance the burdens borne by males and females. . . .

Mississippi has made no showing that women lacked opportunities to obtain training in the field of nursing or to attain positions of leadership in that field when the MUW School of Nursing opened its door or that women currently are deprived of such opportunities. In fact, in 1970, the year before the School of Nursing's first class enrolled, women earned 94 percent of the nursing baccalaureate degrees conferred in Mississippi and 98.6 percent of the degrees earned nationwide. . . . That year was not an aberration; one decade earlier, women had earned all the nursing degrees conferred in Mississippi and 98.9 percent of the degrees conferred

nationwide. As one would expect, the labor force reflects the same predominance of women in nursing. When MUW's School of Nursing began operation, nearly 98 percent of all employed registered nurses were female.

Rather than compensate for discriminatory barriers faced by women, MUW's policy of excluding males from admission to the School of Nursing tends to perpetuate the stereotyped view of nursing as an exclusively woman's job. By assuring that Mississippi allots more openings in its state-supported nursing schools to women than it does to men, MUW's admissions policy lends credibility to the old view that women, not men, should become nurses, and makes the assumption that nursing is a field for women a self-fulfilling prophecy. Thus, we conclude that, although the State recited a "benign, compensatory purpose," it failed to establish that the alleged objective is the actual purpose underlying the discriminatory classification.

The policy is invalid also because it fails the second part of the equal protection test, for the State has made no showing that the gender-based classification is substantially and directly related to its proposed compensatory objective. To the contrary, MUW's policy of permitting men to attend classes as auditors fatally undermines its claim that women, at least those in the School of Nursing, are adversely affected by the presence of men. . . .

Thus, considering both the asserted interest and the relationship between the interest and the methods used by the State, we conclude that the State has fallen far short of establishing the "exceedingly persuasive justification" needed to sustain the gender-based classification. Accordingly, we hold that MUW's policy of denying males the right to enroll for credit in its School of Nursing violates the Equal Protection Clause of the Fourteenth Amendment.[17] . . .

---

[17]Justice Powell's dissent suggests that a second objective is served by the gender-based classification in that Mississippi has elected to provide women a choice of educational environments. Since any gender-based classification provides one class a benefit or choice not available to the other class, however, that argument begs the question. The issue is not whether the benefited class profits from the classification, but whether the State's decision to confer a benefit only upon one class by means of a discriminatory classification is substantially related to achieving a legitimate and substantial goal.

Because we conclude that the State's policy of excluding males from MUW's School of Nursing violates the Equal Protection Clause of the Fourteenth Amendment, we affirm the judgment of the Court of Appeals.

It Is So Ordered.

Study Questions

1. What standard of review did the Court use here? Did the Court simply accept the claimed objective or require the state to show that the legislature actually attempted to further

that aim? If the statute in *Michael M.* had been subjected to the same degree of searching analysis as was used in *Hogan*, would the result there have been different?

2. How narrow is the rationale for this decision? Under it, could Joe Hogan be denied admission to a state medical school for women? Could a state open a nursing school for men only? How about a graduate school of business administration limited to women students? Under this decision, could a state provide "separate but equal" high schools for boys and girls?

A number of interesting and crucial points were made in *Hogan*. The obvious one is that men are also protected against sex discrimination under the Equal Protection Clause. After *Michael M.*, the extent of that protection was in doubt. Another substantial point in *Hogan* is that the Court again asserted that when it applies an intermediate test, that test has teeth. Whether that standard is referred to in the language of *Craig* or merely as "heightened scrutiny," it requires that sex-based laws have an "exceedingly persuasive justification." In reiterating this point, the Court relieved the suspicion that the standard had been weakened in *Michael M.*

In a more recent application, the Supreme Court reiterated the views expressed in *Hogan* with respect to the applicable standard of scrutiny to be applied to a sex-based program. In *U.S. v. Virginia*, 518 U.S. 515 (1996), one of the issues considered by the Court was whether Virginia's exclusion of women from the educational opportunities provided by the Virginia Military Institute (VMI) violated the Equal Protection Clause of the Fourteenth Amendment. Justice Ginsberg, speaking for the majority, summarized the Court's current position on the applicable standard of scrutiny in cases of official classification by gender:

> . . . Focusing on the differential treatment or denial of opportunity for which relief is sought, the reviewing court must determine whether the proffered justification is "exceedingly persuasive." The burden of justification is demanding and rests entirely on the State. . . . The State must show "at least that the [challenged] classification serves 'important governmental objectives and that the discriminatory means employed' are 'substantially related to the achievement of those objectives.'" . . . The justification must be genuine, not hypothesized or invented *post hoc* in response to litigation. And it must not rely on overbroad generalizations about the different talents, capacities, or preferences of males and females. . . . (Citations omitted)

The Court, in measuring the record against its enunciated standard, concluded that Virginia had not shown "exceedingly persuasive justification" for excluding all women from admission to VMI, and affirmed the Fourth Circuit's initial judgment that Virginia had violated the Fourteenth Amendment's Equal Protection Clause.

The Court's decision in *U.S. v. Virginia* also underscored its prior view, enunciated in *Hogan*, that the compensatory objective of a sex-based program must be genuine, and that "the mere recitation of a benign, compensatory purpose is not an automatic shield which protects against any inquiry into the actual purposes underlying a statutory scheme." In *Hogan*, Justice O'Connor found that Mississippi University's program tended to perpetuate the sex-role stereotype of nursing being an exclusively women's job, rather than to compensate women for past discrimination. In *U.S. v. Virginia*, Justice Ginsburg stated that:

> "Inherent differences" between men and women, we have come to appreciate, remain cause for celebration, but not for denigration of the members of either sex or for artificial constraints on an individual's opportunity. Sex classifications may be used to compensate women "for particular economic disabilities [they have] suffered," . . . to "promot[e] equal opportunity," . . . to advance full development of the talent and capacities of our Nation's people. . . . But such classifications may not be used, as they once were, . . . to create or perpetuate the legal, social, and economic inferiority of women. (Citations and footnote omitted)

After *U.S. v. Virginia*, the Court continues to stand ready to separate out latent cultural stereotypes from genuine compensatory goals, and place the burden of proof on the government to justify any purported compensatory purpose for a sex-based classification.

V. THE CONSTITUTIONAL AMENDMENT ALTERNATIVE

Within the U.S. legal system, those interested in abolishing laws and government practices that assign rights and responsibilities on the basis of sex may rely on one or more of three main strategies. First, they may appeal to the legislative and executive branches of government at the various levels in order to revise existing statutes, regulations, programs, and practices individually or in small packages of related measures. This piecemeal approach has been in use at least since the adoption of the Married Women's Property Acts of the mid-nineteenth century. A second strategy involves challenging sex-based laws and practices under the various guarantees of the federal and state constitutions. This approach has been widely used since the *Reed* decision in 1971. As we have seen, however, the Supreme Court appears willing to apply heightened scrutiny to sex-based laws only in a limited range of situations. The third strategy is that of amending federal and state constitutions. It was this approach that finally accomplished the extension of the franchise to women. The drive to erect a constitutional guarantee of equal rights for women and men is popularly thought to have been an episode mainly of the 1970s that focused solely on an amendment to the federal constitution. In fact, this strategy has been deployed since 1923 and also affects state constitutions. In this section, we briefly explore the experience and lessons of the strategy.

The Federal ERA Experience

When the Congress passed the ERA on March 22, 1972, it was understood to have fairly specific objectives. The operative provision of the ERA read: "Equality of rights under the law shall not be denied or abridged by the United States or by any State on account of sex." The leading analysis of the ERA argued for securing an equal rights amendment in addition to equal protection litigation and statutory reform because it would be, relative to the other alternatives, swift, economical, and thorough. Unlike the other strategies, a constitutional amendment would express a permanent, uniform, and national standard for eliminating sex discrimination by government at all levels.

Under that analysis, the ERA would absolutely bar the use of sex-based classifications by governmental bodies, except in rare and readily identifiable situations involving either physical characteristics unique to one sex or privacy rights independently protected by the Constitution. Unlike the views expressed by Justice Powell in his concurring opinion in *Frontiero*, this analysis called for a standard of review even more stringent than the strict scrutiny test developed by the Court for race-based classifications. This analysis anticipated that the ERA would work major changes in the way government programs and agencies were structured, programs such as Social Security and agencies such as the Department of Defense. It also anticipated that the ERA would require the states to make major adjustments in family and criminal law and to eliminate protective labor laws that had proliferated from the early years of the twentieth century. (See Brown, Emerson, Falk, and Freeman, "The Equal Rights Amendment: A Constitutional Basis for Equal Rights for Women," 80 *Yale Law Journal* 871 (1971).)

As we noted earlier in this chapter, the 1970s saw an expansion of constitutional protections under the equal protection guarantee. During that same period, the implementation of statutory protections improved as well. These developments undercut the arguments advanced by both ERA proponents and opponents. The following selection sketches the history of the ERA at the federal level, from its beginnings in the 1920s through the mid-1980s.

THE ERA EXPERIENCE AND ITS LESSONS

Jane J. Mansbridge

Why We Lost the ERA. Chicago: University of Chicago Press, 1986, pp. 8–14, 187–99.

The major women's organizations were able to persuade two-thirds of the states to approve women's suffrage in 1920. In the same year these organizations began to discuss an Equal Rights Amendment. Alice Paul and her militant National Woman's Party had gained national notoriety by picketing the White House and staging hunger strikes for women's suffrage. Now the same group proposed a constitutional amendment, introduced in Congress in 1923, that read: "Men and women shall have equal rights throughout the United States and in every place subject to its jurisdiction. Congress shall have power to enforce this article by appropriate legislation."

From the beginning, "equal rights" meant "ending special benefits." An ERA would have made unconstitutional the protective legislation that socialists and social reformers like Florence Kelley, frustrated by the lack of a strong working-class movement in America, had struggled to erect in order to protect at least women and children from the worst ravages of capitalism. Against Kelley and women like her, the

National Woman's Party leaders, primarily professional and upper- or upper-middle-class women, argued that "a maximum hour law or a minimum wage law which applied to women but not to men was bound to hurt women more than it could possibly help them." Kelley in turn dubbed the ERA "topsy-turvy feminism," and declared that "women cannot achieve true equality with men by securing identity of treatment under the law."

After a 1921 meeting between Alice Paul, Florence Kelley, and others, the board of directors of the National Consumers' League voted to oppose the Equal Rights Amendment. The League, a powerful Progressive organization of which Kelley was general secretary, thereafter made opposition to the ERA a consistent plank in its program. The strong opposition of Progressive and union feminists meant that when the Equal Rights Amendment was introduced in Congress in 1923 it was immediately opposed by a coalition of Progressive organizations and labor unions. And although the Amendment was introduced in every subsequent Congress for the next twenty years, opposition from this coalition and from most conservatives ensured its repeated defeat.

During the 1930s, the National Association of Women Lawyers and the National Federation of Business and Professional Women's Clubs (BPW) decided to sponsor the ERA, and in 1940 the Republican party revitalized the ERA by placing it in the party's platform. In 1944, despite strong opposition from labor, the Democratic party followed suit. Nonetheless, the ERA never came close to passing until 1950 and 1953, when the U.S. Senate passed it, but with the "Hayden rider," which provided that the Amendment "shall not be construed to impair any rights, benefits, or exemptions now or hereinafter conferred by law upon persons of the female sex." In both years the House of Representatives recessed without a vote. Because the women's organizations supporting the ERA knew that special benefits were incompatible with equal rights, they had tried to block the amended ERA in the House and were relieved when their efforts succeeded.

Support widened during the 1950s—primarily among Republicans, although among the Democrats Eleanor Roosevelt and some other prominent women dropped their opposition to the ERA in order to support the United Nations charter, which affirmed the "equal rights of men and women." In 1953 President Dwight Eisenhower replaced the unionist head of the Federal Women's Bureau with a Republican businesswoman who, having sponsored Connecticut's equal pay law, moved the bureau from active opposition into a neutral position regarding the ERA. In later speeches Eisenhower also stressed the pro-ERA planks of both parties and stated his support for "equal rights" for women. In 1963, however, labor struck back when President John Kennedy's Commission on the Status of Women—created under labor influence partly to siphon off pressure for an ERA—concluded that "a constitutional amendment need not now be sought in order to establish this principle [equal rights for women]."

The crucial step in building progressive and liberal support for the ERA was the passage of Title VII of the Civil Rights Act of 1964, which prohibited job discrimination on the basis of sex. Title VII had originally been designed to prevent discrimination against blacks, but a group of southern congressmen added a ban on discrimination against women in a vain effort to make the bill unacceptable to northern conservatives. Initially, Title VII had no effect on "protective" legislation. Unions, accordingly, continued to oppose the ERA because they thought it would nullify such legislation. In 1967, when the newly formed National Organization for Women (NOW) gave the ERA first place on its Bill of Rights for Women, several union members immediately resigned. But by 1970 both the federal courts and the Equal Employment Opportunity Commission (EEOC) had interpreted Title VII as invalidating protective legislation, and had extended most traditional protections to men rather than removing them for women. With their long-standing concern now for the most part made moot, union opposition to the ERA began to wane.

In 1970, the Pittsburgh chapter of NOW took direct action. The group disrupted Senator Birch Bayh's hearings on the nineteen-year-old vote, getting Bayh to promise hearings on the ERA the following spring. This was the moment. Labor opposition was fading, and, because few radical claims had been made for the ERA, conservatives had little ammunition with which to oppose it. In April, the United Auto Workers' convention voted to endorse the ERA. In May, Bayh began Senate hearings on the ERA, and for the first time in its history the U.S. Department of Labor supported the ERA. In June, Representative Martha Griffiths succeeded in collecting enough signatures on a discharge petition to pry the ERA out of the House Judiciary Committee, where for many years the liberal chair of the committee, Emanuel Celler, had refused to schedule hearings because of the persistent opposition by labor movement traditionalists. After only an hour's debate, the House of Representatives passed the ERA by a vote of 350 to 15. . . .

. . . On March 22, 1972, the ERA passed the Senate of the United States with a vote of 84 to 8.

. . . [O]n the very day that the U.S. Senate passed the ERA, Hawaii became the first state to ratify. Delaware, Nebraska, and New Hampshire ratified the next day, and on the third day Idaho and Iowa ratified. Twenty-four more states ratified in 1972 and early 1973. The very earliest states to ratify were all unanimous, and in the other early states the votes were rarely close. . . .

By late 1973, however, the ERA's proponents had lost control of the ratification process. While the national offices of the various pro-ERA organizations could relatively easily coordinate their Washington activities to get the ERA through Congress, they were slow in organizing coalitions in the states. At the end of the 1973 state legislative sessions, only a few states even had active ERA coalitions.

Moreover, in 1973 the Supreme Court decided, in *Roe v. Wade*, that state laws forbidding abortion violated the "right to privacy" implicit in the Constitution. Although the ERA had no obvious direct bearing on whether "abortion is murder," the two issues nonetheless became politically linked. The *Roe* decision took power out of the hands of relatively parochial, conservative state legislators and put it in the hands of a relatively cosmopolitan, liberal U.S. Supreme Court. The ERA would have done the same thing. Furthermore, both were sponsored by what was at that time still called the "women's liberation" movement. Traditionalists saw the "women's libbers" both as rejecting the notion that motherhood was a truly important task and as endorsing sexual hedonism instead of moral restraint. The *Roe* decision seemed to constitute judicial endorsement for these values: Since NOW was not only the leading sponsor of the ERA but the leading defender of abortion on demand, conservative activists saw abortion and the ERA as two prongs of the "libbers'" general strategy for undermining traditional

American values. Unable to overturn the *Roe* decision directly, many conservatives sought to turn the ERA into a referendum on that decision. To a significant degree, they succeeded. The opponents began to organize and convinced the first of several states to rescind ratification—a move that had no legal force but certainly made a political difference in unratified states.

Three more states ratified in 1974, one in 1975, and one—Indiana—in 1977, bringing the total to thirty-five of the required thirty-eight. No state ratified after 1977 despite the triumph of ERA proponents in 1978 in getting Congress to extend the original 1979 deadline until 1982. In 1982 this extension ran out, and the Amendment died. Alabama, Arizona, Arkansas, Florida, Georgia, Illinois, Louisiana, Mississippi, Missouri, Nevada, North Carolina, Oklahoma, South Carolina, Utah, and Virginia had not ratified. All were Mormon or southern states, except Illinois, which required a three-fifths majority for ratifying constitutional amendments and which had a strongly southern culture in the third of the state surrounded by Missouri and Kentucky. . . .

In January 1983, the ERA was reintroduced in the U.S. House of Representatives. After hearings in the spring, Republican representatives proposed a series of amendments to the ERA, providing that it would not require public funding for abortion, would not draft women, would not send women into combat, and would not jeopardize the tax-exempt status of all-male and all-female schools and colleges. To avoid discussing or voting on these amendments, the Democratic Speaker of the House suspended normal rules when the issue came to the floor in November, limited debate to forty minutes, and barred any modifications of the measure on the floor. The Speaker took this action because, he said, he "doubted very, very much" that all of the proposed amendments could have been defeated. In these circumstances the ERA garnered 278 votes for passage and 147 against. It thus fell six votes short of the two-thirds majority needed for a constitutional amendment. Since the Senate is currently more conservative than the House, and since state legislators are far more conservative than Congress on this issue, it seems clear that an ERA of the kind Congress passed in 1972 has virtually no chance of being ratified in the near future.

The political demise of the ERA poses a number of questions. First, with the wisdom born of hindsight, feminists must ask themselves a strategic question: Was the struggle worth the enormous effort they poured into it? Second, anyone involved in the political process can fruitfully ask tactical questions about the struggle: Were any "mistakes" made in the campaign from which all political activists can learn? Finally, there is the question of what to do in the future: Should feminists continue the struggle for the ERA, or abandon it, at least for the moment? . . .

Although the ERA provoked little informed or subtle debate regarding its own impact, it did foster discussion of women's issues more generally. For ten years the ERA focused public attention on women's disadvantage in the workplace, the home, and the streets. The effect was probably greatest in those states that did not ratify, for issues like these had not previously had a large role in the public life of these states. . . .

The ERA ratification campaign brought many women on the Left and the Right into active politics for the first time in their lives. It more than trebled the membership of NOW, making it stronger today than its counterpart in almost any other country. . . .

The attempt to put an ERA in the Constitution also produced important changes in political and judicial practice. At the federal level, the fact that Congress passed the ERA almost certainly encouraged the Supreme Court to interpret the Fourteenth Amendment as barring many varieties of discrimination against women, although uncertainty about the ERA's prospects for ratification may have later discouraged the Court from making gender a suspect classification.

On the state level, the campaign's impact varied greatly from one state to another. In many states, adopting a state ERA, or sometimes even ratifying the federal ERA, led the legislators to review state laws and rewrite them in "gender-neutral" form. . . .

The campaign had costs, but they were not excessive. Because the ratification campaign lost, feminists perhaps lost some political credibility. But the defeat came by a very narrow margin. At least in the key unratified states, legislators were impressed by the duration and intensity of the political effort that both sides mounted. . . .

While the decade of agitation for and against the ERA on balance raised the consciousness of many Americans on matters relating to women as well as producing significant concrete gains, continuing this particular struggle now would probably yield diminishing returns and might become counterproductive.

During this moratorium, feminists will need to discuss what would be best for all women in the realms of combat, school athletics, prisons, and sex-blind legislation generally. Since about 1980, as more women have experienced the results of gender-neutral legislation like no-fault divorce laws and joint custody, some feminists have begun to articulate a critique of egalitarianism that looks much like Marx's critique of bourgeois equality. They argue that in a society where one group hold most of the power, "neutral" laws usually benefit the powerful group. . . .

. . . Whatever the reasons, the years immediately after 1982 saw the start of a lively, thought-provoking debate among feminist lawyers on among other issues, how thoroughly the law should embrace strict gender neutrality. It also saw the publication of several books by feminists that took seriously the concerns of those who opposed traditional feminist positions. . . .

. . . In ten or twenty years it may be possible to pass an ERA that expresses the principle of equality between the sexes in language as simple and unadorned as that of the Bill of Rights and the Fourteenth Amendment. It may even be possible at that time to develop a different legislative history that would extend the Amendment to prohibit some of the laws that discriminate in fact, and not just in intent, against women. But if this book indicates anything, it is that persuading state legislators to vote for such an Amendment would require a major change in political climate.

STUDY QUESTIONS

1. According to this account, what were the reasons that the ERA was initially opposed? What subsequent developments undercut that opposition? Did those same developments also undercut the need for an ERA?

2. In what way did the pro-ERA coalition lose control of the ratification process? Had it been more astute organizationally, would that have changed the outcome?

3. In what ways was the ratification drive worthwhile? What lessons does the ERA experience hold for us?

As Mansbridge noted, when the Senate passed the ERA, state ratification began at a swift pace. In the first year, the ERA received twenty-two out of the needed thirty-eight state ratifications.[1] But, as opposition began to develop, the rate of state ratifications slowed. In 1973, the ERA was ratified by eight states: Connecticut, Minnesota, New Mexico, Oregon, South Dakota, Vermont, Washington, and Wyoming. In 1974 Maine, Montana, and Ohio ratified the ERA, followed by North Dakota in 1975. There were no state ratifications in 1976. After Indiana became the thirty-fifth state to ratify the ERA in 1977, there were no further state ratifications.

In order to continue the drive toward successful ratification of the ERA, a number of pro-ERA groups lobbied Congress for an indefinite extension of the original 1979 time limit for ratification. As a result of public pressure, Congress did grant an extension, but only until June 30, 1982. The three additional required state ratifications were not obtained before the new deadline.

The ERA was reintroduced in Congress on July 14, 1982, and at every session since that date. During the 111th Session of Congress (2008–09) H.J. Res. 31 was introduced in the House of Representatives by Representative Jesse Jackson of Illinois (on March 3, 2009). This bill contains no set deadline for obtaining ratification by the required thirty-eight states. Interestingly, this bill also contains a provision relating to reproductive rights for women. The resolution reads as follows:

JOINT RESOLUTION

Proposing an amendment to the Constitution of the United States relating to equality of rights and reproductive rights.

Resolved by the Senate and House of Representatives of the United States of America in Congress assembled (two-thirds of each House concurring therein), That the following article is proposed as an amendment to the Constitution of the United States, which shall be valid to all intents and purposes as part of the Constitution when ratified by the legislatures of three-fourths of the several States:

'Article—

'Section 1. Equality of rights under the law shall not be denied or abridged by the United States or by any State on account of sex.

---

[1]Those states ratifying the ERA were: Alaska, California, Colorado, Delaware, Hawaii, Idaho, Iowa, Kansas, Kentucky, Maryland, Massachusetts, Michigan, Nebraska, New Hampshire, New Jersey, New York, Pennsylvania, Rhode Island, Tennessee, Texas, West Virginia, and Wisconsin.

'Section 2. Reproductive rights for women under the law shall not be denied or abridged by the United States or any State.

'Section 3. Congress shall have power to enforce and implement this article by appropriate legislation.

'Section 4. This amendment shall take effect two years after the date of ratification.'

Most recently, in 2009, there has been some pro-ratification activity in Florida, Illinois, Missouri, and Arkansas. The activity is grounded in the belief that Congress has the power to both accept state ratifications after the 1982 deadline and maintain the viability of the thirty-five existing ratifications. This strategy is unlikely to be tested, however, until a state actually ratifies the ERA. In addition, should Congress pass this new version of the ERA it is likely that the ratification process would have to begin anew. The previous version of the ERA that was ratified by thirty-five states did not contain the language found in Section 2 concerning the protection of women's reproductive rights.

The State ERA Experience

One by-product of the federal ERA ratification drive, as Mansbridge noted, was the adoption of equal rights amendments to several state constitutions. During the 1970s, nine states added amendments to their constitutions nearly identical to the proposed federal ERA. These states were Pennsylvania (1971), Colorado, Hawaii, Maryland, Texas, Washington (1972), New Mexico (1973), New Hampshire (1974), and Massachusetts (1976). A total of twenty-two (22) states have adopted a form of an equal rights amendment to their respective state constitutions. The other thirteen states are Alaska, California, Connecticut, Florida, Illinois, Iowa, Louisiana, Montana, New Jersey, Rhode Island, Utah, Virginia, and Wyoming. Eight of these states include equal rights on the basis of sex in their Declaration of Rights or Bill of Rights. Virginia states in its Due Process provision that there will be no discrimination by the government on the basis of sex. New Jersey defines "persons" in its Constitution as meaning both sexes. Rhode Island specifically excludes from its equal rights guarantee " . . . any right relating to abortion or the funding thereof." And Utah, interestingly, includes the following provision in its Constitution:

Article IV, Elections and Right of Suffrage

Section 1. [Equal political rights]
    The rights of citizens of the State of Utah to vote and hold office shall not be denied or abridged on account of sex. Both male and female citizens of this State shall enjoy equally all civil, political and religious rights and privileges.

It is also interesting to note that of the twenty-two states that have adopted some form of equal rights protection in their state constitutions, five did not vote to ratify the federal ERA. They are Florida, Illinois, Louisiana, Utah, and Virginia. These amendments to state constitutions are of interest for three reasons: they show how additional avenues can be used to vindicate the rights of victims of sex discrimination; they shed light on the likely consequences of adopting the ERA at the federal level; and they suggest what an ERA can accomplish that an Equal Protection Clause cannot.

ON-LINE RESOURCES

Access Supreme Court Opinions at:
supct.law.cornell.edu/supct/

To track information on bills pending in Congress, go to:
thomas.loc.gov/

CHAPTER 3

EQUAL EMPLOYMENT OPPORTUNITY

FROM THE BEGINNING, one of the principal grievances of feminists has been sex discrimination in employment. In 1848, the Seneca Falls Conference denounced sex segregation in the workplace and the devaluation of work done by women: "He [man] has monopolized nearly all the profitable employments and from those she is permitted to follow, she receives but a scanty remuneration" (*Declaration of Sentiments*; see Chapter 1).

The participation of women in the paid labor force has been restricted by a variety of techniques. During the nineteenth and early twentieth centuries, laws excluded women from particular occupations and limited the hours and times they could work. As discussed in Chapter 1, these restrictions were justified by the separate spheres ideology and later by the protective rationale. Throughout that period, women's participation in the labor force was largely limited to low-paying jobs in textile manufacturing, offices, teaching, and domestic service. Short-lived exceptions to this pattern occurred during the two world wars, when the economy experienced personnel shortages in other labor sectors. Even then, however, women generally earned substantially lower wages than did men in comparable positions.

Sex segregation in the workplace and devaluation of the work done by women have a devastating impact. Although ancient in origin, these practices were not widely acknowledged until the 1950s, when women's participation in the paid labor force dramatically increased. Only 28 percent of adult women worked outside the home in 1950, and half of them on a part-time basis. Within four decades, a revolution in the employment patterns of adult women occurred. By 1990, over 57 percent of adult women worked outside the home, over 70 percent of them full-time. Whereas only about 10 percent of women with preschool-age children were employed in 1950, over two-thirds of such women were in the labor force in the early 1990s.

With this massive change in the rate at which adult women participate in the labor force, the impact of sex discrimination in employment became recognized as a problem of acute proportions. That problem is threefold. The first issue is the "earnings gap." As of 2007, the ratio of women's and men's median annual earnings was about 78 for full-time, year-round workers, despite the change in labor force participation by women and despite major legal measures adopted in the 1960s and 1970s. The second dimension is sex segregation in the workplace. According to the U.S. Department of Labor, Bureau of Labor Statistics, Annual Averages 2008, the twenty leading occupations of full-time employed women (both wage and salary) include high percentages of women in stereotypically female occupations such as secretary, administrative assistant, registered nurse, elementary school teacher, cashier, nursing and home health aide, waitress, receptionist, bookkeeper, accounting and auditing clerk, maid and housekeeping cleaner, and childcare worker. The "feminization of poverty" is the final dimension of the problem. Due to a number of factors, including increases in the divorce rate, families with children are increasingly headed by single females. Conditions in the early 1990s were captured in a number of statistical measures. Over 37 percent of families with children were headed by women—more than three times the rate reported in 1960. This phenomenon, combined with the continuing segregation of women into low-paying, dead-end jobs, has served to produce the feminization of poverty. In 2007, the poverty rate for households headed by women was more than twice that for households headed by men. The poverty effect of sex discrimination in employment is not restricted to women with children. Since Social Security and pensions generally are keyed to past income levels, elderly women are also affected. The poverty rate for women sixty-five years and older was almost twice that for men in the same age bracket. Elderly Black and Hispanic women were especially hard hit; they were more than four times as likely to be living in poverty as white, non-Hispanic men.

These effects of sex discrimination in employment, discussed at greater length in Chapter 4, received attention by the legislative and executive branches of government at the state and federal levels in the 1960s and early 1970s. The statutes enacted are usually referred to as fair employment practice (FEP) laws. State FEP laws were generally understood to be patterned after those at the federal level. There, the main measures were the Equal Pay Act of 1963 and Title VII of the Civil Rights Act of 1964. Of these, Title VII has been the bulwark of antisex-bias practices in employment. This chapter will introduce the principal features of that statute. The other measures will be discussed in Chapter 4.

I. AN INTRODUCTION TO TITLE VII

The History of Title VII

Title VII of the Civil Rights Act of 1964 (42 U.S.C. § 2000e) is the most comprehensive equal employment opportunity statute ever adopted by the federal government. The struggle to enact it was long and bitter. Its proponents sought to eliminate the effects of racial bias from hiring and promotion decisions in private-sector employment. Bills similar to Title VII had been introduced and routinely defeated since 1943—often by means of a Senate filibuster.

The main impetus to the passage of the 1964 bill came only a month after President John F. Kennedy was assassinated in November 1963. President Johnson dedicated the Civil Rights Act, then a series of bills in Congress, to the memory of his predecessor, saying: "We have talked long enough in this country about equal rights . . . it is time now to write the next chapter, and to write it in the book of laws." The following June, President Johnson announced that the Senate filibuster had been broken. The Civil Rights Act was signed into law a month later and went into effect in July 1965.

The story of how gender came to be included in Title VII as a prohibited basis of employment discrimination is anything but edifying. An amendment to the original bill adding "sex" to "race, color, religion and national origin" as a prohibited employment criterion was first proposed on the floor of the House of Representatives on the last day of debate on the bill. It was proposed by Representative Howard Smith of Virginia, Chairman of the House Rules Committee, evidently for the purpose of blocking passage of the entire act. The only arguments favoring the amendment at the time were that sex discrimination was wrong and without the amendment, white women would be at a disadvantage in relation to African American women. The amendment was opposed by the President's Commission on the Status of Women, the Women's Bureau of the Department of Labor, and the American Association of University Women. Even so, the amended bill passed. Representative Smith's ploy failed. One of the most powerful remedies for sex discrimination available today owes its origin to a misfired political tactic on the part of opponents of the act.

Title VII has been amended four times since it was initially enacted. The amendments of 1972 extended the powers of the Equal Employment Opportunity Commission (EEOC), expanded the coverage of the act to include public employers and educational institutions, and clarified a number of its terms and provisions. In 1978, the Pregnancy Discrimination Act (PDA) amended Title VII by adding what is now section 701(k), which declares that classifications based on pregnancy and pregnancy-related disabilities fall within the meaning of "sex" as used in Title VII. The Civil Rights Act (CRA) of 1991 amended Title VII to reverse a series of recent Supreme Court decisions that threatened to cripple the enforcement of the civil rights protected by the statute. It also added several new provisions affecting remedies. Recently, the Lilly Ledbetter Fair Pay Act of 2009 amended Title VII and the Age Discrimination in Employment Act and modified the Americans with Disabilities Act and the Rehabilitation Act to clarify that a discriminatory compensation decision that is unlawful under these acts occurs each time compensation is paid pursuant to the discriminatory compensation decision. Many of these changes will be mentioned in the course of this chapter.

Coverage

Title VII may be conveniently analyzed in three ways. In terms of its coverage, to whom are the statutes' prohibitions addressed? Who are the potential defendants in actions under this statute? Second, in terms of its scope, what behaviors are forbidden? Third, in terms of its remedies, what relief does the statute provide for the victims of prohibited behavior? This chapter and the next will focus on the scope of the statute. Remedies under Title VII will be discussed later in this chapter.

In Chapter 2, we noted that the Equal Protection Clause of the federal Constitution applies only where "state action" is found. That restriction does not apply to the statutes under discussion here. They extend to both the public and private sectors. Title VII prohibits discriminatory practices by employers, employment agencies, labor organizations, and training programs. Since similar principles apply to all these potential defendants, for purposes of clarity we will confine our attention to employers. An employer is defined in 701(b) as "a person engaged in an industry affecting commerce who has fifteen or more employees. . . ." Section 701(a) defines "persons" as including governments, corporations, and partnerships as well as individuals. The Supreme Court ruled in 1984 that a law partnership is an employer under Title VII, *Hishon v. King & Spaulding*, 467 U.S. 69.

Having identified employers, the statute goes on to declare that some employers are nevertheless exempt from the statute's prohibitions. Two of these are relevant to our discussion of sex discrimination. An employer is exempt from coverage under Title VII if it is a bona fide private membership club (701(b)). Finally, an employer is exempt from coverage of Title VII in the employment of aliens outside the United States (section 702). The CRA of 1991 amended the statute to make clear that U.S. citizens working abroad for U.S.-based employers are included within the coverage of Title VII.

Scope

The main prohibitions of the statute are stated in section 703(a).

> It shall be an unlawful employment practice for an employer—
>
> (1) to fail or refuse to hire or to discharge any individual, or otherwise to discriminate against any individual with respect to his compensation, terms, conditions, or privileges of employment, because of such individual's race, color, religion, sex, or national origin: or
>
> (2) to limit, segregate, or classify his employees or applicants for employment in any way which would deprive or tend to deprive any individual of employment opportunities or otherwise adversely affect his status as an employee, because of such individual's race, color, religion, sex, or national origin.

Although attention will be concentrated on the prohibitions of section 703, those in 704(a) should not be ignored. There, the statute makes retaliation against those who oppose unlawful discrimination or make a charge, testify, assist, or participate in an investigation, proceeding, or hearing under Title VII a separate offense. Although the language of section 704(a) makes it clear that employees are protected from retaliation, the lower courts were divided on whether the same protection extended to former employees. In 1997, the Supreme Court addressed this issue in a case brought by a former employee who challenged his firing under Title VII and received a negative reference when applying to another employer for a job. In *Robinson v. Shell Oil Company*, 519 U.S. 337 (1997), the Supreme Court unanimously held that former employees are also covered by section 704(a). The circuit courts also disagreed on whether the challenged retaliatory action had to be employment or workplace related and about how harmful the action must be to constitute retaliation. In *Burlington Northern & Santa Fe Railway Co. v. White*, 548 U.S. 53 (2006), a case brought by a female employee for alleged retaliatory reassignment of her duties, surveillance and monitoring of her daily activities, and a 37-day suspension, the Supreme Court resolved the circuits' conflict. The Court held that the anti-retaliation provision of Title VII, unlike its substantive provision, is not limited to discriminatory actions that affect the terms and conditions of employment. Interpreting the provision to provide broad protection from retaliation ensures the cooperation of employees willing to file complainants and act as witnesses, which is necessary to the enforcement of Title VII. In addition, the Court determined that "a plaintiff must show that a reasonable employee would have found the challenged action materially adverse," *that is*, "it well might have 'dissuaded a reasonable worker from making or supporting a charge of discrimination.'" According to the Court, "material adversity" means the harms must be significant, and "reasonable employee" requires use of an objective standard for judging harm. Finally, the standard is tied to the challenged retaliatory act, not the underlying conduct that forms the basis of the Title VII complaint.

Just as there are exemptions from the coverage, there are exceptions to the scope of the prohibitions. The main exception relevant to sex discrimination is the bona fide occupational qualification (BFOQ) (703(e)(1)). This exception will be discussed at some length later in this chapter. Others include veterans' preference (712); differential treatment based upon seniority, merit systems, productivity, and professionally developed ability tests (703(h)); and wage differentials authorized by the Equal Pay Act (703(h)). Other exceptions include the personal staff or policy-level appointees of elected political officials (701(f)) and individuals not covered for national security reasons (703(g)).

II. Two Concepts of Discrimination

The Basic Ingredients

Title VII does not define the terms *discrimination* or *because of sex*. Congress left the task of interpreting the meaning of these expressions to the courts. It should be noted that the word *sex* was added to Title VII only one day before the House passed the Act. There is some thought that the word *sex* was added in an attempt to defeat the entire Act, which of course failed; the Civil Rights Act of 1964, including the provision protecting against discrimination on the basis of sex, ultimately passed. Because the amendment was last minute, there were no legislative hearings and little discussion upon which the courts could rely to explain what Congress meant by *sex*. Although the scant legislative history indicates that the one-word amendment adding the term *sex* was originally intended to protect women, the Supreme Court in *Newport News Shipbuilding & Dry Dock Co. v. EEOC*, 462 U.S. 669, 682 (1983), subsequently held that Title VII protects men as well.

Discrimination against women and men takes many forms and is most often directed toward enforcement of social norms that are keyed to the biological sex of individuals. Courts have understood Title VII to extend its protection to only some of these forms of discrimination. Historically, courts have interpreted "sex" to mean gender and not sexual orientation. In light of the Supreme Court's decisions in *Oncale v. Sundowner Offshore Services, Inc.*, 523 U.S. 75 (1998), and *Price Waterhouse v. Hopkins*, 490 U.S. 228 (1989), however, the clear demarcation between what is and is not discrimination "because of sex" has been blurred. We will consider *Oncale* in more detail in the discussion of sexual harassment in Chapter 4. It is important to note here that the Supreme Court, in the context of Mr. Oncale's same-sex sexual harassment claim, discussed the meaning of Title VII's prohibition of discrimination "because of . . . sex" and concluded that, ". . . nothing in Title VII necessarily bars a claim of discrimination 'because of . . . sex' merely because the plaintiff and the defendant (or the person charged with acting on behalf of the defendant) are of the same sex." In *Price Waterhouse*, the Supreme Court indicated that the plaintiff could show gender played a part in an adverse employment decision based on the employer's gender stereotyping of her.

In light of these Supreme Court decisions, some federal courts have reconsidered their prior rejection of claims of discrimination "because of sex" that concerned sexual orientation. The following is just such a case.

Nichols v. Azteca Restaurant Enterprises, Inc.

United States Court of Appeals,
Ninth Circuit, 2001.
256 F.3d 864.

GOULD, Circuit Judge.

Antonio Sanchez (footnote omitted) brought this action against his former employer, Azteca Restaurant Enterprises, Inc., alleging, among other claims, sexual harassment and retaliation in violation of Title VII of the Civil Rights Act of 1964 ("Title VII") and its state law counterpart, the Washington Law Against Discrimination ("WLAD"). Sanchez claimed that he was verbally harassed by some male co-workers and a supervisor because he was effeminate and did not meet their views of a male stereotype. Sanchez further asserted that he was terminated in retaliation for opposing the harassment. Following a bench trial, the district court entered judgment in favor of Azteca on all claims. . . .

We agree with Sanchez that the behavior of his co-workers and supervisor violated Title VII and WLAD. We further agree that Azteca failed to take adequate steps to remedy the harassment. We therefore reverse the judgment of the district court with respect to Sanchez's hostile work environment claim, and remand for further proceedings consistent with our opinion. We affirm the judgment of the district court with respect to Sanchez's retaliation claim.

I

Azteca operates a chain of restaurants in Washington and Oregon. It employed Sanchez from October 1991 to July 1995. Sanchez at first worked as a host in Azteca's Burien restaurant, and later worked as a food server at the South-center restaurant.

Throughout his tenure at Azteca, Sanchez was subjected to a relentless campaign of insults, name-calling, and vulgarities. Male co-workers and a supervisor repeatedly referred to Sanchez in Spanish and English as "she" and "her." Male co-workers mocked Sanchez for walking and carrying his serving tray "like a woman," and taunted him in Spanish and English as, among other things, a "faggot" and a "fucking female whore." The remarks were not stray or isolated. Rather, the abuse occurred at least once a week and often several times a day. . . .

Following a bench trial, the district court concluded that Sanchez had not been subjected to a hostile environment. . . . [T]he court concluded that . . . the alleged harassment did not take place "because of sex." . . . Sanchez timely appealed. . . .

III

Under Title VII, it is unlawful for an employer "to discriminate against any individual with respect to his compensation, terms, conditions, or privileges of employment, because of . . . sex." 42 U.S.C. § 2000e-2(a)(1).

To prevail on his hostile environment claim, . . . Sanchez was required to prove that any harassment took place "because of sex." *Oncale v. Sundowner Offshore Servs., Inc.*, 523 U.S. 75, 79 (1998); *Schonauer*, 905 P.2d at 400.

The district court ruled against Sanchez on each of these elements, concluding that: (1) Sanchez's workplace was not objectively hostile; (2) Sanchez did not perceive his workplace to be hostile; and (3) the alleged conduct did not occur because of sex. We disagree with each of these conclusions and, where applicable, the clearly erroneous findings upon which they are based. . . .

C. Because of Sex

Sexual harassment is actionable under Title VII to the extent it occurs "because of" the plaintiff's sex. *Oncale*, 523 U.S. at 79; *see also Schonauer*, 905 P.2d at 400. Sanchez asserts that the verbal abuse at issue was based upon the perception that he is effeminate and, therefore, occurred because of sex. In short, Sanchez contends that he was harassed because he failed to conform to a male stereotype.

Sanchez's theory derives from *Price Waterhouse v. Hopkins*, 490 U.S. 228 (1989), in which the Supreme Court held that a woman who was denied partnership in an accounting firm because she did not match a sex stereotype had an actionable claim under Title VII. Hopkins, the plaintiff in *Price Waterhouse*, was described by various partners as "macho," in need of "a course in charm school," "a lady using foul language," and someone who had been "a tough-talking somewhat masculine hard-nosed manager." *Id.* at 235. Hopkins was advised that she could improve her partnership chances if she would "walk more femininely, talk more femininely, dress more femininely, wear make-up, have her hair styled, and wear jewelry." *Id.* (internal quotation marks omitted.) Writing for the plurality, Justice Brennan held that "[i]n the specific context of sex stereotyping, an employer who acts on the basis of a belief that a woman cannot be aggressive, or that she must not be, has acted on the basis of gender." *Id.* at 250; *see also id.* at 272–73 (O'Connor, J., concurring in the judgment) (characterizing "failure to conform to [sex] stereotypes" as criterion of discrimination).

Sanchez contends that the holding in *Price Waterhouse* applies with equal force to a man who is discriminated against for acting too feminine. We agree. *See Oncale*, 523 U.S. at 78 ("Title VII's prohibition of discrimination 'because of . . . sex' protects men as well as women."); *see also Schwenk v. Hartford*, 204 F.3d 1187, 1202 (9th Cir. 2000) (comparing the scope of the Gender Motivated Violence Act with the scope of Title VII, which forbids "[d]iscrimination because one fails to act in the way expected of a man or woman"); *Higgins v. New Balance Athletic Shoe, Inc.*, 194 F.3d 252, 261 n.4 (1st Cir. 1999) ("[J]ust as a woman can ground an action on a claim that men discriminated against her because she did not meet stereotyped expectations of femininity, a man can ground a claim on evidence that other men discriminated against him because he did not meet stereotyped expectations of masculinity") (citing *Price Waterhouse*, 490 U.S. at 250–51).

At its essence, the systematic abuse directed at Sanchez reflected a belief that Sanchez did not act as a man should act. Sanchez was attacked for walking and carrying his tray "like a woman"—i.e., for having feminine mannerisms. Sanchez was derided for not having sexual intercourse with a waitress who was his friend. Sanchez's male co-workers and one of his supervisors repeatedly reminded Sanchez that he did not conform to their gender-based stereotypes, referring to him as "she" and "her." And, the most vulgar name-calling directed at Sanchez was cast in female terms. We conclude that this verbal abuse was closely linked to gender.

Price Waterhouse sets a rule that bars discrimination on the basis of sex stereotypes. That rule squarely applies to preclude the harassment here.[7] The only potential difficulty arises out of a now faint shadow cast by our decision in *DeSantis v. Pacific Telephone & Telegraph Co., Inc.*, 608 F.2d 327 (9th Cir. 1979). *DeSantis* holds that discrimination based on a stereotype that a man "should have a virile rather than an effeminate appearance" does not fall within Title VII's purview. *Id.* at 331–32. This holding, however, predates and conflicts with the Supreme Court's decision in *Price Waterhouse*. And, in this direct conflict, *DeSantis* must lose. To the extent it conflicts with *Price Waterhouse*, as we hold it does, *DeSantis* is no longer good law. Under *Price Waterhouse*, Sanchez must prevail.

Following *Price Waterhouse*, we hold that the verbal abuse at issue occurred because of sex.[8] Because we hold that Sanchez has established each element of his hostile environment claim, we further hold that the conduct of Sanchez's co-workers and supervisor constituted actionable harassment under both Title VII and WLAD,[9] and reverse the district court's contrary conclusion. . . .

Study Questions

1. What type of behavior was complained of by the plaintiff? Do you think this constituted discrimination? Why or why not?
2. What reasons did the court give for finding that the discrimination suffered by the plaintiff was within the scope of Title VII? How did the court deal with a prior decision that drew the opposite conclusion? Was the court correct in overruling its prior decision?

---

[7]We do not imply that all gender-based distinctions are actionable under Title VII. For example, our decision does not imply that there is any violation of Title VII occasioned by reasonable regulations that require male and female employees to conform to different dress and grooming standards.

[8]The district court's finding that "Sanchez testified that the harassment was unrelated to his sex or gender" is clearly erroneous. Sanchez did not so testify.

[9]There is no Washington state law authority regarding same-sex sexual harassment or harassment based on sex stereotyping. Absent such authority, we may reasonably hold that Sanchez established a hostile environment claim under WLAD as "decisions interpreting [Title VII] are persuasive authority for the construction of [WLAD]." *Xieng v. Peoples Nat'l Bank*, 844 P.2d 389, 392 (Wash. 1993).

In the *Nichols* decision, the Ninth Circuit concluded, pursuant to the Supreme Court's decision in *Price Waterhouse*, that gender discrimination based on sexual stereotyping is actionable under Title VII. Some federal courts have found similar facts implicate discrimination "because of sex" rather than because of sexual orientation. For example, in *Centola v. Potter*, 183 F. Supp. 2d 403 (D. Mass. 2002), the District Court rejected a homosexual employee's claim of sexual orientation discrimination under Title VII. It concluded, however, that the employee could proceed with his claim of sex discrimination on the basis that sex stereotyping can constitute discrimination "because of sex" under Title VII. In that case, the employee's co-workers harassed him because of his perceived "effeminate" behavior.

Other federal courts have continued to hold that the factual allegations by plaintiffs demonstrate purported discrimination based on sexual orientation, which is not actionable under Title VII. In *Bibby v. Philadelphia Coca Cola Bottling Company*, 260 F.3d 257 (3rd Cir. 2001), the Court found there are at least three ways a plaintiff alleging same-sex sexual harassment could demonstrate discrimination "because of sex"—motivation by sexual desire, general hostility to the presence of one sex in the workplace, or punishment of victim for noncompliance with gender stereotypes. In *Bibby*, however, the male (homosexual) plaintiff's claim failed because it ". . . was pure and simple, that he was discriminated against because of his sexual orientation." And, with respect to transsexuals, courts have uniformly held that Title VII does not afford them protection. In *Oiler v. Winn Dixie Stores, Inc.*, E.D. La. No. 00-3114, Sept. 16, 2002, the District Court for the Eastern District of Louisiana granted summary judgment in favor of the employer. The male plaintiff had alleged that his termination for dressing as a woman off-duty amounted to sex (gender) discrimination under Title VII; he was fired because his behavior did not conform to sex stereotypes. In its decision, the court stated that nothing in the language or legislative history of Title VII demonstrated that Congress meant "sex" to mean anything other than "biological sex." Furthermore, until very recently, courts have uniformly held that Title VII does not prohibit discrimination based on sexual orientation, transvestism, transsexualism, or gender identity issues. In 2008, however, in *Schroer v. Billington*, the U.S. District Court for the District of Columbia seemingly departed from that course. Judge James Robertson determined that a man who was offered a terrorism analyst position by the Library of Congress only to have that offer revoked after he told a library official that he was having surgery to change his gender to female demonstrated that the Library had violated Title VII. The judge found that the Library's refusal to hire Schroer was premised on both unlawful sex stereotyping (because Schroer did not comport with the Library's sex stereotype of how men and women should act and appear) and unlawful discrimination on the basis of sex. *Schroer v. Billington*, D. D. C. Civil Action No. 05-1090, September 19, 2008 (". . . [T]he Library's refusal to hire Schroer after being advised that she planned to change her anatomical sex by undergoing sex reassignment surgery was *literally* discrimination 'because of . . . sex.'").

Title VII prohibits discrimination in employment "because of sex." Regardless of the varied factual scenarios presented, the case law clearly demonstrates that "sex" means gender. It is not enough, however, that women or men are victims of discrimination in the workplace. To establish a violation of Title VII, they must show that they have been victimized "because of" their sex.

The "because of" component can be understood in a variety of ways. Courts have considered two of these, rejecting the one and accepting the other. On one reading, an employment practice is prohibited by the statute where the sex of the victim is a sufficient condition for being treated in a discriminatory manner. In this "sufficient condition" interpretation, a discriminatory practice affecting women is prohibited only if all women are eligible for discriminatory treatment under it. The Supreme Court rejected that interpretation in 1971, in *Phillips v. Martin Marietta Corp.*, 400 U.S. 542. There, the employer attempted to defend a policy of refusing to hire women for selected positions if they had preschool-age children at home. The employer unsuccessfully argued that because not all women were affected, the policy was not prohibited by Title VII.

A second interpretation of "because of" has been widely accepted by the courts. In that reading, an employment practice is prohibited by the statute where the sex of the victim is a necessary condition for being treated in a discriminatory manner. In this "necessary condition" interpretation, a discriminatory practice affecting women or men is prohibited only if they would not have been victimized had they not been female or male. In legal jargon, these people would not have been victims "but for" their gender. The following case illustrates the way the "necessary condition" or "but for" interpretation functions in a case and the type of evidence needed to support the claim of discrimination "because of sex."

EEOC v. BROWN & ROOT, INC.
United States Court of Appeals, Fifth Circuit, 1982.
688 F.2d 338.

ALVIN B. RUBIN, Circuit Judge:

. . . The following facts are undisputed: Sarah Joan Boyes was employed by Brown & Root as an electrician's helper. Brown & Root is a construction company and Ms. Boyes was assigned to work on an overhead steel beam that was part of a structure being erected at Escatawpa, Mississippi. She became paralyzed by fear and was unable to move, a condition known as "freezing." It was necessary physically to assist her to climb down. Brown & Root discharged Ms. Boyes from her job for the stated reason that she was "not capable of performing assigned work." After she was fired, another female worker was hired to fill the position of electrician's helper.

What is disputed is whether men who manifested the same acrophobia were also discharged. In opposition to the motion for summary judgment, the Equal Employment Opportunity Commission offered the affidavit of its investigator. To this were attached copies of statements taken from four male employees, each of whom stated that he or some other worker had at some prior time frozen on the beams, could not get down without help, and was not discharged. One statement referred also to a male worker who was kept on the ground because he was afraid of heights. There was also attached an "EEOC affidavit" from a male employee

stating that he had "frozen" and had not been discharged. [The district court granted summary judgment for the defendant.]

While neither the pleadings nor the proof in opposition to the motion for summary judgment frame the issue as directly as would be desirable, the disputed issue was not whether Ms. Boyes was unable to work at heights, a fact that was, indeed, undisputed, or whether she was replaced by a male, another fact that was not disputed, but whether, had she been a man, she would have suffered dismissal as a result of her phobia. . . .

If an employee is discharged under circumstances in which an employee of another sex would not have been discharged, an inference of discrimination arises irrespective of the gender of the employee's replacement. . . .

The summary judgment is REVERSED and the case is REMANDED for further proceedings consistent with this opinion.

STUDY QUESTIONS

1. Why was the plaintiff fired? Does it appear that defendant was merely using the episode as an excuse to keep women out of the electricians' trade?
2. Had defendant also fired acrophobic men, would the decision in this case have been different?

Men and women are treated differently in many ways in employment settings. The reasons offered in justification frequently give expression to ancient, often tradition-based, stereotypes. The objective of Title VII is to counteract the impact of these cultural stereotypes. Employer decisions that work to the disadvantage of women, however, are sometimes based upon true generalizations about differences between men and women. Does Title VII bar employment decisions that treat men and women workers differently if those decisions are based not on outmoded stereotypes but on true generalizations? In the decision that follows, the Supreme Court addressed that question.

LOS ANGELES DEPT. OF WATER & POWER V. MANHART

Supreme Court of the United States, 1978.
435 U.S. 702, 98 S. Ct. 1370, 55 L.Ed.2d 657.

Mr. Justice STEVENS delivered the opinion of the Court.

As a class, women live longer than men. For this reason, the Los Angeles Department of Water and Power required its female employees to make larger contributions to its pension fund than its male employees. We granted certiorari to decide whether this practice discriminated against individual female employees because of their sex in violation of § 703 (a) (1) of the Civil Rights Act of 1964, as amended.

For many years the Department has administered retirement, disability, and death-benefit programs for its employees. Upon retirement each employee is eligible for a monthly retirement benefit computed as a fraction of his or her salary multiplied by years of service. The monthly benefits for men and women of the same age, seniority, and salary are equal. Benefits are funded entirely by contributions from the employees and the Department, augmented by the income earned on those contributions. No private insurance company is involved in the administration or payment of benefits.

Based on a study of mortality tables and its own experience, the Department determined that its 2,000 female employees, on the average, will live a few years longer than its 10,000 male employees. The cost of a pension for the average retired female is greater than for the average male retiree because more monthly payments must be made to the average woman. The Department therefore required female employees to make monthly contributions to the fund which were 14.84% higher than the contributions required of comparable male employees. Because employee contributions were withheld from paychecks, a female employee took home less pay than a male employee earning the same salary.[5]

. . . On a motion for summary judgment, the District Court held that the contribution differential violated § 703 (a) (1) and ordered a refund of all excess contributions made before the amendment of the plan. The United States Court of Appeals for the Ninth Circuit affirmed. . . .

There are both real and fictional differences between women and men. It is true that the average man is taller than the average woman; it is not true that the average woman driver is more accident prone than the average man. Before the Civil Rights Act of 1964 was enacted, an employer could fashion his personnel policies on the

---

[5]The significance of the disparity is illustrated by the record of one woman whose contributions to the fund (including interest on the amount withheld each month) amounted to $18,171.40; a similarly situated male would have contributed only $12,843.53.

basis of assumptions about the differences between men and women, whether or not the assumptions were valid.

It is now well recognized that employment decisions cannot be predicated on mere "stereotyped" impressions about the characteristics of males or females. Myths and purely habitual assumptions about a woman's inability to perform certain kinds of work are no longer acceptable reasons for refusing to employ qualified individuals, or for paying them less. This case does not, however, involve a fictional difference between men and women. It involves a generalization that the parties accept as unquestionably true: Women, as a class, do live longer than men. The Department treated its women employees differently from its men employees because the two classes are in fact different. It is equally true, however, that all individuals in the respective classes do not share the characteristic that differentiates the average class representatives. Many women do not live as long as the average man and many men outlive the average woman. The question, therefore, is whether the existence or nonexistence of "discrimination" is to be determined by comparison of class characteristics or individual characteristics. A "stereotyped" answer to that question may not be the same as the answer that the language and purpose of the statute command.

The statute makes it unlawful "to discriminate against any *individual* with respect to his compensation, terms, conditions, or privileges of employment, because of such *individual's* race, color, religion, sex, or national origin." The statute's focus on the individual is unambiguous. It precludes treatment of individuals as simply components of a racial, religious, sexual, or national class. If height is required for a job, a tall woman may not be refused employment merely because, on the average, women are too short. Even a true generalization about the class is an insufficient reason for disqualifying an individual to whom the generalization does not apply.

That proposition is of critical importance in this case because there is no assurance that any individual woman working for the Department will actually fit the generalization on which the Department's policy is based. Many of those individuals will not live as long as the average man. While they were working, those individuals received smaller paychecks because of their sex, but they will receive no compensating advantage when they retire.

It is true, of course, that while contributions are being collected from the employees, the Department cannot know which individuals will predecease the average woman. Therefore, unless women as a class are assessed an extra charge, they will be subsidized, to some extent, by the class of male employees. It follows, according to the Department, that fairness to its class of male employees justifies the extra assessment against all of its female employees.

But the question of fairness to various classes affected by the statute is essentially a matter of policy for the legislature to address. Congress has decided that classifications based on sex, like those based on national origin or race, are unlawful. Actuarial studies could unquestionably identify differences in life expectancy based on race or national origin, as well as sex. But a statute that was designed to make race irrelevant in the employment market could not reasonably be construed to permit a take-home-pay differential based on a racial classification.

Even if the statutory language were less clear, the basic policy of the statute requires that we focus on fairness to individuals rather than fairness to classes. Practices that classify employees in terms of religion, race, or sex tend to preserve traditional assumptions about groups rather than thoughtful scrutiny of individuals. The generalization involved in this case illustrates the point. Separate mortality tables are easily interpreted as reflecting innate differences between the sexes; but a significant part of the longevity differential may be explained by the social fact that men are heavier smokers than women.

Finally, there is no reason to believe that Congress intended a special definition of discrimination in the context of employee group insurance coverage. It is true that insurance is concerned with events that are individually unpredictable, but that is characteristic of many employment decisions. Individual risks, like individual performance, may not be predicted by resort to classifications proscribed by Title VII. Indeed, the fact that this case involves a group insurance program highlights a basic flaw in the Department's fairness argument. For when insurance risks are grouped, the better risks always subsidize the poorer risks. Healthy persons subsidize medical benefits for the less healthy; unmarried workers subsidize the pensions of married workers; persons who eat, drink, or smoke to excess may subsidize pension benefits for persons whose habits are more temperate. Treating different classes of risks as though they were the same for purposes of group insurance is a common practice that has never been considered inherently unfair. To insure the flabby and the fit as though they were equivalent risks may be more common than treating men and women alike; but nothing more than habit makes one "subsidy" seem less fair than the other. . . .

Although we conclude that the Department's practice violated Title VII, we do not suggest that the statute was intended to revolutionize the insurance and pension industries. All that is at issue today is a requirement that men and women make unequal contributions to an employer-operated pension fund. Nothing in our holding implies that it would be unlawful for an employer to set aside equal retirement contributions for each employee and let each retiree purchase the largest benefit which his or her accumulated contributions could command in the open market. Nor does it call into question the insurance industry practice of considering the composition of an employer's work force in determining the probable cost of a retirement or death benefit plan. Finally, we recognize that in a case of this kind it may be necessary to take special care in fashioning appropriate relief.

There can be no doubt that the prohibition against sex-differentiated employee contributions represents a marked departure from past practice. Although Title VII was enacted in 1964, this is apparently the first litigation challenging contribution differences based on valid actuarial tables. Retroactive liability could be devastating for a pension fund. The harm would fall in large part on innocent third parties. If, as the courts below apparently contemplated, the plaintiffs' contributions are recovered from the pension fund, the administrators of the fund will be forced to meet unchanged obligations with diminished assets. If the reserve proves inadequate, either the expectations of all retired employees will be disappointed or current employees will be forced to pay not only for their own future security but also for the unanticipated reduction in the contributions of past employees.

. . . [I]t was error to grant such relief in this case. Accordingly, although we agree with the Court of Appeals' analysis of the statute, we vacate its judgment and remand the case for further proceedings consistent with this opinion.

It Is So Ordered.

STUDY QUESTIONS

1. Was the pension plan unfair to women as a class or only to those women who outlive the average woman? What question did the Court regard as central to this case?
2. Explain the department's complaint that the Court's solution would be unfair to its male employees. Is that a valid complaint?
3. What reason did the Court offer in support of its decision here? Do you think it reached the correct decision? Suppose that white males have greater life expectancy than black males. Would Title VII permit differentiation in pension payments for them?

The *Manhart* decision, however sweeping its endorsement of the principle of fairness to individuals, was limited in two respects. It dealt only with pension plans that provide for equal payments to women and men after retirement but require unequal payments by participating men and women workers prior to retirement. Most pension plans work the other way around (i.e., they require equal payments into the plan by all workers but provide lower payments to female than male retirees). After *Manhart,* the status of those pension plans remained in doubt. That doubt was removed in 1983 when the Court held in *Arizona Governing Committee v. Norris,* 463 U.S. 1073, that an employer-sponsored pension plan of the latter description violates Title VII.

The *Manhart* decision is also limited in that it applies only to employer-sponsored pension or insurance plans. This limitation is implicit in Title VII, which, you will recall, only covers conduct by employers, employment agencies, labor organizations, and training programs. Insurance and pension plans sponsored and marketed independently of employers and other parties who fall within the coverage of Title VII are not affected by this act.

The Equal Protection Clause affords no protection against sex-based rate schedules in privately issued insurance and pension programs because no state action is involved. It is worth noting once again that state law sometimes affords a remedy where federal law does not. For example, in 1988, a Pennsylvania appellate court found that the sex-based rate schedules used by a private automobile insurance company were in violation of the Equal Rights Amendment to that state's constitution, even though no state action was involved (*Bartholomew v. Foster,* 541 A.2d 393 (1988)).

Title VII bars discrimination in employment on five bases, including sex. When drafting Title VII, Congress did not define the term "discrimination." That task was left to the courts. The meaning of that term emerges from court decisions relating to questions of proof—what is sufficient to establish a violation of the statute?—and questions of procedure—what order of proof is used when analyzing Title VII cases? In the course of addressing these questions, the Supreme Court recognized two concepts of discrimination. These were first explicitly formulated in a footnote to an important race discrimination decision:

> "Disparate treatment". . . is the most easily understood type of discrimination. The employer simply treats some people less favorably than others because of their race, color, religion, sex, or national origin. Proof of discriminatory motive is critical, although it can in some situations be inferred from the mere fact of differences in treatment. . . . Claims of disparate treatment may be distinguished from claims that stress "disparate impact." The latter involve employment practices that are facially neutral in their treatment of different groups but that in fact fall more harshly on one group than another and cannot be justified by business necessity. Proof of discriminatory motive; we have held, is not required under a disparate impact theory. . . .
> International Brotherhood of Teamsters v. U.S., *431 U.S. 324, fn. 15 (1977).*

Disparate Treatment

Discrimination in the disparate treatment sense is, as the Court indicated, similar to the everyday notion of biased or prejudiced treatment, differential treatment that is motivated by prejudice. Sometimes discrimination in this sense can be directly inferred from the employer's behavior (e.g., *EEOC v. Brown & Root*). More often, however, discrimination is not so easily proven. Employment decisions that affect only one or a few persons present especially difficult problems of proof. One such situation was faced by the Supreme Court in the following case. There, the Court summarized its instructions on how proof of discrimination must proceed in disparate treatment cases.

TEXAS DEPT. OF COMMUNITY AFFAIRS V. BURDINE
Supreme Court of the United States, 1981.
450 U.S. 248, 101 S. Ct. 1089, 67 L.Ed.2d 207.

Justice POWELL delivered the opinion of the Court.

. . . Petitioner, the Texas Department of Community Affairs (TDCA), hired respondent, a female, in January 1972, for the position of accounting clerk in the Public Service Careers Division (PSC). PSC provided training and employment opportunities in the public sector for unskilled workers. When hired, respondent possessed several years' experience in employment training. She was promoted to Field Services Coordinator in July 1972. Her supervisor resigned in November of that year, and respondent was assigned additional duties. Although she applied for the supervisor's position of Project Director, the position remained vacant for six months. . . .

After consulting with personnel within TDCA [B. R. Fuller, then Executive Director of TDCA], hired a male from another division of the agency as Project Director. In reducing the PSC staff, he fired respondent along with two other employees, and retained another male, Walz, as the only professional employee in the division. It was undisputed that respondent had maintained her application for the position of Project Director and had requested to remain with TDCA. Respondent soon was rehired by TDCA and assigned to another division of the agency. She received the exact salary paid to the Project Director at PSC, and the subsequent promotions she has received have kept her salary and responsibility commensurate with what she would have received had she been appointed Project Director.

Respondent filed this suit in the United States District Court for the Western District of Texas. She alleged that the failure to promote and the subsequent decision to terminate her had been predicated on gender discrimination in violation of Title VII. After a bench trial, the District Court held that neither decision was based on gender discrimination. . . .

. . . The Court of Appeals, however, reversed the District Court's finding that Fuller's testimony sufficiently had rebutted respondent's prima facie case of gender discrimination in the decision to terminate her employment at PSC. The court reaffirmed its previously announced views that the defendant in a Title VII case bears the burden of proving by a preponderance of the evidence the existence of legitimate nondiscriminatory reasons for the employment action and that the defendant also must prove by objective evidence that those hired or promoted were better qualified than the plaintiff. The court found that Fuller's testimony did not carry either of these evidentiary burdens. It, therefore, reversed the judgment of the District Court and remanded the case for computation of backpay. . . .

In *McDonnell Douglas Corp. v. Green,* we set forth the basic allocation of burdens and order of presentation of proof in a Title VII case alleging discriminatory treatment. First, the plaintiff has the burden of proving by the preponderance of the evidence a prima facie case of discrimination. Second, if the plaintiff succeeds in proving the prima facie case, the burden shifts to the defendant "to articulate some legitimate, nondiscriminatory reason for the employee's rejection." Third, should the defendant carry this burden, the plaintiff must then have an opportunity to prove by a preponderance of the evidence that the legitimate reasons offered by the defendant were not its true reasons, but were a pretext for discrimination.

The nature of the burden that shifts to the defendant should be understood in light of the plaintiff's ultimate and intermediate burdens. The ultimate burden of persuading the trier of fact that the defendant intentionally discriminated against the plaintiff remains at all time with the plaintiff. . . .

The burden of establishing a prima facie case of disparate treatment is not onerous. The plaintiff must prove by a preponderance of the evidence that she applied for an available position, for which she was qualified, but was rejected under circumstances which give rise to an inference of unlawful discrimination.[6] The prima facie case serves an important function in the litigation: it eliminates the most common nondiscriminatory reasons for the plaintiff's rejection. As the Court explained in *Furnco Construction Co. v. Waters*, the prima facie case "raises an inference of discrimination only because we presume these acts, if otherwise unexplained, are more likely than not based on the consideration of impermissible factors." Establishment of the prima facie case in effect creates a presumption that the employer unlawfully discriminated against the employee. If the trier of fact believes the plaintiff's evidence, and if the employer is silent in the face of the presumption, the court must enter judgment for the plaintiff because no issue of fact remains in the case.

The burden that shifts to the defendant, therefore, is to rebut the presumption of discrimination by producing evidence that the plaintiff was rejected, or someone else was preferred, for a legitimate, nondiscriminatory reason. The defendant need not persuade the court that it was actually motivated by the proffered reasons. It is sufficient if the defendant's evidence raises a genuine issue of fact as to whether it discriminated against the plaintiff. To accomplish this, the defendant must clearly set forth, through

the introduction of admissible evidence, the reasons for the plaintiff's rejection. The explanation provided must be legally sufficient to justify a judgment for the defendant. If the defendant carries this burden of production, the presumption raised by the prima facie case is rebutted, and the factual inquiry proce[e]ds to a new level of specificity. Placing this burden of production on the defendant thus serves simultaneously to meet the plaintiff's prima facie case by presenting a legitimate reason for the action and to frame the factual issue with sufficient clarity so that the plaintiff will have a full and fair opportunity to demonstrate pretext. The sufficiency of the defendant's evidence should be evaluated by the extent to which it fulfills these functions.

The plaintiff retains the burden of persuasion. She now must have the opportunity to demonstrate that the proffered reason was not the true reason for the employment decision. This burden now merges with the ultimate burden of persuading the court that she has been the victim of intentional discrimination. She may succeed in this either directly by persuading the court that a discriminatory reason more likely motivated the employer or indirectly by showing that the employer's proffered explanation is unworthy of credence. . . .

The Court of Appeals has misconstrued the nature of the burden that *McDonnell Douglas* and its progeny place on the defendant. . . .

The court placed the burden of persuasion on the defendant apparently because it feared that "[i]f an employer need only *articulate*—not prove—a legitimate,

[6]In *McDonnell Douglas* we described an appropriate model for a prima facie case of racial discrimination. The plaintiff must show: "(i) that he belongs to a racial minority; (ii) that he applied and was qualified for a job for which the employer was seeking applicants; (iii) that, despite his qualification, he was rejected; and (iv) that, after his rejection, the position remained open and the employer continued to seek applicants from persons of complainant's qualifications."

We added, however, that this standard is not inflexible, as "[t]he facts necessarily will vary in Title VII cases, and the specification above of the prima facie proof required from respondent is not necessarily applicable in every respect in differing factual situations."

In the instant case, it is not seriously contested that respondent has proved a prima facie case. She showed that she was a qualified woman who sought an available position, but the position was left open for several months before she finally was rejected in favor of a male, Walz, who had been under her supervision.

nondiscriminatory reason for his action, he may compose fictitious, but legitimate, reasons for his actions." We do not believe, however, that limiting the defendant's evidentiary obligation to a burden of production will unduly hinder the plaintiff. First, as noted above, the defendant's explanation of its legitimate reasons must be clear and reasonably specific. This obligation arises both from the necessity of rebutting the inference of discrimination arising from the prima facie case and from the requirement that the plaintiff be afforded "a full and fair opportunity" to demonstrate pretext. Second, although the defendant does not bear a formal burden of persuasion, the defendant nevertheless retains an incentive to persuade the trier of fact that the employment decision was lawful. Thus, the defendant normally will attempt to prove the factual basis for its explanation. Third, the liberal discovery rules applicable to any civil suit in federal court are supplemented in a Title VII suit by the plaintiff's access to the Equal Employment Opportunity Commission's investigatory files concerning her complaint. Given these factors, we are unpersuaded that the plaintiff will find it particularly difficult to prove that a proffered explanation lacking a factual basis is a pretext. We remain confident that the *McDonnell Douglas* framework permits the plaintiff meriting relief to demonstrate intentional discrimination. . . .

In summary, the Court of Appeals erred by requiring the defendant to prove by a preponderance of the evidence the existence of nondiscriminatory reasons for terminating the respondent and that the person retained in her stead had superior objective qualifications for the position. When the plaintiff has proved a prima facie case of discrimination, the defendant bears only the burden of explaining clearly the nondiscriminatory reasons for its actions. The judgment of the Court of Appeals is vacated and the case is remanded for further proceedings consistent with this opinion.

It Is So Ordered.

STUDY QUESTIONS

1. Women who work in environments where men are predominately the supervisors often suspect that they are being discriminated against because of their sex. Most frequently, such suspicions are discounted and dismissed as misunderstandings on their own part. How should women who find themselves in Burdine's position evaluate such suspicions? What role might networking play in situations like these?
2. Burdine was certain that her suspicions were true. How should a court decide whether her allegations are true? What additional difficulties does that present?

As we saw, the disparate treatment concept of discrimination bears upon differential treatment that is motivated by biased intentions. In *Burdine*, the Court indicated how discriminatory intent can be proven. It is worth noting that the understanding of intent that the Court relies on here is not nearly as narrow as was used in *Feeney* when interpreting the Equal Protection Clause. (See Chapter 2.) There, to establish that a course of action was intentional, the complainant had to show that it was undertaken "at least in part 'because of,' not merely 'in spite of,' its adverse effects upon an identifiable group." In *Burdine*, the demands on the plaintiff are considerably less prodigious. The Court indicated the three-step pattern of proof that is typically required under Title VII. In the first step, called the prima facie case, the courts consider whether the plaintiff has "eliminated the most common reasons for plaintiff's rejection." The plaintiff succeeds in establishing her prima facie case if she raises an inference of discrimination. In footnote 6, the Court recalled from an earlier decision a typical way of establishing a prima facie case. Two points about this step should be kept in mind. The requirement of raising the inference of discrimination is not difficult to satisfy. In the Court's words, it is not "onerous." The other point is that the four-stage model outlined in *McDonnell Douglas* is one way, but not the only way, to meet that requirement.

Once they are satisfied that the plaintiff has raised an inference of discrimination, the courts take the second step and look to the defendant for rebuttal. To meet that burden, the employer must articulate a legitimate, nondiscriminatory reason for the employment decision. In *Burdine*, the Court was at pains to indicate that the employer need not show that it was "actually motivated by the proffered reasons." Rather, the defendant needs only introduce evidence that the decision could have been based upon legitimate, non-discriminatory grounds. The Court carefully noted, however, that this must be done with sufficient clarity to give the plaintiff a fair opportunity to show that the proffered reasons were a pretext.

When they are satisfied that the defendant has articulated legitimate, nondiscriminatory reasons for the challenged employment decision, the courts' third step is to consider whether the plaintiff has shown that those reasons represent a pretext (i.e., that they are used as a ploy to mask discriminatory intent). The plaintiff may show pretext in either of two ways. She may do so "either directly by persuading the court that a discriminatory reason more likely motivated the employer or indirectly by showing that the employer's proffered explanation is unworthy of credence." Although, as we shall see, not all disparate treatment cases turn on a showing of pretext, this is often the crux of the disparate treatment approach to proving discrimination. Table 3-1 may help to organize the elements of a disparate treatment case. After the Civil Rights Act of 1991 was passed, the Supreme Court reaffirmed the *McDonnell Douglas* and *Burdine* model of burden and order of proof. See *St. Mary's Honor Center v. Hicks*, 509 U.S. 502 (1993).

When enacting the Civil Rights Act of 1991, Congress established a commission to study the effects of "the glass ceiling." This initiative followed through on a Department of Labor (DOL) report issued in August 1991. This initiative, and the findings and recommendations of the Federal Glass Ceiling Commission, are discussed at length at the end of Chapter 4. In the DOL report, "glass ceiling" was defined as "artificial barriers based upon attitudinal or organizational bias that prevent qualified minorities and women from advancing into mid- and senior-management positions." Some aspects of the organizational dynamics that contribute to the denial of promotions to well-qualified women and minorities have been identified by means of litigation. Title VII plaintiffs often allege that they are passed over for promotion into management positions because of their sex. These claims are frequently analyzed as disparate treatment. Where that pattern is followed, the decisions most frequently turn on the establishment of pretext. Accordingly, the following cases illustrate both the dynamics of the glass ceiling and the various ways in which pretext is established under the disparate treatment approach to discrimination under Title VII.

TABLE 3-1 Order of Proof in Disparate Treatment Cases

STAGE	BURDEN ON	TO
Prima facie case	Plaintiff	Prove by a preponderance of the evidence that the employer treats qualified members of different sexes differently because of their sex
Rebuttal	Defendant	Articulate a nondiscriminatory reason that may have motivated the decision
Pretext	Plaintiff	Show, either, directly or indirectly, that the explanation proposed by the defendant was not the true reason for the employment decision

As indicated in *Burdine*, pretext can be shown either directly or indirectly. Direct methods attempt to persuade the court that a discriminatory reason was more likely to have motivated the employer than the nondiscriminatory reason that was offered in rebuttal. Indirect methods attempt to discredit the nondiscriminatory explanation that was offered by the employer. The following cases illustrate each of these techniques—*Hopkins*, the direct; *Lindahl*, the indirect.

PRICE WATERHOUSE V. HOPKINS
Supreme Court of the United States, 1989.
490 U.S. 228, 104 L.Ed.2d 268, 109 S. Ct. 1775.

Justice BRENNAN announced the judgment of the Court and delivered an opinion, in which Justice MARSHALL, Justice BLACKMUN, and Justice STEVENS join. [Justice WHITE and Justice O'CONNOR filed opinions concurring in the judgment.] . . .

At Price Waterhouse, a nationwide professional accounting partnership, a senior manager becomes a candidate for partnership when the partners in her local office submit her name as a candidate. All of the other partners in the firm are then invited to submit written comments on each candidate. . . . After reviewing the comments and interviewing the partners who submitted them, the firm's Admissions Committee makes a recommendation to the Policy Board. This recommendation will be either that the firm accept the candidate for partnership, put her applicant on "hold," or deny her the promotion outright. . . .

Ann Hopkins had worked at Price Waterhouse's Office of Government Services in Washington, D.C., for five years when the partners in that office proposed her as a candidate for partnership. Of the 662 partners at the firm at that time, 7 were women. Of the 88 persons proposed for partnership that year [1982], only 1—Hopkins—was a woman. Forty-seven of these candidates were admitted to the partnership, 21 were rejected, and 20—including Hopkins—were "held" for reconsideration the following year. Thirteen of the 32 partners who had submitted comments on Hopkins supported her bid for partnership. Three partners recommended that her candidacy be placed on hold, eight stated that they did not have an informed opinion about her, and eight recommended that she be denied partnership.

In a jointly prepared statement supporting her candidacy, the partners in Hopkins' office showcased her successful 2-year effort to secure a $25 million contract with the Department of State, labeling it "an outstanding performance" and one that Hopkins carried out "virtually at the partner level.". . .

The partners in Hopkins' office praised her character as well as her accomplishments, describing her in their joint statement as "an outstanding professional" who had a "deft touch," a "strong character, independence and integrity." Clients appear to have agreed with these assessments. . . .

On too many occasions, however, Hopkins' aggressiveness apparently spilled over into abrasiveness. Staff members seem to have borne the brunt of Hopkins' brusqueness. . . . Both "[s]upporters and opponents of her candidacy," stressed [District Court] Judge Gesell, "indicated that she was sometimes overly aggressive, unduly harsh, difficult to work with and impatient with staff."

There were clear signs, though, that some of the partners reacted negatively to

Hopkins' personality because she was a woman. One partner described her as "macho"; another suggested that she "overcompensated for being a woman"; a third advised her to take "a course at charm school." Several partners criticized her use of profanity; in response, one partner suggested that those partners object to her swearing only "because it[']s a lady using foul language." Another supporter explained that Hopkins "ha[d] matured from a tough-talking somewhat masculine hard-nosed mgr to an authoritative, formidable, but much more appealing lady ptr candidate." But it was the man who, as Judge Gesell found, bore responsibility for explaining to Hopkins the reasons for the Policy Board's decision to place her candidacy on hold who delivered the coup de grace: in order to improve her chances for partnership, Thomas Beyer advised, Hopkins should "walk more femininely, talk more femininely, dress more femininely, wear make-up, have her hair styled, and wear jewelry.". . .

In previous years, other female candidates for partnership also had been evaluated in sex-based terms. As a general matter, Judge Gesell concluded, "[c]andidates were viewed favorably if partners believed they maintained their femin[in]ity while becoming effective professional managers"; in this environment, "[t]o be identified as a 'women's lib[b]er' was regarded as [a] negative comment." In fact, the judge found that in previous years "[o]ne partner repeatedly commented that he could not consider any woman seriously as a partnership candidate and believed that women were not even capable of functioning as senior managers—yet the firm took no action to discourage his comments and recorded his vote in the overall summary of the evaluations."

Judge Gesell found that Price Waterhouse legitimately emphasized interpersonal skills in its partnership decisions, and also found that the firm had not fabricated its complaints about Hopkins' interpersonal skills as a pretext for discrimination.

Moreover, he concluded, the firm did not give decisive emphasis to such traits only because Hopkins was a woman; although there were male candidates who lacked these skills but who were admitted to partnership, the judge found that these candidates possessed other, positive traits that Hopkins lacked.

The judge went on to decide, however, that some of the partners' remarks about Hopkins stemmed from an impermissibly cabined view of the proper behavior of women, and that Price Waterhouse had done nothing to disavow reliance on such comments. He held that Price Waterhouse had unlawfully discriminated against Hopkins on the basis of sex by consciously giving credence and effect to partners' comments that resulted from sex stereotyping. Noting that Price Waterhouse could avoid equitable relief by proving by clear and convincing evidence that it would have placed Hopkins' candidacy on hold even absent this discrimination, the judge decided that the firm had not carried this heavy burden.

The Court of Appeals affirmed the District Court's ultimate conclusion. . . .

The District Court found that sex stereotyping "was permitted to play a part" in the evaluation of Hopkins as a candidate for partnership. Price Waterhouse disputes both that stereotyping occurred and that it played any part in the decision to place Hopkins' candidacy on hold. In the firm's view, in other words, the District Court's factual conclusions are clearly erroneous. We do not agree. . . .

. . . It takes no special training to discern sex stereotyping in a description of an aggressive female employee as requiring "a course at charm school." Nor, turning to Thomas Beyer's memorable advice to Hopkins, does it require expertise in psychology to know that, if an employee's flawed "interpersonal skills" can be corrected by a soft-hued suit and a new shade of lipstick, perhaps it is the employee's sex and not her interpersonal skills that had drawn the criticism.

Price Waterhouse appears to think that we cannot affirm the factual findings of the trial court without deciding that, instead of being overbearing and aggressive and curt, Hopkins is in fact kind and considerate and patient. If this is indeed its impression, petitioner misunderstands the theory on which Hopkins prevailed. The District Judge acknowledged that Hopkins' conduct justified complaints about her behavior as a senior manager. But he also concluded that the reactions of at least some of the partners were reactions to her as a *woman* manager. Where an evaluation is based on a subjective assessment of a person's strengths and weaknesses, it is simply not true that each evaluator will focus on, or even mention, the same weaknesses. Thus, even if we knew that Hopkins had "personality problems," this would not tell us that the partners who cast their evaluations of Hopkins in sex-based terms would have criticized her as sharply (or criticized her at all) if she had been a man. It is not our job to review the evidence and decide that the negative reactions to Hopkins were based on reality; our perception of Hopkins' character is irrelevant. We sit not to determine whether Ms. Hopkins is nice, but to decide whether the partners reacted negatively to her personality because she is a woman.

We hold that when a plaintiff in a Title VII case proves that her gender played a motivating part in an employment decision, the defendant may avoid a finding of liability only by proving by a preponderance of the evidence that it would have made the same decision even if it had not taken the plaintiff's gender into account. Because the courts below erred by deciding that the defendant must make this proof by clear and convincing evidence, we reverse the Court of Appeals' judgment against Price Waterhouse on liability and remand the case to that court for further proceedings.

It Is So Ordered.

STUDY QUESTIONS

1. What nondiscriminatory reason did Price Waterhouse propose as motivating its decision to put Hopkins' promotion on hold? In what language did the partners describe Hopkins' interpersonal skills?
2. How did Hopkins show that discriminatory reasons also motivated the decision? The court spoke of stereotyping that affected the partners' decision. Discuss what stereotyping involves and why it is not permitted under Title VII.

Hopkins addressed what is often called the "mixed motive" situation (i.e., one in which an employment decision is motivated both by discriminatory and nondiscriminatory considerations). The Court held that such employment decisions are permitted only if the employer can show that the same decision would have been made in the absence of the discriminatory considerations. The Civil Rights Act of 1991 overturned that decision. The key language in the statute makes clear that "an unlawful employment practice has been established when the complaining party demonstrates that race, color, religion, sex, or national origin was a motivating factor for any employment practice, even though other factors also motivated the practice." Once the unlawful employment practice has been established, the employer cannot avoid all liability by demonstrating that it had another, nondiscriminatory motive for its actions. If, however, the employer can show that it would have made the same adverse employment decision in the absence of discrimination, it can limit its liability. Under the Civil Rights Act of 1991, if the employer demonstrates this, the court is limited to awarding declaratory relief and attorneys' fees and costs. The court may not award back pay or damages, or require that the plaintiff be hired, promoted, or reinstated, unless the employer fails to make this showing. In addition, while a plaintiff is required to prove her/his case "by a preponderance of the evidence," Title VII is silent as to the type of evidence required. Recently, the Supreme Court determined that the statute does not require a heightened showing through direct evidence; the plaintiff's burden may be met by using either direct or circumstantial evidence. *Desert Palace Inc. v. Costa,* 539 U.S. 90 (2003).

Like *Hopkins,* the following case also illustrates the glass ceiling, the ways that attitudinal factors limit the upward mobility of talented women. Here, the plaintiff used an indirect method of showing pretext by arguing that the employer's explanation was unworthy of credence. When studying this case, consider what factors brought these biased attitudes to light. Had Lindahl not seized the initiative and pressed for satisfactory explanations, would Air France have even noticed its own biases?

LINDAHL V. AIR FRANCE
United States Court of Appeals,
Ninth Circuit, 1991.
930 F.2d 1434.

RYMER, Circuit Judge:

Michelle Lindahl . . . worked as a Customer Promotion Agent in Air France's Los Angeles office. The office had two groups of employees to handle sales activities, Customer Promotion Agents and Sales Representatives. Sales Representatives worked mostly in the field promoting sales, while the Customer Promotion Agents worked inside, providing backup to the Sales Representatives.

In 1982, the District Manager, Karl Kershaw, told the Customer Promotion Agents that Air France was planning to create a new position of Senior Customer Promotion Agent and invited all of them to apply for the position. After considering their qualifications, Kershaw told Lindahl that she was the most qualified and would be given the promotion. Subsequently, however, Air France decided not to create the position, and Lindahl did not get the promotion.

In 1987, without any prior notification to the Customer Promotion Agents, Kershaw announced that he had chosen Edward Michels to fill a new Senior Customer Promotion Agent position. At that time, there were four eligible candidates: two women over age 40 (including Lindahl), and two men under age 40 (including Michels).

Lindahl, upset about the decision, decided to pursue Air France's grievance procedure. First, she asked Kershaw to give an explanation. After about six weeks, he responded that Michels had the "best overall qualifications." Unsatisfied, she wrote to Regional Manager Robert Watson. Watson responded by affirming Kershaw's decision. Finally, Lindahl had her attorney take her grievance to Personnel Services Manager Eugene Carrara. At this time, she made clear that she felt that the decision was the product of age and sex discrimination. Carrara held a hearing and decided to reject her claim because he believed the promotion decision was reasonable. In his decision, he stated that Michels's computer expertise was the principal reason for selecting him. . . .

. . . After exhausting her administrative remedies, she filed suit in the district court, alleging age and sex discrimination. . . . Air France moved for summary judgment on both causes of action.

The district court granted summary judgment on the ground that Lindahl had not raised a genuine issue of material fact as to whether Air France's legitimate, nondiscriminatory explanations are pretexts for discrimination. . . . She now appeals. . . .

The district court concluded, and the parties do not dispute, that Lindahl made out a prima facie case of discrimination. She is a woman over age 40 who, in effect, applied for a promotion, was qualified for it, but lost it to a man under age 40. The parties also do not dispute that Air France met its burden of producing legitimate, nondiscriminatory reasons for promoting Michels and not Lindahl. Air France points to the deposition testimony of Watson and Kershaw, indicating that their reasons for promoting Michels were (1) his computer proficiency, and (2) his leadership abilities as they related to Air France's need to establish order, rules, and regulations in a chaotic office. . . .

As to Air France's explanation that Michels was chosen for his computer proficiency, Lindahl argues that it is not credible because neither Kershaw nor Watson (the ones most closely associated with the decision) mentioned it as the reason for choosing Michels. Kershaw had said only that Michels had "the best overall qualifications to lead the group," and Watson had simply affirmed Kershaw's decision. The computer explanation did not come out until Personnel Services Manager Carrara, who was not involved with the decision, mentioned it four months later in response to a letter from Lindahl's attorney. . . .

Moreover, computer expertise was not clearly related to the leadership position. Indeed, computer proficiency had never been listed as a qualification for the position of Senior Customer Promotion Agent. While Michels's computer knowledge might have been helpful to Air France generally, it is not clear that it made him a better candidate to lead the Customer Promotion Group.

Lindahl also challenges the credibility of Air France's explanation that Michels was chosen for his leadership abilities. Kershaw testified in his deposition that "being accepted" is an important part of being a leader, but he admitted that Michels "was not well liked by the group." By contrast, Kershaw described Lindahl as having "a good relationship with the staff."

Lindahl also stated that Michels was preoccupied with the computer and neglected his duties backing up the Sales Representatives and that these backup duties were traditionally part of the Customer Promotion Group's responsibilities. Finally, the record shows that Michels was the most junior member of the Customer Promotion Group. . . .

Moreover, even if Kershaw did make his decision based on leadership abilities, other evidence could suggest that his evaluation of leadership ability was itself sexist. Lindahl points out that Kershaw made statements about the candidates' relative qualifications that reflect male/female stereotypes. Kershaw testified in his deposition that he believed that both female candidates get "nervous" and that the other female candidate "gets easily upset [and] loses control." By contrast, Kershaw described Michels's leadership qualities as "not to back away from a situation, to take hold immediately of the situation, to attack the situation right away, to stay cool throughout the whole process." He went on to comment that "sitting and griping and getting emotional is not contributing to, No. 1, getting the job done, number two, to the morale and atmosphere of the group."

The Supreme Court has made clear that sex stereotyping can be evidence of sex discrimination, especially when linked to the employment decision. *Price Waterhouse v. Hopkins.* Kershaw apparently saw Michels as aggressive and cool (in addition to being the one who could impose order), while he saw the female candidates as nervous and emotional. His comments could suggest that Kershaw made his decision on the basis of stereotypical images of men and women, specifically that women do not make good leaders because they are too "emotional."

Finally, Lindahl points to evidence showing that Air France handled the promotion decision differently when only women were eligible than when young men were eligible. In 1982, when the possibility of an opening for Senior Customer Promotion Agent position first arose, the only eligible candidates for the position were women. Kershaw told all of them about the possible opening and that they would have to take a test. Air France abandoned the idea to add the position. In 1987, two men under age 40 and two women over age 40 were eligible. Kershaw did not tell the candidates about the position, and Michels got the promotion without taking a test or having an interview. This difference in treatment might further support an inference that Air France was discriminating against older women.

While not overwhelming, Lindahl's evidence of discriminatory motive is sufficient to raise a genuine issue of fact. She has pointed to facts that could call into question the credibility of Air France's nondiscriminatory explanations and could suggest discriminatory motives. Whether the facts do indicate discrimination is a question that should ordinarily be resolved by a fact-finder, and we believe it is possible that a reasonable trier of fact could find that Air France discriminated against Lindahl in promoting Michels. We therefore conclude that summary judgment should not have been granted.

Reversed and Remanded.

Study Questions

1. Did Lindahl's immediate supervisor give her a specific explanation of why she was denied the promotion? Who did give her a specific explanation? Why do you suppose that the employer felt compelled to give a specific explanation for its decision?

2. What circumstances surrounding the promotion decision persuaded this court that the employer's nondiscriminatory explanation of its decision was not credible? Have you noticed any similar circumstances in jobs that you or your friends have held?

The courts in *Hopkins* and *Lindahl* found that the employers had relied on stereotypes when denying promotions to women professionals. Here is an especially clever comparison of common stereotypes about men and women office workers. Can you think of other stereotypes that work to the disadvantage of women who work in blue-collar jobs? What stereotypes work to the disadvantage of men who work in the health professions? What stereotypes work to the disadvantage of women of color, single mothers, and divorced women?

HE WORKS, SHE WORKS
Natasha Josefowitz
"Impressions from an Office."
Paths to Power. Addison-Wesley Publishing Co., 1980, p. 60.

The family picture is on HIS desk:
Ah, a solid, responsible man.

The family picture is on HER desk:
Umm, her family will come before her career.

HIS desk is cluttered:
He's obviously a hard worker and a busy man.

HER desk is cluttered:
She's obviously a disorganized scatterbrain.

HE is talking with his co-workers:
He must be discussing the latest deal.

SHE is talking with her co-workers:
She must be gossiping.

HE's not at his desk:
He must be at a meeting.

SHE's not at her desk:
She must be in the ladies' room.

HE's not in the office:
He's meeting customers.

SHE's not in the office:
She must be out shopping.

HE's having lunch with the boss:
He's on his way up.

SHE's having lunch with the boss:
They must be having an affair.

The boss criticized HIM:
He'll improve his performance.

The boss criticized HER:
She'll be very upset.

HE got an unfair deal:
Did he get angry?

She got an unfair deal:
Did she cry?

HE's getting married:
He'll get more settled.

SHE's getting married:
She'll get pregnant and leave.

HE's having a baby:
He'll need a raise.

SHE's having a baby:
She'll cost the company money in maternity benefits.

HE's going on a business trip:
It's good for his career.

SHE's going on a business trip:
What does her husband say?

HE's leaving for a better job:
He knows how to recognize a good opportunity.

SHE's leaving for a better job:
Women are undependable.

Reprinted with permission.

Disparate Impact

One type of discrimination because of sex prohibited by Title VII is the familiar and straightforward "disparate treatment" discussed in preceding text. Early in Title VII litigation, the Supreme Court distinguished a second: the disparate impact concept of discrimination. This type of discrimination involves "employment practices that are facially neutral in their treatment of different groups, but that, in fact, fall more harshly on one group than another and cannot be justified by business necessity."

The basic idea behind the disparate impact concept of discrimination derives from elementary statistics. Random selection procedures yield samples that tend to replicate the composition of the populations from which they were drawn. Selection procedures that do not produce such samples are said to be biased. Suppose that you want to estimate the proportion of blue marbles in a pail. One easy way to do that is to use a color-blind technique to select a certain number of marbles from the pail. Once that is done, inspect the sample, determine the proportion of blue marbles in it, and infer that blue marbles are present in that same proportion in the pail.

Like the sampling technique, the statistical concept at the root of disparate impact analysis involves three elements: the general population, the sample population, and the selection procedure. If you know the value of any two of these elements, you can infer the value of the other. In the marble example, we knew the value of the sample population and the selection procedure and inferred the value of the general population. The point of interest for the law of sex discrimination is that if we know the value of the general and the sample populations, we can infer the value of the selection procedure (i.e., we can determine whether it is biased).

Bias is the common element of the two concepts of discrimination used in Title VII analysis. The disparate treatment concept is the more familiar because it is quite similar to the everyday concept of discrimination—the motive of the person who makes the selections is biased. The disparate impact concept of discrimination relies upon a statistical concept of bias. It is not the motive but the selection procedure that is biased. The disparate impact concept of discrimination was developed and endorsed by a unanimous Supreme Court in the following case.

When studying *Griggs,* take note of the contrast between the Court's rulings under Title VII and those under the Equal Protection Clause. We saw in the *Feeney* decision in Chapter 2 that it is discriminatory intent that renders differential treatment of women and men to be a violation of our equal protection rights. In that case, the Court explicitly rejected the extension of the disparate impact concept of discrimination to constitutional interpretation. In *Griggs,* the argument that later prevailed in *Feeney* was endorsed by the lower courts only to be rejected by a unanimous Supreme Court in favor of the disparate impact concept of discrimination. As you study this case, notice the factors that motivated the Court to adopt this interpretation of the statute. Also try to imagine what employers such as the Duke Power Company would probably have done had the Court affirmed the interpretation developed by the circuit court.

GRIGGS V. DUKE POWER CO.
Supreme Court of the United States, 1971.
401 U.S. 424, 91 S. Ct. 849, 28 L.Ed.2d 158.

Mr. Chief Justice BURGER delivered the opinion of the Court.

We granted the writ in this case to resolve the question whether an employer is prohibited by the Civil Rights Act of 1964, Title VII, from requiring a high school education or passing of a standardized general intelligence test as a condition of employment in or transfer to jobs when (a) neither standard is shown to be significantly related to successful job performance, (b) both requirements operate to disqualify Negroes at a substantially higher rate than white applicants, and (c) the jobs in question formerly had been filled only by white employees as part of a longstanding practice of giving preference to whites.

Congress provided, in Title VII of the Civil Rights Act of 1964, for class actions for enforcement of provisions of the Act and this proceeding was brought by a group of incumbent Negro employees against Duke Power Company. All the petitioners are employed at the Company's Dan River Steam Station, a power generating facility located at Draper, North Carolina. At the time this action was instituted, the Company had 95 employees at the Dan River Station, 14 of whom were Negroes; 13 of these are petitioners here.

The District Court found that prior to July 2, 1965, the effective date of the Civil Rights Act of 1964, the Company openly discriminated on the basis of race in the hiring and assigning of employees at its Dan River plant. The plant was organized into five operating departments: (1) Labor, (2) Coal Handling, (3) Operations, (4) Maintenance, and (5) Laboratory and Test. Negroes were employed only in the Labor Department where the highest paying jobs paid less than the lowest paying jobs in the other four "operating" departments in which only whites were employed. Promotions were normally made within each department on the basis of job seniority. Transferees into a department usually began in the lowest position.

In 1955 the Company instituted a policy of requiring a high school education for initial assignment to any department except Labor, and for transfer from the Coal Handling to any "inside" department (Operations, Maintenance, or Laboratory). When the Company abandoned its policy of restricting Negroes to the Labor Department in 1965, completion of high school also was made a prerequisite to transfer from Labor to any other department. From the time the high school requirement was instituted to the time of trial, however, white employees hired before the time of the high school education requirement continued to perform satisfactorily and achieve promotions in the "operating" departments. Findings on this score are not challenged.

The Company added a further requirement for new employees on July 2, 1965, the date on which Title VII became effective. To qualify for placement in any but the Labor Department it became necessary to register satisfactory scores on two professionally prepared aptitude tests, as well as to have a high school education. . . . In September 1965 the Company began to permit incumbent employees who lacked a high school education to qualify for transfer from Labor or Coal Handling to an "inside" job by passing two tests—the Wonderlic Personnel Test, which purports to measure general intelligence, and the Bennett Mechanical Comprehension Test. Neither was directed or intended to measure the ability to learn to perform a particular job or category of jobs. The requisite scores used for both initial hiring and transfer approximated the national median for high school graduates.

The District Court had found that while the Company previously followed a policy of overt racial discrimination in a period prior to the Act, such conduct had ceased. . . .

The Court of Appeals was confronted with a question of first impression, as are we, concerning the meaning of Title VII. After careful analysis a majority of that court concluded that a subjective test of the employer's intent should govern, particularly in a close case, and that in this case there was no showing of a discriminatory purpose in the adoption of the diploma and test requirements. On this basis, the Court of Appeals concluded there was no violation of the Act. . . .

The objective of Congress in the enactment of Title VII is plain from the language of the statute. It was to achieve equality of employment opportunities and remove barriers that have operated in the past to favor an identifiable group of white employees over other employees. Under the Act, practices, procedures, or tests neutral on their face, and even neutral in terms of intent, cannot be maintained if they operate to "freeze" the status quo of prior discriminatory employment practices.

The Court of Appeals' opinion . . . agreed that, on the record in the present case, "whites register far better on the Company's alternative requirements" than Negroes. This consequence would appear to be directly traceable to race. Basic intelligence must have the means of articulation to manifest itself fairly in a testing process. Because they are Negroes, petitioners have long received inferior education in segregated schools. . . . Congress did not intend by Title VII, however, to guarantee a job to every person regardless of qualifications.

In short, the Act does not command that any person be hired simply because he was formerly the subject of discrimination, or because he is a member of a minority group. Discriminatory preference for any group, minority or majority, is precisely and only what Congress has proscribed. What is required by Congress is the removal of artificial, arbitrary, and unnecessary barriers to employment when the barriers operate invidiously to discriminate on the basis of racial or other impermissible classification.

Congress has now provided that tests or criteria for employment or promotion may not provide equality of opportunity merely in the sense of the fabled offer of milk to the stork and the fox. On the contrary, Congress has now required that the posture and condition of the job-seeker be taken into account. It has—to resort again to the fable—provided that the vessel in which the milk is proffered be one all seekers can use. The Act proscribes not only overt discrimination but also practices that are fair in form, but discriminatory in operation. The touchstone is business necessity. If an employment practice which operates to exclude Negroes cannot be shown to be related to job performance, the practice is prohibited.

On the record before us, neither the high school completion requirement nor the general intelligence test is shown to bear a demonstrable relationship to successful performance of the jobs for which it was used. Both were adopted, as the Court of Appeals noted, without meaningful study of their relationship to job-performance ability. Rather, a vice president of the Company testified, the requirements were instituted on the Company's judgment that they generally would improve the overall quality of the work force. . . .

The Court of Appeals held that the Company had adopted the diploma and test requirements without any "intention to discriminate against Negro employees." We do not suggest that either the District Court or the Court of Appeals erred in examining the employer's intent; but good

intent or absence of discriminatory intent does not redeem employment procedures or testing mechanisms that operate as "built-in headwinds" for minority groups and are unrelated to measuring job capability.

The Company's lack of discriminatory intent is suggested by special efforts to help the undereducated employees through Company financing of two-thirds the cost of tuition for high school training. But Congress directed the thrust of the Act to the *consequences* of employment practices, not simply the motivation. More than that, Congress has placed on the employer the burden of showing that any given requirement must have a manifest relationship to the employment in question.

The facts of this case demonstrate the inadequacy of broad and general testing devices as well as the infirmity of using diplomas or degrees as fixed measures of capability. History is filled with examples of men and women who rendered highly effective performance without the conventional badges of accomplishment in terms of certificates, diplomas, or degrees. Diplomas and tests are useful servants, but Congress has mandated the commonsense proposition that they are not to become masters of reality. . . .

Nothing in the Act precludes the use of testing or measuring procedures; obviously they are useful. What Congress has forbidden is giving these devices and mechanisms controlling force unless they are demonstrably a reasonable measure of job performance. Congress has not commanded that the less qualified be preferred over the better qualified simply because of minority origins. Far from disparaging job qualifications as such, Congress has made such qualifications the controlling factor, so that race, religion, nationality, and sex become irrelevant. What Congress has commanded is that any tests used must measure the person for the job and not the person in the abstract.

The judgment of the Court of Appeals is, as to that portion of the judgment appealed from, reversed.

STUDY QUESTIONS

1. What did the Supreme Court understand to be the objective of Title VII? Precisely what does it proscribe? What does it require? Is that a fair reading of the statute? Should an employer be found in violation of an antidiscrimination statute where there is no proof of prejudice or biased motives?

2. Were the requirements of a high school education and satisfactory scores on two aptitude tests job-related? Why or why not?

3. What does "business necessity" mean? What is its role in the order of proof discussed here? Did the employer prove business necessity here?

4. Critics have argued that the disparate impact analysis of Title VII implicitly obligates employers to use employment quotas. Under that analysis, so the critics argue, employment policies that do not grant benefits to people of color and whites in a given pattern place the employer at risk of liability. On the Court's reading of Title VII, are employers required to hire, promote, and so forth, people of color, even though better qualified whites are available?

Following the *Griggs* decision, the courts found many facially neutral employment policies and practices in violation of Title VII on the grounds of disparate impact. These include using subjective employment and promotion criteria, imposing various educational requirements, and rejecting applicants with criminal records.

Minimum height and weight requirements are among the most common work requirements that exclude women to a much greater extent than men. Just such a requirement was challenged in the following case. This was the first time that the Supreme Court applied disparate impact analysis in a sex case. The Court developed a three-step approach to disparate impact analysis that parallels the one developed for disparate treatment cases. In this case, the Court addressed two aspects of Title VII that are of central importance, viz., the disparate impact challenge and a challenge based on the BFOQ exception. The latter will be discussed in section III of this chapter.

DOTHARD V. RAWLINSON

Supreme Court of the United States, 1977.
433 U.S. 321, 97 S. Ct. 2720, 53 L.Ed.2d 786.

Mr. Justice STEWART delivered the opinion of the Court.

Appellee Dianne Rawlinson sought employment with the Alabama Board of Corrections as a prison guard, called in Alabama a "correctional counselor." After her application was rejected, she brought this class suit under Title VII of the Civil Rights Act of 1964 . . . alleging that she had been denied employment because of her sex in violation of federal law. A three-judge Federal District Court for the Middle District of Alabama decided in her favor. . . .

At the time she applied for a position as correctional counselor trainee, Rawlinson was a 22-year-old college graduate whose major course of study had been correctional psychology. She was refused employment because she failed to meet the minimum 120-pound weight requirement established by an Alabama statute. The statute also establishes a height minimum of 5 feet 2 inches. . . .

In enacting Title VII, Congress required "the removal of artificial, arbitrary, and unnecessary barriers to employment when the barriers operate invidiously to discriminate on the basis of racial or other impermissible classification." *Griggs v. Duke Power Co.* The District Court found that the minimum statutory height and weight requirements that applicants for employment as correctional counselors must meet constitute the sort of arbitrary barrier to equal employment opportunity that Title VII forbids. The appellants assert that the District Court erred both in finding that the height and weight standards discriminate against women, and in its refusal to find that, even if they do, these standards are justified as "job related."

The gist of the claim that the statutory height and weight requirements discriminate against women does not involve an assertion of purposeful discriminatory motive. It is asserted, rather, that these facially neutral qualification standards work in fact disproportionately to exclude women from eligibility for employment by the Alabama Board of Corrections. We dealt in *Griggs v. Duke Power Co.*, and *Albemarle Paper Co. v. Moody*, with similar allegations that facially neutral employment standards disproportionately excluded Negroes from employment, and those cases guide our approach here.

Those cases make clear that to establish a prima facie case of discrimination, a plaintiff need only show that the facially neutral standards in question select applicants for hire in a significantly discriminatory pattern. Once it is thus shown that the employment standards are discriminatory in effect, the employer must meet "the burden of showing that any given requirement [has] . . . a manifest relationship to the employment in question." *Griggs.* If the employer proves that the challenged requirements are job related, the plaintiff may then show that other selection devices without a similar discriminatory effect would also "serve the employer's legitimate interest in 'efficient and trustworthy workmanship.'"

Although women 14 years of age or older compose 52.75% of the Alabama population and 36.89% of its total labor force, they hold only 12.9% of its correctional counselor positions. In considering the effect of the minimum height and weight standards on this disparity in rate of hiring between the sexes, the District Court found that the 5' 2" requirement would operate to exclude 33.29% of the women in the United States between the ages of 18–79, while excluding only 1.28% of men between the same ages. The 120-pound weight restriction would exclude 22.29% of the women and 2.35% of the men in this age group. When the height and weight restrictions are combined, Alabama's statutory standards would exclude 41.13% of the female population while excluding less than 1% of the male population. Accordingly, the District Court found that Rawlinson had made out a prima facie case of unlawful sex discrimination. . . .

For these reasons, we cannot say that the District Court was wrong in holding that the statutory height and weight standards had a discriminatory impact on women applicants. . . .

We turn, therefore, to the appellants' argument that they have rebutted the prima facie case of discrimination by showing that the height and weight requirements are job related. These requirements, they say, have a relationship to strength, a sufficient but unspecified amount of which is essential to effective job performance as a correctional counselor. In the District Court, however, the appellants produced no evidence correlating the height and weight requirements with the requisite amount of strength thought essential to good job performance. Indeed, they failed to offer evidence of any kind in specific justification of the statutory standards.

If the job-related quality that the appellants identify is bona fide, their purpose could be achieved by adopting and validating a test for applicants that measures strength directly. Such a test, fairly administered, would fully satisfy the standards of Title VII because it would be one that "measure[s] the person for the job and not the person in the abstract." But nothing in the present record even approaches such a measurement.

For the reasons we have discussed, the District Court was not in error in holding that Title VII of the Civil Rights Act of 1964, as amended, prohibits application of the statutory height and weight requirements to Rawlinson and the class she represents.

STUDY QUESTIONS

1. How did Rawlinson establish a prima facie case here?
2. Suppose that the state of Alabama had introduced convincing evidence that the statutory requirements were job-related. What could Rawlinson have argued in order to prevail?

Disparate impact cases are often class actions (i.e., actions brought by representative members of a protected group on behalf of all members of that group). These cases are analyzed by the courts in three stages that bear a surface resemblance to the three stages of analysis under disparate treatment (see *Burdine*). In the prima facie case, the plaintiff class has the burden of proving that the challenged employment practice disproportionately disadvantages women or men. Often, as in *Dothard*, straightforward statistical analysis is sufficient to establish a prima facie case.

Once a court is satisfied that the plaintiff class has shown that the practice has disparate impact, it looks to the defendant for rebuttal. The employer has the burden of persuading the court that the challenged practice is a "business necessity" (i.e., "has . . . a manifest relationship to the employment in question").

If the defendant succeeds in showing that the challenged policy or practice is a business necessity, rather than merely a "business convenience," the court considers whether the plaintiff class has shown that there exist "other selection devices without similar discriminatory effect [that] would also 'serve the employer's legitimate interest in efficient and trustworthy workmanship.'" In *Dothard*, the Court indicated that a test that measures the strength of individuals would be a less discriminatory alternative. Table 3-2 shows the elements of a disparate impact case.

In the years following these decisions, the federal courts have handed down some decisions in disparate impact cases that eroded the very strong stance taken in *Griggs* and *Dothard*. Some lower courts weakened the business necessity requirements out of consideration for the interests of employers in avoiding the costs of accommodating women. One circuit court approved a minimum height requirement for airline pilots not because being over five-foot-seven tall bears a manifest relation to the safe and efficient operation of an airplane but because airplane cockpits were designed for people whose physical stature is

TABLE 3-2   Order of Proof in Disparate Impact Cases

STAGE	BURDEN ON	TO SHOW
Prima facie case	Plaintiff	The facially neutral practice disproportionately disadvantages women or men
Rebuttal	Defendant	Job-related (i.e., the practice has a manifest relationship to the employment in question and is consistent with business necessity)
Pretext	Plaintiff	Equally efficient but less discriminatory alternatives are available to the employer

that of the average male. Instead of requiring the employer to reconfigure the physical layout of the workplace to accommodate qualified women, the court lightened the business necessity burden (*Boyd v. Ozark Air Lines, Inc.*, 568 F.2d 50 (8th Cir. 1977)). Another circuit court approved an employer policy limiting the coverage of the employer's medical insurance to heads of households, even though 89 percent of male and only 13 percent of female employees qualified. The reason given was that the policy was a cost-saving measure for the employer (*Wambheim v. J. C. Penney Co.*, 705 F.2d 1492 (9th Cir. 1983), *cert. denied*, 467 U.S. 1255 (1984)).

After these decisions, the most devastating blows to Title VII came a few years after Justice Kennedy joined the Court, filling the vacancy left by the retirement of Justice Powell in 1987. A series of decisions handed down during the 1988–1989 term substantially reversed two decades of positive enforcement of civil rights laws. The decision that did the most to cripple Title VII came in the case of *Wards Cove Packing Co. v. Antonio*, 490 U.S. 642 (1989). In that decision, the Court substantially altered its unanimous 1971 *Griggs v. Duke Power Co.* decision establishing the disparate impact approach to employment discrimination. In *Wards Cove*, the Court ruled that no matter how extreme the impact on a protected class, an employer has no obligation to establish the need for the challenged practice; indeed, the victims of discrimination were required to prove that no legitimate reason justifies its use.

Both of these judicial trends were reversed by Congress. On November 21, 1991, President George Bush signed into law the Civil Rights Act of 1991, ending a two-and-a-half year campaign by civil rights advocates to reverse *Wards Cove* and other decisions that threatened to gut Title VII and other civil rights laws. Until then, the Bush administration had resisted such efforts under the guise of opposing any measures that would promote the use of quotas. In the end, civil rights advocates asserted, the president relented because of the political climate created in part by the Anita Hill-Clarence Thomas hearings and the surprisingly strong showing by past Klu Klux Klan leader David Duke in the Republican primary election in Louisiana.

The CRA went into effect on the day it was signed. One of its effects was to reverse *Wards Cove* and the drift toward a lighter standard of business necessity, as was noted in preceding text, in the lower courts. Section 105 of the act reaffirms the integrity of the disparate impact analysis as it had developed from *Griggs* and other decisions prior to *Wards Cove*. The key language in this section provides that an unlawful practice is established when "a complaining party demonstrates that a respondent uses a particular employment practice that causes a disparate impact on the basis of race, color, religion, sex, or national origin and the respondent fails to demonstrate that the challenged practice is job related for the position in question and consistent with business necessity." Like all statutory provisions, this section, too, is subject to judicial interpretation. Future decisions alone will show whether the CRA ended the erosion of civil rights enforcement.

III. BONA FIDE OCCUPATIONAL QUALIFICATIONS

When discussing the ways that violations of Title VII can be established, the Supreme Court typically distinguishes three patterns of litigation. Two were discussed in the preceding section, viz., disparate treatment and disparate impact. These involve differential treatment of men and women that stems from biased motives and differential treatment that stems from the use of biased selection procedures. There is yet another pattern, one that the Court usually calls *overt* or *facial discrimination*. Employer practices are overtly discriminatory if by their very terms they establish one policy for employees or applicants for employment who are women and another for those who are men, regardless of whether they were motivated by benign or prejudiced motive.

Where a case is analyzed as one of overt discrimination, there is no need to pause over what would be a phase parallel to the prima facie case in disparate treatment and disparate impact cases. In facially discriminatory situations, either the employers concede that they discriminate because of sex or it is evident from their policies and practices that they do. In these cases, the courts move directly to the phase that parallels that of rebuttal or business necessity. The only way that an employer engaging in overt discrimination can escape liability under Title VII is by successfully establishing that the policy is a "bona fide occupational qualification" (BFOQ). Congress established this exception by adding the following language to the statute. Note that this exception does not extend to facial racial discrimination.

> Notwithstanding any other provision of this title . . . it shall not be an unlawful employment practice for an employer . . . to hire and employ employees . . . on the basis of his religion, sex, or national origin in those certain instances where religion, sex, or national origin is a bona fide occupational qualification reasonably necessary to the normal operation of that particular business or enterprise . . . (703(e)(1)).

The Equal Employment Opportunity Commission (EEOC) quickly recognized that, like any exception, this one, too, could defeat the rule if understood broadly. If interpreted to include a wide spectrum of situations, it could, in the EEOC's words, "swallow the rule." To forestall that result, the commission urged that the BFOQ be interpreted quite narrowly.

29 C.F.R. § 1604.2. SEX AS A BONA FIDE OCCUPATIONAL QUALIFICATION

(a) The Commission believes that the bona fide occupational qualification exception as to sex should be interpreted narrowly. Label—"Men's jobs" and "Women's jobs"—tend to deny employment opportunities unnecessarily to one sex or the other.

(1) The Commission will find that the following situations do not warrant the application of the bona fide occupational qualification exception:

(i) The refusal to hire a woman because of her sex based on assumptions of the comparative employment characteristics of women in general. For example, the assumption that the turnover rate among women is higher than among men.

(ii) The refusal to hire an individual based on stereotyped characterizations of the sexes. Such stereotypes include, for example, that men are less capable of assembling intricate equipment, that women are less capable of aggressive salesmanship. The principle of nondiscrimination requires that individuals be considered on the basis of individual capacities and not on the basis of any characteristics generally attributed to the group.

(iii) The refusal to hire an individual because of the preferences of coworkers, the employer, clients or customers except as covered specifically in paragraph (a)(2) of this section.

(2) Where it is necessary for the purpose of authenticity or genuineness, the Commission will consider sex to be a bona fide occupational qualification (e.g., an actor or actress).

The courts have generally heeded that counsel, but not without some difficulty. New stereotypes as well as old ones in unexpected contexts continue to be uncovered by litigants claiming and contesting BFOQs. In this section, we will explore some of the more interesting and important aspects of that litigation.

Developing the Standard

Before the courts could confidently apply this exception, they first had to agree on the meaning of the statutory language. By what standard were the courts to interpret "reasonably necessary to the normal operation of that particular business . . . "? A second preliminary issue was the burden of proof. Who must prove that this exception applies or does not apply to the situation? The following case shows how the lower courts reached preliminary accord on the meaning of that language as well as the burden of proof. In *Cheatwood*, the court considered the merits of two interpretations. One was endorsed by the Fifth Circuit Court of Appeals in *Weeks v. Southern Bell Telephone & Telegraph Co.* The other was adopted by another district court in the case of *Bowe v. Colgate-Palmolive Co.* As you read this case, consider what would probably have happened to the frequency of sex discrimination had the *Bowe* standard been widely adopted by the courts.

CHEATWOOD v. SO. CENT. BELL TEL. & TEL. CO.
United States District Court, Northern District of Alabama, 1969.
303 F. Supp. 754.

FRANK M. JOHNSON, Jr., Chief Judge. In this action Mrs. Claudine B. Cheatwood charges her employer, South Central Bell Telephone & Telegraph Company, with discrimination on the basis of sex in filling a vacancy for the job classification of commercial representative in Montgomery, Alabama, in violation of Title VII. . . .

It is admitted that the plaintiff and two other female employees submitted timely bids for the vacancy, that Employer declined to consider the bids of the female employees without considering their individual qualifications, and that the job was awarded to the only male applicant. . . .

Employer has, in effect, admitted a prima facie violation . . . [but] has consistently contended, however, that the position of commercial representative fits within the [BFOQ] exception. . . .

In a recent case quite similar to the one *sub judice*, the Court of Appeals for the Fifth Circuit made clear that the burden of proof is on the employer to demonstrate that a given position fits within the bona fide occupational qualification exception. *Weeks v. Southern Bell Telephone & Telegraph Co.*, 408 F.2d 228 (5th Cir. 1969).

The court in *Weeks* went on to explain the extent of the showing required to satisfy that burden:

> "In order to rely on the bona fide occupational qualification exception, an employer has the burden of proving that he had reasonable cause to believe, that is, a factual basis for believing, that all or substantially all women would be unable to perform safely and efficiently the duties of the job involved."

The only issues in this case, then, are determining the duties of a commercial representative and determining whether or not all or substantially all women would be unable to perform those duties safely and efficiently.

The official job description in effect at the time this dispute arose provides:

> "COMMERCIAL REPRESENTATIVE— (9/49) Handles commercial matters primarily outside the Company's office, such as visits to customers' premises in connection with criticisms, facilities, securing signed applications where required, credit information, deposits, advance payments, coin telephone inspections, and visits in connection with live and final account

treatment work. May also be assigned to work inside the office pertaining to service and collections."

The testimony at trial produced more specific descriptions of these duties and revealed certain additional duties that go with the job in Montgomery, Alabama:

1. Rural canvassing for new customers and mileage checks for billing purposes.
2. Relief of the coin telephone collector on an average of about two days per week.
3. Destroying certain of employer's records on a monthly and annual basis.
4. Handling current record of billing stubs and handling supply requisitions in the office.
5. Performing the biennial furniture inventory.

Defendant contends that several features of these duties make them inappropriate for performance by women. With respect to the rural canvassing, it suggests the possibilities that tires will need to be changed and that restroom facilities are occasionally inaccessible. These contentions can be regarded as little more than makeweights. There is no proof that all or nearly all women would be unable to cope with these difficulties. They do, of course, render the position somewhat unromantic. But as was said in *Weeks*, Title VII "vests individual women with the power to decide whether or not to take on unromantic tasks.".

Employer also contends that the duties of commercial representative would subject a female employee to harassment and danger. This is based partly on problems arising from the collection of overdue bills and partly on the fact that when acting as a substitute coin collector, the employee must make collections in bars, poolrooms, and other such locations. Again, however, there is nothing in the record to indicate that these features of the position are functionally related to sex. They mean nothing more than that some women, and some men, might not wish to perform such tasks. Here, however, the record is clear

that one obtains this position by bidding for it and that if one is dissatisfied it is possible to request a transfer or a return to the former position.

Employer has consistently placed principal reliance on the fact that certain aspects of the job as performed in Montgomery require lifting of weights. Although other aspects of the job require occasional lifting, the alleged strenuousness of the position relates primarily to the work involved in relieving the coin collector. The evidence reflects that other commercial representatives in Montgomery have spent an average of two days per week on this relief work. In a normal day of this work a commercial representative would collect approximately 45 coin boxes from pay stations on his route. As they are collected, these coin boxes are placed in a small metal case which is compact and relatively easy to handle. Each case will hold up to nine coin boxes. A case weighs approximately 6 pounds empty, and the estimates of its weight when full varied from 45 to 80 pounds. An actual random sample indicated that the average on a particular day in Montgomery was 60¾ pounds. Occasionally, a case will weigh over 90 pounds. In a given day, from five to nine cases must be handled, and each case must be lifted and/or carried full in, out or around the collection truck four times a day. . . .

. . . Employer relies upon a statement in *Bowe v. Colgate-Palmolive Co.*, 272 F. Supp. 332, 365 (S.D.Ind.1967), for the proposition that such a showing is sufficient to rely upon the bona fide occupational qualification exception:

> "Generally recognized physical capabilities and physical limitations of the sexes may be made the basis for occupational qualifications in generic terms."

As indicated above, however, Employer faces a more substantial burden. The language quoted from *Bowe* was specifically rejected in *Weeks* for the Fifth Circuit and the [EEOC] is urging on appeal that it be rejected by the Seventh Circuit—in both instances for the very good reason that if it were followed the bona fide occupational exception would swallow the rule against discrimination. . . .

Weeks requires Employer to show that all or substantially all women would be unable to perform safely and efficiently the duties of the position involved. While it may be that, in terms of lifting weights, the duties of this position begin to approach the outer limits of what women should undertake, this Court firmly concludes that Employer has not satisfied its burden of proof. . . . Nor is the fact that pregnant women should not perform the job of crucial importance. Employer can have a rule against pregnant women being considered for this position, but Title VII surely means that all women cannot be excluded from consideration because some of them may become pregnant. . . .

Accordingly, this Court now specifically finds and concludes that the male sex is not a bona fide occupational qualification for the position of commercial representative in Montgomery, Alabama.

STUDY QUESTIONS

1. What is the difference between the *Weeks* and *Bowe* standards for interpreting the BFOQ? What reason did the court give for preferring the *Weeks* standard?
2. Why did the court discount the employer's solicitude for women being inconvenienced by the unavailability of restrooms and its concern for the safety of its women employees? Does Title VII require that employers stop being gallant? How can the convenience and safety of women workers be protected?
3. Why did the court reject the argument of weight lifting ability? How can an employer, without relying on size and gender, decide who is capable of safely lifting sixty to ninety pounds? What accommodation for pregnancy did the court indicate would be acceptable? Would that accommodation be acceptable after the adoption of the PDA?

The district court in *Cheatwood* and the Fifth Circuit Court of Appeals in *Weeks* placed the burden of proof on the employer who claims a BFOQ to produce a factual basis for believing that all or substantially all women will be unable to safely and efficiently perform the job in question. That approach was also followed by the Ninth Circuit Court of Appeals in *Rosenfeld v. Southern Pacific Co.*, 444 F.2d 1219 (1971). There, the employer attempted to defend a policy of excluding women from selected jobs on two grounds: the jobs were deemed unsuitable for women because they involved irregular hours and lifting weights of up to twenty-five pounds; and state laws limited the maximum hours and weight lifting that an employer was permitted to require of female employees. The court decided that neither ground established a BFOQ. That decision is widely regarded as having established that "protective" labor laws similar to those that survived constitutional challenges from *Muller v. Oregon* onward (see Chapter 1) violate Title VII. They violate the statute because, by relying upon gender stereotypes, they discriminate against individuals because of their sex.

These decisions effectively rejected the use of stereotypes relating to the relative preferences and abilities of women and men as a basis for this exception. We saw in *Manhart* that the scope of Title VII prohibitions is not restricted to decisions rooted in stereotyping. They also extend to true generalizations about a sexual group that do not apply to the individuals affected by the employer's decisions. The following case addressed a BFOQ defense based not on stereotyped assumptions but on factual findings.

DIAZ V. PAN AM. WORLD AIRWAYS, INC.

United States Court of Appeals, Fifth Circuit, 1971.
442 F.2d 385, cert. denied, 404 U.S. 950 (1971).

TUTTLE, Circuit Judge:

. . . The facts in this case are not in dispute. Celio Diaz applied for a job as flight cabin attendant with Pan American Airlines in 1967. He was rejected because Pan Am had a policy of restricting its hiring for that position to females. . . .

Pan Am admitted that it had a policy of restricting its hiring for the cabin attendant position to females. Thus, both parties stipulated that the primary issue for the District Court was whether, for the job of flight cabin attendant, being a female is a "bona fide occupational qualification (hereafter BFOQ) reasonably necessary to the normal operation" of Pan American's business.

The trial court found that being a female was a BFOQ. . . .

We note, at the outset, that there is little legislative history to guide our interpretation. The amendment adding the word "sex" to "race, color, religion and national origin" was adopted one day before House passage of the Civil Rights Act. It was added on the floor and engendered little relevant debate. In attempting to read Congress' intent in these circumstances, however, it is reasonable to assume, from a reading of the statute itself, that one of Congress' main goals was to provide equal access to the job market for both men and women. Indeed, as this court in *Weeks v. Southern Bell Telephone and Telegraph Co.*, 5 Cir., 408 F.2d 228 at 235 clearly stated, the purpose of the Act was to provide a foundation in the law for the principle of nondiscrimination. Construing the statute as embodying such a principle is based on the assumption that Congress sought a formula that would not only achieve the optimum use of our labor resources but, and more importantly, would enable individuals to develop as individuals.

Attainment of this goal, however, is, as stated above, limited by the bona fide occupational qualification exception in section 703(e). In construing this provision, we feel, as did the court in *Weeks*, *supra*, that it would be totally anomalous to do so in a manner that would, in effect, permit the exception to swallow the rule. Thus, we adopt the EEOC guidelines which state that "the Commission believes that the bona fide occupational qualification as to sex should be interpreted narrowly.". . .

[T]he trial court's conclusion was based upon (1) its view of Pan Am's history of the use of flight attendants; (2) passenger preference; (3) basic psychological reasons for the preference; and (4) the actualities of the hiring process.

Having reviewed the evidence submitted by Pan American regarding its own experience with both female and male cabin attendants it had hired over the years, the trial court found that Pan Am's current hiring policy was the result of a pragmatic process, "representing a judgment made upon adequate evidence acquired through Pan Am's considerable experience, and designed to yield under Pan Am's current operating conditions better *average* performance for its passengers than would a policy of mixed male and female hiring." (emphasis added) The performance of female attendants was *better* in the sense that they were *superior* in such nonmechanical aspects of the job as "providing reassurance to anxious passengers, giving courteous personalized service and, in general, making flights as pleasurable as possible within the limitations imposed by aircraft operations."

The trial court also found that Pan Am's passengers overwhelmingly preferred to be served by female stewardesses. Moreover, on the basis of the expert testimony of a psychiatrist, the court found that an airplane cabin represents a unique environment in which an air carrier is required to take account of the special psychological needs of its passengers. These psychological needs are better attended to by females. This is not to say that there are no males who would not have the necessary qualities to perform these non-mechanical functions, but the trial court found that the actualities of the hiring process would make it more difficult to find these few males. Indeed, "the admission of men to the hiring process, in the present state of the art of employment selection, would have increased the number of unsatisfactory employees hired, and reduced the average levels of performance of Pan Am's complement of flight attendants.". . .

Because of the narrow reading we give to section 703(e), we do not feel that these findings justify the discrimination practiced by Pan Am.

We begin with the proposition that the use of the word "necessary" in section 703(e) requires that we apply a business *necessity* test, not a business *convenience* test. That is to say, discrimination based on sex is valid only when the *essence* of the business operation would be undermined by not hiring members of one sex exclusively.

The primary function of an airline is to transport passengers safely from one point to another. While a pleasant environment, enhanced by the obvious cosmetic effect that female stewardesses provide as well as, according to the finding of the trial court, their apparent ability to perform the non-mechanical functions of the job in a more effective manner than most men, may all be important, they are tangential to the essence of the business involved. No one has suggested that having male stewards will so seriously affect the operation of an airline as to jeopardize or even minimize its ability to provide safe transportation from one place to another. Indeed the record discloses that many airlines including Pan Am have utilized both men and women flight cabin attendants in the past and Pan Am, even at the time of this suit, has 283 male stewards employed on some of its foreign flights. . . .

While we recognize that the public's expectation of finding one sex in a particular role may cause some initial difficulty, it would be totally anomalous if we were to allow the preferences and prejudices of the customers to determine whether the sex discrimination was valid. Indeed, it was, to a large extent, these very prejudices the Act was meant to overcome. Thus, we feel that customer preference may be taken into account only when it is based on the company's inability to perform the primary function or service it offers.

Of course, Pan Am argues that the customers' preferences are not based on "stereotyped thinking," but the ability of women stewardesses to better provide the non-mechanical aspects of the job. Again, as stated above, since these aspects are tangential to the business, the fact that customers prefer them cannot justify sex discrimination.

The judgment is reversed and the case is remanded for proceedings not inconsistent with this opinion.

STUDY QUESTIONS

1. Would the four reasons offered in support of the restriction here have satisfied the *Weeks* standard? Why did this court reject those reasons?

2. How did the court interpret the word "necessary"? Are courts qualified to decide what the "essence of the business operation" is and to draw a line between it and "tangential" operations? What is the alternative?

3. Assuming that it was right about the preferences of its customers, was Pan Am likely to lose customers to other airlines as a result of this decision? Did this decision affect only Pan Am?

Ten years later, the airline industry again attempted to assert that sex was a BFOQ for flight attendants. This time, Southwest Airlines tried to justify its policy of hiring only attractive women as flight attendants and ticket agents. The airline had, as a marketing strategy, dressed its all-female personnel in hot pants and high boots, and promised to take its passengers to the sky "with love." Apparently, the marketing ploy was very successful in attracting male customers to the airline. The district court determined, however, that the preferences of Southwest's customers did not overcome Congress's intent in enacting Title VII of preventing employers from making employment decisions based on sexual stereotypes. The court held that hiring both sexes would not undermine the essential function of Southwest's business, which was to transport customers. *Wilson v. Southwest Airlines Co.*, 517 F. Supp. 292 (N.D. TX 1981).

In the mid-1990s, another type of company attempted to assert that sex was a BFOQ essential for its business. Seven men brought a class action suit in federal court in Chicago against Hooters, an Atlanta-based restaurant chain, claiming that Hooters discriminated against them on the basis of sex when it failed to hire them as waiters. The restaurant, which employs scantily clad female wait staff called "Hooter Girls," argued that its business is selling female sex appeal; therefore, being female is a BFOQ. Unfortunately, we will never find out if the argument that the essence of Hooters' business is serving sex appeal, not food, would have "tasted" right in court; in 1997, Hooters settled the matter for $3.75 million. The settlement allowed Hooters to continue to use its exclusively female wait staff of Hooter Girls, but did provide that some support jobs, such as host and bartender, would be filled without regard to sex.

The question of the meaning of the BFOQ first reached the Supreme Court in the following case. There, the Court endorsed the narrow standard developed by lower courts in earlier BFOQ cases but appeared to find a factual basis for concluding that all, or substantially all, otherwise qualified women would be unable to safely and efficiently perform the duties of a guard in Alabama maximum-security prisons housing male inmates. The Court's decision, although limited to the facts of this particular situation, is highly controversial. The more controversial points are reviewed by Justice Marshall in his dissenting opinion.

In *Dothard*, the Court addressed two important aspects of Title VII: the BFOQ exception and the disparate impact theory of discrimination. Those elements of the decision relating to the disparate impact theory were discussed in section II of this chapter.

DOTHARD V. RAWLINSON
Supreme Court of the United States, 1977.
433 U.S. 321, 97 S. Ct. 2720, 53 L.Ed.2d 786.

Mr. Justice STEWART delivered the opinion of the Court.

Appellee Dianne Rawlinson sought employment with the Alabama Board of Corrections as a prison guard, called in Alabama a "correctional counselor." After her application was rejected, she brought this class suit under Title VII of the Civil Rights Act of 1964 . . . alleging that she had been denied employment because of her sex in violation of federal law. A three-judge Federal District Court for the Middle District of Alabama decided in her favor. . . .

At the time she applied for a position as correctional counselor trainee, Rawlinson was a 22-year-old college graduate whose major course of study had been correctional psychology. She was refused employment because she failed to meet the minimum 120-pound weight requirement established by an Alabama statute. The statute also establishes a height minimum of 5 feet 2 inches.

After her application was rejected because of her weight, Rawlinson filed a charge with the Equal Employment Opportunity Commission, and ultimately received a right-to-sue letter. She then filed a complaint in the District Court on behalf of herself and other similarly situated women, challenging the statutory height and weight minima as violative of Title VII and the Equal Protection Clause of the Fourteenth Amendment. A three-judge court was convened. While the suit was pending, the Alabama Board of Corrections adopted Administrative Regulation 204, establishing gender criteria for assigning correctional counselors to maximum-security institutions for "contact positions," that is, positions requiring continual close physical proximity to inmates of the institution. Rawlinson amended her class-action complaint by adding a challenge to Regulation 204 as also violative of Title VII and the Fourteenth Amendment.

Like most correctional facilities in the United States, Alabama's prisons are segregated on the basis of sex. . . . The Julia Tutwiler Prison for Women and the four male penitentiaries are maximum-security institutions. Their inmate living quarters are for the most part large dormitories, with communal showers and toilets that are open to the dormitories and hallways. . . .

A correctional counselor's primary duty within these institutions is to maintain security and control of the inmates by continually supervising and observing their activities. . . .

Unlike the statutory height and weight requirements, Regulation 204 explicitly discriminates against women on the basis of their sex. In defense of this overt discrimination, the appellants rely on § 703 (e). . . .

The District Court rejected the bona-fide-occupational-qualification (bfoq) defense, relying on the virtually uniform view of the federal courts that § 703 (e) provides only the narrowest of exceptions to the general rule requiring equality of employment opportunities. This view has been variously formulated. In *Diaz v. Pan American World Airways*, the Court of Appeals for the Fifth Circuit held that "discrimination based on sex is valid only when the essence of the business operation would be undermined by not hiring members of one sex exclusively." In an earlier case, *Weeks v. Southern Bell Telephone and Telegraph Co.*, the same court said that an employer could rely on the bfoq exception only by proving "that he had reasonable cause to believe, that is, a factual basis for believing, that all or substantially all women would be unable to perform safely and efficiently the duties of the job involved." But whatever the verbal formulation, the federal courts have agreed that it is impermissible under Title VII to refuse to hire an individual woman or man on the basis of stereotyped characteristics of the sexes, and the District Court in the present case held in effect that Regulation 204 is based upon just such stereotyped assumptions.

We are persuaded—by the restrictive language of § 703 (e), the relevant legislative history, and the consistent interpretation of the Equal Employment Opportunity Commission—that the bfoq exception was in fact meant to be an extremely narrow exception to the general prohibition of discrimination on the basis of sex. In the particular factual circumstances of this case, however, we conclude that the District Court erred in rejecting the State's contention that Regulation 204 falls within the narrow ambit of the bfoq exception.

The environment in Alabama's penitentiaries is a peculiarly inhospitable one for human beings of whatever sex. Indeed, a Federal District Court has held that the conditions of confinement in the prisons of the State, characterized by "rampant violence" and a "jungle atmosphere," are constitutionally intolerable. *Pugh v. Locke*. The record in the present case shows that because of inadequate staff and facilities, no attempt is made in the four maximum-security male penitentiaries to classify or segregate inmates according to their offense or level of dangerousness—a procedure that, according to expert testimony, is essential to effective penological administration. Consequently, the estimated 20% of the male prisoners who are sex offenders are scattered throughout the penitentiaries' dormitory facilities.

In this environment of violence and disorganization, it would be an oversimplification to characterize Regulation 204 as an exercise in "romantic paternalism." In the usual case, the argument that a particular job is too dangerous for women may appropriately be met by the rejoinder that it is the purpose of Title VII to allow the individual woman to make that choice for herself. More is at stake in this case, however, than an individual woman's decision to weigh and accept the risks of employment, in a "contact" position in a maximum-security male prison.

The essence of a correctional counselor's job is to maintain prison security. A woman's relative ability to maintain order in a male, maximum-security, unclassified penitentiary of the type Alabama now runs could be directly reduced by her womanhood. There is a basis in fact for expecting that sex offenders who have criminally assaulted women in the past would be moved to do so again if access to women were established within the prison. There would also be a real risk that other inmates, deprived of a normal heterosexual environment, would assault women guards because they were women.[22] In a prison system where violence is the order of the day, where inmate access to guards is facilitated by dormitory living arrangements, where every institution is understaffed, and where a substantial portion of the inmate population is composed of sex offenders mixed at random with other prisoners, there are few visible deterrents to inmate assaults on women custodians.

Appellee Rawlinson's own expert testified that dormitory housing for aggressive inmates poses a greater security problem than single-cell lockups, and further testified that it would be unwise to use women as guards in a prison where even 10% of the inmates had been convicted of sex crimes and were not segregated from the other prisoners.[23] The likelihood that inmates would assault a woman because she was a woman would pose a real threat not only to the victim of the assault but also to the basic control of the penitentiary and protection of its inmates and the other security personnel. The employee's very womanhood would thus directly undermine her capacity to provide the security that is the essence of a correctional counselor's responsibility.

There was substantial testimony from experts on both sides of this litigation that the use of women as guards in "contact" positions under the existing conditions in Alabama maximum-security male penitentiaries would pose a substantial security problem, directly linked to the sex of the prison guard. On the basis of that evidence, we conclude that the District Court was in error in ruling that being male is not a bona fide occupational qualification for the job of correctional counselor in a "contact" position in an Alabama male maximum-security penitentiary.

The judgment is accordingly affirmed in part and reversed in part, and the case is remanded to the District Court for further proceedings consistent with this opinion.

It Is So Ordered.

Mr. Justice MARSHALL, with whom Mr. Justice BRENNAN joins, concurring in part and dissenting in part.

[22]The record contains evidence of an attack on a female clerical worker in an Alabama prison, and of an incident involving a woman student who was taken hostage during a visit to one of the maximum-security institutions.
[23]Alabama's penitentiaries are evidently not typical. Appellee Rawlinson's two experts testified that in a normal, relatively stable maximum-security prison—characterized by control over the inmates, reasonable living conditions, and segregation of dangerous offenders—women guards could be used effectively and beneficially. Similarly, an *amicus* brief filed by the State of California attests to that State's success in using women guards in all-male penitentiaries.

. . . The Court is unquestionably correct when it holds "that the bfoq exception was in fact meant to be an extremely narrow exception to the general prohibition of discrimination on the basis of sex." I must, however, respectfully disagree with the Court's application of the bfoq exception in this case. . . .

What would otherwise be considered unlawful discrimination against women is justified by the Court, however, on the basis of the "barbaric and inhumane" conditions in Alabama prisons, conditions so bad that state officials have conceded that they violate the Constitution. To me, this analysis sounds distressingly like saying two wrongs make a right. It is refuted by the plain words of § 703 (e). The statute requires that a bfoq be "reasonably necessary to the normal operation of that particular business or enterprise." But no governmental "business" may operate "normally" in violation of the Constitution. Every action of government is constrained by constitutional limitations. While those limits may be violated more frequently than we would wish, no one disputes that the "normal operation" of all government functions takes place within them. A prison system operating in blatant violation of the Eighth Amendment is an exception that should be remedied with all possible speed, as Judge Johnson's comprehensive order in *Pugh v. Locke* is designed to do. In the meantime, the existence of such violations should not be legitimatized by calling them "normal." Nor should the Court accept them as justifying conduct that would otherwise violate a statute intended to remedy age-old discrimination.

The Court's error in statutory construction is less objectionable, however, than the attitude it displays toward women. Though the Court recognizes that possible harm to women guards is an unacceptable reason for disqualifying women, it relies instead on an equally speculative threat to prison discipline supposedly generated by the sexuality of female guards. There is simply no evidence in the record to show that women guards would create any danger to security

in Alabama prisons significantly greater than that which already exists. All of the dangers—with one exception discussed below—are inherent in a prison setting, whatever the gender of the guards.

The Court first sees women guards as a threat to security because "there are few visible deterrents to inmate assaults on women custodians." In fact, any prison guard is constantly subject to the threat of attack by inmates, and "invisible" deterrents are the guard's only real protection. No prison guard relies primarily on his or her ability to ward off an inmate attack to maintain order. Guards are typically unarmed and sheer numbers of inmates could overcome the normal complement. Rather, like all other law enforcement officers, prison guards must rely primarily on the moral authority of their office and the threat of future punishment for miscreants. As one expert testified below, common sense, fairness, and mental and emotional stability are the qualities a guard needs to cope with the dangers of the job. Well qualified and properly trained women, no less than men, have these psychological weapons at their disposal.

The particular severity of discipline problems in the Alabama maximum-security prisons is also no justification for the discrimination sanctioned by the Court. The District Court found in *Pugh v. Locke* that guards "must spend all their time attempting to maintain control or to protect themselves." If male guards face an impossible situation, it is difficult to see how women could make the problem worse, unless one relies on precisely the type of generalized bias against women that the Court agrees Title VII was intended to outlaw. For example, much of the testimony of appellants' witnesses ignores individual differences among members of each sex and reads like "ancient canards about the proper role of women." The witnesses claimed that women guards are not strict disciplinarians; that they are physically less capable of protecting themselves and subduing unruly inmates; that inmates take advantage of them as they did their mothers, while male guards are strong father figures who easily maintain discipline, and so on. Yet the record shows that the presence of women guards has not led to a single incident amounting to a serious breach of security in any Alabama institution. And, in any event, "[g]uards rarely enter the cell blocks and dormitories," *Pugh v. Locke*, where the danger of inmate attacks is the greatest.

It appears that the real disqualifying factor in the Court's view is "[t]he employee's very womanhood." The Court refers to the large number of sex offenders in Alabama prisons, and to "[t]he likelihood that inmates would assault a woman because she was a woman." In short, the fundamental justification for the decision is that women as guards will generate sexual assaults. With all respect this rationale regrettably perpetuates one of the most insidious of the old myths about women—that women, wittingly or not, are seductive sexual objects. The effect of the decision, made I am sure with the best of intentions, is to punish women because their very presence might provoke sexual assaults. It is women who are made to pay the price in lost job opportunities for the threat of depraved conduct by prison inmates. . . .

The Court points to no evidence in the record to support the asserted "likelihood that inmates would assault a woman because she was a woman." Perhaps the Court relies upon common sense, or "innate recognition." But the danger in this emotionally laden context is that common sense will be used to mask the "romantic paternalism" and persisting discriminatory attitudes that the Court properly eschews. To me, the only matter of innate recognition is that the incidence of sexually motivated attacks on guards will be minute compared to the "likelihood that inmates will assault" a *guard* because he or she is a *guard*.

The proper response to inevitable attacks on both female and male guards is not to limit the employment opportunities of law-abiding women who wish to contribute to their community, but to take swift and sure punitive action against the inmate offenders. Presumably, one of the goals of the Alabama prison system is the eradication of inmates' antisocial behavior patterns so that prisoners will be able to live one day in free society. Sex offenders can begin this process by learning to relate to women guards in a socially acceptable manner. To deprive women of job opportunities because of the threatened behavior of convicted criminals is to turn our social priorities upside down.[5]

Although I do not countenance the sex discrimination condoned by the majority, it is fortunate that the Court's decision is carefully limited to the facts before it. I trust the lower courts will recognize that the decision was impelled by the shockingly inhuman conditions in Alabama prisons, and thus that the "extremely narrow [bfoq] exception" recognized here, . . . will not be allowed "to swallow the rule" against sex discrimination. Expansion of today's decision beyond its narrow factual basis would erect a serious roadblock to economic equality for women.

---

[5]The appellants argue that restrictions on employment of women are also justified by consideration of inmates' privacy. It is strange indeed to hear state officials who have for years been violating the most basic principles of human decency in the operation of their prisons suddenly become concerned about inmate privacy. It is stranger still that these same officials allow women guards in contact positions in a number of nonmaximum security institutions, but strive to protect inmates' privacy in the prisons where personal freedom is most severely restricted. I have no doubt on this record that appellants' professed concern is nothing but a feeble excuse for discrimination.

As the District Court suggested, it may well be possible, once constitutionally adequate staff is available, to rearrange work assignments so that legitimate inmate privacy concerns are respected without denying jobs to women. Finally, if women guards behave in a professional manner at all times, they will engender reciprocal respect from inmates, who will recognize that their privacy is being invaded no more than if a woman doctor examines them. The suggestion implicit in the privacy argument that such behavior is unlikely on either side is an insult to the professionalism of guards and the dignity of inmates.

1. What did Regulation 204 provide? On what grounds was it defended?
2. What reasons were cited for allowing a BFOQ in this case? What would have been lost by following the rationale indicated in *Cheatwood* and allowing the individual job applicant to balance the risk of injury against the benefits of the job?
3. What objections were raised by the dissenters to the Court's willingness to view a guard's "very womanhood" as an impediment to her safe and efficient performance of her job?
4. Does this decision reject the standard developed by the lower courts for interpreting the BFOQ exception or only authorize a narrow departure from that standard in this case?

The decision in *Dothard* concerning the BFOQ exception can be confusing on first reading. The result of the decision was that Alabama was permitted to discriminate against qualified women who applied for the positions at issue here, at least until the unconstitutionally violent conditions of its prisons were corrected. In this respect, several points should be noted. One is that the Court itself emphasized that its ruling here was limited to those unusual circumstances. Another is that very few other prisons have been successful in enlisting the ruling in *Dothard* in support of excluding women from security positions.

More important, however, the Court in *Dothard* approved the narrow interpretation given by the EEOC and the lower courts to the BFOQ exception. In the longer term, therefore, *Dothard* can be understood as indicating that, although there can very well be situations in which differential treatment of women and men in an employment setting is "reasonably necessary to the normal operation of that particular business," those situations are likely to be very rare.

That such situations, however rare they may be, must be tolerated is surely regrettable. The justification offered for the facially discriminatory practices that were present in the Alabama prisons, as Justice Marshall correctly observed, "sounds distressingly like saying two wrongs make a right." Even if it were true that Alabama could not give reasonable assurances to inmates of their safety in part because it could not control those who are prone to violence, it surely does not follow that denial of equal employment opportunities to qualified women who elect to contribute their services in such circumstances is acceptable. This line of justification is reminiscent of traditional attitudes and strategies—woman as temptress and blaming the victim. In the end, the only consolation there may be for accommodating ourselves to such practices is that they are few and far between.

Accommodating Safety, Efficiency, and Privacy Interests

The language of the statute allows overt sex discrimination by an employer where it is "reasonably necessary to the normal operation of that particular business or enterprise." The EEOC specifically rejected "the preferences of coworkers, the employer, clients or customers" (except for the purposes of authenticity or genuineness) as grounds for a BFOQ. In *Dothard*, the Court approved the narrow emphasis recommended by the EEOC, as well as the *Weeks* and *Diaz* standards for interpreting the language of the BFOQ exception. In *Weeks*, the circuit court placed the burden on the employer that invokes a BFOQ defense of proving that "he had reasonable cause to believe, that is, a factual basis for believing, that all or substantially all women would be unable to perform safely and efficiently the duties of the job involved." The Court has since repeated that commitment on several occasions. Several issues remain unclear. How closely must the sex of an employee be related to the job that she performs? Would increased costs to the employer's overall operation suffice as a justification? What type of considerations give an employer reasonable cause to believe that sex is related to job performance? Must such a belief be documented by empirical evidence? Are all types of third party preferences for being served by people of one sex to be rejected as grounds for a BFOQ? Are there no circumstances in which the customary standards of modesty carry sufficient weight to excuse sex discrimination in employment? The following cases illustrate the state of the questions on these issues.

In *Johnson Controls*, the Supreme Court addressed the BFOQ in the context of a safety issue. The safety concern here was not like that in *Cheatwood*, where the employer argued that the safety of the employee was at risk. Here, as in *Dothard*, the risk was to the safety of potential third parties (i.e., to fetuses of women who conceived while working in toxic environments created by the employer).

U. A. W. v. JOHNSON CONTROLS, INC.

United States Supreme Court, 1991.
499 U.S. 187, 111 S. Ct. 1196, 113 L.Ed.2d 158.

Justice BLACKMUN delivered the opinion of the Court.

. . . Respondent Johnson Controls, Inc., manufactures batteries. In the manufacturing process, the element lead is a primary ingredient. Occupational exposure to lead entails health risks, including the risk of harm to any fetus carried by a female employee. . . .

. . . [I]n 1982, Johnson Controls . . . announc[ed] a broad exclusion of women from jobs that exposed them to lead: ". . . [I]t is [Johnson Controls'] policy that women who are pregnant or who are capable of bearing children will not be placed into jobs involving lead exposure or which could expose them to lead through the exercise of job bidding, bumping, transfer or promotion rights." The policy defined "women . . . capable of bearing children" as "[a]ll women except those whose inability to bear children is medically documented.". . .

The District Court granted summary judgment for defendant-respondent Johnson Controls. . . . The Court of Appeals for the Seventh Circuit, sitting en banc, affirmed the summary judgment by a 7-to-4 vote. [This was the first ruling by a Circuit Court] to hold that a fetal-protection policy directed exclusively at women could qualify as a BFOQ. . . .

The bias in Johnson Controls' policy is obvious. Fertile men, but not fertile women, are given a choice as to whether they wish to risk their reproductive health for a particular job. . . . Respondent's fetal-protection policy explicitly discriminates against women on the basis of their sex. The policy excludes women with childbearing capacity from lead-exposed jobs and so creates a facial classification based on gender. . . .

. . . [T]he Court of Appeals assumed . . . that sex-specific fetal-protection policies do not involve facial discrimination. [It] analyzed the policies as though they were facially neutral, and had only a discriminatory effect upon the employment opportunities of women. Consequently, the [court] looked to see [the] employer . . . had established that its policy was justified as a business necessity. The business necessity standard is more lenient for the employer than the statutory BFOQ defense. . . . The court assumed that because the asserted reason for the sex-based exclusion (protecting women's unconceived offspring) was ostensibly benign, the policy was not sex-based discrimination. That assumption, however, was incorrect.

. . . . Johnson Controls' policy is facially discriminatory because it requires only a female employee to produce proof that she is not capable of reproducing.

. . . . We hold that Johnson Controls' fetal-protection policy is sex discrimination forbidden under Title VII unless respondent can establish that sex is a "bona fide occupational qualification" [BFOQ]. . . .

Johnson Controls argues that its fetal-protection policy falls within the so-called safety exception to the BFOQ. Our cases have stressed that discrimination on the basis of sex because of safety concerns is allowed only in narrow circumstances. . . .

Our case law [*Dothard* and other of our decisions] makes clear that the safety exception is limited to instances in which sex or pregnancy actually interferes with the employee's ability to perform the job. This approach is consistent with the language of the BFOQ provision itself, for it suggests that permissible distinctions based on sex must relate to ability to perform the duties of the job. Johnson Controls suggests, however, that we expand the exception to allow fetal-protection policies that mandate particular standards for pregnant or fertile women. We decline to do so. Such an expansion contradicts not only the language of the BFOQ and the narrowness of its exception but the plain language and history of the Pregnancy Discrimination Act.

The PDA's amendment to Title VII contains a BFOQ standard of its own: unless pregnant employees differ from others "in their ability or inability to work," they must be "treated the same" as other employees "for all employment-related purposes." This language clearly sets forth Congress' remedy for discrimination on the basis of pregnancy and potential pregnancy. Women who are either pregnant or potentially pregnant must be treated like others "similar in their ability . . . to work." In other words, women as capable of doing their jobs as their male counterparts may not be forced to choose between having a child and having a job. . . .

We have no difficulty concluding that Johnson Controls cannot establish a BFOQ. Fertile women, as far as appears in the record, participate in the manufacture of batteries as efficiently as anyone else. Johnson Controls' professed moral and ethical concerns about the welfare of the next generation do not suffice to establish a BFOQ of female sterility. Decisions about the welfare of future children must be left to the parents who conceive, bear, support, and raise them rather than to the employers who hire those parents. Congress has mandated this choice through Title VII, as amended by the Pregnancy Discrimination Act. . . .

The judgment of the Court of Appeals is reversed and the case is remanded for further proceedings consistent with this opinion.

Study Questions

1. Compare the issues raised in this case with those raised in *Muller*, as well as the way they were decided. In both, women and men risked safety hazards. In both, job opportunities were denied to women. In both, the asserted motivation is to protect the interests of some individuals from the hazards of particular workplaces. Who has Congress entrusted with the prerogative of deciding whether the risk is to be undertaken where the hazard is to the employee? Who is entrusted with that prerogative where the hazard is to future possible children? Do you agree with that decision? What are the alternatives?

2. The Court decided here that no sex-specific fetal-protection policy can be defended as a BFOQ. The Court noted in the course of its decision that the employer had not examined evidence showing that fetal damage can result from the exposure of male as well as female parents to lead. Had the employer imposed this job restriction on anyone capable of reproducing, would the outcome have been different? Would you approve of that result?

The decision in *Johnson Controls* was unanimous. The lower courts' decision to grant summary judgment to the employer was overturned without a dissenting vote. Notwithstanding, this was a close decision on one issue of lasting significance. Just how narrow an exception is the BFOQ? Justice Blackmun, writing for a majority of five justices, declared that it is narrowly focused on the ability to perform the specific job in question. An important part of the rationale supporting that view was introduced through the discussion of the PDA.

Four justices disagreed. Justices White and Kennedy and Chief Justice Rehnquist declared that the PDA has to do with the definition of "because of sex" and is not relevant to determining the scope of the BFOQ exception. These justices, along with Justice Scalia, rejected the view that BFOQs can be justified only by the linkage of employee ability to the specific job. According to these four justices, the contribution of employees to the employer's cost of doing business is also germane and could sometimes be controlling. Thus, Justice Scalia indicated, "I think, for example, that a shipping company may refuse to hire pregnant women as crew members on long voyages because the on-board facilities for foreseeable emergencies, though quite feasible, would be inordinately expensive." As several justices who voted in the majority in this case have since retired from the Court, the balance of the justices on the delicate question of whether the scope of the BFOQ exception is the same or narrower than that of "business necessity" in the disparate impact pattern of litigation is far from settled.

In the years since *Dothard*, a number of social scientists have studied the consequences of employing women as correctional officers in all-male prisons. These show that where women held these jobs, the male inmates believed that their presence increased the livability of the institutions and also improved the behavior of the inmates. A recent study found similar results for male officers guarding female inmates. Linda Zupan concluded her study by pointing out that all but two of the sixty-four maximum- and medium-security women's prisons in her study employed men as correctional officers and in all but eight, "men were routinely assigned to supervise female inmates in the housing units."

> In regard to reaction of female prisoners to the presence of male officers in the living units, the findings of this study suggest that inmate resistance is minimal. In general, female inmates at the women's prisons in this study expressed a preference for supervision by male officers. The inmates also noted a change in the behavior of other residents in the presence of male officers. They observed that the appearance and grooming of some inmates improved and that inmates were more obedient to the commands of male officers than they were to the commands of female officers.
> *Linda L. Zupan, "Men Guarding Women." 20* Journal of Criminal Justice *297–309 (1992), 308.*

Another of Zupan's findings was that both male and female inmates object strongly to the deployment of opposite-sexed guards in assignments that require direct physical contact or visual observation of a personal nature (e.g., pat or strip searches and supervision of toilet areas). This leads to a third major area of BFOQ decisions, viz., those that relate to privacy interests. These arise in institutional settings involving intimate care and/or close, round-the-clock observation. Prisons, hospitals, and nursing facilities are most frequently the employers that invoke the privacy interests of their clients as grounds for BFOQs. Here, the issue is whether demands for a same-sex service provider based on customs of personal modesty are to be regarded as a protected interest that is closely enough involved in the essence of the business to warrant a BFOQ or as just another type of customer preference that is not permitted to interfere with the equal employment opportunities of qualified women and men.

The privacy interest was raised in footnote 5 of Justice Marshall's dissent in *Dothard*. He endorsed the customer preference approach to these claims and dismissed such complaints as "an insult to the professionalism of guards and the dignity of inmates." Thereafter, the decisions of the lower courts have gone both ways as regards prison inmates. Then, in 1984, the Supreme Court ruled that prisoners do not have a reasonable expectation of privacy in their cells that is sufficient to entitle them to Fourth Amendment protection against unreasonable searches. According to the Court, the interest of prisoners in privacy must give way to the interest of society in the security of its penal institutions, *Hudson v. Palmer,* 468 U.S. 517 (1984). That decision makes it unlikely that prisons can justify single-sex BFOQs by invoking a privacy interest on behalf of inmates.

Prisons are not the only institutional settings in which asserted privacy interests can come into conflict with equal employment opportunity. The following case addresses that same conflict in a hospital setting. It illustrates the rationale and result that lower courts typically reach when hospitals and nursing facilities assert a BFOQ on the basis of patient privacy interests.

HEALEY V. SOUTHWOOD PSYCHIATRIC HOSPITAL
United States Court of Appeals, Third Circuit, 1996.
78 F.3d 128.

COWEN, Circuit Judge.

Brenda L. Healey appeals the order of the district court granting Southwood Psychiatric Hospital's motion for summary judgment on her sex discrimination claim brought under Title VII of the Civil Rights Act of 1964, *codified as amended at* 42 U.S.C. §2000e *et. seq.* Because we find that Southwood has established a bona fide occupational qualification defense to Healey's Title VII claim, we will affirm the order of the district court.

The following facts are not substantially disputed. Healey was hired as a child care specialist at Southwood in October 1987. In this capacity, she was responsible for developing and maintaining a therapeutic environment for the children and adolescents hospitalized at Southwood. Southwood's patients are emotionally disturbed, and some have been sexually abused. In November 1992, Healey was assigned to the night shift at Southwood as a result of a staff reorganization. The reorganization was necessitated by reason of a decline in the patient population. The night shift is a less desirable shift, requiring more housekeeping chores and less patient interaction and responsibility.

Southwood has a policy of scheduling both males and females to all shifts, and considers sex in making its assignments. In November 1992, Southwood assigned Healey to the night shift because it needed a female child care specialist on that shift. Southwood maintains that its gender-based policy is necessary to meet the therapeutic needs and privacy concerns of its mixed-sex patient population. Healey counters that gender should not play any role in the hiring and scheduling of employees, and Southwood's actions towards her constitute sex discrimination in violation of Title VII. The district court granted Southwood's motion for summary judgment from which Healey appeals. . . .

. . . Southwood uses sex as an explicit factor in assigning its staff to the various shifts, and Healey was assigned to the night shift because of her sex. . . . Here, Southwood's staffing policy is facially discriminatory,[1] rather than facially neutral. . . .

---

[1]Judge Sarokin would describe Southwood's scheduling policy as "facially gender-based" rather than "facially discriminatory" for the following reason. Use of the term "discriminatory" connotes that the policy is "characterized by or exhibiting prejudices, racial bias, or the like," *The Random House College Dictionary* 379 (revised ed. 1980); it connotes intent. Because the court concludes that Southwood's policy is motivated not by a discriminatory intent but by a bona fide occupational qualification, Judge Sarokin believes that referring to the policy as "discriminatory" is inappropriate.

. . . On Healey's disparate treatment claim, . . . [she] has shown sex discrimination by establishing the existence of a facially discriminatory employment policy. Title VII expressly states that "[it] shall be an unlawful employment practice for an employer . . . to discriminate against any individual with respect to [her] compensation, terms, conditions, or privileges of employment, because of such individual's . . . sex[.]" 42 U.S.C. § 2000(e). Thus, Title VII sets forth a sweeping prohibition against overt gender-based discrimination in the workplace. *See, e.g., City of Los Angeles Dep't of Water and Power v. Manhart*, 435 U.S. 702, 98 S. Ct. 1370 (1978). When open and explicit use of gender is employed, as is the case here, the systematic discrimination is in effect "admitted" by the employer, and the case will turn on whether such overt disparate treatment is for some reason justified under Title VII. *See* RODNEY A. SMOLLA, *supra*, at §9.03[6] [a]. A justification for overt discrimination may exist if the disparate treatment is part of a legally permissible affirmative action program, or based on a BFOQ. *Id.*

Southwood asserts that its gender-based staffing policy is justified as a bona fide occupational qualification, and therefore is exempt under Title VII. Under the BFOQ defense, overt gender-based discrimination can be countenanced if sex "is a bona fide occupational qualification reasonably necessary to the normal operation of [a] particular business or enterprise[.]" 42 U.S.C. § 2000e-2 (e) (1). The BFOQ defense is written narrowly, and the Supreme Court has read it narrowly. *See Johnson Controls*, 499 U.S. at 201, 111 S. Ct. at 1204. The Supreme Court has interpreted this provision to mean that discrimination is permissible only if those aspects of a job that allegedly require discrimination fall within the "'essence' of the particular business." *Id.* at 206, 111 S. Ct. at 1207. Alternatively, the Supreme Court has stated that sex discrimination "is valid only when the essence of the business operation would be undermined" if the business eliminated its discriminatory policy. *Dothard v. Rawlinson*, 433 U.S. 321, 332, 97 S. Ct. 2720, 2729 (1977) (quoting

Diaz v. Pan American World Airways, Inc., 442 F.2d 385, 388 (5th Cir.), *cert. denied,* 404 U.S. 950, 92 S. Ct. 275 (1971)).

The employer has the burden of establishing the BFOQ defense. *Johnson Controls,* 499 U.S. at 200, 111 S. Ct. at 1204. The employer must have a "basis in fact" for its belief that no members of one sex could perform the job in question. *Dothard,* 433 U.S. at 335, 97 S. Ct. at 2730. . . . The employer must also demonstrate that it "could not reasonably arrange job responsibilities in a way to minimize a clash between the privacy interests of the [patients], and the non-discriminatory principle of Title VII." *Gunther v. Iowa State Men's Reformatory,* 612 F.2d 1079, 1086 (8th Cir.), *cert. denied,* 466 U.S. 966, 100 S. Ct. 2942 (1980). *See Hardin v. Stynchcomb,* 691 F.2d 1364, 1369 (11th Cir. 1982).

With these precepts in mind, we may now turn to the facts of this case. The "essence" of Southwood's business is to treat emotionally disturbed and sexually abused adolescents and children. Southwood has presented expert testimony that staffing both males and females on all shifts is necessary to provide therapeutic care. "Role modeling," including parental role modeling, is an important element of the staff's job, and a male is better able to serve as a male role model than a female and vice versa. A balanced staff is also necessary because children who have been sexually abused will disclose their problems more easily to a member of a certain sex, depending on their sex and the sex of the abuser. If members of both sexes are not on a shift, Southwood's inability to provide basic therapeutic care would hinder the "normal operation" of its "particular business." Therefore, it is reasonably necessary to the normal operation of Southwood to have at least one member of each sex available to the patients at all times.

There is authority for the proposition that a business that has as its "essence" a therapeutic mission requires the consideration of gender in making employment decisions. In *City of Philadelphia v. Pennsylvania Human Relations Commission,* 300 A.2d 97 (Pa. Commw. Ct. 1973), the court determined that gender may be considered in order to treat and supervise children with emotional and social problems, and approved the youth center's gender-based staffing policy under the BFOQ defense. The *City of Philadelphia* court stated that "[i]t is common sense that a young girl with a sexual or emotional problem will usually approach someone of her own sex, possibly her mother, seeking comfort and answers." *Id.* at 103. . . . In this case, Southwood has established a basis in fact through expert opinion that the therapeutic aspects of the child care specialist job require the consideration of gender.

In addition to therapeutic goals, privacy concerns justify Southwood's discriminatory staffing policy. Southwood established that adolescent patients have hygiene, menstrual, and sexuality concerns which are discussed more freely with a staff member of the same sex. Child patients often must be accompanied to the bathroom, and sometimes must be bathed. The Supreme Court has explicitly left open the question whether sex constitutes a BFOQ when privacy interests are implicated, *Johnson Controls, Inc.*, 499 U.S. at 206 n.4, 111 S. Ct. 1207, and the issue has been raised but not yet decided by our court. *See Rider v. Commonwealth of Pennsylvania*, 850 F.2d 982 (3d Cir.), *cert. denied*, 488 U.S. 993, 109 S. Ct. 556 (1988). We note that other circuits have discussed privacy concerns as the basis of a BFOQ defense. However, those cases involve an inmate's right to privacy which is balanced against the state's legitimate penological interest. *See Nina Jordon v. Booth Gardner et. al.*, 986 F.2d 1521, 1524 (9th Cir. 1993) ("prisoners' legitimate expectations of bodily privacy from persons of the opposite sex are extremely limited"); *Kent v. Johnson*, 821 F.2d 1220, 1226 (6th Cir. 1987) (balancing privacy interests of inmates with state's interest in prison security); *Gunther v. Iowa State Men's Reformatory*, 612 F.2d 1079, 1086 (8th Cir. 1980) (same).

In the non-prison context, other courts have held that privacy concerns may justify a discriminatory employment policy.

See AFSCME v. Michigan Council 25, 635 F. Supp. 1010 (E.D. Mich. 1986) (privacy rights of mental health patients can justify a BFOQ to provide for same-sex personal hygiene care); *Fesel v. Masonic Home of Delaware*, 447 F. Supp. 1346, 1353 (D. Del. 1978) (retirement home patients), *aff'd mem.*, 591 F.2d 1334 (3d Cir. 1979); *Backus v. Baptist Medical Center*, 510 F. Supp. 1191 (E.D. Ark. 1981) (essence of obstetrics nurse's business is to provide sensitive care for patient's intimate and private concerns), *vacated as moot*, 671 F.2d 1100 (8th Cir. 1982). . . .

We conclude that due to both therapeutic and privacy concerns, Southwood is an institution in which the sexual characteristics of the employee are crucial to the successful performance of the job of child care specialist. Southwood cannot rearrange job responsibilities in order to spare Healey or another female from working the night shift because at least one female and male should be available at all times in order for Southwood to conduct its business. Accordingly, we hold that the essence of Southwood's business would be impaired if it could not staff at least one male and female child care specialist on each shift. . . .

We conclude that Southwood has established a BFOQ which justifies its discriminatory employment practice. Accordingly, we will affirm the February 7, 1995, order of the district court granting summary judgment in favor of Southwood Psychiatric Hospital.

Study Questions

1. What is the "essence" of Southwood's business? Did this "essence" play a role in the court's determination? If so, how?
2. What did Judge Cowen say about the relevance of privacy concerns with respect to a BFOQ defense? What privacy concerns were present in this case? Did the court find these concerns sufficient to justify Southwood's asserted BFOQ? Do you agree or disagree with the court's view of the privacy concerns?

IV. REMEDIES

A paramount practical concern of parties who litigate disputes under fair employment practices (FEP) laws is the sanctions that courts are likely to impose once violations are found. It is the prospect of benefiting from such sanctions that provides the motivation for aggrieved parties to bring actions and carry them through to completion. It is the prospect of being burdened by such sanctions that provides the motivation for employers to vigorously defend themselves in these actions.

The sanctions that courts are authorized to impose for discrimination in an employment context differ somewhat depending on the statute or statutes under which the violation is found. There are, as we have seen, a number of statutes prohibiting employment discrimination at both federal and state levels. Our discussion will focus primarily on the sanctions available under Title VII. Success in obtaining remedies available under Title VII requires compliance with the particular procedures set out in the statute.

Three themes run through those subsections of the statute that deal with procedure. First, they give high priority to resolving complaints by means of conciliation, rather than litigation. For this reason, a person is not permitted to file a Title VII action in federal court until the EEOC has had the opportunity to investigate the charge and to eliminate the problem by means of persuasion. The second is one of accommodation to the interests of states in promoting equal employment opportunity. Thus, those states that have their own FEP laws must be allowed the opportunity to act on their own FEP laws before the EEOC can assert jurisdiction. The third theme concerns timeliness. All steps have deadlines. For example, a victim has 180 days to file a charge with the EEOC (300 if it occurred in a state with its own FEP laws). The CRA of 1991 added a provision clarifying when the clock begins to run on some of these deadlines. An intentionally discriminatory seniority system can be challenged within 180 (300) days either of its initial adoption, when it becomes applicable to the complaining party, or when the complaining party is injured by its application. A victim may demand a "right to sue letter" 180 days after the charge is filed with the EEOC, even if the EEOC has not taken action on it, but must generally file a suit in federal court within 90 days of receipt of that letter.

One of the most important procedural points to remember is where to file a complaint. If the employer suspected of violating a provision of Title VII is the federal government, the complaint must be filed with the Civil Service Commission. If the employer is not a unit of the federal government, the complaint must be filed with the EEOC. Initiation of a complaint with the EEOC requires the completion of a simple form by the person who claims to have been victimized. Although this phase of proceedings under Title VII may be completed without the assistance of a lawyer, that assistance is often helpful.

The primary source of the authority of the courts to impose sanctions under Title VII is section 706(g). The original language of that section is as follows:

> If the court finds that the respondent has intentionally engaged in or is intentionally engaging in an unlawful employment practice charged in the complaint, the court may enjoin the respondent from engaging in such unlawful employment practice, and order such affirmative action as may be appropriate, which may include, but is not limited to, reinstatement or hiring of employees, with or without back pay . . . or any other equitable relief as the court deems appropriate.

In general, the sanctions imposed under Title VII are designed to offset the harm suffered as a result of violations. Although the language of section 706(g) restricts remedies to "intentional" violations, in this context, the term "intentional" has been interpreted to mean simply that the practice was not accidental, *Rowe v. General Motors Corp.*, 457 F.2d

348 (5th Cir. 1972). The type of sanction imposed corresponds to the type of violation found: where the defendant has refused to hire the plaintiff on unlawful grounds, the courts have ordered that the plaintiff be hired; where the plaintiff has been fired on discriminatory grounds, the courts have ordered reinstatement; and where the employer has paid the plaintiff at a lower rate in violation of the statute, the courts have ordered back pay. Where the plaintiff has unlawfully been denied a promotion to a better paying job, but promotion cannot be ordered because the position is filled, the courts have ordered front pay (i.e., a cash award equal to the difference between the victim's future earnings in her present job and what she would have earned in the position unlawfully denied her). For plaintiffs unlawfully denied seniority, the courts have ordered these rights restored. As indicated in section 706(g), the courts may issue court orders or injunctions to prevent unlawful employment practices from occurring and from continuing. These are the main forms of relief granted by courts in Title VII cases where the plaintiff prevails. Others will be discussed in the course of this section.

Sanctions imposed by the law are sometimes discussed in terms of the purposes they are designed to serve. Three such purposes are often distinguished. As we will see, a given form of relief might be ordered for more than one of these purposes. The first purpose is to compensate the victim of wrongdoing, to make the victim whole, to restore the victim to her or his "rightful place" (i.e., the status that the victim would have enjoyed had she or he not been wronged). Back pay is often ordered for a compensatory purpose. Other types of compensatory remedies include monetary awards for emotional stress and humiliation or actual expenses incurred as a result of discrimination. Another form of monetary relief regularly awarded to plaintiffs who prevail under Title VII is attorney's fees. This type of remedy requires the defendant to pay the reasonable attorney's fees incurred by the plaintiff. These awards are specifically provided by the statute in section 706(k).

A second purpose for imposing sanctions is to penalize a wrongdoer. Examples of sanctions imposed for this purpose are usually found in the context of criminal law, although punitive damages are sometimes awarded in civil contexts. These remedies are ordinarily not available under Title VII or most state antidiscrimination laws.

The third purpose for imposing legal sanctions is the one least familiar to the general public. It is to prevent a wrong from occurring. Remedies imposed for that purpose are called "prophylactic remedies." The best example of such a remedy is the traditional equitable remedy, an injunction. This is a court order directing the employer to avoid engaging in the challenged practice. These orders may bind the employer either temporarily until the dispute is settled at trial or permanently. Permanent injunctions are imposed after a trial on the merits. Injunctions are regularly issued under Title VII and state fair employment provisions.

Just as legal sanctions can be understood from the perspective of the purposes for which they are imposed, they can also be understood from the perspective of the consequences they produce. The consequences provide incentives for future behavior. The concept of prophylactic remedies relies on this. Unless the prospect of being held in contempt of court provides an incentive for a party to comply with an injunction, such a remedy will not prevent the occurrence of wrongful acts. The same can be said for at least one theory of punitive remedies as well, viz., the deterrence theory of punishment.

Compensatory remedies also create incentives. In *Albermarle Paper Co. v. Moody*, 422 U.S. 405 (1975), the Supreme Court indicated how back pay remedies available under Title VII are to be awarded for both compensatory and prophylactic purposes. The Court indicated that the expectation of a back pay award provides an incentive, "a spur or catalyst," for employers to examine their practices and to eliminate those that might lay them open to liability under Title VII. It should also be noted that the expectation of back pay provides incentive for victims of employment discrimination to complain to the EEOC and to bring suit under Title VII. Such remedies provide an answer to the "What's in it for me?" question, whether asked by employer or employee. Indeed, it is the availability of remedies that makes a practical difference in the type and frequency of discriminatory behavior.

The courts have broad discretion under the authority of section 706(g) in fashioning remedies for the relief of those who have been unlawfully denied employment opportunities. The term "equitable relief" in the statute refers to a longstanding distinction between "legal" remedies and "equitable" remedies dating back to early English practices. Legal remedies, for example, awards of money damages, are those that have historically been available in the King's "law courts," while equitable remedies, for example, injunctions, are those that have historically been available "in equity," that is, from the King's Chancellor. Equity traditionally was more flexible and more concerned with doing justice. Today, most American jurisdictions have combined their law and equity courts. The distinction, nevertheless, continues to have important consequences. One of these is that the right of a jury trial guaranteed by the Constitution is limited to claims that would traditionally have been tried in law courts. Claims for equitable relief are heard by judges sitting alone.

One deficiency in the original design of Title VII was that it provided for the award of make-whole remedies but not monetary damages. In this respect, it contrasted unfavorably with the 1866 Civil Rights Act (section 1981), which afforded compensatory and punitive damages to individuals who successfully claimed that they had suffered from intentional racial discrimination in employment settings. The CRA of 1991 partially removed that asymmetry by providing that a victim of intentional discrimination on the basis of race, color, religion, sex, or national origin who cannot recover damages under section 1981 may recover compensatory and punitive damages under Title VII in addition to make-whole relief.

The 1991 act placed a cap on the amount of monetary damages available to those victims, depending on the size of the employer's workforce. These range from fifty thousand dollars where the business employs one hundred or fewer people (95 percent of all businesses) to a maximum of three hundred thousand dollars for those that employ over five hundred. No such cap affects damage awards under section 1981.

At the same time, the CRA of 1991 provided for trial by jury in Title VII cases where intentional discrimination is claimed and damages are demanded. Some knowledgeable practitioners believe that, of all the provisions of the CRA, this one will have the most favorable impact on the interests of complaining parties. The expectation is that the jury trial option will make favorable findings both as to liability and amount of damages much more likely.

It seems that this expectation is being borne out. In 1993, Peggy Kimzey sued Wal-Mart for compensatory and punitive damages on her hostile work environment and constructive discharge claims. The jury returned a verdict of $35,000 for compensatory damages, $1.00 for back pay, and $50,000,000 for punitive damages. After trial, however, the District Court for the Western District of Missouri reduced the punitive damages award to $5,000,000. Upon cross-appeal, the Eighth Circuit Court of Appeals ordered a further reduction of punitive damages to $350,000. *Kimzey v. Wal-Mart Stores, Inc.*, 107 F.3d 568 (8th Cir. 1997). In June 1997, Mitsubishi Motors agreed with the EEOC to resolve charges by its female employees at the company's Normal, Illinois, plant by paying $34 million to more than 300 aggrieved female employees. This is the largest sexual harassment settlement that the EEOC has ever obtained. Given the tendency of juries to award high punitive damages, and in light of the EEOC's vigorous pursuit of class action charges for sexual harassment, it is not surprising that in April of 2003, the Dial Company entered into a joint consent decree for $10 million to settle claims brought by the EEOC alleging sexual harassment at Dial's Montgomery, Illinois, facility, rather than face the prospect of a jury determination of punitive damages on a class basis.

V. CLASS ACTIONS

As stated in preceding text, Title VII permits individuals to vindicate their rights through private lawsuits as well as through the EEOC. And, individuals may bring an action individually or as a class action. The class action is form of private lawsuit that can be used to combat systematic gender discrimination, that is, an individual alleges that her employer engaged in disparate treatment toward her that is part of a pattern or practice of general discriminatory treatment of members of her protected class. To initiate a class action, a suit is usually filed by one or more named plaintiffs on behalf of a proposed class, consisting of a group of individuals who have suffered a common injury. After the complaint is filed, the plaintiff(s) file a motion to have the class certified pursuant to Federal Rule of Civil Procedure 23(a), which delineates the certification prerequisites. The defendant (employer) will likely object and the court in which the suit was filed must then decide if the proposed class has met the prerequisites necessary for certification of the class. Class actions offer the advantage of aggregating claims against a single defendant who is alleged to have engaged in widespread harm, thereby conserving plaintiffs' resources and potentially reducing their expenses, strengthening the impact on the defendant by aggregating recoveries, and avoiding the potential of inconsistent court rulings. They also have disadvantages, such as increasing the cost and time needed to pursue class certification or the suit in general, causing a loss of control over the litigation, and creating procedural or settlement difficulties. Whether a lawsuit will be entitled to proceed as a class action depends, however, on whether the characteristics of the class seeking certification can withstand analysis under Rule 23(a)'s prerequisites, as explained by the U.S. Supreme Court in the following case.

GENERAL TELEPHONE COMPANY OF THE SOUTHWEST V. FALCON
United States Supreme Court, 1982.
457 U.S. 147, 102 S. Ct. 2364, 72 L.Ed.2d 740.

Justice STEVENS delivered the opinion of the Court.

The question presented is whether respondent Falcon, who complained that petitioner did not promote him because he is a Mexican-American, was properly permitted to maintain a class action on behalf of Mexican-American applicants for employment whom petitioner did not hire. . . . Without conducting an evidentiary hearing, the District Court certified a class including Mexican-American employees and Mexican-American applicants for employment who had not been hired. [Footnote omitted]

Following trial of the liability issues, the District Court entered separate findings of fact and conclusions of law with respect first to respondent and then to the class. The District Court found that petitioner had not discriminated against respondent in hiring, but that it did discriminate against him in its promotion practices. . . . The court reached converse conclusions about the class, finding no discrimination in promotion practices, but concluding that petitioner had discriminated against Mexican-Americans at its Irving facility in its hiring practices. . . .

Both parties appealed. . . .

. . . [W]e granted certiorari to decide whether the class action was properly maintained on behalf of both employees who were denied promotion and applicants who were denied employment.

II

The class action device was designed as "an exception to the usual rule that litigation is conducted by and on behalf of the individual named parties only.". . . Class relief is "peculiarly appropriate" when the "issues involved are common to the class as a whole" and when they "turn on questions of law applicable in the same manner to each member of the class.". . . For in such cases, "the class action device saves the resources of both the courts and the parties by permitting an issue potentially affecting every [class member] to be litigated in an economical fashion under Rule 23.". . .

Title VII of the Civil Rights Act of 1964, as amended, authorizes the Equal Employment Opportunity Commission to sue in its own name to secure relief for individuals aggrieved by discriminatory practices forbidden by the Act. *See* 42 U.S.C. § 2000e-5(f)(1). In exercising this enforcement power, the Commission may seek relief for groups of employees or applicants for employment without complying with the strictures of Rule 23. . . . Title VII, however, contains no special authorization for class suits maintained by private parties. An individual litigant seeking to maintain a class action under Title VII must meet "the prerequisites of numerosity, commonality, typicality, and adequacy of representation" specified in Rule 23(a). . . . These requirements effectively "limit the class claims to those fairly encompassed by the named plaintiff's claims.". . .

We have repeatedly held that "a class representative must be part of the class and possess the same interest and suffer the same injury as the class members.". . .

We cannot disagree with the proposition underlying the across-the-board rule—that racial discrimination is, by definition, class discrimination. [Footnote omitted] But the allegation that such discrimination has occurred neither determines whether a class action may be maintained in accordance with Rule 23 nor defines the class that may be certified. Conceptually, there is a wide gap between (a) an individual's claim that he has been denied a promotion on discriminatory grounds and his otherwise unsupported allegation that the company has a policy of discrimination, and (b) the existence of a class of persons who have suffered the same injury as that individual, such that the individual's claim and the class claims will share common questions of law or fact and that the individual's claim will be typical of the class claims. [Footnote omitted] . . .

The trial of this class action followed a predictable course. Instead of raising common questions of law or fact, respondent's evidentiary approaches to the individual and class claims were entirely different. He attempted to sustain his individual claim by proving intentional discrimination. He tried to prove the class claims through statistical evidence of disparate impact. Ironically, the District Court rejected the class claim of promotion discrimination, which conceptually might have borne a closer typicality and commonality relationship with respondent's individual claim, but sustained the class claim of hiring discrimination. As the District Court's bifurcated findings on liability demonstrate, the individual and class claims might as well have been tried separately. It is clear that the maintenance of respondent's action as a class action did not advance "the efficiency and economy of litigation which is a principal purpose of the procedure.". . .

We do not, of course, judge the propriety of a class certification by hindsight. The District Court's error in this case, and the error inherent in the across-the-board rule, is the failure to evaluate carefully the legitimacy of the named plaintiff's plea that he is a proper class representative under Rule 23(a). As we noted in *Coopers & Lybrand v. Livesay,* . . . "the class determination generally involves considerations that are 'enmeshed in the factual and legal issues comprising the plaintiff's cause of action.'". . . Sometimes the issues are plain enough from the pleadings to determine whether the interests of the absent parties are fairly encompassed within the named plaintiff's claim, and sometimes it may be necessary for the court to probe behind the pleadings before coming to rest on the certification question. Even after a certification order is entered, the judge remains free to modify it in the light of subsequent developments in the litigation [Footnote omitted]. For such an order, particularly during the period before any notice is sent to members of the class, "is inherently tentative.". . . This flexibility enhances the usefulness of the class action device; actual, not presumed, conformance with Rule 23(a) remains, however, indispensable.

III

The need to carefully apply the requirements of Rule 23(a) to Title VII class actions was noticed by a member of the Fifth Circuit panel that announced the across-the-board rule. In a specially concurring opinion in *Johnson v. Georgia Highway Express, Inc.*, [citation omitted], Judge Godbold emphasized the need for "more precise pleadings,". . . for, "without reasonable specificity, the court cannot define the class, cannot determine whether the representation

is adequate, and the employer does not know how to defend," [citation omitted]. He termed as "most significant" the potential unfairness to the class members bound by the judgment if the framing of the class is overbroad. . . . And he pointed out the error of the "tacit assumption" underlying the across-the-board rule that "all will be well, for surely the plaintiff will win and manna will fall on all members of the class." [Citation omitted] With the same concerns in mind, we reiterate today that a Title VII class action, like any other class action, may only be certified if the trial court is satisfied, after a rigorous analysis, that the prerequisites of Rule 23(a) have been satisfied.

The judgment of the Court of Appeals affirming the certification order is reversed, and the case is remanded for further proceedings consistent with this opinion.

It Is So Ordered.

STUDY QUESTIONS

1. What are the prerequisites of Rule 23(a)? What is the purpose of applying these requirements to both the framing of a class and the determination of whether to certify that class?
2. What is the potential unfairness to class members if the class certified is overly broad? What is the potential unfairness to the employer?

Although *Falcon* dealt with claims of race and ethnic discrimination, the test enunciated by the U.S. Supreme Court is equally applicable to a case of sex discrimination in which class certification is sought. In the past ten years there have been a number of private gender discrimination cases in which certification for a large class has been achieved or sought. For example, a class action suit was filed against Home Depot in 1994, alleging that the company discriminated against women in hiring for sales and management positions, job assignments, promotions, and compensation in its West Coast Division stores. Three years later, the employer settled the suit by agreeing to: pay $65 million to a class of over 25,000 women; pay $22.5 million in attorney's fees to the class' lawyers; create a system for employees to register their interest in moving into sales and management positions in that Division's stores; develop and implement training for managers and supervisors on equal employment opportunity; refine its internal gender discrimination complaint procedure; and provide self-study product knowledge training.

More recently, there has been ongoing litigation over certification of the class in suits against Wal-Mart and Costco. In June of 2001, a class action lawsuit was filed in the U.S. District Court for the District of San Francisco on behalf of Betty Dukes and five other current or former Wal-Mart and Sam's Club employees alleging that Wal-Mart discriminates against female employees in making promotions, job assignments, pay decisions, and training, and retaliates against women who complain about these practices. In April of 2003, the plaintiffs filed a motion to certify a class of all women who worked for Wal-Mart in the U.S. at any time since December 26, 1998. This proposed class includes approximately 1.5 million women and, if certification is granted, would comprise the largest civil rights class action lawsuit in U.S. history. In June of 2004, the Court certified the class and Wal-Mart appealed that decision. In February of 2007, a three-judge panel of the U.S. Court of Appeals for the Ninth Circuit affirmed the district court's class certification. Wal-Mart promptly requested a rehearing en banc (a quorum of the full Court bench, rather than a smaller panel of judges). In December of 2007, the three-judge panel withdrew its initial opinion and issued a superseding opinion that still permitted the class certification. In doing so, the panel dismissed Wal-Mart's petition for rehearing on the grounds that the revised opinion addressed the legal errors Wal-Mart claimed, but gave Wal-Mart leave to refile its petition. Wal-Mart did refile, and in February of 2009, the Ninth Circuit granted its petition for a rehearing en banc on the class action certification. In light of this, the three-judge panel's December 2007 opinion was no longer decisive. On March 24, 2009, the parties presented oral arguments before an en banc panel of eleven Ninth Circuit judges. It is expected that the en banc panel will take several months to issue an opinion on class certification. If the en banc panel affirms the class' certification, Wal-Mart will probably appeal that decision to the U.S. Supreme Court. So, an ultimate decision on the fate of the 1.5 million Wal-Mart women class may not be decided for quite awhile.

The fate of the Wal-Mart women's class will have an impact beyond their gender discrimination class action. In August of 2004, an employment class action lawsuit was filed in the U.S. District Court for the District of San Francisco against Costco Wholesale Corporation by a then current (now former) female assistant manager on behalf of herself and all current and former female Costco employees in the United States who have been subjected to gender discrimination in promotion to store management positions. Subsequently, two additional named plaintiffs were added to the lawsuit. The suit alleges that Costco operates a "glass ceiling" at the store-management level, which prevents women from being promoted to assistant manager and general manger positions. In August of 2006, the plaintiffs filed a motion asking the district court to certify a class of more than 750 current and former Costco employees. In January of 2007, the class was certified, and the three named plaintiffs were allowed to represent all women employed by Costco in the United States who had been denied promotion to assistant and/or general manager positions since January 3, 2002. Costco appealed that decision to the U.S. Court of Appeals for the Ninth Circuit. After a three-judge panel from the Ninth Circuit heard oral arguments in April of 2008, the judges decided to hold Costco's appeal in abeyance until Wal-Mart's appeal in its gender discrimination class action in concluded. The Ninth Circuit's determination in the Wal-Mart class action will, therefore, directly affect its decision in both the Costco class action and any subsequent class actions filed in its jurisdiction. Furthermore, if the Ninth Circuit's decision in Wal-Mart is appealed and the U.S. Supreme Court decides to consider the case, its decision will shape the outcome for future gender discrimination class actions throughout the United States.

ON-LINE RESOURCES

For information and statistics from the Department of Labor (DOL), including the Women's Bureau, go to the DOL web site:
www.dol.gov

For information on federal EEO law and Equal Employment Opportunity Commission (EEOC) regulations, as well as information on sex discrimination and sexual harassment, and access to task force reports, go to the EEOC web site:
www.eeoc.gov

For information on research conducted by the Institute for Women's Policy Research, including the gender wage gap, go to:
www.iwpr.org/index.cfm

To keep abreast with developments in the Dukes v. Wal-Mart case, go to the Wal-Mart class action web site:
www.walmartclass.com

To keep abreast with developments in the Ellis v. Costco Wholesale Corporation case, go to the Costco class action web site:
www.genderclassactionagainstcostco.com

To read the District Court for the District of Columbia's full "Findings of Fact and Conclusions of Law" in *Schroer v. Billington*, go to:
https://ecf.dcd.uscourts.gov/cgi-bin/show_public_doc?2005cv1090-70

CHAPTER 4

WORKING CONDITIONS AND COMPENSATION

THIS CHAPTER TREATS two strategically important problem areas. These problems, sexual harassment on the job and the earnings gap, are well known. Both affect us all, men as well as women, directly or indirectly, whether we are in the full-time labor force or not. This chapter reviews the principal legal methods and strategies that have been developed over the past three decades for dealing with these forms of sex discrimination.

The principal legal instruments for combating sex discrimination in employment are statutes. At the federal level, the base of the push for more equal employment opportunities is Title VII of the Civil Rights Act of 1964. The main aspects of that statute, the principles used by courts to interpret it, and remedies available to victims of unlawful employment practices under it were discussed in Chapter 3.

I. SEXUAL HARASSMENT

Discussions of this topic often founder on the way that the phrase is used. For now, we can adopt a working definition of sexual harassment simply as any unwelcome sexual attention. A moment's reflection reveals that sexual harassment is everywhere and extends over a broad spectrum of behavior from forcible rape and unwanted touching to rude inquiries and crude boasting. As in other contexts, sexual harassment in the workplace can be blatant—"have sex with me or you're fired"—or more subtle—comments on the anatomy of one's fellow workers. Although debate persists about the magnitude of the problem, an increasing body of information supports the contention that the frequency of sexual harassment in the workplace is very significant.

HOW PERVASIVE IS SEXUAL HARASSMENT?

Charles S. Clark

"Sexual Harassment." 1 *CQ Researcher* 539, 542–3 (1991).

Gauging the actual incidence of sexual harassment is difficult, both because definitions of the term are mercurial and, according to some critics, because the problem's seriousness may be exaggerated by ideologues or management consultants who specialize in sexual harassment cases.

Several surveys covering disparate sectors of society have varied widely in their findings. The first broadscale effort to measure sexual harassment was conducted by *Redbook* magazine, which surveyed 9,000 women in 1976. Eighty-eight percent of the respondents said they had been victims of harassment and 52 percent said they had been fired or induced to quit a job because of it.

In 1980, a survey was conducted among 20,000 federal workers by the U.S. Merit Systems Protection Board (MSPB), the grievance arbitration board for government employees. Forty-two percent of the females and 15 percent of the males responding said they had been sexually harassed. (An updated, smaller survey conducted by the board in 1987 produced nearly identical results.) According to the MSPB, victims of harassment tended to be young, not married, college-educated, members of a minority racial or ethnic group (if male), in a trainee position (or office/clerical positions, if male), in a non-traditional position (female law enforcement officers or male secretaries), to have an immediate supervisor of the opposite sex or to have an immediate work group composed predominantly of the opposite sex.

The most recent large-scale survey of sexual harassment was released in September 1990 by the Department of Defense. Of 20,000 U.S. military respondents around the world, 64 percent of the females reported having been sexually harassed, some directly, others in subtler ways such as being subjected to catcalls, dirty looks and teasing. (Only 17 percent of the males reported being harassed.) Of those women reporting direct harassment, 38 percent said they had been touched or "cornered," 15 percent said they had been pressured for sexual favors (compared with only 2 percent of males) and 5 percent said they had been victims of rape or attempted rape.

In the corporate world, recent surveys indicate that 15 percent of women have been sexually harassed within the past year, according to Freada Klein, an organizational development expert who specializes in sexual harassment.

Surveys on college campuses show the number of respondents reporting to have been sexually harassed ranging from 40–70 percent. Bernice R. Sandler, a college specialist at the Center for Women Policy Studies in Washington, says only 2 percent of campus harassment cases involve a professor demanding sex in return for a good grade. Most sexual harassment on campus involves male and female students, she says. On several campuses recently, college men have been taken to task for a practice known as "scoping"—loudly rating the physical attributes of women as they walk by. Sometimes the men will surround a woman and demand that she bare her breasts.

The steadiest barometer of the ebbs and flows of sexual harassment is the number of such complaints filed with EEOC offices. The number of complaints (of which those found to have merit is a fraction) has risen slightly in recent years, reaching 5,557 in 1990. The 1986 Supreme Court decision expanding the definition of sexual harassment to include incidents that create a hostile work environment may account for some of the increase. . . .

Women's groups and others who favor an activist approach to combating sexual harassment say the incidence is significantly underreported. "Women used to think there was nothing they could do about it," says Isabelle Katz Pinzler, director of the women's rights project at the ACLU. Many women decline to file charges for fear of confronting superiors, being labeled a troublemaker or subjecting their personal lives to scrutiny.

The American population at large does not appear to believe that sexual harassment is rampant. Only 26 percent of the women responding to a national survey conducted in September 1986 said they had experienced sexual harassment at work. Only 17 percent of the women and 16 percent of the men thought sexual harassment was "a big problem"; 67 percent of both men and women said it was "somewhat of a problem."

STUDY QUESTIONS

1. What proportion of women employees reported to the MSPB that they were victims of sexual harassment? How did that survey characterize the typical victim? Does the MSPB survey hold any surprises for you?
2. What forms do harassing behaviors take in the military? On college and university campuses?
3. As of August 1986, what proportion of the public thought that sexual harassment was a "big problem"?

Although sexual harassment is commonplace, it had not been widely acknowledged, even among those whose lives were most severely affected by it. It was one of the dirty secrets of our culture. That changed on October 11, 1991. On that day, law professor Anita Hill broke the silence. Testifying at a nationally televised hearing of the all-male Senate Judiciary Committee, Hill alleged in vivid detail how Supreme Court nominee Clarence Thomas had sexually harassed her in the early 1980s when he was her supervisor in the Department of Education and the EEOC.

The sharp contrast between the poise and courage shown by Hill and the obtuse and often mean-spirited response of committee members staggered a great many viewers, both women and men. It was clear that the senators did not comprehend the seriousness and pervasiveness of sexual harassment. Two types of reactions were common among viewers. "They just don't get it, the men, they just don't get it!" was a widespread sentiment. Women and men apparently do not perceive sexual harassment in the same way. Another common reaction took the form of self-examination. Has this happened to me? Have I done this to someone else? As these questions were pursued, the nation began to glimpse the dimensions of the problem.

A second watershed event affecting the nation's consciousness of sexual harassment took place in 1991. The annual convention of the Tailhook Association, a professional organization of active duty and retired Navy flying officers, held that year in a Las Vegas hotel from September 4th to 7th, was the scene of massive sexual harassment. After repeated attempts to hide the ugly details by Navy officials at various levels, the Pentagon's inspector general released the final report of his investigation in April 1993. According to the report, eighty-three women and seven men were sexually assaulted during the drunken revel. The report said that as many as 175 officers may face disciplinary action as a result of their involvement and suggested that the cases of thirty Navy admirals and two Marine generals present at the meeting be reviewed. The adverse publicity received by the Navy and the military generally over the two-year period leading up to the final report prompted a commitment on the part of the Clinton administration to fundamentally change the culture of the military from one that condones, if not encourages, sexual harassment of women to one that respects and values women who serve their country in the uniform of the military services. According to the 1995 Department of Defense (DOD) survey, the percentage of servicewomen reporting harassment dropped from 9 percentage points from 1998, and the percentage of men reporting such incidents dropped from 3 percentage points. In the DOD's 2002 survey, the rate of reported sexual harassment of active-duty members dropped yet again—from 46 percent to 24 percent for women and from 8 percent to 3 percent for men. In addition, 77 percent of women and 79 percent of men reported that they had received sexual harassment training at least once in the 12 months prior to taking the survey and the majority of women (76 percent) and men (83 percent) indicated the training made them feel it was safe to complain about sexual harassment. Hopefully, this is an indication of the change in culture and attitude of the military toward women in uniform.

Clark noted that sexual harassment in the workplace was not widely acknowledged as "a big problem" as of September 1986. Since the Hill-Thomas hearings and the Tailhook scandal, that status has changed sharply. One measure is the volume of complaints alleging sexual harassment filed with the EEOC. These doubled in the six months following the hearing. Another indication of changed attitudes is political activity. In November 1992, a record eleven women stood for election to the U.S. Senate. In addition, 107 women were on the ballot for the House of Representatives, a 54 percent increase over 1990.

A review of more recent versions of some of the statistics Clark discusses demonstrates that although we are now better at recognizing sexual harassment, we have not made great strides in eradicating the problem. For example, the MSPB conducted a second study in 1987, and a third one in 1994. The 1987 survey reported the same percentage of women and 1 percent fewer men stating that they had experienced sexual harassment. The 1994 survey reported a slight increase; 44 percent of women and 19 percent of men responding to that survey indicated that they had experienced some sexual harassment at work. Even more telling are the data from the EEOC, Clark's "barometer" of sexual harassment. Between 1990 and 2002 the number of sexual harassment complaints filed with EEOC offices increased, averaging almost 15,000 complaints a year for the ten-year period between 1993 and 2002. It is interesting to note that for that same period, the percentage of those complaints filed by men steadily increased from 9.1 percent to 14.9 percent. This may have been a reflection of our understanding of male and same-sex sexual harassment after *Oncale*. More recently the average number of complaints filed with the EEOC has dropped; for the six-year period from 2003 through 2008, complaints averaged about 13,000 a year, and the number of complaints filed by men remained fairly constant, increasing by only 1 percent to 15.9 percent. The decrease in complaints filed may be a reflection of the fact that more and more companies now offer sexual harassment training programs and have adopted written sexual harassment policies.

Although high-profile cases helped put sexual harassment in the spotlight, they appear to have polarized society's discomfort with the subject rather than realign its views. The following selection suggests that although the law, in theory, affords protection against sexual harassment, how the public assesses the conduct of the purported male harasser and female victim still works against women.

HOSTILE ENVIRONMENT

Gwendolyn Mink

Hostile Environment: The Political Betrayal of Sexually Harassed Women
Ithaca: Cornell University Press, 2000. From Chapter One, pp. 1–7.

When Anita Hill recounted how then-Judge Clarence Thomas had sexually harassed her, the *Wall Street Journal* speculated that she was motivated to make such a claim by her ideological opposition to the judge's conservative views. [footnote omitted] On Capitol Hill, key Republican strategists questioned not only her motives but also her sanity. [footnote omitted] At the Judiciary Committee hearings, one senator accused her of "flat-out perjury," while another suggested she had concocted her testimony with the help of case law and excerpts from the novel *The Exorcist*. [footnote omitted]

When Paula Jones told the nation that she had been sexually harassed in a Little Rock hotel room by then-Governor Bill Clinton, Michael Isikoff (who later became famous for his access to Linda Tripp and her audiotapes) reasoned in the *Washington Post* that Jones had "smelled money" in leveling charges against the President of the United States. [footnote omitted] At the White House, presidential strategists portrayed Jones as a gold-digging "trailer-park floozy" who was the pawn of the Republican right wing. [footnote omitted] Many of the president's friends insisted that Jones and her supporters were the *real* harassers: Jesse Jackson, for example, suspected that conservatives "want him to drop his pants in public. Paula Jones's lawyers are hardly masking their gratification at the demand for him to expose his body parts in a deposition." [footnote omitted] Fighting fire with fire, meanwhile, the president's lawyer, Robert Bennett, threatened to excavate and expose Jones's sexual history, presumably to diminish her credibility and to show that even if the president did expose himself and tell her to "kiss it," she couldn't possibly have been offended.

The vicious personal attacks weathered by Anita Hill and Paula Jones are no different from those endured by many women who bring sexual harassment claims, although the attacks against Hill and Jones were far louder and more visible than most. It is disappointing but not surprising that alleged harassers try to defend themselves by discrediting the women who bring charges against them. More surprising is how ecumenical this strategy can be. On the left as well as the right, friends of alleged harassers have propagated ugly speculations about women who have been brave enough to vindicate their injuries. Speculations about the motives and character of the women who use sexual harassment law, in turn, have fueled attacks on the law itself—most often by right-wingers who think the law is a boondoggle for disreputable women, but more recently also by liberals who chafe when the law is deployed against their own men. Solidarity with alleged harassers against women and against the law may be par for the course among conservatives. Among liberals—and feminists—however, it is a disturbing new development. When the law's putative champions deprive even one sexually harassed woman of its protections, they betray all sexually harassed women. When they redefine the law to exclude even one woman's injury, they betray feminism's signal legal accomplishment and compromise its future.

Sexual harassment targets first began to seek legal redress in the mid-1970s. By the mid-1980s, their right to legal redress was firmly established. The law now recognizes that unwanted, demeaning, or threatening sexual conduct can limit women's opportunities, ambitions, and rewards in workplaces and in schools—that such conduct at work or in school substitutes a woman's sex for her personhood, interposing sex between a woman and her job or education. Following this, courts consider employers vicariously liable when a supervisor (or higher authority) harasses a subordinate; [footnote omitted] large groups of women have won significant settlements against pervasively hostile work environments; [footnote omitted] and a sexually harassed worker whose only viable alternative is to give up her job can claim that she was "constructively discharged" by her employer.

The law not only recognizes the objective wrongs of sexual harassment but also proceeds from the assumption that a woman's subjective experience of sexual harassment may impair her civil rights. It permits women to tell what happened and how they were affected. A woman's account of her harassment is not proof that harassment occurred, of course: her account must be weighed against her alleged harasser's claim that he didn't do it or that she was not harmed. Yet importantly, the law begins with a woman's word.

The Paula Jones case made clear, however, that while the law of sexual harassment may begin by taking at face value a woman's description of her own harassment, the politics of sexual harassment begins by questioning whether a particular woman is to be believed. Conservatives' support for Paula Jones created the possibility that for once an alleged harassment target might enjoy the presumption of credibility among a wide public. But almost from the moment Paula Jones filed her lawsuit against Bill Clinton in May 1994, many of the feminists and liberals who had championed the development of sexual harassment law joined the chorus against her.

Comparing Paula Jones to Anita Hill, feminist columnist Anna Quindlen determined that Hill was more credible than Jones, in part because Hill had been "forced" to come forward while Jones did so voluntarily. [footnote omitted] Ellen Goodman, another feminist columnist, cautioned that "you don't have to check your skepticism at the door of feminism . . . [Paula Jones's] original coming out party at a conservative press conference, her earlier

attempt to trade money for silence . . . don't make for a perfect profile." [footnote omitted] Attorney Deborah Katz, who represents plaintiffs in sexual harassment cases, warned that "whenever you look at someone bringing a case you have to look at the motives that the person may have." [footnote omitted] In a similar vein, National Organization for Women President Patricia Ireland told *Time* that feminists would not "rise to the right wing's bait" and must "assess the credibility of the witness." [footnote omitted] Feminists thus sent a strong signal to Paula Jones that unless she proved herself credible politically they would doubt the legal credibility of her claim. Feminist groups such as NOW did aver that Paula Jones had a right to her day in court, and NOW loudly rebuked the president's lawyer when he threatened to scour Jones's sex life for discrediting information. [footnote omitted] Feminist groups and leaders, however, also stoked public speculation about Jones's motivations, truthfulness, and political associations, sending a discouraging message to women who need to use sexual harassment law. [footnote omitted]

If the law now will listen to a woman's experience, it does not shield her from promiscuous public scrutiny that distorts the experience she describes. It does not defend her from suspicion that her character flaws might have led to the harassment ("Just because we're making men accountable for what goes on in hotel rooms or offices doesn't mean that women should be absolved of all responsibility," wrote Susan Estrich in *USA Today*). [footnote omitted] It doesn't protect her from the charge that her harassment must be invented because her friends aren't very nice ("It's a right-wing plot," Eleanor Smeal told Larry King). [footnote omitted] And it doesn't prevent allegations that her motives are entirely mercenary ("This is about money and book contracts," Robert Bennett told *Time*). [footnote omitted]

Notwithstanding advances in the law, casuistry controls how we talk about sexual harassment when it involves real people. Our casuistry works against women who complain of harassment, dampening the effects of improved legal rules and remedies on women's lives. We spend more time wondering why a woman complains of harassment than why the harasser felt entitled to harass her. We second-guess her choices—why did she agree to meet her boss for a drink? why was she alone in his office?—rather than examining how he used his power. We measure her actions and reactions against what we imagine we would have done, rather than against what she tells us her situation permitted her to do.

Sexual harassment law has brought predatory, intimidating, and humiliating sexual conduct under the scrutiny of laws that are supposed to promote equality. Rescuing such conduct from the cover of private behavior, women plaintiffs, feminist lawyers, and courts have demonstrated how certain sexual conduct enforces women's (and sometimes men's) inequality. Expanding the concept of discrimination to encompass sexual dimensions of inequality, they have forged legal weapons for fighting sexual imposition and shame. But these weapons are costly, often requiring women to pay for redress with their reputations.

Although feminists and women have won important battles in law, we have not won them where reputations are won and lost: in politics. The political premise of feminism is that we should each take seriously what women say about their lives. We may come to disbelieve a particular woman or to consider her feelings to be misdirected, but we should start by listening to her story and we should fight for a legal process that permits her to tell it fully. Following this premise, feminists distinguished themselves in 1991 by "believing Anita Hill" and by demanding that the United States Senate

hear her out. [footnote omitted] The Hill-Thomas hearings increased public attention to sexual harassment but did not increase public support for the feminist premise. Indeed, feminists' hostility toward Paula Jones suggests that not even feminists are willing to take seriously what *all* women say about their lives or to fight for all women to receive a fair hearing.

Sexual harassment law promises remedies to complainants who can convince juries that they have been harmed. It provides assistance from the Office for Civil Rights or from the Equal Employment Opportunity Commission to complainants whose schools or employers will not help. It also rewards preventive measures by schools and employers so that girls and women will not be exposed to harm. But sexual harassment law is not self-enforcing and will not by itself end sexualized inequality in workplaces and schools. Its remedies are available only to women who successfully state a legal claim. It inspires preventive action only because employers or schools fear exposure to the law's remedies. In other words, the law gains strength from the women who use it.

If we now have laws to help us fight back against our harassers, we have to dare to use them. Few women do. [footnote omitted] Who would want to endure what Anita Hill had to, even on a microcosmic scale? Who would want to be Paula Jones? . . .

STUDY QUESTIONS

1. How did high-profile cases help bring the phenomenon of "sexual harassment" to public awareness? How did feminists respond to these high-profile plaintiffs? Politicians?
2. What role do activists play in framing and pressing the legal issues? What about politicians? Feminists? Society?

Catherine MacKinnon's book, *The Sexual Harassment of Working Women* (New Haven, Conn.: Yale University Press, 1979), helped to focus attention on legal and conceptual advances already worked out by others. In particular, she drew attention to a distinction that feminist activists had made between two types of sexual harassment. The first, quid pro quo harassment, "is defined by the more or less explicit exchange: the woman must comply [with a demand for a sexual service] or forfeit an employment benefit" (p. 32). In these situations, a supervisor makes submission to his sexual demands a prerequisite for an employment benefit, such as being hired, promoted, given a wage increase, or even simply retained. The other, most frequently called the hostile environment form of harassment, "is the situation in which sexual harassment simply makes the work environment unbearable" (p. 40). In these cases, the harasser, who may be a supervisor, a co-worker, or even a customer, engages in sexual advances or other verbal or physical conduct of a sexual nature that is so unwelcome as to create an intimidating, hostile, or offensive working environment.

As Mink indicated, the main impetus for the legal developments came as a result of litigation by sexual harassment targets in the 1970s. When the issue was first raised, the courts refused to recognize unwanted sexual attentions toward women such as ogling, patting, brushing against, propositioning, grabbing, and so forth, by supervisors, co-workers, and customers, as violations of Title VII. This resistance reflected male attitudes on the part of the courts. First, such behavior was seen as a private matter, an innocent intrusion of sexual byplay into the workplace. It was viewed as an innocuous, if unproductive, interlude. Second, even if working women sustained harm as a result of such treatment, the courts could not bring themselves to make employers liable for it. They believed this form of maltreatment almost invariably occurred without the knowledge of higher management and contrary to its policies. Finally, the courts were concerned lest they adopt a legal doctrine that would be ridiculed by their peers. In particular, they were slow to acknowledge that sexual harassment is imposed "because of sex." One common worry was that a defense of bisexuality would become available (i.e., the claim that the plaintiff would have been subject to the same treatment even if she had been a man). *See, for example, Corne v. Bausch & Lomb,* 390 F. Supp. 161 (D. Ariz. 1975).

Courts first held that the sexual harassment of employees violates Title VII in the mid-1970s. *Tomkins* was one of the first of these decisions. Over the next ten years, culminating in the Supreme Court's decision in *Vinson,* a number of the key features of Title VII law as it relates to sexual harassment were established. One is the distinction between the quid pro quo and the hostile environment types of sexual harassment. *Tomkins* illustrates the quid pro quo type of sexual harassment.

TOMKINS V. PUBLIC SERVICE ELECTRIC & GAS CO.
United States Court of Appeals,
Third Circuit, 1977.
568 F.2d 1044.

ALDISERT, Circuit Judge.

. . . Taken as true, the facts set out in appellant's complaint demonstrate that Adrienne Tomkins was hired by PSE&G in April 1971, and progressed to positions of increasing responsibility from that time until August 1973, when she began working in a secretarial position under the direction of a named supervisor. On October 30, 1973, the supervisor told Tomkins that she should have lunch with him in a nearby restaurant, in order to discuss his upcoming evaluation of her work, as well as a possible job promotion. At lunch, he made advances toward her, indicating his desire to have sexual relations with her and stating that this would be necessary if they were to have a satisfactory working relationship. When Tomkins attempted to leave the restaurant, the supervisor responded first by threats of recrimination against Tomkins in her employment, then by threats of physical force, and ultimately by physically restraining Tomkins. During the incident, he told her that no one at PSE&G would help her should she lodge a complaint against him. . . .

Tomkins's complaint alleges that PSE&G and certain of its agents knew or should have known that such incidents would occur, and that they nevertheless "placed [Tomkins] in a position where she would be subjected to the aforesaid conduct of [the supervisor] and failed to take adequate supervisory measures to prevent such incidents from occurring." It further alleged that on the day following the lunch, Tomkins expressed her intention to leave PSE&G as a result of the incident. She agreed to continue work only after being promised a transfer to a comparable position elsewhere in the company. A comparable position did not become available, however, and Tomkins was instead placed in an inferior position in another department. There, she was subjected to false and adverse employment evaluations, disciplinary lay-offs, and threats of demotion by various PSE&G employees. Tomkins maintains that as a result of the supervisor's conduct and the continued pattern of harassment by PSE&G personnel, she suffered physical and emotional distress, resulting in absenteeism and loss of income.

In January 1975, PSE&G fired Tomkins. Following her dismissal, she filed an employment discrimination complaint with the Equal Employment Opportunity Commission, which ultimately issued a Notice of Right to Sue. After Tomkins filed suit in

district court, PSE&G moved to dismiss the complaint. . . . [T]he company's motion to dismiss Tomkins's claim against PSE&G for his actions was granted for failure to state a claim. The latter judgment was determined final by the district court . . . and this appeal followed. . . .

Tomkins claims that the sexual demands of her supervisor imposed a sex-based "term or condition" on her employment. She alleges that her promotion and favorable job evaluation were made conditional upon her granting sexual favors, and that she suffered adverse job consequences as a result of this incident. In granting appellees' motion to dismiss, however, the district court characterized the supervisor's acts as "abuse of authority . . . for personal purposes." The court thus overlooked the major thrust of Tomkins's complaint, i.e., that her employer, either knowingly or constructively, made acquiescence in her supervisor's sexual demands a necessary prerequisite to the continuation of or advancement in, her job.

The facts as alleged by appellant clearly demonstrate an incident with employment ramifications, one within the intended coverage of Title VII. The context within which the sexual advances occurred is itself strong evidence of a job-related condition: Tomkins was asked to lunch by her supervisor for the express purpose of discussing his upcoming evaluation of her work and possible recommendation of her for a promotion. But one need not infer the added condition from the setting alone. It is expressly alleged that the supervisor stated to Tomkins that her continued success and advancement at PSE&G were dependent upon her agreeing to his sexual demands. The demand thus amounted to a condition of employment, an additional duty or burden Tomkins was required by her supervisor to meet as a prerequisite to her continued employment. . . .

. . . The courts have distinguished between complaints alleging sexual advances of an individual or personal nature and those alleging direct employment consequences flowing from the advances, finding Title VII violations in the latter category.

This distinction recognizes two elements necessary to find a violation of Title VII: first, that a term or condition of employment has been imposed and second, that it has been imposed by the employer, either directly or vicariously, in a sexually discriminatory fashion. Applying these requirements to the present complaint, we conclude that Title VII is violated when a supervisor, with the actual or constructive knowledge of the employer, makes sexual advances or demands toward a subordinate employee and conditions that employee's job status—evaluation, continued employment, promotion, or other aspects of career development—on a favorable response to those advances or demands, and the employer does not take prompt and appropriate remedial action after acquiring such knowledge. . . .

We do not agree with the district court that finding a Title VII violation on these facts will result in an unmanageable number of suits and a difficulty in differentiating between spurious and meritorious claims. The congressional mandate that the federal courts provide relief is strong; it must not be thwarted by concern for judicial economy. More significant, however, this decision in no way relieves the plaintiff of the burden of proving the facts alleged to establish the required elements of a Title VII violation.

Although any theory of liability may be used in vexatious or bad faith suits, we are confident that traditional judicial mechanisms will separate the valid from the invalid complaints.

The judgment of the district court will be reversed and the cause remanded for further proceedings.

STUDY QUESTIONS

1. In what sense were the advances Tomkins allegedly endured a "condition of employment"? Would they have been a condition of employment if no job-related consequences were threatened?
2. What standard did the court use for establishing employer liability? If Tomkins's supervisor had not threatened reprisal if she refused, would she have prevailed in this court? If the person who took her to lunch on the fateful day had not been Tomkins's supervisor but rather a co-worker, would she have prevailed?
3. Answer the critic who proclaims that: "This has gone too far! After all, no one was hurt. There's no harm in asking, right? Only a prude would advocate the removal of all sexual give and take from the workplace. Hey, loosen up."

When first confronted with complaints alleging that sexual harassment violates Title VII, the courts did not treat them seriously. They continued to perceive such situations as innocuous until the plight of the victims was made abundantly clear. They then recognized that sexual harassment in an employment setting is very harmful to its victims. The early cases, such as *Tomkins*, focused primarily upon the harm suffered in terms of income, job security, and career advancement. These are substantial harms, but they are not the entire story.

Stress is another direct consequence of sexual harassment. The Working Women's Institute analyzed letters from victims of sexual harassment on the job and found that the resulting stress affected the work performance, the psychological well-being, and the physical health of the victims.

> Even though women express pride at being able to do their jobs despite harassment, 46 percent of the 518 cases said it interfered with their work performance. The two most common effects on work performance were that the women were distracted from their tasks and dreaded coming to work. . . .

The negative effects of sexual harassment are not limited to the work setting. They invade every aspect of the woman's life and often are manifested as general psychological stress symptoms. At least one negative effect was reported by over 94 percent of the women in our sample. The reaction most often mentioned was excessive tension. . . .

About 36 percent of the women involved in our study pointed out physical ailments they thought had been brought about by sexual harassment. The most prevalent ones were nausea, tiredness (a frequent sign of depression), and headaches. . . .

Peggy Crull. "Sexual Harassment and Women's Health." In Double Exposure: Women's Health Hazards on the Job and in the Home, edited by W. Chavkin. New York: Monthly Review Press, 1983, pp. 107–109.

Beyond the financial, career, and stress effects of sexual harassment in the workplace, there is the perhaps even more crushing emotional harm occasioned by the message such treatment inevitably conveys in our culture. The attorney who argued Tomkins's case described that harm as follows:

Sexual references, as well as explicit demands for sexual cooperation, convey the message that a woman is a sexual object before she is a contributing worker, and whether it is consciously undertaken or not, such behavior serves to reinforce woman's sexual role. Indeed, such behavior is probably the quintessential expression of stereotypic role expectations. Like other expressions of stereotypic expectations occurring at the work place, it is dysfunctional in two respects. Whether or not perceived as flattering by women, sexual advances remind women of a societally-imposed incongruity between their role as worker and as woman. By thus arousing role conflict in women, advances interfere with their performance. By underscoring their sexual identity in the eyes of male supervisors, sexual advances make it less likely that women will be viewed as persons capable of performing a demanding task, and consequently, less likely that they will have the opportunity to try to do so. . . .

The situation in which a person is asked to exchange sexual services for continued employment is uniquely disturbing to women. It is a reminder, a badge or incident of a servile status, which women are striving to leave behind.

Nadine Taub. "Keeping Women in Their Place: Stereotyping Per Se as a Form of Employment Discrimination." 21 Boston College Law Review 345, 361, 368 (1980).

In order to prevail under Title VII, a plaintiff who alleges sexual harassment on the job must show that the employer is responsible for the imposition of a special condition of employment upon the plaintiff because of her sex. *Tomkins* and similar decisions during the late 1970s laid the foundations for later refinements by the EEOC and the federal courts.

The court in *Tomkins* took the view that sexual harassment on the job is "a condition of employment" in the sense of a "prerequisite" for some employment benefit. This no doubt resulted from the fact that Tomkins's harassment was of that nature. Still, until that conception of "condition of employment" was expanded, harassment by co-workers and other dimensions of this problem were beyond the reach of Title VII.

Tomkins also addressed the issue of employer liability. There, the court held the employer responsible for the sexual harassment of female employees by their male supervisors on the basis of something like a *negligence standard* (the employer knew or should have known of the conduct and taken immediate and appropriate corrective action). Other courts facing quid pro quo situations at about the same time used a stricter standard of employer liability. In *Miller v. Bank of America*, 600 F.2d 211 (9th Cir. 1979), the court used what appears to be a *strict liability standard* (the employer is unconditionally responsible for the torts that employees commit in the course of their employment). After these decisions, the courts were faced with the question of which standard of responsibility applies to employers in Title VII actions alleging sexual harassment. The next major step came in November 1980, when the EEOC, then under the leadership of Eleanor Holmes Norton, published its Guidelines on Sexual Harassment.

29 C.F.R. § 1604.11 SEXUAL HARASSMENT

(a) Harassment on the basis of sex is a violation of Sec. 703 of Title VII. Unwelcome sexual advances, requests for sexual favors, and other verbal or physical conduct of a sexual nature constitute sexual harassment when (1) submission to such conduct is made either explicitly or implicitly a term or condition of an individual's employment, (2) submission to or rejection of such conduct by an individual is used as the basis for employment decisions affecting such individual, or (3) such conduct has the purpose or effect of unreasonably interfering with an individual's work performance or creating an intimidating, hostile, or offensive working environment.

(b) In determining whether alleged conduct constitutes sexual harassment, the Commission will look at the record as a whole and at the totality of the circumstances such as the nature of the sexual advances and the context in which the alleged incidents occurred. The determination of the legality of a particular action will be made from the facts, on a case by case basis.

(c) Applying general Title VII principles, an employer, employment agency, joint apprenticeship committee or labor organization (hereinafter collectively referred to as "employer") is responsible for its acts and those of its agents and supervisory employees with respect to sexual harassment regardless of whether the specific acts complained of were authorized or even forbidden by the employer and regardless of whether the employer knew or should have known of their occurrence. The Commission will examine the circumstances of the particular employment relationship and the job functions performed by the individual in determining whether an individual acts in either a supervisory or agency capacity.

(d) With respect to conduct between fellow employees, an employer is responsible for acts of sexual harassment in the workplace where the employer (or its agents or supervisory employees) knows or should have known of the conduct, unless it can show that it took immediate and appropriate corrective action.

(e) An employer may also be responsible for the acts of non-employees, with respect to sexual harassment of employees in the workplace, where the employer (or its agents or supervisory employees) knows or should have known of the conduct and fails to take immediate and appropriate corrective action. In reviewing these cases the Commission will consider the extent of the employer's control and any other legal responsibility which the employer may have with respect to the conduct of such non-employees.

(f) Prevention is the best tool for the elimination of sexual harassment. An employer should take all steps necessary to prevent sexual harassment from occurring, such as affirmatively raising the subject, expressing strong disapproval, developing appropriate sanctions, informing employees of their right to raise and how to raise the issue of harassment under Title VII, and developing methods to sensitize all concerned.

(g) Other related practices. Where employment opportunities or benefits are granted because of an individual's submission to the employer's sexual advances or requests for sexual favors, the employer may be held liable for unlawful sex discrimination against other persons who were qualified for but denied that employment opportunity or benefit.

The EEOC guidelines provided bold leadership in formulating the main elements of Title VII law as it relates to sexual harassment. They are regularly cited with approval by the courts and relied upon by employers. The definition set out in section (a) is widely used in both the public and the private sectors. It incorporates both the quid pro quo and the hostile environment forms of harassment. In section (d) the EEOC endorsed the negligence standard for hostile environment situations. Section (c), the standard of employer liability for harassment by supervisors, was rescinded by the EEOC as no longer valid after the U.S. Supreme Court issued its decisions in *Burlington Industries, Inc. v. Ellerth* and *Faragher v. City of Boca Raton* (discussed later in this chapter). Instead, the EEOC issued a policy document that examined those decisions and provided guidance on the issue of vicarious liability for harassment by supervisors: *EEOC Enforcement Guidance: Vicarious Employer Liability for Unlawful Harassment by Supervisors (6/18/99)* (available on the EEOC Web site).

The guidelines also broke new ground in sections (e) and (g). In the former, the EEOC recommended treating the sexual harassment of employees by customers and clients as a form of hostile environment and therefore subject to the negligence standard. The advance in section (g) was even more subtle. Sometimes people who resist sexual advances in an employment setting fear that they will lose advancement opportunities to others who are less qualified but more sexually accommodating. Although the number of people who "get ahead on their backs" and the advancement achieved in that way is greatly exaggerated by office mythology, the fear of that type of competition is real and extensive. The guidelines made provision for allaying those fears by making the employer liable for granting employment benefits in those situations.

Shortly after the EEOC guidelines were issued, the Circuit Court of Appeals for the District of Columbia handed down a decision that gave effect to the approach to the hostile environment type of sexual harassment endorsed by these guidelines.

BUNDY V. JACKSON
United States Court of Appeals for the District of Columbia, 1981.
641 F.2d 934.

J. SKELLY WRIGHT, Chief Judge.

In *Barnes v. Costle,* we held that an employer who abolished a female employee's job to retaliate against the employee's resistance of his sexual advances violated Title VII of the Civil Rights Act of 1964. . . . [A]ppellant asks us to extend *Barnes* by holding that an employer violates Title VII merely by subjecting female employees to sexual harassment, even if the employee's resistance to that harassment does not cause the employer to deprive her of any tangible job benefits.

The District Court in this case made an express finding of fact that in appellant's agency "the making of improper sexual advances to female employees [was] standard operating procedure, a fact of life, a normal condition of employment," and that the director of the agency, to whom

she complained of the harassment, failed to investigate her complaints or take them seriously. Nevertheless, the District Court refused to grant appellant any declaratory or injunctive relief, concluding that sexual harassment does not in itself represent discrimination "with respect to. . . terms, conditions, or privileges of employment" within the meaning of Title VII. . . .

Appellant Sandra Bundy is now, and was at the time she filed her lawsuit, a Vocational Rehabilitation Specialist, level GS–9, with the District of Columbia Department of Corrections (the agency). . . . In recent years Bundy's chief task has been to find jobs for former criminal offenders.

The District Court's finding that sexual intimidation was a "normal condition of employment" in Bundy's agency finds ample support in the District Court's own chronology of Bundy's experiences there. Those experiences began in 1972 when Bundy, still a GS–5, received and rejected sexual propositions from Delbert Jackson, then a fellow employee at the agency but now its Director and the named defendant in this lawsuit in his official capacity. It was two years later, however, that the sexual intimidation Bundy suffered began to intertwine directly with her employment when she received propositions from two of her supervisors, Arthur Burton and James Gainey.

Burton became Bundy's supervisor when Bundy became an Employment Development Specialist in 1974. Shortly thereafter Gainey became her first-line supervisor and Burton her second-line supervisor, although Burton retained control of Bundy's employment status. Burton began sexually harassing Bundy in June 1974, continually calling her into his office to request that she spend the workday afternoon with him at his apartment and to question her about her sexual proclivities. Shortly after becoming her first-line supervisor Gainey also began making sexual advances to Bundy, asking her to join him at a motel and on a trip to the Bahamas. Bundy complained about these advances to Lawrence Swain, who supervised both Burton and Gainey. Swain casually dismissed Bundy's complaints, telling her that "any man in his right mind would want to rape you," and then proceeding himself to request that she begin a sexual relationship with him in his apartment. Bundy rejected his request.

We add that, although the District Court made no explicit findings as to harassment of other female employees, its finding that harassment was "standard operating procedure" finds ample support in record evidence that Bundy was not the only woman subjected to sexual intimidation by male supervisors.

In denying Bundy any relief, the District Court found that Bundy's supervisors did not take the "game" of sexually propositioning female employees "seriously," and that Bundy's rejection of their advances did not evoke in them any motive to take any action against her. The record, however, contains nothing to support this view, and indeed some evidence directly belies it. . . .

We thus readily conclude that Bundy's employer discriminated against her on the basis of sex. What remains is the novel question whether the sexual harassment of the sort Bundy suffered amounted by itself to sex discrimination with respect to the "*terms, conditions, or privileges of employment.*" Though no court has as yet so held, we believe that an affirmative answer follows ineluctably from numerous cases finding Title VII violations where an employer created or condoned a substantially discriminatory work *environment*, regardless of whether the complaining employees lost any tangible job benefits as a result of the discrimination.

Bundy's claim on this score is essentially that "conditions of employment" include the psychological and emotional work environment—that the sexually stereotyped insults and demeaning propositions to which she was indisputably subjected and which caused her anxiety and debilitation, illegally poisoned that environment. . . .

The employer can thus implicitly and effectively make the employee's endurance of sexual intimidation a "condition" of her employment. The woman then faces a "cruel trilemma." She can endure the harassment. She can attempt to oppose it, with little hope of success, either legal or practical, but with every prospect of making the job even less tolerable for her. Or she can leave her job, with little hope of legal relief and the likely prospect of another job where she will face harassment anew.

Bundy proved that she was the victim of a practice of sexual harassment and a discriminatory work environment permitted by her employer. Her rights under Title VII were therefore violated. We thus reverse the District Court's holding on this issue and remand it to that court so it can fashion appropriate injunctive relief.

STUDY QUESTIONS

1. What did the district court mean when it said that the supervisors did not take the "game" of sexually propositioning female employees seriously? If they didn't take it seriously, why did Bundy?
2. Was Judge Wright correct in describing this behavior as "sexual intimidation"? Is being subjected to such treatment likely to affect one's job performance? Is that apt to affect one's success in a career? Is it likely to affect the employer's productivity?
3. What was the "cruel trilemma" that faced Bundy? What enabled the others to place her in that position? Who was best situated to prevent such manipulation from occurring?

The standards applying Title VII to allegations of sexual harassment in the workplace were developed over the course of a decade by the federal circuit courts and the EEOC. In its first decision on a sexual harassment case under Title VII, the Supreme Court unanimously signaled general approval of these standards. Of particular interest was its approval of the "hostile environment" theory of liability and the centrality of "unwanted" in the definition of sexual harassment. The decision in *Vinson*, however, reserved judgment on the standards of employer liability developed by the EEOC and the lower courts.

MERITOR SAVINGS BANK V. VINSON
Supreme Court of the United States, 1986.
477 U.S. 57, 106 S. Ct. 2399, 91 L.Ed.2d 49.

Justice REHNQUIST delivered the opinion of the Court. . . .

In 1974, respondent Mechelle Vinson met Sidney Taylor, a vice president of what is now petitioner Meritor Savings Bank (the bank) and manager of one of its branch offices. When respondent asked whether she might obtain employment at the bank, Taylor gave her an application, which she completed and returned the next day; later that same day Taylor called her to say that she had been hired. With Taylor as her supervisor, respondent started as a teller-trainee, and thereafter was promoted to teller, head teller, and assistant branch manager. She worked at the same branch for four years, and it is undisputed that her advancement there was based on merit alone. In September 1978, respondent notified Taylor that she was taking sick leave for an indefinite period. On November 1, 1978, the bank discharged her for excessive use of that leave.

Respondent brought this action against Taylor and the bank, claiming that during her four years at the bank she had "constantly been subjected to sexual harassment" by Taylor in violation of Title VII. She sought injunctive relief, compensatory and punitive damages against Taylor and the bank, and attorney's fees.

At the 11-day bench trial, the parties presented conflicting testimony about Taylor's behavior during respondent's employment. Respondent testified that during her probationary period as a teller-trainee, Taylor treated her in a fatherly way and made no sexual advances. Shortly thereafter, however, he invited her out to dinner and, during the course of the meal, suggested that they go to a motel to have sexual relations. At first she refused, but out of what she described as fear of losing her job she eventually agreed. According to respondent, Taylor thereafter made repeated demands upon her for sexual favors, usually at the branch, both during and after business hours; she estimated that over the next several years she had intercourse with him some 40 or 50 times. In addition, respondent testified that Taylor fondled her in front of other employees, followed her into the women's restroom when she went there alone, exposed himself to her, and even forcibly raped her on several occasions. These activities ceased after 1977, respondent stated, when she started going with a steady boyfriend. . . .

Taylor denied respondent's allegations of sexual activity, testifying that he never fondled her, never made suggestive remarks to her, never engaged in sexual intercourse with her and never asked her to do so. He contended instead that respondent made her accusations in response to a business-related dispute. The bank also denied respondent's allegations and asserted that any sexual harassment by Taylor was unknown to the bank and engaged in without its consent or approval.

The District Court denied relief, but did not resolve the conflicting testimony about the existence of a sexual relationship between respondent and Taylor. It found instead that

> "If [respondent] and Taylor did engage in an intimate or sexual relationship during the time of [respondent's] employment with [the bank], that relationship was a voluntary one having nothing to do with her continued employment at [the bank] or her advancement or promotions at that institution."

The court ultimately found that respondent "was not the victim of sexual harassment and was not the victim of sexual discrimination" while employed at the bank.

Although it concluded that respondent had not proved a violation of Title VII, the District Court nevertheless went on to address the bank's liability. After noting the bank's express policy against discrimination, and finding that neither respondent nor any other employee had ever lodged a complaint about sexual harassment by Taylor, the court

ultimately concluded that "the bank was without notice and cannot be held liable for the alleged actions of Taylor."

The Court of Appeals for the District of Columbia Circuit reversed.

Respondent argues, and the Court of Appeals held, that unwelcome sexual advances that create an offensive or hostile working environment violate Title VII. Without question, when a supervisor sexually harasses a subordinate because of the subordinate's sex, that supervisor "discriminate[s]" on the basis of sex. Petitioner apparently does not challenge this proposition. It contends instead that in prohibiting discrimination with respect to "compensation, terms, conditions, or privileges" of employment, Congress was concerned with what petitioner describes as "tangible loss" of "an economic character," not "purely psychological aspects of the workplace environment."

We reject petitioner's view. First, . . . [p]etitioner has pointed to nothing in the Act to suggest that Congress contemplated the limitation urged here.

Second, in 1980 the EEOC issued guidelines specifying that "sexual harassment," as there defined, is a form of sex discrimination prohibited by Title VII. The EEOC guidelines fully support the view that harassment leading to noneconomic injury can violate Title VII. . . .

Since the guidelines were issued, courts have uniformly held, and we agree, that a plaintiff may establish a violation of Title VII by proving that discrimination based on sex has created a hostile or abusive work environment. As the Court of Appeals for the Eleventh Circuit wrote in *Henson v. Dundee:*

> "Sexual harassment which creates a hostile or offensive environment for members of one sex is every bit the arbitrary barrier to sexual equality at the workplace that racial harassment is to racial equality. Surely, a requirement that a man or woman run a gauntlet of sexual abuse in return for the privilege of being allowed to work and make a living can be as demeaning and disconcerting as the harshest of racial epithets." . . .

The question remains, however, whether the District Court's ultimate finding that respondent "was not the victim of sexual harassment," effectively disposed of respondent's claim. The Court of Appeals recognized, we think correctly, that this ultimate finding was likely based on one or both of two erroneous views of the law. First, the District Court apparently believed that a claim for sexual harassment will not lie absent an *economic* effect on the complainant's employment. . . . Since it appears that the District Court made its findings without ever considering the "hostile environment" theory of sexual harassment, the Court of Appeals' decision to remand was correct.

Second, the District Court's conclusion that no actionable harassment occurred might have rested on its earlier "finding" that "[i]f [respondent] and Taylor did engage in an intimate or sexual relationship . . ., that relationship was a voluntary one." But the fact that sex-related conduct was "voluntary," in the sense that the complainant was not forced to participate against her will, is not a defense to a sexual harassment suit brought under Title VII. The gravamen of any sexual harassment claim is that the alleged sexual advances were "unwelcome." 29 CFR § 1604.11(a) (1985). While the question whether particular conduct was indeed unwelcome presents difficult problems of proof and turns largely on credibility determinations committed to the trier of fact, the District Court in this case erroneously focused on the "voluntariness" of respondent's participation in the claimed sexual episodes. The correct inquiry is whether respondent by her conduct indicated that the alleged sexual advances were unwelcome, not whether her actual participation in sexual intercourse was voluntary. . . .

Although the District Court concluded that respondent had not proved a violation of Title VII, it nevertheless went on to consider the question of the bank's liability. Finding that "the bank was without notice" of Taylor's alleged conduct, and that notice to Taylor was not the equivalent of notice to the bank, the court

concluded that the bank therefore could not be held liable for Taylor's alleged actions. The Court of Appeals took the opposite view, holding that an employer is strictly liable for a hostile environment created by a supervisor's sexual advances, even though the employer neither knew nor reasonably could have known of the alleged misconduct: . . .

[The] debate over the appropriate standard for employer liability has a rather abstract quality about it given the state of the record in this case. We do not know at this stage whether Taylor made any sexual advances toward respondent at all, let alone whether those advances were unwelcome. . . .

We therefore decline the parties' invitation to issue a definitive rule on employer liability, but we do agree with the EEOC that Congress wanted courts to look to agency principles for guidance in this area. While such common-law principles may not be transferable in all their particulars to Title VII, Congress' decision to define "employer" to include any "agent" of an employer, surely evinces an intent to place some limits on the acts of employees for which employers under Title VII are to be held responsible. For this reason, we hold that the Court of Appeals erred in concluding that employers are always automatically liable for sexual harassment by their supervisors. For the same reason, absence of notice to an employer does not necessarily insulate that employer from liability. . . .

Accordingly, the judgment of the Court of Appeals reversing the judgment of the District Court is affirmed, and the case is remanded for further proceedings consistent with this opinion.

STUDY QUESTIONS

1. What reason did the Court give for rejecting voluntariness as a defense in sexual harassment suits brought under Title VII? How would the Court have strengthened the position of would-be harassers had it allowed this defense?

Think about the cruel trilemmas faced by the plaintiffs in the foregoing cases.

2. The District Court held that employer liability is limited to situations of which it has actual notice. What standard of employer liability was adopted by the Court of Appeals for the type of situation described in Vinson's testimony? By the Supreme Court? Which do you favor?

After *Vinson*, a key issue that remained to be worked out was the standard of employer liability in cases alleging quid pro quo or hostile environment harassment.

One of the major achievements of the Supreme Court's 1997–98 term was to introduce order into the standards by which courts decide whether employers are liable under Title VII for sexual harassment by their supervisory employees. In addition, the Court ruled on the standard applicable to the liability of school districts under Title IX for sexual harassment of students by teachers. The latter is a less demanding standard and will be discussed in Chapter 5. The Title VII standard endorsed by the Court was developed and stated in two cases. The statement of the standard in the cases is identical. In *Burlington Industries, Inc. v. Ellerth*, 524 U.S. 742 (1998), Justice Kennedy, writing for a seven-justice majority, discouraged courts from seeing the employer liability issue as turning on the distinction between quid pro quo and hostile environment harassment. "The terms quid pro quo and hostile work environment are helpful, perhaps, in making a rough demarcation between cases in which threats are carried out and those where they are not or are absent altogether, but beyond this are of limited utility." Instead, both *Ellerth* and the case that follows develop the standard for employer liability in such cases based on detailed examination of the interests affected and the traditional standards for awards of damages. The following focuses on the standard itself.

FARAGHER V. CITY OF BOCA RATON
Supreme Court of the United States, 1998.
524 U.S. 775

Justice SOUTER delivered the opinion of the Court.

. . . Between 1985 and 1990, while attending college, petitioner Beth Ann Faragher worked part time and during the summers as an ocean lifeguard for the Marine Safety Section of the Parks and Recreation Department of respondent, the City of Boca Raton, Florida (City). During this period, Faragher's immediate supervisors were Bill Terry, David Silverman, and Robert Gordon. In June 1990, Faragher resigned.

In 1992, Faragher brought an action against Terry, Silverman, and the City, asserting claims under Title VII, and Florida law. So far as it concerns the Title VII claim, the complaint alleged that Terry and Silverman created a "sexually hostile atmosphere" at the beach by repeatedly subjecting Faragher and other female lifeguards to "uninvited and offensive touching," by making lewd remarks, and by speaking of women in offensive terms. . . .

In February 1986, the City adopted a sexual harassment policy, which it stated in a memorandum from the City Manager addressed to all employees. In May, the City revised the policy and reissued a statement of it. Although the City may actually have circulated the memos and statements to some employees, it completely failed to disseminate its policy among employees of the Marine Safety Section, with the result that Terry, Silverman, Gordon, and many lifeguards were unaware of it. . . .

Faragher did not complain to higher management about Terry or Silverman. Although she spoke of their behavior to Gordon, she did not regard these discussions as formal complaints to a supervisor but as conversations with a person she held in high esteem. Other female lifeguards had similarly informal talks with Gordon, but because Gordon did not feel that it was his place to do so, he did not report these complaints to Terry, his own supervisor, or to any other city official. Gordon responded to the complaints of one lifeguard by saying that "the City just [doesn't] care."

In April 1990, however, two months before Faragher's resignation, Nancy Ewanchew, a former lifeguard, wrote to Richard Bender, the City's Personnel Director, complaining that Terry and Silverman had harassed her and other female lifeguards. Following investigation of this complaint, the City found that Terry and Silverman had behaved improperly, reprimanded them, and required them to choose between a suspension without pay or the forfeiture of annual leave.

. . . [T]he District Court concluded that the conduct of Terry and Silverman was discriminatory harassment sufficiently serious to alter the conditions of Faragher's employment and constitute an abusive working environment. The District Court then ruled . . . the City liable for the harassment of its supervisory employees. . . .

A panel of the Court of Appeals for the Eleventh Circuit reversed the judgment against the City. Although the panel had "no trouble concluding that Terry's and Silverman's conduct . . . was severe and pervasive enough to create an objectively abusive work environment," it overturned the District Court's conclusion that the City was liable. The panel ruled that Terry and Silverman

were not acting within the scope of their employment when they engaged in the harassment, that they were not aided in their actions by the agency relationship, and that the City had no constructive knowledge of the harassment by virtue of its pervasiveness or Gordon's actual knowledge.

In a 7-to-5 decision, the full Court of Appeals, sitting en banc, adopted the panel's conclusion. . . .

II

A

. . . While indicating the substantive contours of the hostile environments forbidden by Title VII, our cases have established few definite rules for determining when an employer will be liable for a discriminatory environment that is otherwise actionably abusive. . . .

. . . [T]his Court's only discussion to date of standards of employer liability, in *Meritor*, which involved a claim of discrimination by a supervisor's sexual harassment of a subordinate over an extended period. In affirming the Court of Appeals' holding that a hostile atmosphere resulting from sex discrimination is actionable under Title VII, we also anticipated proceedings on remand by holding agency principles relevant in assigning employer liability and by rejecting three per se rules of liability or immunity. We observed that the very definition of employer in Title VII, as including an "agent," expressed Congress's intent that courts look to traditional principles of the law of agency in devising standards of employer liability in those instances where liability for the actions of a supervisory employee was not otherwise obvious, and although we cautioned that "common-law principles may not be transferable in all their particulars to Title VII," . . . with general approval.

We then proceeded to reject two limitations on employer liability, while establishing the rule that some limitation was intended. We held that neither the existence of a company grievance procedure nor the absence of actual notice of the harassment on the part of upper management would be dispositive of such a claim; while either might be relevant to the liability, neither would result automatically in employer immunity. Conversely, we held that Title VII placed some limit on employer responsibility for the creation of a discriminatory environment by a supervisor, and we held that Title VII does not make employers "always automatically liable for sexual harassment by their supervisors." . . .

Meritor's statement of the law is the foundation on which we build today. . . .

II

B

. . . The proper analysis here, then, calls not for a mechanical application of indefinite and malleable factors . . ., but rather an enquiry into the reasons that would support a conclusion that harassing behavior ought to be held within the scope of a supervisor's employment, and the reasons for the opposite view. . . .

[After a lengthy discussion of factors, both pro and con, Justice Souter concluded that i]n sum, there are good reasons for vicarious liability for misuse of supervisory authority. That rationale must, however, satisfy one more condition. We are not entitled to recognize this theory under Title VII unless we can square it with *Meritor*'s holding that an employer is not "automatically" liable for harassment by a supervisor who creates the requisite degree of discrimination. . . .

Although Title VII seeks "to make persons whole for injuries suffered on account of unlawful employment discrimination," its "primary objective," like that of any statute meant to influence primary conduct, is not to provide redress but to avoid harm. . . . It would therefore implement clear statutory policy and complement the Government's Title VII enforcement efforts to recognize the employer's affirmative obligation to prevent violations and give credit here to employers who make reasonable efforts to discharge their duty. Indeed, a theory of vicarious liability for misuse of supervisory power would

be at odds with the statutory policy if it failed to provide employers with some such incentive.

The requirement to show that the employee has failed in a coordinate duty to avoid or mitigate harm reflects an equally obvious policy imported from the general theory of damages, that a victim has a duty "to use such means as are reasonable under the circumstances to avoid or minimize the damages" that result from violations of the statute. An employer may, for example, have provided a proven, effective mechanism for reporting and resolving complaints of sexual harassment, available to the employee without undue risk or expense. If the plaintiff unreasonably failed to avail herself of the employer's preventive or remedial apparatus, she should not recover damages that could have been avoided if she had done so. If the victim could have avoided harm, no liability should be found against the employer who had taken reasonable care, and if damages could reasonably have been mitigated no award against a liable employer should reward a plaintiff for what her own efforts could have avoided.

In order to accommodate the principle of vicarious liability for harm caused by misuse of supervisory authority, as well as Title VII's equally basic policies of encouraging forethought by employers and saving action by objecting employees, we adopt the following holding in this case and in *Burlington Industries, Inc. v. Ellerth*, also decided today. An employer is subject to vicarious liability to a victimized employee for an actionable hostile environment created by a supervisor with immediate (or successively higher) authority over the employee. When no tangible employment action is taken, a defending employer may raise an affirmative defense to liability or damages, subject to proof by a preponderance of the evidence. The defense comprises two necessary elements: (a) that the employer exercised reasonable care to prevent and correct promptly any sexually harassing behavior, and (b) that the plaintiff employee unreasonably failed to take advantage of any preventive or corrective opportunities provided by the employer or to avoid harm otherwise. While proof that an employer had promulgated an anti-harassment policy with complaint procedure is not necessary in every instance as a matter of law, the need for a stated policy suitable to the employment circumstances may appropriately be addressed in any case when litigating the first element of the defense. And while proof that an employee failed to fulfill the corresponding obligation of reasonable care to avoid harm is not limited to showing an unreasonable failure to use any complaint procedure provided by the employer, a demonstration of such failure will normally suffice to satisfy the employer's burden under the second element of the defense. No affirmative defense is available, however, when the supervisor's harassment culminates in a tangible employment action, such as discharge, demotion, or undesirable reassignment.

Applying these rules here, we believe that the judgment of the Court of Appeals must be reversed. The District Court found that the degree of hostility in the work environment rose to the actionable level and was attributable to Silverman and Terry. It is undisputed that these supervisors "were granted virtually unchecked authority" over their subordinates, "directly controll[ing] and supervis[ing] all aspects of [Faragher's]

day-to-day activities." It is also clear that Faragher and her colleagues were "completely isolated from the City's higher management." The City did not seek review of these findings. . . .

III

The judgment of the Court of Appeals for the Eleventh Circuit is reversed, and the case is remanded for reinstatement of the judgment of the District Court.

STUDY QUESTIONS

1. The District Court held that the City was liable for the harassment of its supervisory employees. Did the Court of Appeals agree or disagree with that holding? Explain.
2. Upon what case's prior statement of law did the Supreme Court build on in this case to create the standard for assessing employer liability? What was the Court's holding with respect to employer liability in that prior case?
3. What was the Court's holding, in both *Burlington Industries, Inc. v. Ellerth* and this case, with respect to the standard for employer liability? Can the employer assert any affirmative defense and, if so, what must the employer show to prevail?

The Court's decisions in *Faragher* and *Ellerth* were immediately hailed by both the corporate and feminist communities as fair and effective. Most encouraging, lawyers who advised the country's major corporations were recommending that their clients take steps to adopt, promulgate, and enforce the very types of sexual harassment guidelines and grievance procedures that the EEOC had been recommending for decades. If employers wanted to minimize their liability, they needed to establish clear sexual harassment policies; distribute them to their workforce; and make sure their employees received those policies, understood the compliance procedures, and knew precisely to whom they should make their complaints. In light of this ruling, it also behooved feminist litigators to advise their clients to use their employer's grievance procedure, provided it was available to the employee without undue risk or expense and contained an effective mechanism to report, investigate, and attempt to resolve sexual harassment complaints.

The Supreme Court, in its *Faragher* and *Ellerth* decisions, enunciated two categories of sexual harassment claims: those alleging a "tangible employment action" for which an employer could be held strictly liable; and those that did not allege a tangible employment action, where an employer could assert an affirmative defense. In *Pennsylvania State Police v. Suders*, 542 U.S. 129 (2004), the Court considered the application of the *Ellerth/Faragher* affirmative defense in the context of a constructive discharge claim. In that case, Suders, a female police communications operator for a Pennsylvania State Police (PSP) barracks, complained that her male supervisors subjected her to a continuous barrage of sexual harassment. She contacted the PSP EEO Officer on two occasions: once to say she might need help (neither she nor the EEO Officer followed up on the call); and two months later to report she was being harassed and was afraid, at which time she was told to file a complaint but was not told how to get the necessary form. Two days after the second call Suders' supervisors arrested her for the theft of her own computer-skills exam papers. Suders took them because she believed her supervisors had falsely reported that she had failed repeatedly, but her exams had never been sent for grading. Suders resigned from the force and sued the PSP, alleging that she had been subjected to sexual harassment and constructively discharged in violation of Title VII of the Civil Rights Act of 1964. The federal district court granted the PSP's motion for summary judgment; although Suders' testimony would permit a trier of fact to conclude her supervisors had created a hostile work environment, the PSP was not vicariously liable for the supervisors' conduct because Suders had unreasonably failed to avail herself of its internal harassment resolution procedures. The District Court did not address the constructive discharge claim. On appeal, the Court of Appeals for the Third Circuit reversed and remanded for trial. The Third Circuit found that even if the PSP could assert the *Ellerth/Faragher* affirmative defense, there existed genuine issues of material fact (the standard used to defeat a summary judgment motion) about the effectiveness of the PSP's program to address sexual harassment claims. In addition, the Third Circuit held that the District Court erred in failing to recognize that Suders had stated a claim of constructive discharge due to hostile work environment. The Third Circuit also determined that a constructive discharge, if proven, constitutes a "tangible employment action" that renders an employer strictly liable and precludes recourse to the *Ellerth/Faragher* affirmative defense.

The U.S. Supreme Court granted *certiorari* to resolve a disagreement among the Circuits on the issue of whether a constructive discharge caused by a supervisor's harassment rises to the level of a "tangible employment action" and, therefore, precludes assertion of the *Ellerth/Faragher* affirmative defense. This was also the first opportunity the Court had to state, in agreement with the lower courts and the EEOC, that Title VII encompasses employer liability for a constructive discharge. With respect to *Suders'*, the Court determined that the Third Circuit erred when it stated that the *Ellerth/Faragher* affirmative defense is never available in a constructive discharge case. Rather, the Court held that an employer cannot avail itself of the affirmative defense " . . .when a supervisor's official act precipitates the constructive discharge." . . . In cases where a supervisor's harassment does not culminate in a "tangible employment action," however, the defense is available to the employer. The victim has a duty to use reasonable means under the circumstances to avoid or minimize harm, and the defendant has the burden of proving that the plaintiff unreasonably failed to avoid or reduce the harm.

In *Vinson*, the Court also outlined the pattern of proof for hostile environment situations. To establish a prima facie case, the plaintiff must show that: (1) she was subjected to unwelcome sexual conduct; (2) these were based on her sex; (3) they were sufficiently pervasive or severe to create an abusive or hostile work environment; and (4) the employer knew or should have known of the harassment and failed to take prompt and appropriate remedial action. Fashioning a test for these elements poses special problems. Subsequent decisions by lower courts have clarified the first and third of these elements.

When assessing whether the plaintiff, in the words of the Court, "by her conduct indicated that the alleged sexual advances were unwelcome" and whether the harassment is so pervasive and abusive as to create a hostile environment, courts usually applied a reasonableness test from the perspective of the actor. Would a "reasonable person" in the harasser's position have known that the behavior was unwelcome? In practice, this approach typically trivializes the seriousness of sexual harassment because harassers ordinarily are men, and men, as we have seen, have had great difficulty in appreciating the harm done to female victims of sexual harassment. The feminist bar has long argued that harassing conduct must be assessed from the victim's perspective. The emphasis on harassment as "unwelcome" behavior in *Vinson* was an advance in that direction. The next advance came when circuit courts began to apply the reasonableness standard from the perspective of the victim. Would "a reasonable person" in the victim's position have regarded the behavior as unwelcome? The court in the following case took that approach in endorsing the "reasonable victim" standard.

ELLISON V. BRADY
United States Court of Appeals,
Ninth Circuit, 1991.
924 F.2d 872

BEEZER, Circuit Judge:

. . . Kerry Ellison worked as a revenue agent for the Internal Revenue Service [IRS] in San Mateo, California. During her initial training in 1984 she met Sterling Gray, another trainee, who was also assigned to the San Mateo office. The two co-workers never became friends, and they did not work closely together.

. . . In June of 1986 when no one else was in the office, Gray asked Ellison to lunch. She accepted. . . .

Ellison alleges that after the June lunch Gray started to pester her with unnecessary questions and hang around her desk. [Over the next four months, Gray's unwelcome attentions escalated. He continued to ask Ellison out and to send her notes and letters that expressed affection for her. She rejected all of Gray's attentions.] . . .

Explaining her reaction [to a three-page letter], Ellison stated: "I just thought he was crazy. I thought he was nuts. I didn't know what he would do next. I was frightened."

She immediately telephoned [Bonnie] Miller [who supervised both Ellison and

Gray]. Ellison told her supervisor that she was frightened and really upset. She requested that Miller transfer either her or Gray because she would not be comfortable working in the same office with him. . . .

. . . Gray subsequently transferred to the San Francisco office. . . .

After three weeks in San Francisco, Gray filed union grievances requesting a return to the San Mateo office. The IRS and the union settled the grievances in Gray's favor, agreeing to allow him to transfer back to the San Mateo office provided that he spend four more months in San Francisco and promise not to bother Ellison. On January 28, 1987, Ellison first learned of Gray's request in a letter from Miller explaining that Gray would return to the San Mateo office. The letter indicated that management decided to resolve Ellison's problem with a six-month separation, and that it would take additional action if the problem recurred.

After receiving the letter, Ellison was "frantic." She filed a formal complaint alleging sexual harassment on January 30,

1987 with the IRS. She also obtained permission to transfer to San Francisco temporarily when Gray returned. . . .

[The Treasury Department, the EEOC, and the district court all found in favor of the government, and Ellison appealed.]

The parties ask us to determine if Gray's conduct, as alleged by Ellison, was sufficiently severe or pervasive to alter the conditions of Ellison's employment and create an abusive working environment. The district court, with little Ninth Circuit case law to look to for guidance, held that Ellison did not state a prima facie case of sexual harassment due to a hostile working environment. It believed that Gray's conduct was "isolated and genuinely trivial." We disagree.

. . . The Supreme Court in *Meritor* explained that courts may properly look to guidelines issued by the Equal Employment Opportunity Commission (EEOC) for guidance when examining hostile environment claims of sexual harassment. The EEOC guidelines describe hostile environment harassment as "conduct [which] has the purpose or effect of unreasonably interfering with an individual's work performance or creating an intimidating, hostile, or offensive working environment." The EEOC, in accord with a substantial body of judicial decisions, has concluded that "Title VII affords employees the right to work in an environment free from discriminatory intimidation, ridicule, and insult."

The Supreme Court cautioned, however, that not all harassment affects a "term, condition, or privilege" of employment within the meaning of Title VII. For example, the "mere utterance of an ethnic or racial epithet which engenders offensive feelings in an employee" is not, by itself, actionable under Title VII. To state a claim under Title VII, sexual harassment "must be sufficiently severe or pervasive to alter the conditions of

the victim's employment and create an abusive working environment." . . .

[W]e believe that in evaluating the severity and pervasiveness of sexual harassment, we should focus on the perspective of the victim. If we only examined whether a reasonable person would engage in allegedly harassing conduct, we would run the risk of reinforcing the prevailing level of discrimination. Harassers could continue to harass merely because a particular discriminatory practice was common, and victims of harassment would have no remedy. . . .

In order to shield employers from having to accommodate the idiosyncratic concerns of the rare hyper-sensitive employee, we hold that a female plaintiff states a prima facie case of hostile environment sexual harassment when she alleges conduct which a reasonable woman[11] would consider sufficiently severe or pervasive to alter the conditions of employment and create an abusive working environment.[12]

We adopt the perspective of a reasonable woman primarily because we believe that a sex-blind reasonable person standard tends to be male-biased and tends to systematically ignore the experiences of women. The reasonable woman standard does not establish a higher level of protection for women than men. Instead, a gender-conscious examination of sexual harassment enables women to participate in the workplace on an equal footing with men. By acknowledging and not trivializing the effects of sexual harassment on reasonable women, courts can work toward ensuring that neither men nor women will have to "run a gauntlet of sexual abuse in return for the privilege of being allowed to work and make a living."

We note that the reasonable victim standard we adopt today classifies conduct as unlawful sexual harassment even when harassers do not realize that their

[11] Of course, where male employees allege that co-workers engage in conduct which creates a hostile environment, the appropriate victim's perspective would be that of a reasonable man.

[12] We realize that the reasonable woman standard will not address conduct which some women find offensive. Conduct considered harmless by many today may be considered discriminatory in the future. Fortunately, the reasonableness inquiry which we adopt today is not static. As the views of reasonable women change, so too does the Title VII standard of acceptable behavior.

conduct creates a hostile working environment. Well-intentioned compliments by co-workers or supervisors can form the basis of a sexual harassment cause of action if a reasonable victim of the same sex as the plaintiff would consider the comments sufficiently severe, or pervasive to alter a condition of employment and create an abusive working environment.[13]

We cannot say as a matter of law that Ellison's reaction was idiosyncratic or hypersensitive. We believe that a reasonable woman could have had a similar reaction. . . .

We next must determine what remedial actions by employers shield them from liability under Title VII for sexual harassment by co-workers. . . .

Ellison maintains that the government's remedy was insufficient because it did not discipline Gray and because it allowed Gray to return to San Mateo after only a six-month separation. Even though the hostile environment had been eliminated when Gray began working in San Francisco, we cannot say that the government's response was reasonable under Title VII. The record on appeal suggests that Ellison's employer did not express strong disapproval of Gray's conduct, did not reprimand Gray, did not put him on probation, and did not inform him that repeated harassment would result in suspension or termination. Apparently, Gray's employer only told him to stop harassing Ellison. Title VII requires more than a mere request to refrain from discriminatory conduct. Employers send the wrong message to potential harassers when they do not discipline employees for sexual harassment. If Ellison can prove on remand that

Gray knew or should have known that his conduct was unlawful and that the government failed to take even the mildest form of disciplinary action, the district court should hold that the government's initial remedy was insufficient under Title VII. At this point, genuine issues of material fact remain concerning whether the government properly disciplined Gray. . . .

We reverse the district court's decision that Ellison did not allege a prima facie case of sexual harassment due to a hostile working environment, and we remand for further proceedings consistent with this opinion. . . .

STUDY QUESTIONS

1. The court here intended to shield employers from liability by not accommodating the sensibilities of idiosyncratic and hypersensitive individuals. Do you think the reactions of Kerry Ellison were extreme and unreasonable? Do the men and women in your class agree about that? To what do you attribute that disagreement? In your discussions of this case, has anyone's views changed? How did that come about?

2. If it is true, for now at least, that men and women often do not agree that some forms of sexual conduct are deeply offensive, why should the law adopt the perspective of the victim? Why not adopt the perspective of the "reasonable harasser" instead? Which perspective are employers likely to prefer? Is employee productivity apt to be affected even if the men "don't get it"?

---

[13] If sexual comments or sexual advances are in fact welcomed by the recipient, they, of course, do not constitute sexual harassment. Title VII's prohibition of sex discrimination in employment does not require a totally desexualized workplace.

One of the concerns left by the *Ellison* decision is how courts are to determine what the reasonable person in the plaintiff's circumstances would have felt. At about the same time that the Ninth Circuit Court of Appeals decided the *Ellison* case, a district court in Florida, using the same standard, handed down its ruling in the following case. Two features are significant about the *Robinson* case. It is the first sexual harassment case in which expert witnesses played an important role. It is also the first case in which the display of pornography in the workplace was found to have created a sufficiently hostile working environment to violate Title VII. Apparently the impact of pornography in the workplace is quite different when viewed from the perspective of the reasonable woman as opposed to that of the "reasonable harasser."

ROBINSON V. JACKSONVILLE SHIPYARDS, INC.
United States District Court, Florida, 1991.
760 F. Supp. 1486.

MELTON, D.J.

This action was commenced by plaintiff Lois Robinson pursuant to Title VII of the Civil Rights Act of 1964, as amended. . . . Plaintiff asserts defendants created and encouraged a sexually hostile, intimidating work environment. Her claim centers around the presence in the workplace of pictures of women in various stages of undress and in sexually suggestive or submissive poses, as well as remarks by male employees and supervisors which demean women. Defendants dispute plaintiff's description of the work environment and maintain that, to the extent the work environment may be found to satisfy the legal definition of a hostile work environment, they are not liable for the acts that give rise to such a description. . . .

Plaintiff Lois Robinson ("Robinson") is a female employee of Jacksonville Shipyards, Inc. ("JSI"). She has been a welder since September 1977. Robinson is one of a very small number of female skilled craftworkers employed by JSI. Between 1977 and the present, Robinson was promoted from third-class welder to second-class welder and from second-class welder to her present position as a first-class welder. . . .

Pictures of nude and partially nude women appear throughout the JSI workplace in the form of magazines, plaques on the wall, photographs torn from magazines and affixed to the wall or attached to calendars supplied by advertising tool supply companies ("vendors' advertising calendars"). Two plaques consisting of pictures of naked women, affixed to wood and varnished, were introduced into evidence and identified by several witnesses as having been on display for years at JSI in the fab[rication] shop area under the supervision of defendant Lovett. . . .

Robinson's testimony provides a vivid description of a visual assault on the sensibilities of female workers at JSI that did not relent during working hours. She credibly testified that the pervasiveness of the pictures left her unable to recount every example, but those pictures which she did describe illustrate the extent of this aspect of the work environment at JSI. She testified to seeing in the period prior to April 4, 1984, the three hundredth day prior to the filing of her EEOC charge: (a) a picture of a woman, breasts and pubic area exposed, inside a dry-dock area in 1977 or 1978. (b) a picture of a nude Black woman, pubic area exposed to reveal her labia, seen in the public locker room. (c) drawings and graffiti on the walls, including a drawing depicting a frontal view of a nude female torso with the words "USDA Choice" written on it, at the Commercial Yard in the late 1970's or early 1980's, in an area where Robinson was assigned to work. (d) a picture of a woman's pubic area with a meat spatula pressed on it, observed on a wall next to the sheetmetal shop at Mayport in the late 1970's. . . .

Robinson's testimony concerning visual harassment in the period commencing April 4, 1984, includes: (a) a picture of a nude woman with long blonde hair wearing high heels and holding a whip, waved around by a coworker, Freddie Dixon, in 1984, in an enclosed area where Robinson and approximately six men were working. Robinson testified she felt particularly targeted by this action because she has long blonde hair and works with a welding tool known as a whip. . . .

Robinson also testified about comments of a sexual nature she recalled hearing at JSI from coworkers. In some instances these comments were made while she also was in the presence of the pictures of nude or partially nude women. Among the remarks Robinson recalled are: "Hey pussycat, come here and give me a whiff"; "The more you lick it, the harder it gets"; "I'd like to get in bed with that"; "I'd like to have some of that"; "Black women taste like sardines," . . .

Robinson testified concerning the presence of abusive language written on the walls in her working areas in 1987 and 1988. Among this graffiti were the phrases "lick me you whore dog bitch," "eat me," and "pussy." This first phrase appeared on the wall over a spot where Robinson had left her jacket. The second phrase was freshly painted in Robinson's work area when she observed it. The third phrase appeared during a break after she left her work area to get a drink of water. . . .

The Court heard testimony from two of Robinson's female coworkers, Lawanna Gail Banks ("Banks") and Leslie Albert ("Albert"), concerning incidents of sexual harassment to which they were subjected, including incidents that did not occur in Robinson's presence. . . .

Based on the foregoing, the Court finds that sexually harassing behavior occurred throughout the JSI working environment with both frequency and intensity over the relevant time period. Robinson did not welcome such behavior. . . .

. . . To affect a "term, condition, or privilege" of employment within the meaning of Title VII, the harassment "must be sufficiently severe or pervasive 'to alter the conditions of [the victim's] employment and create an abusive working environment.' " "This test may be satisfied by a showing that the sexual harassment was sufficiently severe or persistent 'to affect seriously [the victim's] psychological well being.' " This "is a question to be determined with regard to the totality of the circumstances." . . .

Element four must be tested both subjectively and objectively. Regarding the former, the question is whether Robinson has shown she is an "affected individual," that is, she is at least as affected as the reasonable person under like circumstances. The evidence reflects the great upset that Robinson felt when confronted with individual episodes of harassment and the workplace as a whole. Further, the impact on her work performance is plain. . . .

The objective standard asks whether a reasonable person of Robinson's sex, that is, a reasonable woman, would perceive that an abusive working environment has been created. The severity and pervasiveness aspects form a structure to test this hypothesis. . . .

A reasonable woman would find that the working environment at JSI was abusive. This conclusion reaches the totality of the circumstances, including the sexual remarks, the sexual jokes, the sexually-oriented pictures of women, and the non-sexual rejection of women by co-workers. The testimony by Dr. Fiske and Ms. Wagner [expert witnesses for the plaintiff] provides a reliable basis upon which to conclude that the cumulative, corrosive effect of this work environment over time affects the psychological well-being of a reasonable woman placed in these conditions. . . .

This Court must "render a decree which will so far as possible eliminate the discriminatory effects of the past as well as bar like discrimination in the future." *Albemarle Paper Co.* Ms. Wagner endorsed plaintiff's proposed sexual harassment policy and procedures as an effective remedy for the work environment at JSI. The Court agrees with her assessment. The Court notes the use of education, training and the development of effective complaint procedures as an appropriate remedy in prior hostile work environment sexual harassment cases. The Court adopts the policy and procedures proposed by plaintiff. . . .

STUDY QUESTIONS

1. Do you agree that the reasonable person in the plaintiffs' circumstances would have found this working environment to be hostile and offensive? Do the men and women in your class agree on this?

2. Do you find the observations of Dr. Fiske and Ms. Wagner credible? If it had been shown that Lois Robinson was as tolerant of pornography in other settings as the average person, would your views of her complaints here be any different? Does the social context in which pornography is viewed affect the extent to which it is taken as threatening?

The reasonable woman standard was used by these courts to alter, not reinforce, prevailing stereotypes—to combat generally tolerated, if not accepted, discriminatory practices. Their decisions declare that even if the form of harassment is commonplace, it nevertheless violates Title VII if it is sufficiently severe or pervasive in the eyes of the reasonable woman. The hope here is that this process will contribute to changing the prevailing stereotypes and customary practices of those in power in the workplaces of the nation. The hope is that one day, soon, the men will "get it."

In *Harris v. Forklift Systems, Inc.*, 510 U.S. 17 (1993), the Supreme Court considered what factors are necessary to prove the third prong of the *Vinson* test. In that case, Teresa Harris, a manager, was subjected to insults because of her gender and was targeted for unwanted sexual innuendos by Charles Hardy, the company president. Harris complained to Hardy about his behavior. He apologized and promised to stop. Shortly thereafter, Hardy renewed his objectionable behavior. Harris quit about a month later and sued Forklift, claiming that Hardy's conduct created an abusive work environment for her because of her gender. The District Court found this to be a close case, but held that Hardy's conduct did not create an abusive environment. Although the District Court found that some of Hardy's comments offended Harris and would offend a "reasonable woman," they were not "so severe as to be expected to seriously affect [Harris'] psychological well being. A reasonable woman manager under like circumstances would have been offended by Hardy, but his conduct would not have risen to the level of interfering with that person's work performance." The District Court's decision was affirmed in an unpublished opinion by the Sixth Circuit.

The Supreme Court then granted certiorari to resolve a conflict among the Circuits on whether conduct to be actionable as "abusive work environment" sexual harassment must "seriously affect [an employee's] psychological well being" or cause the employee to "suffe[r] injury." The Court determined that "[w]hen the workplace is permeated with 'discriminatory intimidation, ridicule, and insult' . . . that is 'sufficiently severe or pervasive to alter the conditions of the victim's employment and create an abusive working environment,' . . . Title VII is violated." The Court took this "middle path between making actionable any conduct that is merely offensive and requiring the conduct to cause a tangible psychological injury." According to the Court, Title VII protections arise "before the harassing conduct leads to a nervous breakdown." While not a "mathematically precise test," the Court stated that "whether an environment is 'hostile' or 'abusive' can be determined only by looking at all the circumstances," including the frequency of the discriminatory conduct, whether it is physically threatening or humiliating rather than merely offensive, and whether it unreasonably interferes with work performance. Although the effect on an employee's psychological well-being may be relevant to the determination, the Court held that no single factor is required to make a showing of hostile work environment.

Five years later, the Supreme Court decided *Oncale v. Sundowner Offshore Services, Inc.*, 523 U.S. 75 (1998), a same-sex sexual harassment case. As discussed in Chapter 3, the Supreme Court concluded that Title VII did not bar a claim of discrimination "because of . . . sex" merely because the plaintiff and the harasser(s) were of the same sex. In this context, the Court again considered what factors are necessary to demonstrate that conduct is so "severe or pervasive" it creates an "objectively hostile or abusive work environment—an environment a reasonable person would find hostile or abusive." According to the Court, this standard will ensure that ordinary socializing, such as "male-on-male horseplay or intersexual flirtation," will not be mistakenly viewed as conduct violating Title VII. The Court also noted that, as in *Harris*, the objective severity of the harassment should be judged from the perspective of a reasonable person in the victim's position, considering "all the circumstances." Furthermore, in same-sex harassment cases, just as in all harassment cases, the social context in which the behavior occurs is important. "Common sense and an appropriate sensitivity to social context will enable courts and juries to distinguish between simple teasing or roughhousing among members of the same sex, and conduct which a reasonable person in the plaintiff's position would find severely hostile or abusive." Whether the Court's guidance in these two cases is sufficient to help would be harassers of either sex, in heterosexual or same sex situations, "get it" remains to be seen.

After *Oncale*, the Ninth Circuit had the opportunity to consider the question of " . . . whether an employee who alleges he was subjected to severe, pervasive, and unwelcome 'physical conduct of a sexual nature' in the workplace asserts a viable claim of discrimination based on sex under title VII if the Civil Rights Act, . . . even if that employee also alleges that the motivation for that discrimination was his sexual orientation." In *Rene v. MGM Grand Hotel, Inc.*, 305 F.3d 1061 (9th Cir. 2002), Medina Rene, an openly gay man filed a charge of discrimination with the Nevada Equal Rights Commission, alleging that he was discriminated against because of his sex "male" and alleged his gender was a factor in the adverse treatment he received. He subsequently filed an action in federal district court alleging that he had been unlawfully sexually harassed in violation of Title VII, and attached a copy of his Nevada Equal Rights Commission charge. MGM moved for summary judgment on the grounds that "claims of discrimination based on sexual orientation are not cognizable under title VII." The District Court granted summary judgment and Rene appealed. The Ninth Circuit, in an *en banc* opinion, determined that Rene had stated a cause of action under Title VII and reversed the District Court's grant of summary judgment and remanded the case. It held that an employee's sexual orientation, as well as the harasser's motivation, is irrelevant for purposes of Title VII. What matters is whether the harasser has engaged in severe or pervasive unwelcome physical conduct "of a sexual nature." The Ninth Circuit noted that it had surveyed many cases concerning offensive touching of the genitalia, buttocks, or breasts of women where a Title VII violation was found, and none of those cases denied relief because the victim was or might have been a lesbian. It surmised that if sexual orientation was irrelevant for a female victim, it should also be irrelevant for a male victim. On numerous occasions, Rene's supervisor and fellow butlers grabbed his crotch and poked their fingers in his anus through his clothing. The court stated that "the physical attacks to which Rene was subjected, which targeted body parts clearly linked to his sexuality, were 'because of . . . sex.' Whatever else those attacks may, or may not, have been 'because of' has no legal consequence." Pursuant to the Supreme Court's decision in *Oncale*, severe or pervasive same-sex offensive sexual touching is prohibited under Title VII. In addition, offensive sexual touching is actionable discrimination even in a same-sex workforce. Discrimination "because of sex" can occur among men where some men are subjected to the offensive sexual touching while others are not; it is sufficient to demonstrate that there was discrimination "in comparison to other men."

And, lest we think that men can only be victims if the harasser is also male, consider the matter involving the popular weight-loss clinic, Jenny Craig. In 1993, eight men from the Boston area made public charges of sex discrimination and sexual harassment against their former employer. Six of the men filed charges with the Massachusetts Commission Against Discrimination (MCAD). In 1994, five of the men brought suit in Massachusetts Superior Court. One male employee claimed that female co-workers sexually harassed him by complimenting him on his impressive biceps, nice eyes, and "tight buns." He also complained that "girl talk," such as discussions on menstrual cycles, whom to marry, and who was pregnant or how to get pregnant, was offensive. Finally, he asserted it was sexist to ask the male employees to shovel the snow. The MCAD found probable cause for gender bias and ordered mediation. The state superior court case had a convoluted procedural history; the first case brought by the five men was removed to federal district court by Jenny Craig only to be remanded to state court where summary judgment was eventually granted in favor of the employer. In 1995, a second superior court action was instituted by three of the men after they withdrew their case from the MCAD. That case was also removed to federal district court, ultimately remanded to state court where summary judgment was also granted, and appealed to the Massachusetts Appeals Court, which reversed the summary judgment. Interestingly, although the EEOC statistics for sexual harassment claims filed around that time period showed that less than 10 percent of the claims made were filed by men, the Jenny Craig matter was reported in the *Wall Street Journal* (front page) the day after filing. Furthermore, the eight men were sought out for appearances on national television shows such as *Today*. Although we might expect that, as women gain prominence and power in business, there will be instances of inappropriate behavior similar to those committed by their male counterparts, we should not expect these cases to generate more sympathy than those in which women are the victims.

Over the past three decades, feminists have worked to eliminate sexual harassment from our culture and in particular from our workplaces. The focus in this section has been on litigative approaches to that goal. The following selection identifies additional ways to advance the same objective.

Techniques for Preventing Sexual Harassment
Kathryn Abrams
"Gender Discrimination and the Transformation of Workplace Norms."
42 *Vanderbilt Law Review* 1183, 1215–20 (1989).

. . . Although revising Title VII standards is a crucial step toward reshaping the norms governing personal exchange in the workplace, it would be unwise to rely on litigation as the sole, or even primary, means of reform. Litigation is vastly disruptive of the plaintiffs' relations with others in the workplace. . . . The sexual harassment plaintiff typically is subjected to further or intensified harassment as she pursues her claim, and her relationships with both men and women in the workplace may be severed beyond repair, a form of damage that even legal victory cannot undo. Moreover, changes

Reprinted by permission of Vanderbilt Law Review.

in behavior that are compelled by judicial decree, rather than voluntarily introduced and advocated by the employer, may produce lingering resentment among male workers that affects not only their receptivity to subsequent female coworkers, but also their behavior toward the other women in their lives. Strategies to end sexual harassment should not require all women to make the difficult choice between enduring continued harassment and seeking costly victory in the courts.

Litigation can also be a comparatively blunt tool for producing changes in workplace norms. Judgments—and even opinions—in sexual harassment cases give employers only an anecdotal notion of what behavior is unacceptable, and otherwise fail to direct employers toward more satisfactory behavior. Nor do these decisions, in and of themselves, organize or educate employees to produce the necessary changes in conduct. An adverse judgment also may put supervisors on the defensive, rather than engaging them as participants in bringing about change. For the protection of women and the education of those who victimize them, it is necessary to explore less coercive means of normative change.

Reliance on nonadjudicative means should not, and need not, alter the focus of enforcement against sexual harassment. Two nonadjudicative strategies might offer an even more effective means of targeting and ameliorating devaluative sexual conduct in the workplace. First, enforcement efforts by the EEOC provide an avenue for reform that is less adversarial in nature than a full-blown private action. Were the EEOC to conciliate . . ., it could investigate devaluative sexual conduct and seek agreements to reform workplace behavior that would provide a comprehensive education to members of the defendant's workforce. Conciliation . . . also would be less coercive than judicial intervention, and would produce few of the costs to the complaint that arise from pressing and testifying in her own litigation.

Another promising approach is for employers to implement the proposed Title VII standards through voluntary compliance programs. Compliance programs have been adopted widely by large and small firms in areas such as antitrust, in which the consequences of legal liability are potentially great. Although treble damages and criminal sanctions do not threaten defendants in Title VII cases, other factors might make compliance programs attractive to employers. . . . A well-administered compliance program reduces the likelihood that an employer will be held liable for harassing conduct, and should reduce the likelihood that such harassment will occur at all. Moreover, a well-publicized program could be an effective recruitment tool for an employer seeking to increase the number of women in its workforce, notwithstanding the possible ambivalence of some of its male employees. An effective compliance program might also bring broader competitive advantages, as it would reduce a source of tension that saps employees' productivity, and might improve the position of the firm in the labor market and among certain groups of consumers.

Although compliance programs do not carry the force of legal sanctions, they have several features that better enable them to modify those norms giving rise to sexual harassment. First, they can provide guidelines for employees regarding proper and improper behavior in a context less emotionally charged, and more accessible to employees, than a court battle. . . .

Perhaps the greatest asset of a compliance program is the opportunity it provides for sustained re-education of a workforce. A judicial decree awards only reinstatement, back pay, or attorney's fees; the preceding litigation may highlight only a few offensive practices. Neither the decree nor the litigation helps employers or employees understand the injury that the legal standard is intended to prevent, nor do they help workers learn more acceptable forms of conduct. Most authors of legal compliance programs insist that the element most important to the programs' success is a face-to-face education of the workforce at their inception. Thorough introductions accompanied by small-group question and answer sessions can provide new perspectives on widely accepted conduct. Readings, films, or simulations—varying perhaps with the background of the workforce—can help perpetrators to recognize potential violations and help victims to stand firm in their resistance. These opportunities for exchange can be of crucial value when the goal is to create an awareness of divergent viewpoints.

While a change in the adjudicative approach to sexual harassment is essential, it need not be the only arrow in the quiver of feminists advocating change. The precise guidelines, shared responsibility, and comprehensive education that compliance programs can provide make them a nondivisive, fine-tuned supplement to adjudicative enforcement.

Study Questions

1. What reasons were given against complete reliance on litigation to eliminate sexual harassment from workplaces? What alternative techniques were discussed?
2. What incentives do employers have for implementing voluntary compliance programs designed to end sexual harassment in their workplaces? What interest do victims and potential victims have in supporting such programs? Are such programs likely to escape the problems faced by the litigative approach?

II. Pay Equity

Of all the issues that have arisen in the area of sex discrimination in employment, the most heated and enduring relates to the compensation differential between men and women. In this section, we will explore some of the many dimensions of that issue and examine the main legal responses available under federal law.

The Earnings Gap

> The Lord said to Moses, "Say to the people of Israel, When a man makes a special vow of persons to the Lord at your valuation, then your valuation of a male from twenty years old up to sixty years old shall be fifty shekels of the sanctuary. If the person is a female, your valuation shall be thirty shekels."
> *Lev. 27: 1–4.*

Over the past four decades, the gender composition of the labor force has undergone an unprecedented transformation. What has occurred might be called the "feminization" of the workforce. The U.S. Department of Labor (DOL) reported that in 1960, one in three full-time workers was a woman. In 2004, women made up approximately 59 percent of the total U.S. workforce. From 1975 to 2000, the workforce participation of mothers with children under eighteen rose from 47 percent to 73 percent but decreased slightly by 2004 to 71 percent. According to the DOL's May 2005 report, *Women in the Labor Force: A Datebook*, mothers with older children (six to seventeen years old) are more likely to participate in the workforce than mothers of younger children (under six) and unmarried mothers have higher participation rates than do married mothers.

Of course, other changes occurred during that same period. In 1960, one in ten households, just over 5 million families, was maintained by women—no spouse present. By 1991, 18 percent of all households were headed by women. One of the consequences of these developments is reflected in the poverty rates. According to the 2000 U.S. Census, 12.9 million women ran households with no husband present. One of the groups to feel the impact of this was our children. According to the 2000 U.S. Census, over 16 percent of children in the United States live in poverty. As Figure 4.1 shows, in 2000, people in female-householder families had a poverty rate at least four-and-one-half times greater than those in married-couple families.

Certainly, one of the principal factors that generates these poverty effects from the feminization of the labor force is what has come to be known as the "earnings gap." As Figure 4.2 indicates, the pattern has been fairly consistent.

We saw in Chapter 3 that a much larger proportion of adult women is in the work force in the mid-1980s than in the mid-1950s, when only about one in three worked outside the home. Now a little more than half are in the work force. During those three decades, however, the differential between male and female earnings remained the same as the one mentioned by Moses. Throughout that period, women earned three-fifths as much as men. The constancy of that differential over these decades is startling: Even today, women's median full-time weekly earnings are only about 80 cents of every dollar earned by men.

One of the dimensions of the earnings gap that is frequently overlooked when considering such gross measures is the different ways it affects minority women and men. As Figure 4.3 shows, men in each racial/ethnic category earn more than women in the same category. However, compare the earnings of white women to men in different racial/ethnic groups.

What explains the earnings gap? Why does it exist at all, and what makes it so persistent? One of the most frequently voiced explanations is that women bring a different and less-valued set of personal characteristics, such as skills and work experience, to the

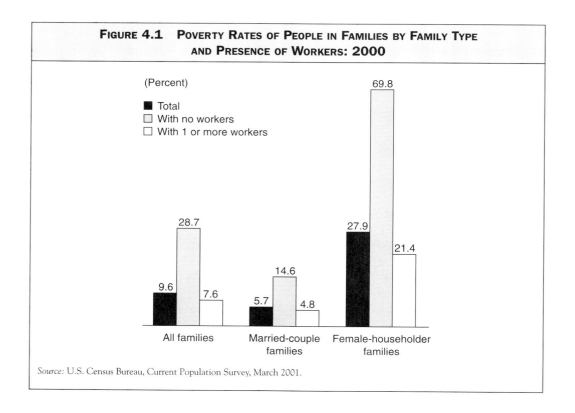

FIGURE 4.1   POVERTY RATES OF PEOPLE IN FAMILIES BY FAMILY TYPE
AND PRESENCE OF WORKERS: 2000

(Percent)

■ Total
▢ With no workers
▢ With 1 or more workers

Source: U.S. Census Bureau, Current Population Survey, March 2001.

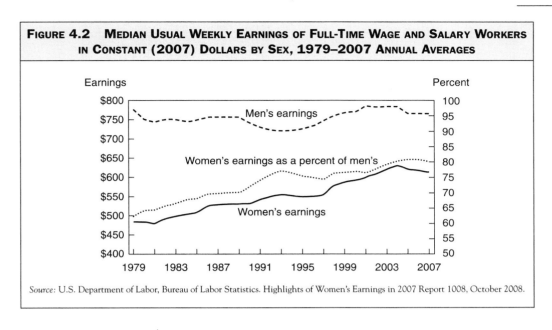

FIGURE 4.2   MEDIAN USUAL WEEKLY EARNINGS OF FULL-TIME WAGE AND SALARY WORKERS IN CONSTANT (2007) DOLLARS BY SEX, 1979–2007 ANNUAL AVERAGES

Source: U.S. Department of Labor, Bureau of Labor Statistics. Highlights of Women's Earnings in 2007 Report 1008, October 2008.

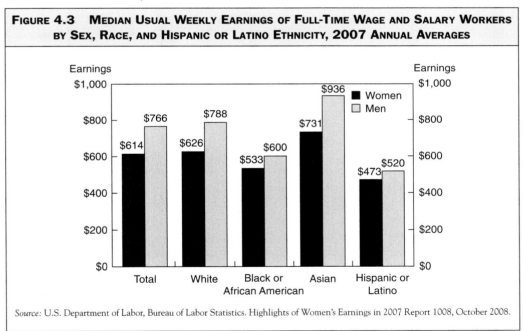

FIGURE 4.3   MEDIAN USUAL WEEKLY EARNINGS OF FULL-TIME WAGE AND SALARY WORKERS BY SEX, RACE, AND HISPANIC OR LATINO ETHNICITY, 2007 ANNUAL AVERAGES

Source: U.S. Department of Labor, Bureau of Labor Statistics. Highlights of Women's Earnings in 2007 Report 1008, October 2008.

workplace than do men. Educational attainment is also frequently cited as one of the differences between males and females, as groups, in the labor force. Many who urge women to seek ever more education at ever more advanced levels proceed on this premise—the thought being that education is the great equalizer. According to the U.S. Department of Labor, Bureau of Labor Statistics data on earnings sorted by gender and levels of education, although women fared better than men with respect to earnings growth from 1979 to 2007, this has less resulted in about an 8 percent gain in women's earnings as a percent of men's.

The Equal Pay Act

Wage and salary discrimination is a second explanation that is commonly advanced to account for the earnings gap. In this view, a substantial proportion of the remaining wage gap might be explained by sex discrimination on the part of employers. Even though the language of Title VII includes such discrimination within the scope of its prohibitions, the main burden of preventing pay discrimination based on sex has been assumed by the Equal Pay Act.

The first major legal measure at the federal level attempting to remedy the substantial and unexplained wage differential was the Equal Pay Act of 1963 (29 U.S.C. § 206(d)(1)). As originally enacted, the act contained an exemption for "employees employed in a bona fide executive, administrative, or professional capacity. . . ." This exemption was removed by an amendment added by the 92nd Congress in 1972. The full text of the amended act reads as follows:

> *No employer* having employees subject to any provisions of this section *shall* discriminate, within any establishment in which such employees are employed, between employees on the basis of sex by paying wages to employees in such establishment at a rate less than the rate at which he pays wages to employees of the opposite sex in such establishment for equal work on jobs the performance of which requires equal skill, effort, and responsibility, and which are performed under similar working conditions,
>
> *except where* such payment is made pursuant to (i) a seniority system; (ii) a merit system; (iii) a system which measures earnings by quantity or quality of production; or (iv) a differential based on any other factor other than sex:
>
> *Provided,* That an employer who is paying a wage rate differential in violation of this subsection shall not, in order to comply with the provisions of this subsection, reduce the wage rate of any employee. (Emphasis added.)

As you can see, the statute contains three main provisions. These are ordinarily referred to as the equal pay for equal work formula, the four affirmative defenses, and the limitation on remedies. The "equal pay for equal work" provision of the act prohibits employers from paying employees of opposite sexes at different rates for jobs that are equivalent in terms of skill, effort, responsibility, and working conditions. The violation envisioned by this provision is paying women in a job classification less than men in the same classification. Such practices are banned by the act, whether blatantly exploitive of women or rationalized as granting preference to men as the alleged primary providers for the nation's households. In this sense, the act directly confronted the most blatant and overt instances of sex discrimination in matters of compensation.

Congress, however, carefully limited the scope of this prohibition. The prohibition applies only where the jobs held by women and those held by better-paid men are "equal." The prohibition of the Equal Pay Act does not reach differentiation in the rates of pay among different job classifications. The courts, however, have interpreted this prohibition to include jobs in distinct classifications where the work performed by women workers is "substantially equal" to that performed by better-paid men in the respects listed in the act. (*Shultz v. Wheaton Glass Co.* 421 F.2d 259 (3d Cir. 1970).) This extension was evidently intended to thwart more subtle forms of wage discrimination in which refinements of job descriptions are used to mask sex discrimination.

In *Wheaton Glass,* the appellate court extended the reach of the act to include "substantially equal" work. In 1974, the Supreme Court followed a similar approach in the decision that follows. In the course of upholding a judgment against an employer, the Court also clarified the order of proof used in the analysis of equal pay litigation.

CORNING GLASS WORKS V. BRENNAN
Supreme Court of the United States, 1974.
417 U.S. 188, 94 S. Ct. 2223,
41 L.Ed.2d 1.

Mr. Justice MARSHALL delivered the opinion of the Court.

These cases arise under the Equal Pay Act of 1963 which added to the Fair Labor Standards Act the principle of equal pay for equal work regardless of sex. The principal question posed is whether Corning Glass Works violated the Act by paying a higher base wage to male night shift inspectors than it paid to female inspectors performing the same tasks on the day shift, where the higher wage was paid in addition to a separate night shift differential paid to all employees for night work. In No. 73–29, the Court of Appeals for the Second Circuit, in a case involving several Corning plants in Corning, New York, held that this practice violated the Act. In No. 73–695, the Court of Appeals for the Third Circuit, in a case involving a Corning plant in Wellsboro, Pennsylvania, reached the opposite conclusion. We granted certiorari and consolidated the cases to resolve this unusually direct conflict between two circuits. . . .

Prior to 1925, Corning operated its plants in Wellsboro and Corning only during the day and all inspection work was performed by women. Between 1925 and 1930, the company began to introduce automatic production equipment which made it desirable to institute a night shift. During this period, however, both New York and Pennsylvania law prohibited women from working at night. As a result, in order to fill inspector positions on the new night shift, the company had to recruit male employees from among its male dayworkers. The male employees so transferred demanded and received wages substantially higher than those paid to women inspectors engaged on the two day shifts. During this same period, however, no plant-wide shift differential existed and male employees working at night, other than inspectors, received the same wages as their day shift counterparts. Thus a situation developed where the night inspectors were all male, the day inspectors all female, and the male inspectors received significantly higher wages.

In 1944, Corning plants at both locations were organized by a labor union and a collective-bargaining agreement was negotiated for all production and maintenance employees. This agreement for the first time established a plant-wide shift differential, but this change did not eliminate the higher base wage paid to male night inspectors. Rather, the shift differential was superimposed on the existing difference in base wages between male night inspectors and female day inspectors.

Prior to June 11, 1964, the effective date of the Equal Pay Act, the law in both Pennsylvania and New York was amended to permit women to work at night. It was not until some time after the effective date of the Act, however, that Corning initiated efforts to eliminate the differential rates for male and female inspectors. Beginning in June 1966, Corning started to open up jobs on the night shift to women. Previously separate male and female seniority lists were consolidated and women became eligible to exercise their seniority, on the same basis as men, to bid for the higher paid night inspection jobs as vacancies occurred.

On January 20, 1969, a new collective-bargaining agreement went into effect, establishing a new "job evaluation" system for setting wage rates. The new agreement abolished for the future the separate base wages for day and night shift inspectors and imposed a uniform base wage for inspectors exceeding the wage rate for the night shift previously in effect. All inspectors hired after January 20, 1969, were to receive the same base wage, whatever their sex or shift. The collective-bargaining agreement further provided, however, for a higher "red circle" rate for employees hired prior to January 20, 1969, when working as inspectors on the night shift. This "red circle" rate served essentially to perpetuate the differential in base wages between day and night inspectors.

The Secretary of Labor brought these cases to enjoin Corning from violating the Equal Pay Act and to collect back wages allegedly due female employees because of past violations. Three distinct questions are presented: (1) Did Corning ever violate the Equal Pay Act by paying male night shift inspectors more than female day shift inspectors? (2) If so, did Corning cure its violation of the Act in 1966 by permitting women to work as night shift inspectors? (3) Finally, if the violation was not remedied in 1966, did Corning cure its violation in 1969 by equalizing day and night inspector wage rates but establishing higher "red circle" rates for existing employees working on the night shift?

Congress' purpose in enacting the Equal Pay Act was to remedy what was perceived to be a serious and endemic problem of employment discrimination in private industry—the fact that the wage structure of "many segments of American industry has been based on an ancient but outmoded belief that a man, because of his role in society, should be paid more than a woman even though his duties are the same." The solution adopted was quite simple in principle: to require that "equal work will be rewarded by equal wages."

The Act's basic structure and operation are similarly straightforward. In order to make out a case under the Act, the Secretary must show that an employer pays different wages to employees of opposite sexes "for equal work on jobs the performance of which requires equal skill, effort, and responsibility, and which are performed under similar working conditions." Although the Act is silent on this point, its legislative history makes plain that the Secretary has the burden of proof on this issue, as both of the courts below recognized.

The Act also establishes four exceptions—three specific and one a general catchall provision—where different payment to employees of opposite sexes "is made pursuant to (i) a seniority system; (ii) a merit system; (iii) a system which measures earnings by quantity or quality of production; or (iv) a differential based on any other factor other than sex." Again, while the Act is silent on this question, its structure and history also suggest that once the Secretary has carried his burden of showing that the employer pays workers of one sex more than workers of the opposite sex for equal work, the burden shifts to the employer to show that the differential is justified under one of the Act's four exceptions. . . .

While a layman might well assume that time of day worked reflects one aspect of a job's "working conditions," the term has a different and much more specific meaning in the language of industrial relations. As Corning's own representative testified at the hearings, the element of working conditions encompasses two subfactors: "surroundings" and "hazards." "Surroundings" measures the elements, such as toxic chemicals or fumes, regularly encountered by a worker, their intensity, and their frequency. "Hazards" takes into account the physical hazards regularly encountered, their frequency, and the severity of injury they can cause. This definition of "working conditions" is not only manifested in Corning's own job evaluation plans but is also well accepted across a wide range of American industry.

Nowhere in any of these definitions is time of day worked mentioned as a relevant criterion. The fact of the matter is that the concept of "working conditions," as used in the specialized language of job evaluation systems, simply does not encompass shift differentials. . . . We agree with the Second Circuit that the inspection work at issue in this case, whether performed during the day or night, is "equal work" as that term is defined in the Act. . . .

. . . [The next] question is whether the company remedied the specific violation of the Act which the Secretary proved. We agree with the Second Circuit, as well as with all other circuits that have had occasion to consider this issue, that the company could not cure its violation except by equalizing the base wages of female day inspectors with the higher rates paid the night inspectors. This result is implicit in the Act's language, its statement of purpose, and its legislative history. . . .

The Equal Pay Act is broadly remedial, and it should be construed and applied so as to fulfill the underlying purposes which Congress sought to achieve. If, as the Secretary proved, the work performed by women on the day shift was equal to that performed by men on the night shift, the company became obligated to pay the women the same base wage as their male counterparts on the effective date of the Act. To permit the company to escape that obligation by agreeing to allow some women to work on the night shift at a higher rate of pay as vacancies occurred would frustrate, not serve, Congress' ends. . . .

The judgment in No. 73–29 is affirmed. The judgment in No. 73–695 is reversed and the case remanded to the Court of Appeals for further proceedings consistent with this opinion.

It Is So Ordered.

STUDY QUESTIONS

1. What did the Court declare to have been Congress's purpose in enacting the Equal Pay Act?
2. On what grounds did the Court find that the jobs of day inspector and night inspector were performed under "similar working conditions"?

In *Corning Glass*, the Court indicated the order of proof to be followed in Equal Pay Act cases. If the government shows that the employer used different wage rates for employees of opposite sexes for jobs that are substantially equal in skill, effort, responsibility, and working conditions, the burden of proof shifts to the employer to show that one of the four affirmative defenses listed in the statute applies to the situation. If the employer does not succeed, the government prevails.

As indicated at the beginning of this section, the bulk of litigation regarding pay inequity has been governed by the Equal Pay Act. This resulted from an exception to Title VII known as the "Bennett Amendment" (section 703(h)), which provides:

> It shall not be an unlawful employment practice under this subchapter for any employer to differentiate upon the basis of sex in determining the amount of the wages or compensation paid or to be paid to employees of such employer if such differentiation is authorized by the provisions of section 206 (d) of Title 29 [The Equal Pay Act] . . . .

In its 1981 decision in *County of Washington v. Gunther* (452 U.S. 161), the Supreme Court declared that the Bennett Amendment is to be understood as incorporating not the equal pay for equal work formula but only the four affirmative defenses of the Equal Pay Act into Title VII. This decision has the effect of making any of these four defenses a complete shield against liability for pay discrimination under Title VII.

The affirmative defenses afforded employers by the Act function as exceptions to the rule stated in the "equal pay for equal work" provision. As such, they create the same concern as those created by Title VII (i.e., that the exceptions might be interpreted so broadly as to "swallow the rule"). This is especially important for the fourth affirmative defense—"any other factor other than sex."

Occupational Segregation

So far, we have considered two possible explanations of the earnings gap. The first was that women workers, as a group, possess a different and less valuable set of employment skills than do men workers as a group. We saw that research shows that this can explain less than half the difference in the average earnings of women and men. The second was that the difference was the result of overt sex discrimination on the part of employers that pay their women employees less than their men employees who do the same kind of work. The experience with the Equal Pay Act, which targets exactly that type of discrimination, suggests that this hypothesis has little explanatory power.

Although the earnings gap has gotten somewhat smaller, it has not significantly changed in the forty-six years since the Equal Pay Act went into effect. That might be interpreted in several ways. One might suspect that the act has not been vigorously enforced—it's only been window dressing. Not even the harshest critics suggest that this is the entire explanation.

An alternative explanation is that the Equal Pay Act does not reach the principal factors responsible for the wage differential. One popular version of this theory proposes that working women as a group earn substantially less than working men as a group primarily because women workers tend to be concentrated in lower-paying occupations than men. If this is the principal explanation of the earnings gap, the act will not help because it applies only to jobs that are substantially equal.

The occupational segregation explanation of the earnings gap has two parts, each of which is well supported by Labor Department data. First, women and men are concentrated in different occupations. The second part of the occupational segregation explanation of the earnings gap is that the occupations in which women cluster are lower paid than are those in which men predominate. This too is amply supported by Labor Department data (see Table 4-1).

Since the mid-1970s, feminists have insisted on the centrality of occupational segregation as a key factor in the eradication of the earnings gap. Since then, researchers have shown that occupational segregation accounts for a sizable portion of the earnings gap. Jerry Jacobs, in *Revolving Doors: Sex Segregation and Women's Careers* (Stanford, Calif.: Stanford University Press, 1989), reported that between 25 and 40 percent of the gap is explained by the direct effects of the sex-segregated labor force. When the indirect effects are included, its explanatory power exceeds 50 percent.

The issue of interest in the context of this book is whether legal remedies are available where earnings differences are attributable to occupational segregation. This question has ordinarily been posed in the context of Title VII and resolved differently by different courts, depending, as law professor Vicki Schultz points out, on the story that is told about why women tend to be concentrated in different occupations than men.

TABLE 4-1   Twenty Leading Occupations of Employed Women 2008 Annual Averages (employment in thousands)

Occupation	Total Employed Women	Total Employed (Men and Women)	Percent Women	Women's Median Weekly Earnings
Total, 16 years and older (all employed women)	67,876	145,362	46.7	$638
Secretaries and administrative assistants	3,168	3,296	96.1	614
Registered Nurses	2,548	2,778	91.7	1,011
Elementary and middle school teachers	2,403	2,958	81.2	871
Cashiers	2,287	3,031	75.5	349
Retail salespersons	1,783	3,416	52.2	440
Nursing, psychiatric, and home health aides	1,675	1,889	88.7	424
First-line supervisors/managers of retail sales workers	1,505	3,471	43.3	556
Waiters and waitresses	1,471	2,010	73.2	367
Receptionists and information clerks	1,323	1,413	93.6	502
Bookkeeping, accounting, and auditing clerks	1,311	1,434	91.4	603
Customer service representatives	1,302	1,908	68.3	568
Maids and housekeeping cleaners	1,287	1,434	89.7	371
Childcare workers	1,256	1,314	95.6	393
Managers, all others	1,244	3,473	35.8	1,010
First-line supervisors/managers of office and administrative support	1,169	1,641	71.2	688
Accountants and auditors	1,077	1,762	61.1	908
Office clerks, general	993	1,176	84.4	582
Teacher assistants	936	1,020	91.8	413
Cooks	801	1,997	40.1	363
Personal and home care aides	744	871	85.4	404

Source: U.S. Department of Labor, Bureau of Labor Statistics, Annual Averages 2008.

Telling Stories about Women and Work

Vicki Schultz

103 *Harvard Law Review* 1749 (1990).

How do we make sense of that most basic feature of the world of work, sex segregation on the job? That it exists is part of our common understanding. Social science research has documented, and casual observation confirmed, that men work mostly with men, doing "men's work," and women work mostly with women, doing "women's work." We know also the serious negative consequences segregation has for women workers.

Work traditionally done by women has lower wages, less status, and fewer opportunities of advancement than work done by men. Despite this shared knowledge, however, we remain deeply divided in our attitudes toward sex segregation on the job. What divides us is how we interpret this reality, the stories we tell about its origins and meaning. Why does sex segregation on the job exist? Who is responsible for it? Is it an injustice, or an inevitability?

In *EEOC v. Sears, Roebuck & Co.*, the district court interpreted sex segregation as the expression of women's own choice. The Equal Employment Opportunity Commission (EEOC) sued Sears under Title VII of the Civil Rights Act of 1964. The EEOC claimed that Sears had engaged in sex discrimination in hiring and promotion into commission sales jobs, reserving these jobs mostly for men while relegating women to much lower-paying noncommission sales jobs. Like most employment discrimination plaintiffs, the EEOC relied heavily on statistical evidence to prove its claims. The EEOC's statistical studies showed that Sears had significantly underhired women sales applicants for the more lucrative commission sales positions, even after controlling for potential sex differences in qualifications.

Although the statistical evidence exposed a long-standing pattern of sex segregation in Sears' salesforce, the judge refused to attribute this pattern to sex discrimination. The judge concluded that the EEOC's statistical analyses were "virtually meaningless," because they were based on the faulty assumption that female sales applicants were as "interested" as male applicants in commission sales jobs. Indeed, the EEOC had "turned a blind eye to reality," for Sears had proved that women sales applicants preferred lower-paying noncommission sales jobs. The judge credited various explanations for women's "lack of interest" in commission sales, all of which rested on conventional images of women as "feminine" and nurturing, unsuited for the vicious competition in the male-dominated

world of commission selling. In the court's eyes, Sears had done nothing to segregate its salesforce; it had merely honored the preexisting employment preferences of working women themselves. . . .

[Professor Schultz characterized this court and others that rely on the "lack of interest" explanation of work force sex segregation as "conservative." She went on to contrast that analysis with those of other "liberal" courts that rejected the "lack of interest" explanation.] Even though both explanations rest in a common evidentiary framework, each of them also stands as a separate narrative that justifies a different legal outcome. I refer to the rhetorical justification used by courts who have accepted the lack of interest argument. . . .as the conservative story of choice, and to the one used by courts who have rejected that argument as the liberal story of coercion. . . .

The critical assumption that binds the two stories within a single interpretive universe is the assumption that women form stable job preferences, independently of employer action, in early social realms. In the conservative story, this assumption is accompanied by a naturalized, totalizing account of gender. Sex segregation exists because women are "feminine," and the feminine role is so all-encompassing that it implies by definition a preference for "feminine" work. In the liberal story of coercion, by contrast, the assumption that women's job preferences are fixed before they begin working means that gender difference must be suppressed. Liberal courts can justify holding employers liable only to the extent that judges can represent women as "ungendered" subjects who emerge from a gender-free social order with the same aspirations and values as men.

That these two stories constitute the entire interpretive universe creates problems for plaintiffs challenging sex segregation. By accepting the premise that only women who escape early sex-role socialization can aspire to nontraditional jobs, the liberal story reinforces the conservative one. By failing to develop an account of how employers create jobs and job aspirations along gendered lines, both stories ultimately assume away the major problem Title VII should be addressing: the organization of work structures and workplace cultures disempower large numbers of women from aspiring to and succeeding in more highly rewarded nontraditional work. . . .

. . . The partial truth of the conservative story is that people and jobs are gendered. But they are not naturally or inevitably so. To provide an adequate explanation for sex segregation, one must account for how employers arrange work systems so as to construct work and work aspirations along gendered lines. The liberal story fails to develop such an account because it shares the conservative assumption that women form their work preferences exclusively in early pre-work realms. This assumption, in turn, leads the liberal approach to adopt an overly restrictive view of the role Title VII can play in dismantling sex segregation in the workplace. If women have already formed their job preferences before seeking work, the most the law can do is to ensure that employers do not erect formal barriers to prevent women from realizing their pre-existing preferences.

There is a need for a new story to make sense of sex segregation in the workplace. Gender conditioning in pre-work realms is too slender a reed to sustain the weight of sex segregation. To explain sex segregation, the law needs an account of how employers actively construct gendered job aspirations—and jobs—in the workplace itself. . . .

The current judicial framework proceeds from the view that women bring to the labor market stable, fixed preferences for certain types of work. . . .

[This conviction] . . . depends on two different sets of assumptions. The first is the assumption that young women emerge from early life experiences articulating preferences for different types of work than young men. This assumption is correct. There is, however, nothing "natural" about the process through which young people

come to express gendered job aspirations. Girls and boys are regularly subjected to sex-role conditioning in the family, the schools, and other early realms of life; they are constantly bombarded with messages that link "femininity" or "masculinity" to sex-appropriate work. It is therefore unsurprising that numerous studies have documented sex differences in the vocational aspirations of children, adolescents, teenagers, and young adults.

This evidence alone, however, is insufficient to support the claim that workplace segregation exists because women have been socialized to prefer traditionally female jobs. . . .

Recent sociological research has demonstrated the weakness of this link. In his book *Revolving Doors*, sociologist Jerry Jacobs presents the most comprehensive quantitative analyses of these issues to date. Jacobs' research presents three propositions that refute the claim that workplace segregation is attributable to women's pre-labor market preferences. First, the sex-type of the work to which young women initially aspire does not remain stable over time, but changes substantially after they start working. For the more than eighty percent of young women who changed their aspirations between 1970 and 1980, the sexual composition of the occupation to which they aspired in 1970 was only very weakly associated with the sexual composition of the occupation to which they aspired ten years later. Second, the sex-type of the work to which young women initially aspire does not predict the sex-type of the work they do as their careers unfold. For the eighty percent of young women who changed occupations, the sexual composition of the occupations they said they desired in 1970 was not correlated with the sexual composition of the occupations they actually held in 1980. Third, the sex-type of women's early work does not predict the type of work they do later in life. For those who changed occupations, there was no correlation between the sexual composition of the occupations in which they began and the sexual composition of the occupations in which they were employed a decade later.

. . . Furthermore, not only young women change the sex-type of their occupations over time; older women do also. Mature women who move into nontraditional occupations mid-career are almost equally likely to move into them from male-dominated, female-dominated, and more sexually integrated occupations.

Taken together, Jacobs' analyses provide strong evidence that workplace segregation cannot be attributed solely to women's prelabor market preferences. Even if young women's early preferences perfectly predicted the sex-type of their first jobs, the sex-type of the occupations to which they aspire changes substantially over time. . . .

. . . Even if the main thrust of women's early training is to reward them for appropriate sex-role behavior, socialization is not a straitjacket that predetermines that adult women will aspire only to work defined by the dominant culture as feminine.

[Schultz next reviewed the results of sociological research bearing on career choice among women workers and concluded that] the sociological literature provides an alternative to the pre-labor market explanation for sex segregation in the workplace. This alternative perspective begins from the premise that people's work aspirations are shaped by their experiences in the workworld. It examines how structural features of work organizations reduce women's incentive to pursue nontraditional work and encourage them to display the very work attitudes and behavior that come to be viewed as preexisting gender attributes. . . .

This perspective sheds light on the workplace dynamics that limit women's ability to claim higher-paid nontraditional work as their own. Women's patterns of occupational movement suggest that there are powerful disincentives for women to move into and to remain in nontraditional occupations. The mobility studies show that women in higher-paying, male-dominated occupations are much less likely

to remain in such occupations over time than are women in lower-paying, female-dominated occupations, who are more likely to stay put. Thus, just as employers appear to have begun opening the doors to nontraditional jobs to women, almost as many women have been leaving those jobs as have been entering them. To the extent that women have been given the formal opportunity to do nontraditional work, something is preventing them from realizing that opportunity.

[This new] perspective instructs us to look beyond formal labor market opportunity and to ask what it is about the workplace itself that disempowers women from permanently seizing that opportunity. . . . [Schultz goes on to analyze] two structural features of work organizations that discourage women from pursuing nontraditional work. These two structural features interact dynamically to construct work and workers along gendered lines—the first on the "female" side and the second on the "male" side.

It is an old insight that people who are placed in jobs that offer little opportunity for growth or upward mobility will adapt to their situations by lowering their work aspirations and turning their energies elsewhere. Decades ago, researchers documented this phenomenon among male workers. Indeed, men in low-mobility positions display orientations toward work that conventional stereotypes reserve for women. . . .

While separate-but-unequal job structures encourage women to lower their work aspirations, they also imply that segregation is natural in a way that encourages male workers to adopt proprietary attitudes toward "their" jobs. These attitudes encapsulate male-dominated jobs in a web of social relations that are hostile and alienating to women who dare to upset the "natural" order of segregation. I refer to the entire bundle of practices and processes through which these relations are created and sustained as harassment. Overtly sexual behavior is only the tip of a tremendous iceberg that confronts women in nontraditional jobs. They face a wide-ranging set of behaviors and attitudes by their male supervisors and co-workers that make the culture of nontraditional work hostile and alienating. . . .

This analysis of the relationship between harassment and the "masculinity" of nontraditional work makes clear why many women are reluctant to apply for such work. Women understand that behind the symbolism of masculinized job descriptions lies a very real force: the power of men to harass, belittle, ostracize, dismiss, marginalize, discard, and just plain hurt them as workers. . . .

The legal system thus places women workers in a Catch-22 situation. Women are disempowered from pursuing or staying in higher-paid nontraditional jobs because of the hostile work cultures. The only real hope for making those work cultures more hospitable to women lies in dramatically increasing the proportion of women in those jobs. Eliminating those imbalances is, of course, what Title VII lawsuits challenging segregation promise. But when women workers bring these suits, too often the courts tell them that they are under-represented in non-traditional jobs not because the work culture is threatening or alienating, but rather because their own internalized sense of "femininity" has led them to avoid those jobs.

And so the cycle continues. A few women continue to move in and out the "revolving door," with little being done to stop them from being shoved back out almost as soon as they enter. The majority of working women stand by as silent witnesses, their failure to enter used to confirm that they "chose" all along to remain on the outside. There is no need for a sign on the door. Women understand that they enter at their own risk. . . .

I have elaborated a new account of the dynamics of job segregation in the hope of challenging—but also offering something positive to replace—the images of women and work that inform this fatalistic choice explanation. . . .

The central insight of the new account is that working women do not bring with them to the workworld fixed preferences for traditionally female or traditionally male work. Rather, the workplace is a central site of development for women's aspirations and identities as workers. In a very real sense, employers create women's job preferences. Once judges realize that women's preferences are unstable and always potentially in transition depending on work conditions, it will no longer do to imagine that women have a static set of "true" preferences independent of employer action that courts can discover as a factual matter and use to ground legal decision-making. Indeed, the notion that women have stable preferences for traditional or nontraditional work becomes a legal fiction that is plausible only by accepting as given the very structural features of the workplace that women seek to challenge through the lawsuit. . . .

STUDY QUESTIONS

1. What are the "lack of interest" and the "coercion" stories about why women workers tend to be concentrated in lower-paying occupations? What objections did Schultz raise to each of these explanations? Do you find her objections persuasive?

2. What story does she propose in their place? In this account, what factors inhibit women from moving out of female-intensive, lower-paying jobs? What factors encourage women to leave better-paying, male-intensive occupations? Might the presence of any of these factors constitute a violation of Title VII?

3. Review the cases of EEOC v. Brown & Root, Inc. and Price Waterhouse v. Hopkins in Chapter 3. Are these examples of what Professor Schultz refers to as "attitudes by [women's] male supervisors and co-workers that make the culture of nontraditional work hostile and alienating"? Why or why not?

According to the AAUW Educational Foundation's 2007 report, *Behind the Pay Gap*, occupational gender segregation is a leading contributor to the pay gap existence. Even when women choose majors such as mathematics, their choice of career can adversely affect their earning potential. A mathematics major who chooses a career in business or computer science will earn more than one who decides to teach. Women are also more likely than men to take positions in a nonprofit or local government agency, both of which pay less than forprofits or federal government jobs. The report posits that gender segregation in the classroom and in the workplace must be reduced in order to combat this situation. It suggests this can be accomplished by better integrating girls' education with women's career path, supporting mothers in the workplace, and ending discrimination. In the following selection, the authors consider the effects of the "Mommy Track."

WORKING WHILE MOTHER: THE MOMMY PENALTY

Evelyn F. Murphy with E. J. Graff

GETTING EVEN: Why Women Don't Get Paid Like

Men—And What to Do About It

New York: A Touchstone Book, Published by Simon & Schuster, 2005.

From Chapter 9, pp. 195, 199, 200-203, 205, 210–213.

. . . For the past ten years, public discussion about working women's careers has been shorthanded into a single phrase: the "mommy track." Women—especially those in high-end careers—are said to "choose" to drop out rather than run themselves to death on the gerbil wheel of corporate advancement. They'd rather oversee homework than head count. They'd rather take their children to piano lessons than take a meeting. This simplistic, outdated explanation is a media favorite, making it into the influential *New York Times Magazine* twice in recent years: once in 1998 and again (this time on its cover) in 2003. [footnote omitted] But is this how women themselves see the "mommy track"?

Perhaps some do—especially those with husbands so wealthy that, even if the marriage is one of the 49 percent that ends in divorce, the woman and her child are guaranteed a good cushion for years to come. But most of the women I've spoken to discovered that they had been "mommy-tracked" without being asked. When they got pregnant or had a child, these women found they were no longer considered for promotion—because, without asking, their manager automatically assumed that the new moms would soon be working part-time, would refuse to travel overnight, or would no longer show up reliably at important meetings. Or, when these women returned from maternity leave, they discovered that they were kept off important (read: promotion-track) projects, since managers assumed their "work-family conflict" would slow them down. And if they did ask to work part-time for awhile, their salaries and career possibilities were penalized far out of proportion to the time they put into their kids. When they returned to full-time work, their salaries were lower than when they'd left. . . .

Just Say the Words: The Mommy Penalty and the Daddy Bonus

. . . According to law professor Joan Williams, the mother stereotype gets triggered at three points in a woman's parental life. The first is when she tells her boss or others at work that she's pregnant. Her body soon becomes a constant reminder, triggering coworkers to stereotype her every move. What's more visibly and exaggeratedly female than that swollen belly (or, in a later phase, the expressed milk stored in the office fridge)? Pregnancy and nursing can both dramatically amplify otherwise latent stereotypes of women as overly emotional and irrational, arbitrary and whimsical, ruled by their (sexual) bodies rather than their minds. No wonder one study of female managers found that their performance ratings "plummeted" after their pregnancies started to show. [footnote omitted] And when a manager's performance ratings drop, so do her bonuses, raises, and promotions—which means that simply being visibly pregnant is costing her in real dollars and cents. "[M]ost women, like my wife, have enough stress in their lives just with being pregnant, so after being fired, they do not challenge an employer by filing a complaint with the EEOC," wrote law professor Samuel Joyner after his wife lost her job after letting it be known that she was pregnant. (footnoted omitted)

The second trigger moment for the mother stereotype comes when a woman returns from maternity leave. In chapters 5 and 8, there are stories in which women returned from maternity leave—only to find that, while they were out, they were laid off or their jobs were reorganized out of existence. That's illegal. Some women are so outraged that they sue. Remember, for instance, the state cop who took her employer to court because pregnant officers had been sidelined for no good reason. She and her fellow officers won that lawsuit. But most new mothers don't have the time, energy, or willingness to go into court, get a reputation as a troublemaker, and perhaps jeopardize their jobs.

The third moment comes when a mother asks for any accommodation, however temporary or slight, for her family responsibilities. That accommodation can be flextime, telecommuting, a temporary part-time schedule, or just two days of coming to work an hour late because, as happened to the journeywoman pile driver, the school required a parent's presence. Even if women aren't fired, they're sidelined and financially penalized far out of proportion to their time out.

Why? Because the American stereotype of mothering is left over from the 1950s: unlike a father, a mother is someone who is available to respond to her child at any moment of the day or night. If being a mom is a twenty-four-hour-a-day job and being a *worker* involves a full-time commitment to a job, too, the two roles are mutually exclusive. The insurance firm The Hartford, Inc., based in Connecticut, was sued when one manager said he wouldn't consider an employee for a promotion because, as he put it, "women are not good planners, especially women with kids," adding that women cannot be both good mothers and good workers, since "I don't see how you can do either job well." [footnote omitted] A comment like that is not just discriminatory; it reveals attitudes and behaviors that may be illegal and actionable. The Hartford settled the lawsuit.

But that manager's crude statement is useful, because it perfectly captures the double bind conveyed by the phrase "working mother." This label implies that if a worker so much as *thinks* about anything but the production line or the bottom line, he (yes, he) will be forever rendered useless on the job. A lawyer might be able to juggle the demands of many complex cases in various stages of research and negotiation, or a grocery manager might be able to juggle dozens of delivery deadlines and worker schedules—but should she have so much as a fleeting thought about a pediatrician's appointment, her on-the-job reliability will evaporate. In this way, the phrase "working mother" is heard as something similar to "deadbeat dad": both phrases suggest people who are not fulfilling their "God-given responsibilities." Such stereotypes click into place invisibly, the way carbon monoxide can poison a room without anyone noticing. And they hold back women's paychecks.

An entirely different stereotype kicks in for working fathers. A father at his desk is a serious, hardworking provider, a go-getter, a responsible breadwinner, a family man, a reliable guy. If he also tries to "help out" at home, he's exceptional and ought to be rewarded. Take the case of Illinois governor Rod Blagojevich, who, during a budget crisis in the fall of 2003, flew home every night (from Springfield, the state capital, to Chicago) to kiss his kids good night—on the taxpayers' tab. He took a little flak, but he didn't face anything like the vituperation spewed at Massachusetts Lieutenant Governor Jane Swift two years earlier, when she flew home across the state to see a sick child. Swift was eviscerated; Blagojevich was a good guy. "I wanted to go home and see my seven-year-old and kiss my baby," Blagojevich was quoted as saying. "If you're asking me if I'm guilty of that, I plead guilty. And I did it and that's what I'll continue to do." Can you imagine a woman saying such a thing and getting away with it? . . .

Working While Mother: Performance, Pay, and Promotion

. . . [S]imply because they are working while female, women are held to different (read: double) standards to get raises and recognition for top performance. When the mother stereotype *also* clicks into the boss's mind, women suddenly have that much more to overcome—and that much less likelihood of getting paid fairly. . . .

. . . Until now, our society has tackled these issues as questions of "work family" balance, as if women were making personal choices to be underpaid in order to be happy. But women who are now hitting the workforce know that that's not so, and they're outraged at getting shunted aside just because they have a child at home. An earlier generation of women, who were just entering the workforce, pushed the discussion of equality as far as they could. Fixing this illegal treatment of mothers as lesser workers is an essential part of getting women even.

It's essential—because all these women needed every penny they could bring home. Surely their bosses did not intend to force families to forgo music lessons, to get by on rice and beans instead of roast beef, or to skip contributing to Mom's retirement account in order to pay for braces. Those employers' stereotypes probably clicked in without reflection. And as we'll see in the next

section of this book, that's the problem: the failure to examine and flush out outdated stereotypes. Until we make sure that "working mother" is no longer heard as a synonym for "frazzled" and "unreliable," hardworking mothers (and their children) will continue to pay the price. [footnote omitted] And the wage gap will continue. . . .

The (Extra) Mommy Wage Gap

. . . Average together the paychecks of . . . all . . . women who are working while mothers, and then compare it to the average of all those full-time working men who've received their "daddy bonus." Here's what you find: mothers who work full-time earn only 60 cents to a working father's dollar. [footnote omitted]

Overall, working mothers earn 73 cents compared to the average male dollar. That means they're missing another 4 cents—money that's badly needed by their families. [footnote omitted] Imagine the hardship divorced moms face: trying to pay for rent, food, child care, and clothing with that much less in every dollar to cover these basics.

The "mommy wage gap" is commonly accepted by women and men alike as the price women pay for juggling their work and family responsibilities. A whole consulting industry has grown up in the last dozen years to help companies design "family-friendly" benefits for their employees. The hitch is, with rare exceptions, that only women use these. Men know that they're just too costly in real wages; taking the "family-friendly" track would disproportionately hold back their careers.

Over the last twenty years or so, social scientists have tested their favorite theories about why working mothers earn much less than other working women. Their theories are based on their own assumptions about how working moms should reasonably behave. For instance, they presume that mothers choose less demanding (read: lower-paying) work so that they have more energy for their family responsibilities. Or they propose that women choose to drop in and out of the workforce to have children,

gender roles still present in division of work

setting back their experience and seniority. Or that mothers choose to earn less than their husbands, because the pair has sensibly divided up work and family responsibilities, assigning him to bring in the higher paycheck while she brings in the groceries and laundry. Or that mothers choose flexible hours instead of higher pay. All these assume that women knowingly set themselves back financially in order to be mothers.

But is it so? Or are working mothers coerced-forced off the job when they get pregnant, treated as if they've had a lobotomy when they come back from maternity leave, condescended to insultingly no matter how well they perform, passed over for promotion without being told? Their "choices" are so bad as to fail to be real choices at all.

If there's a choice to be made, *the working mother* is the person who should make the choice. Ask yourself or ask a few working mothers you know whether their dollars-and-cents options were laid out to them fairly or they simply realized one day that they'd been financially mommy-tracked. Too often, bosses unilaterally—and patronizingly—decide to "accommodate" mothers instead of paying them equally. Women's wallets suffer as a result.

Sometimes employers, supervisors, or managers think that paying mothers less is fair because those moms just aren't putting in the time at work that it takes to get ahead. Don't believe it. Time at work is falsely considered a proxy for ambition and dedication. Some men put in extra hours just for others to notice. This overtime may not be especially productive. Maybe a man will drop by the boss's office at the end of the day or go out for a drink after hours with colleagues—in theory to "discuss work" but in practice just to socialize. Maybe he'll return a low-priority telephone call after hours (since important ones would have been returned during the workday). Maybe he'll

just stop by another over-timer's office to commiserate about their awful work hours.

Rather than hang around at work late to be seen, many women take work home. They may leave the office precisely at 5:00 or 6:00 to pick up the dry cleaning, shop for groceries, pick up children, and cook dinner—while returning phone calls on the way. Then, after the kids are in bed, they'll pull out the computer and finish a spreadsheet, catch up on e-mail, or finalize a report. Maybe they'll even have *more* measurable productivity than the guys, as happened to the lawyer who wasn't put up for partner even though she had more billable hours than her male colleague. But even extremely hardworking moms lose "credit" because they're not hanging around after hours—the kind of credit that registers in the boss's mind as round-the-clock dedication—even if they are actually contributing more to the bottom line. If pay and promotion decisions are being made subjectively, based on "gut instinct"—the famous "tap on the shoulder" method—guess who will be paid more?

. . . Employers make a host of everyday decisions based on their "instinctive"—read "stereotypical" and often "discriminatory"—notions of what mothers can and cannot do. All those biased decisions take a financial toll on working mothers. That's the mommy wage gap.

STUDY QUESTIONS

1. What is the "mommy track"? What is the "mommy penalty"? What is the "mommy wage gap"? How are these related?
2. What is the "mother stereotype"? When, according to Professor Joan Williams, in a woman's parental life is this stereotype triggered? Why?
3. How, according to Murphy and Graff, are fathers stereotyped? What effect do the mother and father stereotypes have on women's and men's careers?

Within two years after *Getting Even* was published, some major business journals reported on "the new mommy track." According to these publications, some employers now offer their female employees a variety of services to help them transition back into the workforce from maternity leave. These include flexible work schedules, private lactation rooms, on-site day care facilities, and opportunities to work from home. Although these accommodations do help women return to and remain in the workforce after having a child, the number of companies providing such support is small. And, not every company offers the complete array of services. While the existence of flexible schedules and on-site support services do make working easier for mothers, the effects of the "mommy track," "mommy penalty," and "mommy wage gap" will continue to be felt until this type of support becomes the norm in the workplace.

III. BENEFITS

Family and Medical Leave Act

The Family and Medical Leave Act (FMLA) was enacted in 1993. The FMLA applies to all public agencies, including state, local, and federal employers, local schools, and private-sector employers who employ fifty or more employees within seventy-five miles of the worksite. The statute states that a covered employer must grant an eligible employee (an employee who has been employed by the employer at least twelve months—not consecutive—and worked at least 1,250 hours during the twelve-month period) up to a total of twelve workweeks of *unpaid* leave during any twelve-month period for one of the following reasons: the birth or care of the employee's newborn, newly adopted, or newly placed foster child; the care of the employee's spouse, child, or parent who has a serious health condition; because the employee is unable to work because of a serious health condition; or for qualifying exigencies arising because the employee's spouse, son, daughter, or parent is on active duty or called to active duty status as a member of the National Guard or Reserves in support of a contingency operation. Although FMLA leave is unpaid, the statute provides that employees may take, or employers may require employees to take, any accrued paid vacation, personal, family or medical or sick leave, as permitted by the employer's normal leave policy, concurrently with FMLA leave. A new Department of Labor (DOL) Wage and Hour Division Final Rule, effective January 16, 2009, clarifies that all forms of paid leave offered by an employer (including generic "paid time off") are to be treated the same regardless of which type of paid leave is substituted for unpaid FMLA leave; however, an employee is always entitled to unpaid FMLA leave if she does not meet the employer's requirements for taking paid leave, and an employer may waive any procedural requirement for taking any type of paid leave.

The one impediment to utilizing FMLA leave is that this leave is unpaid. Many workers cannot afford to take leave that is not paid or partially paid. According to a report summarizing a meeting co-hosted by the Institute for Women's Policy Research and the Institute of Industrial relations of the University of California Berkeley in March of 2002, most workers who use FMLA leave (66 percent) receive some pay during their leave (be it paid sick, vacation, personal, or parental leave, temporary disability insurance, or other benefits); however, millions of other workers either cannot afford to take FMLA leave or have difficulty meeting their financial obligations while on leave without full pay (*Estimating the Benefits of Paid Family and Medical Leave: A Colloquium Report*, Vicky Lovell, PhD).

The ability to balance work and family is one of the greatest challenges facing people today. Studies show that there is a disparate impact on women as women continue to be the primary caretakers of children and, now more recently, of elderly parents. FMLA relieves some of the burden; however, many people cannot access the benefit because they cannot afford to take unpaid leave. In 2000 the DOL conducted surveys on the family and medical leave experiences of employees and employers in that year, seven years after the enactment of the FMLA. According to the survey of employees, more than half the leave-takers were concerned about not having sufficient funds to pay bills. Overall, about one-third of the leave-takers received no pay during their FMLA leave: 37.5 percent of the women leave-takers, as compared to 29.6 percent of the men. To date, three states have enacted laws aimed at filling the gap left by the FMLA and similar state laws that allow employees to take unpaid leave to care for a child or permitted family member. California's law has been in effect since 2004. In 2007 Washington became the second state to pass such a law; it will go into effect in October of 2009. And, under New Jersey's law, which was passed in 2008, benefits became available after July 1, 2009. California and New Jersey provide partial pay for time off to care for a seriously ill child, parent, spouse, or domestic partner (New Jersey also covers care for a civil union partner), or to bond with a new child. Washington's law applies only to parental leave. And, on June 5, 2009, the U.S. House of Representatives voted in favor of the Federal Paid Parental Leave Act, which will provide four weeks of paid parental leave to federal employees after the birth or adoption of a child. If the Senate approves the bill, President Obama is expected to sign it into law. Perhaps these actions are harbingers of change for the United States, which has lagged behind other countries in terms of providing financial support for parental leave.

Pregnancy Discrimination Act of 1978

As stated in Chapter 3, the Pregnancy Discrimination Act (PDA) amended Title VII to include within the meaning of "sex" pregnancy, childbirth, and pregnancy-related medical conditions. This amendment was enacted to reverse the effect of the Supreme Court's decision in *General Electric. v. Gilbert*, 429 U.S. 125 (1976), which held a disability plan that did not cover pregnancy did not violate Title VII, and to ensure that employers would not treat pregnancy leaves different from other disability leaves. Unfortunately, Congress did not make the PDA retroactive and now the impact of that decision is being felt.

In *AT&T Corp. v. Hulteen, et al*, No. 07-543 (May 18, 2009), the Supreme Court considered the issue of whether an employer violates the PDA when it pays pension benefits calculated in part under an accrual rule, applied only prior to the PDA, that gave less credit for pregnancy leave than for other medical leave. The Court held that there was no violation because the benefit calculation rule was part of a *bona fide* seniority system under Title VII, which insulates it from challenge. In this case, AT&T employees on "disability" leave in the 1960s and early to mid-1970s were given full credit for the entire period of absence, while employees who took "personal" leave received a maximum service credit of thirty days. Leave for pregnancy was treated as personal, not disability until AT&T adopted its Maternity Payment Plan (MPP) in 1977. The MPP entitled pregnant employees to disability benefits and service credit for up to six weeks of leave, but any absence after that was treated as personal leave for which there were no benefits or credit. Employees on disability continued to receive full-service credit for the entire absence. After the PDA was passed, AT&T adopted its Anticipated Disability Plan, which replaced the MPP and provided service credit for pregnancy leave on the same basis as leave for other temporary disabilities. AT&T did not make any retroactive adjustments to service credit calculation for female employees who had been subjected to pre-PDA personnel policies. Four women employees who had received less service credit for pregnancy than would have accrued for disability and their union filed charges with the EEOC alleging discrimination on the basis of sex and pregnancy in violation of Title VII. The EEOC issued a Letter of Determination finding reasonable cause to believe AT&T had discriminated against Hulteen and a "class of other similarly-situated female employees," and issued a notice of right to sue for the four women and the union. A suit was brought in the U.S. District Court for the Northern District of California. Both sides filed summary judgment motions and the Court found it was bound by a Ninth Circuit decision that found a Title VII violation where post-PDA retirement eligibility calculations incorporated pre-PDA accrual rules that differentiated on the basis of pregnancy. Because the Ninth Circuit's decision was in direct conflict with holdings in two other circuits, the Supreme Court granted certiorari to resolve the split and held the women did not have the right to sue. As a result of this decision, the women retires will bear the brunt of the employer's pre-PDA differentiation on the basis of pregnancy in their retirement checks.

Same-Sex Benefits

As we will learn in Chapter 6, the definition of what constitutes a family is expanding from the original concept of a heterosexual nuclear family. The recognition of domestic partnerships, civil unions, and same-sex marriages, whether done legally or voluntarily, is affecting the provision of benefits in employment. Federal law neither prohibits nor requires that private-sector employers offer benefits to domestic partners, so the decision by private-sector employers to offer or not offer domestic partner benefits is voluntary. In its *State of the Workplace Report*, the Human Rights Campaign Foundation, a gay, lesbian, bisexual, and transgendered civil rights organization, reported that 83 percent of *Fortune* 100, 57 percent of *Fortune* 500, and 39 percent of *Fortune* 1,000 companies offered domestic partner benefits in 2008.

Because there is no uniform legal standard in the fifty states governing recognition of same-sex relationships, there is no one legal standard regarding the provision of same-sex benefits in state or municipal employment. A few states have faced this issue through litigation, but these decisions' reach is limited to their respective states. And, while some states voluntarily afford such benefits, others have moved to prohibit them. For example, in *National Pride at Work, Inc. v. Governor of Michigan*, 748 N.W.2d 524 (Mich. 2008), the Michigan Supreme Court considered the issue of whether the state's marriage amendment, which states "the union of one man and one woman in marriage shall be the only agreement recognized as a marriage or similar union for any purpose," prohibited public employers from providing health insurance benefits to their employees' qualified same-sex domestic partners. The court, in a 5–2 decision, held that providing these benefits violates the language of Michigan's marriage amendment. And, in Arizona, legislators have included a provision in the proposed state budget that legally defines "dependents" of state employees who are entitled to insurance coverage as a spouse or a child younger than 19, or younger than 23 if a full-time student. This would override regulations adopted in 2008 that added domestic partners and their children to those eligible for this insurance.

Currently, six states recognize same-sex marriage: Massachusetts (2006); Connecticut (2008); Iowa (2009); Vermont (2009); Maine (2009); and New Hampshire (2009). And, Canada, our contiguous neighbor to the north, also recognizes same-sex marriage. What happens, then, when couples legally married in another state or country, seek the protection afforded by employment benefits in a state where same-sex marriage is not performed? The following case considers this issue.

MARTINEZ V. COUNTY OF MONROE

N.Y. App. Div., 4th Dept., 2008.
50 A.D.3d 189, 850 N.Y.S.2d 740

Opinion by PERADOTTO, J.

On July 5, 2004, plaintiff, an employee of defendant Monroe Community College (MCC), married her same-sex partner, Lisa Ann Golden, in the Province of Ontario, Canada. Defendants do not dispute that the marriage is valid under the laws of Canada and the Province of Ontario. On the basis of that marriage, plaintiff applied to MCC on July 7, 2004 for spousal health care benefits for Golden. MCC admittedly provided health care benefits for the opposite-sex spouses of its employees. On November 24, 2004, defendant MCC Director of Human Resources Sherry Ralston denied plaintiff's application for spousal health care benefits.

Plaintiff commenced this action seeking, inter alia, a declaration that defendants' failure to recognize her marriage for purposes of her spousal health care benefits application violated her rights under the Equal Protection Clause of the New York State Constitution and Executive Law § 296 and damages incurred as a result of those violations. Defendants moved for summary judgment dismissing the first amended complaint, and plaintiff cross-moved for partial summary judgment on the first amended complaint. Supreme Court granted defendants' motion to the extent of granting judgment in favor of defendants declaring that plaintiff's marriage is not entitled to recognition in New York and that defendants did not violate the Equal Protection Clause or Executive Law § 296 in refusing to recognize plaintiff's marriage for the purposes of plaintiff's application for spousal health care benefits. On appeal, plaintiff contends that her valid Canadian marriage is entitled to recognition in New York. We agree.

II

For well over a century, New York has recognized marriages solemnized outside of New York unless they fall into two categories of exception: (1) marriage, the recognition of which is prohibited by the "positive law" of New York and (2) marriages involving incest or polygamy, both of which fall within the prohibitions of "natural law" (citations omitted). Thus, if a marriage is valid in the place where it was entered, "it is to be recognized as such in the courts of this State, unless contrary to the prohibitions of natural law or the express prohibitions of a statute" (citations omitted). Under that "marriage-recognition" rule, New York has recognized a marriage between an uncle and his niece "by the half blood" (citation omitted), common-law marriages valid under the laws of other states (citation omitted), a marriage valid under the law of the Province of Ontario, Canada of a man and a woman both under the age of 18 (citation omitted), and a "proxy marriage" valid in the District of Columbia (citation omitted), all of which would have been invalid if solemnized in New York.

We conclude that plaintiff's marriage does not fall within either of the two exceptions to the marriage-recognition rule. "[A]bsent any New York statute expressing clearly the Legislature's intent to regulate within this State marriages of its domiciliaries solemnized abroad, there is no positive law in this jurisdiction" to prohibit recognition of a marriage that would have been invalid if solemnized in New York (citations omitted). The Legislature has not enacted legislation to prohibit the recognition of same-sex marriages validly entered into outside of New York, and we thus conclude that the positive law exception to the general rule of foreign marriage recognition is not applicable in this case.

The natural law exception also is not applicable. That exception has generally been limited to marriages involving polygamy or incest or marriages "offensive to the public sense of morality to a degree regarded generally with abhorrence" (citation omitted), and that cannot be said here.

Defendants nevertheless contend that recognition of plaintiff's same-sex marriage is contrary to the public policy of New York, as articulated by the Court of Appeals in *Hernandez v. Robles*, 7 N.Y.3d 338, 821 N.Y.S.2d 770, 855 N.E.2d 1, and thus falls within an exception to the rule requiring recognition of valid foreign marriages. We reject that contention. Hernandez does not articulate the public policy for which it is cited by defendants, but instead holds merely that the New York State Constitution does not compel recognition of same-sex marriages solemnized in New York (citation omitted). The Court of Appeals noted that the Legislature may enact legislation recognizing same-sex marriages (citation omitted) and, in our view, the Court of Appeals thereby indicated that the recognition of plaintiff's marriage is not against the public policy of New York. It is also worth noting that, unlike the overwhelming majority of states, New York has not chosen, pursuant to the federal Defense of Marriage Act (28 USC § 1738C), to enact legislation denying full faith and credit to same-sex marriages validly solemnized in another state.

Thus, we conclude that plaintiff's marriage to Golden, valid in the Province of Ontario, Canada, is entitled to recognition in New York in the absence of express legislation to the contrary. As the Court of Appeals indicated in Hernandez, the place for the expression of the public policy of New York is in the Legislature, not the courts (citation omitted). The Legislature may decide to prohibit the recognition of same-sex marriages solemnized abroad. Until it does so, however, such marriages are entitled to recognition in New York.

III

Having concluded that plaintiff's marriage to Golden is entitled to recognition in New York, we further conclude that, by refusing to recognize plaintiff's valid Canadian marriage, defendants violated Executive Law § 296(1)(a), which forbids an employer from discriminating against an employee "in compensation or in terms, conditions or privileges of employment" because of the employee's sexual orientation. Defendants' contention that the discrimination to which plaintiff was subject is based not on her sexual orientation but on her marital status is circular in its reasoning. The sole reason for defendants' rejection of the marital status of plaintiff is her sexual orientation, and defendants thus violated Executive Law § 296(1)(a). In light of our decision, we need not, and do not, consider plaintiff's contention that defendants also violated the Equal Protection Clause of the New York State Constitution (citations omitted).

IV

. . .

V

. . . Accordingly, we conclude that the judgment should be reversed, defendants' motion for summary judgment denied in its entirety, plaintiff's cross motion for partial summary judgment granted in part, and judgment granted in favor of plaintiff declaring that plaintiff's marriage to Lisa Ann Golden in the Province of Ontario, Canada is entitled to recognition in New York.

STUDY QUESTIONS

1. What are the two exceptions to New York State recognition of "foreign" marriages? Why did plaintiff's marriage not fall within either exception?
2. On what basis did the Appellate Division determine that recognizing plaintiff's marriage was not contrary to public policy? Why was it important that New York had not enacted legislation pursuant to the federal Defense of Marriage Act?

3. What is meant by "full faith and credit"? What would have convinced the Appellate Division not to extend full faith and credit to plaintiff's Canadian same-sex marriage?

4. What was the plaintiff ultimately seeking in this case? How would recognition of her Canadian same-sex marriage assist her in achieving the result she sought?

IV. AFFIRMATIVE ACTION

We previously saw that much, if not most, of the disparity between the earnings of women and men workers results from occupational segregation. Two strategies have been used over the past two decades to lessen the impact of occupational segregation on the earnings of women. One, comparable worth, was specifically fashioned for this purpose. It aimed at increasing the earnings of workers in female-intensive occupations. Supporters of the comparable worth theory argued that women whose jobs are different or distinct from the jobs performed by male employees should be compensated on a comparable basis with those male employees if the women's jobs are of comparable worth/value to their employer. The other, affirmative action, was fashioned for other purposes, but has its applications in this context as well. Here it is used to promote outward mobility from the "pink-collar ghetto." Because the comparable worth theory has not been accepted by the courts (see, for example, *AFSCME v. Washington*, 770 F.2d 1401 (9th Cir. 1985)), the viability of affirmative action has once again come into focus.

Affirmative action is a technical legal expression with a long history in the labor law of the early years of the twentieth century. In general, affirmative action consists of extra steps taken to ensure that a legally required result is actually produced. In ordinary terms, one takes affirmative action when one "goes the extra mile" to ensure that, for example, equal employment opportunities are available to all employees. Under this concept, employers would remedy discriminatory practices in the hiring of non-whites and women. Affirmative action plans (AAPs) were designed to eradicate existing and continuing discrimination, eliminate any effects of past discrimination, and prevent future discrimination. In order to effectively combat a history of racism and sexism, employers would give special consideration to minorities and women.

When Title VII went into effect in 1965, President Lyndon B. Johnson signed the first executive order requiring businesses that had contracts with the federal government to implement affirmative action by hiring and promoting racial minorities. Women were not covered by this executive order. Two years later, President Johnson amended his order to require that businesses with federal contracts include women in their AAPs.

In its 1971 decision in *Griggs v. Duke Power Co.*, set out in more detail in Chapter 3, the Supreme Court enunciated its position on discriminatory preferences and Title VII. It stated that Congress's intent in enacting Title VII was to "achieve equality of employment opportunities and remove barriers" that had favored white employees over others. The Supreme Court recognized, however, that Congress did not intend Title VII to "guarantee a job to every person regardless of qualifications." The Court stated that:

> [Title VII] does not command that any person be hired simply because he was formerly the subject of discrimination, or because he is a member of a minority group. Discriminatory preference for any group, minority or majority, is precisely and only what Congress has proscribed. What is required by Congress is the removal of artificial, arbitrary, and unnecessary barriers to employment when the barriers operate invidiously to discriminate on the basis of racial or other impermissible classification.

During the period from the late 1970s through the 1980s, the Supreme Court endorsed the use of affirmative action remedies in Title VII contexts. In *United Steel Workers v. Weber,* 443 U.S. 193 (1979), the Court held that Title VII permits private employers who have not been found to have violated the act to adopt voluntary race-conscious AAPs to eliminate a manifest racial imbalance in traditionally segregated job categories. The Supreme Court considered the same issue with respect to public employers in *Johnson v. Transportation Agency, Santa Clara City,* 480 U.S. 616 (1987), the first affirmative action case to involve gender. In that case, the Supreme Court held that the county's AAP, which allowed the agency to remedy the "manifest imbalance" of men and women in "traditionally segregated job categories," was legal.

Up through the mid-1990s, the Supreme Court debated the applicable standard for considering constitutional challenges to AAPs using race. The decision in *Adarand Constructors, Inc. v. Peña,* 515 U.S. 200 (1995) put that matter to rest; the Court, in a 5–4 decision, held that strict scrutiny is the appropriate standard for assessing all government AAPs based on race, including "benign" classifications. The federal or state entity defending against an equal protection challenge must, therefore, demonstrate that the AAP is narrowly tailored to serve a compelling governmental interest.

In 2003, the Supreme Court was provided with an opportunity to both address the use of affirmative action in higher education (the first time since its decision in *University of California Bd. of Regents v. Bakke,* 438 U.S. 265 (1978)) and apply the strict scrutiny standard enunciated in *Adarand.* This opportunity was presented through two cases involving two different programs at the University of Michigan: *Grutter v. Bollinger* concerned a challenge to the law school's admissions program, while *Gratz v. Bollinger* dealt with a challenged undergraduate admissions program. In both cases, the university asserted that its admission policies were aimed at achieving a diverse student body including a wide range of social, ethnic, and racial backgrounds. The opponents in both cases argued that this was not a compelling interest. In the law school case, the Court held that the use of race in admission decisions was constitutional; the admissions program furthered the compelling interest in obtaining educational benefits from a diverse student body and was narrowly tailored. *Grutter v. Bollinger,* 539 U.S. 306 (2003). In the undergraduate case, the Court rejected the argument that diversity cannot constitute a compelling state interest, but found that the admissions policy was not narrowly tailored to achieve educational diversity. *Gratz v. Bollinger,* 539 U.S. 244 (2003). As you read the excerpts from the *Grutter* Opinion, consider the law school's race-conscious admissions program in the context of the Court's discussion of quotas, "plus" factors, and race-neutral criteria.

Grutter v. Bollinger
United States Supreme Court, 539 U.S. 306 (2003).

Justice O'CONNOR delivered the Opinion of the Court.

This case requires us to decide whether the use of race as a factor in student admissions by the University of Michigan Law School (Law School) is unlawful.

I

A

. . .

I

B

. . . We granted certiorari, 537 U.S. 1043 (2002), to resolve the disagreement among the Courts of Appeals on a question of national importance: Whether diversity is a compelling interest that can justify the narrowly tailored use of race in selecting applicants for admission to public universities. Compare *Hopwood v. Texas*, 78 F. 3d 932 (CA5 1996) (*Hopwood* I) (holding that diversity is not a compelling state interest), with *Smith v. University of Wash. Law School*, 233 F. 3d 1188 (CA9 2000) (holding that it is).

II

A

We last addressed the use of race in public higher education over 25 years ago. In the landmark *Bakke* case, we reviewed a racial set-aside program that reserved 16 out of 100 seats in a medical school class for members of certain minority groups. 438 U.S. 265 (1978). The decision produced six separate opinions, none of which commanded a majority of the Court. Four Justices would have upheld the program against all attack on the ground that the government can use race to "remedy disadvantages cast on minorities by past racial prejudice." *Id.*, at 325 (joint opinion of Brennan, White, Marshall, and Blackmun, JJ., concurring in judgment

in part and dissenting in part). Four other Justices avoided the constitutional question altogether and struck down the program on statutory grounds. *Id.*, at 408 (opinion of STEVENS, J., joined by Burger, C. J., and Stewart and REHNQUIST, JJ., concurring in judgment in part and dissenting in part). Justice Powell provided a fifth vote not only for invalidating the set-aside program, but also for reversing the state court's injunction against any use of race whatsoever. The only holding for the Court in *Bakke* was that a "State has a substantial interest that legitimately may be served by a properly devised admissions program involving the competitive consideration of race and ethnic origin." *Id.*, at 320. Thus, we reversed that part of the lower court's judgment that enjoined the university "from any consideration of the race of any applicant." *Ibid.*

Since this Court's splintered decision in *Bakke*, Justice Powell's opinion announcing the judgment of the Court has served as the touchstone for constitutional analysis of race-conscious admissions policies. Public and private universities across the Nation have modeled their own admissions programs on Justice Powell's views on permissible race-conscious policies. . . . For the reasons set out below, today we endorse Justice Powell's view that student body diversity is a compelling state interest that can justify the use of race in university admissions.

B

The Equal Protection Clause provides that no State shall "deny to any person within its jurisdiction the equal protection of the laws." U.S. Const., Amdt. 14, §2. Because the Fourteenth Amendment "protect[s] *persons, not groups*," all "governmental action based on race—a *group* classification long recognized as in most circumstances irrelevant and therefore prohibited—should be subjected to detailed judicial inquiry to ensure that the *personal* right to equal protection of the laws has not been infringed." *Adarand Constructors, Inc. v. Peña*, 515 U.S. 200, 227 (1995) (emphasis in original; internal quotation marks and citation omitted). We are a "free people whose institutions are founded upon the doctrine of equality." *Loving v. Virginia*, 388 U.S. 1, 11 (1967) (internal quotation marks and citation omitted). It follows from that principle that "government may treat people differently because of their race only for the most compelling reasons." *Adarand Constructors, Inc. v. Peña*, 515 U.S., at 227.

We have held that all racial classifications imposed by government "must be analyzed by a reviewing court under strict scrutiny." *Ibid.* This means that such classifications are constitutional only if they are narrowly tailored to further compelling governmental interests. "Absent searching judicial inquiry into the justification for such race-based measures," we have no way to determine what "classifications are 'benign' or 'remedial' and what classifications are in fact motivated by illegitimate notions of racial inferiority or simple racial politics." *Richmond v. J. A. Croson Co.*, 488 U.S. 469, 493 (1989) (plurality opinion). We apply strict scrutiny to all racial classifications to " 'smoke out' illegitimate uses of race by assuring that [government] is pursuing a goal important enough to warrant use of a highly suspect tool." *Ibid.*

Strict scrutiny is not "strict in theory, but fatal in fact." *Adarand Constructors, Inc. v. Peña, supra*, at 237 (internal quotation marks and citation omitted). Although all governmental uses of race are subject to strict scrutiny, not all are invalidated by it. As we have explained, "whenever the government treats any person unequally because of his or her race, that person has suffered an injury that falls squarely within the language and spirit of the Constitution's guarantee of equal protection." 515 U.S., at 229–230. But that observation "says nothing about the ultimate validity of any particular law; that determination is the job of the court applying strict scrutiny." *Id.*, at 230. When race-based action is necessary to further a compelling governmental interest, such action does not violate the constitutional guarantee of equal protection so long as the narrow-tailoring requirement is also satisfied.

Context matters when reviewing race-based governmental action under the Equal Protection Clause. See *Gomillion v. Lightfoot*, 364 U.S. 339, 343–344 (1960) (admonishing that, "in dealing with claims under broad provisions of the Constitution, which derive content by an interpretive process of inclusion and exclusion, it is imperative that generalizations, based on and qualified by the concrete situations that gave rise to them, must not be applied out of context in disregard of variant controlling facts"). In *Adarand Constructors, Inc. v. Peña*, we made clear that strict scrutiny must take " 'relevant differences' into account." 515 U.S., at 228. Indeed, as we explained, that is its "fundamental purpose." *Ibid.* Not every decision influenced by race is equally objectionable and strict scrutiny is designed to provide a framework for carefully examining the importance and the sincerity of the reasons advanced by the governmental decisionmaker for the use of race in that particular context.

III

A

With these principles in mind, we turn to the question whether the Law School's use of race is justified by a compelling state interest. Before this Court, as they have throughout this litigation, respondents assert only one justification for their use of race in the admissions process: obtaining "the educational benefits that flow from a diverse student body." Brief for Respondents Bollinger et al. i. In other words, the Law School asks us to recognize, in the context of higher education, a compelling state interest in student body diversity.

We first wish to dispel the notion that the Law School's argument has been foreclosed, either expressly or implicitly, by our affirmative-action cases decided since *Bakke*. It is true that some language in those opinions might be read to suggest that remedying past discrimination is the only permissible justification for race-based governmental action. See, e.g., *Richmond v. J. A. Croson Co., supra*, at 493 (plurality opinion) (stating that unless classifications based on race are "strictly reserved for remedial settings, they may in fact promote notions of racial inferiority and lead to a politics of racial hostility"). But we have never held that the only governmental use of race that can survive strict scrutiny is remedying past discrimination. Nor, since *Bakke*, have we directly addressed the use of race in the context of public higher education. Today, we hold that the Law School has a compelling interest in attaining a diverse student body.

The Law School's educational judgment that such diversity is essential to its educational mission is one to which we defer. The Law School's assessment that diversity will, in fact, yield educational benefits is substantiated by respondents and their *amici*. Our scrutiny of the interest asserted by the Law School is no less strict for taking into account complex educational judgments in an area that lies primarily within the expertise of the university. Our holding today is in keeping with our tradition of giving a degree of deference to a university's academic decisions, within constitutionally prescribed limits [citations omitted].

. . . We have repeatedly acknowledged the overriding importance of preparing students for work and citizenship, describing education as pivotal to "sustaining our political and cultural heritage" with a fundamental role in maintaining the fabric of society. *Plyler v. Doe*, 457 U.S. 202, 221 (1982). This Court has long recognized that "education . . . is the very foundation of good citizenship." *Brown v. Board of Education*, 347 U.S. 483, 493 (1954). For this reason, the diffusion of knowledge and opportunity through public institutions of higher education must be accessible to all individuals regardless of race or ethnicity. The United States, as *amicus curiae*, affirms that "[e]nsuring that public institutions are open and available to all segments of American society, including people of all races and

ethnicities, represents a paramount government objective." Brief for United States as *Amicus Curiae* 13. And, "[n]owhere is the importance of such openness more acute than in the context of higher education." *Ibid.* Effective participation by members of all racial and ethnic groups in the civic life of our Nation is essential if the dream of one Nation, indivisible, is to be realized. . . .

B

Even in the limited circumstance when drawing racial distinctions is permissible to further a compelling state interest, government is still "constrained in how it may pursue that end: [T]he means chosen to accomplish the [government's] asserted purpose must be specifically and narrowly framed to accomplish that purpose." *Shaw v. Hunt*, 517 U.S. 899, 908 (1996) (internal quotation marks and citation omitted). The purpose of the narrow tailoring requirement is to ensure that "the means chosen 'fit' . . . th[e] compelling goal so closely that there is little or no possibility that the motive for the classification was illegitimate racial prejudice or stereotype." *Richmond v. J. A. Croson Co.*, 488 U.S., at 493 (plurality opinion).

Since *Bakke*, we have had no occasion to define the contours of the narrow-tailoring inquiry with respect to race-conscious university admissions programs. That inquiry must be calibrated to fit the distinct issues raised by the use of race to achieve student body diversity in public higher education. Contrary to JUSTICE KENNEDY's assertions, we do not "abandon[] strict scrutiny," see *post*, at 8 (dissenting opinion). Rather, as we have already explained, *ante*, at 15, we adhere to *Adarand*'s teaching that the very purpose of strict scrutiny is to take such "relevant differences into account." 515 U.S., at 228 (internal quotation marks omitted).

To be narrowly tailored, a race-conscious admissions program cannot use a quota system—it cannot "insulat[e] each category of applicants with certain desired qualifications from competition with all other applicants." *Bakke, supra*, at 315 (opinion of Powell, J.). Instead, a university may consider race or ethnicity only as a " 'plus' in a particular applicant's file," without "insulat[ing] the individual from comparison with all other candidates for the available seats." *Id.*, at 317. In other words, an admissions program must be "flexible enough to consider all pertinent elements of diversity in light of the particular qualifications of each applicant, and to place them on the same footing for consideration, although not necessarily according them the same weight." *Ibid.*

We find that the Law School's admissions program bears the hallmarks of a narrowly tailored plan. . . .

. . . Properly understood, a "quota" is a program in which a certain fixed number or proportion of opportunities are "reserved exclusively for certain minority groups." *Richmond v. J. A. Croson Co., supra,* at 496 (plurality opinion). Quotas " 'impose a fixed number or percentage which must be attained, or which cannot be exceeded,' " *Sheet Metal Workers v. EEOC,* 478 U.S. 421, 495 (1986) (O'CONNOR, J., concurring in part and dissenting in part), and "insulate the individual from comparison with all other candidates for the available seats." *Bakke, supra,* at 317 (opinion of Powell, J.). In contrast, "a permissible goal . . . require[s] only a good-faith effort . . . to come within a range demarcated by the goal itself," *Sheet Metal Workers v. EEOC, supra,* at 495, and permits consideration of race as a "plus" factor in any given case while still ensuring that each candidate "compete[s] with all other qualified applicants," *Johnson v. Transportation Agency, Santa Clara Cty.,* 480 U.S. 616, 638 (1987).

. . . The Law School's goal of attaining a critical mass of underrepresented minority students does not transform its program into a quota. . . . " [S]ome attention to numbers," without more, does not transform a flexible admissions system into a rigid quota. . . .

That a race-conscious admissions program does not operate as a quota does not, by itself, satisfy the requirement of individualized consideration. When using race as a "plus" factor in university admissions, a university's admissions program must remain flexible enough to ensure that each applicant is evaluated as an individual and not in a way that makes an applicant's race or ethnicity the defining feature of his or her application. The importance of this individualized consideration in the context of a race-conscious admissions program is paramount. See *Bakke, supra,* at 318, n. 52 (opinion of Powell, J.) (identifying the "denial . . . of th[e] right to individualized consideration" as the "principal evil" of the medical school's admissions program).

Here, the Law School engages in a highly individualized, holistic review of each applicant's file, giving serious consideration to all the ways an applicant might contribute to a diverse educational environment. The Law School affords this individualized consideration to applicants of all races. There is no policy, either *de jure* or *de facto,* of automatic acceptance or rejection based on any single "soft" variable. Unlike the program at issue in *Gratz v. Bollinger, ante,* the Law School awards no mechanical, predetermined diversity "bonuses" based on race or ethnicity. . . . [T]he Law School's admissions policy "is flexible enough to consider all pertinent elements of diversity in light of the particular qualifications of each applicant, and to place them on the same footing for consideration, although not necessarily according them the same weight" [citation omitted].

We also find that, like the Harvard plan Justice Powell referenced in *Bakke,* the Law School's race-conscious admissions program adequately ensures that all factors that may contribute to student body diversity are meaningfully considered alongside race in admissions decisions. With respect to the use of race itself, all underrepresented minority students admitted by the Law School have been deemed qualified. By virtue of our Nation's struggle with racial inequality, such students are both likely to have experiences of particular importance to the Law School's mission, and less likely to be admitted in meaningful numbers on criteria that ignore those experiences. See App. 120.

The Law School does not, however, limit in any way the broad range of qualities and experiences that may be considered valuable contributions to student body diversity. To the contrary, the 1992 policy makes clear "[t]here are many possible bases for diversity admissions," and provides examples of admittees who have lived or traveled widely abroad, are fluent in several languages, have overcome personal adversity and family hardship, have exceptional records of extensive community service, and have had successful careers in other fields. *Id.*, at 118–119. The Law School seriously considers each "applicant's promise of making a notable contribution to the class by way of a particular strength, attainment, or characteristic—e.g., an unusual intellectual achievement, employment experience, nonacademic performance, or personal background." *Id.*, at 83–84. All applicants have the opportunity to highlight their own potential diversity contributions through the submission of a personal statement, letters of recommendation, and an essay describing the ways in which the applicant will contribute to the life and diversity of the Law School.

What is more, the Law School actually gives substantial weight to diversity factors besides race. The Law School frequently accepts nonminority applicants with grades and test scores lower than underrepresented minority applicants (and other nonminority applicants) who are rejected. See Brief for Respondents Bollinger et al. 10; App. 121–122. This shows that the Law School seriously weighs many other diversity factors besides race that can make a real and dispositive difference for nonminority applicants as well. By this flexible approach, the Law School sufficiently takes into account, in practice as well as in theory, a wide variety of characteristics besides race and ethnicity that contribute to a diverse student body. . . .

Petitioner and the United States argue that the Law School's plan is not narrowly tailored because race-neutral means exist to obtain the educational benefits of student body diversity that the Law School seeks. We disagree. Narrow tailoring does not require exhaustion of every conceivable race-neutral alternative. Nor does it require a university to choose between maintaining a reputation for excellence or fulfilling a commitment to provide educational opportunities to members of all racial groups. . . . Narrow tailoring does, however, require serious, good faith consideration of workable race-neutral alternatives that will achieve the diversity the university seeks. . . .

We agree with the Court of Appeals that the Law School sufficiently considered workable race-neutral alternatives. The District Court took the Law School to task for failing to consider race-neutral alternatives such as "using a lottery system" or "decreasing the emphasis for all applicants on undergraduate GPA and LSAT scores." App. to Pet. for Cert. 251a. But these alternatives would require a dramatic sacrifice of diversity, the academic quality of all admitted students, or both.

The Law School's current admissions program considers race as one factor among many, in an effort to assemble a student body that is diverse in ways broader than race. Because a lottery would make that kind of nuanced judgment impossible, it would effectively sacrifice all other educational values, not to mention every other kind of diversity. So too with the suggestion that the Law School simply lower admissions standards for all students, a drastic remedy that would require the Law School to become a much different institution and sacrifice a vital component of its educational mission. . . . We are satisfied that the Law School adequately considered race-neutral alternatives currently capable of producing a critical mass without forcing the Law School to abandon the academic selectivity that is the cornerstone of its educational mission.

We acknowledge that "there are serious problems of justice connected with the idea of preference itself." *Bakke*, 438 U.S., at 298 (opinion of Powell, J.). Narrow tailoring, therefore, requires that a race-conscious admissions program not unduly harm members of any racial group. Even remedial race-based governmental action generally "remains subject to continuing oversight to assure that it will work the least harm possible to other innocent persons competing for the benefit." *Id.*, at 308. To be narrowly tailored, a race-conscious admissions program must not "unduly burden individuals who are not members of the favored racial and ethnic groups." *Metro Broadcasting, Inc. v. FCC*, 497 U.S. 547, 630 (1990) (O'CONNOR, J., dissenting).

We are satisfied that the Law School's admissions program does not. Because the Law School considers "all pertinent elements of diversity," it can (and does) select nonminority applicants who have greater potential to enhance student body diversity over underrepresented minority applicants. See *Bakke, supra*, at 317 (opinion of Powell, J.). As Justice Powell recognized in *Bakke*, so long as a race-conscious admissions program uses race as a "plus" factor in the context of individualized consideration, a rejected applicant

> "will not have been foreclosed from all consideration for that seat simply because he was not the right color or had the wrong surname.... His qualifications would have been weighed fairly and competitively, and he would have no basis to complain of unequal treatment under the Fourteenth Amendment." 438 U.S., at 318.

We agree that, in the context of its individualized inquiry into the possible diversity contributions of all applicants, the Law School's race-conscious admissions program does not unduly harm nonminority applicants.

We are mindful, however, that "[a] core purpose of the Fourteenth Amendment was to do away with all governmentally imposed discrimination based on race." *Palmore v. Sidoti*, 466 U.S. 429, 432 (1984). Accordingly, race-conscious admissions policies must be limited in time. This requirement reflects that racial classifications, however compelling their goals, are potentially so dangerous that they may be employed no more broadly than the interest demands. Enshrining a permanent justification for racial preferences would offend this fundamental equal protection principle. We see no reason to exempt race-conscious admissions programs from the requirement that all governmental use of race must have a logical end point. The Law School, too, concedes

that all "race-conscious programs must have reasonable durational limits." Brief for Respondents Bollinger et al. 32....

The requirement that all race-conscious admissions programs have a termination point "assure[s] all citizens that the deviation from the norm of equal treatment of all racial and ethnic groups is a temporary matter, a measure taken in the service of the goal of equality itself."...

We take the Law School at its word that it would "like nothing better than to find a race-neutral admissions formula" and will terminate its race-conscious admissions program as soon as practicable. See Brief for Respondents Bollinger et al. 34; *Bakke, supra*, at 317–318 (opinion of Powell, J.) (presuming good faith of university officials in the absence of a showing to the contrary). It has been 25 years since Justice Powell first approved the use of race to further an interest in student body diversity in the context of public higher education. Since that time, the number of minority applicants with high grades and test scores has indeed increased. See Tr. of Oral Arg. 43. We expect that 25 years from now, the use of racial preferences will no longer be necessary to further the interest approved today.

IV

In summary, the Equal Protection Clause does not prohibit the Law School's narrowly tailored use of race in admissions decisions to further a compelling interest in obtaining the educational benefits that flow from a diverse student body.... The judgment of the Court of Appeals for the Sixth Circuit, accordingly, is affirmed.

It Is So Ordered.

STUDY QUESTIONS

1. What type of affirmative action programs were being challenged in the two Michigan University cases? What factor received preferential treatment and why?
2. What is a quota? What is a "plus" factor? What are race-neutral criteria? According to the Court majority, which

did the law school use in its admissions program?

3. What standard of scrutiny did the Supreme Court apply? What are the elements of this standard? Do you think the Supreme Court correctly applied this standard? Why or why not?

4. These cases involved challenges to racial preferences. What standard of scrutiny has traditionally been used when reviewing constitutional challenges concerning gender? Do you think the Court should apply the same standard of scrutiny if an AAP preference is based on gender? Why or why not?

As previously stated, the Supreme Court's most recent pronouncements in the affirmative action area concerned racial preferences in public university admissions. The *Grutter* decision relied on reasoning from prior decisions concerning affirmative action in both education and employment settings. Naturally, one wonders how the Court will consider affirmative action programs in employment after *Grutter,* especially ones that contain a preference based on gender. In November of 2003, the Court declined to grant certiorari in a case from the Tenth Circuit that approved the use of both racial and gender preferences in public contracting. *See Concrete Works of Colorado, Inc. v. City and County of Denver, Colorado,* 86 F. Supp.2d 1042 (D. Colo, 2000), *rev'd* 321 F.3d 950 (10th Cir. 2003), *cert. denied,* 540 U.S. 1027 (2003). In February of 2004, the U.S. District Court for the Northern District of Florida, which is in the Eleventh Circuit, declared unconstitutional Governor Jeb Bush's One Florida plan to eliminate affirmative action because it required agencies to consider race and gender rather than "race-neutral" criteria for awarding state contracts, however, the parties then settled the matter by agreeing, among other things, not to award state construction contracts on the basis of race, ethnicity, or gender. The appropriate vehicle for bringing the subject of gender-based AAPs in employment before the Supreme Court has yet to appear.

As we indicated at the beginning of this discussion, affirmative action takes a variety of forms. The use of numerical goals is only one of them, the most controversial form. In the early 1990s, the DOL initiated another form of affirmative action aimed at identifying factors that inhibit the advancement of women into upper managerial positions in private industry: The Glass Ceiling Initiative. The following selection contains the recommendations of the Federal Glass Ceiling Commission, whose creation followed the DOL's report on the Glass Ceiling Initiative.

RECOMMENDATIONS OF THE FEDERAL GLASS CEILING COMMISSION
A Solid Investment: Making Full Use of the Nation's Human Capital,
Federal Glass Ceiling Commission
U.S. Government Printing Office,
Washington, D.C., November 1995.

INTRODUCTION

Title II of the Civil Rights Act of 1991 created the 21-member, bipartisan Federal Glass Ceiling Commission. The Commission's mandate is to study the barriers to the advancement of minorities and women within corporate hierarchies (the problem known as the glass ceiling), to issue a report on its findings and conclusions, and to make recommendations on ways to dismantle the glass ceiling.

The Commission undertook an extensive research and information gathering effort, including public hearings, surveys of chief executive officers, and interviews with focus groups. This work culminated with the spring 1995 release of the Commission's report, *Good For Business: Making Full Use of the Nation's Human Capital*. The Commission now completes its work, with the release of its recommendations in *A Solid Investment: Making Full Use of the Nation's Human Capital*.

The glass ceiling is a reality in corporate America. Glass ceiling barriers continue to deny untold numbers of qualified people the opportunity to compete for and hold executive level positions in the private sector. The relationship between glass ceilings, equal opportunity and affirmative action is complex, as the findings contained in *Good for Business* demonstrate. Minorities and women are still consistently underrepresented and under utilized at the highest levels of corporate America. For example, 97 percent of the senior managers of *Fortune* 1000 Industrial and *Fortune* 500 companies are white, and 95 to 97 percent are male; in the *Fortune* 2000 industrial and service companies, only 5 percent of senior managers are women, and almost all of them are white; African American men with professional degrees earn 21 percent less than their white counterparts holding the same degrees in the same job categories. But women and African Americans are not the only ones kept down by the glass ceiling. Only 0.4 percent of managers are Hispanic, although Hispanics make up eight percent of America's workforce. Asian and Pacific Islander Americans earn less than whites in comparable positions and receive fewer promotions, despite more formal education than other groups. Generally, the lack of educational opportunity drastically reduces the available pool of American Indian candidates and CEOs rarely consider them for management jobs. These numbers are put in context by the fact that in our society,

two-thirds of the population—and 57 percent of workers—are women, minorities or both.

Corporate leaders increasingly are cognizant of both the existence of the glass ceiling and the value of workforce diversity at the management and decisionmaking levels. What motivates companies that have begun to take steps to break glass ceiling barriers? The bottom line. Business leaders see the changes taking place in the demographics of national consumer markets and the labor force, and the rapid globalization of the marketplace. They know that these conditions affect the ability of their companies to survive and prosper—and that the existence of the glass ceiling keeps them from adapting to these conditions efficiently and effectively.

The glass ceiling can affect the bottom line in other ways, too. Companies that make full use of diverse human resources at home will be better prepared for the challenges involved in managing even more diverse workforces in the emerging global economy. Companies with strong records for developing and advancing minorities and women will find it easier to recruit members of those groups. Companies whose cultures are hospitable to minorities and women will find it easier to retain those employees, or incur additional recruitment and training costs due to turnover. Increasing the number of minorities and women in areas such as product development, marketing and advertising allows companies to maximize their ability to tap into many segments of the consumer market. Overall, a poor diversity track record can make companies vulnerable to activist consumer groups.

To compete successfully at home and abroad, businesses must make full use of the resources embodied in our people—all of our people. Individuals of all races and both genders are entering our workforce in increasing numbers. By the year 2000, two-thirds of new labor force entrants will be minorities and women, yet the glass ceiling prevents qualified people of diverse backgrounds from achieving top management positions. Over the past 30 years government and business have taken steps to provide access for minorities and women to all levels of employment. These efforts must continue, but business must take the initiative to go beyond what it has achieved to date. Successful companies will be those that seize the opportunity presented by increased diversity, to create a world in which inclusion is elicited and not coerced, and work to increase both the diversity of their workforces and the opportunities available to all members of their workforce.

The Recommendations

True to its mandate, the Commission offers its recommendations as a strategy for shattering the glass ceiling once and for all. The glass ceiling is, in the first instance, a business issue, and we must look for solutions in the world of business. The recommendations begin with steps businesses can take to dismantle barriers within their corporate structures.

Business does not operate in a vacuum. It reflects the attitudes and conditions of society as a whole, and other segments of society must also contribute to ending the glass ceiling. The recommendations turn, then, to ways in which government can most effectively play a part in delivering for its customers—the citizens—by breaking glass ceiling barriers. Finally, the report discusses societal initiatives to enlist schools, the media, community organizations and other institutions in helping to bring down the glass ceiling.

But the recommendations offered by the Commission can only be the beginning. There must be an open and continuing dialogue on how to move this issue to the forefront, with business leading, not following. Business-to-business communications— peer-to-peer CEO sessions, roundtables and industry forums—must play a central role in the process to break the glass ceiling.

The Commission believes that every member of our society should have the opportunity to strive for positions of responsibility and leadership, regardless of their gender, race or ethnic background. The concept of upward mobility needs to be kept alive in our culture; it is vital to our nation's future. These recommendations are submitted in

the belief that they will help to shatter the glass ceiling in American business and in so doing enable business to fully utilize our most precious resource—our people.

Summary of Recommendations

Business

Demonstrate CEO Commitment

Eliminating the glass ceiling requires that the CEO communicate visible and continuing commitment to workforce diversity throughout the organization. The Commission recommends that all CEOs and boards of directors set companywide policies that actively promote diversity programs and policies that remove artificial barriers at every level.

Include Diversity in All Strategic Business Plans and Hold Line Managers Accountable for Progress

Businesses customarily establish short- and long-term objectives and measure progress in key business areas. The Commission recommends that all corporations include in their strategic business plans efforts to achieve diversity both at the senior management level and throughout the workforce. Additionally, performance appraisals, compensation incentives and other evaluation measures must reflect a line manager's ability to set a high standard *and* demonstrate progress toward breaking the glass ceiling.

Use Affirmative Action as a Tool

Affirmative action is the deliberate undertaking of positive steps to design and implement employment procedures that ensure the employment system provides equal opportunity to all. The Commission recommends that corporate America use affirmative action as a tool ensuring that all *qualified* individuals have equal access and opportunity to compete based on ability and merit.

Select, Promote and Retain Qualified Individuals

Traditional prerequisites and qualifications for senior management and board of director positions focus too narrowly on conventional sources and experiences. The Commission recommends that organizations expand their vision and seek candidates from non-customary sources, backgrounds and experiences, and that the executive recruiting industry work with businesses to explore ways to expand the universe of qualified candidates.

Prepare Minorities and Women for Senior Positions

Too often, minorities and women find themselves channeled into staff positions that provide little access and visibility to corporate decisionmakers, and removed from strategic business decisions. The Commission recommends that organizations expand access to core areas of the business and to various developmental experiences, and establish formal mentoring programs that provide career guidance and support to prepare minorities and women for senior positions.

Educate the Corporate Ranks

Organizations cannot make members of society blind to differences in color, culture or gender, but they can demand and enforce merit-based practice and behavior internally. The Commission recommends that companies provide formal training at regular intervals on company time to sensitize and familiarize all employees about the strengths and challenges of gender, racial, ethnic and cultural differences.

Initiate Work/Life and Family-Friendly Policies

Work/life and family-friendly policies, although they benefit all employees, are an important step in an organization's commitment to hiring, retaining and promoting both men and women. The Commission recommends that organizations adopt policies that recognize and accommodate the balance between work and family responsibilities that impact the lifelong career paths of all employees.

Adopt High Performance Work-Place Practices

There is a positive relationship between corporate financial performance, productivity and the use of high performance workplace practices. The Commission recommends that all companies adopt high performance workplace practices, which fall under the categories of skills and information; participation, organization and partnership; and compensation, security and work environment.

Government

Lead by Example

Government at all levels must be a leader in the quest to make equal opportunity a reality for minorities and women. The Commission recommends that all government agencies, as employers, increase their efforts to eliminate internal glass ceilings by examining their practices for promoting qualified minorities and women to senior management and decisionmaking positions.

Strengthen Enforcement of Anti-Discrimination Laws

Workplace discrimination presents a significant glass ceiling barrier for minorities and women. The Commission recommends that Federal enforcement agencies increase their efforts to enforce existing laws by expanding efforts to end systemic discrimination and challenging multiple discrimination. The Commission also recommends evaluating effectiveness and efficiency and strengthening interagency coordination as a way of furthering the effort. Additionally, updating anti-discrimination regulations, strengthening and expanding corporate management reviews and improving the complaint processing system play major roles in ending discrimination. Finally, the Commission recommends making sure that enforcement agencies have adequate resources to enforce anti-discrimination laws.

Improve Data Collection

Accurate data on minorities and women can show where progress is or is not being made in breaking glass ceiling barriers. The Commission recommends that relevant government agencies revise the collection of data by refining existing data categories and improving the specificity of data collected. All government agencies that collect data must break it out by race and gender, and avoid double counting of minority women, in order to develop a clear picture of where minorities and women are in the workforce.

Increase Disclosure of Diversity Data
Public disclosure of diversity data—specifically, data on the most senior positions—is an effective incentive to develop and maintain innovative, effective programs to break glass ceiling barriers. The Commission recommends that both the public and private sectors work toward increased public disclosure of diversity data.

STUDY QUESTIONS

1. What is meant by the "glass ceiling"? What evidence is there that a glass ceiling exists in American businesses?
2. What would motivate a company to act to break through the glass ceiling barriers?
3. What recommendations does the Commission make to businesses to shatter the glass ceiling? What recommendations does it make to all levels of government? Do you agree or disagree with these recommendations? Why?

According to Catalyst, a nonprofit membership organization that works with businesses to expand opportunities for women in business, as of 2009 fifteen CEOs of *Fortune* 500 companies and thirteen CEOs of *Fortune* 1,000 companies are women. In 2008, women held 15.7 percent of the *Fortune* 500 corporate officer positions, but seventy-five companies had no women corporate officers. In addition, women held 15.2 percent of the *Fortune* 500 directorships, but sixty-six companies had no women board directors. Women have certainly improved their corporate standing since the Glass Ceiling Commission issued its report in 1995, but considering that in 2008 they comprised 46.5 percent of the total U.S. workforce and the largest percentage of women—39 percent—worked in management, professional, and related occupations, they have barely scratched the *Fortune* 500 companies' glass.

ON-LINE RESOURCES

For information and statistics from the Department of Labor (DOL), including the Bureau of Labor Statistics, go to the DOL Web site:
www.dol.gov

For information on the 2000 U.S. Census, go to the U.S. Census Home page:
www.census.gov

To read more about the Family and Medical Leave Act (FMLA), go to:
www.dol.gov/esa/whd/fmla

To find the most recent U.S. Supreme Court Opinions go to the U.S. Supreme Court's Web site:
www.supremecourtus.gov

To read the entire Federal Glass Ceiling Commission's Recommendations report, go to:
www.ilr.cornell.edu/library/downloads/keyWorkplaceDocuments/
GlassCeilingRecommendations.pdf

To read the entire Federal Glass Ceiling Commission's Report, go to:
www.arts.cornell.edu/wrc/GCRpt.pdf

CHAPTER 5

EQUAL EDUCATIONAL OPPORTUNITY

Many Of The Instances of sex discrimination discussed in the preceding chapters have their roots in stereotyped attitudes toward what an earlier era called the nature, place, and proper destiny of men and women. The resilience of these attitudes in the face of changes in the law and feminist critique is remarkable.

Schools are widely recognized as a central vehicle of culture in our country today. Undoubtedly, schools have contributed to the resilience of attitudes that cast men and women in different roles. Schools contribute to the process of sex-role socialization, however, not so much by initiating such roles and patterns of expectation as by reinforcing the attitudes already learned outside the school.

I. The Social and Legal Context

Since the early 1970s, courts and legislatures have become increasingly aware of the role that the schools play in denying girls and women equal access to important educational opportunities. The legal response to this increasing awareness came in the form of constitutional litigation in federal and state courts and new legislation from state legislatures and Congress. The courts began to apply the new *Reed* standard in equal protection cases to the schools. The main contribution by Congress is popularly known as Title IX. This chapter traces some of the more significant of these legal developments. Before turning to those, we consider the dimensions of the problem in historical context and briefly introduce Title IX.

GENDER GAMES

David Sadker

The Washington Post, July 30, 2000.

Remember when your elementary school teacher would announce the teams for the weekly spelling bee? "Boys against the girls!" There was nothing like a gender showdown to liven things up. Apparently, some writers never left this elementary level of intrigue. A spate of recent books and articles takes us back to the "boys versus girls" fray but this time, with much higher stakes.

May's *Atlantic Monthly* cover story, "Girls Rule," is a case in point. The magazine published an excerpt from *The War Against Boys* by Christina Hoff Sommers, a book advancing the notion that boys are the real victims of gender bias while girls are soaring in school.

Sommers and her supporters are correct in saying that girls and women have made significant educational progress in the past two decades. Females today make up more than 40 percent of medical and law school students, and more than half of college students. Girls continue to read sooner and write better than boys. And for as long as anyone can remember, girls have received higher grades than boys.

But there is more to these selected statistics than meets the eye. Although girls continue to receive higher report card grades than boys, their grades do not translate into higher test scores. The same girls who beat boys in the spelling bees score below boys on the tests that matter: the PSATs crucial for scholarships, the SATs and the ACTs needed for college acceptances, the GREs for graduate school and even the admission tests for law, business and medical schools.

Many believe that girls' higher grades may be more a reflection of their manageable classroom behavior than their intellectual accomplishment. Test scores are not influenced by quieter classroom behavior.

Girls may in fact be trading their initiative and independence for peer approval and good grades, a trade-off that can have costly personal and economic consequences.

The increase in female college enrollment catches headlines because it heralds the first time that females have outnumbered males on college campuses. But even these enrollment figures are misleading. The female presence increases as the status of the college decreases. Female students are more likely to dominate two-year schools than the Ivy League. And wherever they are, they find themselves segregated and channeled into the least prestigious and least costly majors.

In today's world of e-success, more than 60 percent of computer science and business majors are male, about 70 percent of physics majors are male, and more than 80 percent of engineering students are male. But peek into language, psychology, nursing and humanities classrooms, and you will find a sea of female faces.

Higher female enrollment figures mask the "glass walls" that separate the sexes and channel females and males into very different careers, with very different paychecks. Today, despite all the progress, the five leading occupations of employed women are secretary, receptionist, bookkeeper, registered nurse and hairdresser/cosmetologist.

Add this to the "glass ceiling" (about 3 percent of *Fortune* 500 top managers are women) and the persistence of a gender wage gap (women with advanced degrees still lag well behind their less-educated male counterparts) and the crippling impact of workplace and college stereotyping becomes evident.

Even within schools, where female teachers greatly outnumber male teachers,

The writer is Professor Emeritus at American University and co-author of a number of books, including *Failing at Fairness: How Our Schools Cheat Girls* (Touchstone, 1995). Reprinted by permission of the author.

school management figures remind us that if there is a war on boys, women are not the generals. More than 85 percent of junior and senior high school principals are male, while 88 percent of school superintendents are male.

Despite sparkling advances of females on the athletic fields, two-thirds of athletic scholarships still go to males. In some areas, women have actually lost ground. When Title IX was enacted in 1972, women coached more than 90 percent of intercollegiate women's teams. Today women coach only 48 percent of women's teams and only 1 percent of men's teams.

If some adults are persuaded by the rhetoric in such books as *The War Against Boys* be assured that children know the score. When more than 1,000 Michigan elementary school students were asked to describe what life would be like if they were born a member of the opposite sex, more than 40 percent of the girls saw positive advantages

to being a boy: better jobs, more money and definitely more respect. Ninety-five percent of the boys saw no advantage to being a female.

The War Against Boys attempts to persuade the public to abandon support for educational initiatives designed to help girls and boys avoid crippling stereotypes. I hope the public and Congress will not be taken in by the book's misrepresentations. We have no time to wage a war on either our boys or our girls.

STUDY QUESTIONS

1. In what ways has the access of women to education changed in the past twenty years? In what ways has the meaning of education for women remained the same?
2. Despite women's progress, into what roles is education channeling women?
3. How does college stereotyping of women affect their status in the workplace?

In 1997, the AAUW Educational Foundation commissioned the American Institutes of Research to assess the progress toward equity in education since 1992. As a result, a new report, "Gender Gaps: Where Schools Still Fail Our Children," was published in 1998. This report looks at what is different for girls in American schools and what gaps remain to be addressed. The report concludes that schools have made some progress toward equity. "In critical areas such as math and science, the answer for girls is a definitive yes, although as [the report] makes clear, some troubling gaps remain. The field of public education is ever-changing. And so, even as we narrow historic gaps, new ones emerge; technology is the prime example." The report goes on to explain, "[e]ven as girls narrow many gaps in math and science, new disciplines—like computer science, biotechnology, and environmental science—could produce new gender gaps. For girls to achieve economic independence and participate fully in the boom industries of the twenty-first century, educators will need to ensure that girls are included in these fields." With respect to boys, the reports states, ". . .as we enter a more information-based global economy, boys will need to be encouraged to pursue and develop communications skills."

Under the impact of such legal measures as Title IX, the practice of overtly steering women students into traditional fields has declined. As Sadker notes in his article, however, the result has not been a burgeoning enrollment of women in nontraditional courses of study. Part of the continued concentration of women in the more traditional fields can be explained by their own preferences. Student educational preferences continue to be formed by factors outside the control of schools and colleges. Nonetheless, differential treatment of students, even in mixed classrooms, continues to reinforce cultural stereotypes about the appropriate skills and aspirations of women and men. The following selection discusses how well our nation's colleges and universities are doing in eliminating gender bias in education.

TITLE IX AT 30
Report Card on Gender Equity
National Coalition for Women and Girls in Education, June 2002,
excerpts, pp. 6–12.

PROGRESS REPORTS

The National Coalition for Women and Girls in Education *Report Card* examines the state of gender equity in education in 10 key areas: access to higher education, athletics, career education, employment, learning environment, math and science, sexual harassment, standardized testing, technology, and treatment of pregnant and parenting students.

The progress reports grade the nation's efforts to implement Title IX based on a variety of indicators, such as women's participation rates, the federal government's enforcement actions, and legal developments. Based on these indicators, the progress reports assess how far the nation has come in realizing Title IX's goal of eliminating sex discrimination in education—first compared to before Title IX, and then compared to Title IX at 25.

Progress Toward Gender Equity

SUBJECT	2002	1997
Access to Higher Education	B	B–
Athletics	C+	C
Career Education	D	C
Employment	C–	C–
Learning Environment	C–	C–
Math and Science	B–	C+
Sexual Harassment	C	D+
Standardized Testing	C	C
Technology	D+	Not Graded
Treatment of Pregnant and Parenting Teens	C+	C+

The grading scale is as follows:

A—Equitable: Gender and other areas of diversity respected and affirmed
B—Substantial Progress: Most gender-based barriers eliminated

C—Some Progress: Some barriers addressed, but more improvement necessary
D—Little Progress: Significant barriers remain
F—Failure: No progress
How did the nation fare? . . .

ACCESS TO HIGHER EDUCATION

B

Since its passage in 1972, Title IX has dramatically expanded women's access to higher education. The increased representation of women in degree-granting programs has contributed to the economic progress of women and their families. Title IX has helped reduce sex discrimination, most notably in admissions standards, to the benefit of women and men alike. But other barriers to higher education persist, including sex segregation by academic subject and disparities in financial aid awards.

Admissions

Until the 1970s a great many of the nation's colleges and universities—private and public—simply excluded women outright. Institutions that admitted women welcomed them with a maze of obstacles including quotas, requirements to live in limited on-campus housing, and admissions criteria tougher than those for men. Based on the assumption that women were most interested in marriage and children, other colleges and universities scrutinized whether women applicants were serious about pursuing a degree. In college interviews, female applicants to doctoral programs often had to explain how they would combine a career with a family. Admissions policies too frequently were guided by traditional attitudes about the "proper" place of women and the widespread belief that women would drop out of school to take their "rightful" place in the home. As a result, many colleges and universities limited women's entry to ensure that only the most "committed" students—men—would have access to educational opportunities.

TITLE IX SNAPSHOT

- Harvard University, which opened its doors in 1636, did not admit women until 1943.
- The University of Virginia excluded women until 1970.
- Before Title IX, the University of North Carolina limited the number of women students by requiring them to live on campus, where there was little housing. Men, in contrast, could live anywhere.
- Women seeking admission to the New York State College of Agriculture in the early 1970s needed SAT scores 30 to 40 points higher than those of men.

Thirty years later, such overt practices have mostly been eliminated throughout higher education. Women have taken advantage of these new opportunities to earn degrees at astonishing rates. Women still lag behind their male counterparts, however, in earning doctoral and professional degrees, which is especially striking in light of the number of women receiving bachelor's degrees. Women also receive far fewer math and science bachelor's degrees, which typically offer greater earning potential.

Financial Aid

With the ever-increasing cost of college, financial aid has never been more important to providing access to higher education. Prior to Title IX, many colleges and universities kept women from receiving this critical assistance by

- Restricting the most prestigious scholarships, such as the Rhodes Scholarship, to men
- Giving preference to men in the award of other scholarships, fellowships, and loans
- Withholding financial aid from women who were married, pregnant, or parenting
- Withholding financial aid from part-time students, who were more likely to be women
- Failing to allow for child care expenses
- Tracking women into low-paying work-study jobs

Title IX meant an end to many policies and practices denying women financial aid. Over the past thirty years, financial aid programs have been modified to facilitate women's access into higher education, recognizing that many women pursuing degrees must support not only themselves but also their families. Women make up almost 60 percent of part-time students and 58 percent of students over age twenty-four. Compared to men, women who attend a postsecondary institution are twice as likely to have dependents and three times as likely to be single parents. To make higher education more accessible to these students, Congress enacted several key provisions in the 1986 reauthorization of the Higher Education Act. For example, Pell Grants and campus-based aid are now awarded to part-time as well as full-time students. Moreover, to determine eligibility for financial aid, students can waive the value of their homes in the calculation of expected family contributions.

Despite these advances, disparities still exist in the distribution of financial aid. Financial aid budgets include little or no allowance for dependent care, forcing many student parents to rely on friends and family, reduce their course loads, or leave school altogether. In the 1999–2000 school year, the National Collegiate Athletic Association (NCAA) reported that women athletes received as little as 40 percent of scholarship dollars in some athletic divisions, although this number reflects a steady increase over the last nine years. In addition, although Title IX allows education institutions to take affirmative steps to remedy past discrimination, the law also allows colleges and universities to exclude women from certain scholarships that have no remedial purpose.

Percentage of Degrees Awarded to Women

Degree (Projected)	1971–72	1996–97	1997–98
Associate of Arts	45	60	61
Bachelor of Arts	44	56	56
Master of Arts	41	51	57
Doctorate	16	39	42
First Professional	6	40	43

Title IX's implementing regulation permits schools to administer scholarships created under a will, bequest, or other legal instrument that is sex specific. For example, scholarships exist for men from New Jersey, male engineering students who are members of the Sigma Chi Fraternity, or men who attended certain high schools. Unlike many scholarships targeting women and people of color, these scholarships do not remedy past discrimination; in fact, they reinforce the gender disparities in many fields, conferring advantages from one generation of men to the next.

Sex Segregation in Courses

Even though women have made progress at all levels of education, they continue to be underrepresented in traditionally male fields that lead to greater earning power upon graduation. Women continue to be clustered in areas traditional for their gender. Undergraduate data from the 1997–98 academic year show that women received 75 percent of the education degrees, 74 percent of psychology degrees, and 67 percent of English degrees, all fields in which women have traditionally participated. In contrast, women earned only 39 percent of physical science degrees, 27 percent of bachelor's degrees in computer and information sciences (a gain of just 1 percent from five years earlier), and 18 percent of engineering degrees. This pattern of sex segregation directly limits women's earning power because careers in math and the sciences frequently result in higher pay. For example, in 2001 engineers had median weekly earnings of $1,142; in contrast, elementary school teachers' median weekly earnings were $774, about 30 percent less.

Sex segregation by academic concentration is even more acute in doctoral degree programs, where women already are underrepresented. For 1997–98 women received only 26 percent of doctorate degrees in mathematics, 16 percent of doctorates awarded in computers and information sciences, and 12 percent of doctorates awarded in engineering. Women received none of the doctoral degrees awarded in engineering-related technologies. Even in areas where women are strongly represented among undergraduate students, women's numbers drop at the doctoral level. In 1997–98, for example, women earned 63 percent of education doctoral degrees and 59 percent of English doctoral degrees.

Women's underrepresentation in math- and science-related fields has a cyclic effect, depriving girls and young women of role models and mentors, in effect further discouraging women and girls from pursuing degrees in those fields.

The hostile environment many women encounter in science, mathematics, and engineering no doubt plays a great role in women's underrepresentation in these fields. Research has shown that women pursuing math and sciences in higher education face outright hostility in many instances, including

- Deliberate sabotaging of female students' experiments
- Constant comments that women do not belong in certain departments or schools
- Slide presentations interspersed with pictures of nude women, purportedly to "liven up" the classroom
- Sexual harassment in laboratory or field work, causing women to avoid these settings altogether

Less blatant forms of sexism also are commonplace and make the environment equally unpleasant. Examples follow:

■ Male faculty may be reluctant to work with women because they question women's competence.
■ Male students may exclude women from study groups and project teams.
■ Male students who do work with women may try to dominate projects.
■ Many faculty refuse to incorporate the work of women in math and science in the curriculum, reinforcing women's invisibility in these areas.

The "chilly" climate for women coupled with the small number of female faculty in math, science, and engineering effectively limits women's access to these fields and, in so doing, closes off important career alternatives for women.

ROOM FOR IMPROVEMENT

• Women still lag behind men in earning doctoral and professional degrees.
• Some scholarships still are reserved for men.
• Women are underrepresented in math and science, in large part because of the hostile environment many confront in these fields.
• Education institutions are moving to dismantle affirmative action programs that have increased access for women and students of color.
• Low-income women have lost an avenue to higher education under the new welfare law.

Limiting Access in the Future

Despite the progress made over the last thirty years of Title IX enforcement, even today new policy developments threaten women's progress in higher education. In 1996 Congress and President Clinton approved a new welfare law that prohibits women receiving public assistance from meeting their work requirement by attending a postsecondary institution. Prior to this

law, welfare recipients could, at the states' discretion, attend a two- or four-year college. As this report goes to press, Congress is deliberating the reauthorization of the welfare law. While several proposals could expand welfare recipients' access to higher education, partisan entrenchment may prevent these proposals from becoming a reality, preventing many women from pursuing their dreams of a college degree and a means to support their families.

Currently changes are being made to the Department of Education's research division. While many of these changes could be productive, there is some concern that the department will shift its focus from the research that has been so important to advocates working to make higher education more equitable and accessible. For instance, department data that disaggregate student information by race and gender—essential to monitoring the effects of Title IX and other equity measures—are being reconsidered.

In addition, recent assaults on affirmative action could mean the end of programs that have helped women redress past sex discrimination and enhanced their educational opportunities, particularly in areas where women have been and continue to be underrepresented, such as math and science. Although Congress defeated legislative proposals to dismantle affirmative action in the last reauthorization of the Higher Education Act, more attempts may be proposed in the upcoming reauthorization. The 1996 passage of California Proposition 209 and the *Hopwood v. State of Texas* and *Johnson v. University of Georgia* decisions led many colleges and universities to dismantle affirmative action policies to avoid lawsuits, impeding access to higher education for women and people of color. Most recently, in *Gratz v. University of Michigan*, the U.S. Court of Appeals in Cincinnati heard arguments regarding the constitutionality of the university's affirmative action admissions plan at the undergraduate level for students of color. A decision from that court is pending. In May 2002, however, the Sixth Circuit

Court of Appeals upheld the constitutionality of the use of affirmative action in the law school's admissions process. It is widely believed that one of these cases will ultimately be heard by the Supreme Court and determine the future of affirmative action in higher education. . . .

STUDY QUESTIONS

1. According to the Report Card for Access to Higher Education, overt discriminatory admissions practices directed toward women have mostly been eliminated. What practices remain, however, that may effectively exclude women from higher education or limit their educational options if they are able to matriculate?

2. Review in Chapter 4 the U.S. Supreme Court's decisions in *Grutter* and *Gratz* (decided after this report was issued). In light of these decisions, what do you think the findings of this report would now be with respect to affirmative action?

3. Where can you go for assistance in your college or university if you believe you have encountered a gender-biased practice?

In 2008, the National Coalition for Women and Girls in Education (NCWGE) issued a new report "Title IX at 35: Beyond the Headlines." This report "sets forth the facts behind the headlines in six areas covered by title IX that have been focused on in recent years: athletics in schools; education in the "STEM" subjects—science, technology, engineering, and mathematics; career and technical education; employment in educational institutions; sexual harassment of students; and single-sex education." One of those headlines concerned a remark made by then Harvard University President, Lawrence Summers, during a speech at a January 2005 National Bureau of Economic Research conference in Cambridge, MA. Summers was reported to have said that innate differences between men and women might be one of the reasons fewer women succeed in science and math careers. NCWGE posits that the ensuing media storm diverted attention from ". . . the all too real culprits: socialization and discrimination while girls are still in school." Indeed, the statistics cited in this report concerning women undergraduate degrees in the sciences reflects a lingering gap at the college level. According to the report, women ". . . comprise nearly 60% of all undergraduate college students, and nearly half of all master's doctoral, law and medical students." Even so, women's share of STEM-subject bachelor degrees continues to lag behind that of men, particularly in physics, computer science, and engineering. It appears, therefore, that even though women's opportunity for education has increased, the pathways to study in technology and the sciences remain at least partially blocked.

Title IX

Over the past thirty years, the courts have applied constitutional provisions as well as the provisions of and regulations under Title IX to combat sex discrimination in education. We are already familiar, from Chapter 2, with the relevant developments in equal protection analysis and in state ERAs. Title IX, however, requires an introduction.

Title IX of the Educational Amendments of 1972, 20 U.S.C. Sec. 1681, was one of the first major legal steps taken to eliminate sex discrimination from schools. It was passed by both houses of Congress after hearings, held in 1970, that documented the pervasiveness, perniciousness, and long-range consequences of sex discrimination in educational policy, practices, and attitudes. Regulations that interpret Title IX were issued three years later.

Since the enactment of Title IX, other federal statutes guaranteeing students equal educational opportunities without regard to their sex have been adopted. These include the Equal Educational Opportunities Act of 1974 and Title II of the Educational Amendments of 1976. Although some states have more stringent requirements, Title IX has served as a model for federal and state efforts to provide equal educational opportunities for men and women. The language of Title IX parallels that of Title VI of the Civil Rights Act of 1964, which prohibits racial discrimination in programs or activities receiving federal financial assistance.

Scope

Just as we found it helpful in Chapter 3 to analyze Title VII in terms of its coverage, scope, and remedies, so it is useful here to approach Title IX in the same way. In terms of its scope (i.e., what behaviors it prohibits), the statute provides:

> No person in the United States shall, on the basis of sex, be excluded from participation in, be denied the benefits of, or be subjected to discrimination under any education program or activity receiving Federal financial assistance . . .

Regulations issued in support of Title IX amplify statutory requirements regarding admissions and recruitment and develop standards applicable to curriculum, research, extracurricular activities, student aid, student services, counseling and guidance, financial aid, housing, and athletics. Most observers agree that during the 1970s, performance in these areas by educational institutions vastly improved, and they credit Title IX with providing the impetus for that improvement. Between 1980 and 1988, the Reagan administration cut back on Title IX enforcement efforts, with the result that much of the earlier momentum was lost. Interest in enforcement efforts was revived, however, with the passage of the Civil Rights Restoration Act of 1988 and the Supreme Court decision in *Franklin v. Gwinnett*, 503 U.S. 60 (1992).

Exceptions to the general prohibition of Title IX were included in both the statute itself and in the interpretative regulations. The main exception included in the statute relates to sex-based admission policies. The statute specifies eight types of educational institutions: (1) preschool; (2) elementary school; (3) secondary school; (4) vocational school; (5) private institution of undergraduate higher education; (6) public institution of undergraduate higher education; (7) professional school; and (8) graduate school. As a result of the exceptions written into the statute, the general prohibition against sex-based admissions policies applies only to four of these, viz., 4, 6, 7, and 8. The clear bar to sex-based admissions policies in vocational, professional, and graduate schools is generally credited as a significant move toward the integration of traditionally all-male fields, such as law, medicine, engineering, and so forth. Title IX, however, does not prohibit sex-based admissions in any public or private preschool, any public or private elementary school, any public or private secondary school, or any private college.

Two other statutory exceptions pertain to material addressed in this chapter. One specifically declares that the sex-based admissions policies of any "public institution of undergraduate higher education which is an institution that traditionally and continually from its establishment has had a policy of admitting only students of one sex . . ." do not violate the prohibition of sex-based admissions policies. Another statutory exception to the general prohibition against sex discrimination in educational programs relates to social clubs. The statute excludes the membership policies of social fraternities and sororities from coverage under Title IX.

Title IX regulations introduce additional exceptions to the general prohibition against sex discrimination in educational programs. The regulations permit the provision of separate housing on the basis of sex with the caveat that separate housing, when compared to that provided to students of the other sex, is as a whole proportional in quantity to the number of students of that sex applying for housing as well as comparable in quality and cost to the student. In addition, the regulations permit separate locker rooms, shower facilities, and toilets on the basis of sex as long as the facilities provided for students of one sex are comparable to the facilities provided for students of the other sex. These exceptions may be justified by appeal to considerations of personal privacy. Few would consider them to be departures from the principle of equal educational opportunity.

The treatment of school athletics (34 C.F.R. §106.41) is a different matter. The section opens with a sweeping prohibition:

> No person shall, on the basis of sex, be excluded from participation in, be denied the benefits of, be treated differently from another person, or otherwise be discriminated against in any interscholastic, intercollegiate, club, or intramural athletics offered by a recipient, and no recipient shall provide any such athletics separately on such basis.

The section, however, immediately introduces a number of major exceptions to this general prohibition. Single-sex teams are permitted in the case of "contact sports" (e.g., boxing, wrestling, rugby, football, basketball, and ice hockey). Schools are not required to sponsor female teams for contact sports. Single-sex teams are also permitted for noncontact sports if a team for the excluded sex is also sponsored in that sport. Thus, a male tennis team is permitted if a female tennis team is also sponsored. The regulations, qualified in this way, require schools to permit females to try out for athletic teams previously dominated by males only in the case of noncontact sports and then only where an equal athletic opportunity (i.e., a separate team for the other sex) is not provided.

Coverage

The prohibitions of Title IX are generally addressed to all educational institutions, including public and private preschool, elementary, secondary, vocational, graduate, and professional schools, as well as colleges and universities, that receive federal financial assistance. The latter restriction is the key to grasping an important feature of Title IX, viz., that it imposes a contractual obligation upon recipients of federal largesse. The obligation to eliminate sex discrimination in educational institutions is a legal string that is attached to the funds that the schools receive from the federal government.

Several actions, taken by the Supreme Court and Congress since the passage of Title IX, have clarified the coverage of this statute. In 1984, the Supreme Court handed down two rulings in a case of key importance for the coverage of Title IX. On the one hand, it ruled that a private college that accepts no direct aid from the federal government but enrolls students who do receive federal grants that are used to defray tuition and fees at the school is a "recipient of federal financial assistance" for the purposes of Title IX and therefore is obligated to conform to its requirements (*Grove City College v. Bell*, 465 U.S. 555). On the other hand, and in the same decision, the Court ruled that only the "educational program or activity" that benefits directly from the receipt of federal funds is under that obligation. In *Grove City*, that was the financial aid office of the college.

This latter aspect of the Court's decision in *Grove City* brought Title IX enforcement to a standstill for the next four years. The narrow construction given to the "program or activity" language of Title IX had an immediate chilling effect not only on Title IX but also on other civil rights statutes governing recipients of federal funds. Title VI, prohibiting discrimination on the basis of race and national origin; Section 504 of the Rehabilitation Act of 1973, protecting handicapped persons; and the Age Discrimination Act of 1975 are all severely impeded because the reach of these statutes is also limited by "program or activity" language. The decision in *Grove City* relating to that language was overturned by the

Civil Rights Restoration Act. At the urging of the Reagan administration, the Republican-controlled Senate of the 98th and 99th Congresses rejected the act. In March 1988, it was passed by the Democrat-controlled 100th Congress over President Ronald Reagan's veto. Thereafter, enforcement efforts began to recover their earlier vigor.

Remedies

We saw in preceding text that the obligations imposed by Title IX are contractual in nature. Accordingly, the principal remedy initially envisioned for violations was the withholding of federal funds. Those schools that fail to avoid practices that discriminate on the basis of sex in the education of students or in dealing with employees are in jeopardy of having their federal funding cut off. In *Franklin v. Gwinnett Cty. Public Schools*, the Supreme Court made clear that another remedy available to individuals who bring action under Title IX against schools is monetary damages. Observers expect that the availability of damages will be a powerful incentive for schools to take more initiative in identifying and eliminating discriminatory practices in the future.

In the remainder of this chapter, we take up a number of themes that run through both litigation and legislation bearing on sex discrimination in the schools. Each illustrates that a variety of legal standards are frequently available to those who seek to enforce equality of educational opportunity.

II. SINGLE-SEX SCHOOLS

Title IX prohibits the segregation by sex of vocational, professional, and graduate schools and of those public undergraduate colleges and universities that have not barred admission to one sex continually from their founding. As indicated earlier, this prohibition was enormously influential in opening opportunities to women in these types of schools. Notwithstanding, many schools were not reached by Title IX because of specific statutory exclusions. As a result, the debate during the past several decades over whether sex segregation in schools should be permitted has been framed mainly in terms of whether the Equal Protection Clause of the Fourteenth Amendment permits governments to support single-sex schools.

The leading arguments, pro and con, on equality of education and separate educational opportunities were first addressed in connection with racial segregation in the schools. The Supreme Court first endorsed the "separate but equal" doctrine as it applied to racial segregation in *Plessy v. Ferguson*, 163 U.S. 537 (1896). In that case, the Court rejected an equal protection challenge to a Louisiana statute that provided for separate railway coaches for whites and blacks. The challenge was predicated upon the assumption that "the enforced separation of the two races stamps the colored race with a badge of inferiority." Applying the rational relation test, the Court rejected that argument and held that states are "at liberty to act with reference to the established usages, customs and traditions of the people, and with a view to the promotion of their comfort, and the preservation of the public peace and good order."

The "separate but equal" doctrine approved in *Plessy* permitted segregation of schools by race when the separate schools provided substantially equal facilities. The doctrine withstood over fifty years of argument and litigation. It was eaten away as part of a legal campaign by the National Association for the Advancement of Colored People through intermediate decisions and was finally rejected outright in the landmark decision of *Brown v. Board of Education*, 347 U.S. 483 (1954). There, statutes of four states that provided for racially segregated public schools were challenged on equal protection grounds. The challenge was the same as the one that was rejected by the *Plessy* Court (i.e., enforced segregation imposes a stigma on the minority group).

Specifically, the question addressed by the *Brown* Court was: "Does segregation of children in public schools on the basis of race, even though the physical facilities and other 'tangible' factors may be equal, deprive the children of the minority group of equal educational opportunities?" A unanimous Court replied: "We believe that it does." "We conclude," wrote Chief Justice Warren, "that in the field of public education the doctrine of 'separate but equal' has no place. Separate educational facilities are inherently unequal."

Racially segregated schools were found in violation of the Equal Protection Clause because they enforce a larger social point about the inferior social place of racial minorities. Like so many other practices associated with the system of racial segregation in the United States—practices such as separate bathrooms, separate sleeping quarters, and separate sports leagues—separate schools also "imposed a badge of inferiority."

Sexually segregated schools, too, were once commonplace. Like racially segregated schools, those schools also make a larger social point about boys and girls. Although sexually segregated schools were not as overtly hostile as those that were racially segregated, there is an important similarity. In this section, we consider the rationales used to justify sex segregation in the schools.

At first, the courts addressed equal protection challenges to single-sex schools by applying the same line of reasoning that was used in *Plessy*. The plaintiff had the burden of showing that the practice was arbitrary. That burden was not met where a usage, custom, or tradition of maintaining such schools could be cited. Equal facilities, however, had to be provided for all.

In *Williams v. McNair*, 316 F. Supp. 134 (D.S.C. 1970), *aff'd. without opinion*, 410 U.S. 951 (1971), which was decided before the Supreme Court handed down its decision in *Reed v. Reed*, the Court applied the rational relation test. After *Reed*, which held that sex-based classifications are subject to heightened scrutiny under the Equal Protection Clause, the rational relation test used in *Williams* no longer sufficed. Six years later, a circuit court upheld sex-segregated public high schools against an equal protection challenge assertedly applying a more stringent standard of review.

Judge Weis in *Vorchheimer v. Sch. Dist. of Philadelphia*, 532 F.2d 880 (3rd Cir. 1976), *aff'd.*, 430 U.S. 703 (1977), reminded us of another element of the ideology that supports the social system of sex segregation. The presence of girls in the same classroom as adolescent boys presents a distraction for the boys. That element, too, has a long history. When sex-segregated schools are viewed in the light of this social system and its ideology, we can easily see how it implies the inferiority of females: it too imposes "a badge of inferiority." The courts, however, have been reluctant to draw this parallel and address the question of whether "separate educational facilities are inherently unequal" where segregation is based on sex rather than race.

The segregation of Central and Girls high schools in Philadelphia was successfully challenged on equal protection and state ERA grounds in 1983 (*Newberg v. Board of Education*, 26 Pa. D. & C.3d 682). A trial-level court ruled that the educational opportunities afforded by the two schools were quite unequal and that the "theory that adolescents may study more effectively in single-sex schools" was contradicted by the actual experience of the Boston Latin School, which had recently admitted girls for the first time. In so ruling, the judge showed that sex-segregated schools can be found in violation even of the old "separate but equal" doctrine and that traditional theories lauding the merit of sex-segregated schools can be discredited when confronted with factual evidence.

The Supreme Court affirmed *Vorchheimer* by a 4-4 vote, without issuing an opinion. Six years later, in *Miss. Univ. for Women v. Hogan*, the Court addressed another case involving sex segregation in an educational context. This time, it struck down the arrangement, although, as we noted in Chapter 2, on quite narrow grounds. Incorporated into the opinions in *Hogan* was a discussion of the merit and relevance of the arguments in support of sex-segregated colleges.

The debate between Justices O'Connor, who wrote the Opinion, and Powell, who wrote a dissent, in *Hogan* resurfaced in the 1990s, when the courts were called upon to decide an Equal Protection challenge to the all-male admissions policy of Virginia Military Institute (VMI). VMI and the Citadel are exempt from coverage of Title IX's bar of single sex admissions policies because both have been male-only schools continually from their founding. Echoing the arguments of Justice Powell, as well as those advanced in *McNair* and *Vorchheimer*, the District Court initially declared that the maintenance of educational diversity was a sufficiently important government objective to justify the male-only admissions policy. On appeal, the Fourth Circuit Court of Appeals found the admission policy in violation of the Equal Protection Clause, vacated the District Court's order, and returned the matter with instructions that Virginia elect to require VMI to admit qualified women or establish a parallel institution for women, or abandon public support of VMI. The Supreme Court had left open in *Hogan* the question of whether the "separate but equal doctrine" is still viable as regards gender-segregated public schools. Virginia elected the "separate but equal course" of action, establishing the Virginia Women's Institute for Leadership (VWIL) at nearby Mary Baldwin College as a "parallel institution." The District Court approved that plan as a sufficient remedy, as did the Fourth Circuit. The Supreme Court, by a 7 to 1 vote, rejected that plan, thereby leaving VMI to choose between admitting qualified women or transforming itself into a completely private institution.

UNITED STATES V. VIRGINIA
518 U.S. 515 (1996).

JUSTICE GINSBURG delivered the opinion of the Court.

Virginia's public institutions of higher learning include an incomparable military college, Virginia Military Institute (VMI). The United States maintains that the Constitution's equal protection guarantee precludes Virginia from reserving exclusively to men the unique educational opportunities VMI affords. We agree.

Founded in 1839, VMI is today the sole single-sex school among Virginia's 15 public institutions of higher learning. VMI's distinctive mission is to produce "citizen-soldiers," men prepared for leadership in civilian life and in military service. VMI pursues this mission through pervasive training of a kind not available anywhere else in Virginia. Assigning prime place to character development, VMI uses an "adversative method" modeled on English public schools and once characteristic of military instruction. VMI constantly endeavors to instill physical and mental discipline in its cadets and impart to them a strong moral code. The school's graduates leave VMI with heightened comprehension of their capacity to deal with duress and stress, and a large sense of accomplishment for completing the hazardous course.

VMI has notably succeeded in its mission to produce leaders; among its alumni are military generals, Members of Congress, and business executives. The school's alumni overwhelmingly perceive that their VMI training helped them to realize their personal goals. VMI's endowment reflects the loyalty of its graduates; VMI has the largest per-student endowment of all undergraduate institutions in the Nation.

Neither the goal of producing citizen-soldiers nor VMI's implementing methodology is inherently unsuitable to women. And the schools' impressive record in producing leaders has made admission desirable to some women. Nevertheless, Virginia has elected to preserve exclusively for men the advantages and opportunities a VMI education affords. . . .

In 1990, prompted by a complaint filed with the Attorney General by a female high-school student seeking admission to VMI, the United States sued the Commonwealth of Virginia and VMI, alleging that VMI's exclusively male admission policy violated the Equal Protection Clause of the Fourteenth Amendment. . . .

The District Court ruled in favor of VMI, however, and rejected the equal protection challenge pressed by the United States. . . .

The District Court reasoned that education in "a single-gender environment, be it male or female," yields substantial benefits. VMI's school for men brought diversity to an otherwise coeducational Virginia system, and that diversity was "enhanced by VMI's unique method of instruction." If single-gender education for males ranks as an important governmental objective, it becomes obvious, the District Court concluded, that the only means of achieving the objective "is to exclude women from the all-male institution—VMI.". . .

The Court of Appeals for the Fourth Circuit disagreed and vacated the District Court's judgment. The appellate court held: "The Commonwealth of Virginia has not . . . advanced any state policy by which it can justify its determination, under an announced policy of diversity, to afford VMI's unique type of program to men and not to women.". . .

. . . Remanding the case, the appeals court assigned to Virginia, in the first instance, responsibility for selecting a remedial course. The court suggested these options for the State: Admit women to VMI; establish parallel institutions or programs; or abandon state support, leaving VMI free to pursue its policies as a private institution. . . .

In response to the Fourth Circuit's ruling, Virginia proposed a parallel program for women: Virginia Women's Institute

for Leadership (VWIL). The 4-year, state-sponsored undergraduate program would be located at Mary Baldwin College, a private liberal arts school for women, and would be open, initially, to about 25 to 30 students. Although VWIL would share VMI's mission—to produce "citizen-soldiers"—the VWIL program would differ, as does Mary Baldwin College, from VMI academic offerings, methods of education, and financial resources. . . .

The average combined SAT score of entrants at Mary Baldwin is about 100 points lower than the score for VMI freshmen. Mary Baldwin's faculty holds "significantly fewer Ph.D.'s than the faculty at VMI" and receives significantly lower salaries. While VMI offers degrees in liberal arts, the sciences, and engineering, Mary Baldwin, at the time of trial, offered only bachelor of arts degrees. A VWIL student seeking to earn an engineering degree could gain one, without public support, by attending Washington University in St. Louis, Missouri, for two years, paying the required private tuition. . . .

Experts in educating women at the college level composed the Task Force charged with designing the VWIL program; Task Force members were drawn from Mary Baldwin's own faculty and staff. Training its attention on methods of instruction appropriate for "most women," the Task Force determined that a military model would be "wholly inappropriate" for VWIL. . . .

VWIL students would participate in ROTC programs and a newly established, "largely ceremonial" Virginia Corps of Cadets, but the VWIL House would not have a military format, and VWIL would not require its students to eat meals together or to wear uniforms during the school day. In lieu of VMI's adversative method, the VWIL Task Force favored "a cooperative method which reinforces self-esteem." In addition to the standard bachelor of arts program offered at Mary Baldwin, VWIL students would take courses in leadership, complete an off-campus leadership externship, participate in community service projects, and assist in arranging a speaker series. . . .

Virginia returned to the District Court seeking approval of its proposed remedial plan, and the court decided the plan met the requirements of the Equal Protection Clause. . . .

A divided Court of Appeals affirmed the District Court's judgment. This time, the appellate court determined to give "greater scrutiny to the selection of means than to the [State's] proffered objective." The official objective or purpose, the court said, should be reviewed deferentially. Respect for the "legislative will," the court reasoned, meant that the judiciary should take a "cautious approach," inquiring into the "legitima[cy]" of the governmental objective and refusing approval for any purpose revealed to be "pernicious.". . .

The court recognized that, as it analyzed the case, means merged into end, and the merger risked "bypass[ing] any equal protection scrutiny." The court therefore added another inquiry, a decisive test it called "substantive comparability." The key question, the court said, was whether men at VMI and women at VWIL would obtain "substantively comparable benefits at their institution or through other means offered by the [S]tate." Although the appeals court recognized that the VWIL degree "lacks the historical benefit and prestige" of a VMI degree, it nevertheless found the educational opportunities at the two schools "sufficiently comparable.". . .

The cross-petitions in this case present two ultimate issues. First, does Virginia's exclusion of women from the educational opportunities provided by VMI—extraordinary opportunities for military training and civilian leadership development—deny to women "capable of all of the individual activities required of VMI cadets," the equal protection of the laws guaranteed by the Fourteenth Amendment? Second, if VMI's "unique" situation—as Virginia's sole single-sex public institution of higher education—offends the Constitution's

equal protection principle, what is the remedial requirement?. . .

The Fourth Circuit initially held that Virginia had advanced no state policy by which it could justify, under equal protection principles, its determination "to afford VMI's unique type of program to men and not to women." Virginia challenges that "liability" ruling and asserts two justifications in defense of VMI's exclusion of women. First, the Commonwealth contends, "single-sex education provides important educational benefits," and the option of single-sex education contributes to "diversity in educational approaches." Second, the Commonwealth argues, "The unique VMI method of character development and leadership training," the school's adversative approach, would have to be modified were VMI to admit women. We consider these two justifications in turn.

Single-sex education affords pedagogical benefits to at least some students, Virginia emphasizes, and that reality is uncontested in this litigation. Similarly, it is not disputed that diversity among public educational institutions can serve the public good. But Virginia has not shown that VMI was established, or has been maintained, with a view to diversifying, by its categorical exclusion of women, educational opportunities within the State. In cases of this genre, our precedent instructs that "benign" justifications proffered in defense of categorical exclusions will not be accepted automatically; a tenable justification must describe actual state purposes, not rationalizations for actions in fact differently grounded. . . .

Neither recent nor distant history bears out Virginia's alleged pursuit of diversity through single-sex educational options. In 1839, when the State established VMI, a range of educational opportunities for men and women was scarcely contemplated. Higher education at the time was considered dangerous for women; reflecting widely held views about women's proper place, the Nation's first universities and colleges—for example, Harvard in Massachusetts, William and Mary in Virginia—admitted only men. VMI was not at all novel in this respect: In admitting no women, VMI followed the lead of the State's flagship school, the University of Virginia, founded in 1819. [The court summarized the long struggle to open publicly supported higher education in Virginia to women, which culminated in the gender integration of the University of Virginia only in 1972.]. . .

In sum, we find no persuasive evidence in this record that VMI's male-only admission policy "is in furtherance of a state policy of 'diversity.'" No such policy, the Fourth Circuit observed, can be discerned from the movement of all other public colleges and universities in Virginia away from single-sex education. . . .

Virginia next argues that VMI's adversative method of training provides educational benefits that cannot be made available, unmodified, to women. . . .

The District Court forecast from expert witness testimony, and the Court of Appeals accepted, that coeducation would materially affect "at least these three aspects of VMI's program—physical training, the absence of privacy, and the adversative approach." And it is uncontested that women's admission would require accommodations, primarily in arranging housing assignments and physical training programs for female cadets. It is also undisputed, however, that "the VMI methodology could be used to educate women." The District Court even allowed that some women may prefer it to the methodology a women's college might pursue. "[S]ome women, at least, would want to attend [VMI] if they had the opportunity," the District Court recognized, and "some women," the expert testimony established, "are capable of all of the individual activities required of VMI cadets." The parties, furthermore, agree that "some women can meet the physical standards [VMI] now impose[s] on men." In sum, as the Court of Appeals stated, "neither the goal of producing citizen soldiers," VMI's raison d'etre, "nor VMI's implementing methodology is inherently unsuitable to women.". . .

The notion that admission of women would downgrade VMI's stature, destroy the adversative system and, with it, even the school, is a judgment hardly proved, a prediction hardly different from other "self-fulfilling prophec[ies]," once routinely used to deny rights or opportunities. When women first sought admission to the bar and access to legal education, concerns of the same order were expressed. . . .

Women's successful entry into the federal military academies, and their participation in the Nation's military forces, indicate that Virginia's fears for the future of VMI may not be solidly grounded. The State's justification for excluding all women from "citizen-soldier" training for which some are qualified, in any event, cannot rank as "exceedingly persuasive," as we have explained and applied that standard. . . .

In the second phase of the litigation, Virginia presented its remedial plan—maintain VMI as a male-only college and create VWIL as a separate program for women. . . .

A remedial decree, this Court has said, must closely fit the constitutional violation; it must be shaped to place persons unconstitutionally denied an opportunity or advantage in "the position they would have occupied in the absence of [discrimination]." The constitutional violation in this case is the categorical exclusion of women from an extraordinary educational opportunity afforded men. A proper remedy for an unconstitutional exclusion, we have explained, aims to "eliminate [so far as possible] the discriminatory effects of the past" and to "bar like discrimination in the future."

Virginia chose not to eliminate, but to leave untouched, VMI's exclusionary policy. For women only, however, Virginia proposed a separate program, different in kind from VMI and unequal in tangible and intangible facilities. Having violated the Constitution's equal protection requirement, Virginia was obliged to show that its remedial proposal "directly address[ed] and relate[d] to" the violation, i.e., the equal protection denied to women ready, willing, and able to benefit from educational opportunities of the kind VMI offers. Virginia described VMI as a "parallel program," and asserted that VWIL shares VMI's mission of producing "citizen-soldiers" and VMI's goals of providing "education, military training, mental and physical discipline, character . . . and leadership development." If the VWIL program could not "eliminate the discriminatory effects of the past," could it at least "bar like discrimination in the future"? A comparison of the programs said to be "parallel" informs our answer. In exposing the character of, and differences in, the VMI and VWIL programs, we recapitulate facts earlier presented.

VWIL affords women no opportunity to experience the rigorous military training for which VMI is famed. Instead, the VWIL program "deemphasize[s]" military education, and uses a "cooperative method" of education "which reinforces self-esteem.". . .

In myriad respects other than military training, VWIL does not qualify as VMI's equal. VWIL's student body, faculty, course offerings, and facilities hardly match VMI's. Nor can the VWIL graduate anticipate the benefits associated with VMI's 157-year history, the school's prestige, and its influential alumni network. . . .

Virginia, in sum, while maintaining VMI for men only, has failed to provide any "comparable single-gender women's institution." Instead, the Commonwealth has created a VWIL program fairly appraised as a "pale shadow" of VMI in terms of the range of curricular choices and faculty stature, funding, prestige, alumni support and influence. . . .

The Fourth Circuit plainly erred in exposing Virginia's VWIL plan to a deferential analysis, for "all gender-based classifications today" warrant "heightened scrutiny." Valu-

able as VWIL may prove for students who seek the program offered, Virginia's remedy affords no cure at all for the opportunities and advantages withheld from women who want a VMI education and can make the grade. In sum, Virginia's remedy does not match the constitutional violation; the State has shown no "exceedingly persuasive justification" for withholding from women qualified for the experience premier training of the kind VMI affords. . . .

For the reasons stated, the initial judgment of the Court of Appeals, is affirmed, the final judgment of the Court of Appeals, is reversed, and the case is remanded for further proceedings consistent with this opinion.

It Is So Ordered.

STUDY QUESTIONS

1. What was VMI's educational mission? Why were women excluded from VMI?
2. Although VWIL shared VMI's mission, VWIL's academic program, methods of education, and financial resources were different. Explain how they were different and what, if any, effect this had on VWIL's comparability to VMI.
3. Why did the Fourth Circuit originally remand the case to the district court? What did the district court determine on remand? The second time, the Fourth Circuit affirmed the district court's decision. Why?
4. Two issues were presented to the Supreme Court. What were they? How did the Supreme Court rule on each of these issues and why?
5. What level of scrutiny did the Supreme Court state is applicable to all gender-based classifications? Applying that standard, what did the Court conclude?

Two days after the *U.S. v. Virginia* decision was issued, The Citadel announced that it would immediately and "enthusiastically" begin admitting qualified women into its corps of cadets. Within a month, VMI would do the same. Since VMI and The Citadel were the only remaining single-sex public institutions of higher education, that decision effectively settled the question of gendered admissions policies at that level of public schools. Because the decision did not directly address the question of whether the "separate but equal doctrine" survived in the area of sex discrimination, the future of single-sex elementary and secondary public schools or gender-segregated special classes at those schools was not clear.

On January 8, 2002, the No Child Left Behind Act of 2001 was signed into law by President Bush. That act reauthorized the Elementary and Secondary Education Act, and allowed federal education funds to be used for single-sex schools and classrooms as long as comparable courses, services, and facilities were made available to both sexes. On October 24, 2006, the Secretary of Education announced the release of the final Title IX single-sex regulations applicable to non-vocational single-sex classes, extracurricular activities, and schools at the elementary and secondary levels (34 C.F.R. §106). These regulations, which were published in the Federal Register on October 25, 2006, and became effective on November 24, 2006, provided more flexibility for offering such single-sex programs in public schools.

The implementation of the new regulations heightened the debate over the appropriateness of single-sex schools. Title IX's original intent was to "level the playing field" for women in education. Armed with the protection of Title IX, barriers for girls in public education were breached. Now proponents of single-sex education argue that such schools and classes are necessary because there is a crisis for boys in education. They argue that boys are not doing as well and assert the same arguments seen in prior cases—boys and girls learn differently and girls in the classroom are a distraction for adolescent boys. Opponents express fear that a resurgence of single-sex schools or classes will result in the erosion of girls' gains under Title IX and return girls to "separate" but "unequal" classrooms.

It is questionable whether a "boys" crisis exists and, if it does, whether single-sex schools are the answer. In 2008, the AAUW issued a report entitled "Where the Girls Are: The Facts About Gender Equity in Education" that reviewed girls' educational achievements over the past thirty-five years and paid particular attention to the relationship between girls' and boys' progress. It stated, "Educational achievement is not a zero-sum game, in which a gain for one group results in a corresponding loss for the other." Furthermore, the report said, "Family income level and race/ethnicity are closely associated with academic performance." The findings reviewed in the AAUW report concerning standardized tests, such as the NAEP, SAT, and ACT, demonstrated that children from the lowest-income families had the lowest average test scores. In addition, there was also a strong correlation between race/ethnicity and test scores; African American and Hispanic girls and boys scored lower than white and Asian American children. Gender differences in educational achievement varied by race, ethnicity, and family level; the gender gap was most consistent for white students, less so for African American students, and least among Hispanic students. The report concluded that girls' gains have not come at boys' expense; on average, both genders' educational performance has improved. If there is a crisis in educational achievement, therefore, it is not a crisis for boys, but rather one for both male and female students from African American, Hispanic, and lower-income families.

Under the new Title IX regulations, single-sex non-vocational classes and extracurricular activities are permitted in non-vocational, coeducational elementary or secondary schools if the class or extracurricular activity is based on an "important objective," such as improving students' educational achievement through an established policy to provide diverse educational opportunities or to meet a particular, identified educational need of students, provided the single-sex nature of the class or activity is "substantially related to achieving the important objective." If a single-sex class or extracurricular activity is offered under this section of the regulations, the recipient of federal funds *may* be required to provide a "substantially equal single-sex class or extracurricular activity" for students of the excluded sex. With respect to single-sex schools, a recipient that operates a single-sex public non-vocational elementary or secondary school *must* provide a "substantially equal school" to students excluded from the single-sex school based on sex, but that "substantially equal school" may be either single-sex or coeducational. The new regulations also exempt from the "substantially equal school" requirement a non-vocational public charter school that is a single-school local educational agency (LEA) under state law. Some of the factors (individually or in the aggregate) the Department of Education will consider in determining whether a class or school is "substantially equal" are:

> . . . the policies and criteria of admission, the educational benefits provided, including the quality, range, and content of curriculum and other services and the quality and availability of books, instructional materials, and technology, the qualifications of faculty and staff, geographic accessibility, the quality, accessibility, and availability of facilities and resources provided to the class, and intangible features, such as reputation of faculty.

Bolstered by the flexibility granted under these new regulations, many states seem intent to return to the concept of separating students by gender in elementary and secondary public schools.

Indeed, the National Association for Single Sex Public Education (NASSPE) reports that as of March of 2009, there were at least 540 U.S. public schools offering single-sex educational opportunities. And, although most of these appear to be coed schools with single-sex classrooms and some coed activities (in some instances only coed lunch and 1–2 electives) at least 95 of the 540 schools NASSPE lists on its Web site are single-sex schools, that is, all school activities (including lunch and electives) are all-boy or all-girl. According to NASSPE, the new Title IX regulations give school districts some incentive to offer single-sex schools instead of single-sex classrooms within coed schools. Certainly, these new regulations lay to rest most fears of single-sex schools being shut down, so long as they meet the requirements set forth in the Title IX regulations. In some states, however, single-sex schools may still face obstacles. For example, Massachusetts laws make it difficult for public, non-charter schools to offer single-sex classes, and for school districts to establish single-sex schools. On January 14, 2009, Bill No. 2262 was filed in the Massachusetts House of Representatives, entitled "An Act Providing for Opportunities for Single-Sex School and Classes"; however, its chance for success seems remote given that this is the fourth year in a row that such a bill has been filed in the Commonwealth's House of Representatives. Furthermore, a bill filed on January 5, 2009, entitled "An Act Relative to Gender Based Discrimination and Hate Crimes" seems to take aim at the purpose of Bill No. 2262 by seeking to amend the same statutes relating to both charter schools and public schools to ensure that no one will be excluded from admission to either type of school on the basis of sex.

Although there is a resurgence of interest in single-sex schools in the public sector at the primary and secondary levels, in the private sector, single-sex schools are quickly becoming a rarity. At the college level, these schools are succumbing to financial pressures that have resulted from an overall decline in the numbers of college-age students and from changing educational preferences among high school graduates. In 2008, only three private all-men colleges remained in the United States: Hampden-Sydney College (Virginia); Morehouse (Georgia); and Wabash College (Indiana). The picture for all-women schools is almost as extreme. Although there were 298 women's colleges in 1960, approximately sixty remained at the end of 2008. And, of the seven sister colleges, only five—Barnard (New York); Bryn Mawr (Pennsylvania); and Mount Holyoke, Smith, and Wellesley (Massachusetts)— remain women's colleges; Vassar has admitted men since 1969, and Radcliffe merged with Harvard in 1977 and became the Radcliffe Institute for Advanced Study at Harvard (a non-degree-granting part of Harvard University) upon its complete integration in 1999.

The question of whether women-only schools ought to be encouraged is hotly debated among feminists as well as the educational community. Advocates of all-women schools emphasize the educational benefits available to women in supportive single-sex settings, in contrast with the "chilly climate" that so pervades coeducational schools. These arguments were stressed by Justice Powell in his *Hogan* dissent. The learning environment of women's colleges fosters self-confidence, intellectual self-esteem, and high aspirations among their students. They prepare women to assume positions of leadership in society. They encourage young women to pursue nontraditional fields of study, such as mathematics and the natural sciences. They provide resources that enable women to go on, after graduation, to promote equity for women in all walks of life. Studies showing that elite women's colleges have been historically more successful at producing career-oriented women graduates than have coeducational colleges and universities are adduced in support of these claims. Given the resurgence of interest in single-sex primary and secondary schools and classes, it will be interesting to see what the future now holds for private single-sex colleges.

III. SCHOOL SPORTS

The same "sex-role socialization" that adversely affected girls in the pre-1970s also worked to the disadvantage of female students in school athletic programs. Title IX and its interpretative regulations prohibited discrimination in many aspects of school sport programs. The enforcement of Title IX, however, was lax, especially during the Reagan and Bush administrations. As a result, the debate over sex discrimination in this area, like that over single-sex schools, has taken place within the framework of constitutional litigation. Once again, a review of the role that gender has played in schools affords the context for the legal discussion.

WOMEN AND SPORTS
Susan L. Morse
2 *CQ Researcher* 194–215 (1992).

The ancient Greeks didn't just exclude women from Olympic competition. They barred them from even viewing the games on pain of death. According to legend, those caught disobeying were hurled off the cliffs. But some plucky women established their own counterpart—the all-female Herean Games at Olympia, held a month before the Olympics. Females in Sparta, another macho Greek society, were encouraged to train from girlhood in running, jumping and javelin throwing, on the theory that athletics built better breeders.

It would be many grim centuries later before large numbers of women would experience such freedom again. In 19th-century America, the well-to-do insisted on women's frailty, even while poor women lived lives of backbreaking toil. The modern concept of sports that formed by the end of the century excluded women. Popular leaders including Teddy Roosevelt glorified men's athleticism to combat what they saw as the "feminizing" effects of a more sedentary, post-industrial way of life. Sports, they said, built character, perseverance, strength and respect for authority—traits considered irrelevant for women.

Title IX led to a new era in athletics for women

But not all women thought so. Such women's colleges as Vassar began incorporating physical education into their curricula. And though critics warned physical exertion would damage women's reproductive capabilities and leave them too tired to fulfill their "womanly duties," students appeared to benefit. Other women followed suit, shedding tight corsets to gain freedom of movement. *yay them!*

For decades, the emphasis in women's gym classes was on play rather than competitive sport. Claiming women were more susceptible than men to heart strain, fatigue and other injury, educators changed game rules to restrict movement and vigorously opposed women's participation in Olympic games and tournaments. Athletic scholarships were rejected as potentially exploitative. "A game for every girl and a girl for every game," proclaimed the motto of the women's division of the National Amateur Athletic Federation in the 1930s. Women physical educators brandished the popular slogan to reassure women that all females would have an opportunity in sports, albeit not at a highly competitive level. The philosophy prevailed well into the 1960s.

In 1971 only 294,000 girls played high school sports, compared with nearly 2 million today. "Don't worry," parents of tomboys consoled one another. "They'll grow out of it." Most did. They had to. At colleges like the University of Michigan, the budget for women's sports was zero, and would-be athletes raised funds by selling apples at football games. Coeds' coaches—nearly all women—were unpaid, the equipment make-do and the practice time catch as catch can. Both in school, where gym classes were sex-segregated, and out, competition with boys was discouraged: Girls were routinely banned from Little League and other playing fields.

But the social revolution that was transforming the workplace, the family and education quickly spread to the gym, spurred by a new fitness craze and a potent federal law. Title IX of the Education Amend-

ments of 1972 outlawed discrimination by sex in all schools receiving federal funds. The floodgates opened, and a new era in sports began.

Women today are roughly a third of all college athletes. They make up the majority of new participants in weight training, running, cycling and basketball. And more females than males swim, exercise aerobically and ride bicycles. Even such physically grueling contests as triathlons have seen jumps in female participation, from 1,200 women in 1982 to 72,000 in 1990.

More girls are exposed to sports at a young age, encouraged by a major shift in social attitudes: Nearly 90 percent of the 1,000 parents interviewed in a 1988 study viewed sports participation as important for their daughters as for their sons.

Female athletes' visibility and credibility have increased, too. While at annual sports rites like the Super Bowl women still appear only as nubile distractions, other audiences are learning that talented female players provide just as good entertainment as the men.

College basketball is a case in point. Last season, some 4 million fans attended women's games, more than double the attendance in 1981–82. CBS cameras followed the thrilling National Collegiate Athletic Association (NCAA) championship game on March 31, 1991, in which Tennessee squeaked past Virginia in triple overtime, 70–67. And just last month [February 1992] No. 2-ranked Virginia stole first place from Maryland before 14,500 fans—the fourth-largest regular season crowd in women's basketball history.

And talk about a steal. American women ran away with the gold this year at the Winter Olympics in Albertville, France, scooping up all five of the American team's first-place medals and nine of 11 U.S. medals overall.

But despite such gains, women's access still is severely limited: The playing field is far from level. "Sports in our society," says Donna Lopiano, director of intercollegiate athletics for women at the University of

Texas at Austin, "is still a right for little boys and a privilege for little girls."

At the university level, equity in sports is regarded as something of a joke. Nationwide, female college athletes routinely get a third of the team spots, less than a third of the scholarship dollars and a mere fifth of the total athletic budget.

At the Olympic level, opportunities also are limited. Women's water polo, weightlifting, ice hockey, wrestling, soccer and pentathlon all have world championships—but no Olympic status, in most cases because the sports can't meet required participation levels. Men compete in all 33 Olympics sports categories, while women only compete in 24 of them. One-third of all events are for men only.

Fewer than ever female student athletes enter careers in physical education, and leadership ranks are shrinking. In 1972 women coached more than 90 percent of college women's sports teams and headed nearly all women's college athletic programs. Female coaches today head less than a quarter of all teams. Female athletic direc-

tors, at 16 percent, are practically an endangered species.

The fight for women's sports is ultimately a fight for greater social access. "Sports has traditionally been used to train males for the competitive world of corporate games," says Lopiano. Sports, she says, teaches "loyalty, playing as a team, playing a role"—all with direct application in business. "When you remove sports from the training of women, you make them less competitive in other activities, including the work world."

STUDY QUESTIONS

1. What is involved in the "modern concept of sports," as articulated by Teddy Roosevelt? Have women's sports programs ever aspired to realizing that concept?
2. What have been some of the major changes in women's sports since the enactment of Title IX? What are some of the hurdles still standing in the way of equal opportunity in school sports?

Participation in athletics is recognized today as an important dimension of any healthy, vigorous lifestyle. Athletics have not always been viewed in that way. From earliest times, sport was represented as a form of combat, with victory over the adversary as the primary measure of accomplishment. Winning, as the best athletes and coaches stress, is not the only thing that is valued about athletics. Boys have traditionally been introduced to sports at an early age not only to urge upon them the skills and attitudes of combat but also so they will learn important lessons about self-discipline, self-confidence, leadership, and teamwork. These lessons are valuable to anyone who strives for achievement in a competitive environment, whether on the playing field or in the boardroom.

In our era, the lessons afforded by participation in sports are increasingly recognized as valuable for both boys and girls. Until quite recently, however, there was little commitment to afford athletic opportunities to girls. Even thirty-five years after the passage of Title IX, equity in school sports is not within sight. The 2002 NCWGE "Report Card on Gender Equity" ("Education Report Card") gave the nation a "C+" in athletics. According to that report, even though women's and girl's participation in high school and college sports had increased dramatically in the thirty years since Title IX was enacted, the amount of resources and benefits colleges provide for women athletes lags far behind that for men (the report noted there is no national data on expenditures for girls' and boys' interscholastic sports, but anecdotal evidence suggests the same holds true for elementary and secondary sports). According to the NCWGE 2008 report, "Title IX at 35: Beyond the Headlines," even though 44 percent of the high school population was female in 2005, they received only 41 percent of the athletic participation opportunities. On the college level the gap was even greater for women: as 57 percent of the student population they received only 43 percent of the athletic opportunities. Furthermore, only 35 percent of the athletic administrators and 19 percent of the athletic directors are women. Finally, between 1971 (the year before Title IX was enacted) and 2006, the number of female head coaches for college women's teams has steadily diminished from a high of 90 percent to 42 percent.

Even so, much has changed in the sports area for girls and women over the past thirty-five years. The accomplishments of women athletes have been widely noted, participation rates of girls have soared, budgets for the programs that serve the interests of girls and women students have improved, and attendance and fan interest in women's athletics have also shown marked increases. Despite these changes, much remains to be done. Legal remedies already exist for taking down some of the remaining barriers. For others, legal remedies are being developed. This section explores some of these remedies.

Sex-Segregated Athletics

We saw in earlier sections of this chapter that, unlike race segregation in the schools, sex segregation can survive an equal protection challenge. In that context, the separate but equal doctrine remains intact provided that single-sex programs can be shown to be substantially related to the advancement of important government interests. Courts have applied the same equal protection standard to sex segregation in school sports.

Sex stereotypes pervade debates over sports equity just as they do other educational contexts. The convictions that permeate discussions of girls and women participating in athletic programs include the following: (1) Girls and women are less athletically talented than boys and men. Thus, in any competition involving both sexes, females as a group will do less well than will males as a group. (2) Girls and women are more likely to sustain injury in athletic competitions than are boys and men. This carries forward the Victorian image of girls and women as frail and delicate. (3) Sport masculinizes girls. This conviction draws on the concept of sport as combat mentioned by Morse, as well as the cultural association of aggressiveness with masculinity. As a result, the femininity of female athletes is placed in doubt, often overtly, as when women sports figures are ridiculed as lesbians. (4) People are not interested in women's sports. The plausibility of this conviction, which rationalized the status quo for decades, is becoming increasingly difficult to maintain in the light of attendance figures reviewed by Morse.

The following case concerns a female member of a male college football team.

MERCER V. DUKE

United States Court of Appeals, Fourth Circuit, 1999. 109 F.3d 643.

LUTTIG, Circuit Judge.

Appellant Heather Sue Mercer challenges the federal district court's holding that Title IX provides a blanket exemption for contact sports and the court's consequent dismissal of her claim that Duke University discriminated against her during her participation in Duke's intercollegiate football program. For the reasons that follow, we hold that where a university has allowed a member of the opposite sex to try out for a single-sex team in a contact sport, the university is, contrary to the holding of the district court, subject to Title IX and therefore prohibited from discriminating against that individual on the basis of his or her sex.

I

Appellee Duke University operates a Division I college football team. During the period relevant to this appeal (1994–98), appellee Fred Goldsmith was head coach of the Duke football team and appellant Heather Sue Mercer was a student at the school.

Before attending Duke, Mercer was an all-state kicker at Yorktown Heights High School in Yorktown Heights, New York. Upon enrolling at Duke in the fall of 1994, Mercer tried out for the Duke football team as a walk-on kicker. Mercer was the first—and to date, only—woman to try out for the team. Mercer did not initially make the team, and instead served as a manager during the 1994 season; however, she regularly attended practices in the fall of 1994 and participated in conditioning drills the following spring.

In April 1995, the seniors on the team selected Mercer to participate in the Blue-White Game, an intrasquad scrimmage played each spring. In that game, Mercer kicked the winning 28-yard field goal, giving the Blue team a 24–22 victory. The kick was subsequently shown on ESPN, the cable television sports network. Soon after the game, Goldsmith told the news media that Mercer was on the Duke football team, and Fred Chatham, the Duke kicking coach, told Mercer herself that she had made the team. Also, Mike Cragg, the Duke sports information director, asked Mercer to participate in a number of interviews with newspaper, radio, and television reporters, including one with representatives from *The Tonight Show*.

Although Mercer did not play in any games during the 1995 season, she again regularly attended practices in the fall and participated in conditioning drills the following spring. Mercer was also officially listed by Duke as a member of the Duke football team on the team roster filed with

the NCAA and was pictured in the Duke football yearbook.

During this latter period, Mercer alleges that she was the subject of discriminatory treatment by Duke. Specifically, she claims that Goldsmith did not permit her to attend summer camp, refused to allow her to dress for games or sit on the sidelines during games, and gave her fewer opportunities to participate in practices than other walk-on kickers. In addition, Mercer claims that Goldsmith made a number of offensive comments to her, including asking her why she was interested in football, wondering why she did not prefer to participate in beauty pageants rather than football, and suggesting that she sit in the stands with her boyfriend rather than on the sidelines.

At the beginning of the 1996 season, Goldsmith informed Mercer that he was dropping her from the team. Mercer alleges that Goldsmith's decision to exclude her from the team was on the basis of her sex because Goldsmith allowed other, less qualified walk-on kickers to remain on the team. Mercer attempted to participate in conditioning drills the following spring, but Goldsmith asked her to leave because the drills were only for members of the team. Goldsmith told Mercer, however, that she could try out for the team again in the fall.

On September 16, 1997, rather than try out for the team again, Mercer filed suit against Duke and Goldsmith, alleging sex discrimination in violation of Title IX of the Education Amendments of 1972, 20 U.S.C. §§ 1681–1688, and negligent misrepresentation and breach of contract in violation of North Carolina law. Duke and Goldsmith filed a motion to dismiss for failure to state a claim under Title IX, and, after discovery was completed, Duke and Goldsmith filed additional motions for summary judgment and a motion to dismiss for lack of subject-matter jurisdiction. On November 9, 1998, the district court granted the motion to dismiss for failure to state a claim under Title IX, and dismissed the state-law claims without prejudice, refusing to exercise supplemental jurisdiction over those claims. The district court declined to rule on any of the other outstanding motions. The district court subsequently denied Mercer's motion to alter judgment.

From the district court's order dismissing her Title IX claim for failure to state a claim upon which relief can be granted and its order denying the motion to alter judgment, Mercer appeals.

II

Title IX prohibits discrimination on the basis of sex by educational institutions receiving federal funding. See 20 U.S.C. § 1681(a) ("No person in the United States shall, on the basis of sex, be excluded from participation in, be denied the benefits of, or be subjected to discrimination under any education program or activity receiving Federal financial assistance. . .."). Soon after enacting Title IX, Congress charged the Department of Health, Education, and Welfare (HEW) with responsibility for developing regulations regarding the applicability of Title IX to athletic programs. See Pub. L. No. 93–380, § 844, 88 Stat. 484 (1974). Acting upon that charge, HEW duly promulgated 34 C.F.R. § 106.41, which reads in relevant part as follows:

ATHLETICS

(a) General. No person shall, on the basis of sex, be excluded from participation in, be denied the benefits of, be treated differently from another person or otherwise be discriminated against in any interscholastic, intercollegiate, club or intramural athletics offered by a recipient, and no recipient shall provide any such athletics separately on such basis.

(b) Separate teams. Notwithstanding the requirements of paragraph (a) of this section, a recipient may operate or sponsor separate teams for members of each sex where selection for such teams is based upon competitive skill or the activity involved is a contact sport. However, where a recipient operates or sponsors a team in a particular sport for members of one sex but operates or sponsors no such team for members of the other sex, and athletic opportunities for members of that

sex have previously been limited, members of the excluded sex must be allowed to try out for the team offered unless the sport involved is a contact sport. For the purposes of this part, contact sports include boxing, wrestling, rugby, ice hockey, football, basketball and other sports the purpose or major activity of which involves bodily contact. . . .

The district court held, and appellees contend on appeal, that, under this regulation, "contact sports, such as football, are specifically excluded from Title IX coverage." We disagree.

Subsections (a) and (b) of section 106.41 stand in a symbiotic relationship to one another. Subsection (a) establishes a baseline prohibition against sex discrimination in intercollegiate athletics, tracking almost identically the language in the parallel statutory provision prohibiting discrimination by federally funded educational institutions. In addition to generally barring discrimination on the basis of sex in intercollegiate athletics, subsection (a) specifically prohibits any covered institution from "provid[ing] any such athletics separately on such basis."

Standing alone, then, subsection (a) would require covered institutions to integrate all of their sports teams. In order to avoid such a result—which would have radically altered the face of intercollegiate athletics—HEW provided an explicit exception to the rule of subsection (a) in the first sentence of subsection (b), allowing covered institutions to "operate or sponsor separate teams for members of each sex where selection for such teams is based upon competitive skill or the activity involved is a contact sport." By its terms, this sentence permits covered institutions to operate separate teams for men and women in many sports, including contact sports such as football, rather than integrating those teams. The first sentence of subsection (b), however, leaves unanswered the question of what, if any, restrictions apply to sports in which a covered institution operates a team for one sex, but operates no corresponding team for the other sex.

HEW addressed this question in the second sentence of subsection (b).

This second sentence is applicable only when two predicate criteria are met: first, that the institution in question "operates or sponsors a team in a particular sport for members of one sex but operates or sponsors no such team for members of the other sex," and second, that "athletic opportunities for members of that sex have previously been limited." In this case, appellees do not dispute that athletic opportunities for women at Duke have previously been limited, and thus we assume that the second condition has been met. Further, we assume, without deciding, that Duke operated its football team "for members of one sex"—that is, for only men—but did not operate a separate team "for members of the other sex," and therefore that the first condition has also been satisfied [footnote omitted]. Thus, insofar as the present appeal is concerned, we consider the predicate conditions to application of the sentence to have been met.

Provided that both of the conditions in the protasis of the second sentence of subsection (b) have been met, the apodosis of the sentence requires that "members of the excluded sex must be allowed to try out for the team offered unless the sport involved is a contact sport." The text of this clause, on its face, is incomplete: it affirmatively specifies that members of the excluded sex must be allowed to try out for single-sex teams where no team is provided for their sex except in the case of contact sports, but is silent regarding what requirements, if any, apply to single-sex teams in contact sports. As to contact sports, this clause is susceptible of two interpretations. First, it could be read to mean that "members of the excluded sex must be allowed to try out for the team offered unless the sport involved is a contact sport, *in which case the anti-discrimination provision of subsection (a) does not apply at all.*" Second, it could be interpreted to mean that "members of the excluded sex must be allowed to try out for the team offered unless the sport involved is a contact sport, *in*

which case members of the excluded sex need not be allowed to try out."

Appellees advocate the former reading, arguing that HEW intended through this clause to exempt contact sports entirely from the coverage of Title IX. We believe, however, that the latter reading is the more natural and intended meaning. The second sentence of subsection (b) does not purport in any way to state an exemption, whether for contact sports or for any other subcategory, from the general anti-discrimination rule stated in subsection (a). And HEW certainly knew how to provide for a complete exemption had it wished, Congress itself having provided a number of such exemptions in the very statute implemented by the regulation. Rather, the sentence says, and says only, that covered institutions must allow members of an excluded sex to try out for single-sex teams in non-contact sports. Therefore, the "unless" phrase at the end of the second clause of the sentence cannot (logically or grammatically) do anything more than except contact sports from the tryout requirement that the beginning of the second clause of the sentence imposes on all other sports.

Contrary to appellees' assertion, this reading of the regulation is perfectly consistent with the evident congressional intent not to require the sexual integration of intercollegiate contact sports. If a university chooses not to permit members of the opposite sex to try out for a single-sex contact-sports team, this interpretation respects that choice. At the same time, however, the reading of the regulation we adopt today, unlike the one advanced by appellees, ensures that the likewise indisputable congressional intent to prohibit discrimination in all circumstances where such discrimination is unreasonable—for example, where the university itself has voluntarily opened the team in question to members of both sexes—is not frustrated. We therefore construe the second sentence of subsection (b) as providing that in non-contact sports, but not in contact sports, covered institutions must allow members of an excluded sex to try out for single-sex teams. Once an institution has allowed a member of one sex to try out for a team operated by the institution for the other sex in a contact sport, subsection (b) is simply no longer applicable, and the institution is subject to the general anti-discrimination provision of subsection (a). To the extent that the Third Circuit intended to hold otherwise in *Williams v. School Dist. of Bethlehem, Pa.*, 998 F.2d 168, 174 (3d Cir. 1993), with its lone unexplained statement that, "[i]f it is determined that [a particular sport] is a contact sport, no other inquiry is necessary because that will be dispositive of the Title IX claim," we reject such a conclusion as inconsistent with the language of the regulation.

Accordingly, because appellant has alleged that Duke allowed her to try out for its football team (and actually made her a member of the team), then discriminated against her and ultimately excluded her from participation in the sport on the basis of her sex, we conclude that she has stated a claim under the applicable regulation, and therefore under Title IX. We take to heart appellees' cautionary observation that, in so holding, we thereby become "the first Court in United States history to recognize such a cause of action." Br. of Appellees at 20. Where, as here, however, the university invites women into what appellees characterize as the "traditionally all-

male bastion of collegiate football," *id.* at 20 n.10, we are convinced that this reading of the regulation is the only one permissible under law.

The district court's order granting appellees' motion to dismiss for failure to state a claim is hereby reversed, and the case is remanded for further proceedings.

Reversed and Remanded

STUDY QUESTIONS

1. Did Duke operate its team for members of one sex (i.e., men)? Did Duke have a women's football team? Why were these facts important to the Fourth Circuit's determination?
2. How did Mercer, a woman, become a member of the Duke football team? What position did she play? What was the discriminatory treatment to which Mercer alleged she was subjected?
3. Review the sections of Title IX cited by the Fourth Circuit. Now review the court's analysis of the facts in this case pursuant to those sections of Title IX. Do you agree with the Fourth Circuit's conclusion that once Duke allowed Mercer to try out for the men's football team, subsection (b) no longer applied and the university was subject to the general anti-discrimination provision of subsection (a)? Why or why not?

Mercer prevailed at the trial upon remand and was awarded compensatory damages of $1, punitive damages of $2 million, and attorney's fees. In an unpublished decision issued on November 15, 2002, the Fourth Circuit vacated the punitive damages award and remanded the case to the district court to determine whether the award of attorney's fees remained appropriate. And, in *Mercer v. Duke*, 401 F.3d 199 (4th Cir. 2005), the Fourth Circuit affirmed the district court's award of almost $350,000 in attorney's fees.

This case appears to support the cause of women athletes who wish to participate in men's contact sports teams. It may, however, operate in the reverse. As noted earlier in this chapter, Title IX permits single-sex teams in contact sports such as football and does not require schools to allow members of the opposite sex to try out for those teams. In addition, Title IX does not require schools to provide a separate-but-equal team for a contact sport. So, schools wishing to avoid litigation and potential exposure may simply prohibit women from playing on men's contact sports teams and the women would have no recourse under Title IX.

Inequitable Availability of Resources

The struggle for equitable treatment in athletics at the college and university level has proven a greater challenge than it was at the primary and secondary level. As Morse intimated, that is due in large part to the insinuation of professional sports interests at the college level. The dimensions and difficulty of this struggle are most evident in such mundane but vital issues as budgets, facilities, schedules, recruiting, and coaching. In these areas, although there has been substantial progress toward equity, much remains to be done.

Morse pointed out that in the early 1970s, many women's college teams had no budget at all. They typically relied on such traditional devices as bake sales to raise money for uniforms. It was not unusual for the coaches of the women's teams to volunteer their time, for the facilities to be unmaintained, and for scholarship aid to be entirely unavailable to women athletes. Just as in an earlier age girls and women were not taken seriously as students, so in the 1970s, they were seldom regarded as serious athletes. Indeed, at the time that Title IX was enacted, the very idea that women's sports should be afforded resources comparable with those provided for men's sports struck many collegiate officials as absurd. As women's sports historian Allen Guttmann reports, "At a time when Father Edmund M. Joyce, an executive vice-president of Notre Dame University, castigated Title IX as 'asinine,' his university allotted over $1 million for financial aid to male athletes and not a penny for the women."

Until quite recently, Title IX has afforded little effective recourse. Under the Reagan administration, and particularly in the wake of the *Grove City College* decision previously discussed, the federal government did little to enforce the act's requirements. With the passage of the Civil Rights Restoration Act in March 1988, the courts became more engaged. Within months, Temple University settled an eight-year-old suit that focused on inequity in its sports programs. With the incentive of a restored Title IX, the university agreed to take a wide range of significant steps to place women's athletics on a par with men's programs. The provisions of the settlement included steps toward budget parity, new teams for women, increased coach and trainer staff serving women athletes, and a full-time publicist for women's programs. Temple's example, however, was not widely imitated. In fact, the NWCGA, in its 2008 report, states that resources for women's teams continue to lag behind; women athletes in college received only 37 percent of the sports-operating dollars and 32 percent of the recruitment dollars during the 2003–04 school year. In addition, equipment, facilities, and publicity are still not allocated equally to women's and men's teams.

Although suits alleging sports-related violations of Title IX have often been filed, by the 1990s, few had been fully litigated. In the first such case to reach the circuit court level, the court signaled its determination to require equitable opportunities for both sexes in school athletics.

COHEN v. BROWN UNIVERSITY
United States Court of Appeals, First Circuit. 1993. 991 F.2d 888.

SELYA, Circuit Judge.

In this watershed case, defendants-appellants Brown University . . . appeal from the district court's issuance of a preliminary injunction ordering Brown to reinstate its women's gymnastics and volleyball programs to full intercollegiate varsity status pending the resolution of a Title IX claim. After mapping Title IX's rugged legal terrain and cutting a passable swath through the factual thicket that over-spreads the parties' arguments, we affirm.

College athletics, particularly in the realm of football and basketball, has traditionally occupied a prominent role in American sports and American society. For college students, athletics offers an opportunity to execute leadership skills, learn teamwork, build self-confidence, and perfect self-discipline. In addition, for many student-athletes, physical skills are a passport to college admissions and scholarships, allowing them to attend otherwise inaccessible schools. These opportunities, and the lessons learned on the playing fields, are invaluable in attaining career and life successes in and out of professional sports.

The highway of opportunity runs in both directions. Not only student-athletes, but universities, too, benefit from the magic of intercollegiate sports. Successful teams generate television revenues and gate receipts which often fund significant percentages of a university's overall athletic program, offering students the opportunity to partake of sports that are not financially self-sustaining. Even those institutions whose teams do not fill the grandstands of cavernous stadiums or attract national television exposure benefit from increased student and alumni cohesion and the support it engenders. Thus, universities nurture the legends, great or small, inhering in their athletic past, polishing the hardware that adorns field-house trophy cases and reliving heroic exploits in the pages of alumni magazines.

In these terms, Brown will never be confused with Notre Dame or the more muscular members of the Big Ten. Although its football team did play in the 1916 Rose Bowl and its men's basketball team won the Ivy League championship as recently as 1986, Brown's athletic program has only occasionally achieved national prominence or, for that matter, enjoyed sustained success. Moreover, at Brown, as at most schools, women are a relatively inconspicuous part of the storied athletic past. Historically, colleges limited athletics to the male sphere, leaving those few women's teams that sprouted to scrounge for resources.

The absence of women's athletics at Brown was, until 1970, an ineluctable consequence of the absence of women; Brown sponsored a women's college—Pembroke—but did not itself admit women. In 1971, Brown subsumed Pembroke. Brown promptly upgraded Pembroke's rather primitive athletic offerings so that by 1977 there were fourteen women's varsity teams. In subsequent years, Brown added only one distaff team winter track. Hence, in the 1991–92 academic year, Brown fielded fifteen women's varsity teams—one fewer than the number of men's varsity teams.

In the spring of 1991, Brown announced that it, like many other schools, was in a financial bind, and that, as a belt-tightening measure, it planned to drop four sports from its intercollegiate varsity athletic roster: women's volleyball and gymnastics, men's golf, and water polo. The University permitted the teams to continue playing as "intercollegiate clubs," a status that allowed them to compete against varsity teams from other colleges, but cut off financial subsidies and support services routinely available to varsity teams (e.g., salaried coaches, access to prime facilities, preferred practice time, medical trainers, clerical assistance, office support, admission preferences, and the like). Brown estimated that eliminating these four varsity teams would save $77,813 per annum, broken down as follows: women's volleyball, $37,127; women's gymnastics, $24,901; men's water polo, $9,250; men's golf, $6,545.

Before the cuts, Brown athletics offered an aggregate of 328 varsity slots for female athletes and 566 varsity slots for male athletes. Thus, women had 36.7% of the athletic opportunities and men 63.3%. Abolishing the four varsity teams took substantially more dollars from the women's athletic budget than from the men's budget, but did not materially affect the athletic opportunity ratios; women retained 36.6% of the opportunities and men 63.4%. At that time (and for a number of years prior thereto), Brown's student body comprised approximately 52% men and 48% women.

Following Brown's announcement of the cutbacks, disappointed members of the women's volleyball and gymnastics teams brought suit. . . . The plaintiffs charged that Brown's athletic arrangements violated Title IX's ban on gender-based discrimination, a violation that was allegedly exacerbated by Brown's decision to devalue the two women's programs without first making sufficient reductions in men's activities or, in the alternative, adding other women's teams to compensate for the loss.

. . . [A]fter hearing fourteen days of testimony from twenty witnesses, the [district court] judge granted a preliminary injunction requiring Brown to reinstate the two women's teams pending the outcome of a full trial on the merits. We stayed execution of the order and expedited Brown's appeal.

Title IX prohibits gender-based discrimination by educational institutions receiving federal financial support—in practice, the vast majority of all accredited colleges and universities. The statute sketches wide policy lines, leaving the details to regulating agencies. . . .

[The court next reviewed the provisions of Title IX and its implementing regulations, focusing in particular upon an HEW policy interpretation that specifies] three major areas of regulatory compliance: "Athletic Financial Assistance (Scholarships)," "Equivalence in Other Athletic Benefits and Opportunities," and "Effective Accommodation of Student Interests and Abilities." The court below . . . adopted this formulation and ruled that a university violates Title IX if it ineffectively accommodates student interests and abilities, regardless of its performance in other Title IX areas.

Equal opportunity to participate lies at the core of Title IX's purpose. Because the third compliance area delineates this heartland, we agree with the district courts that have so ruled and hold that, with regard to the effective accommodation of students' interests and abilities, an institution can violate Title IX even if it meets the "finan-

cial assistance" and "athletic equivalence" standards. . . .

. . . The parties agree that the third compliance area is the field on which this appeal must be fought. In surveying the dimensions of this battleground, that is, whether an athletic program effectively accommodates students' interests and abilities, the Policy Interpretation maps a trinitarian model under which the university must meet at least one of three benchmarks: (1) Whether intercollegiate level participation opportunities for male and female students are provided in numbers substantially proportionate to their respective enrollments; or (2) Where the members of one sex have been and are underrepresented among intercollegiate athletes, whether the institution can show a history and continuing practice of program expansion which is demonstrably responsive to the developing interest and abilities of the members of that sex; or (3) Where the members of one sex are underrepresented among intercollegiate athletes, and the institution cannot show a continuing practice of program expansion such as that cited above, whether it can be demonstrated that the interests and abilities of the members of that sex have been fully and effectively accommodated by the present program. The first benchmark furnishes a safe harbor for those institutions that have distributed athletic opportunities in numbers "substantially proportionate" to the gender composition of their student bodies. Thus, a university which does not wish to engage in extensive compliance analysis may stay on the sunny side of Title IX simply by maintaining gender parity between its student body and its athletic lineup.

The second and third parts of the accommodation test recognize that there are circumstances under which, as a practical matter, something short of this proportionality is a satisfactory proxy for gender balance. For example, so long as a university is continually expanding athletic opportunities in an ongoing effort to meet the needs of the underrepresented gender, and persists in this approach as interest and ability levels in its student body and secondary feeder schools rise, benchmark two is satisfied and Title IX does not require that the university leap to complete gender parity in a single bound. Or, if a school has a student body in which one sex is demonstrably less interested in athletics, Title IX does not require that the school create teams for, or rain money upon, otherwise disinterested students; rather, the third benchmark is satisfied if the underrepresented sex's discernible interests are fully and effectively accommodated.

It seems unlikely, even in this day and age, that the athletic establishments of many coeducational universities reflect the gender balance of their student bodies. Similarly, the recent boom in Title IX suits suggests that, in an era of fiscal austerity, few universities are prone to expand athletic opportunities. It is not surprising, then, that schools more often than not attempt to manage the rigors of Title IX by satisfying the interests and abilities of the underrepresented gender, that is, by meeting the third benchmark of the accommodation test. Yet, this benchmark sets a high standard: it demands not merely some accommodation, but full and effective accommodation. If there is sufficient interest and ability among members of the statistically underrepresented gender, not slaked by existing programs, an institution necessarily fails this prong of the test.

Although the full-and-effective-accommodation standard is high, it is not absolute. Even when male athletic opportunities outnumber female athletic opportunities, and the university has not met the first benchmark (substantial statistical proportionality) or the second benchmark (continuing program expansion) of the accommodation test, the mere fact that there are some female students interested in a sport does not ipso facto require the school to provide a varsity team in order to comply with the third benchmark. Rather, the institution can satisfy the third benchmark by ensuring participatory opportunities at the intercollegiate level when, and to the extent that, there is "sufficient interest and ability among the members of the excluded sex to sustain a viable team and

a reasonable expectation of intercollegiate competition for that team. . . ." Staying on top of the problem is not sport for the short-winded: the institution must remain vigilant, "upgrading the competitive opportunities available to the historically disadvantaged sex as warranted by developing abilities among the athletes of that sex," until the opportunities for, and levels of, competition are equivalent by gender. . . .

. . . In an era where the practices of higher education must adjust to stunted revenues, careening costs, and changing demographics, colleges might well be obliged to curb spending on programs, like athletics, that do not lie at the epicenter of their institutional mission. Title IX does not purport to override financial necessity. Yet, the pruning of athletic budgets cannot take place solely in comptrollers' offices, isolated from the legislative and regulatory imperatives that Title IX imposes.

This case aptly illustrates the point. Brown earnestly professes that it has done no more than slash women's and men's athletics by approximately the same degree, and, indeed, the raw numbers lend partial credence to that characterization. But, Brown's claim overlooks the shortcomings that plagued its program before it took blade in hand. If a school, like Brown, eschews the first two benchmarks of the accommodation test, electing to stray from substantial proportionality and failing to march uninterruptedly in the direction of equal athletic opportunity, it must comply with the third benchmark. To do so, the school must fully and effectively accommodate the underrepresented gender's interests and abilities, even if that requires it to give the underrepresented gender (in this case, women) what amounts to a larger slice of a shrinking athletic-opportunity pie.

The record reveals that the court below paid heed to these realities. It properly recognized that even balanced use of the budget-paring knife runs afoul of Title IX where, as here, the fruits of a university's athletic program remain ill-distributed after the trimming takes place. . . .

The preliminary injunction is affirmed, the temporary stay is dissolved, and the cause is remanded to the district court for further proceedings.

STUDY QUESTIONS

1. What led Brown University to decrease the size of its varsity athletic program? Did that decision disproportionately affect women athletes at Brown?

2. Discuss the three ways that colleges and universities have historically neglected athletic opportunities for women students. Why did the court find that Brown's action fell short when judged by these benchmarks?

3. What course of action is Brown permitted to take during years of shrinking resources?

On remand, the District Court found Brown in violation of Title IX because it could satisfy none of the three prongs of the test identified by the First Circuit Court of Appeals, and in particular had not "demonstrated that the interests and abilities of members of [the underrepresented] sex have been fully and effectively accommodated by the present program." Appealing that decision, Brown asserted that it does satisfy the "relative interests" of its women students to the same extent that it satisfies those of its male students. In rejecting that argument, the First Circuit made an important point that bears repeating.

> Brown has contended throughout this litigation that the significant disparity in athletics opportunities for men and women at Brown is the result of a gender-based differential in the level of interest in sports and that the district court's application of the three-part test requires universities to provide athletics opportunities for women to an extent that exceeds their relative interests and abilities in sports. Thus, at the heart of this litigation is the question whether Title IX permits Brown to deny its female students equal opportunity to participate in sports, based upon its unproven assertion that the district court's finding of a significant disparity in athletics opportunities for male and female students reflects, not discrimination in Brown's intercollegiate athletics program, but a lack of interest on the part of its female students that is unrelated to a lack of opportunities.
>
> We view Brown's argument that women are less interested than men in participating in intercollegiate athletics, as well as its conclusion that institutions should be required to accommodate the interests and abilities of its female students only to the extent that it accommodates the interests and abilities of its male students, with great suspicion. To assert that Title IX permits institutions to provide fewer athletics participation opportunities for women than for men, based upon the premise that women are less interested in sports than are men, is (among other things) to ignore the fact that Title IX was enacted in order to remedy discrimination that results from stereotyped notions of women's interests and abilities.
>
> Interest and ability rarely develop in a vacuum; they evolve as a function of opportunity and experience. The Policy Interpretation recognizes that women's lower rate of participation in athletics reflects women's historical lack of opportunities to participate in sports. . . .
>
> Thus, there exists the danger that, rather than providing a true measure of women's interest in sports, statistical evidence purporting to reflect women's interest instead provides only a measure of the very discrimination that is and has been the basis for women's lack of opportunity to participate in sports. Prong three requires some kind of evidence of interest in athletics, and the Title IX framework permits the use of statistical evidence in assessing the level of interest in sports. Nevertheless, to allow a numbers-based lack-of-interest defense to become the instrument of further discrimination against the underrepresented gender would pervert the remedial purpose of Title IX. We conclude that, even if it can be empirically demonstrated that, at a particular time, women have less interest in sports than do men, such evidence, standing alone, cannot justify providing fewer athletics opportunities for women

than for men. Furthermore, such evidence is completely irrelevant where, as here, viable and successful women's varsity teams have been demoted or eliminated. *Cohen v. Brown University*, 101 F.3d 155, 178-80 (1st Cir. 1996), *cert. denied*, 520 U.S. 1186 (1997).

Subsequent to the Supreme Court's denial of certiorari, the parties submitted a proposed settlement to U.S. District Court Judge Ernest Torres, which was approved in June of 1998. Under the terms of that settlement, Brown must ensure that its women's intercollegiate athletics participation rate is within 3.5 percent of its women undergraduate enrollment rate. This percentage applies as long as Brown continues to offer the full complement of women's university-funded and donor-funded sports in its intercollegiate athletic program at the time of the settlement. If Brown eliminates or downgrades a current women's team, or adds or upgrades a men's team without adding or upgrading a corresponding women's team, the percentage participation rate Brown must ensure changes to within 2.5 percent of women's undergraduate enrollment at the school. In addition, Brown agreed to upgrade women's water polo from club to donor-funded varsity status and to guarantee funding for four teams found to be inadequately funded—gymnastics, fencing, skiing, and water polo.

In the more recent case of *Jackson v. Birmingham Board of Education*, 544 U.S. 167 (2005), which concerned allocation of resources in high school sports, girls' basketball coach Roderick Jackson was removed from his coaching position after complaining unsuccessfully to his supervisors that his team was not receiving equal funding or equal access to athletic equipment and facilities. He brought an action alleging that the school board had retaliated against him because he complained about sex discrimination in the high school's athletic program. The Supreme Court held that Title IX's private right of action encompasses claims of retaliation against an individual because he complained about sex discrimination, and remanded the case for trial. Prior to trial, Jackson reached a settlement with the school board that provided he would remain as the girls' basketball coach and receive $50,000, his attorneys would receive $340,000, and the school board would take all necessary steps to provide female athletes with facilities comparable to those used by male athletes.

Unfortunately, the advances attained through Title IX, the Department of Education's Policy Interpretation of 1979 and relevant case decisions may be undermined by the Department's more recent action. On March 17, 2005, the Department's Office for Civil Rights (OCR) issued a document entitled *Additional Clarification of Intercollegiate Athletics Policy: Three-Part Test—Part Three*, which sought to provide schools with specific guidance on part three of the three-prong test, that is, "the school is fully and effectively accommodating the interests and abilities of the underrepresented sex." According to the Additional Clarification,

> Under part three of the three-part test, an institution may provide proportionally fewer athletic participation opportunities to one sex, as compared to its enrollment rate, if the interests and abilities of the enrolled and admitted students of the underrepresented sex are being fully and effectively accommodated by the institution's current varsity athletics program [footnote omitted]. Merely showing that there is disproportionality in the athletic opportunities provided to male and female athletes is not evidence of unmet interests and abilities of the underrepresented sex. There must be actual evidence of unmet interests and abilities among the underrepresented sex. The burden of proof is on OCR (in the case of an OCR investigation or compliance review), or on students (in the case of a complaint files with the school under its Title IX grievance procedures), to show by a preponderance of the evidence that the institution is not in compliance with part three.
>
> The part three analysis centers on whether there are concrete and viable interests among the underrepresented sex that should be accommodated by the institution's athletic program.

OCR has explained that an institution will be found in compliance with part three unless there exists a sport(s) for the underrepresented sex for which ~~all three~~ of the following conditions are met:

(a) ~~unmet interest sufficient to sustain a varsity team~~ in the sport(s);
(b) ~~sufficient ability~~ to sustain an intercollegiate team in the sport(s); and
(c) ~~reasonable expectation~~ of ~~intercollegiate competition~~ for a team in the sport(s) within the school's normal competitive region.

U.S. Department of Education, Office for Civil Rights, *Additional Clarification of Intercollegiate Athletics Policy: Three-Part Test—Part Three*, Washington, D.C., 2005

According to OCR, scientific validation of assessments of interest under the Policy Interpretation is not required. In fact, OCR provides a web-based Model Survey and User's Guide with recommendations for the survey's administration as an example of a competent method for ascertaining interest in a sport. OCR indicates that a school may effectively assess interest of the underrepresented sex by: using its Model Survey or conducting a census using the Model Survey as long as either is done pursuant to OCR's User's Guide; conducting a census other than the Model Survey that is consistent with its User's Guide; or using some other nondiscriminatory method of the school's choosing that complies with the requirements of the Policy Interpretation. Opponents of the Additional Clarification fear that schools will now be able to meet the requirements of part three by e-mailing a survey to students and asserting that a lack of response demonstrates insufficient interest in a sport.

Discriminatory Hiring Practices—Coaches

As stated in the beginning of this section, women's coaching opportunities have not grown at the same rate as women's participation in school athletics. Although it is not uncommon for men to coach women's teams, it is extremely rare for schools to hire women to coach men's teams. The following case illustrates this point.

FUHR V. SCHOOL DIST. OF CTY. OF HAZEL PARK
United States District Court, Eastern District of Michigan, 2001.
131 F. Supp. 2d 947.

STEEH, District Judge.

Order Denying Defendant's Motion for Summary Judgment

This case arises out of plaintiff Geraldine Fuhr's allegation of sexual discrimination by defendant School District of the City of Hazel Park. Plaintiff's allegation of discrimination stems from the fact that she was passed over for the position of boys' varsity basketball coach in favor of a male teacher. Defendant has filed a motion for summary judgment, which this court DENIES for the reasons stated below.

FACTUAL BACKGROUND

Plaintiff was hired at Hazel Park High School ("HPHS") as a social studies teacher and coach in 1989. Charles Kirkland had been the boys' varsity basketball coach at HPHS for ten years when he decided to give up the position at the end of the 1998–1999 season. Only two candidates applied for the boys' varsity basketball coach position—plaintiff and fellow-teacher John Barnett.

In 1999, at the time of the selection process for boys' varsity basketball coach, plaintiff's experience and credentials included the following:

—16 seasons coaching girls' basketball (including 10 years as varsity coach) and 12 seasons coaching boys' basketball (including 9 years as junior varsity coach),
—8 seasons as assistant varsity coach to Charlie Kirkland,
—many seasons conducting basketball clinics and camps,
—experience managing and coordinating basketball tournaments and tours, both domestic and international, and
—served as social studies department head.

John Barnett's experience at that time was as a junior high gym teacher for four years and coach of the boys' freshman basketball team at HPHS for two years under plaintiff.

The collective bargaining agreement between defendant and its teachers' union provides that individuals who coach sports receive additional pay, which is calculated as a percentage of base pay. In 1999 plaintiff's base salary was approximately $66,000. Plaintiff received an additional 9% of pay for serving as coach of the junior varsity boys' basketball team, and an additional 11% of pay for serving as the coach of the girls' varsity basketball team. The pay for coaching a basketball team is the same, regardless of whether the team is boys or girls.

When Charlie Kirkland announced his resignation in March 1999, a selection committee was put together to hire his replacement. The committee consisted of Jim Anker (Superintendent), Vic Mayo (Assistant Superintendent), Dan Grant (District-wide Athletic Director), Jim Meisinger (HPHS Principal), and Tom Pratt (teacher who had been named HPHS Athletic Director for the following year). The committee was selected by Grant. Plaintiff points out that missing from the committee were the previous coach Charlie Kirkland and the current HPHS Athletic Director Dave Eldred. Kirkland ran the basketball program at HPHS and plaintiff

coached under him. Kirkland's opinion was never sought by the committee. Eldred attended nearly every home sporting event and supervised both candidates. He testified that if plaintiff had been a male, she would have gotten the job. Eldred testified that the natural progression in coaching is freshman, then junior varsity, then varsity. Eldred opined that plaintiff was qualified for and deserved the boys' varsity coach position, and that Barnett should have moved into the boys' junior varsity position. Eldred was initially asked to be on the selection committee, but was then "uninvited" on the day of the interviews by Grant, who told him that Superintendent Anker did not want him there.

Principal Meisinger testified that prior to the interviews he learned that certain Board members and Superintendent Anker were not in favor of plaintiff getting the job, citing "community problems" which Meisinger believed had no validity. Meisinger confirmed that Fuhr had no "community problems" beyond what all coaches have to contend with (parent complaints about their child being disciplined unfairly or denied adequate playing time).

Barnett was interviewed first. Anker remained in the room during his entire interview, but left a few minutes into plaintiff's interview. Teacher Tom Pratt asked plaintiff if she could coach both the Varsity boys and girls teams, to which she answered "absolutely," explaining that she had been coaching boys and girls basketball simultaneously at Hazel Park for the past ten years. There is a potential overlap between the boys' and girls' basketball seasons, depending on how the girls' team fares in the state tournament. For example, in 1999, the girls' tournament began on November 15, the same day as the boys' team began its practice for the upcoming season. The girls' tournament ran until December 4, 1999, ending two days before the first varsity boys' basketball game. Coach Kirkland testified that based on his experience, it would be difficult to coach both varsity girls and varsity boys basketball teams at the same time. "Somebody is going to have to cover for somebody somewhere."

The committee met to discuss the candidates. Meisinger wanted plaintiff. Pratt remained neutral, but agreed that plaintiff was more qualified for the job. The other members supported Barnett, mentioning unspecified "community problems." The issue of gender came up during the committee's discussions, with Anker asking whether it would be a problem to have a female coach in the boy's locker room. No other reasons for not selecting plaintiff were ever mentioned. . . .

ANALYSIS

The parties disagree as to how this case ought to be viewed. According to defendant, plaintiff was denied a transfer from coach of the varsity girls team to the varsity boys team. Defendant argues that the fact plaintiff was not transferred from the varsity girls to the varsity boys team is not actionable because the positions are equivalent and there has been no reduction in plaintiff's pay. Plaintiff, on the other hand, views the facts as presenting a case of failure to hire her in favor of a less qualified male applicant. Additionally plaintiff argues she should have been promoted from coach of boys junior varsity to that of boys varsity.

A plaintiff may establish a prima facie case of discrimination under Title VII and Michigan's Elliott-Larsen Civil Rights Act either by presenting direct evidence of intentional discrimination by the defendant or by showing the existence of circumstantial evidence which creates an inference of discrimination. *Hoffman v. Sebro Plastics*, 108 F. Supp.2d 757 (E. D. Mich,2000). Under the framework set forth by the Supreme Court in *McDonnell Douglas Corp. v. Green*, 411 U.S. 792, 93 S. Ct. 1817, 36 L.Ed.2d 668 (1973), a plaintiff satisfies the burden of establishing a prima facie case of discrimination by proving (1) membership in a protected class; (2) that she suffered an adverse action; (3) that she was qualified for the position; and (4) that she was replaced by, or treated differently than, someone outside the protected class. *Id.* at 802, 93 S. Ct. 1817. As modified for a "failure to promote" case, the test is whether plaintiff can show she belongs to a protected group, was qualified and applied for the promotion, and that another employee with similar qualifications who was not in the protected group was promoted to the position sought by plaintiff. *Brown v. State of Tennessee*, 693 F.2d 600, 603 (6th Cir.1982).

Once a plaintiff establishes a prima facie case, an inference of discrimination arises. The burden of proof then shifts to the employer to articulate a legitimate, nondiscriminatory reason for the employer's action. Once established, the burden shifts back to the plaintiff to prove that the employer's articulated nondiscriminatory reason for its action was merely pretextual. *Texas Dept. of Community Affairs v. Burdine*, 450 U.S. 248, 252-53, 101 S. Ct. 1089, 67 L.Ed.2d 207 (1981).

Defendant argues that there has been no adverse action in this case because plaintiff could not have retained her position as girls' varsity coach and held the boys' varsity coaching position at the same time. Based on this premise, and because both positions had the same rate of pay, defendant argues that plaintiff did not suffer any adverse employment action when she was not chosen to coach the boys' varsity basketball team.

The reason defendant contends plaintiff could not coach both varsity teams is because there is an overlap between the boys' and girls' basketball seasons. The length of the overlap depends on the performance of the girls' team in the state tournament. In 1999, the girls' season finished on December 4, 1999 with the tournament finals, while the boys' first practice began on November 15—a potential overlap of three weeks. Defendant offers the opinion of Charles Kirkland, who had been the boys' varsity basketball coach at HPHS for ten years. According to Mr. Kirkland, during the preseason, he put in three hours a day for fifteen days, plus six hours for a scrimmage day after Thanksgiving. In the regular season he would have three days of practice, totaling seven hours, each week. Games were twice a week, for a total of ten hours, plus 1 1/2 to 2 hours after each game to review and get ready for the next day's practice. During Christmas and winter break he had practices, scrimmages and games. It is only the preseason that would overlap with the girls' varsity tournament schedule. Kirkland opined that if the same person coached the girls' and boys' varsity basketball teams it would detract from at least one program. "If you're working with the girls and you've got to finish that one up, then somebody's got to deal with the boys until, you know, whoever is coaching them can get there."

Defendant maintains that it has an established non-discriminatory practice of not allowing a single individual to coach two major sports when there is an overlap in the seasons. In support, defendant provides affidavits from Tom Pratt and Dan Grant, along with a chart identifying the coaches and schedules from 1990 to the present. Plaintiff contends that other individuals at HPHS have been permitted to coach two varsity sports. However, according to defendant, each of these instances involve sports which are played during different parts of the school year, with no overlap. For example, while Amy Houser coaches girls' and boys' varsity soccer, the seasons do not overlap at all.

Plaintiff highlights the example of Frank Stagg who was coach of varsity football and wrestling. The football season ran from August 9 until November 27 including the tournament finals, while the wresting season began November 15. Plaintiff provides the deposition testimony of James Anker, who identifies Frank Stagg as the one exception to defendant's practice of not having a person be head coach of two major sports. Defendant does not respond to plaintiff's allegation that Frank Stagg was permitted to coach two varsity sports with overlapping seasons. It would appear that this occurred prior to the 1990–1991 season, as it is not included in Exhibit B to defendant's supplemental brief.

Recognizing the overlap in the girls' and boys' basketball seasons, plaintiff points out that she handled the overlap for ten years while she coached the girls' varsity and boy's junior varsity teams. She testifies that in applying for the boys' varsity basketball position, she "wanted to be both the varsity girls and the varsity boys coach. . . . No one told me that I couldn't be both. If it ever came to the point where they said you had to choose one, not because I love girls basketball any less, but because I have—I've never coached the varsity boys, I would have done that if I had to, but I didn't want to and I could have handled both and I should have been both." According to plaintiff, nobody ever told her that if she was offered the boys' varsity position she would have to choose one varsity team over the other.

In addition to relying on its alleged non-discriminatory practice of treating all varsity coaches alike, defendant cites to a number of cases from the Sixth Circuit for the proposition that something more than a slight reduction in employment level is required before finding an adverse employment action. *Bowman v. Shawnee State University*, 220 F.3d 456 (6th Cir.2000); *Hatcher v. General Electric*, 2000 WL 245515, 2000 U.S. App. LEXIS 2837 (6th Cir. 2000); *Orsini v. East Detroit Public Schools*, 1995 WL 428426, 1995 U.S. App. LEXIS 20538 (6th Cir. 1995). According to defendant, a plaintiff must suffer a loss of seniority, salary or other benefits as a result of a reduction in her employment level in order to state a cause of action. Defendant contends that in this case, if plaintiff had been appointed to the position of boys' varsity coach, she would have had to give up her boys' junior varsity position as well as her girls' varsity position, and would have suffered a reduction in her total pay. Therefore, defendant maintains that its refusal to transfer plaintiff actually preserved her existing rate of pay.

However, each of the cases relied on by defendant involved an employer-imposed job transfer where the employee was required to show that the transfer was in some way adverse. In the present case, plaintiff's adverse job action was not an employer-imposed job transfer, but rather the denial of an employee-sought job transfer or promotion. The Seventh Circuit has stated that when a plaintiff applies for a transfer, "[w]hether the new position is equivalent to or better than her current job is irrelevant to whether she was qualified for, applied for, and was rejected from the position while a less qualified male was selected. The fact that she was denied a position she applied for is adverse in and of itself." *Parker v. State, Dept. of Public Safety*, 11 F. Supp.2d 467, 477 (D.Del.1998).

Plaintiff has successfully raised a question of fact whether defendant in fact had an established policy of not permitting the same person to coach two varsity sports with overlapping seasons. Such a policy was never communicated to plaintiff when she applied for the boys' varsity position. Plaintiff was not asked to choose between the boys' and girls' varsity teams. Finally, defendant has no explanation for Frank Stagg being able to coach two varsity sports with overlapping schedules.

The court does not agree with defendant's characterization of plaintiff's claim as being one of discriminatory failure to transfer. Rather, the court will analyze plaintiff's claim as one of discriminatory failure to hire or promote. Plaintiff argues that the denial of the boys' varsity coach position was an adverse action whether viewed as a failure to promote case or a failure to hire case. Plaintiff argues that defendant failed to promote her from boys' junior varsity coach to varsity/head coach, where she would have been in charge of the entire boys' basketball program, providing direction to and supervising the junior varsity and ninth-grade coaches. In this way, the job was clearly a promotion with higher visibility, a more distinguished title, and higher pay. In employment law, adverse action includes the failure to promote. *Board of County Com'rs, Wabaunsee County, KS v. Umbehr*, 518 U.S. 668, 116 S. Ct. 2342, 135 L.Ed.2d 843 (1996). If viewed as a failure to hire case, the denial of a sought-after position is also clearly an adverse action.

Plaintiff has successfully made out a prima facie case of discrimination in this case. The burden then shifts to defendant to articulate a legitimate, nondiscriminatory reason for its action. In this case, defendant has explained that it had an established policy of not permitting anybody to coach two varsity sports with overlapping seasons. Plaintiff, however, has provided sufficient evidence to raise an issue of fact that the defendant's articulated nondiscriminatory reason for its action was pretext for discrimination. Plaintiff, therefore, survives defendant's motion for summary judgment.

CONCLUSION

For the Reasons Stated, Defendant's Motion for Summary Judgment Is DENIED.

STUDY QUESTIONS

1. For what position had Geraldine Fuhr applied? What were her qualifications? Who else was being considered for the job? How did Fuhr's qualifications compare to the other applicant?

2. Under what federal statute did Fuhr bring suit? What did the school district argue in defense of its decision not to select Fuhr?

3. Remember that this was a summary judgment motion. What did the court find with respect to the burden of proof in this case?

After the defendant's summary judgment motion was denied, the matter went to trial. In August of 2001, an eight-member jury found the school district had discriminated against Geraldine Fuhr and awarded her $455,000 in damages, more than double the amount she had sought. On October 10, in response to a motion by Fuhr's attorney, District Court

Judge George Steeh ordered that Fuhr be appointed boys' varsity coach and let Fuhr decide whether to take the job or the full amount of damages. On October 31, Fuhr opted to take the job and the judge reduced her damages to $245,000 ($210,000 of the original award was meant to compensate her for reduced future earnings).

As we learned in Chapter 3, Title VII prohibits hiring and firing based on gender. It encourages that employment decisions be made on the basis of qualifications, not gender stereotyping. It applies equally to women and men. And, there are occasions when men must seek its protection and redress. Jim Babyak, former basketball and soccer coach for Smith College, had such an occasion. Babyak had helped build Smith's athletics program and had received good performance evaluations through 1995. When he was fired in 1996, the basketball team had set a school record for wins and the soccer team won its sixth conference championship. Babyak sued for sex and age discrimination; he claimed the college wanted a female coach. Although the college claimed that Babyak tried to force his student athletes to give him good reviews through manipulation and bribery, the facts did not support its claim. In December of 2001, a jury found in favor of Babyak on his claims of sex and age discrimination and awarded $1.6 million.

IV. SEXUAL HARASSMENT OF STUDENTS

In Chapter 4, we explored at length the forms and consequences of sexual harassment and the main legal remedies available for coping with it in an employment context. There we saw that the problem is widespread, serious, and unlawful. In this section, we will again consider the problem of sexual harassment, but this time in the context of our schools. According to the NCWGE's 2002 "Report Card on Gender Equity," in the area of sexual harassment, we merit a "C." The following selection explains why.

TITLE IX AT 30
Report Card on Gender Equity
National Coalition for Women and Girls in Education, June 2002,
excerpts, pp. 40–44.

SEXUAL HARASSMENT

C

Although some gains have been made in this area since 1997, when *Title IX at 25* was published, sexual harassment continues to plague our nation's schools and students—both boys and girls. Sexual harassment is unwanted and unwelcome sexual behavior that creates a hostile environment, limiting full access to education and work. Legal developments since the law's 25th anniversary confirm that schools have an obligation under Title IX to respond to sexual harassment in school. But in too many cases, sexual harassment continues to undermine equal opportunity for students and school employees.

Legal Changes Since 1997

It has been clear for more than a decade that Title IX prohibits the sexual harassment of students. In 1992, in its unanimous decision in *Franklin v. Gwinnett County Public Schools,* the Supreme Court held that a student could bring a Title IX claim for damages for a sexually hostile environment created by a teacher.

And in 1999 the court announced, in *Davis v. Monroe County Board of Education*, that schools may also be liable under Title IX if one student sexually harasses another student in a school program. These decisions have made clear that schools have a legal responsibility to take steps to prevent sexual harassment and to respond appropriately to any sexual harassment that occurs.

Although no legal developments have undermined this fundamental principle, recent case law has restricted the scope of remedies available for victims of sexual harassment. In 1998, in *Gebser v. Lago Vista Independent School District*, the Supreme Court held that school districts are not liable for damages for the sexual harassment of students by teachers unless an appropriate official had actual notice of, and demonstrated deliberate indifference to, the teacher's misconduct. *Davis* adopted the same standard for evaluating school liability for damages for student-on-student harassment. In these cases, the court rejected application of the standards of Title VII of the Civil Rights Act of 1964, which protects employees from sexual harassment by their supervisors and colleagues. As a result, students—who are often more vulnerable to sexual harassment than adults, and who are required to attend school—have fewer protections from sexual harassment than do employees in the workplace.

Importantly, however, both *Gebser* and *Davis* made clear that the liability standards they established are limited to private actions for monetary damages. Nothing in either decision changes a school's obligation to take reasonable steps under Title IX to prevent and eliminate sexual harassment. And nothing in the decisions limits OCR's authority to enforce its regulations and policies, including those provisions that require schools to adopt and publicize a policy against sexual harassment as well as grievance procedures for those subjected to it. OCR has made each of these points clear in its Revised Sexual Harassment Guidance, issued in January 2001.

The Scope of Sexual Harassment

Despite the attention paid to the issue in recent years, sexual harassment remains widespread, hurting girls and boys at every level of their education. This fact is confirmed by a 2001 study by the American Association of University Women (AAUW) Educational Foundation, *Hostile Hallways: Bullying, Teasing, and Sexual Harassment in School*, which followed up a similar Foundation study in 1993. According to the 2001 study—a representative sample of 2,064 public school students in eighth through 11th grades—81 percent of students have experienced some form of sexual harassment. As in 1993, girls in 2001 were more likely than boys were to have experienced sexual harassment at some point (83 percent vs. 79 percent). But boys today were more likely than were those in 1993 to experience sexual harassment often or occasionally (56 percent vs. 49 percent). As in 1993, nearly nine in ten students (85 percent) reported that students sexually harass other students at their schools.

SEXUAL HARASSMENT IN SCHOOLS IS ALL TOO COMMON

- Eight in ten students experience some form of harassment during their school lives, and more than one-quarter of them experience it often.
- Girls are more likely than boys to experience harassment, but boys today are more likely to be harassed than boys in 1993.
- Six in ten students experience physical sexual harassment at some point in their school lives, one-third often or occasionally.
- The most common forms of sexual harassment in school span the nonphysical and physical:
  - ✓ Making sexual comments, jokes, gestures, or looks
  - ✓ Claiming that a person is gay or lesbian

✓ Spreading sexual rumors about a person
✓ Touching, grabbing, or pinching in a sexual way
✓ Intentionally brushing up against someone in a sexual way
✓ Flashing or "mooning"

HOW DID THE HARASSMENT MAKE YOU FEEL?

Girls

- "I was very upset. I cried for someone even thinking that, but I had my friends to help me." (eighth-grader)
- "Angry, embarrassed, hurt feelings." (eighth-grader)
- "I didn't care. It's a joke." (ninth-grader)
- "Like guys like me!" (ninth-grader)
- "Like I have lost most of my respect for the male gender." (10th-grader)
- "Uncomfortable and uneasy." (11th-grader)

Boys

- "Disturbed and generally angry." (eighth-grader)
- "Good." (eighth-grader)
- "Mad and upset." (ninth-grader)
- "It was a joke, and you can just call him fag back and move on with your life." (ninth-grader)
- "I guess uncomfortable, of course. It's not fun for anyone to get harassed." (ninth-grader)
- "Kinda grossed out." (10th-grader)
- "Surprised." (11th-grader)

Moreover, a large number of students (38 percent) still reported that teachers and other school employees sexually harass students.

The Impact of Sexual Harassment

School sexual harassment has a negative impact on students' emotional and educational lives. For example, nearly half (47 percent) of all students who experienced sexual harassment feel very or somewhat upset right after. Those who experienced physical forms of harassment were even more likely to feel very or somewhat upset by the experience. And students' behavior in school was affected by the harassment. Students who experienced sexual harassment were most likely to react by avoiding the person who harassed them (40 percent), talking less in class (24 percent), not wanting to go to school (22 percent), changing their seat in class to get farther away from the harasser (21 percent), and finding it hard to pay attention in school (20 percent). Sexual harassment thus typically exacts high costs from its victims. And students were often quite aware of the feelings that harassment engenders in them, whether negative or more neutral.

Action/Inaction by Education Institutions

Overall, students in 2001 were more aware than were students in 1993 of the definition of sexual harassment and the actions their schools take to raise awareness on the subject. Of the students surveyed in 2001, nearly all (96 percent) understood sexual harassment.

Perhaps one of the most important findings of the AAUW report was that students in 2001 are much more likely than those in 1993 to say that their schools have a policy or distribute literature on sexual harassment. Specifically, 69 percent of students in 2001, compared to just 26 percent in 1993, said their schools have a policy to deal with sexual harassment and complaints. Thirty-six percent of students, compared to 13 percent in 1993, said their schools distribute booklets, handouts, and other literature and materials about sexual harassment.

Despite an increased awareness of schools' distribution of information on sexual harassment, neither girls nor boys necessarily reported actual incidents to adults. While 71 percent of students said they would complain to an adult at school if they were sexually harassed by a teacher or another school employee, only 40 percent of students reported that they were likely to tell an adult at school if they were harassed by another student. Students were six times more likely to tell a friend than a teacher or other school employee about their experience with harassment.

While awareness of school efforts to distribute information to students on sexual harassment have increased along with student knowledge of sexual harassment, student unwillingness to come forward to report incidents of sexual harassment indicates that schools must do more to empower students to take that next step. When asked why they told no one, many students reported that they "didn't know," "didn't want to be a tattletale," or "didn't want to make a mountain out of a molehill." Students who did tell someone about their experience of sexual harassment were most likely to receive the following reactions: The highest percentage of boys said the people they told either laughed or thought it was a joke (21 percent), whereas the highest percentage of girls said they were told to report the incident (23 percent).

WHAT COULD YOUR SCHOOL DO TO ADDRESS SEXUAL HARASSMENT?

- "Maybe if they had an assembly about sexual harassment and expulsion for those who violate the rules." (eighth-grade boy)
- "My school handles the issue of sexual harassment very well." (eighth-grade girl)
- "Stop letting athletes get off easy." (ninth-grade boy)
- "I'd just like them to, if the matter comes up, deal with it swiftly and fairly, taking in all considerations." (ninth-grade girl)
- "Make aware what exactly it is and what to do about it if you are offended." (10th-grade boy)
- "Deal with the problem on the spot." (10th-grade girl)
- "I think that the current policies that deal with that subject are sufficient enough for the quantity and the degree of offense found at my school." (11th-grade boy)
- "Have the same no tolerance policy as knives or guns and make an example of anyone who does commit sexual harassment, so maybe it will stop others." (11th-grade girl)
- Told to go to the authorities and make them aware or tell parents (18 percent)
- Told it was a joke or were laughed at (13 percent)
- Told "Don't worry about it, it's not a big deal, forget about it" (10 percent)

Title IX Enforcement

Complaints of sexual harassment constitute 63 percent of non-sports-related Title IX complaints filed with OCR. Seventy percent of elementary and secondary school and 59 percent of college and university Title IX complaints involve sexual harassment.

OCR's 2001 Revised Sexual Harassment Guidance sets out the standards it will apply in investigating sexual harassment complaints and the steps that educa-tion institutions will be expected to take to comply with Title IX. The guidance makes clear that institutions have an obligation to ensure that sexual harassment is not a part of an education program or activity. Among the strategies OCR recommends to prevent sexual harassment is having and implementing a sexual harassment policy. When sexual harassment does occur, institutions must act promptly and appropriately, including investigating the complaint and taking steps to end the harassing conduct.

STUDY QUESTIONS

1. How pervasive is sexual harassment in the schools? What forms does it take? Who are the harassers? Compare the statistics on female and male victims.

2. What is the impact of sexual harassment on students? How are they affected?

3. What can schools do to make students aware of sexual harassment and the methods to combat this problem? Does your school have a sexual harassment policy? If so, how is that communicated to the school community?

As mentioned in the "Report Card on Gender Equity," in 1992, the Supreme Court determined that a student could bring a suit for damages under Title IX for sexual harassment by a teacher. *See Franklin v. Gwinnett Cty. Public Schools*, 503 U.S. 60 (1992). Six years later, the Supreme Court had occasion to consider what standard of liability applies under Title IX when a teacher is alleged to have sexually harassed a student. In that case, the Court determined that neither the negligence standard endorsed by the Department of Education in its 1997 "Sexual Harassment Guidance" nor the vicarious liability standard endorsed by the Court for Title VII in the *Faragher* and *Burlington* cases, discussed in Chapter 4, applied. Instead, the Court held that where a case is brought under Title IX for harassment of a student by a teacher and damages are sought, the plaintiff must show that the school district had actual notice of the discrimination and was deliberately indifferent to it.

GEBSER V. LAGO VISTA INDEPENDENT SCHOOL DISTRICT
524 U.S. 274, (1998).

Justice O'CONNOR delivered the opinion of the Court. . . .

I

In the spring of 1991, when petitioner Alida Star Gebser was an eighth-grade student at a middle school in respondent Lago Vista Independent School District (Lago Vista), she joined a high school book discussion group led by Frank Waldrop, a teacher at Lago Vista's high school. Lago Vista received federal funds at all pertinent times. During the book discussion sessions, Waldrop often made sexually suggestive comments to the students. Gebser entered high school in the fall and was assigned to classes taught by Waldrop in both semesters. Waldrop continued to make inappropriate remarks to the students, and he began to direct more of his suggestive comments toward Gebser, including during the substantial amount of time that the two were alone in his classroom. He initiated sexual contact with Gebser in the spring, when, while visiting her home ostensibly to give her a book, he kissed and fondled her. The two had sexual intercourse on a number of occasions during the remainder of the school year. Their relationship continued through the summer and into the following school year, and they often had intercourse during class time, although never on school property.

Gebser did not report the relationship to school officials, testifying that while she realized Waldrop's conduct was improper, she was uncertain how to react and she wanted to continue having him as a teacher. In October 1992, the parents of two other students complained to the high school principal about Waldrop's comments in class. The principal arranged a meeting, at which, according to the principal, Waldrop indicated that he did not believe he had made offensive remarks but apologized to the parents and said it would not happen again. The principal also advised Waldrop to be careful about his classroom comments and told the school guidance counselor about the meeting, but he did not report the parents' complaint to Lago Vista's superintendent, who was the district's Title IX coordinator. A couple of months later, in January 1993, a police officer discovered Waldrop and Gebser engaging in sexual intercourse and arrested Waldrop. Lago Vista terminated his employment, and subsequently, the Texas Education Agency revoked his teaching license. During this time, the district had not promulgated or distributed an official grievance procedure for lodging sexual harassment complaints; nor had it issued a formal anti-harassment policy.

Gebser and her mother filed suit against Lago Vista and Waldrop in state court in November 1993, raising claims against the school district under Title IX, and state negligence law, and claims against Waldrop primarily under state law. They sought compensatory and punitive damages from both defendants. After the case was removed, the United States District Court for the Western District of Texas granted summary judgment in favor of Lago Vista on all claims, and remanded the allegations against Waldrop to state court. In rejecting the Title IX claim against the school district, the court reasoned that the statute "was enacted to counter policies of discrimination . . . in federally funded education programs," and that "[o]nly if school administrators have some type of notice of the gender discrimination and fail to respond in good faith can the discrimination be interpreted as a policy of the school district." Here, the court determined, the parents' complaint to the principal concerning Waldrop's comments in class was the only one Lago Vista had received about Waldrop, and that evidence was inadequate

to raise a genuine issue on whether the school district had actual or constructive notice that Waldrop was involved in a sexual relationship with a student.

Petitioners appealed only on the Title IX claim. The Court of Appeals for the Fifth Circuit affirmed. . . .

II

. . . *Franklin [v. Gwinnett Country Public Schools]* . . . establishes that a school district can be held liable in damages in cases involving a teacher's sexual harassment of a student; the decision, however, does not purport to define the contours of that liability.

We face that issue squarely in this case. Petitioners, joined by the United States as amicus curiae, would invoke standards used by the Courts of Appeals in Title VII cases involving a supervisor's sexual harassment of an employee in the workplace. . . .

Specifically, they advance two possible standards under which Lago Vista would be liable for Waldrop's conduct. First, relying on a 1997 "Policy Guidance" issued by the Department of Education, they would hold a school district liable in damages under Title IX where a teacher is "'aided in carrying out the sexual harassment of students by his or her position of authority with the institution,'" irrespective of whether school district officials had any knowledge of the harassment and irrespective of their response upon becoming aware. That rule is an expression of respondeat superior liability, i.e., vicarious or imputed liability, under which recovery in damages against a school district would generally follow whenever a teacher's authority over a student facilitates the harassment. Second, petitioners and the United States submit that a school district should at a minimum be liable for damages based on a theory of constructive notice, i.e., where the district knew or "should have known" about harassment but failed to uncover and eliminate it. Both standards would allow a damages recovery in a broader range of situations than the rule adopted by the Court of Appeals, which hinges on actual knowledge by a school official with authority to end the harassment.

Whether educational institutions can be said to violate Title IX based solely on principles of respondeat superior or constructive notice was not resolved by *Franklin's* citation of *Meritor*. That reference to *Meritor* was made with regard to the general proposition that sexual harassment can constitute discrimination on the basis of sex under Title IX. . . . Moreover, *Meritor's* rationale for concluding that agency principles guide the liability inquiry under Title VII rests on an aspect of that statute not found in Title IX: Title VII, in which the prohibition against employment discrimination runs against "an employer," explicitly defines "employer" to include "any agent." Title IX contains no comparable reference to an educational institution's "agents," and so does not expressly call for application of agency principles.

In this case, moreover, petitioners seek not just to establish a Title IX violation but to recover damages based on theories of respondeat superior and constructive notice. It is that aspect of their action, in our view, which is most critical to resolving the case. Unlike Title IX, Title VII contains an express cause of action, and specifically provides for relief in the form of monetary damages. Congress therefore has directly addressed the subject of damages relief under Title VII and has set out the particular situations in which damages are available as well as the maximum amounts recoverable. With respect to Title IX, however, the private right of action is judicially implied, see *Cannon v. University of Chicago*, and there is thus no legislative expression of the scope of available remedies, including when it is appropriate to award monetary damages. . . .

III

Because the private right of action under Title IX is judicially implied, we have a measure of latitude to shape a sensible remedial scheme that best comports with the statute. That endeavor inherently entails a

degree of speculation, since it addresses an issue on which Congress has not specifically spoken. To guide the analysis, we generally examine the relevant statute to ensure that we do not fashion the parameters of an implied right in a manner at odds with the statutory structure and purpose. . . .

Congress enacted Title IX in 1972 with two principal objectives in mind: "to avoid the use of federal resources to support discriminatory practices" and "to provide individual citizens effective protection against those practices." The statute was modeled after Title VI of the Civil Rights Act of 1964, which is parallel to Title IX except that it prohibits race discrimination, not sex discrimination, and applies in all programs receiving federal funds, not only in education programs. The two statutes operate in the same manner, conditioning an offer of federal funding on a promise by the recipient not to discriminate, in what amounts essentially to a contract between the Government and the recipient of funds.

That contractual framework distinguishes Title IX from Title VII, which is framed in terms not of a condition but of an outright prohibition. Title VII applies to all employers without regard to federal funding and aims broadly to "eradicat[e] discrimination throughout the economy." Title VII, moreover, seeks to "make persons whole for injuries suffered through past discrimination." Thus, whereas Title VII aims centrally to compensate victims of discrimination, Title IX focuses more on "protecting" individuals from discriminatory practices carried out by recipients of federal funds. That might explain why, when the Court first recognized the implied right under Title IX in *Cannon*, the opinion referred to injunctive or equitable relief in a private action, but not to a damages remedy.

Title IX's contractual nature has implications for our construction of the scope of available remedies. When Congress attaches conditions to the award of federal funds under its spending power, as it has in Title IX and Title VI, we examine closely the propriety of private actions holding the recipient liable in monetary damages for noncompliance with the condition. Our central concern in that regard is with ensuring "that the receiving entity of federal funds [has] notice that it will be liable for a monetary award." . . . If a school district's liability for a teacher's sexual harassment rests on principles of constructive notice or respondeat superior, it will likewise be the case that the recipient of funds was unaware of the discrimination. It is sensible to assume that Congress did not envision a recipient's liability in damages in that situation.

. . . Most significantly, Title IX contains important clues that Congress did not intend to allow recovery in damages where liability rests solely on principles of vicarious liability or constructive notice. Title IX's express means of enforcement—by administrative agencies—operates on an assumption of actual notice to officials of the funding recipient. The statute entitles agencies who disburse education funding to enforce their rules implementing the non-discrimination mandate through proceedings to suspend or terminate funding or through "other means authorized by law." Significantly, however, an agency may not initiate enforcement proceedings until it "has advised the appropriate person or persons of the failure to comply with the requirement and has determined that compliance cannot be secured by voluntary means.". . .

Presumably, a central purpose of requiring notice of the violation "to the appropriate person" and an opportunity for voluntary compliance before administrative enforcement proceedings can commence is to avoid diverting education funding from beneficial uses where a recipient was unaware of discrimination in its programs and is willing to institute prompt corrective measures. The scope of private damages relief proposed by petitioners is at odds with that basic objective. . . .

IV

Because the express remedial scheme under Title IX is predicated upon notice to an "appropriate person" and an opportunity to rectify any violation, we conclude, in the absence of further direction from Congress, that the implied damages remedy should be fashioned along the same lines. An "appropriate person" under § 1682 is, at a minimum, an official of the recipient entity with authority to take corrective action to end the discrimination. Consequently, in cases like this one that do not involve official policy of the recipient entity, we hold that a damages remedy will not lie under Title IX unless an official who at a minimum has authority to address the alleged discrimination and to institute corrective measures on the recipient's behalf has actual knowledge of discrimination in the recipient's programs and fails adequately to respond.

We think, moreover, that the response must amount to deliberate indifference to discrimination. The administrative enforcement scheme presupposes that an official who is advised of a Title IX violation refuses to take action to bring the recipient into compliance. The premise, in other words, is an official decision by the recipient not to remedy the violation. That framework finds a rough parallel in the standard of deliberate indifference. Under a lower standard, there would be a risk that the recipient would be liable in damages not for its own official decision but instead for its employees' independent actions. . . .

Applying the framework to this case is fairly straightforward, as petitioners do not contend they can prevail under an actual notice standard. The only official alleged to have had information about Waldrop's misconduct is the high school principal. That information, however, consisted of a complaint from parents of other students charging only that Waldrop had made inappropriate comments during class, which was plainly insufficient to alert the principal to the possibility that Waldrop was involved in a sexual relationship with a student. Lago Vista, moreover, terminated Waldrop's employment upon learning of his relationship with Gebser.

Petitioners focus primarily on Lago Vista's asserted failure to promulgate and publicize an effective policy and grievance procedure for sexual harassment claims. They point to Department of Education regulations requiring each funding recipient to "adopt and publish grievance procedures providing for prompt and equitable resolution" of discrimination complaints, and to notify students and others "that it does not discriminate on the basis of sex in the educational programs or activities which it operates." Lago Vista's alleged failure to comply with the regulations, however, does not establish the requisite actual notice and deliberate indifference. And in any event, the failure to promulgate a grievance procedure does not itself constitute "discrimination" under Title IX. Of course, the Department of Education could enforce the requirement administratively: Agencies generally have authority to promulgate and enforce requirements that effectuate the statute's non-discrimination mandate, even if those requirements do not purport to represent a definition of discrimination under the statute. We have never held, however, that the implied private right of action under Title IX allows recovery in damages for violation of those sorts of administrative requirements.

V

The number of reported cases involving sexual harassment of students in schools confirms that harassment unfortunately is an all too common aspect of the educational experience. No one questions that a student suffers extraordinary harm when subjected to sexual harassment and abuse by a teacher, and that the teacher's conduct is reprehensible and undermines the basic purposes of the educational system. The issue in this case, however, is whether the independent misconduct of a teacher is attributable to the school district that employs him under a specific federal statute designed primarily to prevent recipients of federal financial assistance from using the funds in a discriminatory manner. Our decision does not affect any right of recovery that an individual may have against a school district as a matter of state law or against the teacher in his individual capacity under state law or under 42 U.S.C. § 1983. Until Congress speaks directly on the subject, however, we will not hold a school district liable in damages under Title IX for a teacher's sexual harassment of a student absent actual notice and deliberate indifference. We therefore affirm the judgment of the Court of Appeals.

It Is So Ordered.

Justice Stevens, with Whom Justice Souter, Justice Ginsburg, and Justice Breyer Join, Dissenting.

IV

. . . It is not clear to me why the well-settled rules of law that impose responsibility on the principal for the misconduct of its agents should not apply in this case. As a matter of policy, the Court ranks protection of the school district's purse above the protection of immature high school students that those rules would provide. Because those students are members of the class for whose special benefit Congress enacted Title IX, that policy choice is not faithful to the intent of the policymaking branch of our Government.

I respectfully dissent.

STUDY QUESTIONS

1. What was the issue before the Supreme Court in this case? How did the Court rule? What was its rationale?
2. What avenues of recovery were not affected by the Court's decision? Do you think these avenues are sufficient for a student who was harassed by a teacher?
3. What did Justice Stevens say with respect to the majority's decision? Do you agree with his statement?

Justice O'Connor, writing for the majority, explained the justification for taking such a restrained view of school board liability for acts of its agents under Title IX. The operative factor appears to have been a commitment to judicial restraint. Congress arguably authorized agency-based liability in crafting Title VII, but did not in the case of Title IX. The majority in this case evidently felt that endorsing the availability of damages was as far as the Court should go absent further Congressional authorization. The majority, however, was not insensitive to the issues raised in the quoted portion of Justice Stevens's dissent. Indeed, the majority explicitly encouraged Congress and the Department of Education to take the initiative in adjusting the law to counter the effects of this decision.

In 1999, the Court heard a case involving a claim for damages under Title IX for student-on-student harassment. In that case, the Court applied the same standard for assessing a school's liability for damages as it used in *Gebser*. *See Davis v. Monroe County Board of Education*, 526 U.S. 629 (1999).

In January of 2001, the Department of Education did exactly what the Court had suggested in *Gebser*: it issued a "Revised Sexual Harassment Guidance: Harassment of Students by School Employees, Other Students, or Third Parties." That document's Preamble clearly explains the purpose and scope of the revised guidance, as well as its adherence to the principles enunciated in the 1997 guidance:

PREAMBLE

SUMMARY

The Assistant Secretary for Civil Rights, U.S. Department of Education (Department), issues a new document (revised guidance) that replaces the 1997 document entitled "Sexual Harassment Guidance: Harassment of Students by School Employees, Other Students, or Third Parties," issued by the Office for Civil Rights (OCR) on March 13, 1997 (1997 guidance). We revised the guidance in limited respects in light of subsequent Supreme Court cases relating to sexual harassment in schools.

The revised guidance reaffirms the compliance standards that OCR applies in investigations and administrative enforcement of Title IX of the Education Amendments of 1972 (Title IX) regarding sexual harassment. The revised guidance re-grounds these standards in the Title IX regulations, distinguishing them from the standards applicable to private litigation for money damages and clarifying their regulatory basis as distinct from Title VII of the Civil Rights Act of 1964 (Title VII) agency law. In most other respects the revised guidance is identical to the 1997 guidance. Thus, we intend the revised guidance to serve the same purpose as the 1997 guidance. It continues to provide the principles that a school[1] should use to recognize and effectively respond to sexual harassment of students in its program as a condition of receiving Federal financial assistance.

PURPOSE AND SCOPE OF THE REVISED GUIDANCE

In March 1997, we published in the *Federal Register* "Sexual Harassment Guidance: Harassment of Students by School Employees, Other Students, or Third Parties." 62 FR 12034. We issued the guidance pursuant to our authority under Title IX, and our Title IX implementing regulations, to eliminate discrimination based on sex in education programs and activities receiving Federal financial assistance. It was grounded in longstanding legal authority establishing that sexual

---

[1] As in the 1997 guidance, the revised guidance uses the term "school" to refer to all schools, colleges, universities, and other educational institutions that receive Federal funds from the Department.

harassment of students can be a form of sex discrimination covered by Title IX. The guidance was the product of extensive consultation with interested parties, including students, teachers, school administrators, and researchers. We also made the document available for public comment.

Since the issuance of the 1997 guidance, the Supreme Court (Court) has issued several important decisions in sexual harassment cases, including two decisions specifically addressing sexual harassment of students under Title IX: *Gebser v. Lago Vista Independent School District* (*Gebser*), 524 U.S. 274 (1998), and *Davis v. Monroe County Board of Education* (*Davis*), 526 U.S. 629 (1999). The Court held in *Gebser* that a school can be liable for monetary damages if a teacher sexually harasses a student, an official who has authority to address the harassment has actual knowledge of the harassment, and that official is deliberately indifferent in responding to the harassment. In *Davis*, the Court announced that a school also may be liable for monetary damages if one student sexually harasses another student in the school's program and the conditions of *Gebser* are met.

The Court was explicit in *Gebser* and *Davis* that the liability standards established in those cases are limited to private actions for monetary damages. See, e.g., *Gebser*, 524 U.S. 283, and *Davis*, 526 U.S. at 639. The Court acknowledged, by contrast, the power of Federal agencies, such as the Department, to "promulgate and enforce requirements that effectuate [Title IX's] nondiscrimination mandate," even in circumstances that would not give rise to a claim for money damages. See, *Gebser*, 524 U.S. at 292.

In an August 1998 letter to school superintendents and a January 1999 letter to college and university presidents, the Secretary of Education informed school officials that the *Gebser* decision did not change a school's obligations to take reasonable steps under Title IX and the regulations to prevent and eliminate sexual harassment as a condition of its receipt of Federal funding. The Department also determined that, although in most important respects the substance of the 1997 guidance was reaffirmed in *Gebser* and *Davis*, certain areas of the 1997 guidance could be strengthened by further clarification and explanation of the Title IX regulatory basis for the guidance.

On November 2, 2000, we published in the *Federal Register* a notice requesting comments on the proposed revised guidance (62 FR 66092). A detailed explanation of the *Gebser* and *Davis* decisions, and an explanation of the proposed changes in the guidance, can be found in the preamble to the proposed revised guidance. In those decisions and a third opinion, *Oncale v. Sundowner Offshore Services, Inc.* (*Oncale*), 523 U.S. 75 (1998) (a sexual harassment case decided under Title VII), the Supreme Court confirmed several fundamental principles we articulated in the 1997 guidance. In these areas, no changes in the guidance were necessary. A notice regarding the availability of this final document appeared in the *Federal Register* on January 19, 2001.

ENDURING PRINCIPLES FROM THE 1997 GUIDANCE

It continues to be the case that a significant number of students, both male and female, have experienced sexual harassment, which can interfere with a student's academic performance and emotional and physical well-being. Preventing and remedying sexual harassment in schools is essential to ensuring a safe environment in which students can learn. As with the 1997 guidance, the revised guidance applies to students at every level of education. School personnel who understand their obligations under Title IX, e.g., understand that sexual harassment can be sex discrimination in violation of Title IX, are in the best position to prevent harassment and to lessen the harm to students if, despite their best efforts, harassment occurs.

One of the fundamental aims of both the 1997 guidance and the revised guidance has been to emphasize that, in addressing allegations of sexual harassment, the good judgment and common sense of teachers and school administrators are important elements of a response that meets the requirements of Title IX.

A critical issue under Title IX is whether the school recognized that sexual harassment has occurred and took prompt and effective action calculated to end the harassment, prevent its recurrence, and, as appropriate, remedy its effects. If harassment has occurred, doing nothing is always the wrong response. However, depending on the circumstances, there may be more than one right way to respond. The important thing is for school employees or officials to pay attention to the school environment and not to hesitate to respond to sexual harassment in the same reasonable, commonsense manner as they would to other types of serious misconduct.

It is also important that schools not overreact to behavior that does not rise to the level of sexual harassment. As the Department stated in the 1997 guidance, a kiss on the cheek by a first grader does not constitute sexual harassment. School personnel should consider the age and maturity of students in responding to allegations of sexual harassment.

Finally, we reiterate the importance of having well-publicized and effective grievance procedures in place to handle complaints of sex discrimination, including sexual harassment complaints. Nondiscrimination policies and procedures are required by the Title IX regulations. In fact, the Supreme Court in *Gebser* specifically affirmed the Department's authority to enforce this requirement administratively in order to carry out Title IX's nondiscrimination mandate. 524 U.S. at 292. Strong policies and effective grievance procedures are essential to let students and employees know that sexual harassment will not be tolerated and to ensure that they know how to report it.

ON-LINE RESOURCES

To read the entire Department of Education "Revised Sexual Harassment Guidance: Harassment of Students by School Employees, Other Students, or Third Parties," go to: www.ed.gov/offices/OCR/archives/pdf/shguide.pdf

To read the entire text of the new Title IX regulations, go to: www.ed.gov/policy/rights/reg/ocr/edlite-34cfr106.html

To review the NCWGE's various reports, including its report entitled "Title IX at 35: Beyond the Headlines," go to: www.ncwge.org

Through the American Association of University Women's Web site, you can access that organization's research publications: www.aauw.org/research/index.cfm

The NASSPE's Web site is: www.singlesexschools.org

To read the entire U.S. Department of Education, Office for Civil Rights, Additional Clarification of Intercollegiate Athletics Policy: Three-Part Test—Part Three, Washington, D.C., 2005, go to: www.ed.gov/about/offices/list/ocr/docs/title9guidanceadditional.pdf

CHAPTER 6

THE FAMILY

UNLIKE THE PUBLIC sphere of government and the marketplace, the family has long been considered an appropriate focus for women's interests and activities. Religion, culture, and law have routinely assigned family roles on the basis of sex, relegating women to a disproportionate share of child care and other domestic work.

Recall, for example, Blackstone's rendering of the common law doctrine of coverture and its consequences (see Chapter 1). Blackstone reported that at common law, the husband was accorded the role of head and master in the family. He owned the property, was entitled to the custody and labors of the children, owed support to the wife, and was responsible not only for her debts but also for her discipline. The wife, in turn, owed service and sexual fidelity to her husband.

As we saw in Chapter 1, some of these problems were remedied by the Married Women's Property Acts enacted in most states between 1840 and 1900. These laws made it possible for a woman to retain her wages from work outside the home, to manage and control her real property, and to sue and be sued.

The legal developments that began in the early 1900s dispelled a number of disadvantages associated with coverture and also made it easier for women to escape from intolerable marriages. Though problems still persist, during the 1990s, the legal system began to address some of the more onerous issues, such as domestic violence and adequate child support. A woman's "role" has begun to change into one of relative equality in certain areas. As you will see, however, some of these changes brought with them a new set of challenges.

This chapter will address the issues associated with women's roles in the family and the interplay between gender and family issues in the marital relationship. We will examine how the laws impact the marital relation and the care and custody of children. We will also examine the emerging law surrounding the new definition of family, including domestic partnerships, same-sex marriage, and the dissolution of those relationships. As you read each section, think about how women's roles have changed and whether—and to what extent—"equality" has been achieved.

I. THE MARITAL RELATION

The Heritage of Coverture

Marriage under the common law meant the imposition of fixed obligations on both spouses. These differences in duties and vulnerabilities continued long after many of the consequences of marriage were softened by the Married Women's Property Acts. The nature of these continuing marital obligations, the ways they can and cannot be enforced, and their continuing vitality are addressed in the next several cases. The first demonstrates the difficulties a wife faces in attempting to enforce the duty of support owed to her during marriage.

McGUIRE V. McGUIRE
Supreme Court of Nebraska, 1953.
157 Neb. 226, 59 N.W.2d 336.

MESSMORE, Justice.

The plaintiff, Lydia McGuire, brought this action in equity in the district court for Wayne County against Charles W. McGuire, her husband, as defendant, to recover suitable maintenance and support money, and for costs and attorney's fees. Trial was had to the court and a decree was rendered in favor of the plaintiff. . . . [P]laintiff had been previously married. Her first husband died in October 1914, leaving surviving him the plaintiff and two daughters. He died intestate, leaving 80 acres of land in Dixon County. The plaintiff and each of the daughters inherited a one-third interest therein. At the time of the marriage of the plaintiff and defendant the plaintiff's daughters were 9 and 11 years of age. By working and receiving financial assistance from the parties to this action, the daughters received a high school education in Pender. One daughter attended Wayne State Teachers College for 2 years and the other daughter attended a business college in Sioux City, Iowa, for 1 year. Both these daughters are married and have families of their own.

On April 12, 1939, the plaintiff transferred her interest in the 80 acre farm to her two daughters. The defendant signed the deed.

At the time of trial plaintiff was 66 years of age and the defendant nearly 80 years of age. No children were born to these parties. The defendant had no dependents except the plaintiff.

The plaintiff testified that she was a dutiful and obedient wife, worked and saved, and cohabited with the defendant until the last 2 or 3 years. She worked in the fields, did outside chores, cooked, and attended to her household duties such as cleaning the house and doing the washing. For a number of years she raised as high as 300 chickens, sold poultry and eggs, and used the money to buy clothing, things she wanted, and for groceries. She further testified that the defendant was the boss of the house and his word was law, that: he would not tolerate any charge accounts and would not inform her as to his finances or business; and that he was a poor companion. The defendant did not complain of her work, but left the impression to her that she had not done enough. On several occasions the plaintiff asked the defendant for money. He would give her very small amounts; and for the last 3 or 4 years he had not given her any money nor provided her with clothing, except a coat about 4 years previous. The defendant had purchased the groceries the last 3 or 4 years, and permitted her to buy groceries, but he paid for them by check. There is apparently no complaint about the groceries the defendant furnished. The defendant had not taken her to a motion picture show during the past 12 years. They did not belong to any organizations or charitable institutions, nor did he give her money to make contributions to any charitable institutions. The defendant belongs to the Pleasant Valley Church which occupies about 2 acres of his farm land. At the time of trial there was no minister for this church so there were no services. For the past 4 years or more, the defendant had not given the plaintiff money to purchase furniture or other household necessities. Three years ago he did purchase an electric, wood-and-cob combination stove which was installed in the kitchen, also linoleum floor covering for the kitchen. The plaintiff further testified that the house is not equipped with a bathroom, bathing facilities, or inside toilet. The kitchen is not modern. She does not have a kitchen sink. Hard and soft water is obtained from a well and cistern. She has a mechanical Servel refrigerator, and the house is equipped with electricity. There is a pipeless furnace which she testified had not been in good working order for 5 or 6 years, and she testified she was tired of scooping coal and ashes. She had requested a new furnace but the defendant believed the one they had to be satisfactory. She related that the furniture was old and she would like to replenish it, at least to be comparable with some of her neighbors; that her silverware and dishes were old and were primarily gifts, outside of what she purchased; that one of her daughters was good about furnishing her clothing, at least a dress a year, or sometimes two; that the defendant owns a 1929 Ford coupé equipped with a heater which is not efficient, and on the average of every 2 weeks he drives the plaintiff to Wayne to visit her mother; and that he also owns a 1927 Chevrolet pickup which is used for different purposes on the farm. The plaintiff was privileged to use all of the rent money she wanted to from the 80-acre farm, and

when she goes to see her daughters, which is not frequent, she uses part of the rent money for that purpose, the defendant providing no funds for such use. The defendant ordinarily raised hogs on his farm, but the last 4 or 5 years has leased his farm land to tenants, and he generally keeps up the fences and the buildings. At the present time the plaintiff is not able to raise chickens and sell eggs. She has about 25 chickens. The plaintiff has had three abdominal operations for which the defendant has paid. She selected her own doctor, and there were no restrictions placed in that respect. When she has requested various things for the home or personal effects, defendant has informed her on many occasions that he did not have the money to pay for the same. She would like to have a new car. She visited one daughter in Spokane, Washington, in March 1951 for 3 or 4 weeks, and visited the other daughter living in Fort Worth, Texas, on three occasions for 2 to 4 weeks at a time. She had visited one of her daughters when she was living in Sioux City some weekends. The plaintiff further testified that she had very little funds, possibly $1,500 in the bank which was chicken money and money which her father furnished her, he having departed this life a few years ago; and that use of the telephone was restricted, indicating that defendant did not desire that she make long distance calls, otherwise she had free access to the telephone.

It appears that the defendant owns 398 acres of land with 2 acres deeded to a church, the land being of the value of $83,960; that he has bank deposits in the sum of $12,786.81 and government bonds in the amount of $104,500; and that his income, including interest on the bonds and rental for his real estate, is $8,000 or $9,000 a year. There are apparently some Series E United States Savings Bonds listed and registered in the names of Charles W. McGuire or Lydia M. McGuire purchased in 1943, 1944, and 1945, in the amount of $2,500. Other bonds seem to be in the name of Charles W. McGuire, without a beneficiary or co-owner designated. The plaintiff has a bank account of $5,960.22. This account includes deposits of some $200 and $100 which the court required the defendant to pay his wife as temporary allowance during the pendency of these proceedings. One hundred dollars was withdrawn on the date of each deposit.

The facts are not in dispute. . . .

In the instant case the marital relation has continued for more than 33 years, and the wife has been supported in the same manner during this time without complaint on her part. The parties have not been separated or living apart from each other at any time. In the light of the . . . cases it is clear, especially so in this jurisdiction, that to maintain an action such as the one at bar, the parties must be separated or living apart from each other.

The living standards of a family are a matter of concern to the household, and not for the courts to determine, even though the husband's attitude toward his wife, according to his wealth and circumstances, leaves little to be said in his behalf. As long as the home is maintained and the parties are living as husband and wife it may be said that the husband is legally supporting his wife and the purpose of the marriage relation is being carried out. Public policy requires such a holding. It appears that the plaintiff is not devoid of money in her own right. She has a fair-sized bank account and

is entitled to use the rent from the 80 acres of land left by her first husband, if she so chooses. . . .

For the reasons given in this opinion, the judgment rendered by the district court is reversed and the cause remanded with directions to dismiss the cause.

Reversed and Remanded with Directions to Dismiss.

STUDY QUESTIONS

1. According to the court, what is the purpose of the marriage relation? When is it being carried out? Do you agree? Why? Why not?

2. What is the basis for the court's refusal to grant relief? Do you suppose Charles McGuire would have obtained any relief had he complained that his wife was not attending to her household duties? Would a court be likely to consider housekeeping and cooking part of a family's "living standards" that are "of concern to the household and not for courts to determine"?

3. Why are courts unwilling to intervene when married couples are still living together? Should they be? Would your answer be affected in any way by knowing that, after the court case, the McGuires continued living together until Charles McGuire's death?

The *McGuire* case illustrates two important features of family law: the judicial reluctance to intervene in intact families and the traditional allocation of family roles. Even today, *McGuire* is routinely cited for the proposition that courts will not intervene in ongoing marriages to enforce spousal obligations. Although this rule is neutral in form, its impact has been far from neutral. Historically, the control that husbands were given over their wives' persons and property allowed them sufficient leverage to coerce their wives into complying with their obligations. Wives, however, were dependent on their husbands economically and thus lacked the means to enforce the obligations due them. Although the law no longer enables men to control their wives property, women's obligations combined with the difficulties they face in the workplace may often have the same effect.

The *McGuire* case also illustrates the traditional allocation of roles in operation. By virtue of his support duty, the husband was obliged to be the breadwinner, and by virtue of her duty to provide services, the wife was obliged to be the homemaker. The services provided by Lydia McGuire clearly contributed to the economic worth of the household and are easily recognizable as work. As the next two cases demonstrate, wives owe their husbands other services as well. These involve social and sexual activities and are far less likely to be seen as work.

The first case, *Glover v. Glover*, concerns a wife's petition for support in the context of divorce. Under New York statutes applicable until the 1970s, the trial court could refuse to award support where it considered the petitioner's conduct highly improper, even if the conduct did not endanger the physical or mental well-being of the other spouse. In finding that the wife's conduct was so reprehensible as to justify a denial of support, the court revealed its view of proper wifely conduct.

GLOVER V. GLOVER
New York Family Court, 1970.
64 Misc.2d 374, 314 N.Y.S.2d 873.

ISIDORE LEVINE, Judge.

Petitioner, a most attractive, articulate and youthful looking woman, apparently in her forties, but fiery, volatile, ruthless, self-centered, cunning and uncompromising, sues the respondent herein contending that since November, 1969 he has refused and neglected to provide fair and reasonable support for her. Petitioner also contends that respondent was physically abusive to her and in particular on June 6, 1970 when without provocation he allegedly kicked her in the lower part of her spine, requiring X-Rays and medical treatment, when all she did, she claims, was to ask him for her weekly allowance.

Respondent, a practicing attorney for 30 years, vehemently denies these allegations and claims that petitioner has been guilty of such gross misconduct that she is not entitled to support from him on a means basis.

Petitioner and respondent were married on May 20, 1962, approximately eight years ago. There are no children of the marriage.

While much of the testimony was in sharp contradiction between the parties, some critical issues were admitted by petitioner. The court, however, has had the special advantage of seeing, hearing and observing the manner of the witnesses on the stand, and evaluating their credibility.

From the credible evidence, adduced at the trial, the court credits the testimony of respondent, and his witnesses, including respondent's version of the alleged assault on petitioner on June 6, 1970, and finds that the petitioner did indeed grossly misconduct herself toward her husband.

The court finds that petitioner, who was obsessed with the desire to be in business for herself despite the respondent's repeated requests to her to give up her business ventures and take care of the home, and despite the fact that he had already yielded to petitioner and given her no less than $2,000, for her business ventures which he opposed, went behind respondent's back and approached several of his legal clients and friends to loan her money or co-sign loans for her. (Petitioner admitted approaching at least five whose names are in the record.)

In addition and most reprehensibly the court finds that petitioner told a number of respondent's clients that he was not a good lawyer and that they should not do business with him. (Petitioner admitted that she may have made deprecating remarks about her husband as a lawyer.)

Two witnesses, both in the real estate business, professionally engaged with respondent, testified to specific instances of professional deprecation of respondent by petitioner.

Petitioner further provoked and exacerbated deteriorating relationships with her husband by failing to keep several appointments with her husband which were vital to his business relationships with clients. On several occasions respondent was compelled to entertain clients alone at his home and cook the dinner for them, since petitioner, who was aware of the social engagements, came home several hours late, and on two occasions, corroborated by a witness for respondent who was present as a guest, came home at about midnight. The testimony evidences further social and business relationships outside the home when petitioner failed to show up on time and respondent was required to entertain his clients and their wives alone.

Further exacerbations of the marital strain between the parties were the result of petitioner's pre-occupation with animals which resulted in dispossess proceedings against her and respondent because of charges of barking emanating from the apartment at all hours of the day and night, because of the urination and defecation by the dogs on the terrace of this apartment (one of the respondent's witnesses testified that petitioner's home was a mess and that the dogs vomited in the living room when he was present in the apartment on August 14, 1970, corroborating in part testimony by respondent that the apartment was constantly in a mess).

Adding up all of this testimony, together with other testimony in the record, the court concludes that the petitioner's misconduct has been so gross as to warrant a denial of her support by respondent on a means basis. One who would destroy her husband professionally and hence financially ought not to be permitted to look to him for support and share in his income on a means basis. . . .

Having denied petitioner support on a means basis, the court now turns to consideration of support of petitioner on a public charge basis, should this eventuate, despite the court's finding that the petitioner is fully able to support herself. It will be noted that the petitioner has had excellent background as a sales representative, interior decorator, and real estate saleswoman, and is attractive, articulate and youthful. However, since at the moment petitioner claims not to have any income, the court directs her support by respondent on a public charge basis for a period not to exceed four weeks from the date hereof for which purpose the attorneys for both sides are directed to confer with the Department of Social Services to agree upon a sum. Should the attorneys fail to come to agreement within one week after receipt of the decision and order herein, either attorney may petition the court for fixing of this sum. Should petitioner not be gainfully employed after four weeks from date, she may petition the court for the continuance of this order of support on a public charge basis.

Notify attorneys for parties.

Study Questions

1. In what way did the court consider that Karen Glover had "grossly misconduct[ed] herself toward her husband?" By being obsessed with the desire to be in business? By attempting to obtain loans or loan guarantees from her husband's clients and friends? By deprecating her husband?
2. How do you suppose the judge would have reacted to testimony to the effect that George Glover constantly left his clothes and other belongings strewn about their home? That the dogs had been his?
3. Are you likely to hear the same criticisms of a wife's conduct today?

The court in this divorce case seems to have seen Karen Glover's misconduct as putting her own interests and tastes ahead of her husband's, thereby neglecting her duties to him. These duties apparently included supporting her husband's professional life by entertaining his clients and their wives and refraining from making deprecating remarks about his professional capabilities. Although courts are probably less likely to cite reasons of this sort today when they withhold support or alimony, similar expectations may well continue to influence the way they exercise their discretion in such matters.

The next case involves a man's right to recover damages from another man who has had sexual relations with his wife. Such actions, although actually civil in nature, are called actions "for criminal conversation." Derived from the common law, they have historically been available only to men. In confronting such a sex-based cause of action, the Maryland Court of Appeals was inevitably required to reflect on the nature of the marital relation today.

KLINE V. ANSELL
Maryland Court of Appeals, 1980.
287 Md. 585, 414 A.2d 929.

DAVIDSON, Judge.

We shall here consider the question whether the common law cause of action for criminal conversation is viable in Maryland. . . .

At common law, the cause of action for criminal conversation was available only to a man. III Blackstone, *Commentaries on the Laws of England*, 139 40 (Lewis's ed. 1898). The gravamen of this action was adultery. Its elements consisted of a valid marriage and an act of sexual intercourse between a married woman and a man other than her husband. The fact that the wife consented, that she was the aggressor, that she represented herself as single, that she was mistreated or neglected by her husband, that she and her husband were separated through no fault of her own, or that her husband was impotent, were not valid defenses. *See* Prosser, *The Law of Torts*, § 124 (4th ed. 1971). The only valid defense to this action was the consent of the husband.

The cause of action for criminal conversation evolved from the action for enticing away a servant and depriving a master of his proprietary interest in the servant's services. Because at common law the status of a wife was that of a servant, that action was extended to include the deprivation of the wife's services. Prosser, § 124 at 873. The husband was regarded as having a property right in the body of his wife and an exclusive right to the personal enjoyment of her. The wife's adultery was therefore considered to be an invasion of the husband's property rights. A husband could maintain an action for criminal conversation even if his wife was a willing participant, because under the common law, she was considered incapable of giving her consent to what was regarded as an injury to her husband.

While the action for criminal conversation was founded on the services which the wife owed to her husband, the underlying basis of recovery was the injury to the husband's feelings and particularly to his sense of his own and his family's honor. Many of the early cases held "that the essential injury to the husband consists in the defilement of the marriage bed, in the invasion of his exclusive right to marital intercourse with his wife and to beget his own children." This right was recognized as "a right of the highest kind, upon the thorough maintenance of which the whole social order rests, and . . . [for the purpose of] the maintenance of the action it may properly be described as a property right." Thus, while these cases recognized that the essence of the action was an injury to the husband's personal feelings arising from an interference with the marital relationship, they nonetheless continued to describe the basis of the action as an interference with a property right.

Over the years, there has been a gradual shift of emphasis away from the concepts of services and property rights toward a recognition of the more intangible elements of the marital relationship, such as companionship and affection. Prosser, § 124 at 873. Greater emphasis is now placed upon the concept that the wife's act of adultery is an injury to the feelings and the marital rights of the husband, and is therefore an invasion of his personal rights. Thus, an interference with the continuance of the personal rights associated with the marital relationship is becoming recognized as the basis for this action.

In more recent years, the action for criminal conversation has come under attack. In some jurisdictions, it has been abolished by the Legislature. In others, it has been abolished by the courts. A variety of rationales have been relied upon to justify this result. The action for criminal conversation is notorious for affording a fertile field for blackmail and extortion because it involves an accusation of sexual misbehavior. Criminal conversation actions may frequently be brought, not for the purpose of preserving the marital relationship, but rather for purely mercenary or vindictive motives. An award of damages does not constitute an effective deterrent to the act of adultery, and it does not effectively help to preserve or restore a marital relationship in which adultery has already occurred. Indeed, a contested trial may destroy a chance to restore a meaningful relationship. In addition, this action, which eliminates all defenses except the husband's consent and which imposes liability without any regard to the quality of the marital relationship, is incompatible with today's sense of fairness. Most important, today's sense of the increasing personal and sexual freedom of women is incompatible with the rationale underlying this

action. For all of these reasons, this harsh cause of action has been considered to be unreasonable and anachronistic.

In 1972, Art. 46 of the Maryland Declaration of Rights, Maryland's Equal Rights Amendment (ERA), was adopted. It provides:

> "Equality of rights under the law shall not be abridged or denied because of sex." . . .

At common law, the action for criminal conversation provided different benefits to and imposed different burdens upon men and women. Only a man could sue or be sued for criminal conversation. These facts remain unchanged under the common law as it exists in Maryland today. A man has a cause of action for criminal conversation, but a woman does not. Moreover, a man who engages in an act of sexual intercourse with another man's wife is civilly liable for damages, but a woman who engages in a similar activity with another woman's husband is not. Thus, Maryland's law provides different benefits for and imposes different burdens upon its citizens based solely upon their sex. Such a result violates the ERA. Any previous implicit approval by this Court of the action for criminal conversation is eradicated by the existence of the ERA. The common law cause of action for criminal conversation is a vestige of the past. It cannot be reconciled with our commitment to equality of the sexes.

We now hold that in Maryland the cause of action for criminal conversation is unconstitutional and is no longer viable. Accordingly, we shall reverse that portion of the judgment relating to criminal conversation.

STUDY QUESTIONS

1. At common law, who could bring an action for criminal conversation against whom? What was the original basis for the action? What did it become? How could the person being sued defend against the action?

2. What expectations concerning sexual fidelity in marriage are reflected in this

cause of action? Do these expectations apply only to the wife or to both the wife and the husband? Do you think people generally have similar expectations today?

3. Was abolition of the cause of action the only remedy available to the court? Like suits for criminal conversation, suits for loss of consortium (loss of a spouse's services or support, companionship and sexual attentions resulting from negligent injury to the spouse) were historically only available to husbands. Yet as courts recognize this gender classification is unconstitutional or otherwise improper, they generally make the cause of action available to wives as well as husbands. Why do you suppose the Maryland court declined to extend the right to sue wives in this case?

The decision in *Kline v. Ansell* to eliminate the cause of action for criminal conversation reflects some changes in attitude toward wives' duties of fidelity in marriage. The decision should not necessarily be read as a sign that extramarital sexual conduct is totally acceptable, however, since adultery is still a ground for divorce in many jurisdictions. It may, instead, indicate an unwillingness to see women as responsible for the seduction of adulterous husbands in the same way that men have been seen as responsible for the seduction of adulterous wives.

In discussing the shift of emphasis in marriage away from services and property rights toward companionship and affection, the courts have allowed us to see how new rationales evolve to justify the continuation of sex-based doctrines rooted in coverture. Like *Kline v. Ansell*, the next case involves the durability of a traditional attribute associated with coverture. At issue here is the continued vitality of a Louisiana provision awarding husbands the power to control property held jointly by a married couple. The case also introduces one of the forms of marital property arrangements treated at greater length in the next subsection. For now, it is enough to understand that under community property, the arrangement at issue here, all income and property acquired during the marriage generally belongs to both spouses, though the man might have control over it. By contrast, under the common law system, income or property generally goes to the spouse who has title to it.

KIRCHBERG V. FEENSTRA
United States Supreme Court, 1981.
450 U.S. 455, 101 S. Ct. 1195, 67. L. Ed.2d 428.

Justice MARSHALL delivered the opinion of the Court.

In this appeal we consider the constitutionality of a now superseded Louisiana statute that gave a husband, as "head and master" of property jointly owned with his wife, the unilateral right to dispose of such property without his spouse's consent. Concluding that the provision violates the Equal Protection Clause of the Fourteenth Amendment, we affirm the judgment of the Court of Appeals for the Fifth Circuit invalidating the statute.

I

In 1974, appellee Joan Feenstra filed a criminal complaint against her husband, Harold Feenstra, charging him with molesting their minor daughter. While incarcerated on that charge, Mr. Feenstra retained appellant Karl

Kirchberg, an attorney, to represent him. Mr. Feenstra signed a $3,000 promissory note in prepayment for legal services to be performed by appellant Kirchberg. As security on this note, Mr. Feenstra executed a mortgage in favor of appellant on the home he jointly owned with his wife. Mrs. Feenstra was not informed of the mortgage, and her consent was not required because a state statute . . . gave her husband exclusive control over the disposition of community property.

Mrs. Feenstra eventually dropped the charge against her husband . . . [who] obtained a legal separation from his wife and moved out of the State. Mrs. Feenstra first learned of the existence of the mortgage in 1976, when appellant Kirchberg threatened to foreclose on her home unless she paid him the amount outstanding on the promissory note executed by her husband. After Mrs. Feenstra refused to pay the obligation, Kirchberg obtained an order of executory process directing the local sheriff to seize and sell the Feenstra home.

. . . Kirchberg in March 1976 filed this action . . . seeking a declaratory judgment against Mrs. Feenstra that he was not liable under the Truth in Lending Act, 15 U.S.C. § 1601 *et seq.*, for any nondisclosures concerning the mortgage he held on the Feenstra home. In her answer to Kirchberg's complaint, Mrs. Feenstra . . . included a . . . counterclaim challenging the constitutionality of the statutory scheme that empowered her husband unilaterally to execute a mortgage on their jointly owned home . . .

While Mrs. Feenstra's appeal from the District Court's order was pending before the Court of Appeals for the Fifth Circuit, the Louisiana Legislature completely revised its code provisions relating to community property. In so doing, the State abandoned the "head and master" concept embodied in Art 2404, and instead granted spouses equal control over the disposition of community property. . . . These provisions, however, did not take effect until January 1, 1980, and the Court of Appeals was therefore required to consider whether Art. 2404, the Civil Code provision which had authorized

Mr. Feenstra to mortgage his home in 1974 without his wife's knowledge or consent, violated the Equal Protection Clause of the Fourteenth Amendment. . . .

[The appellate court] concluded that Art. 2404 violated the Equal Protection Clause. . . .

II

By granting the husband exclusive control over the disposition of community property, Art. 2404 clearly embodies the type of express gender-based discrimination that we have found unconstitutional absent a showing that the classification is tailored to further an important governmental interest. In defending the constitutionality of Art. 2404, appellant Kirchberg does not claim that the provision serves any such interest. Instead, appellant attempts to distinguish this Court's decisions in cases such as *Craig v. Boren* and *Orr v. Orr*, which struck down similar gender-based statutory classifications, by arguing that appellee Feenstra, as opposed to the disadvantaged individuals in those cases, could have taken steps to avoid the discriminatory impact of Art. 2404. Appellant notes that under Art. 2334 of the Louisiana Civil Code, in effect at the time Mr. Feenstra executed the mortgage, Mrs. Feenstra could have made a "declaration by authentic act" prohibiting her husband from executing a mortgage on her home without her consent. By failing to take advantage of this procedure, Mrs. Feenstra, in appellant's view, became the "architect of her own predicament" and therefore should not be heard to complain of the discriminatory impact of Art. 2404.

By focusing on steps that Mrs. Feenstra could have taken to preclude her husband from mortgaging their home without her consent, however, appellant overlooks the critical question: Whether Art. 2404 substantially furthers an important government interest. As we have previously noted, the "absence of an insurmountable barrier" will not redeem an otherwise unconstitutionally discriminatory law. Instead the burden remains on the party seeking to uphold a statute that expressly discriminates on the basis of sex to advance an "exceedingly persuasive justification" for the challenged classification. Because appellant has failed to offer such a justification, and because the State, by declining to appeal from the decision below, has apparently abandoned any claim that an important government objective was served by the statute, we affirm the judgment of the Court of Appeals invalidating Art. 2404.

Accordingly, the judgment of the Court of Appeals is affirmed.

So Ordered.

STUDY QUESTIONS

1. Is Joan Feenstra's experience unusual in your view? Are women often damaged by the type of law challenged here? In what ways?
2. Why don't the procedures that allow wives to stop their husbands from disposing of property without their consent take care of the problem posed by the statute?
3. Can you see any reason why the power to manage and control property should reside only in one spouse?

Joan Feenstra had won at the appellate level, and Louisiana had amended the law while the case was pending. In taking the *Feenstra* case, the Supreme Court went out of its way to make clear that legally imposed inequalities in the marital relation cannot persist in the absence of an "exceedingly persuasive justification." In so holding, the Court followed its earlier decision in *Orr v. Orr* (see Chapter 2), which invalidated Alabama's statute making husbands, but not wives, liable for alimony. There, as in *Feenstra*, the Court found no compelling reason for continuing unequal marital obligations. Indeed, the *Orr* Court explicitly rejected a state preference for traditional allocation of roles as an acceptable justification for such inequalities.

Male management of property was an important aspect of the civil death or loss of identity women experienced under coverture. Perhaps the most conspicuous symbol of that loss of identity that endures today is a woman's assumption of her husband's name. Refusing to comply with this practice has been a form of feminist protest at least since suffragist Lucy Stone married Henry Blackwell in 1855. With the second wave of feminism, women have, on occasion, retained or reverted to their own names or have even chosen, at times with their husbands, a new name on marrying. Initially, these women encountered unofficial resistance from commercial enterprises and other private entities and official resistance from voter registrars, motor vehicle departments, and the like. As a result, a number of legal challenges were instituted in the early 1970s. Asserting violations of the First and Fourteenth Amendments, women argued that use of their own names was an important expression of their independent identity and that requiring women, but not men, to change their names on marriage was an obvious gender classification. Courts generally rejected these claims. They did, however, recognize that name changes on marriage were simply examples of the general common law principle that individuals may change their names by usage. Thus, they have held that as long as there is no criminal purpose or intent to defraud creditors, a married woman, like anyone else, may use any name she chooses.

Although it is now clear that women may retain their names on marriage, they may still lack the power to give their children their name. Some states have explicit provisions allowing parents to give children their mothers' surname, but problems arise when parents do not agree. At times, courts have acknowledged that legal rules for awarding and changing names may be premised on theories of inequality. In *Marriage of Shiffman*, 620 P.2d 579 (1980), for example, the California Supreme Court recognized the father's common law right to name his child as "part of that system, wherein he was sole legal representative of the marriage, its property, and its children." Courts that now allow mothers and fathers equal rights to determine which name their children bear are likely to look to extenuating circumstances and the children's best interests in determining which name the children will take.

Legal domicile rules are even clearer remnants of women's loss of legal identity on marriage. A legal domicile is one's official residence for such purposes as voting and being taxed. In most states, women are automatically assigned their husband's domicile when they marry. As a result, they may be required to pay higher taxes or tuition or to vote in a new place. Apart from their symbolic impact, such rules can have a considerable practical effect today on couples who spend substantial periods of time apart. Consider, for example, the problems of students attending different state universities or employees of different states or localities that maintain residency requirements. In a few circumstances involving state university residency requirements, the courts have held that rigid rules attributing husbands' domiciles to women violate equal protection guarantees. In other cases, courts have carved out exceptions to permit women living apart from their husbands to acquire separate domiciles. As a general matter, however, courts have yet to recognize the right of married women to choose their own domicile.

Thus, remnants of common law notions of marriage lasted well into the twentieth century. In exchange for the obligation to support their spouses, men have been entitled to their wives' personal and sexual services. The law has recognized husbands as the heads of households empowered to determine family names and domiciles and to control marital property.

Contemporary Marriage Models

Although cases like *Orr v. Orr* and *Kirchberg v. Feenstra* rule out legal forms that impose a sex-based hierarchy on the marital relation, they leave open the question of what new legal models will replace the old. It is possible to envision many different types of relationships that satisfy the requirements of equal protection. Two basic models are often considered. One pictures marriage as a bonding of two parties into a new unit, a unit in which the parties' interests and identities truly merge. This is often referred to as the "partnership model." The other picture of marriage is a more flexible alliance between two independent individuals who have many common interests. We will call this the "alliance model."

Though remnants of common law notions of marriage continued well into the twentieth century, courts and legislatures are now engaged in a process of revising the laws to reflect more modern views of the marital relation. Much of this process is taking place in the context of determining the economic rights of marital partners.

Economic Arrangements & Division of Property

A little background will be helpful in understanding the different views of marriage that are inherent in legal rules that relate to property arrangements within marriage. In the United States, two basic systems have determined the property rights of married couples: the "community property" system and the "common law" system. Rooted in the civil law systems of the European continent, the community property system generally provides that income or assets (other than gifts or inheritance) acquired by either spouse during the marriage belong to both spouses. Historically, as we saw in Louisiana, male spouses were often given the right to manage and control the property. The common law system derives from English law and came into use with the enactment of the Married Women's Property Acts giving wives the right to own and control their own income and assets. Under the common law system, property belongs to the spouse who holds the title to it. There are, however, several forms of ownership that permit couples to own property together. The two systems differ in their theoretical emphasis: in merging the couple's assets, the community property system emphasizes the couple's unity or partnership, while the common law system underscores the independence of the two spouses by allowing them to hold their property individually. At present, ten states—Alaska, Arizona, California, Idaho, Louisiana, Nevada, New Mexico, Texas, Washington, and Wisconsin—and the commonwealth of Puerto Rico have a community property system.

The legal rules governing marital property are no more evident than at the time of a divorce. In a community property state, marital assets are divided equally between the parties. This reflects the system's assumption that each party contributed equally to the marriage. In a common law state, each piece of property goes to the party in whose name it is titled. The result of the common law system is to effectively dispossess women of property at the breakup of a marriage because, in most cases, property was titled to the husband. As a result of the divorce reform movement of the early 1980s in response to this result, most common law states developed a system of division of property known as "equitable distribution." Under equitable distribution, property obtained after the marriage (with certain exceptions such as inheritances and gifts) is considered marital property and subject to a fair distribution, regardless of the name on the title and "who paid for the property." Assets in a divorce are allocated based on a list of factors that examine what may be deemed as "fair" or "equitable." In both community property and equitable distribution states, decisions regarding the division of property are based on case law precedent or statutory regulation. In all but sixteen states, the courts are guided by statutory factors in dividing property. In most states, nonmonetary contributions and economic misconduct, such as wasting or transferring assets, are considered in the distribution of property.

Much of the litigation involving equitable distribution revolves around whether certain property is marital and whether it is "property" subject to distribution. So, for example, in some states deferred compensation (pensions) acquired during the marriage are divided as marital property, as is the value in a business. In some states, a professional degree and the income derived there from is considered marital property subject to equitable distribution.

Legal rules regarding alimony or spousal support also reveal different concepts of marriage. Historically, alimony has been awarded for a variety of purposes: to ensure the wife's support until she died or remarried and became the responsibility of another man; to reward virtue and punish wrongdoing; to maintain the status or standard of living the wife attained by marriage; and, some say, to compensate the wife for her labor during the marriage. Alimony also came to be a means of adjusting equities, especially after property was distributed, to ensure that wives shared in the fruits of the marriage.

Almost all states still retain provisions for alimony or spousal support in their divorce statutes. The principles for awarding alimony have changed somewhat in recent years, however. Though provisions vary somewhat from state to state, there is generally a much greater emphasis on demonstrated need and the spouse's potential for becoming self-supporting. In other words, alimony awards—certainly permanent awards—are now disfavored, and the burden is on the spouse seeking support to show need. Although some states still take fault into consideration, alimony awarded now is generally thought of as temporary, transitional support to allow a period of adjustment and retraining.

While some states acknowledge the contributions and the services of the party seeking support as a spouse, parent, wage earner, and homemaker and their contributions to the career potential of the other party, in practice most states seem to emphasize future needs and ability to pay. There is some recognition that a divorced woman's earning capacity has often been impaired by her time out of the job market and that after long marriages, some women will be permanently incapable of supporting themselves. Though most states now have statutory factors that courts must consider in determining maintenance, unlike child support, there is no statutory standard that is employed. Maintenance awards are largely based on the discretion of the trial court and the concept of what is fair "compensation." To that end, in over half of the states, marital fault is relevant in whether or not to award maintenance.

Many advocates for divorced wives argue that they are entitled to more alimony, particularly when they have put their husbands through professional school or enhanced the value of their businesses through entertaining or other efforts. Here, too, the different ways of valuing these past contributions reflect different views of the marital relation. The husband's degree or business may be valued and split by the marital partners the same way business partners would divide their assets if their partnership dissolved. A second approach would simply reimburse the wife for her actual contributions (such as her husband's support and educational or business expenses) as though the two spouses were separate individuals who, in essence, made a deal. Courts are beginning to follow both approaches.

In evaluating the pluses and minuses of these different views of marriage, one should consider how they might affect people in traditional, nontraditional, and transitional roles. Women in traditional homemaker roles have the most to gain from the partnership view of marriage, as they usually do not have an independent source of income and have foregone opportunities to develop their earning potential, often with permanent effect. The situation is less clear for women who work outside the home. Often their earnings are limited by their family obligations, and they benefit from a view of marriage that involves pooling finances. However, such a view means that they are no more able to exercise independent control over their resources than are their husbands. Such control may be an important consideration for women who are in the process of establishing identities for themselves other than as wives and mothers, just as it is for the unusual women who earn more than their husbands. Thus, no one view may be appropriate for all marriages. In sum, while it is clear that the heritage of coverture with its notion of marital unity and male dominance has not faded, it is not yet clear what model of the marital relation should or will replace it in the context of economic arrangements.

A common thread so far in this chapter is that marriage is shaped by legal rules that embody the marital relationship. Marriage has increasingly been viewed in terms of a contract between two parties. One need look no further than the grounds for the dissolution of a marriage or the annulment of a marriage to see how marriage is considered contractual. An annulment often looks at proof of the inability to contract (age or mental illness) and divorce at the violation of the marriage contract (cruel and inhuman treatment). Marriage is within the domain of the states to regulate, keeping in mind the overall federal constitutional requirements. States can set the rules as to who and how one can marry, as long as those requirements are not "improper" in that there is no constitutional violation. Based on these constitutional requirements, states cannot prohibit interracial marriages. However, states can and do prohibit same-sex marriages. Is this any different than interracial marriage?

Issues of Marital Discord and Marriage Policies of Today

Most would not dispute that some regulation of marriage is valid; setting the age a person can marry, for example, is not without merit. But as we enter the twenty-first century, a new phenomenon is taking hold. Amid a skyrocketing divorce rate that some find shocking, many states, led by the federal government, are now stepping in to require pre-marriage education and counseling. An area previously relegated to religious institutions, the government is addressing issues of marriage permanency by attempting to require educational courses prior to issuing a marriage license. Further, under the welfare reform policies of the Bush Administration, marriage is viewed as worthy of special compensation and incentive. Thus, the Bush Administration had made it a priority that some states use part of their welfare funding to develop initiatives that promote getting married and staying married. Is it the role of the government to enter into this realm? Many advocates for the poor and women's advocates strongly disagree with these propositions. Foremost is the very real concern that promoting marriage will force battered women to stay in violent relationships. Though proponents of these policies do not intend for this to happen, it is clear to most advocates that it will happen. Batterers will have another means to keep their victims in the relationship. Further, funding marriage promotion initiatives will divert already diminishing funds and lessen necessary safety net services such as health care and child care.

The remaining sections of this chapter will examine these and other issues that impact the family, both in its creation and in its dissolution.

Intimate Partner Violence

Intimate partner violence under the guise of "domestic chastisement" has been permitted under the laws of most governments since the early days of the Roman Empire. Blackstone reported that just as the common law gave husbands the right to discipline their children, it gave husbands the right to discipline their wives as long as they used "moderation." Though "wife-beating" per se became illegal in most states by the late 1800s, it was not until the mid-1970s, in many states, that a wife could prosecute her husband in criminal court for assault or other crimes against her. The Battered Women's Movement, an outgrowth of the Feminist Movement of the 1960s, gained momentum in the early 1970s, when the first battered women's shelters opened in communities across the nation. Advocates for battered women recognized that, in order to eradicate domestic violence from our homes, our culture, laws, and attitudes must change.

Battered women's advocates demanded a tougher stance toward domestic violence, including training of judges and law enforcement on the manner in which they addressed the issues and the litigants in domestic violence cases. Among their proposals were legislation that provided for mandatory arrest programs, pro-arrest programs, and simultaneous prosecution in both Family and Criminal Court.

One of the provisions sought by some advocates was *mandatory arrest*; that is, laws that require the police to arrest regardless of the wishes of the victim. Mandatory arrest proposals have been controversial, not only within the general community but also among domestic violence advocates themselves. The controversy stems from a different approach to deal with this issue. There are those who believe that when law enforcement responds to an assault between strangers, the victim is not asked whether she wants to file charges, so should one ask a victim of intimate partner violence? Many believe that by taking the decision away from the victim, she is made safer. Others believe that mandatory arrest disempowers women and puts them in danger because they know that an arrest will result in more violence.

MANDATORY ARREST AND PROSECUTION POLICIES FOR DOMESTIC VIOLENCE

A Critical Literature Review and the Case for More Research to Test
Victim Empowerment Approaches

Reviewed by David M. Heger, Policy Analyst, University of Missouri–St.
Louis, from an article of the same title by:
Linda G. Mills, University of California–Los Angeles. Published:
Criminal Justice & Behavior, 1998, 25, 3, Sept., pp. 306–18.

The criminal justice system has only recently begun to consider violence between adult intimate partners a public matter worthy of legal concern. Advocates lobbied successfully to change the way perpetrators and victims are treated within the system. As a result, new laws have proliferated, including pro-arrest and mandatory, or no-drop, prosecution policies. Mandatory arrest approaches direct police to detain a perpetrator when there is probable cause that a domestic assault has occurred, regardless of the victim's wishes. Mandatory prosecution requires government attorneys to bring criminal charges against batterers.

More than one-third of U.S. police departments reported adopting pro-arrest policies because of empirical data showing arrest to be a deterrent against future spousal violence. Recent data suggest that arrest may actually increase abuse for some women. The number of jurisdictions implementing mandatory prosecution has increased, even though data on the benefits and drawbacks of the policy are scarce.

MANDATORY ARREST

Early studies showed mandatory arrest to be the most effective policy in deterring batterers from future violence. Sherman and Berk (1984a, 1984b) were the first to study mandatory arrest, with numerous studies to follow. They examined 314 cases of misdemeanor assault over six months and found mandatory arrest to be a significantly more effective deterrent than either physical separation or officer mediation. Each of the several studies in the United States that replicated Sherman and Berk produced varying results on the efficacy of mandatory arrest.

An investigation of the combined data from all the mandatory arrest studies found that the policy's success is tied to whether an offender is "good risk" or "bad risk" (Berk et al., 1992). Good risk batterers are defined as having ties to the community through marriage, employment, etc. (Berk, 1993). They are likely to suffer embarrassment and stigmatization as a result of being arrested and are therefore less inclined to reoffend. Bad risk offenders do not possess the same community attachments, are less likely to be embarrassed by detainment, and are prone to future violence.

Overall, mandatory arrest studies indicate a need to individualize intervention strategies based on local demographics. Based on their review of mandatory arrest studies, Sherman, Schmidt, and Rogan (1992) suggest jurisdictions replace mandatory arrest policies with mandatory action or police action chosen from a list of possibilities. Such options could include transportation to a shelter, transportation to a detoxification center, victim-driven arrest, and providing counsel for victim protection.

MANDATORY PROSECUTION

Few studies have examined mandatory prosecution policies. In fact, Ford and Regoli (1993) conducted the only randomized study of no-drop prosecution. They found that the type of prosecution strategy used (drop-permitted versus no-drop) has a significant effect on the future behavior of the batterer. Victims who chose to file charges against the perpetrator under a drop-permitted policy were less likely to experience future violence than were victims whose batterers were prosecuted without their input. However, the opposite was true for victims who chose to drop charges against their batterers; they were more likely to experience abuse again than those dealt with under mandatory prosecution.

Ford and Regoli hypothesize that the preventative impact in drop-permitted cases comes from a victim's personal empowerment. They suggest this power derives from women using prosecution as a bargaining chip with their partners, allying with law enforcement, and being provided with a voice in determining sanctions.

The Effect of Empowerment on Recidivism

Sherman and Berk (1984a) briefly addressed victim empowerment in their examination of mandatory arrest (although the replication studies failed to do so). They found a relationship between police concern and batterer recidivism. When batterers were arrested, victims experienced repeat abuse in 26 percent of the cases. When batterers were arrested and the victim perceived the police as concerned and willing to listen, the repeat abuse rate dropped to [9] percent. Sherman and Berk hypothesized that the rate of recidivism dropped with police concern because victims felt empowered by the interaction. . . .

Study Questions

1. Under what circumstances must the police arrest?
2. Do police generally ask a victim whether he or she wants to arrest the perpetrator of other crimes, such as burglary?
3. Do you think that mandatory arrest empowers battered women? Why or why not?

Since the implementation of mandatory arrest policies in the early 1990s, experts have had the opportunity to study the effect of the policy on continued violence. Though the studies have come under fire, one conclusion is that mandatory arrest must be accompanied by vigorous prosecution and changes in state laws that further criminalize acts of domestic violence. For example, in New York State, the acts of punching, slapping, knocking down, biting, and kicking a person are *not* considered assault unless there is some physical injury more severe than scratches or bruises. These acts, though physical in nature, are considered harassment. Harassment is a violation, not a crime, and is punishable by no more than fifteen days in jail. Mandatory arrest must be accompanied by a tougher stand on the criminality of domestic violence.

To those who would criticize mandatory arrest, further research drew the following conclusions.

MANDATORY ARREST OF BATTERERS
A Reply to Its Critics
Evan Stark

Purpose of Research

To review and critique the assumptions, methods, and findings of the literature concluding that mandatory arrest policies are ineffective, including the Minneapolis police experiment and the five studies designed to replicate it, which attempted to test the deterrent effect on domestic violence of arrests and other police responses.

CONCLUSIONS

The author offers several conclusions regarding "pro-arrest" or mandatory arrest strategies:

- [A] pro-arrest strategy should be thought of as a "package of goods" that may include everything from a mere warning, handcuffing, or an arrest warrant through a weekend in jail, mandated treatment, a stalker's law, community intervention programs, the provision of court-based advocates, and real prison time.
- In addition to repeated physical abuse, woman battering typically includes a range of coercive strategies designed to dominate a partner. Many offenders respond to sanctions against physical abuse by isolating, intimidating, and controlling their partners. Therefore, mandatory arrest policies are best assessed by their overall effect on the victim's subordination rather than by the incidence of violence alone.
- There are reasons beyond deterrence for mandatory arrest policy. These include:

- Providing a standard against which to judge variation in police response.
- Providing immediate protection from current violence and giving victims time to consider their options.
- Reducing the overall incidence of domestic violence both directly (because arrest might deter recidivism), and by sending a clear message that battering is unacceptable.
- Acknowledging a special social interest in redressing the legacy of discriminatory treatment of women by law enforcement.
- Serving a "redistributive" function by acknowledging that police service is a resource previously not available to women on an egalitarian basis.
- Providing victims access to services and protection that would not be available outside the criminal justice system.

STUDY QUESTIONS

1. According to this study, what purpose does mandatory arrest serve?
2. Considering both articles, do you agree? Why or why not?

Violence Against Women Act of 1994

The landmark legislation enacted by Congress in 1994 represented a major shift in this country's response to domestic violence. Officially known as the Violence Against Women Act (VAWA), Title IV of the Violent Crime Control and Law Enforcement Act of 1994 (Public Law 103-322), VAWA brought sweeping changes in the way the legal system and government dealt with issues of domestic violence. It was the first recognition at a federal level that domestic violence was a plague on our society.

The provisions of VAWA were widespread. They included mandatory changes to the way states addressed issues of domestic violence; made certain acts of domestic violence a federal crime; provided for training of law enforcement and judiciary; provided millions of dollars of funding to agencies and municipalities to help fight domestic violence; established domestic violence protocols for law enforcement, district attorneys, and the court system; and created a civil remedy for gender-motivated violence.

Gender-motivated violence is violence against people because of their gender (i.e., because they are women). Much like hate crimes directed toward a particular race, gender-motivated violence has a devastating effect not only on the individual but also on society as a whole. The civil remedy that was part of VAWA permitted the commencement of a private federal civil rights action for gender-motivated crime that included rape, sexual assault, stalking, and domestic violence. The statute provided for compensatory and punitive damages, as well as injunctive and declaratory relief.

In 2000, the civil remedy was called into question on constitutional grounds in a case known as *U.S. v. Morrison.* The following is an excerpt of the U.S. Supreme Court decision which found the provisions of a civil action for gender-motivated violence unconstitutional.

UNITED STATES, Petitioner, v. Antonio J. MORRISON, et al. Christy Brzonkala, Petitioner, v. Antonio J. Morrison et al.

Supreme Court of the United States,
May 15, 2000.

Chief Justice REHNQUIST delivered the opinion of the Court.

In these cases we consider the constitutionality of [section of the Violence Against Women Act—VAWA] which provides a federal civil remedy for the victims of gender-motivated violence. The United States Court of Appeals for the Fourth Circuit, sitting en banc, struck down [the section] because it concluded that Congress lacked constitutional authority to enact the section's civil remedy. We affirm.

Petitioner Christy Brzonkala enrolled at Virginia Polytechnic Institute (Virginia Tech) in the fall of 1994. In September of that year, Brzonkala met respondents Antonio Morrison and James Crawford, who were both students at Virginia Tech and members of its varsity football team. Brzonkala alleges that, within 30 minutes of meeting Morrison and Crawford, they assaulted and repeatedly raped her. After the attack, Morrison allegedly told Brzonkala, "You better not have any . . . diseases." In the months following the rape, Morrison also allegedly announced in the dormitory's dining room that he "like[d] to get girls drunk and . . . " The omitted portions, quoted verbatim in the briefs on file with this Court, consist of boasting, debased remarks about what Morrison would do to women, vulgar remarks that cannot fail to shock and offend.

Brzonkala alleges that this attack caused her to become severely emotionally disturbed and depressed. She sought assistance from a university psychiatrist, who prescribed antidepressant medication. Shortly after the rape Brzonkala stopped attending classes and withdrew from the university.

. . . Brzonkala sued Morrison, Crawford, and Virginia Tech in the United States District Court for the Western District of Virginia. Her complaint alleged that Morrison's and Crawford's attack violated VAWA. . . . The full Court of Appeals vacated the panel's opinion and . . . then issued an opinion affirming the District Court's conclusion that Brzonkala stated a claim under [VAWA civil remedy] because her complaint alleged a crime of violence and the allegations of Morrison's crude and derogatory statements regarding his treatment of women sufficiently indicated that his crime was motivated by gender animus. Nevertheless, the court by a divided vote affirmed the District Court's conclusion that Congress lacked constitutional authority to enact VAWA's civil remedy.

Section 13981 was part of the Violence Against Women Act of 1994, § 40302, 108 Stat. 1941–1942. It states that "[a]ll persons within the United States shall have the right to be free from crimes of violence motivated by gender" . . . a "crime[e] of violence motivated by gender" as "a crime of violence committed because of gender or on the basis of gender, and due, at least in part, to an animus based on the victim's gender."

Petitioners assert that [the civil remedy] can be sustained under Congress' commerce power as a regulation of activity that substantially affects interstate commerce. . . . The Commerce Clause does not provide Congress with authority to enact [the section's] federal civil remedy. A congressional enactment will be invalidated only upon a plain showing that Congress has exceeded its constitutional bounds. First, . . . gender-motivated crimes of violence are not, in any sense, economic activity. Second, [the section] contains no jurisdictional element establishing that the federal cause of action is in pursuance of Congress' regulation of interstate commerce. . . . Third, although [the section] *is* supported by numerous findings regarding the serious impact of gender-motivated violence on victims and their families, these findings are substantially weakened by the fact that they rely on reasoning that this Court has rejected, namely, a but-for causal chain from the initial occurrence of violent crime to every attenuated effect upon interstate commerce. If accepted, this reasoning would allow Congress to regulate any crime whose nationwide, aggregated impact has substantial effects on employment, production, transit, or consumption. Moreover, such reasoning will not limit Congress to regulating violence, but may be applied equally as well to family law and other areas of state regulation since the aggregate effect of marriage, divorce, and childrearing on the national economy is undoubtedly significant.

The Constitution requires a distinction between what is truly national and what is truly local, and there is no better example of the police power, which the Founders undeniably left reposed in the States and denied the central Government, than the suppression of violent crime and vindication of its victims. Congress therefore may not regulate noneconomic, violent criminal conduct based solely on the conduct's aggregate effect on interstate commerce.

. . . Because we conclude that the Commerce Clause does not provide Congress with authority to enact [the civil remedy] we address petitioners' alternative argument that the section's civil remedy should be upheld as an exercise of Congress' remedial power under . . . the Fourteenth Amendment. As noted above, Congress expressly invoked the Fourteenth Amendment as a source of authority to enact [this section].

[Section 5 of] the Fourteenth Amendment, which permits Congress to enforce by appropriate legislation the constitutional guarantee that no State shall deprive any person of life, liberty, or property without due process, or deny any person equal protection of the laws, also does not give Congress the authority to enact the [VAWA civil remedy]. Petitioners' assertion that there is pervasive bias in various state justice systems against victims of gender-motivated violence is supported by a voluminous congressional record. However, the Fourteenth Amendment places limitations on the manner in which Congress may attack discriminatory conduct. Foremost among them is the principle that the Amendment prohibits only state action, not private conduct. . . . Assuming that there has been gender-based disparate treatment by state authorities in these cases, it would not be enough to save [VAWA's] civil remedy, which is directed not at a State or state actor but at individuals who have committed criminal acts motivated by gender bias. [The civil remedy] visits no consequence on any Virginia public official involved in investigating or prosecuting Brzonkala's assault, and it is thus unlike any of the [section 5 of the 14th Amendment] remedies that this Court has previously upheld.

The Decision Below Is Affirmed.

STUDY QUESTIONS

1. What was the basis of the Supreme Court's holding?
2. With what sort of gender bias was VAWA concerned?
3. Do state courts have the power to create this remedy under the court's analysis? Should they?

One aspect of VAWA is that, for the first time, local and federal governments are gathering data on domestic violence in a systemic fashion. To understand whether the programs and policies are having any effect, a large part of VAWA includes resources for statistical analysis and research. Though declining, statistics surrounding domestic violence continue to be astounding. Victims of intimate partner violence are overwhelmingly women. According to the Department of Justice, Bureau of Justice Statistics report (February 2003), nearly 85 percent of incidents were against women. Intimate partner violence made up 20 percent of all violent crime against women in 2001, compared to 3 percent against men. In 2000, 1247 women were killed by an intimate partner. The number of violent crimes by intimate partners against females declined from 1993 to 2001. In 1993 women experienced 1.1 million nonfatal violent crimes by an intimate; in 2001, there were about 588,490 such crimes.

According to the Center for Disease Control Each year, women experience about 4.8 million intimate partner related physical assaults and rapes. In 2004 intimate partner violence resulted in 1,544 deaths. Of these deaths, 25% were males and 75% were females. The cost of IPV was an estimated $5.8 billion in 1995. Updated to 2003 dollars, that's more than $8.3 billion. This cost includes medical care, mental health services, and lost productivity (e.g., time away from work).

The impact of this violence is overwhelming, affecting women victims and their children. Though laws dealing with domestic violence have been strengthened, barriers remain and violence continues. Many victims become desperate, afraid that the system will fail them and that they or their children may be subjected to more severe violence. They often make decisions that appear irrational, staying with the batterer or, in some cases, killing their batterer. The theory that attempts to address this is often referred to as "battered woman syndrome." As a legal defense to justify the actions of battered women who kill, battered woman syndrome has been largely unsuccessful. Recent research has expanded this theory and provided a different perspective on the effect of domestic violence on women.

VALIDITY OF "BATTERED WOMAN SYNDROME" IN CRIMINAL CASES INVOLVING BATTERED WOMEN
Selected Findings and Implications
Malcolm Gordon[18]

FINDINGS

The term "battered woman syndrome" wrongly implies that all battered women respond similarly to being battered and that the common response includes inability to defend themselves, posttraumatic stress distress, and a pathological or maladjusted mental state. In fact, battered women may experience a wide range of traumatic psychological reactions to being battered, which may affect:

- Continued involvement in an abusive relationship.
- Use of physical aggression toward the abuser.
- Future appraisal of the threat of violence.

[18] From an edited version of a review paper prepared by Mary Ann Dutton, *The Validity and Use of Evidence Concerning Battering and Its Effects in Criminal Trials: A Report to Congress Under the Violence Against Women Act*, Research Report, Washington, D.C.: U.S. Department of Justice, National Institute of Justice and the U.S. Department of Health and Human Services, National Institute of Mental Health, May 1996, NCJ 160972.

- Involvement in other criminal activity.
- Refusal or reluctance to cooperate in prosecuting the abuser because of fear of retaliation.

Battered women also experience negative psychological consequences of domestic violence, which may include:

- Amnesia.
- Re-experiencing the trauma (e.g., flashbacks).
- Absence of emotional reactions.
- Hostile or angry reactions.
- Depression.

Additional findings included that:

- Battered women may continue their involvement in abusive relationships because of:
  - Economic factors.
  - Fear that violence will escalate if there is an attempt to leave.
  - Fear that the abuser might retaliate by legally or illegally taking the children.
  - Emotional attachment to the abuser.
- It is a myth that battered women are passive about their victimization; many do fight back either physically or verbally, or engage in other active efforts to resist, avoid, escape, and stop the violence against them.
- A battered woman's appraisal of the threat implicit in a batterer's behavior is based on the pattern of the batterer's prior violence and abuse, the actual threat, the timing of the threat, and the victim's state of mind at the time of the threat.
- There is no one pattern that characterizes all batterers' behavior. Several recognized patterns include:
  - A "cycle of violence" with a series of stages with differing levels of positive and negative emotional engagement, coercion, and physical aggression. These stages may include tension-building, acute-battering, and contrite-loving phases.
  - A long period of time between acute battering episodes.
  - "Separation abuse" where the batterer threatens violence or retaliates violently if the victim separates from the batterer either physically or by making herself unavailable (e.g., becoming involved in a new relationship or beginning divorce proceedings).

- Battered women may fail to cooperate with prosecution as a way to avoid retaliation by their abusers or as a way of avoiding painful and distressing emotions that cooperation would entail.
- Because battering and the effects of battering vary from case to case, there is no "battered woman defense" *per se*.
- Nevertheless, evidence and expert testimony about battering and its effects can assist the factfinder in putting battered women's actions in context in criminal proceedings involving:
  - Self-defense or insanity defense of a battered woman who has murdered or assaulted her batterer.
  - Charging or sentencing a battered woman who has murdered or assaulted her batterer.
  - Duress defense of a battered woman who has committed criminal or illegal conduct through the instigation or coercion of a perpetrator.
  - Prosecution of alleged perpetrators of domestic violence.

Such testimony can also dispel misconceptions about domestic violence that might be held by a judge or jury.

- Expert testimony about battering may be either general (providing information about the scientific and clinical knowledge about battering without relating the information to a specific individual) or specific (based on an evaluation of a specific individual).

IMPLICATIONS FOR DEFENSE ATTORNEYS

Expert testimony on domestic violence may be useful in supporting a plea of self-defense, an insanity defense, or a duress defense. It may also be used to support mitigating factors in charging and sentencing and to explain misconceptions about domestic violence to judges and juries.

IMPLICATIONS FOR PROSECUTORS

Expert testimony may be useful in supporting the prosecution of defendants accused of domestic violence by explaining the victim's recantation of previous statements, refusal or unwillingness to proceed and other behavior that might otherwise be detrimental to the prosecution, and by explaining misconceptions about domestic violence to judges and juries.

STUDY QUESTIONS

1. What effect does repeated violence have on women?
2. How can battered woman syndrome be used in court?
3. What are some of the reasons women stay in relationships with their batterer?

With a better understanding of the impact that abuse has on victims, communities are better able to fashion an appropriate response to intimate partner violence. Most communities across the United States currently look for coordination in their response. A "coordinated community response" brings together all aspects of the system to address violence: police, courts, legal providers, shelters, and domestic violence providers. Domestic violence not only affects its intended partner victim, but also has widespread implications in matters involving the family, in particular children.

Divorce Today

As we have seen, courts have historically been unwilling to enforce agreements between marital partners or to otherwise interfere in ongoing marriages. Nevertheless, in setting and applying the rules governing divorce, courts have made clear their expectations of the two partners during marriage. The rules governing divorce have changed in recent years—generally as a result of legislative action. The next selection describes these changes and helps us understand their impact both before and after the divorce.

BEYOND NO-FAULT
Herma Hill Kay
Divorce Reform at the Crossroads, edited by Stephen D. Sugarman and
Herma Hill Kay. New Haven: Yale University Press, 1990, pp. 6–11.

During the past twenty years, the United States has experienced a period of rapid change in the laws governing divorce. Touched off in 1969 by California's adoption of the nation's first divorce code that dispensed entirely with traditional fault-based divorce grounds and completed in 1985 when South Dakota added a no-fault provision to its list of fault-based grounds, the concept that marriage failure is itself an adequate reason for marital dissolution has been accepted by every state. Viewed from a broader historical perspective, however, the shift from fault to no-fault as a statutory basis for divorce did not begin in 1969, nor was it fully completed in 1985. The history of divorce in Anglo-American law shows a movement from the total unavailability of permanent divorce under the jurisdiction of the ecclesiastical courts in England prior to the reign of King Henry VIII, through a limited traffic in parliamentary divorces during the latter part of the seventeenth and eighteenth centuries, to the conferral of divorce jurisdiction upon the civil courts in 1857 in England and even earlier in some American states. From this perspective, the recognition of divorce for marital fault was itself a liberalizing repudiation of the earlier doctrine that marriage was indissoluble. By the early twentieth century, all American states (except South Carolina, which did not permit permanent divorce until 1948) had enacted laws authorizing courts to dissolve marriages for cause. The most widely recognized statutory grounds were adultery, cruelty, and desertion. A few states unwittingly anticipated the subsequent no-fault ground of marriage breakdown by granting courts discretion to terminate a marriage for a cause deemed "sufficient," so long as the judge was "satisfied" that the parties could "no longer live together," while others recognized grounds for divorce that did not involve fault, such as incurable insanity or voluntary separation for a specified period of time. Max Rheinstein characterized these early no-fault grounds as providing, an "opening wedge" for the more modern recognition that marriage breakdown is itself a sufficient basis for dissolution.

Formidable religious, social, political, and economic barriers had to be overcome before these modest wedges successfully pried open the door that led to no-fault divorce. Between 1966 and 1970, however, four influential groups concluded, after respectively studying the contemporary divorce laws in England, California, and the United States, that divorce based on fault no longer represented wise social or legal policy. . . . Despite the respect these reports commanded, however, none of them enjoyed full legislative acceptance. Opposition to such a complete

shift in the basis for divorce led in each case to uneasy compromise. The final product to emerge from each of these studies—the English Divorce Reform Act [of] 1969, the California Family Law Act of 1969, and the 1973 version of the Uniform Marriage and Divorce Act (UMDA)—all differed from the original proposals, chiefly by retaining marital fault as a factor that could be considered in determining whether the marriage had broken down. The controversy and compromise are reflected in the reception of the recommendations for change in the grounds for divorce among the American states. Although the no-fault principle is firmly established in all states as a statutory basis for divorce, its formulation varies across the states, and it forms the exclusive basis for divorce only in a minority of states. Nevertheless, the impasse that had for so many years prevented meaningful reform of the grounds for divorce in both countries had been broken, and the new approach continues to spread among the American states.

. . . The no-fault principle is most intuitively appealing when it is invoked to permit the legal termination of a marriage that both spouses agree has ended in fact. In that context, the recognition of marriage breakdown is tantamount to legalization of divorce by mutual consent, and the elimination of fault as a basis for resolving the related issues of property, support, and child custody appears appropriate. Family dissolution has been analogized in such cases to the winding up of a partnership; much of the emotional work of terminating the marriage relationship may have been accomplished before the case goes to court.

As Lawrence Friedman has pointed out, however, "No-fault goes beyond consensual divorce. Either partner can end a marriage simply by asserting that the marriage has broken down." Divorce by unilateral fiat is closer to desertion than to mutual separation. Unlike divorce based on mutual consent, unilateral divorce is apt to produce unexpected emotional stress and financial dislocation that exacerbates the upheaval accompanying family breakdown. The fault doctrine may have served to lend emotional vindication to the rejected spouse, as well as a measure of financial protection and status as the preferred custodian of children. If so, greater justification may be required in those cases for eliminating that doctrine from the related core areas of support, property distribution, and child custody.

Adequate justification may be found in the ideal of marriage as a relationship characterized by the continuing existence of a mutual loving commitment between the spouses. It follows that once the marriage is no longer viable, neither its legal existence nor its related legal incidents should become weapons used to obtain revenge for the breakdown or to extort a favorable settlement. But if fault is withdrawn, the party formerly able to invoke that doctrine may be left in a vulnerable position both when negotiating a dissolution agreement and when litigating the matter in court. This vulnerability may be lessened or avoided if the elimination of fault is accompanied by a clear specification of appropriate substantive standards capable of ensuring fair treatment to both parties to replace the punitive philosophy inherent in the former approach. . . .

Instead, as Mary Ann Glendon has pointed out, the prevailing approach in the United States has been to rely on judicial discretion to decide contested cases under general standards without requiring any meticulous judicial scrutiny of the private agreements negotiated by the parties in noncontested cases. And as Lenore Weitzman has demonstrated in her award-winning study of practice under the California no-fault law, many judges exercised their discretion in ways that failed to protect the vulnerable party, thus impoverishing many dependent women and the children in their custody. Drawing on Weitzman's study and those of others, Glendon concludes that "more than any other country among those examined here, the United States

has accepted the idea of no-fault, no-responsibility divorce.". . .

I have suggested elsewhere that, although the law should not penalize women at divorce whose earlier marital choices left them financially dependent upon their husbands, neither should we perpetuate a legal framework for marriage and divorce that encourages couples to choose gender roles that are financially disabling for women in the event of divorce. Yet, even if we imagine that many or most future marital unions will be composed of economically self-sufficient individuals, the presence of children normally entails periods of dependency for caretaking parents that may impair their financial security if divorce ensues. It seems necessary, therefore, that divorce law must provide what Jeremy Waldron has termed the "fallback" rights that marital partners can rely on for protection if their mutual affection fades.

The fall-back rights we create during this next phase of contemporary divorce reform should be designed for a society in which the context of family life is changing rapidly. Today, it is normal for family life to occur outside of marriage, and marriage itself may be expected to continue its present trend toward norms of greater equality between husband and wife. Some observers expect that marriage may eventually be redefined to become available to homosexual as well as heterosexual couples. We need to create a legal framework sufficiently flexible to permit the flourishing of a human intimacy that is the basis of loving commitment in all its variety and that, in turn, fosters the nurturance and guidance of children. . . .

STUDY QUESTIONS

1. How did the modern concept of no-fault divorce come about? Does the no-fault principle change the meaning of marriage? How so?
2. As compared to prior law, what problems does the no-fault approach make for divorcing partners?

The divorce reform Kay describes reflects a view that ideally, marriage should continue only so long as the partners have a loving commitment to each other and that the partners should not be blamed for their failure to feel this commitment. As she points out, however, this view and the laws that embody it have consequences for the formerly "innocent" party. In recent times, no-fault divorce has become the subject of criticism from two sources. The conservative right criticizes no-fault divorce for making divorce too easy. They are concerned with the imposition of the more traditional model of marriage and preserving the traditional nuclear family. This has implications not only for keeping marriages together but also for what is meant by a traditional nuclear family. On the other side of the divide, women's advocates are moving away from no-fault divorce and toward fault as a way to give women more leverage and bargaining power in divorce litigation. The conflict is palpable, as more and more people seek to exert more control over their personal choices and find simpler ways to extricate themselves from bad relationships. Others have concerns that some of the restrictions promoting marriage and restricting divorce can have grave consequences on women, particularly women in violent relationships.

Economic Impact of Divorce on Women

Many divorce experts specializing in women's issues believe that the trade-off in the change to community property or equitable distribution resulted in the courts treating alimony less as an automatic way to compensate the non-monied spouse after divorce and more of a transitional way to support that spouse until he or she found full-time work or completed some schooling. Alimony is not an absolute. Awards are made on a case-by-case basis, with judges bound by case law precedence, not statute. People of moderate means are further jeopardized as courts often do no award maintenance or alimony because there is not enough money to "go around."

The following article excerpted from the NOW Legal Defense Fund's Guide to Divorce provides a good overview of alimony today and how it is treated by courts across the country.

Divorce Planning: A Guide for Women
Seeking and Getting Alimony
Legal Momentum (formerly NOW Legal Defense Fund)

Alimony (also called spousal support or maintenance) is a financial payment made by one spouse to another, more financially dependent spouse after a divorce. Virtually all states have statutes permitting alimony awards in appropriate cases, although states may use different reasons in determining such awards. Originally, alimony was awarded to enable an ex-wife to continue living at the same standard she had enjoyed during the marriage, especially if she had been a loyal wife, married a long time, and had no marketable skills. Increasingly, courts award alimony to enable an economically disadvantaged spouse to acquire marketable skills and become self-supporting. There are many different reasons why alimony might be justified:

- To provide further family support;
- To prevent the dependent spouse from becoming a public charge;

Reprinted with permission of Legal Momentum (formerly known as NOW Legal Defense and Education Fund).

- To compensate a spouse for contributing faithful service to the marriage (particularly as a homemaker);
- To compensate a spouse for enabling the education or training of the other spouse and to enable the one who gave up educational or work opportunities during the marriage to become rehabilitated (i.e., financially independent).

Alimony can be awarded to either spouse as a one-time, lump sum payment; periodic payments for a temporary amount of time; or periodic payments for an indefinite time (usually until the death or remarriage of the recipient). Courts often use factors similar to those governing the division of property in determining alimony awards. The factors most used include: length of the marriage; the respective earning capacities of the parties; the needs of each party; and whether one party sacrificed career opportunities for the sake of the family. Some courts will order a spouse to pay alimony (temporary or permanent) to reimburse the other spouse who lost income and opportunities by agreement of the parties (for example, to stay home with the children or to forego college and support a spouse advancing his career). Modest awards are the present day norm and some states will award only short-term, rehabilitative alimony to enable a spouse to establish a career or to obtain the necessary training, education, job skills, or experience. This is true even if a spouse had marketable skills before the marriage, but stayed home (or worked part-time menial jobs) for ten to fifteen years to raise the children. Some states permit only short-term alimony awards even if the results are very unfair.

Twenty-nine states permit the court to consider marital misconduct or fault generally in considering whether to grant alimony. A small number of states prohibit alimony to an adulterous wife or spouse. Some judges will not order husbands to pay alimony to adulterous wives or ex-wives who live with another partner. (A few state appellate courts have ruled that a judge cannot automatically prohibit an alimony award for a cohabiting former spouse, but must look to see if the new cohabitant is contributing to the support of the former spouse). Even in states that do not end alimony payments for a spouse who lives with a new partner, many men insist on including a provision in the separation or divorce agreement that the alimony payments end if the dependent spouse lives with a new partner.

In equitable distribution states, an alternative to alimony is to award a spouse a larger share of the marital property in lieu of alimony (as it is often better to receive property at the time of the divorce than to have to fight to get alimony each month). Courts can also order a spouse to pay health insurance or reasonable medical expenses otherwise not reimbursed as a form of alimony. (If [a] spouse's employer has twenty or more employees, [the other spouse] can obtain medical insurance through her/his workplace for up to three years after the divorce).

STUDY QUESTIONS

1. Under what circumstances might alimony be justified?
2. What factors do courts consider in determining alimony awards?
3. Do courts consider fault? Should they?

The development of no-fault divorce grew from dissatisfaction with the need to prove grounds that one might not be able to prove, and a desire to eliminate the stigma of divorce as suggested by Herma Hill Kay in her article that we reviewed earlier in this chapter. Perhaps the remedy to this issue lies more in the elimination of economic inequities that women bear and in the provision of adequate financial support after divorce than it does in making divorce more difficult to achieve. If women worked at adequate jobs that provided a living wage, or received appropriate child support and maintenance awards, *how* they obtain the divorce would take on far less significance than *what* they obtained in the divorce.

A 2008 study showed that a greater number of women who are divorced are living in poverty, in particular older women. The Population Reference Bureau (PRB) (www.prb.org) finds that elderly woman are "highly vulnerable" to becoming poor. Many outlive their partners and run out of resources as they age. Divorced or separated older women are even more likely to be poor. According to the PRB 37% of poor elderly women are divorced or separated compared to 10% who are married. Divorced women oftentimes lose assets as a result of the divorce and lost earning potential during the marriage. Many find themselves without health care coverage and without access to assets and funds. Many advocates look to balance no-fault laws by seeking standardized maintenance formulas like what are used in child support cases or permitting proof of fault for equitable distribution purposes to ensure that women do not become vulnerable to poverty as a result of the divorce.

As we will see in the next sections, in addition to financial consequences, fault in a divorce may also greatly impact issues of custody.

II. CUSTODY AND CARE OF CHILDREN

Just as courts were historically unwilling to intervene in ongoing marriages to enforce spousal obligations or to attempt to control violence between spouses, they were reluctant to intervene in ongoing families to designate caretakers for children. Nevertheless, the law reflects and reinforces societal views regarding gender-appropriate behavior in caring for children in the same way it reinforces societal views of the marital relation. Views about the proper allocation of child care duties and the proper behavior for caretakers are often expressed when the law resolves custody conflicts between former spouses and between the state or third parties, and in government programs affecting the family.

Custody Disputes Between Parents

The rules for awarding custody have evolved from sex-based doctrines favoring fathers to sex-based doctrines favoring mothers to nominally sex-neutral standards. In considering these more modern doctrines, think about whether they, in fact, operate in a neutral way. Are they likely to be applied in a biased fashion? Are they based on traditional breadwinner and caretaker roles? Do their delineations of proper caretaker behavior reflect sex stereotypes? Think finally about whether the Seneca Falls complaint—that divorce laws pertaining to guardianship of children are "wholly regardless of the happiness of women"—is still valid.

The Tender Years Presumption

In the case that follows, the Alabama Supreme Court considered the mother-oriented tender years presumption that began to replace the rigid father-oriented custody rule in the mid-nineteenth century. That presumption required either that the mother be given custody of young children unless she was found unfit or that she be given a preference where all other factors were equal. By the mid-twentieth century, that presumption was found throughout the country.

EX PARTE DEVINE

Supreme Court of Alabama, 1981.
398 So.2d 686.

MADDOX, Justice.

We granted certiorari to review the question of whether the tender years presumption, as applied in child custody proceedings, violates the Fourteenth Amendment to the United States Constitution. In the present case, the Court of Civil Appeals affirmed the trial court's usage of that presumption in awarding custody of the parties' two minor children to the respondent, Alice Beth Clark Devine. For the reasons hereinafter set forth, we reverse and remand. . . .

At common law, it was the father rather than the mother who held a virtual absolute right to the custody of their minor children. This rule of law was fostered, in part, by feudalistic notions concerning the "natural" responsibilities of the husband at common law. The husband was considered the head or master of his family, and, as such, responsible for the care, maintenance, education and religious training of his children. By virtue of these responsibilities, the husband was given a corresponding entitlement to the benefits of his children, i.e., their services and association. It is interesting to note that in many instances these rights and privileges were considered dependent upon the recognized laws of nature and in accordance with the *presumption* that the father could best provide for the necessities of his children. . . .

By contrast, the wife was without any rights to the care and custody of her minor children. By marriage, husband and wife became one person with the legal identity of the woman being totally merged with that of her husband. As a result, her rights were often subordinated to those of her husband and she was laden with numerous marital disabilities. As far as any custodial rights were concerned, Blackstone stated the law to be that the mother was "entitled to no power [over her children], but only to reverence and respect." 1 W. Blackstone, *Commentaries on the Law of England* 453 (Tucker ed. 1803).

By the middle of the 19th century, the courts of England began to question and qualify the paternal preference rule. This was due, in part, to the "hardships, not to say cruelty, inflicted upon unoffending mothers by a state of law which took little account of their claims or feelings." W. Forsyth, *A Treatise on the Law Relating to the Custody of Infants in Cases of Difference Between Parents or Guardians* 66 (1850). Courts reacted by taking a more moderate stance concerning child custody, a stance which conditioned a father's absolute custodial rights upon his fitness as a parent. Ultimately, by a series of statutes culminating with Justice Talfourd's Act, 2 and 3 Vict. c. 54 (1839), Parliament affirmatively extended the rights of mothers, especially as concerned the custody of young children. Justice Talfourd's Act expressly provided that the chancery courts, in cases of divorce and separation, could award the custody of minor children to the mother *if the children were less than seven years old*. This statute marks the origin of the tender years presumption in England.

In the United States the origin of the tender years presumption is attributed to the 1830 Maryland decision of *Helms v. Franciscus*. In *Helms*, the court, while recognizing the general rights of the father, stated that it would violate the laws of nature to "snatch" an infant from the care of its mother:

> The father is the rightful and legal guardian of all his infant children; and in general, no court can take from him the custody and control of them, thrown upon him by the law, not for his gratification,

but on account of his duties, and place them against his will in the hands even of his wife. . . . Yet even a court of common law will not go so far as to hold nature in contempt, and snatch helpless, puling infancy from the bosom of an affectionate mother, and place it in the coarse hands of the father. The mother is the softest and safest nurse of infancy, and with her it will be left in opposition to this general right of the father.

Thus began a "process of evolution, perhaps reflecting a change in social attitudes, [whereby] the mother came to be the preferred custodian of young children and daughters. . . . " Foster, *Life with Father, 1978*, 11 Fam.L.Q.327 (1978).

In Alabama, the first noticeable discussion of the tender years presumption appears in the case of *Cornelius v. Cornelius* [in 1858]. In that case the court awarded custody of a young male child to the mother because the father was found to be guilty of certain "fixed intemperate habits"; however, the court qualified its decision by stating that the father could later recover the custody of his child by presenting credible evidence that he had reformed. . . .

The attitude expressed in *Cornelius* was not readily accepted. Alabama courts continued to award custody to the father, even in cases involving very young children. . . .

As late as 1946, this Court continued to recognize the paternal preference rule; however, by that time the rule was no longer a formidable factor in resolving child custody disputes. The influence of the paternal preference rule had been gradually replaced by a growing adherence to the tender years presumption.

At the present time, the tender years presumption is recognized in Alabama as a rebuttable factual presumption based upon the inherent suitability of the mother to care for and nurture young children. All things being equal, the mother is presumed to be best fitted to guide and care for children of tender years. To rebut this presumption the father must present clear and convincing evidence of the mother's positive unfitness. Thus, the tender years presumption affects the resolution of child custody disputes on both a substantive and procedural level. Substantively, it requires the court to award custody of young children to the mother when the parties, as in the present case, are equally fit parents. Procedurally, it imposes an evidentiary burden on the father to prove the positive unfitness of the mother.

In recent years, the tender years doctrine has been severely criticized by legal commentators as an outmoded means of resolving child custody disputes. Several state courts have chosen to abandon or abolish the doctrine, noting that the presumption "facilitates error in an arena in which there is little room for error.". . .

The appellate courts of this state have held that the tender years presumption is "not a classification based upon gender, but merely a factual presumption based upon the historic role of the mother." These statements indicate that the courts in the forties had not developed the sensitivity to gender-based classifications which the courts by the seventies had developed. . . .

Having reviewed the historical development of the presumption as well as its modern status, and having examined the presumption in view of the holdings in *Reed, Frontiero, Orr* and *Caban*, we conclude that the tender years presumption represents an unconstitutional gender-based classification which discriminates between fathers and mothers in child custody proceedings solely on the basis of sex. Like the statutory presumption in *Reed*, the tender years doctrine creates a presumption of fitness and suitability of one parent without any consideration of the actual capabilities of the parties. The tender years presumption, like the statutory schemes in *Frontiero* and *Orr*, imposes legal burdens upon individuals according to the "immutable characteristic" of sex. By requiring

fathers to carry the difficult burden of affirmatively proving the unfitness of the
mother, the presumption may have the effect of depriving some loving fathers of the
custody of their children, while enabling
some alienated mothers to arbitrarily obtain temporary custody. *Cf. Caban.* Even
so, a gender-based classification, although
suspect, may be justified if it is substantially related to a significant state interest.
See, Reed, Frontiero and *Caban,* supra.

Admittedly, the State has a significant
interest in overseeing the care and custody
of infants. In fulfilling this responsibility
in child custody proceedings, the courts of
this state, in custody determinations, have
applied the "best interests of the child"
rule. We are convinced that the tender
years presumption rejects the fundamental
proposition asserted in *Caban* that "maternal and paternal roles are not invariably
different in importance." Even if mothers
as a class were closer than fathers to young
children, this presumption concerning parent-child relations becomes less acceptable
as a basis for judicial distinctions as the age
of the child increases. Courts have come to
rely upon the presumption as a substitute
for a searching factual analysis of the relative parental capabilities of the parties, and
the psychological and physical necessities
of the children. . . .

The trial court's custody decree conclusively shows that the tender years
presumption was a significant factor underlying the court's decision. The cause is due
to be remanded to the trial court with
directions that the court consider the individual facts of the case. The sex and age
of the children are indeed very important
considerations; however, the court must
go beyond these to consider the characteristics and needs of each child, including
their emotional, social, moral, material
and educational needs, the respective
home environments offered by the parties; the characteristics of those seeking

custody, including age, character, stability,
mental and physical health; the capacity and interest of each parent to provide
for the emotional, social, moral, material
and educational needs of the children; the
interpersonal relationship between each
child and each parent; the interpersonal
relationship between the children; the
effect on the child of disrupting or continuing an existing custodial status; the
preference of each child, if the child is of
sufficient age and maturity; the report and
recommendation of any expert witnesses
or other independent investigator; available alternatives; and any other relevant
matter the evidence may disclose.

Reversed and Remanded with Directions.

STUDY QUESTIONS

1. At common law, which parent had the "virtually absolute" right to custody of the children of a marriage? What was the rationale for this doctrine?
2. What does the tender years doctrine provide? Does it always result in the mother being awarded custody? What do you suppose accounts for the change in doctrine? Do you think that there is any truth to the notion that the doctrine changed to give women an edge in custody cases only after children ceased making an eco-nomic contribution to the household and became an economic liability instead?
3. Who benefits from the tender years presumption? Who is harmed by it? Do you think the presumption has any effect on a woman who is considering whether to relinquish custody of her children to their father? Does it affect a man considering relinquishing cus-tody of his children to their mother? Do you think it has any effect on how women's and men's roles are perceived generally?

Modern Custody Doctrines: The Trend Towards Gender Neutrality

Today all states have rejected the tender years presumption as an automatic standard for awarding custody. The majority of courts apply what is known as the "best interests of the child" standard. The best interests test permits the courts to make stylized decisions based on what is best for individual families and does not look at the gender of the parent and the determining issue in awarding custody. The best interests test often looks at a child's psychological and developmental well-being. The critics of the best interests test view it as too vague and are concerned that it is inconsistently applied. To address this criticism, some states have adopted specific factors to consider in determining custody. According to American Bar Association statistics, forty-two states currently have statutory guidelines to determine custody. Other states have established criteria based on case law.

The countervailing theory to best interests, most often put forth by women's rights advocates, is called the "primary caretaker" standard. This standard looks at who was the primary caretaker during the marriage and continues custody with that person. Although this standard recognizes that either parent can be the primary caretaker, some argue that it maintains the status quo—whoever was the caretaker remains the caretaker. The belief is that it often precludes fathers who wish to maintain a relationship with the child from obtaining custody. Critics of this standard believe that it fails to look at the quality of the relationship that the child has with the caretaker, in favor of number of hours spent with the child. To date, West Virginia and Washington are the only states that favor the primary caretaker standard.

In addition to the two standards set forth above, there are other factors that certain courts consider in arriving at decisions of custody. One is the wish of the child. If a child is of sufficient age and maturity, courts will take into account what the child desires. This is expressed either by the child at a special hearing conducted by the judge or through an attorney for the child called a guardian or law guardian. According to the American Bar Association, all but four states (Arkansas, Massachusetts, Mississippi, and Vermont) consider a child's wishes.

Another factor that has recently been statutorily added in some states is the existence of domestic violence between the parents. The heightened awareness of domestic violence has also brought with it the recognition that violence in the home affects the well-being of children even if they are not the subjects of abuse. As of 2001, all but three states—Utah, Connecticut, and Massachusetts—considered the existence of domestic violence in the determination of custody matters. Unfortunately this awareness has also had a backlash effect on battered women. They may be accused of neglect for not leaving their batterer or parental alienation for seeking to limit contact between the child and an abusive father.

Joint Custody

Until recently, rules for deciding disputes have assumed that custody could be awarded to one parent only. More recently, courts have begun to consider shared or joint custody arrangements, which give both parents the opportunity to participate in raising their children. The term *joint custody* refers to joint legal custody (i.e., arrangements giving both parents equal legal rights to make important decisions affecting the child's life), and to joint physical custody (i.e., arrangements for parents alternately living with and taking physical care of that child). As of 2001, according to American Bar Association statistics, forty-seven states have statutes in which joint custody is either an option or a preference. The remaining states recognize joint custody as an option by case law.

The following decision of the New Jersey Supreme Court, though rendered in 1981, still provides a good overview of how Courts analyze joint custody as an option in determining custody.

BECK V. BECK

Supreme Court of New Jersey, 1981.
432 A.2d 63.

CLIFFORD, J.

The parties to this matrimonial action have been granted joint legal and physical custody of their two adopted female children. Although neither party requested joint custody, the trial court nevertheless found such an arrangement to be in the best interests of the children. On appeal by defendant-wife, the Appellate Division found in her favor, reversing and remanding the joint custody decree with directions to award sole custody to her as the children's mother and liberal visitation rights to their father, and to make an appropriate upward adjustment of child support. . . .

The initial issue is whether courts are authorized to decree the joint custody of children. The pertinent statute . . . evinces a legislative intent to grant courts wide latitude to fashion creative remedies in matrimonial custody cases. . . .

Moreover, parents involved in custody controversies have by statute been granted both equal rights and equal responsibilities regarding the care, nurture, education and welfare of their children. Although not an explicit authorization of joint custody, this clearly related statute indicates a legislative preference for custody decrees that allow both parents full and genuine involvement in the lives of their children following a divorce. This approach is consonant with the common law policy that "in promoting the child's welfare, the court should strain every effort to attain for the child the affection of both parents rather than one." . . .

In recent years the concept of joint custody has become topical, due largely to the perceived inadequacies of sole custody awards and in recognition of the modern trend toward shared parenting in marriage. Sole custody tends both to isolate children from the noncustodial parent and to place heavy financial and emotional burdens on the sole caretaker, usually the mother, although awards of custody to the father, especially in households where both parents are employed outside the home, are more common now than in years past. Moreover, because of the absolute nature of sole custody determinations, in which one parent "wins" and the other "loses," the children are likely to become the subject of bitter custody contests and post-decree tension. The upshot is that the best interests of the child are disserved by many aspects of sole custody.

Joint custody attempts to solve some of the problems of sole custody by providing the child with access to both parents and granting parents equal rights and responsibilities regarding their children. Properly analyzed, joint custody is comprised of two elements[:] legal custody and physical custody. Under a joint custody arrangement legal custody, the legal authority and responsibility for making "major" decisions regarding the child's welfare, is shared at all times by both parents. Physical custody, the logistical arrangement whereby the parents share the companionship of the child and are responsible for "minor" day-to-day decisions, may be alternated in accordance with the needs of the parties and the children.

At the root of the joint custody arrangement is the assumption that children in a unified family setting develop attachments to both parents and the severance of either of these attachments is contrary to the child's best interest. . . . Through its legal custody component joint custody seeks to maintain these attachments by permitting both parents to remain decision-makers in the lives of their children. Alternating physical custody enables the children to share with both parents the intimate day-to-day contact necessary to strengthen a true parent-child relationship.

Joint custody, however, is not without its critics. The objections most frequently voiced include contentions that such an arrangement creates instability for children, causes loyalty conflicts, makes maintaining parental authority difficult, and aggravates the already stressful divorce situation by requiring interaction between hostile ex-spouses. . . .

Because we are persuaded that joint custody is likely to foster the best interests of the child in the proper case, we endorse its use as an alternative to sole custody in matrimonial actions. We recognize, however, that such an arrangement will prove acceptable in only a limited class of cases, as set forth more particularly [later in] this opinion. But . . . despite our belief that joint custody will be the preferred disposition in some matrimonial actions, we decline to establish a presumption in its favor or in favor of any particular custody determination. Our concern is that a presumption of this sort might serve as a disincentive for the meticulous fact-finding required in custody cases. [That] is particularly important in these cases because the very interplay of parents and children that gives joint custody its potential value also creates complications different from those found in sole custody arrangements. Some of those complications are dramatized by the instant case.

The parties were married in July 1963. Their two daughters, Lauren, now age twelve, and Kirsten, now age ten, were adopted in infancy. Plaintiff-husband is a successful commercial photographer. Defendant-wife works as a part-time student teacher supervisor at a local college. Since February 14, 1976, when Mr. Beck left the marital residence, the girls have resided with their mother subject to periodic visitation by their father.

In September 1977 plaintiff-husband filed a complaint for divorce based on eighteen months separation. He sought liberal visitation rights but not custody of the children. Defendant answered and counterclaimed for divorce on grounds of desertion.

The initial proceeding was concerned solely with financial matters pertaining to alimony, child support and equitable distribution. The issue of custody appeared to be settled by the pleadings until April 12, 1979 when in the course of its decision the trial court decreed sua sponte that both legal and physical custody would be shared by the parties.

. The court supported the decree with reference to the "uniqueness" of this case. It found the parties to be "sophisticated," with a generally "positive attitude between themselves with regard to the girls"; that plaintiff's income is sufficient to support two households; that the children's ages presented no obstacle; that the proximity of the residences would enable continuity of schooling despite changes in physical custody; that the prior visitation arrangement had been maintained "with no difficulty whatever" between the parties; and, finally, that because the girls were adopted, they needed "the benefit, contact, and security of both parents."

Shortly thereafter, defendant moved for an order amending the findings and judgment of the trial court on the issue of joint custody. Plaintiff opposed the motion and both parties filed lengthy certifications. After reviewing the certifications and hearing argument, the trial court ordered a plenary hearing on the issue of custody. At the hearing defendant testified and also produced a child psychiatrist to testify on her behalf. Plaintiff chose not to testify himself, although he had done so extensively during the first proceeding; but offered three experts in support of his lately-adopted position favoring joint custody: a school psychologist, a clinical psychologist, and a psychiatric social worker. Also, in the course of the hearing the court for the first time met privately with the girls. . . .

At the conclusion of the plenary hearing the trial court reiterated its prior findings and modified its original decision. Viewing the issue in terms of the importance of fatherhood in the lives of the two girls, it concluded that the lack of real contact with the father would have negative developmental effects, particularly because the girls are adopted. . . .

The trial court stressed that although defendant's care of the girls was more than adequate, she is limited by an inability to be both a mother and a father. It found Mrs. Beck to be a "sensible" person, but also somewhat bitter and "stiff lipped" and more partisan than plaintiff, whom he described as "a rather . . . relaxed type of man." Noting that Mrs. Beck "honestly objects to the plan because she contends she cannot cooperate with her former husband," the court concluded, based on the testimony of Dr. Greif, that an amicable relationship between the parties is "comparatively unimportant and not essential" as long as the parties "are looking out for the best interests of the children."

The Appellate Division reversed. . . .

The question of whether a trial court may make a sua sponte custody determination need not long detain us. The paramount consideration in child custody cases is to foster the best interests of the child. This standard has been described as one that protects the "safety, happiness, physical, mental and moral welfare of the child." . . . It would be incongruous and counterproductive to restrict application of this standard to the relief requested by the parties to a custody dispute. Accordingly, a sua sponte custody determination is properly within the discretion of the trial court provided it is supported by the record. . . .

The factors to be considered by a trial court contemplating an award of joint custody require some elaboration. As indicated heretofore, we perceive that the necessary elements will coalesce only infrequently.

First, . . . the court must determine whether the children have established such relationships with both parents that they would benefit from joint custody. For such bonds to exist the parents need not have been equally involved in the child rearing process. Rather, from the child's point of view it is necessary only that the child recognize both parents as sources of security and love and wish to continue both relationships.

Having established the joint custody arrangement's potential benefit to the children, the court must focus on the parents in order to determine, whether they qualify for such an arrangement. . . . In addition [to being "fit" physically and psychologically], they must each be willing to accept custody, although their opposition to joint custody does not preclude the court from ordering that arrangement. Rather, even if neither party seeks joint custody, as long as both are willing to care for the children, joint custody is a possibility.

The most troublesome aspect of a joint custody decree is the additional requirement that the parent exhibit a potential for cooperation in matters of child rearing. This feature does not translate into a requirement that the parents have an amicable relationship. . . .

. . . [T]he judge need only determine if the parents can separate and put aside any conflicts between them to cooperate for the benefit of their child. The judge must look for the parents' ability to cooperate and if the potential exists, encourage its activation by instructing the parents on what is expected of them.

The necessity for at least minimal parental cooperation in a joint custody arrangement presents a thorny problem of judicial enforcement in a case such as the present one, wherein despite the trial court's determination that joint custody is in the best interests of the child, one parent (here, the mother) nevertheless contends that cooperation is impossible and refuses to abide by the decree. Traditional enforcement techniques are singularly inappropriate in a child custody proceeding for which the best interests of the child is our polestar. Despite the obvious unfairness of allowing an uncooperative parent to flout a court decree, we are unwilling to sanction punishment of a recalcitrant parent if the welfare of the child will also suffer. However, when the actions of such a parent deprive the child of the kind of relationship with the other parent that is deemed to be in the child's best interests, removing the child from the custody of the uncooperative parent may well be appropriate as a remedy of last resort. . . .

In addition to the factors set forth above, the physical custody element of a joint custody award requires examination of practical considerations such as the financial status of the parents, the proximity of their respective homes, the demands of parental employment, and the age and number of the children. Joint physical custody necessarily places an additional financial burden on the family. Although exact duplication of facilities and furnishings is not necessary, the trial court should [e]nsure that the children can be adequately cared for in two homes. The geographical proximity of the two homes is an important factor to the extent that it impinges on school arrangements, the children's access to relatives and friends (including visitation by the noncustodial parent), and the ease of travel between the two homes. Parental employment is significant for its effect on a parent's ability properly to care for the children and maintain a relationship with them. The significance of the ages and number of the children is somewhat unclear at present, and will probably vary from case to case, requiring expert testimony as to their impact on the custody arrangement.

If joint custody is feasible except for one or more of these practical considerations, the court should consider awarding legal custody to both parents with physical custody to only one and liberal visitation rights to the other. Such an award will preserve the decision making role of both parents and should approximate, to the extent practicable, the shared companionship of the child and non-custodial parent that is provided in joint physical custody.

Finally, as in all custody determinations, the preference of the children of "sufficient age and capacity" must be accorded "due weight." N.J.S.A. 9:2–4 . . .

The judgment of the Appellate Division is reversed and the case remanded to the trial court [for a speedy but thorough determination of the current appropriateness of joint custody] . . .

court may make decisions about the status, custody of children

STUDY QUESTIONS

1. How do you think the joint custody order will work in this case? How will it affect the relations between all the parties?

2. What enforcement orders did the New Jersey Supreme Court envision? What do you think will be the effects of such orders? How will the parent most concerned about keeping custody be likely to respond to the other parent's misconduct?

3. What effect do you think the decision in this case will have on other divorcing couples and their negotiations over financial matters, child custody, and visitation?

Like other approaches to resolving custody disputes, joint custody is currently the subject of a great deal of controversy. Although there is general agreement that joint custody should be available as a legal option for parents who are able to cooperate, many question whether judges should have the power to impose such arrangements on parents who do not agree. In such cases, men may avoid some of their responsibilities for support without actually performing their share of parenting, and some women may be coerced into "agreeing" to joint custody for fear that their failure to agree will be held against them at a subsequent trial to determine sole custody. Presumptions in favor of joint custody also undercut the type of case-by-case determination that is necessary to identify cases truly suited to joint custody.

Some of the states that do not recognize a presumption of joint custody will not award joint custody absent parental agreement or a finding that the parents' relationship is not acrimonious. Advocates for battered women raise serious concerns about imposing a presumption of joint custody or preference for joint custody in cases where there has been abuse between the parties.

Joint custody poses particular dangers for battered spouses and children, since they are designed to promote and continue contact between parties. The pattern of abuse revolves around issues of power and control. In essence, joint custody forces parents to continue to maintain a relationship and to negotiate with each other. That puts a battered woman in the untenable position of having to *negotiate* with the batterer from a position of where she has no power. In some cases, battered women have lost custody because of these beliefs. Using a theory of parental alienation, or "friendly parent," some courts have taken custody from battered women, claiming they have alienated the child from the other parent. The next article examines the interplay between domestic violence and custody determinations.

CHILD CUSTODY AND VISITATION DECISIONS IN DOMESTIC VIOLENCE CASES: LEGAL TRENDS, RESEARCH FINDINGS, AND RECOMMENDATIONS

Daniel G. Saunders, Ph.D.
University of Michigan, School of Social Work.
Publication Date: August 1998
Revision Date: October 1998

INTRODUCTION

It may be hard to believe an abusive partner can ever make good on his threat to take the children away from his victim. After all, he has a history of violent behavior and she almost never does. Unfortunately, a surprising number of battered women lose custody of their children. The actual number is not known and offenders appear to be no more successful in gaining custody than non-offenders (Liss & Stahly, 1993). However, violence against one parent by another is often considered in custody-determination proceedings (Family Violence Project, 1995). This document describes some of the legal and cultural trends surrounding custody and visitation decisions and the social science evidence supporting a need to consider domestic violence in these decisions.

LEGAL TRENDS

Over the past 200 years, the bases for child custody decisions have changed considerably. The patriarchal doctrine of fathers' ownership of children gave way in the 1920s and 30s to little preference for one parent or the other obtaining custody. When given such broad discretion, judges tended to award custody to mothers, especially of young children. The mother-child bond during the early, "tender years" was considered essential for children's development. In the 1970s, "the best interests of the children" became the predominant guideline (Fine & Fine, 1994) and presumably was neutral regarding parental rights. Exposure to domestic violence was not originally included in the list of factors used to determine the child's best interest.

Source: Reprinted by permission of Daniel G. Saunders. Retrieved from www.minicava.umn.edu on October 28, 2003.

States recently came to recognize that domestic violence needs to be considered in custody decisions (Cahn, 1991; Hart, 1992; for a review of state laws see *Family Violence Project*, NCJFCJ, 1995, and legislative updates for 1996, 1997, and 1998). While a growing number of states specifically mention domestic violence as a factor to be considered, most of them allow wide discretion and do not give it special weight. It is simply one additional factor when considering the best interests of the child. By the end of the 1997 legislative session, 13 states had adopted the Model Code of the Family Violence Project of the National Council of Juvenile and Family Court Judges (NCFCJ, 1998). These statutes specify that there is a "rebuttable presumption that it is detrimental to the child and not in the best interest of the child to be placed in sole custody, joint legal custody, or joint physical custody with the perpetrator of family violence" (p. 33).

Statutes now address other concerns related to custody and the recent proliferation of legislation seems likely to continue. Statutes in some states now cover the prevention of child abduction by the perpetrator through supervised visitation and similar safeguards (Girdner & Hoff, 1996; Hart, 1990), providing a defense against child abduction charges if battered women flee with their children, exempting battered women from mandated mediation (Girdner, 1996), protecting battered women from charges of "child abandonment" if they flee for safety without their children (Cahn, 1991), and allowing parents to check on the criminal charges against a divorce partner (Pennsylvania's Jen & Dave's law). Recent case law makes it easier for battered women to relocate far away from their abusers (Dunford-Jackson, in press). Unfortunately, courts may apply psychological pressures that keep women tied to their abusers. "Friendly parent" statutes ask courts to assess each parent's willingness to co-parent when making custody decisions (Zorza, 1992). Despite their reasonable reluctance to co-parent, battered women may end up being labeled "uncooperative," with an increased risk of losing their children. Along with legal changes, training and resource manuals for judges and court managers have recently been published, including guidelines for selecting custody evaluators and guardian ad litems (Goelman, Lehrman, & Valente, 1996; Lemon, Jaffe, & Ganley, 1995; NCJFCJ, 1995; National Center for State Courts, 1997).

RECOMMENDATIONS FOR CUSTODY AND VISITATION

Despite the dearth of sound research in this area, some tentative recommendations can be made from practice wisdom and the research that does exist. There is general agreement that joint custody has many advantages when a woman has good financial resources and an ex-partner who is nonabusive and supportive as a co-parent. However, the past and potential behavior of men who batter means that joint custody (or sole custody to him) is rarely the preferred option for these families. In addition to their propensity for violence, these men are likely to abuse alcohol (Tolman & Bennett, 1990) and communicate in a hostile, manipulative manner (Holtzworth-Munroe & Stuart, 1994).

As stated earlier, the model state statute of the National Council of Juvenile and Family Court Judges clearly states that there should be a presumption that it is detrimental to the child to be placed in sole or joint custody with a perpetrator of family violence (NCJFCJ, 1993). The model statute emphasizes that the safety and well-being of the child and the parent who is the victim must be primary. The perpetrator's history of causing fear as well as physical harm should be considered. A parent's absence or relocation in an attempt to escape violence by the other parent should not be used as a factor to determine custody. Courts sometimes label battered women as "impulsive" or "uncooperative" if they leave suddenly to find safety in another city or state. The model statute specifies that it is in the best interest of the child to reside with the nonviolent parent and that this parent should be able to choose the location of the residence, even if it is in another state. The non-custodial parent may also be denied access to the child's medical and educational records if such information could be used to locate the custodial parent.

Visitation guidelines should be based on the following general principles: a) contact between child and parent should be structured in a way that limits the child's exposure to parental conflict; b) transitions should be infrequent in cases of ongoing conflict and the reasonable fear of violence; and c) substantial amounts of time with both parents may not be advisable (Johnston, 1992). Ideally, a court order should detail the conditions of supervised visitation, including the role of the supervisor (NCJFCJ, 1995). Unsupervised visitation should be allowed only after the abuser completes a specialized program for men who batter and does not threaten or become violent for a substantial period of time. Practitioners need to be aware of the strong likelihood that men who batter will become violent in a new relationship and that they often use nonviolent tactics that can harm the children. Rather than rely on official records of recidivism, the best way to establish that the perpetrator is nonviolent is to interview current and past partners.

Visitation should be suspended if there are repeated violations of the terms of visitation, the child is severely distressed in response to visitation, or there are clear indications that the violent parent has threatened to harm or flee with the child. Even with unsupervised visitation, it is best to have telephone contact between parents only at scheduled times, to maintain restraining orders to keep the offender away from the victim, and to transfer the child in a neutral, safe place with the help of a third party (Johnston, 1992). Hart (1990) describes a number of safety planning strategies that can be taught to children in these situations.

The model statute (NCJFCJ, 1993) states that visitation should only be awarded to the perpetrator if adequate safety provisions for the child and adult victim can be made. Orders of visitation can specify, among other things: the exchange of the child in a protected setting, supervised visitation by a person or agency, completion by the perpetrator of "a program of intervention for perpetrators," and no overnight visitation. If the court allows a family or household member to supervise the visitation, the court can set the conditions to be followed during visitation. For example, an order might specify that the batterer not use alcohol prior to or during a visit and that the child be allowed to call the mother at any time.

Visitation centers are expanding across North America in response to the need for safe access and visitation (Straus, 1995). The approaches of these centers vary. For example, most of them provide some form of observational records of the visit, but the role of these programs in evaluating parents and reporting to courts differs. The experience of the visitation center in Duluth, Minnesota, shows the difficulty of keeping a neutral stance given the traditional biases in our social systems (McMahon & Pence, 1995). The Duluth center found that the traditional over-emphasis on parental rights and child welfare may block from view the harm of domestic violence to both battered women and their children.

In conclusion, although there is a need for further practice experience and research, our current knowledge of risk factors for continued abuse of women and children means that decision-makers must exercise great caution in awarding custody or visitation to perpetrators of domestic violence. If custody or visitation is granted, careful safety planning and conditions attached to the court order are important to help lower the risk of harm to the children and their mothers.

STUDY QUESTIONS

1. What does the research say are the dangers of joint custody in abuse situations?
2. What is proposed as a better way to determine custody in abuse situations?
3. Do you agree or do you believe that the danger is exaggerated?

In cases other than abuse cases, the trend is toward co-parenting, shared custody, and a belief that children suffer in divorce when there is conflict between parents. To address the conflict inherent in the breakup of a marriage, parent education programs have begun to be the norm in many states. These education programs are designed to provide parents with information regarding the effects of conflict on children and communication techniques to teach parents how to keep children out of the middle of these disputes. A good description of these programs is found in an article by Joan B. Kelly, "The Determination of Child Custody" (*Children and Divorce* Vol. 4. No. 1, Spring 1994). These programs are offered through not-for-profits, churches, and in some cases, by the courts. Some states, like New York State, have made these programs mandatory, except in cases of domestic violence. Another method to reach resolution of custody with the minimum of acrimony is mandatory mediation of the dispute. Mediation involves the parties achieving an agreement with the assistance of a trained neutral mediator outside of the litigation system. The intent of mediation is that parents themselves can fashion a fairer and more appropriate custodial arrangement than a court. Research focuses more on the needs of the children and what is best for children when parents determine to separate and dissolve their relationship.

Economic Support of Children: Child Support Standards

Unlike alimony, child support has in recent years taken a huge leap forward toward adequate and appropriate awards. Prompted by increasing welfare costs, the federal government intervened by requiring states to amend the manner in which they handle child support awards and collections. This push for stronger child support enforcement was driven by inadequate child support awards and enforcement, which resulted in more children receiving welfare.

The legislation that followed included provisions for special child support enforcement units, the ability to enforce orders and collect child support across state lines, and standardized formulas to calculate child support. Congress was able to mandate these changes in each state by making the states eligible for federal welfare reimbursement dependent on state law changes.

Today, all states have child support formulas to guide the courts in decision making. Though there may be differences from state to state, essentially the court bases child support on a percentage of income based on the number of children and then proportionately allocates that required amount between the parents based on their income. The formula is designed to consider the basic needs of the child, including food, shelter, and clothing and considers the standard of living of the family. The amount of support awarded is directly based on the income of the parties. Other expenses such as health insurance, uncovered health expenses, child care, and education are considered add-ons and are proportionately allocated between the parties and added to the child support award.

Although the child support statutes have made the calculation of child support and the enforcement of orders more uniform, they still do not address a remaining gap in child support collection. The formula is easily applied to wage earners who have a set income upon which to base a child support award and to garnish if there is no payment. The difficulty is with self-employed parents who have no set income or income to garnish, the chronically unemployed, or those who refuse to work. In those cases, unless parents are willing to cooperate and pay appropriate child support, children suffer because the courts are virtually without remedy. While most parents would pay support rather than go to jail—the potential result of violating a court order—there are those who would rather sit in jail while their children suffer inadequate food, clothing, housing, and health care.

Governmental Programs to Aid in the Care of Children

Assistance to Families

Until 1996, the Aid to Families with Dependent Children (AFDC) program played a major role in helping women and their children subsist. Although the states varied in the particulars of their programs, each state was required to meet federal standards. Moreover, AFDC programs provided assistance to every person meeting the eligibility criteria. In effect for over sixty years, the AFDC program came to an end in 1996 with the passage by Congress of the Personal Responsibility and Work Opportunity and Reconciliation Act (PRWORA), replacing AFDC with the Temporary Assistance for Needy Families Program.

The Personal Responsibility Act of 1996 provides for block grants to the states governed by federal provisions designed to ensure recipients work in regular jobs and community work programs or participate in training programs. Essentially, the same single-headed household family requirements still apply, but the work requirement applies to all recipients over sixteen. Exemptions are very limited: custodians of children up to twelve weeks, persons up to eighteen years enrolled in high school or the equivalent, hardship exemptions (up to the time limit only), and, as explained below, a Family Violence Option (FVO), which the state can choose to implement. There is a five-year time limit on the receipt of benefits.

As a result of court challenges, employment programs in a few states have been required to pay "prevailing" wages. Other cases have succeeded in enjoining work in unsafe conditions and work that fills jobs normally performed by regular workers. Work requirements that interfere with college students' education have been enjoined in at least one case.

Some states have also adopted durational residency provisions. Under these requirements, welfare recipients who move from states paying lower benefits would be required to wait for a specified period before receiving welfare benefits in their new home state. These provisions have been invalidated. Another state regulation, upheld in several jurisdictions, denies a later-born child (but not existing children) assistance if the later-born child was conceived while a parent was on welfare.

Included in the federal welfare bill is the FVO. About half the states have taken the option. The FVO allows the states to help poor women who are victims of domestic violence by: (1) screening for domestic violence in their welfare caseloads; (2) offering domestic violence support services; and (3) waiving program requirements that would penalize these victims or make it more difficult for them to escape violence (e.g., work requirements and time limits). In June 1997, Congress issued a sense of Congress resolution, making clear that these waivers were supposed to be individual and temporary, something different from the more limited hardship exemption. Women's advocates are making efforts to ensure that the FVO is actually implemented. Early reports, for example, indicated that states adopting the FVO on average gave only seven to eight waivers per month.

In short, today's public assistance program is built on very different premises than AFDC. Assistance is now temporary. Moreover, many recipients are expected to work. Work outside the home is deemed necessary, even for mothers of young children. Child care is no longer recognized as "work."

Government Regulation of Parenting: Termination of Parental Rights

The next group of cases involves state efforts to limit parental rights, usually to permit a third party to adopt. In such cases, parents may be seeking custody or simply the right to see their children. The legal issues in such cases may turn on common law, statutes, or constitutional provisions. Our focus is primarily on constitutional questions and, in particular, due process and equal protection. In terms of due process, the courts have two concerns in this context: (1) what procedures must be followed before a parent may be deprived of such rights as custody and contact with a child; and (2) what must be shown as a matter of substance before such rights are terminated.

Like the intrafamily custody cases, these materials illustrate the ways that judicial and societal expectations of parents vary according to their gender. As compared to intrafamily custody cases, however, adoption and termination cases continue to rely on sex-based classifications to a much greater extent. In studying these materials, consider whether there is a biological basis for the role expectations these classifications embody. Consider also how the roles ascribed to parents differ from the roles ascribed to other figures in a child's life. Consider, finally, the ways in which altering our conceptions of parenting might transform the lives of women whose options have been so sharply defined by their roles as mothers.

The first case to deal with the relations between unwed fathers and their children, *Stanley v. Illinois*, 405 U.S. 645 (1972), was decided only months after *Reed v. Reed*. There, the Court did reject a presumption that parents are unfit for custody of their own children if they are unwed fathers but not if they are unwed mothers. However, despite the fact that the issues in *Stanley* were in many respects the same as those addressed in *Reed*, the Court elected to decide the case under the Due Process rather than the Equal Protection Clause. There is little chance that we will ever know precisely why the Supreme Court relied on due process arguments and avoided the equal protection issue in *Stanley* at a time when it was obviously willing to hold some sex-based classifications unconstitutional. The justices' due process approach suggests, however, that they were less clear about the acceptability of sex-based generalizations in the area of parenting. Nevertheless, they did face the equal protection issue seven years later in *Caban v. Mohammed*, 441 U.S. 380 (1979), a case involving a New York statute that required the consent of an unwed mother, but not an unwed father, for adoption. By a narrow 5–4 vote, they rejected the statute as "another example of overbroad generalizations in gender-based classifications."

> Contrary to appellees' argument and to the apparent presumption underlying § 111, maternal and paternal roles are not invariably different in importance. Even if unwed mothers as a class were closer than unwed fathers to their newborn infants, this generalization concerning parent-child relations would become less acceptable as a basis for legislative distinctions as the age of the child increased. The present case demonstrates that an unwed father may have a relationship with his children fully comparable to that of the mother. Appellant Caban, appellee Maria Mohammed, and their two children lived together as a natural family for several years. As members of this family, both mother and father participated in the care and support of their children. There is no reason to believe that the Caban children—aged 4 and 6 at the time of the adoption proceedings—had a relationship with their mother unrivaled by the affection and concern of their father. We reject, therefore, the claim that the broad, gender-based distinction of § 111 is required by any universal difference between maternal and paternal relations at every phase of a child's development.
>
> *Id. at 389.*

The state had sought to justify the sex-based distinction by arguing that requiring unmarried fathers' consent to adoption impedes adoptions because it is often impossible to locate the fathers, whereas mothers are likely to remain with the children. In rejecting this argument, the Court again pointed to Caban's specific circumstances:

> Even if the special difficulties attendant upon locating and identifying unwed fathers at birth would justify a legislative distinction between mothers and fathers of newborns, these difficulties need not persist past infancy. When the adoption of an older child is sought, the State's

interest in proceeding with adoption cases can be protected by means that do not draw such an inflexible gender-based distinction as that made in § 111. In those cases where the father never has come forward to participate in the rearing of his child, nothing in the Equal Protection Clause precludes the State from withholding from him the privilege of vetoing the adoption of that child. Indeed, under the statute as it now stands the surrogate may proceed in the absence of consent when the parent whose consent otherwise would be required never has come forward or has abandoned the child. But in cases such as this, where the father has established a substantial relationship with the child and has admitted his paternity, a State should have no difficulty in identifying the father even of children born out of wedlock. Thus, no showing has been made that the different treatment afforded unmarried fathers and unmarried mothers under § 111 bears a substantial relationship to the proclaimed interest of the State in promoting the adoption of illegitimate children.

Id. at 392.

The Court thus rested its decision on equal protection grounds. Yet, by focusing so pointedly on Caban's particular relationship with his children, it suggested its discomfort with a broad equal protection analysis in the unwed parent situation. Indeed, the Court hinted that some distinctions may be made between unwed mothers and fathers. The narrow nature of the Court's approach is apparent when we contrast this case, for example, with *Reed v. Reed* (see Chapter 2), in which the Court was totally unconcerned with Sally Reed's ability to administer an estate. The Court simply found the statute's gender-based classification impermissible. Nothing in the opinion suggested that a statute that gave certain rights to all men and to those women who could show competence in estate administration would be constitutional. In *Caban*, however, the Court intimated that just such a distinction may be permissible with regard to unwed mothers and fathers.

Subsequent developments have borne out the intimations from *Caban*. In *Lehr v. Robertson*, the Court upheld a New York adoption that was granted without notice to or consent of the unwed father. The adoption at issue took place under the same New York law as was before the Court in *Caban*.

LEHR V. ROBERTSON
United States Supreme Court, 1983.
463 U.S. 248, 103 S. Ct. 2985, 77 L.Ed.2d 614.

Justice STEVENS delivered the opinion of the Court.

The question presented is whether New York has sufficiently protected an unmarried father's inchoate relationship with a child whom he has never supported and rarely seen in the two years since her birth. The appellant, Jonathan Lehr, claims that the Due Process and Equal Protection Clauses of the Fourteenth Amendment, as interpreted in *Stanley v. Illinois* and *Caban v. Mohammed* give him an absolute right to notice and an opportunity to be heard before the child may be adopted. We disagree.

Jessica M. was born out of wedlock on November 9, 1976. Her mother, Lorraine Robertson, married Richard Robertson eight months after Jessica's birth. On December 21, 1978, when Jessica was over two years old, the Robertsons filed an adoption petition in the Family Court of Ulster County, New York. The court heard their testimony and received a favorable report from the Ulster County Department of Social Services. On March 7, 1979, the court entered an order of adoption. In this proceeding, appellant contends that the adoption order is invalid because he, Jessica's putative father, was not given advance notice of the adoption proceeding.

The State of New York maintains a "putative father registry." A man who files with that registry demonstrates his intent to claim paternity of a child born out of wedlock and is therefore entitled to receive notice of any proceeding to adopt that child. Before entering Jessica's adoption order, the Ulster County Family Court had the putative father registry examined. Although appellant claims to be Jessica's natural father, he had not entered his name in the registry.

In addition to the persons whose names are listed on the putative father registry, New York law requires that notice of an adoption proceeding be given to several other classes of possible fathers of children born out of wedlock—those who have been adjudicated to be the father, those who have been identified as the father on the child's birth certificate, those who live openly with the child and the child's mother and who hold themselves out to be the father, those who have been identified as the father by the mother in a sworn written statement, and those who were married to the child's mother before the child was six months old. Appellant admittedly was not a member of any of those classes. He had lived with appellee prior to Jessica's birth and visited her in the hospital when Jessica was born, but his name does not appear on Jessica's birth certificate. He did not live with appellee or Jessica after Jessica's birth, he has never provided them with any financial support, and he has never offered to marry appellee. Nevertheless, he contends that [his initiation of a separate proceeding to determine paternal support and visitation] gave him a constitutional right to notice and a hearing before Jessica was adopted. . . .

Appellant has now invoked our appellate jurisdiction. He offers two alternative grounds for holding the New York statutory scheme unconstitutional. First, he contends that a putative father's actual or potential relationship with a child born out of wedlock is an interest in liberty which may not be destroyed without due process of law;

he argues therefore that he had a constitutional right to prior notice and an opportunity to be heard before he was deprived of that interest. Second, he contends that the gender-based classification in the statute, which both denied him the right to consent to Jessica's adoption and accorded him fewer procedural rights than her mother, violated the Equal Protection Clause. . . .

When an unwed father demonstrates a full commitment to the responsibilities of parenthood by "com[ing] forward to participate in the rearing of his child," *Caban,* 441 U.S. at 392, his interest in personal contact with his child acquires substantial protection under the due process clause. At that point it may be said that he "act[s] as a father toward his children." *Id.,* at 389, n. 7. But the mere existence of a biological link does not merit equivalent constitutional protection. . . .

The legislation at issue in this case, sections 111 and 111a of the New York Domestic Relations Law, is intended to establish procedures for adoptions. Those procedures are designed to promote the best interests of the child, protect the rights of interested third parties, and ensure promptness and finality. To serve those ends, the legislation guarantees to certain people the right to veto an adoption and the right to prior notice of any adoption proceeding. The mother of an illegitimate child is always within that favored class, but only certain putative fathers are included. Appellant contends that the gender-based distinction is invidious.

As we noted above, the existence or nonexistence of a substantial relationship between parent and child is a relevant criterion in evaluating both the rights of the parent and the best interests of the child. In *Quilloin v. Walcott* [434 U.S. 246, 256 (1978)] we noted that the putative father, like appellant, "ha[d] never shouldered any significant responsibility with respect to the daily supervision, education, protection, or care of the child. Appellant does not complain of his exemption from these responsibilities . . . " We therefore found that a Georgia statute that always required a mother's consent to the adoption of a child born out of wedlock, but required the father's consent only if he had legitimated the child, did not violate the Equal Protection Clause. Because, like the father in *Quilloin*, appellant has never established a substantial relationship with his daughter, the New York statutes at issue in this case did not operate to deny appellant equal protection.

We have held that these statutes may not constitutionally be applied in that class of cases where the mother and father are in fact similarly situated with regard to their relationship with the child. In *Caban v. Mohammed*, the Court held that it violated the Equal Protection Clause to grant the mother a veto over the adoption of a four-year-old girl and a six-year-old boy, but not to grant a veto to their father, who had admitted paternity and had participated in the rearing of the children. The Court made it clear, however, that if the father had not "come forward to participate in the rearing of his child, nothing in the Equal Protection Clause [would] preclude the State from withholding from him the privilege of vetoing the adoption of that child."

Jessica's parents are not like the parents involved in *Caban*. Whereas appellee had

a continuous custodial responsibility for Jessica, appellant never established any custodial, personal, or financial relationship with her. If one parent has an established custodial relationship with the child and the other parent has either abandoned or never established a relationship, the Equal Protection Clause does not prevent a state from according the two parents different legal rights.

The judgment of the New York Court of Appeals is

Affirmed.

STUDY QUESTIONS

1. If Jonathan Lehr had married and petitioned to adopt his child, would Lorraine Robertson have been given notice? Why the difference?
2. As a factual matter, how did Lehr's relationship to his child differ from Caban's relationship to his children?
3. Do New York and the Court presume that an unwed mother automatically establishes a substantial relationship with her child? Is that true? Is it true that an unwed father invariably, or even typically, does not? To the extent that the generalization is valid, does it reflect biological necessities or social realities?

More recently, in the case of *Michael H. v. Gerald D*, 491 U.S. 110 (1989), the Supreme Court upheld a law that permitted only a husband or a wife to rebut a state statute's presumption that a child born during the marriage was legitimate. In finding that this statute did not violate the due process rights of another man seeking to establish paternity, the Court used a sex-neutral analysis. Nevertheless, it is apparent that most decisions involving unwed parents assume women and men play very different roles as parents. Women are viewed as automatically responsible for the care of their out-of-wedlock children, while men must affirmatively establish a custodial, legal, or financial relationship before the law will recognize their parental role. Although judges at times suggest sex-based legal rules reflect physical differences between the sexes, it is simply not true that all unwed mothers (and no unwed fathers) assume responsibility for their children. Most differences in parenting behavior are thus better understood as a product of social expectations rather than biological fact. However, as we have seen, even among feminists, such sex-based classifications are controversial. Some feminists support them on the ground that it is not fair to give an uninvolved father custody of a woman's child when, in reality, she most often bears the day-to-day responsibility for a child borne out-of-wedlock. Others believe that men must be encouraged to become involved in child care and that it is harmful to reinforce the stereotype of women as always being responsible for their children. Thus, the debates over adoption statutes mirror the debates over custody standards.

III. The New Definition of Family: Emerging Issues related to the non-traditional family

As the preceding sections have suggested, governmental policies and judicial decisions frequently assume that people do and should live in stable units composed of one breadwinner (the husband), one homemaker (the wife), and their children. These units are generally referred to as "nuclear families."

These early assumptions regarding the nuclear family have become increasingly difficult to justify in light of major changes that have occurred in families during the past several decades. Available statistics show that the traditional nuclear family no longer dominates the American scene, if it ever did. In 1991, households composed of married couples represented only 55 percent of all households. Marriage and remarriage rates are both falling, and, although the divorce rate is now declining, it doubled between 1965 and 1985. As marriage and remarriage rates decline, the number of non-marital living arrangements has grown. Not surprisingly, growing up in a home with two parents is far from a universal experience for children today. In 1991, 72 percent of American children lived with both parents; 25 percent lived with one parent; and the remainder lived in other situations. In 2007 the numbers shift even more. According to the US Census Bureau in their 2007 report *Families and Living Arrangements: 2007*, 73.7 million children younger than eighteen lived in the United States. Of these, 67.8 percent lived with married parents, 2.9 percent lived with two unmarried parents, 25.8 percent lived with one parent and 3.5 percent lived with no parent. Likewise, that report shows that in 2007, of the 67.1 million opposite sex couples who lived together, 60.7 million were married couples, and 6.4 million were unmarried couples.

Slowly, the definition of what constitutes a family is changing. In the early part of the 20th century in the United States, the heterosexual nuclear family was the norm and was closely linked with rigid gender roles and women's dependent status. The husband was expected to provide for the family economically and the wife was expected to take care of her husband and children in the home. Historically, a woman's role in the traditional nuclear family interfered with her equal participation in political and economic life and reinforced her dependence on men. In today's society, a woman's role is changing and the definition of the traditional family is also changing.

As our reality changes, so too must our laws, and change is often fraught with conflict. Countervailing forces are at work shaping the law in this area. One is a conservative force that would deny legal recognition to non-traditional living arrangements that are seen as jeopardizing prevailing moral values. The other is a liberalizing force that calls for legal recognition of different forms of living arrangements so that the affairs of people actually living in those arrangements can be handled in an orderly fashion. The composite effect of these two forces is that legislators and judges have often been unwilling to recognize non-nuclear living arrangements until they perceive that they are widespread and that society has come to view them as morally acceptable. When they do accord legal recognition to non-traditional arrangements, they emphasize the similarities between the new arrangements and the more conventional ones and affirm traditional values.

A case striking down a restriction on marriage illustrates this process. The decision, *Zablocki v. Redhail*, 434 U.S. 374 (1978), invalidated a state prohibition on marriages by non-custodial parents whose children had received or were likely to receive public assistance. One effect of the decision was to ease the way for divorced fathers to remarry, thereby allowing them to start second families and/or legitimize new families they may already have started. In this sense, the decision responded to a societal perception that having a series of families is morally acceptable and also, to a practical need to regularize the legal status of family members in subsequent relationships. In recognizing these relationships, however, the Court reaffirmed the importance of marriage as an institution, as well as the close relationship between marriage and procreation. It made clear that the state retained the power to impose "reasonable" regulations on marriage.

Issues involving legal recognition of different family structures arise in numerous contexts. Many laws govern family relationships directly, specifying, for example, who may marry and when they may divorce. Other statutes and judge-made legal rules establish principles for resolving disputes between individuals who have lived or had children together. Still other legal conflicts involving family forms arise when public bodies attempt to govern living arrangements through restrictions on employment or zoning laws. The resolution of these conflicts often involves the interpretation of a particular statute or legal doctrine. Many times the question is a constitutional one: to what extent does the Constitution afford protection to the individual's or family's choice of living arrangements?

One of the rapidly emerging areas of law is the constitutionality of governmental regulation of what constitutes a marriage and who can marry. The materials in this section first examine the early non-traditional family: heterosexual cohabitation and the emerging domestic partnership laws. The balance of the section will look at the emerging doctrines of same-sex marriage, same-sex adoption, and finally the breakup of same-sex relationships. To understand these materials, it is necessary to look beyond the legal doctrines the courts discuss to the actual impact of the decisions on the parties; the practical pressures on the courts to recognize the particular arrangement; and the extent to which the courts perceive the arrangement to be widespread and acceptable.

Cohabitation and Domestic Partnerships

Although earlier sections of the book recognize that oftentimes the economic affect of divorce on women is negative, when married couples divorce, Courts do require parties to pay child support and/or alimony and to make property settlements with their former spouses. In general, courts have not imposed similar requirements on unmarried cohabitants at the termination of their relationships. Some jurisdictions do recognize actions for "palimony." The following case from 1976 is one of the first decisions authorizing redistribution of property at the time a non-marital relationship is dissolved.

MARVIN V. MARVIN
Supreme Court of California, 1976.
18 Cal.3d 660,
134 Cal. Rptr. 815, 557 P.2d 106.

TOBRINER, Justice.

During the past 15 years, there has been a substantial increase in the number of couples living together without marrying. Such nonmarital relationships lead to legal controversy when one partner dies or the couple separates. . . .

Plaintiff avers that in October of 1964 she and defendant "entered into an oral agreement" that while "the parties lived together they would combine their efforts and earnings and would share equally any and all property accumulated as a result of their efforts whether individual or combined." Furthermore, they agreed to "hold themselves out to the general public as husband and wife" and that "plaintiff would further render her services as a companion, homemaker, housekeeper and cook to . . . defendant."

Shortly thereafter plaintiff agreed to "give up her lucrative career as an entertainer [and] singer" in order to "devote her full time to defendant . . . as a companion, homemaker, housekeeper and cook;" in return defendant agreed to "provide for all of plaintiff's financial support and needs for the rest of her life."

Plaintiff alleges that she lived with defendant from October of 1964 through May of 1970 and fulfilled her obligations under the agreement. During this period the parties as a result of their efforts and earnings acquired in defendant's name substantial real and personal property, including motion picture rights worth over $1 million. In May of 1970, however, defendant compelled plaintiff to leave his household. He continued to support plaintiff until November of 1971, but thereafter refused to provide further support. . . .

Although the past decisions hover over the issue in the somewhat wispy form of the figures of a Chagall painting, we can abstract from those decisions a clear and simple rule. The fact that a man and woman live together without marriage, and engage in a sexual relationship, does not in itself invalidate agreements between them relating to their earnings, property, or expenses. Neither is such an agreement invalid merely because the parties may have contemplated the creation or continuation of a nonmarital relationship when they entered into it. Agreements between nonmarital partners fail only to the extent that they rest upon a consideration of meretricious sexual services. Thus the rule asserted by defendant, that a contract fails if it is "involved in" or made "in contemplation" of a nonmarital relationship, cannot be reconciled with the decisions. . . .

[W]e base our opinion on the principle that adults who voluntarily live together and engage in sexual relations are nonetheless as competent as any other persons to contract respecting their earnings and property rights. Of course, they cannot lawfully contract to pay for the performance of sexual services, for such a contract is, in essence, an agreement for prostitution and unlawful for that reason. But . . . so long as the agreement does not rest upon illicit meretricious consideration, the parties may order their economic affairs as they choose, and no policy precludes the courts from enforcing such agreements.

In the present instance, plaintiff alleges that the parties agreed to pool their earnings, that they contracted to share equally in all property acquired, and that defendant agreed to support plaintiff. The terms of the contract as alleged do not rest upon any unlawful consideration. We therefore conclude that the complaint furnishes a suitable basis upon which the trial court can render declaratory relief. . . .

As we have noted, both causes of action in plaintiff's complaint allege an express contract; neither assert any basis for relief independent from the contract. In *In re Marriage of Cary*, however, the Court of Appeals held that, in view of the policy of the Family Law Act, property accumulated by nonmarital partners in an actual family relationship should be divided equally. . . . Although our conclusion that plaintiff's complaint states a cause of action based on an express contract alone compels us to reverse the judgment for defendant, resolution of the *Cary* issue will serve both to guide the parties upon retrial and to resolve a conflict presently manifest in published Court of Appeals decisions. . . .

If *Cary* is interpreted as holding that the Family Law Act requires an equal division of property accumulated in nonmarital "actual family relationships," then . . . *Cary* distends the act. No language in the Family Law Act addresses the property rights of nonmarital partners, and nothing in the legislative history of the act suggests that the Legislature considered that subject. The delineation of the rights of nonmarital partners before 1970 had been fixed entirely by judicial decision; we see no reason to believe that the Legislature, by enacting the Family Law Act, intended to change that state of affairs. . . .

But, although parties to a nonmarital relationship obviously cannot have based any expectations upon the belief that they were married, other expectations and equitable considerations remain. The parties may well expect that property will be divided in accord with the parties' own tacit understanding and that in the absence of such understanding the courts will fairly apportion property accumulated through mutual effort. We need not treat nonmarital partners as putatively married persons in order to apply principles of implied contract, or extend equitable remedies; we need to treat them only as we do any other unmarried persons. . . .

Although we recognize the well-established public policy to foster and promote the institution of marriage, perpetuation of judicial rules which result in an inequitable distribution of property accumulated during a nonmarital relationship is neither a just nor an effective way of carrying out that policy.

In summary, we believe that the prevalence of nonmarital relationships in modern society and the social acceptance of them, marks this as a time when our courts should by no means apply the doctrine of the unlawfulness of the so-called meretricious relationship to the instant case. As we have explained, the nonenforceability of agreements expressly providing for meretricious conduct rested upon the fact that such conduct, as the word suggests, pertained to an encompassed prostitution. To equate the nonmarital relationship of today to such a subject matter is to do violence to an accepted and wholly different practice. . . .

The mores of the society have indeed changed so radically in regard to cohabitation that we cannot impose a standard based on alleged moral considerations that have apparently been so widely abandoned by so many. Lest we be misunderstood, however, we take this occasion to point out that the structure of society itself largely depends upon the institution of marriage, and nothing we have said in this opinion should be taken to derogate from that institution. The joining of the man and woman in marriage is at once the most socially productive and individually fulfilling relationship that one can enjoy in the course of a lifetime.

Judgment is reversed and the cause remanded for further proceedings consistent with the views expressed herein.

STUDY QUESTIONS

1. According to Michelle Marvin's complaint, why was she entitled to property held by Lee Marvin?
2. When will the California courts enforce agreements between cohabitants? Are all services subject to contract? Does a sexual or emotional component to a relationship preclude a valid contract? Should it?
3. Why did the court decline to interpret the Family Law Act to authorize an equal division of property in "actual family relationships"? Had it done so, would cohabitation have been tantamount to marriage? If so, would individuals be unduly restricted in their ability to order their own affairs? Is it feasible for courts to identify "actual family relationships"?

Though many states have declined to follow the ruling in *Marvin v. Marvin,* it is still good law and has not been overturned by another court. The states that do permit the division of property of separating couples do so with a variety of approaches. Some, like California, use doctrines from a variety of areas to enforce both express and tacit understandings between the parties and to ensure fair results. Others states will make property awards only when they find the parties made an express contract. Still others refuse altogether to intervene in such disputes, at least in part because they are unwilling to give such relationships any legal standing.

Scholars as well as judges and other lawmakers continue to debate the most appropriate way for the law to treat cohabitation. Some see contract law as the best way to settle legitimate claims against non-marital partners while at the same time allowing individuals freedom in shaping their relationships. Others question whether women are sufficiently able to strike fair bargains in light of unequal social and economic conditions. Thus, they would impose a legal status on stable relationships that is akin to marriage and that permits support awards and property divisions on separation.

Another context in which courts determine legal and financial consequences of cohabitation involves the right to continued alimony from a previous marriage. The obligation to pay alimony usually ceases when the spouse receiving support remarries. Often ex-husbands stop making payments when their former spouses begin cohabitating with a paramour, and the courts are then required to decide whether the new relationship suffices to terminate the alimony obligation. Decisions that terminate the alimony obligation, even though the former wife's need for alimony has not ended, have the effect of punishing the woman simply for her choice of living arrangements. Such decisions may also reflect and reinforce the view that having entered into a sexual relationship, the new man has assumed responsibility for her financial support. In any event, most states now permit alimony payments to be reduced or terminated only when the new relationship has changed the supported spouse's financial circumstances.

The courts' approach to these cases, like their approach to *Marvin v. Marvin*-type disputes, suggests that even though courts are not eager to recognize the sexual component of non-marital relationships, they are increasingly willing to resolve the financial disputes that arise as households form, dissolve, and reform. Legal changes making it possible to resolve such financial disputes in the courts may be developing for the same reason that divorce became available: to reflect a commercial need to make clear who owns particular property. Despite the modicum of legal recognition they thus gain, non-marital relationships may nevertheless be the subject of societal oppression.

Despite the conservative lobby to the contrary, the definition of family has expanded from its original nuclear definition to encompass the reality that people have chosen for their lives. Now that we have turned the generational corner into the new millennium, the notion of what constitutes a family is slowly beginning to change. Domestic partnerships in both heterosexual and same-sex relationships are more widely recognized by companies and municipalities for the purposes of health-care coverage and benefits. Although there is no clearinghouse of data that keeps track of the number of employers that extend benefits to domestic partnerships, according to the Human Rights Campaign Foundation, which works on issues related to gay, lesbian, bisexual, and transgender rights, approximately 5,892 employers nationwide recognize domestic partnerships. The majority of those employers are private sector companies.

In the United States, laws regarding domestic partnerships are evolving to create registries and other mechanisms to "legalize" the relationship for purposes of providing benefits to partners. Many states are now also creating a category of "legal relationship" known as a civil union which provides "almost all" of the same rights as a marital relationship. Thirteen states in the United States permit civil unions. Twenty countries ranging from Denmark, the first country to permit civil unions, to Argentina, currently permit civil unions. These legal arrangements apply to same-sex and opposite-sex partners alike. Critics however believe that domestic partnerships and civil unions are simply not enough legally, morally, or emotionally when a couple, same-sex or opposite-sex, wish to marry.

In *Marvin*, the parties *chose* to cohabitate and not marry. For most same-sex couples in the United States, there is no *choice* because they are *not* permitted to marry. Many couples in a same-sex relationship seek a more traditional commitment such as marriage and further seek the legal security and benefit that marriage provides.

The law that applies to same-sex marriage continues to evolve at a rapid pace. As of this writing, there are three states which recognize same-sex marriage and three additional states where laws recognizing same-sex marriage will go into effect by the end of 2009. The next section will explore the legal interplay between same-sex relationships, the family, and the law.

Same-Sex Marriage

As we have seen, the expectation that individuals should be grouped in family units consisting of a man, a woman, and their children has been an important factor in shaping the opportunities open to women and men. In precluding alternative outlets for fulfilling emotional, sexual, and economic needs, this expectation has contributed to the pressure on both sexes to accept marriage on whatever terms were available. It has also had an especially harsh impact on those who wish to establish same-sex relationships. The legal system has been a key mechanism in reinforcing that expectation by denying opportunities to formalize those relationships and by failing to recognize their legitimacy in other contexts.

Same-sex couples have sought to marry for a number of reasons, both emotional and financial. They have sought to adopt children and enjoy sexual freedom in the privacy of their homes absent legal intervention. Up until very recently, most constitutional claims to support same-sex marriage and sexual privacy have failed. Arguments have been made both on equal protection and rights to privacy, and court actions seeking to permit same-sex marriages and to invalidate statutes that criminalize sex between consenting lesbian, gay, bisexual and transgender (LGBT) adults have failed. Though change is slow in coming, the laws that govern same-sex marriage and relationships pertaining to same-sex families have begun to shift.

In 2003, the US Supreme Court struck down as unconstitutional a statute that made it a crime for same-sex couples to engage in certain consensual sex acts. *Lawrence v. Texas* 539 US 558 (2003). In *Lawrence*, the Court found that "This case involve[s] two adults who, with full and mutual consent, engaged in sexual practices common to a homosexual lifestyle. Petitioners' right to liberty under the Due Process Clause gives them the full right to engage in private conduct without government intervention. . . . The Texas statute furthers no legitimate state interest which can justify its intrusion into the individual's personal and private life."

The debate for the legalization of same-sex marriage began in 1993, but has not truly evolved until very recently. In 1993, the Supreme Court in Hawaii, in the case of *Baehr v. Lewin*, 852 P.2d 44 (1993), was one of the first Courts to open the doors to legally sanctioned marriage between same-sex partners. Though the Court did not openly embrace the concept of same-sex marriage, it found the possibility of constitutional violation of the sex-based classification and remanded the case for further hearing on whether the sex-based classification (only a man and woman could marry) was justified by a compelling state interest. In 2000, in a far more direct decision, the Vermont Supreme Court, in *Baker v. State of Vermont* 81 A.L.R. 5th 627, rendered a groundbreaking decision that specifically found that to withstand constitutional scrutiny, Vermont laws must permit same-sex marriage and required the Legislature of that state to make the necessary amendments.

In November 2003, the Massachusetts Supreme Judicial Court, in the case of *Hillary GOODRIDGE v. Department of Health*, made a ruling similar to the Vermont Court and ordered the Legislature to revise the statutes pertaining to marriage within 180 days.

GOODRIDGE V. DEPARTMENT OF PUBLIC HEALTH
440 Mass. 309, 798 N.E.2d 941
November 18, 2003

Background: Same-sex couples denied marriage licenses filed action for declaratory judgment against Department and Commissioner of Public Health, alleging that department policy and practice of denying marriage licenses to same-sex couples violated numerous provisions of state constitution. The Supreme Judicial Court granted parties' requests for direct appellate review

Marshall C.J.

Marriage is a vital social institution. The exclusive commitment of two individuals to each other nurtures love and mutual support; it brings stability to our society. For those who choose to marry, and for their children, marriage provides an abundance of legal, financial, and social benefits. In return it imposes weighty legal, financial, and social obligations. The question before us is whether, consistent with the Massachusetts Constitution, the Commonwealth may deny the protections, benefits, and obligations conferred by civil marriage to two individuals of the same sex who wish to marry. We conclude that it may not. The Massachusetts Constitution affirms the dignity and equality of all individuals. It forbids the creation of second-class citizens. In reaching our conclusion we have given full deference to the arguments made by the Commonwealth. But it has failed to identify any constitutionally adequate reason for denying civil marriage to same-sex couples.

We are mindful that our decision marks a change in the history of our marriage law.

Many people hold deep-seated religious, moral, and ethical convictions that marriage should be limited to the union of one man and one woman, and that homosexual conduct is immoral. Many hold equally strong religious, moral, and ethical convictions that same-sex couples are entitled to be married, and that homosexual persons should be treated no differently than their heterosexual neighbors. Neither view answers the question before us. Our concern is with the Massachusetts Constitution as a charter of governance for every person properly within its reach. "Our obligation is to define the liberty of all, not to mandate our own moral code."

Barred access to the protections, benefits, and obligations of civil marriage, a person who enters into an intimate, exclusive union with another of the same sex is arbitrarily deprived of membership in one of our community's most rewarding and cherished institutions. That exclusion is incompatible with the constitutional principles of respect for individual autonomy and equality under law.

The plaintiffs challenge the marriage statute on both equal protection and due process grounds. With respect to each such claim, we must first determine the appropriate standard of review. Where a statute implicates a fundamental right or uses a suspect classification, we employ "strict judicial scrutiny." For all other statutes, we employ the "rational basis" test. For due process claims, rational basis analysis requires that statutes "bear a real and substantial relation to the public health, safety, morals, or some other phase of the general welfare." . . . For equal protection challenges, the rational basis test requires that "an impartial lawmaker could logically believe that the classification would serve a legitimate public purpose that transcends the harm to the members of the disadvantaged class." The department argues that no fundamental right or "suspect" class is at issue here, and rational basis is the appropriate standard of review. For the reasons we explain[ed] below, we conclude that the marriage ban does not meet the rational basis test for either due process or equal protection. Because the statute does not survive rational basis review, we do not consider the plaintiffs' arguments that this case merits strict judicial scrutiny. The department posits three legislative rationales for prohibiting same-sex couples from marrying: (1) providing a "favorable setting for procreation"; (2) ensuring the optimal setting for child rearing, which the department defines as "a two-parent family with one parent of each sex"; and (3) preserving scarce State and private financial resources.

The department has offered purported justifications for the civil marriage restriction that are starkly at odds with the comprehensive network of vigorous, gender-neutral laws promoting stable families and the best interests of children. It has failed to identify any relevant characteristic that would justify shutting the door to civil marriage to a person who wishes to marry someone of the same sex.

The marriage ban works a deep and scarring hardship on a very real segment of the community for no rational reason. The absence of any reasonable relationship between, on the one hand, an absolute disqualification of same-sex couples who wish to enter into civil marriage and, on the other, protection of public health, safety, or general welfare, suggests that the marriage restriction is rooted in persistent prejudices against persons who are (or who are believed to be) homosexual. "The Constitution cannot control such prejudices but neither can it tolerate them. Private biases may be outside the reach of the law, but the law cannot, directly or indirectly, give them effect. . . . Limiting the protections, benefits, and obligations of civil marriage to opposite-sex couples violates the basic premises of individual liberty and equality under law protected by the Massachusetts Constitution.

We declare that barring an individual from the protections, benefits, and obligations of civil marriage solely because that person would marry a person of the same sex violates the Massachusetts Constitution. Entry of judgment shall be stayed for 180 days to permit the Legislature to take such action as it may deem appropriate in light of this opinion.

In *Goodridge,* the Court articulated numerous statutory benefits afforded by the institution of marriage, which were not available to same-sex couples who are not married. These benefits included: joint state income tax filing; ownership of property by virtue of marriage called tenancy by the entirety; automatic rights to inherit property of deceased spouse who does not leave a will; equitable division of marital property on divorce; temporary and permanent alimony rights; qualification for bereavement or medical leave to care for individuals related by blood or marriage; automatic "family member" preference to make medical decisions for an incompetent or disabled spouse who does not have a contrary health-care proxy.

In response to the Court's decision in *Goodridge,* the Massachusetts Legislature began to draft legislation to address the due process and equal protection issues raised by the Court. In February of 2004, the Massachusetts Senate certified a question to the Supreme Judicial Court seeking their opinion as to whether a bill which prohibits same-sex couples from entering into marriage but allows them to form civil unions with all benefits, protections, rights, and responsibilities of marriage was constitutional.

In re Opinions of the Justices to the Senate
440 Mass. 1201, 802 N.E.2d 565
February 03, 2004

Background: Senate requested opinion on constitutionality of bill which prohibits same-sex couples from entering into marriage, but allows them to form civil unions with all benefits, protections, rights, and responsibilities of marriage.

Holding: The Supreme Judicial Court held as a matter of first impression that the bill violates the equal protection and due process requirements of the state constitution.

The Goodridge decision by the court made no reference to the concept of "civil unions," . . . Rather, it was the lawfulness under the Massachusetts Constitution of the bar to civil marriage itself, "a vital social institution," that the court was asked to decide. The court decided the question after extensively reviewing the government's justifications for the marriage ban.

The order of the Senate plainly reflects that Senate No. 2175 is proposed action in response to the Goodridge opinion. The bill states that the "purpose" of the act is to provide "eligible same-sex couples the opportunity to obtain the benefits, protections, rights and responsibilities afforded to opposite sex couples by the marriage laws of the commonwealth, without entering into a marriage," declares that it is the "public policy" of the Commonwealth that "spouses in a civil union" "shall have all the benefits, protections, rights and responsibilities afforded by the marriage laws," and recites "that the Commonwealth's laws should be revised to give same-sex couples the opportunity to obtain the legal protections, benefits, rights and responsibilities associated with civil marriage, while preserving the traditional, historic nature and meaning of the institution of civil marriage."

The proposed law states that "spouses" in a civil union shall be "joined in it with a legal status equivalent to marriage." The bill expressly maintains that "marriage" is reserved exclusively for opposite-sex couples by providing that "[p]ersons eligible to form a civil union with each other under this chapter shall not be eligible to enter into a marriage with each other under chapter 207." Notwithstanding, the proposed law purports to make the institution of a "civil union" parallel to the institution of civil "marriage." For example, the bill provides that "spouses in a civil union shall have all the same benefits, protections, rights and responsibilities under law as are granted to spouses in a marriage." In addition, terms that denote spousal relationships, such as "husband," "wife," "family," and "next of kin," are to be interpreted to include spouses in a civil union "as those terms are used in any law." Id. The bill goes on to enumerate a nonexclusive list of the legal benefits that will adhere to spouses in a civil union, including property rights, joint State income tax filing, evidentiary rights, rights to veteran benefits and group insurance, and the right to the issuance of a "civil union" license, identical to a marriage license "as if a civil union was a marriage."

. . . [T]he bill, as we read it, does nothing to "preserve" the civil marriage law, only its constitutional infirmity. This is not a matter of social policy but of constitutional interpretation. As the court concluded in Goodridge, the traditional, historic nature and meaning of civil marriage in Massachusetts is as a wholly secular and dynamic legal institution, the governmental aim of which is to encourage stable adult relationships for the good of the individual and of the community, especially its children. The very nature and purpose of civil marriage, the court concluded, renders unconstitutional any attempt to ban all same-sex couples, as same-sex couples, from entering into civil marriage.

The same defects of rationality evident in the marriage ban considered in Goodridge are evident in, if not exaggerated by, Senate No. 2175. Segregating same-sex unions from opposite-sex unions cannot possibly be held rationally to advance or "preserve" what we stated in Goodridge were the Commonwealth's legitimate interests in procreation, child rearing, and the conservation of resources. Because the proposed law by its express terms forbids same-sex couples entry into civil marriage, it continues to relegate same-sex couples to a different status. The holding in Goodridge, by which we are bound, is that group classifications based on unsupportable distinctions, such as that embodied in the proposed bill, are invalid under the Massachusetts Constitution. The history of our nation has demonstrated that separate is seldom, if ever, equal.

STUDY QUESTIONS

1. What benefits does marriage provide that civil unions do not? What if the laws provided those same benefits? Is there still a difference?
2. What basis did the Court used to determine whether there was a legitimate state interest? Why did the Court conclude there was none?
3. What are the three standards of scrutiny a Court uses to assess the state's interest? Which did they chose and why?

Following the Court's decision in the *In Re Opinion*, same-sex marriage was legalized in Massachusetts. In 2006, the New York State Court of Appeals had its first opportunity to decide the same issue. The Court used a constitutional analysis as to whether New York State statutes that permitted marriage between persons of the opposite sex violated either due process or the equal protection clauses. The New York Court found that the question did not require the more difficult constitutional requirement of "strict scrutiny" and that the State had only to show that there was a rational basis for the restrictions against same-sex marriage. Here is an excerpt of the Court's analysis:

HERNANDEZ V. ROBLES
7 N.Y.3d 338, 855 N.E.2d 1
July 06, 2006
R.S. SMITH, J.

We hold that the New York Constitution does not compel recognition of marriages between members of the same sex. Whether such marriages should be recognized is a question to be addressed by the Legislature.

New York's statutory law clearly limits marriage to opposite-sex couples. The more serious question is whether that limitation is consistent with the New York Constitution.

Plaintiffs claim that, by limiting marriage to opposite-sex couples, the New York Domestic Relations Law violates two provisions of the State Constitution: the Due Process Clause and the Equal Protection Clause. We approach plaintiffs' claims by first considering whether the challenged limitation can be defended as a rational legislative decision.

It is undisputed that the benefits of marriage are many. The diligence of counsel has identified 316 such benefits in New York law, of which it is enough to summarize some of the most important: Married people receive significant tax advantages, rights in probate and intestacy proceedings, rights to support from their spouses both during the marriage and after it is dissolved, and rights to be treated as family members in obtaining insurance coverage and making health care decisions. Beyond this, they receive the symbolic benefit, or moral satisfaction, of seeing their relationships recognized by the State.

The critical question is whether a rational legislature could decide that these benefits should be given to members of opposite-sex couples, but not same-sex couples. The question is not, we emphasize, whether the Legislature must or should continue to limit marriage in this way; of course the Legislature may extend marriage or some or all of its benefits to same-sex couples. We conclude, however, that there are at least two grounds that rationally support the limitation on marriage that the Legislature has enacted.

First, the Legislature could rationally decide that, for the welfare of children, it is more important to promote stability, and to avoid instability, in opposite-sex than in same-sex relationships. . . . The Legislature could rationally believe that it is better, other things being equal, for children to grow up with both a mother and a father. Intuition and experience suggest that a child benefits from having before his or her eyes, every day, living models of what both a man and a woman are like. It is obvious that there are exceptions to this general rule—some children who never know their fathers, or their mothers, do far better than some who grow up with parents of both sexes—but the Legislature could find that the general rule will usually hold.

In sum, there are rational grounds on which the Legislature could choose to restrict marriage to couples of opposite sex. Plaintiffs have not persuaded us that this long-accepted restriction is a wholly irrational one, based solely on ignorance and prejudice against homosexuals. This is the question on which these cases turn. If we were convinced that the restriction plaintiffs attack were founded on nothing but prejudice we would hold it invalid, no matter how long its history.

It is true that there has been serious injustice in the treatment of homosexuals also, a wrong that has been widely recognized only in the relatively recent past, and one our Legislature tried to address when it enacted the Sexual Orientation Non-Discrimination Act four years ago. But the traditional definition of marriage is not merely a by-product of historical injustice. Its history is of a different kind.

The idea that same-sex marriage is even possible is a relatively new one. Until a few decades ago, it was an accepted truth for almost everyone who ever lived, in any society in which marriage existed, that there could be marriages only between participants of different sex. A court should not lightly conclude that everyone who held this belief was irrational, ignorant or bigoted. We do not so conclude.

Our conclusion that there is a rational basis for limiting marriage to opposite-sex couples leads us to hold that that limitation is valid under the New York Due Process and Equal Protection clauses, and that any expansion of the traditional definition of marriage should come from the Legislature.

STUDY QUESTIONS

1. What standard of scrutiny did the Court of Appeals apply in this case and why?
2. How does the Court's analysis compare to the Massachusetts Court in *Goodridge* and *In Re Marriage*.
3. Did the New York Court find a legitimate state interest to restrict marriages to between a man and a woman? What did the Court find that interest to be?

Since the New York Court of Appeals decision, the New York State Legislature has begun the debate on the passage of legislation permitting gay marriage. In April of 2009, the legislation was passed by the State Assembly and is being hotly debated in the State Senate.

California's statutes and court opinions regarding this issue have taken a different and—some would say—twisted set of turns. In May of 2008, the California Supreme Court, in *In re Marriage Cases* 43 Cal.4th 757, 183 P.3d 384, held that provisions of California Family Court Code that defined marriage as between a man and a woman were unconstitutional. The question before the Court was whether the failure to designate the official relationship of same-sex couples as marriage violates the California Constitution. The Court in its analysis concluded:

> . . . [I]n view of the substance and significance of the fundamental constitutional right to form a family relationship, the California Constitution properly must be interpreted to guarantee this basic civil right to all Californians, whether gay or heterosexual, and to same-sex couples as well as to opposite-sex couples."

The Court further found a proper basis to use a "strict scrutiny" standard and not the easier, rational basis standard the New York Court used. Using that standard it concluded that:

> [T]he purpose underlying differential treatment of opposite-sex and same-sex couples embodied in California's current marriage statutes—the interest in retaining the traditional and well-established definition of marriage—cannot properly be viewed as a compelling state interest for purposes of the equal protection clause, or as necessary to serve such an interest.

The Court concluded that the language "limiting the designation of marriage to a union 'between a man and a woman' is unconstitutional and must be stricken from the statute" thereby rendering the designation of marriage available both to opposite-sex and same-sex couples.

Following this Court decision, thousands of same-sex couples made the decision to marry in California. But that is not the end of the story. California is a state with a long history of ballot initiatives which permit the voters to easily amend the State Constitution by placing an amendment on the ballot and permitting the voters to decide. An initiative known as Proposition 8 amended the State's Constitution to define marriage to be between a man and a woman and to permit civil unions between same-sex couples. This amendment passed in the November 2008 election and a court action seeking to declare the provision unconstitutional was filed immediately thereafter. The California Supreme Court reached its decision in May of 2009. In what appears to be a 360 degree turn around, the Supreme Court declared Proposition 8 to be a valid constitutional amendment. What follows is an excerpt of that decision. As you review this, think of the Court's analysis in its 2008 decision and how it compares to this decision.

Karen L. Strauss et al., Petitioners, v. Mark B. Horton, as State Registrar of Vital

--- Cal.Rptr.3d ----, 2009 WL 1444655

May 26, 2009

Proposition 8, an initiative measure approved by a majority of voters at the November 4, 2008 election, added a new section—section 7.5—to article I of the California Constitution, providing: "Only marriage between a man and a woman is valid or recognized in California." The measure took effect on November 5, 2008. In the present case, we address the question whether Proposition 8, under the governing provisions of the California Constitution, constitutes a permissible change to the California Constitution, and—if it does—we are faced with the further question of the effect, if any, of Proposition 8 upon the estimated 18,000 marriages of same-sex couples that were performed before that initiative measure was adopted.

It also is necessary to understand that the legal issues before us in this case are entirely distinct from those that were presented in the Marriage Cases . . . the validity (or invalidity) of a statutory provision limiting marriage to a union between a man and a woman under state constitutional provisions that do not expressly permit or prescribe such a limitation. Instead, the principal issue before us concerns the scope of the right of the people, under the provisions of the California Constitution, to change or alter the state Constitution itself through the initiative process so as to incorporate such a limitation as an explicit section of the state Constitution.

In considering this question, it is essential to keep in mind that the provisions of the California Constitution governing the procedures by which that Constitution may be amended are very different from the more familiar provisions of the United States Constitution. . . . The federal Constitution provides that an amendment to that Constitution may be proposed either by two-thirds of both houses of Congress or by a convention called on the application of two-thirds of the state legislatures, and requires, in either instance, that any proposed amendment be ratified by the legislatures of three-fourths of the states. In contrast, the California Constitution provides that an amendment to that Constitution may be proposed either by two-thirds of the membership of each house of the Legislature or by an initiative petition signed by voters numbering at least 8 percent of the total votes cast for all candidates for Governor in the last gubernatorial election and further specifies that, once an amendment is proposed by either means, the amendment becomes part of the state Constitution if it is approved by a simple majority of the voters who cast votes on the measure at a statewide election.

Proposition 8 does not entirely repeal or abrogate the aspect of a same-sex couple's state constitutional right of privacy and due process that was analyzed in the majority opinion in the Marriage Cases—that is, the constitutional right of same-sex couples to "choose one's life partner and enter with that person into a committed, officially recognized, and protected family relationship that enjoys all of the constitutionally based incidents of marriage" (Marriage Cases, supra, 43 Cal. 4th at p. 829). Nor does Proposition 8 fundamentally alter the meaning and substance of state constitutional equal protection principles as articulated in that opinion. Instead, the measure carves out a narrow and limited exception to these state constitutional rights, reserving the official designation of the term "marriage" for the union of opposite-sex couples as a matter of state constitutional law, but leaving undisturbed all of the other extremely significant substantive aspects of a same-sex couple's state constitutional right to establish an officially recognized and protected family relationship and the guarantee of equal protection of the laws.

We emphasize only that among the various constitutional protections recognized in the Marriage Cases as available to same-sex couples, it is only the designation of marriage—albeit significant—that has been removed by this initiative measure.

[A]lthough Proposition 8 eliminates the ability of same-sex couples to enter into an official relationship designated "marriage," in all other respects those couples continue to possess, under the state constitutional privacy and due process clauses, "the core set of basic substantive legal rights and attributes traditionally associated with marriage," including, "most fundamentally, the opportunity of an individual to establish—with the person with whom the individual has chosen to share his or her life—an officially recognized and protected family possessing mutual rights and responsibilities and entitled to the same respect and dignity accorded a union traditionally designated as marriage."

Although the Court upheld the provisions of Proposition 8, it did decline to apply it retroactively which would have invalidated the 18,000 marriages that had occurred between the time their decision was reached in the *Marriage* case and the passage of the ballot amendment.

STUDY QUESTIONS

1. How does the Court's holding in *Strauss* differ from its holding in *In Re Marriages?*
2. Do you think the holdings are consistent or are they opposing holdings?
3. How does this decision compare to the decision in *Hernandez* and *Goodrich?*
4. How is the California Constitutional amendment process different than the Federal Constitutional amendment process?

Currently five states in addition to Massachusetts recognize same-sex marriage. In 2008, Connecticut legalized same-sex marriage, followed by Iowa, Vermont, Maine, and New Hampshire in 2009. Outside of the United States, same-sex marriage is recognized in Canada, Spain, Belgium, Netherlands, Norway, South Africa, and Sweden. One of the emerging issues now before some Courts is to what extent they will recognize or give "full faith and credit" to foreign same-sex marriages even if their state does not permit same-sex marriage. One such case, *Martinez v Monroe County*, 50 AD 3d 189 (2008), was analyzed in Chapter 4 as it applies to employment benefits. Later, you will see how this concept is applied when same-sex couples separate.

Gay and Lesbian Adoptions

Until such time that same-sex marriage is universally permitted, the issue of the parentage of children of the relationship is unsettled. If there is no marriage, then there are no "children of the marriage" or there is no presumption of legitimacy that would attach to children born to married couples. Increasingly, same-sex couples have sought the right to adopt children within their family. Some cases involve a child who is the natural child of one partner and the other partner seeks adoption, and other cases involve an LGBT individual who seeks to adopt a child. The legal decisions surrounding this area vary widely from state to state. The Vermont Supreme Court, in 1993, had the opportunity to review this issue. This decision not only relied on the Vermont Court's interpretation of law and policy but also the laws and policies of other states that have previously grappled with this issue. In this case, one lesbian partner sought to adopt a child born of her partner.

ADOPTIONS OF B.L.V.B. AND E.L.V.B.
Supreme Court of Vermont. June 18, 1993.

JOHNSON, Justice.

The issue we decide today is whether Vermont law requires the termination of a natural mother's parental rights if her children are adopted by a person to whom she is not married. We hold that when the family unit is comprised of the natural mother and her partner, and the adoption is in the best interests of the children, terminating the natural mother's rights is unreasonable and unnecessary. We reverse.

Appellants are two women, Jane and Deborah, who have lived together in a committed, monogamous relationship since 1986. Together, they made the decision to have and raise children, and together, they consulted various sources to determine the best method for them to achieve their goal of starting a family. On November 2, 1988, Jane gave birth to a son, B.L.V.B., after being impregnated with the sperm of an anonymous donor. On August 27, 1992, after being impregnated with sperm from the same donor, she gave birth to a second son, E.L.V.B. Deborah assisted the midwife at both births, and she has been equally responsible for raising and parenting the children since their births.

Appellants sought legal recognition of their existing status as coparents, and asked the probate court to allow Deborah to legally adopt the children, while leaving Jane's parental rights intact. The adoption petitions were uncontested. The Department of Social and Rehabilitation Services conducted a home study, determined the adoptions were in the best interests of the children, and recommended that they be allowed. A clinical and school psychologist who had evaluated the family testified that it was essential for the children to be assured of a continuing relationship with Deborah, and recommended that the adoptions be allowed for the psychological and emotional protection of the children.

Despite the lack of opposition, the probate court denied the adoptions, declining to reach whether the adoptions were in the best interests of the children because the proposed adoptive mother "does not satisfy the statutory prerequisite to adoption."

In interpreting Vermont's adoption statutes, we are mindful that the state's primary concern is to promote the welfare of children, and that application of the statutes should implement that purpose. In doing so, we must avoid results that are irrational, unreasonable or absurd. We must look "not only at the letter of a statute but also its reason and spirit."

Nothing in Vermont law, other than a restrictive interpretation of [the statute] would exclude Deborah from adopting another person. Under [the statute] which broadly grants the right to adopt to "a person or husband and wife together," an unmarried person is permitted to adopt, and the sole limitation—that the adoption of a married person requires the consent of the adoptee's spouse—does not apply here. Because adoptions by same-sex partners were apparently not contemplated when [the statute] was drafted, it cannot be said that they are either specifically prohibited or specifically allowed by the statute. To determine whether such adoptions are consistent with the purpose of the statute, it is necessary to discern what [the statute] was designed to accomplish.

. . . The intent of the legislature was to protect the security of family units by defining the legal rights and responsibilities of children who find themselves in circumstances that do not include two biological parents. Despite the narrow wording of the step-parent exception, we cannot conclude that the legislature ever meant to terminate the parental rights of a biological parent who intended to continue raising a child with the help of a partner. Such a narrow construction would produce the unreasonable and irrational result of defeating adoptions that are otherwise indisputably in the best interests of children.

If this provision were strictly enforced it would require termination of the parental rights of [the biological mother] upon granting the adoption to [the mother's partner]. This would be an absurd outcome which would nullify the advantage sought by the proposed adoption: the creation of a legal family unit identical to the actual family setup.

When social mores change, governing statutes must be interpreted to allow for those changes in a manner that does not frustrate the purposes behind their enactment. To deny the children of same-sex partners, as a class, the security of a legally recognized relationship with their second parent serves no legitimate state interest. . . . It is not the courts that have engendered the diverse composition of today's families. It is the advancement of reproductive technologies and society's recognition of alternative lifestyles that have produced families in which a biological, and therefore a legal, connection is no longer the sole organizing principle. But it is the courts that are required to define, declare and protect the rights of children raised in these families, usually upon their dissolution. At that point, courts are left to vindicate the public interest in the children's financial support and emotional well-being by developing theories of parenthood, so that "legal strangers" who are de facto parents may be awarded custody or visitation or reached for support. Because the probate court rejected these adoptions on legal grounds, it did not make findings on whether the adoptions were, in fact, in the best interests of the children. Ordinarily, this would require a remand to the probate court; however, in light of the fact that the adoptions were unopposed, that all of the evidence stands uncontroverted, that

the adoption was investigated and recommended by the state, through SRS, and that there is not a scintilla of evidence in the record to suggest that the adoptions are not in the best interests of these children, no reason exists to remand for another hearing.

Reversed; Judgment Is Entered Granting the Petitions for Adoption.

STUDY QUESTIONS

1. What is the state's primary concern in statutory interpretation?
2. What would the result have been if the Court had not reversed the lower court's decision?
3. Do you agree that a court must be flexible in interpreting statutes? Can you give an example where courts have not been flexible?

Just as the law has evolved with regard to same-sex relationships and same-sex marriage so has it evolved with regard to adoptions by LGBT persons. In the past decade, most states have permitted LGBT individuals to adopt children. Florida was the only state specifically prohibiting LGBT adoption. Arkansas, Mississippi, and Utah prohibit adoption by unmarried couples, effectively barring adoptions by same-sex couples.

In 2008, the Florida Circuit Court held the statute that prohibited adoptions by a gay person was unconstitutional. In the case of *Adoption of Doe*, two siblings were placed in foster care with the Petitioner who was a gay man. He and his partner petitioned for the right to adopt the children. Their application was denied based on Florida's law prohibiting LGBT individuals from adopting. The Court reviewed in great details the arguments against LGBT adoptions but ultimately concluded such a prohibition lacked a rational basis and therefore was unconstitutional.

In re Adoption of Doe
Not Reported in So.2d, 2008 WL 5006172
Fla.Cir.Ct.,2008.
November 25, 2008

FINAL JUDGMENT OF ADOPTION

THIS MATTER came before the Court on Petitioner's sworn Petition for Adoption of John Doe, born June 15, 2000, and his biological half-brother James Doe, born August 2, 2004. The Department of Children and Families moved to dismiss the Petition based on Petitioner's sexual orientation. The Court, having considered the record, testimony and arguments of counsel, makes the following Findings of Fact and Conclusions of Law.

The Department argues that the homosexual adoption restriction serves the legitimate state interest of promoting the well-being of minor children, as well as broader, societal morality interests. To support their contention, one of the Department's two experts testified that the law should not include a blanket exclusion of homosexuals, rather a case by case judicial determination is more appropriate.

The other expert witness generally testified that the law's restriction serves the best interests of children because when compared to heterosexual behaving individuals, homosexual behaving individuals experience: (1) a lifetime prevalence of significantly increased psychiatric disorders; (2) higher levels of alcohol and substance abuse; (3) higher levels of major depression; (4) higher levels of affective disorder; (5) four times higher levels of suicide attempts; and (6) substantially increased rates of relationship instability and breakup. Such factors, according to the Department, harm children of homosexual parents. Petitioner's expert witnesses countered these conclusions and suggested that: (1) homosexually behaving individuals are no more susceptible to mental health or psychological disorders than their heterosexual counterparts; (2) both heterosexual and homosexual parents can provide nurturing, safe, healthy environments for children; and (3) children of homosexual parents are no more at risk of maladjustment than their counterparts with heterosexual parents.

Based on the evidence presented from experts from all over this country and abroad, it is clear that sexual orientation is not a predictor of a person's ability to parent. Sexual orientation no more leads to psychiatric disorders, alcohol and substance abuse, relationship instability, a lower life expectancy or sexual disorders than race, gender, socioeconomic class or any other demographic characteristic. Qualities indicative of good parenting include attentiveness, involvement in a child's educational development, the ability to sooth, offer comfort, advice and a secure base for a child, the provision of resources and maintaining a warm, harmonious environment. The most important factor in ensuring a well adjusted child is the quality of parenting.

Similarly, a child in need of love, safety and stability does not first consider the sexual orientation of his parent. More importantly, sexual orientation, solely, should not interfere with a child's right to enjoy the accoutrements of a legal family. John and James, due to no fault of their own, were removed from an environment perilous to their physical, emotional and educational well being. Their biological parents relinquished them to the State, which in turn placed them into an environment that allowed them, eventually, to heal, and now flourish.

The quality and breadth of research available, as well as the results of the studies performed about gay parenting and children of gay parents, is robust and has provided the basis for a consensus in the field.

These reports and studies find that there are no differences in the parenting of homosexuals or the adjustment of their children. These conclusions have been accepted, adopted and ratified by the American Psychological Association, the American Psychiatry Association, the American Pediatric Association, the American Academy of Pediatrics, the Child Welfare League of America and the National Association of Social Workers. As a result, based on the robust nature of the evidence available in the field, this Court is satisfied that the issue is so far beyond dispute that it would be irrational to hold otherwise; the best interests of children are not preserved by prohibiting homosexual adoption.

Petitioner attacks the constitutionality of the categorical exclusion of homosexuals as eligible adoptive parents on equal protection and substantive due process grounds. This Court finds merit in the Petitioner and the Children's equal protection claim and further finds that the statute infringes on the Children's right to permanency pursuant to the Adoption and Safe Families Act of 1997, adopted in Chapter 39 of the Florida Statutes.

Florida's statutory framework is explicit that dependent children have the right to permanency and stability in adoptive placements. The law is also explicit that there is a compelling state interest in providing such permanent, adoptive placement as rapidly as possible. Id. Florida's dependency and adoption laws thereby embody the substance of state and federal decisions that declare a child's constitutional right to a true home, and in the case of a foster child, to a permanent adoptive home.

[T]he petition for adoption should be determined on the basis of the fitness of a petitioner who is petitioning to adopt the child and whether the adoptive home that would be provided for the child by that petitioner is suitable for the child so that the child can grow up in a stable, permanent, and loving environment. It is within those criteria that the determination as to the best interests

of the child is to be made with regard to an adoption petition.

Rational Basis Review

This matter does not involve a fundamental right or a suspect class and is thus reviewed under the rational basis test. Therefore, Petitioner and the Children must show that the statute discriminates against homosexuals and children without a rational basis for the discrimination.

While the Court agrees the burden is on Petitioner, a presentation of the State's legitimate governmental interest provides a helpful outline for a discussion of Petitioner's arguments. First, the Department argues that the homosexual adoption restriction serves the legitimate state interests of promoting the well-being of minor children. According to the Department, the law's restriction serves the best interests of children because when compared to heterosexual behaving individuals, homosexual behaving individuals experience higher levels of stressors disadvantageous to children. Second, the State also aims to protect the best interest of children by placing them in an adoptive home which minimizes social stigmatization. A third basis for the State's ban on homosexual adoption is its protection of societal moral interests of the child.

Promoting the well-being of children
In order to be considered rationally related to a governmental interest, the distinctions between individuals may not be based on unsubstantiated assumptions. Based on the statistics, there are no set of facts for which such a stated interest can be reasonably conceived of to justify the legislation.

Social Stigmatization/Necessity of dual gender homes
The Department next claims that best interests of children are served by placing them in an adoptive home which minimizes the social stigmatization they may experience. Again applying rational basis review, this Court rejects the Department's attempt to justify the statute by reference to a

supposed dark cloud hovering over homes of homosexuals and their children.

Morality

The Department's final rationale is that [the statute] rationally relates to Florida's legitimate moral interest to promote public morality. However, public morality per se, disconnected from any separate legitimate interest, is not a legitimate government interest to justify unequal treatment.

Conclusion

This Court finds Fla. Stat. § 63.042(3) violates the Petitioner and the Children's equal protection rights guaranteed by Article 1, § 2 of the Florida Constitution without satisfying a rational basis. Moreover, the statutory exclusion defeats a child's right to permanency as provided by federal and state law pursuant to the Adoption and Safe Families Act of 1997.

Study Questions

1. What arguments did the State put forth to justify why LGBT individuals should not be permitted to adopt?
2. How does this compare to the argument in the preceding case of *Adoptions of B.L.V.B.*
3. What standard of scrutiny did the Court use to review the State's argument? Did the Court find a legitimate state interest in prohibiting adoptions by a gay person? Why not?
4. How does this case and the *Adoption of BLVD* case compare to the same-sex marriage cases?

In addition to permitting adoptions by LGBT people, states are also grappling with the issue of second-parent adoptions, or joint adoptions by a same-sex couple. According to Lamda Legal, a civil rights organization focusing on the civil rights of lesbians, gay men, bisexuals, and transgender people, the adoption laws of about half the states have been held to permit adoption petitions by the unmarried partner of an existing legal parent, so-called "second-parent adoptions." Some states permit "joint adoptions" if a same-sex couple who are not married jointly petition for the right to adopt a child when neither is the legal parent. Although married couples in this situation are generally required to file a joint adoption, same-sex couples are only *permitted* to file a joint petitions in certain states.

Most recently, in January of 2009, a New York Family Court determined that same-sex partners who were married outside of New York State did not have to be pre-certified to adopt their partner's natural child. In *re Donna S.* 871 N.Y.S.2d 883, 2009, Judge Joan Kohout held that "although New York State does not currently permit same-sex couples to marry, recently developing case law has held that the marriage of same-sex couples legally married in other jurisdictions must be recognized by New York." The Court further found that since the non-birth parent was the spouse of the birth parent then under existing laws, she would at the very least be considered a stepparent after the child's birth. Stepparents are not required to be pre-certified as qualified adoptive parents for the purpose of adopting their spouse's children. Further, a child born to a married woman by artificial insemination is deemed the legal child of the husband if both spouses execute a consent to that effect. Given the full faith and credit set forth in the *Martinez* case previously discussed in this book, the Court believed it would seem that by the simple execution of a consent, the birth mother's spouse could become the baby's legal parent without the necessity of an adoption.

But consider the additional legal complications in the case of the "pregnant man" in Oregon. In 2008, Thomas Beatie, a transgender male who had retained his female reproductive organs, announced to the world that he was pregnant. They—Thomas and Linda Beatie—decided that Thomas would become pregnant as she could not. Thomas Beatie identified as a male, and changed his name birth certificate to reflect that after his sex reassignment surgery that he was a man. The pregnant man case was and is hotly debated throughout the United States and the world. In 2009, Thomas Beatie had a second child. In an interview with ABC news 20/20 show, Thomas Beatie said that he and his wife are clear on their parental roles:

"I am my daughter's father, and that's all I'll ever be to her," he said. "Nancy is Susan's mother.

The State of Oregon however had a different opinion when they issued the birth certificate. At first, the Office of Vital Statistics listed Thomas as the baby's mother and Linda as the father. After the couple protested, Oregon relented and used the terminology used for same-sex parents in a domestic partnership, "parent and parent." This however was still not acceptable to the Beaties. The Beaties identify themselves as a *heterosexual* couple and insist that the designation must be Thomas Beatie as Father and Linda as Mother. According to ABC news, they are considering legal action to resolve the conflict. This issue raises interesting questions of gender, gender classification, and sexual orientation, and the manner in which our society and our laws approach these distinctions.

Just as heterosexual relationships end and couples divorce, so to do same-sex couples. As states are now beginning to accept the notion of same-sex "marriage," it is unclear how quickly the notion of "same-sex divorce" will be accepted. As previously discussed in this chapter, the dissolution of relationships can be complicated and difficult. Same-sex divorces are even more complicated as there is very little precedent and law in the area. Resolutions are unclear and unpredictable. As we will see, the result of the cases differ from state to state and can be even more financially and emotionally devastating than traditional divorces.

When Same-Sex Couples Split Up: Same-Sex Divorce and Issues of Custody, Visitation, and Child Support

One of the early cases involving the breakup of a same-sex couple involves the issue of custody and visitation of the parties' minor child. This child was born of one partner and, although raised by the second partner, was never adopted by her. Look at the Court's analysis of the relationship between the child and the non-birth parent and the legal rights of the non-birth parent.

ALISON D. V. VIRGINIA M.
Court of Appeals of New York, 1991
77 NY 2d 651

Per Curiam.

At issue in this case is whether petitioner, a biological stranger to a child who is properly in the custody of his biological mother, has standing to seek visitation with the child under Domestic Relations Law

§ 70. Petitioner relies on both her established relationship with the child and her alleged agreement with the biological mother to support her claim that she has standing . . .

Petitioner Alison D. and respondent Virginia M. established a relationship in

September 1977 and began living together in March 1978. In March 1980, they decided to have a child and agreed that respondent would be artificially inseminated. Together, they planned for the conception and birth of the child and agreed to share jointly all rights and responsibilities of child-rearing. In July 1981, respondent gave birth to a baby boy, A. D. M., who was given petitioner's last name as his middle name and respondent's last name became his last name. Petitioner shared in all birthing expenses and, after A. D. M.'s birth, continued to provide for his support. During A. D. M.'s first two years, petitioner and respondent jointly cared for and made decisions regarding the child.

In November 1983, when the child was 2 years and 4 months old, petitioner and respondent terminated their relationship and petitioner moved out of the home they jointly owned. Petitioner and respondent agreed to a visitation schedule whereby petitioner continued to see the child a few times a week. Petitioner also agreed to continue to pay one half of the mortgage and major household expenses. By this time, the child had referred to both respondent and petitioner as "mommy." Petitioner's visitation with the child continued until 1986, at which time respondent bought out petitioner's interest in the house and then began to restrict petitioner's visitation with the child. In 1987 petitioner moved to Ireland to pursue career opportunities, but continued her attempts to communicate with the child. Thereafter, respondent terminated all contact between petitioner and the child, returning all of petitioner's gifts and letters. No dispute exists that respondent is a fit parent. Petitioner commenced this proceeding seeking visitation rights pursuant to Domestic Relations Law § 70.

Pursuant to Domestic Relations Law § 70 "either parent may apply to the supreme court for a writ of habeas corpus to have

such minor child brought before such court; and [the court] may award the natural guardianship, charge and custody of such child to either parent as the case may require." Although the Court is mindful of petitioner's understandable concern for and interest in the child and of her expectation and desire that her contact with the child would continue, she has no right under Domestic Relations Law § 70 to seek visitation and, thereby, limit or diminish the right of the concededly fit biological parent to choose with whom her child associates. She is not a "parent" within the meaning of section 70.

. . . While one may dispute in an individual case whether it would be beneficial to a child to have continued contact with a nonparent, the Legislature did not in section 70 give such nonparent the opportunity to compel a fit parent to allow them to do so . . .

Accordingly, the order of the Appellate Division [denying visitation] should be affirmed, with costs.

Many cases that followed *Alison D* tracked this Court's reasoning on the issue of visitation and custody, essentially that a non-biological and non-adoptive parent was a "stranger" to the child without regard for the relationship between the child and the party. In New York, *Alison D* is still good law although the issues that developed in that case can be resolved by a second-parent adoption that has been permitted in New York since 1995. Since 2000, other Appellate Courts throughout the country have begun to move away from the strict ruling of *Alison D* and have looked at the second parent in terms "de facto parent" or "in loco parentis," meaning to stand in the place of a parent. One such case from the state of Washington was decided in 2005. The State's highest court determined that the non-biological mother had a *common law* claim of parentage and therefore the legal right to petition the Court for visitation.

SUPREME COURT OF WASHINGTON,

En Banc.

In re the Matter of the PARENTAGE OF L.B.

Sue Ellen ("Mian") CARVIN, Respondent,

v.

Page Britain, Petitioner.

No. 75626-1.

Argued Feb. 15, 2005.

Decided Nov. 3, 2005

Background: Woman brought action against biological mother of minor, seeking to establish her coparentage of minor, who was conceived by artificial insemination during the woman's 12-year intimate domestic relationship with mother. The Superior Court, King County, Michael Trickey, J., ruled that woman had no cause of action and dismissed petition. Woman appealed. The Court of Appeals, 121 Wash. App. 460, 89 P.3d 271, affirmed in part, reversed in part, and remanded. Review was granted.

Holdings: The Supreme Court, Bridge, J., held that:

(1) in matter of first impression, common law claim of de facto parentage existed such that woman had standing to petition for rights and responsibilities of shared parentage, and

(2) woman lacked standing to seek visitation under third party visitation statutes, which had been declared facially unconstitutional.

Court of Appeals affirmed in part and reversed in part; remanded.

The equitable power of the courts to adjudicate relationships between children and families is well recognized, and our legislature has evinced no intent to preclude the application of an equitable remedy in circumstances such as these. Accordingly, we now hold, as did the Court of Appeals, that Washington's common law recognizes the status of de facto parents and grants them standing to petition for a determination of the rights and responsibilities that accompany legal parentage in this state. Therefore, Carvin should have the opportunity to present evidence to the court sufficient to establish her status as a de facto parent of L.B. and if successful to obtain the rights and responsibilities attendant to parentage.

In the face of advancing technologies and evolving notions of what comprises a family unit, this case causes us to confront the manner in which our state, through its statutory scheme and common law principles, defines the terms "parents" and "families." During the first half of Washington's statehood, determinations of the conflicting rights of persons in family relationships were made by courts acting in equity. But over the past half-century, our legislature has established statutory schemes intended to govern various aspects of parentage, child custody disputes, visitation privileges, and child support obligations. Yet, inevitably, in the field of familial relations, factual scenarios arise, which even after a strict statutory analysis remain unresolved, leaving deserving parties without any appropriate remedy, often where demonstrated public policy is in favor of redress.

And so we turn to the question before us: whether our state's common law recognizes de facto parents and, if so, what rights and obligations accompany such recognition. Specifically, we are asked to discern whether, in the absence of a statutory remedy, the equitable power of our courts in domestic matters permits a remedy outside of the statutory scheme, or conversely, whether our state's relevant statutes provide the exclusive means of obtaining parental rights and responsibilities.

Conclusion: Our state's current statutory scheme reflects the unsurprising fact that statutes often fail to contemplate all potential scenarios which may arise in the ever changing and evolving notion of familial relations. Yet, simply because a statute fails to speak to a specific situation should not, and does not in our common law system, operate to preclude the availability of potential redress. This is especially true when the rights and interests of those least able to speak for themselves are concerned. We cannot read the legislature's pronouncements on this subject to preclude any potential redress to Carvin or L.B. In fact, to do so would be antagonistic to the clear legislative intent that permeates this field of law—to effectuate the best interests of the child in the face of differing notions of family and to provide certain and needed economical and psychological support and nurturing to the children of our state. While the legislature may eventually choose to enact differing standards than those recognized here today, and to do so would be within its province, until that time, it is the duty of this court to "endeavor to administer justice according to the promptings of reason and common sense . . . "

Reason and common sense support recognizing the existence of de facto parents and according them the rights and responsibilities which attach to parents in this state. We adapt our common law today to fill the interstices that our current legislative enactment fails to cover in a manner consistent with our laws and stated legislative policy. As [US Supreme Court] Justice O'Connor noted, "[t]he demographic changes of the past century make it difficult to speak of an average American family."

STUDY QUESTIONS

1. Compare this holding to the holding of the New York Court in *Alison D* and Vermont court in *Adoption of B.L.V.B.* earlier in this chapter. How is the reasoning different?

2. Is Justice Kaye right in her dissenting opinion in *Alison D.* that the majority there imposed an old-fashioned and unnecessarily narrow view of families and parenting? Do you agree that such a view ignores reality?

3. What principle did the Washington Court use to support its finding that the non-biological parent had a legal right to file for custody and visitation?

4. In light of the *Martinez* and *Donna S* cases, if the Court were to render this decision, today do you think it would reach the same or different conclusion? What do you think? Which case provides a fairer remedy?

Hand in hand with the rights of custody and visitation comes the responsibility for support of the child. Although Courts in several states have ruled, using the same principles as above, that the non-biological parent has the obligation to pay child support, in 2002, the Appellate Court of Pennsylvania found that the [respondent] acted as a co-parent with the mother in all areas concerning the children's conception, care, and support. In that particular case, the non-biological parent had sought custody during summer and school breaks. The Court believed that a parent could not "blow hot and cold" and that with the assertion of parental rights comes the assumption of parental duties.

In the cases we have seen, the same-sex couples resided together but never married. If they had been married and their relationship dissolved could they get divorced? Is there a remedy for same-sex divorce? Two Courts have recently reviewed this issue with differing results. Next we will review those decisions and examine the analysis each Court used in arriving at its conclusion.

CHAMBERS V. ORMISTON

935 A.2d 956
R.I.,2007.
December 07, 2007

Justice ROBINSON for the Court.

The Family Court, a legislatively created court of limited jurisdiction, has certified the following question to this Court:

"May the Family Court properly recognize, for the purpose of entertaining a divorce petition, the marriage of two persons of the same sex who were purportedly married in another state?"

For the reasons set forth herein, it is our opinion that the certified question must be answered in the negative.

We are sensitive to the fact that our holding on the jurisdictional issue deprives the parties to this case of the opportunity to seek a divorce in our Family Court. (See discussion entitled "A Final Consideration," infra.) Nevertheless, it is our conviction that the pertinent statute does not authorize the Family Court to entertain a divorce petition filed by "two persons of the same sex who were purportedly married in another state."

Upon contemplating the question certified by the Family Court, it became clear to us that the precise issue we must decide is ultimately the following: What is the meaning of the word "marriage" within the Rhode Island statute that empowers the Family Court to grant divorces—or, stated even more precisely, what did the word mean at the time that the members of the General Assembly enacted the statute? It is imperative that we direct our attention to the meaning of this statutory term at that point in time. We are well aware that "[t]his Court is the final arbiter with respect to questions of statutory construction."

Both parties argue in their briefs that the common law concept of "comity" requires us to recognize their status as married for the purpose of granting them a divorce. It is our view, however, that considerations of comity (a largely discretionary and some-what amorphous concept) do not come into play if the court lacks jurisdiction over the case before it. We have also concluded that, because our ruling as to the Family Court's lack of jurisdiction ends our inquiry, the Full Faith and Credit Clause of the United States Constitution is not relevant to these proceedings. Similarly, we have no occasion to address the applicability of the Defense of Marriage Act.

The issue before us is rather narrow, and it can be decided entirely on the statutory level: Does the statute authorizing the Family Court to "hear and determine all petitions for divorce from the bond of marriage," empower that court to grant a divorce to the instant parties, who are described in the certified question as "two persons of the same sex who were purportedly married in another state?"

It is clear to us that in this instance we are not confronted with an ambiguous statute. Therefore we simply must determine what the words in this statute were intended to mean. Once we have done so, our interpretive task is at an end and our role is simply to apply the statute as written. . . . With respect to the case at hand, there is absolutely no reason to believe that, when the act creating the Family Court became law in 1961, the legislators understood the word marriage to refer to any state other than "the state of being united to a person of the opposite sex.". . . The role of the judicial branch is not to make policy, but simply to determine the legislative intent as expressed in the statutes enacted by the General Assembly.

We know that sometimes our decisions result in palpable hardship to the persons affected by them. It is, however, a fundamental principle of jurisprudence that a court has no power to grant relief in the absence of jurisdiction, as is true in the instant case.

Ours is not a policy-making branch of the government. We are cognizant of the fact that this observation may be cold comfort to the parties before us. But, if there is to be a remedy to this predicament, fashioning such a remedy would fall within the province of the General Assembly.

Conclusion

We conclude that the word "marriage" in the statute which empowers the Family Court "to hear and determine all petitions for divorce from the bond of marriage," was not intended by the General Assembly to empower the Family Court to hear and determine petitions for divorce involving "two persons of the same sex who were purportedly married in another state." It necessarily follows that the Family Court, a court of limited statutory jurisdiction, is without jurisdiction over the captioned matter.

The Rhode Island Court based its decision on a very narrow construction of what was meant by "marriage" when the statute permitted the Family court to issue divorce was enacted. See how different this result is compared to the *In re Parentage of LB* above where the Court went beyond the statute and looked at what it deemed "equitable" or fair. Next we turn to a New York Trial Court decision regarding same sex divorce.

C.M. v. C.C.
21 Misc.3d 926, 867 N.Y.S.2d 884
October 14, 2008

ROSALYN H. RICHTER, J.

The parties, a same sex couple, were married in Massachusetts in a civil ceremony on August 26, 2005. At the time of their marriage, they were residents of New York. They have provided this Court with a copy of their Certificate of Marriage which was recorded with a town clerk in Massachusetts.

Earlier this year, the parties filed for divorce in this Court and an inquest on grounds was held. Although there was no opposition to the holding of the inquest, a question arose as to whether this Court had jurisdiction to grant a divorce to the parties since they could not, as a same sex couple, at the time of their marriage or now, get married in New York State. Because the question of subject matter jurisdiction cannot be waived or conferred on the Court by consent and can be raised at any point in the proceeding, see generally, the Court requested briefing on this jurisdictional issue. The parties have submitted a joint memorandum of law requesting that this Court grant a divorce in this matter once the ancillary issues of custody and finances are resolved.

In *Martinez v. County of Monroe*, 50 A.D.3d 189, (2008), the Appellate Division held that the recognition of a same sex marriage solemnized abroad was not contrary to the public policy of this State even if the marriage could not be solemnized in New York. In Martinez, the parties had been married in Canada and were seeking to have their marriage recognized here for the purpose of receiving spousal health benefits. As the Martinez court held, "[I]f a marriage is valid in the place where it was entered, it is to be recognized as such in the courts of this State, unless contrary to the prohibitions of natural law or the express prohibitions of a statute. It is undisputed that the New York State legislature has not enacted any statute that would prohibit recognition of a same sex marriage from another jurisdiction, nor is there any constitutional amendment barring recognition of such marriages. Thus, there is no positive law that would bar granting of a divorce in this case. Moreover, as the Martinez decision correctly notes, the natural law exception "has generally been limited to marriages involving polygamy or incest or marriages offensive to the public sense of morality to a degree regarded generally with abhorrence."

A similar result was reached in *Beth R. v. Donna M.*, 19 Misc.3d 724, (2008), in which a judge of this court concluded in a thoroughly researched decision that the common law doctrine of comity required recognition of a same sex Canadian marriage for divorce purposes. In that decision, the court noted the numerous other types of marriage, including common law marriages, that would not be valid if they occurred in New York, but which are recognized by New York if they are valid out of state marriages. Indeed, it is well-settled that in deciding whether to recognize a marriage that occurred in a sister state, the critical question is whether the marriage would be valid where contracted. This Court concurs with the analysis in *Beth R.* and sees no reason to distinguish between the Canadian marriage in that case and the Massachusetts marriage here.

The decision of the Rhode Island Supreme Court in *Chambers v. Ormiston*, 935 A.2d 956 (2007), is distinguishable from the instant case and in any event, would not be binding on this Court. In Chambers, the court held that the Rhode Island Family Court, as a court of limited statutory jurisdiction, could not grant a divorce petition involving a same sex couple who were married in Massachusetts. The Chambers court concluded that the concepts of full and faith and credit or comity were not applicable because the Family Court as a court of limited jurisdiction could only exercise

the powers granted to it by the legislature, which did not include the power to divorce a same sex couple. The Supreme Court in New York is a court of general jurisdiction and has the power to grant a divorce even if the marriage could not lawfully occur in this State. Moreover, as the dissent in Chambers correctly notes, it is a well established principle that the validity of a marriage is determined by the place where the marriage is celebrated.

The purpose of the full faith and credit provision of the constitution and the doctrine of comity is to accord parties, especially in today's mobile society, the ability to ensure that if they were married in another state, they can enforce the civil contract of marriage in New York. This Court's research and the cases cited by the parties provide no reason to carve out a unique exception for the parties here simply because they are of the same gender or because of their sexual orientation.

Accordingly, for all the reasons set forth above, no basis exists to decline to exercise jurisdiction over the dissolution of the parties' Massachusetts marriage and this New York divorce action can proceed.

STUDY QUESTIONS

1. In the New York case, the Trial Court distinguished its ruling from Rhode Island ruling in the earlier case. How did it justify a different ruling?
2. Should a Court give full Faith and Credit to marriages that are valid in other States or countries?
3. Do you agree that the Court in the Rhode Island case was bound by the limited jurisdiction of the Family Court or could it have applied the doctrine of comity as did the Court in New York.

Throughout this chapter, you have seen the progression of laws that affect woman and the issue of gender. You have also seen some Courts seemingly make it a point to interpret the law based on today's conventions and others that will not deviate from what they perceive to be the express intent of a statute. Courts frequently argue that they are not policy-makers, that they merely interpret the law as written by the policy-makers, the legislatures. Would you agree? Do you think that the Court in Massachusetts in enacting *Goodridge* in fact created the policy that permitted same-sex marriage? What role do you think that the Courts should have in this process? As society evolves, as our families evolve, what role should our legal system play in this evolution?

ON-LINE RESOURCES

Census Bureau
www.census.gov/
This site provides official U.S. Government statistical information.

Child Stats
www.childstats.gov/ac2000/poptxt.asp
Population and Family Characteristics presents data that illustrate the changes in the population and family context in which America's children are being raised.

Lambda Legal
www.lambdalegal.org/cgi-bin/iowa/
Lambda Legal is a national organization committed to achieving full recognition of the civil rights of lesbians, gay men, bisexuals, the transgendered, and people with HIV or AIDS through impact litigation, education, and public policy work.

Legal Information Institute
www.law.cornell.edu/
This is an excellent resource for legal research and information by Cornell Law School.

Legal Momentum (formerly NOW Legal Defense and Education Fund)
www.legalmomentum.org/
Legal Momentum formerly known as the NOW Legal Defense and Education Fund is an invaluable resource for information on gender-related legal and public policy issues.

National Criminal Justice Reference Services
www.ncjrs.org/
Contains research and studies on many aspects of criminal justice issues such as victim services and immigration issues.

Office of Violence Against Women
www.ojp.usdoj.gov/vawo/
This is the official Web site for the Office of Violence Against Women. It contains links to research and information on services, including statistics, findings, and funding opportunities.

VAWnet Domestic Violence
www.vawnet.org/DomesticViolence/
VAWnet is an electronic clearinghouse for information and materials on domestic violence, sexual assault, and related issues.

Violence Against Women Online Resources
www.vaw.umn.edu/
This site provides law, criminal justice, advocacy, and social service professionals with up-to-date information on interventions to stop violence against women.

CHAPTER 7

REPRODUCTION

THIS CHAPTER IS CONCERNED with decisions relating to whether, when, and how people have children. While these matters have a great impact on people of both sexes, the nature of that impact is very different for the two sexes. With present technology, the biological consequences of conception are very different for women and men. Pregnancy has a very real and intrusive impact on women physically. Under present social arrangements, the responsibility for caring for the children that are produced falls overwhelmingly on women. As we have seen throughout the preceding chapters, women's childbearing and child-rearing responsibilities have been the basis for limiting their opportunities to participate in society. Finally, the conditions under which people make their reproductive choices have been shaped by gender. Notions of appropriate social behavior, ability to control one's sexual partner, access to information and services, and influence in shaping the legal rules governing birth control are different for women and men.

As we saw in Chapter 6, regardless of our notions of gender and reproduction, there are those, like the "pregnant man," Thomas Beatie, who continue to challenge our perceptions. As you will recall, Thomas Beatie is a transgender male who had sex reassignment surgery but left his female reproductive organs intact. He married a woman who could not bear children and so the decision was made for Thomas to have the children. Even given this unusual circumstance, the couple assumed "traditional roles" with Thomas as the father and his wife as the mother.

In considering these questions from a legal perspective, it may be helpful to think of the law as establishing a framework that allocates the power to make reproductive choices, rather than determining the actual choices. For example, as we shall see, although the Supreme Court has made clear that the Constitution sets some limits on government's ability to interfere with the ability of women to choose abortions, it did not hold that particular women should or should not get abortions. Courts have often resolved fertility control cases in "privacy" terms, that is, by saying that decisions involving procreation should be made by the individual without State interference. Thus, courts look to see whether governmental action interferes with private decision making, and if so, whether there is adequate justification for that interference. As you consider this approach, think about whether courts seem to appreciate the connection between reproduction and gender sufficiently.

I. DEVELOPING THE RIGHT TO REPRODUCTIVE CHOICES

The Historical Context

The major Supreme Court decisions protecting reproductive choice are quite recent. Constitutional protection for procreation dates from the Court's 1942 decision, *Skinner v. Oklahoma*, 316 U.S. 535, invalidating a State statute authorizing sterilization of persons convicted two or more times of felonies "involving moral turpitude." The *Skinner* Court used heightened scrutiny to invalidate the statute, which only authorized sterilization of embezzlers and certain other criminals, under the Equal Protection Clause on the ground that it "forever deprived [these criminals] of a basic liberty." The *Skinner* holding and the protection it accorded procreation as "fundamental to the very existence and survival of the race" reflect a rather sharp break with the view held of sterilization and reproductive rights earlier in our history. *Griswold v. Connecticut*, 318 U.S. 479, the landmark case striking down Connecticut's ban on the use of contraceptives by married couples, was decided in 1965. *Roe v. Wade*, 410 U.S., 113, the historic decision recognizing a constitutional right to abortion, came in 1973.

Birth control attitudes and practices in the United States have varied considerably over the years. As James C. Mohr explains in his book, *Abortion in America* (Oxford University Press, Oxford, 1978), like contraception, abortion prior to quickening (when the first fetal movement can be perceived) was considered perfectly legal and acceptable prior to 1800. In the early nineteenth century, urbanization and industrialization began to undercut the economic reasons for large families, and the birth rate among whites began to fall, even in rural areas. A rise in abortion, particularly among "respectable" married women, played an important role in this change. By the 1840s, abortion had become a common commercialized practice in most States. Newspapers, for example, routinely advertised pills and midwives' services to help women with "irregular periods." Similarly, a typical circular publicized the availability of "novel inventions" to assist women who did not want children for health or financial reasons.

Although the use of abortion and contraception remained widespread throughout most of the nineteenth century, the legal framework changed significantly during that period. During the first half of the nineteenth century, most jurisdictions followed the English common law rule that held that abortion with a woman's consent prior to quickening was not a crime. Between 1840 and 1860, a number of anti-abortion laws were enacted, but these generally preserved the woman's right to end her pregnancy prior to quickening. However, a doctor's crusade initiated in the 1850s by "regular physicians" led to the enactment of restrictive abortion legislation in the next several decades.

As contrasted with the more experientially oriented populist healers, the "regulars" were predominantly male doctors committed to scientific research and education and organized into medical societies. Their campaign, carried out under the auspices of the American Medical Association, focused on moral and safety concerns about abortions, as well as on white, native-born Protestants' fear of being outbred by Catholic immigrants. Although the Catholic Church had banned abortion for the first time in the mid-nineteenth century, the physicians did not succeed in enlisting the aid of the American religious community. They did, however, find valuable allies in the anti-obscenity movement. Meaningful prohibitions on abortion were widely enacted between 1860 and 1880, but the courts did not enforce them stringently for another twenty years.

As Mohr points out, one important indication of the physicians' effectiveness following the Civil War was the ability to have all abortion-related matters included in the definition of obscenity. The prime mover in the anti-obscenity crusade was Anthony Comstock, head of the New York Society for the Suppression of Vice. In 1873, at Comstock's urging, Congress passed an "Act for the Suppression of Trade in, and Circulation of, Obscene Literature and Articles of Immoral Use." Aimed at the distribution of contraceptive and abortifacient articles and information, as well as more conventionally defined pornography, the law permitted Comstock and his associates to prosecute numerous abortionists for obscenity throughout the decade. Remaining on the books intact until challenged judicially in 1938, the statute also led to birth control advocate Margaret Sanger's prosecution and exile for distributing birth control information in the second decade of the twentieth century. In short, although legal options were ultimately restricted for many people, reproductive decisions during most of the nineteenth century were made in a permissive legal climate.

The legal and economic nature of slavery meant, however, that a special set of constraints governed the reproductive lives of many black women. As historian Herbert Gutman explains in his classic book, *The Black Family in Slavery and Freedom 1750–1925* (Vintage Books, New York, 1979), the system of slavery was plain. It required slave women, especially after the abolition of the overseas slave trade, to reproduce the slave labor force. From the slave-owner's perspective, the birth of a child meant more profits. From the slave-woman's perspective, giving birth might demonstrate her fertility, thereby reducing her chances of being sold and separated from her family. Sexual advances from owners were not always welcome, however, and slave women exercised considerable ingenuity in resisting them. Reports in Southern medical journals and elsewhere suggest that slave women also resorted to home remedies to avoid reproducing. Often they relied on herbal brews rather than mechanical means. Infusions of tansy, rue, and cotton root served as abortifacients, and camphor was used as a contraceptive.

Significant changes for reproductive choice also occurred in the twentieth century. These developments reflect the influences of the three important reproductive control movements of the nineteenth century: a neo-Malthusian movement for population control, a eugenics movement aimed at improving the human race, and a feminist movement for Voluntary Motherhood. Historian Linda Gordon traces these influences and their connection with twentieth-century birth control movements in her article, "Feminism, Reproduction, and the Family" in *Rethinking the Family* (Barrie Thorne and Marilyn Yalom, editors, Longman, New York, 1982).

The neo-Malthusian movement supported contraception as a means to ameliorate social problems by reducing population size on a large scale. Now a recognizable strain in global population control efforts, the movement came later to the United States than to Europe because this country was more preoccupied with under-population than overpopulation until World War II.

The eugenics movement initially sought to improve the human stock by eliminating idiocy, criminality, and drunkenness, all mistakenly thought to be hereditary. As the upper class WASP (white Anglo-Saxon Protestant) elite of the Northeast became increasingly aware of their small-family pattern as opposed to the large-family pattern of immigrants and the rural poor, eugenicists advocated selective use of contraception and sterilization to ensure the survival of the superior stock.

Widespread sterilization became possible in this country at the end of the nineteenth century with the perfection of safe and simple operations for both sexes. The eugenics movement stimulated compulsory sterilization. That movement, which held force during the first three decades of the twentieth century and which was supported by a number of liberals and progressives at the time, attempted to prevent those considered biologically unfit from propagating and to encourage those considered worthy of procreating. By the 1930s, more than thirty States had adopted laws authorizing sterilization of convicted rapists and other criminals, such as those judged "insane," "idiotic," "imbecilic," or "moronic."

Eugenicists made no bones about those they deemed worthy of reproducing, and their movement reflected definite race and class biases. As implemented, the compulsory sterilization laws they inspired also had a definite gender bias. Laws authorizing the sterilization of criminals were directed at men, and there is some evidence that courts were reluctant to order men sterilized under these statutes. Due process and cruel and unusual punishment arguments frequently sufficed to block sterilization in the lower courts, and when the U.S. Supreme Court faced the issue in the 1942 *Skinner v. Oklahoma* decision, it invalidated compulsory sterilization of certain felons on equal protection grounds.

Sterilization of women, however, was thought crucial to ending feeblemindedness, and of those sterilized for that reason, two-thirds were women. In 1927, the U.S. Supreme Court upheld the compulsory sterilization of the feebleminded in *Buck v. Bell*, 274 U.S. 200, the famous decision in which Justice Oliver Wendell Holmes declared, "Three generations of imbeciles are enough." As biologist Stephen Jay Gould showed in his article, "Carrie Buck's Daughter," appearing in *Natural History* (July 1984), that case illustrates a subtler aspect of the gender bias in sterilization abuse. As Gould convincingly demonstrated, there was no evidence that Carrie Buck, her mother, or her daughter were deficient mentally. Rather, Carrie Buck, one of several illegitimate children, was institutionalized to hide the pregnancy that had resulted from her rape by one of her foster relatives. Not only was Carrie Buck blamed for her pregnancy, but, as Gould's article suggests, her improper sexual behavior was considered a key indicator of feeblemindedness.

Unlike the neo-Malthusian and the eugenics movements, the Voluntary Motherhood movement, which dated from the 1840s, advocated birth control through abstinence rather than contraception. Voluntary Motherhood proponents saw birth control as crucial to achieving feminist goals of the day. Abstinence, rather than contraception, however, was best suited to winning the freedom women required from excessive childbearing, marital rape, and other forms of male sexual tyranny without devaluing motherhood. Self-respect and respect for motherhood were, as they saw it, essential to equal rights.

Feminists in the following century took a distinctly different view. The feminists who sparked the twentieth-century birth control movement were radicals—feminist socialists such as Emma Goldman and Margaret Sanger, who argued that free sexual expression and reproductive self-determination were essential to women's liberation. Subsequently, under Margaret Sanger's leadership, the movement sought and gained respectability through professionalization. Activities focused increasingly on opening clinics and lobbying for legislation. Male physicians assumed more visible leadership roles and women generally assumed staff and organizer positions. Eugenics, with its overtones of racial superiority, also became an important theme in the early twentieth-century struggle to legalize contraception and abortion, resulting in the loss of black support.

With the coming of the Depression in the 1930s, social workers also became involved in the birth control movement. Emphasizing contraception as a tool against poverty, and in some locations as a means of limiting the growth of the black population, some State, local, and federal agencies developed small-scale birth control programs. Nevertheless, laws prohibiting contraception and abortion persisted in a number of States. In 1939, the American Birth Control League and the Birth Control Clinical Research Bureau merged to form the Birth Control Federation of America, which in 1942 adopted the name Planned Parenthood Federation of America (PPFA).

During the 1940s, PPFA stressed the importance of family planning in achieving healthier marriages and parenthood. In the 1950s and 1960s, population control on a national and global level assumed greater importance for the birth control movement (including PPFA). Programs and policies advanced by the United States, at times through the United Nations, urged reduction in the birth rate as a way of combating poverty at home and promoting economic development abroad. Family planning thus gained a political acceptability that led ultimately to a transformation of the legal climate surrounding reproduction.

Contraception

From the 1920s on, the birth control movement sought the enactment of measures legalizing contraceptives. When religious and other birth control opponents repeatedly succeeded in blocking legislative reforms, Planned Parenthood sought to challenge bans on contraception in court. *Skinner v. Oklahoma*, the 1942 decision invalidating the compulsory sterilization of certain criminals, prepared the way for these challenges. As noted, the Court there asserted for the first time that the right to reproduce was "one of the basic civil rights of man." It took almost a quarter of a century more for the Court to recognize the right *not* to reproduce.

The Supreme Court twice rejected challenges to Connecticut's prohibitions on birth control on procedural grounds related to the statute not having been enforced against a user or prescribing physician. Finally, in 1965, the Supreme Court reached the statute's merits after the Planned Parenthood affiliate actually provoked arrests by opening a clinic.

GRISWOLD V. CONNECTICUT
U.S. Supreme Court, 1965.
381 U.S. 479, 85 S. Ct. 1678, 14 L.Ed.2d 510.

Mr. Justice DOUGLAS delivered the opinion of the Court.

Appellant Griswold is Executive Director of the Planned Parenthood League of Connecticut. Appellant Buxton is a licensed physician and a professor at the Yale Medical School who served as Medical Director for the League at its Center in New Haven—a center open and operating from November 1 to November 10, 1961, when appellants were arrested.

They gave information, instruction, and medical advice to *married persons* as to the means of preventing conception. They examined the wife and prescribed the best contraceptive device or material for her use. Fees were usually charged, although some couples were serviced free.

The statutes whose constitutionality is involved in this appeal are §§ 53–32 and 54–196 of the General Statutes of Connecticut (1958 rev.). The former provides:

"Any person who uses any drug, medicinal article or instrument for the purpose of preventing conception shall be fined not less than fifty dollars or imprisoned not less than sixty days nor more than one year or be both fined and imprisoned."

Section 54–196 provides:

"Any person who assists, abets, counsels, causes, hires or commands another to commit any offense may be prosecuted and punished as if he were the principal offender."

The appellants were found guilty as accessories and fined $100 each, against the claim that the accessory statute as so applied violated the Fourteenth Amendment. The Appellate Division of the Circuit Court affirmed. The Supreme Court of Errors affirmed that judgment. . . .

Coming to the merits, we are met with a wide range of questions that implicate the Due Process Clause of the Fourteenth Amendment. . . . We do not sit as a super-legislature to determine the wisdom, need, and propriety of laws that touch economic problems, business affairs, or social conditions. This law, however, operates directly on an intimate relation of husband and wife and their physician's role in one aspect of that relation.

The association of people is not mentioned in the Constitution nor in the Bill of Rights. The right to educate a child in a school of the parents' choice—whether public or private or parochial—is also not mentioned. Nor is the right to study any particular subject or any foreign language. Yet the First Amendment has been construed to include certain of those rights. . . .

The right of "association," like the right of belief, is more than the right to attend a meeting; it includes the right to express one's attitudes or philosophies by membership in a group or by affiliation with it or by other lawful means. Association in that context is a form of expression of opinion; and while it is not expressly included in the First Amendment its existence is necessary in making the express guarantees fully meaningful.

The foregoing cases suggest that specific guarantees in the Bill of Rights have penumbras, formed by emanations from those guarantees that help give them life and substance. Various guarantees create zones of privacy. The right of association contained in the penumbra of the First Amendment is one, as we have seen. The Third Amendment in its prohibition against the quartering of soldiers "in any house" in time of peace without the consent of the owner is another facet of that privacy. The Fourth Amendment explicitly affirms the "right of the people to be secure in their persons, houses, papers, and effects, against unreasonable searches and seizures." The Fifth Amendment in its Self-Incrimination Clause enables the citizen to create a zone of privacy which government may not force him to surrender to his detriment. The Ninth Amendment provides: "The enumeration in the Constitution, of certain rights, shall not be construed to deny or disparage others, retained by the people."

The Fourth and Fifth Amendments were described in *Boyd v. United States*, as protection against all governmental invasions "of the sanctity of a man's home and the privacies of life." We recently referred in *Mapp v. Ohio* to the Fourth Amendment as creating a "right to privacy, no less important than any other right carefully and particularly reserved to the people." . . .

We have had many controversies over these penumbral rights of "privacy and repose." These cases bear witness that the right of privacy which presses for recognition here is a legitimate one.

The present case, then, concerns a relationship lying within the zone of privacy created by several fundamental constitutional guarantees. And it concerns a law which, in forbidding the *use* of contraceptives rather than regulating their manufacture or sale, seeks to achieve its goals by means having a maximum destructive impact upon that relationship. Such a law cannot stand in light of the familiar principle, so often applied by this Court, that a "governmental purpose to control or prevent activities constitutionally subject to State regulation may not be achieved by means which sweep unnecessarily broadly and thereby invade the area of protected freedoms." Would we allow the police to search the sacred precincts of marital bedrooms for telltale signs of the use of contraceptives? The very idea is repulsive to the notions of privacy surrounding the marriage relationship.

We deal with a right of privacy older than the Bill of Rights—older than our political parties, older than our school system. Marriage is a coming together for better or for worse, hopefully enduring, and intimate to the degree of being sacred. It is an association that promotes a way of life, not causes; a harmony in living, not political faiths; a bilateral loyalty, not commercial or social projects. Yet it is an association for as noble a purpose as any involved in our prior decisions.

Reversed.

Mr. Justice BLACK, with whom Mr. Justice STEWART joins, dissenting. . . .

One of the most effective ways of diluting or expanding a constitutionally guaranteed right is to substitute for the crucial word or words of a constitutional guarantee another word or words more or less flexible and more or less restricted in meaning. This fact is well illustrated by the use of the term "right of privacy" as a comprehensive substitute for the Fourth Amendment's guarantee against "unreasonable searches and seizures." "Privacy" is a broad, abstract and ambiguous concept which can easily be shrunken in meaning but which can also, on the other hand, easily be interpreted as a constitutional ban against many things other than searches and seizures. . . .

I agree with my Brother Stewart's dissenting opinion. And like him I do not to any extent whatever base my view that this Connecticut law is constitutional on a belief that the law is wise or that its policy is a good one. . . .

There is no single one of the graphic and eloquent strictures and criticisms fired at the policy of this Connecticut law either by the Court's opinion or by those of my concurring Brethren to which I cannot subscribe—except their conclusion that the evil qualities they see in the law make it unconstitutional. . . .

The Court talks about a constitutional "right of privacy" as though there is some constitutional provision or provisions forbidding any law ever to be passed which might abridge the "privacy" of individuals. But there is not. There are, of course, guarantees in certain specific constitutional provisions which are designed in part to protect privacy at certain times and places with respect to certain activities. . . .

I like my privacy as well as the next one, but I am nevertheless compelled to admit that government has a right to invade it unless prohibited by some specific constitutional provision. For these reasons I cannot agree with the Court's judgment and the reasons it gives for holding this Connecticut law unconstitutional.

. . . I think that if properly construed neither the Due Process Clause nor the Ninth Amendment, nor both together, could under any circumstances be a proper basis for invalidating the Connecticut law. I discuss

the due process and Ninth Amendment arguments together because on analysis they turn out to be the same thing—merely using different words to claim for this Court and the federal judiciary power to invalidate any legislative act which the judges find irrational, unreasonable or offensive.

The due process argument . . . is based . . . on the premise that this Court is vested with power to invalidate all State laws that it considers to be arbitrary, capricious, unreasonable, or oppressive, or on this Court's belief that a particular State law under scrutiny has no "rational or justifying" purpose, or is offensive to a "sense of fairness and justice." If these formulas based on "natural justice," or others which mean the same thing, are to prevail, they require judges to determine what is or is not constitutional on the basis of their own appraisal of what laws are unwise or unnecessary. The power to make such decisions is of course that of a legislative body. . . .

I do not believe that we are granted power by the Due Process Clause or any other constitutional provision or provisions to measure constitutionality by our belief that legislation is arbitrary, capricious or unreasonable, or accomplishes no justifiable purpose, or is offensive to our own notions of "civilized standards of conduct." . . .

STUDY QUESTIONS

1. Did Justice Douglas and the majority of the Court find that the statute violated any specific provision of the Constitution? What is the source of the "right to privacy" that was violated by the statute, according to Justice Douglas's opinion?

2. What is the scope of the right of privacy recognized in *Griswold*? May States punish single persons for using contraceptives? May States proscribe the distribution of contraceptives? May States make adultery and fornication crimes?

3. In a concurring opinion, Justice Goldberg made the point that if the Constitution does not protect the right

not to become a parent, it does not protect the right to become a parent, so that a State could subject an individual to compulsory sterilization. Do you agree?

4. What was the basis of Justice Black's dissent? Is he correct that when judges recognize constitutional rights that are not guaranteed by explicit provisions of the Constitution, they inevitably impose their own views of what are wise or necessary laws?

In *Griswold*, the Court struck down a State restriction on the use of contraceptives by married couples. The decision's effect was to reinforce the fundamental right to procreative choice first recognized in *Skinner*, but its reasoning emphasized the privacy rights of married couples. *Griswold* thus left open the question of whether a State may restrict the distribution of contraceptives to *unmarried* persons. In answering that question, the Supreme Court by a plurality of four justices endorsed the view that the right of privacy inheres in individuals as well as married couples.

As Justice Brennan put it for the plurality in *Eisenstadt v. Baird*, 405 U.S. 438, 453 (1972):

> It is true that in *Griswold* the right of privacy in question inhered in the marital relationship. Yet the marital couple is not an independent entity with a heart and mind of its own, but an association of two individuals each with a separate intellectual and emotional makeup. If the right of privacy means anything, it is the right of an *individual*, married or single, to be free from unwanted governmental intrusion into matters so fundamentally affecting a person as the decision whether to bear or beget a child.

As we shall see in the next section, this individual right of privacy first articulated in the contraception context was later developed in the abortion context. *Eisenstadt* is also noteworthy because it extended *Griswold's* prohibition on laws barring the use of contraceptives to laws barring the distribution of contraceptives.

Following *Griswold*, in 1977, the U.S. Supreme Court in *Carey v. Population Services International*, 431 U.S. 678, clearly indicated that the government must justify a restriction on reproductive choice with a compelling State interest. Though the Court in *Carey* recognized that adults engage in sexual activity without procreation, it also raised concerns regarding young people engaging in sexual activity.

Adolescent sexuality poses difficult questions for many people, and there has been much debate in recent years over the appropriate role for government in this troublesome area. Justice Powell's concurring opinion in *Carey* points to "parental" interests in rearing their children as a possible basis for limiting minors' access to contraception. He suggests a requirement of prior parental consultation would be a permissible regulation in this area. Subsequently, the U.S. Department of Health and Human Services (formerly Health, Education, and Welfare) pursued this suggestion by adopting the so-called squeal rule.

The squeal rule required all recipients of federal funding for family planning services under Title X of the Public Health Services Act to notify parents or guardians within ten days of prescribing contraceptives to unemancipated minors and to comply with all State laws requiring parental notification or consent for such services. Although the agency attempted to justify the regulations as required by amendments to Title X that reflected a congressional desire to encourage family participation in preventing unwanted teen pregnancies, the courts rejected these arguments and invalidated the regulations. Rather, the courts found that Congress did not intend to *mandate* family involvement in large part because Congress had found that it was essential to maintain adolescents' confidentiality in order to attract them to family planning clinics. See *Planned Parenthood Federation of America, Inc. v. Heckler*, 712 F.2d 650 (D.C. Cir. 1983) and *New York v. Heckler*, 719 F.2d 1191 (2d Cir. 1983).

Unlike similar State laws, the squeal rule received widespread denunciation by the public, and the episode seems to have ended attempts to enforce notification at the federal level. However, because the decisions were based on statutory grounds, the question of constitutionality of such requirements is still open.

One area involving contraception where there have been some recent legislative developments is the issue of insurance coverage for contraception. Many States have enacted Contraception Coverage Laws mandating that insurance companies that provide coverage for prescription drugs also provide coverage for FDA-approved contraceptive drugs or devices.

In recent case developments, the issue of whether religious employers who provide health insurance can decline to provide coverage for contraceptives has emerged. In 2004, the U.S. Supreme Court declined to overturn a ruling by the California Supreme Court that required the employer Catholic Charities to provide insurance coverage for contraceptive prescriptions and devices. Because the organization was not purely religious in nature and offered such secular services as counseling, housing, and immigration services, it was not deemed exempt under the religious exemption to California's law. *Catholic Charities of Sacramento, Inc. v. California*, 543 U.S. 816, 125 S.Ct. 53, 160 L.Ed.2d 22 (2004). According to a 2009 article from the Guttmacher Institute, there are now twenty-seven States that require insurers that cover prescription drugs in general to provide coverage for FDA-approved contraceptive drugs and devices. There are currently fifteen States that exempt this requirement for religious employers. The issue is one of access to health care and specifically access by women to contraceptive services. The constitutional balance is a balance between the First Amendment right of religious freedom versus the rights of privacy and equal protection.

The National Women's Law Center outlines the argument in their 2007 article "Coverage of Contraceptives in Health Insurance: The Facts You Should Know." The article highlights the disparity to women when insurers do not cover contraception for women:

> The exclusion of prescription contraceptives from health insurance coverage unfairly disadvantages women by singling out for unfavorable treatment a health insurance need that only they have. Failure to cover contraception forces women to bear higher health care costs to avoid pregnancy, and exposes women to the unique physical, economic, and emotional consequences that can result from unintended pregnancy.

Refusing to cover women's contraception not only treats women differently but it also has negative financial affect on women who must cover the costs of prescription medication and devices out of pocket.

Abortion

During the years between *Griswold* (1965) and *Roe v. Wade* (1973), State legislatures considered and adopted a variety of changes in abortion statutes. By 1973, nineteen States had changed their abortion laws. The Supreme Court preempted this process of piecemeal reform when it handed down its decision in *Roe v. Wade*. Drawing on the legal foundation it had laid in *Griswold* and *Eisenstadt*, the Supreme Court explicitly extended the right of reproductive choice to abortion in 1973. As political theorist Rosalind Petchesky argued in her book, *Abortion and Women's Choice* (Longman, New York, 1985), the *Roe v. Wade* decision and the liberalization of abortion laws that preceded it must be seen as the product of social and political forces as well as legal developments. Petchesky identifies the efforts of the women's liberation movement, which stressed the need for women to be able to control their bodies, and the more established population control and medical organizations, which stressed public health concerns and medical control as the immediate factors. However, Petchesky saw the large demand for abortions—legal or illegal—as crucial to stimulating the efforts of both groups. This demand for abortion services was part of the overall drop in fertility that began among women in the United States in the early 1960s. This decline reflected their greater participation in the labor force and college attendance, increasing divorce rates, and their continued responsibility for child care in the absence of adequate government funding for social services.

Although the demand for abortion services persisted through the 1980s and early 1990s, as we shall see, this did not mean that *Roe v. Wade* would remain the law of the land. We look first at the *Roe v. Wade* decision and some of the theory behind it, then at its application, and finally, at the limitations imposed on it.

The Decision

Although abortion law reform was underway as early as the 1960s, the Court's ruling in *Roe v. Wade* proved extremely controversial, both legally and politically. We now consider the decision and the controversies it engendered.

ROE V. WADE

U.S. Supreme Court, 1973.

410 U.S. 113, 93 S. Ct. 705, 35 L.Ed.2d 147.

Mr. Justice BLACKMUN delivered the opinion of the Court.

This Texas federal appeal and its Georgia companion, *Doe v. Bolton*, present constitutional challenges to State criminal abortion legislation. The Texas statutes under attack here are typical of those that have been in effect in many States for approximately a century. The Georgia statutes, in contrast, have a modern cast and are a legislative product that, to an extent at least, obviously reflects the influences of recent attitudinal change, of advancing medical knowledge and techniques, and of new thinking about an old issue.

We forthwith acknowledge our awareness of the sensitive and emotional nature of the abortion controversy, of the vigorous opposing views, even among physicians, and of the deep and seemingly absolute convictions that the subject inspires. One's philosophy, one's experiences, one's exposure to the raw edges of human existence, one's religious training, one's attitudes toward life and family and their values, and the moral standards one establishes and seeks to observe, are all likely to influence and to color one's thinking and conclusions about abortion.

In addition, population growth, pollution, poverty, and racial overtones tend to complicate and not to simplify the problem.

Our task, of course, is to resolve the issue by constitutional measurement free of emotion and of predilection. We seek earnestly to do this, and, because we do, we have inquired into, and in this opinion place some emphasis upon, medical and medical-legal history and what that history reveals about man's attitudes toward the abortive procedure over the centuries. We bear in mind, too, Mr. Justice Holmes' admonition in his now vindicated dissent in *Lochner v. New York*, 198 U.S. 45, 76 (1905): . . .

[The Constitution] is made for people of fundamentally differing views, and the accident of our finding certain opinions natural and familiar or novel and even shocking ought not to conclude our judgment upon the question whether statutes embodying them conflict with the Constitution of the United States.

The Texas statutes . . . make it a crime to "procure an abortion," as therein defined, or to attempt one, except with respect to "an abortion procured or attempted by medical advice for the purpose of saving the life of the mother." Similar statutes are in existence in a majority of the States. . . .

Jane Roe, a single woman who was residing in Dallas County, Texas, instituted this federal action in March 1970 against the District Attorney of the county. . . .

Roe alleged that she was unmarried and pregnant; that she wished to terminate her pregnancy by an abortion "performed by a competent, licensed physician, under safe, clinical conditions"; that she was unable to get a "legal" abortion in Texas because her life did not appear to be threatened by the continuation of her pregnancy; and that she could not afford to travel to another jurisdiction in order to secure a legal abortion under safe conditions. . . .

The principal thrust of appellant's attack on the Texas statutes is that they improperly invade a right, said to be possessed by the pregnant woman, to choose to terminate her pregnancy. Appellant would discover this right in the concept of personal "liberty" embodied in the Fourteenth Amendment's Due Process Clause; or in personal, marital, familial, and sexual privacy said to be protected by the Bill of Rights or its penumbras, see *Griswold v. Connecticut; Eisenstadt v. Baird* (White, J., concurring); or among those rights reserved to the people by the Ninth Amendment, *Griswold v. Connecticut* (Goldberg, J., concurring). Before addressing this claim, we feel it desirable

briefly to survey, in several aspects, the history of abortion, for such insight as that history may afford us, and then to examine the State purposes and interests behind the criminal abortion laws.

It perhaps is not generally appreciated that the restrictive criminal abortion laws in effect in a majority of States today are of relatively recent vintage. Those laws, generally proscribing abortion or its attempt at any time during pregnancy except when necessary to preserve the pregnant woman's life, are not of ancient or even of common law origin. Instead, they derive from statutory changes effected, for the most part, in the latter half of the 19th century. . . .

Gradually, in the middle and late 19th century, the quickening distinction disappeared from the statutory law of most States and the degree of the offense and the penalties were increased. By the end of the 1950's, a large majority of the States banned abortion, however and whenever performed, unless done to save or preserve the life of the mother. The exceptions, Alabama and the District of Columbia, permitted abortion to preserve the mother's health. Three other States permitted abortions that were not "unlawfully" performed or that were not "without lawful justification," leaving interpretation of those standards to the courts. In the past several years, however, a trend toward liberalization of abortion statutes has resulted in adoption, by about one-third of the States, of less stringent laws, most of them patterned after the ALI Model Penal Code. . . .

It is thus apparent that at common law, at the time of the adoption of our Constitution, and throughout the major portion of the 19th century, abortion was viewed with less disfavor than under most American statutes currently in effect. Phrasing it another way, a woman enjoyed a substantially broader right to terminate a pregnancy than she does in most States today. At least with respect to the early stage of pregnancy, and very possibly without such a limitation, the opportunity to make this choice was present in this country well into the 19th century.

Even later, the law continued for some time to treat less punitively an abortion procured in early pregnancy. . . .

Three reasons have been advanced to explain historically the enactment of criminal abortion laws in the 19th century and to justify their continued existence.

It has been argued occasionally that these laws were the product of a Victorian social concern to discourage illicit sexual conduct. Texas, however, does not advance this justification in the present case, and it appears that no court or commentator has taken the argument seriously. . . .

A second reason is concerned with abortion as a medical procedure. When most criminal abortion laws were first enacted, the procedure was a hazardous one for the woman. This was particularly true prior to the development of antisepsis. Antiseptic techniques, of course, were based on discoveries by Lister, Pasteur, and others first announced in 1867, but were not generally accepted and employed until about the turn of the century. Abortion mortality was high. Even after 1900, and perhaps until as late as the development of antibiotics in the 1940's, standard modern techniques such as dilation and curettage were not nearly so safe as they are today. Thus it has been argued that a State's real concern in enacting a criminal abortion law was to protect the pregnant woman, that is, to restrain her from submitting to a procedure that placed her life in serious jeopardy.

Modern medical techniques have altered this situation. Appellants and various amici refer to medical data indicating that abortion in early pregnancy, that is, prior to the end of first trimester, although not without its risk, is now relatively safe. Mortality rates for women undergoing early abortions, where the procedure is legal, appear to be as low as or lower than the rates for normal childbirth. Consequently, any interest of the State in protecting the woman from an inherently hazardous procedure, except when it would be equally dangerous for her to forgo it, has largely disappeared. Of course, important State interests in the

area of health and medical standards do remain. The State has a legitimate interest in seeing to it that abortion, like any other medical procedure, is performed under circumstances that [e]nsure maximum safety for the patient. This interest obviously extends at least to the performing physician and his staff, to the facilities involved, to the availability of after-care, and to adequate provision for any complication or emergency that might arise. The prevalence of high mortality rates at illegal "abortion mills" strengthens, rather than weakens, the State's interest in regulating the conditions under which abortions are performed. Moreover, the risk to the woman increases as her pregnancy continues. Thus the State retains a definite interest in protecting the woman's own health and safety when an abortion is proposed at a late stage of pregnancy.

The third reason is the State's interest— some phrase it in terms of duty—in protecting prenatal life. Some of the argument for this justification rests on the theory that a new human life is present from the moment of conception. The State's interest and general obligation to protect life then extends, it is argued, to prenatal life. Only when the life of the pregnant mother herself is at stake, balanced against the life she carries within her, should the interest of the embryo or fetus not prevail. Logically, of course, a legitimate State interest in this area need not stand or fall on acceptance of the belief that life begins at conception or at some other, point prior to live birth. In assessing the State's interest recognition may be given to the less rigid claim that as long as at least *potential* life is involved, the State may assert interests beyond the protection of the pregnant woman alone. . . .

It is with these interests, and the weight to be attached to them, that this case is concerned. . . .

The Constitution does not explicitly mention any right of privacy. In a line of decisions, however, going back perhaps as far as *Union Pacific R. Co. v. Botsford*, 141 U.S. 250, 251 (1891), the Court has recognized that a right of personal privacy, or a guarantee of certain areas or zones of privacy, does exist under the Constitution. In varying contexts the Court or individual justices have indeed found at least the roots of that right in the First Amendment, in the Fourth and Fifth Amendments, in the penumbras of the Bill of Rights, in the Ninth Amendment, or in the concept of liberty guaranteed by the first section of the Fourteenth Amendment.

This right of privacy, whether it be founded in the Fourteenth Amendment's concept of personal liberty and restrictions upon State action, as we feel it is, or, as the District Court determined, in the Ninth Amendment's reservation of rights to the people, is broad enough to encompass a woman's decision whether or not to terminate her pregnancy. The detriment that the State would impose upon the pregnant woman by denying this choice altogether is apparent. Specific and direct harm medically diagnosable even in early pregnancy may be involved. Maternity, or additional off-spring, may force upon the woman a distressful life and future. Psychological harm may be imminent. Mental and physical health may be taxed by child care. There is also the distress, for all concerned, associated with the unwanted child, and there is the problem of bringing a child into a family already unable, psychologically and otherwise, to care for it. In other cases, as in this one, the additional difficulties and continuing stigma of unwed motherhood may be involved. All these are factors the woman and her responsible physician necessarily will consider in consultation.

On the basis of elements such as these, appellants and some amici argue that the woman's right is absolute and that she is entitled to terminate her pregnancy at whatever time, in whatever way, and for whatever reason she alone chooses. With this we do not agree. Appellants' arguments that Texas either has no valid interest at all in regulating the abortion decision, or no interest strong enough to support any limitation upon the woman's sole determination,

[are] unpersuasive. The Court's decisions recognizing a right of privacy also acknowledge that some State regulation in areas protected by that right is appropriate. As noted above, a State may properly assert important interests in safeguarding health, in maintaining medical standards, and in protecting potential life. At some point in pregnancy, these respective interests become sufficiently compelling to sustain regulation of the factors that govern the abortion decision. The privacy right involved, therefore, cannot be said to be absolute. . . .

Where certain "fundamental rights" are involved, the Court has held that regulation limiting these rights may be justified only by a "compelling State interest," and that legislative enactments must be narrowly drawn to express only the legitimate State interests at stake. . . .

The District Court held that the appellee failed to meet his burden of demonstrating that the Texas statute's infringement upon Roe's rights was necessary to support a compelling State interest, and that, although the [appellee] presented "several compelling justifications for State presence in the area of abortions," the statutes outstripped these justifications and swept "far beyond any areas of compelling State interest." Appellant and appellee both contest that holding. . . .

The appellee and certain amici argue that the fetus is a "person" within the language and meaning of the Fourteenth Amendment. In support of this they outline at length and in detail the well-known facts of fetal development. If this suggestion of personhood is established, the appellant's case, of course, collapses, for the fetus' right to life [would] then [be] guaranteed specifically by the Amendment. The appellant conceded as much on reargument. On the other hand, the appellee conceded on reargument that no case could be cited that holds that a fetus is a person within the meaning of the Fourteenth Amendment.

The Constitution does not define "person" . . . in so many words. Section 1 of the Fourteenth Amendment contains three references to "person."

But in nearly all . . . instances, the use of the word is such that it has application only postnatally. None indicates, with any assurance, that it has any possible pre-natal application.

All this, together with our observation, supra, that throughout the major portion of the 19th century prevailing legal abortion practices were far freer than they are today, persuades us that the word "person," as used in the Fourteenth Amendment, does not include the unborn. This is in accord with the results reached in those few cases where the issue has been squarely presented. . . .

The pregnant woman cannot be isolated in her privacy. She carries an embryo and, later, a fetus, if one accepts the medical definitions of the developing young in the human uterus. See *Dorland's Illustrated Medical Dictionary*, 478–479, 547 (24th ed. 1965). The situation therefore is inherently different from marital intimacy, or bedroom possession of obscene material, or marriage, or procreation, or education, with which *Eisenstadt* and *Griswold, Stanley, Loving, Skinner, Pierce,* and *Meyer* were respectively concerned. As we have intimated above, it is reasonable and appropriate for a State to decide that at some point in time another interest, that of health of the mother or that of potential human life, becomes significantly involved. The woman's privacy is no longer sole and any right of privacy she possesses must be measured accordingly.

Texas urges that, apart from the Fourteenth Amendment, life begins at conception and is present throughout pregnancy, and that, therefore, the State has a compelling interest in protecting that life from and after conception. We need not resolve the difficult question of when life begins. When those trained in the respective disciplines of medicine, philosophy, and theology are unable to arrive at any consensus, the judiciary, at this point in the development of man's knowledge, is not in a position to speculate as to the answer.

It should be sufficient to note briefly the wide divergence of thinking on this most sensitive and difficult question. There has always been strong support for the view that life does not begin until live birth. This was the belief of the Stoics. It appears to be the predominant, though not the unanimous, attitude of the Jewish faith. It may be taken to represent also the position of a large segment of the Protestant community, insofar as that can be ascertained; organized groups that have taken a formal position on the abortion issue have generally regarded abortion as a matter for the conscience of the individual and her family. As we have noted, the common law found greater significance in quickening. Physicians and their scientific colleagues have regarded that event with less interest and have tended to focus either upon conception, upon live birth, or upon the interim point at which the fetus becomes "viable," that is, potentially able to live outside the mother's womb, albeit with artificial aid. Viability is usually placed at about seven months (28 weeks) but may occur earlier, even at 24 weeks. The Aristotelian theory of "mediate animation," that held sway throughout the Middle Ages and the Renaissance in Europe, continued to be official Roman Catholic dogma until the 19th century, despite opposition to this "ensoulment" theory from those in the Church who would recognize the existence of life from the moment of conception. The latter is now, of course, the official belief of the Catholic Church. As one of the briefs amicus discloses, this is a view strongly held by many non-Catholics as well, and by many physicians. Substantial problems for precise definition of this view are posed, however, by new embryological data that purport to indicate that conception is a "process" over time, rather than an event, and by new medical techniques such as menstrual extraction, the "morning-after" pill, implantation of embryos, artificial insemination, and even artificial wombs.

In areas other than criminal abortion, the law has been reluctant to endorse any theory that life, as we recognize it, begins before live birth or to accord legal rights to the unborn except in narrowly defined situations and except when the rights are contingent upon live birth. For example, the traditional rule of tort law had denied recovery for prenatal injuries even though the child was born alive. That rule has been changed in almost every jurisdiction. In most States, recovery is said to be permitted only if the fetus was viable, or at least quick, when the injuries were sustained, though few courts have squarely so held. . . .

In view of all this, we do not agree that, by adopting one theory of life, Texas may override the rights of the pregnant woman that are at stake. We repeat, however, that the State does have an important and legitimate interest in preserving and protecting the health of the pregnant woman, whether she be a resident of the State or a nonresident who seeks medical consultation and treatment there, and that it has still *another* important and legitimate interest in protecting the potentiality of human life. These interests are separate and distinct. Each grows in substantiality as the woman approaches term and, at a point during pregnancy, each becomes "compelling."

With respect to the State's important and legitimate interest in the health of the mother, the "compelling" point, in the light of present medical knowledge, is at approximately the end of the first trimester. This is so because of the now established medical fact that until the end of the first trimester mortality in abortion may be less than mortality in normal childbirth. It follows that, from and after this point, a State may regulate the abortion procedure to the extent that the regulation reasonably relates to the preservation and protection of maternal health. Examples of permissible State regulation in this area are requirements as to the qualifications of the person who is to perform the abortion; as to the licensure of that person, as to the facility in which the procedure is to be performed, that is, whether it must be a hospital or may be a clinic or some other place of less-than-hospital status; as to the licensing of the facility, and the like.

This means, on the other hand, that, for the period of pregnancy prior to this

"compelling" point, the attending physician, in consultation with his patient, is free to determine, without regulation by the State, that, in his medical judgment the patient's pregnancy should be terminated. If that decision is reached, the judgment may be effectuated by an abortion free of interference by the State.

With respect to the State's important and legitimate interest in potential life, the "compelling" point is at viability. This is so because the fetus then presumably has the capability of meaningful life outside the mother's womb. State regulation protective of fetal life after viability thus has both logical and biological justifications. If the State is interested in protecting fetal life after viability, it may go so far as to proscribe abortion during that period, except when it is necessary to preserve the life or health of the mother.

Measured against these standards, Art. 1196 of the Texas Penal Code, in restricting legal abortions to those "procured or attempted by medical advice for the purpose of saving the life of the mother," sweeps too broadly. The statute makes no distinction between abortions performed early in pregnancy and those performed later, and it limits to a single reason, "saving" the mother's life, the legal justification for the procedure. The statute, therefore, cannot survive the constitutional attack made upon it here. . . .

To summarize and to repeat:

1. A State criminal abortion statute of the current Texas type, that excepts from criminality only a *life-saving* procedure on behalf of the mother, without regard to pregnancy stage and without recognition of the other interests involved, is violative of the Due Process Clause of the Fourteenth Amendment.

    a. For the stage prior to approximately the end of the first trimester, the abortion decision and its effectuation must be left to the medical judgment of the pregnant woman's attending physician.

    b. For the stage subsequent to approximately the end of the first trimester, the State, in promoting its interest in the health of the mother, may, if it chooses, regulate the abortion procedure in ways that are reasonably related to maternal health.

  c. For the stage subsequent to viability, the State, in promoting its interest in the potentiality of human life may, if it chooses, regulate, and even proscribe, abortion except where it is necessary, in appropriate medical judgment, for the preservation of the life or health of the mother.

2. The State may define the term "physician," as it has been employed in the preceding numbered paragraphs . . . of this opinion, to mean only a physician currently licensed by the State, and may proscribe any abortion by a person who is not a physician as so defined.

In *Doe v. Bolton*, procedural requirements contained in one of the modern abortion statutes are considered. That opinion and this one, of course, are to be read together.

This holding, we feel, is consistent with the relative weights of the respective interests involved, with the lessons and example of medical and legal history, with the lenity of the common law, and with the demands of the profound problems of the present day. The decision leaves the State free to place increasing restrictions on abortion as the period of pregnancy lengthens, so long as those restrictions are tailored to the recognized State interests. The decision vindicates the right of the physician to administer medical treatment according to his professional judgment up to the points where important State interests provide compelling justifications for intervention. Up to those points, the abortion decision in all its aspects is inherently, and primarily, a medical decision, and basic responsibility for it must rest with the physician. If an individual practitioner abuses the privilege of exercising proper medical judgment, the usual remedies, judicial and intraprofessional, are available. . . .

STUDY QUESTIONS

1. What provision of the Constitution did the Court apply to evaluate the Texas statute? Why? Would another provision be stronger?
2. What reasons did the Court give for asserting that, at least initially, the decision is that of the woman and her physician? To what extent does the Court's decision reflect the fact that women bear the burdens of pregnancy and child rearing?
3. At what points in pregnancy may a State restrict access to abortions, according to the *Roe* Court? What reasons did the Court give for permitting that intervention? Must a State intervene at those points?
4. How did the Court deal with Texas's claims that a fetus is a person protected by the Fourteenth Amendment? Do you find this resolution satisfactory?

After a detailed review of historical and current attitudes toward abortion (much of which is omitted from the version of the case reprinted here), the Court in *Roe* determined that carrying a pregnancy to term so fundamentally affects a woman that her decision, made in consultation with her physician, to terminate her pregnancy is protected by the right of privacy recognized in *Griswold*. For this reason, her decision must be free from governmental intrusion except where a compelling State interest is at stake. The Court went on to identify two such interests and to specify the points at which they become compelling. The Court, however, rejected the State's claim that the fetus is a person within the meaning of the Fourteenth Amendment and that the State has a compelling interest in protecting it by forbidding all abortions.

The decision in *Roe* established that, at least during the first twelve weeks of pregnancy, the State may not prohibit or otherwise regulate abortions so long as they are performed by licensed physicians. *Roe* does, however, permit a State to regulate abortions during the next twelve weeks, but only for the purpose of protecting the health of the woman. After the point when the fetus becomes viable, which the Court defined as the point at which the fetus is capable of meaningful life outside the womb, the State has greater leeway in imposing restrictions. After this point, which the Court placed at the beginning of the third trimester, a State may restrict abortions either to promote the woman's health or to protect the potential life that the fetus represents. Nevertheless, even in this third trimester, the State must permit abortions that are necessary to protect the woman's life or health.

Heated controversy greeted the Court's decision in *Roe*. A number of critics claimed that, rather than applying a previously recognized right, the Court drafted the equivalent of a new constitutional provision. Like Justice Rehnquist dissenting in *Roe* and Justice Black dissenting in *Griswold*, some critics argued that it is wrong for courts to overrule legislative decisions when they can identify no specific provision in the Constitution that guides them in doing so. In the words of John Hart Ely:

> What is so frightening about *Roe* is that this super-protected right [abortion] is not inferable from the language of the Constitution, the Framers' thinking respecting the specific problem in issue, any general value derivable from the provisions they included, or the nation's governmental structure. Nor is it explainable in terms of the usual political importance of the group judicially protected vis-a-vis the interest that legislatively prevailed over it. And that . . . is a charge that can responsibly be leveled at no other decision of the [previous] twenty years.
> *"The Wages of Crying Wolf: A Comment on* Roe v. Wade*." 82 Yale Law Journal 920, 935–36 (1973).*

A number of responses have been made to this criticism. Constitutional scholars have argued that courts, like legislatures, inevitably make value judgments and that it is proper for them to do so. Others, contrary to Ely, have suggested that the Court needed to act in order to correct defects in the political process. For example, in an article published shortly after the decision, Laurence Tribe took the position that judgments concerning abortion are inherently religious and that they therefore should not be made by legislatures. He thus viewed the Court's action as a way of eliminating excessive government entanglement with religion. Kenneth Karst, echoing feminist concerns expressed in the litigation campaign against abortion laws, saw the Court's action as necessary to ensure that women are treated as full and equal citizens.

Several feminist legal scholars have sought to ground the abortion right in the equality principle. Arguing that *Roe v. Wade's* approach obscures the connection between reproductive autonomy and gender equality, Sylvia Law, for example, has written:

> The rhetoric of privacy, as opposed to equality, blunts our ability to focus on the fact that it is *women* who are oppressed when abortion is denied. A privacy right that demands that "the abortion decision . . . be left to the medical judgment of the pregnant woman's attending physician," gives doctors undue power by falsely casting the abortion decision as primarily a medical question.
> *"Rethinking Sex and the Constitution." 132 University of Pennsylvania Law Review 995, 1020 (1984).*

Feminist legal scholars and advocates have also attempted to show that the right to choose abortion is rooted in values well respected in our legal tradition. Focusing on the physical intrusiveness and sheer work of pregnancy, they have argued that the abortion right is essential to the right to bodily integrity safeguarded by the common law and the right to be free of involuntary servitude guaranteed by the Thirteenth Amendment. They have also argued that denying a woman the right to terminate her pregnancy violates equal protection guarantees. Proponents of these equality arguments point both to pregnancy's effect on women's bodily integrity and the limitations childbearing imposes on women's ability to choose their place in society. Thus, they point to both sex-based physical factors that will not change (at least in the foreseeable future) and the theoretically changeable social role that women play as mothers.

Although many people agree that procreative choice and gender equality are closely linked, the argument that denying women reproductive control violates their rights to equal protection is not one that the U.S. Supreme Court is likely to accept in the near future. As we saw in Chapter 2, the Court held in its 1974 decision in *Geduldig v. Aiello* that when women are treated differently because of their unique reproductive functions, they are not being discriminated against on the basis of sex. Like the pregnancy classification at issue in *Geduldig*, the laws that restrict access to abortion are classifications having to do with women's unique reproductive functions and are not, under the *Geduldig* reasoning, denials of equal protection. Moreover, as we shall see, in 1992, three key Supreme Court justices declined to reverse *Roe v. Wade* in large part because they believed so strongly in sustaining earlier decisions and principles. In all probability, then, to the extent that the Court continues to protect the right to choose, it will do so using the liberty and privacy analysis announced in *Griswold*, *Carey*, and *Roe*.

Although opinion polls continued to show that a sizable majority of people in the United States supported legalized abortion, the *Roe* decision prompted considerable political opposition. Initially expressed through restrictive legislation at the State level, this opposition ultimately led to several federal attempts to overrule *Roe v. Wade* through statutes and constitutional amendments. Following its 1973 action, the Supreme Court applied the *Roe* decision to strike down a number of State provisions that impinged on the abortion choice. Among the key decisions were *Planned Parenthood of Central Missouri v. Danforth*, 428 U.S. 52 (1976); *Akron v. Akron Center for Reproductive Rights*, 462 U.S. 416 (1983); and *Thornburgh v. American College of Obstetricians & Gynecologists*, 476 U.S. 747 (1986), which invalidated, among other things, so-called informed consent requirements, mandatory counseling and waiting periods, and spousal consent requirements. Thus, in the *Danforth* case, for example, the Supreme Court struck down State provisions requiring special efforts to save the fetus at any age, notification of parents and spouses, and limitations on the use of saline abortions. Similarly, its 1983 *Akron I* decision invalidated "informed consent" and waiting period requirements, parental consent requirements, and limitations on second- and third-trimester procedures. So, too, in its 1986 *Thornburgh* decision, the Court struck down informed consent and reporting requirements, as well as second physician requirements in certain cases.

Denial of public funding for abortion is a problem that dates back to the late 1970s. Passed by Congress in 1976, the Hyde Amendment excludes abortion from the health care services provided to low-income people through Medicaid. The ban on federal funding has been renewed by Congress every year by amendment to the appropriations bill. The exceptions to the ban have varied over the years. The federal Medicaid law passed in 1997 allows funding only in cases of rape, incest, and physical endangerment of the woman's life.

On the State level, only fifteen States now provide funding for abortion needs comparable to those provided for pregnancy-related needs. Only three of these States pay on a voluntary basis; the other twelve States pay under court order. Although, as we have seen, State constitutional challenges have succeeded in some States, they have been denied in at least four others. All States, however, must provide funding for the exceptions requiring funding in the federal law.

A law Congress passed in 1997 imposed greater burdens on at least some of the States that still include abortion funding in their Medicaid program. For those States that provide medical services through a managed care program, the State must make a separate, additional contract with the managed care providers.

Hyde Amendment–type restrictions have also been included in federal health care and insurance programs—those for Native American women, federal employees and their dependents, Peace Corps volunteers, federal prisoners, military personnel and their dependents, and low-income residents of the District of Columbia. These restrictions have also been added to the Children's Health Insurance Program, which expands health insurance coverage to children nineteen and younger as part of the 1997 Balanced Budget Act and bars abortion with only the same narrow exceptions as are found in the Hyde Amendment.

Starting in 1989, however, the Court did begin to signal that *Roe* was in trouble. In that year, the Court upheld a number of provisions that seemed vulnerable, and a plurality of the Court suggested an interest in reversing *Roe*. Thus, *Webster v. Reproductive Health Services*, 492 U.S. 490 (1989), let stand Missouri's statutory preamble containing its value judgment favoring childbirth over abortion, a bar on public employees and facilities participating in abortion procedures, and a requirement that specified viability tests be performed starting at twenty weeks. Although it found that the case did not afford it the occasion to revisit the precise holding in *Roe*, the Court did modify and narrow *Roe* in succeeding cases.

A year later, in *Hodgson v. Minnesota*, 497 U.S. 417 (1990), and *Ohio v. Akron Center for Reproductive Health*, 497 U.S. 502 (1990), the Court upheld two-parent notification provisions that allowed a minor to avoid the notification requirements by showing a court that she is mature or that an abortion is in her best interest. In finding that such a parental notification requirement "does not impose an undue, or otherwise unconstitutional, burden on a minor seeking an abortion," the Court indicated it was "both rational and fair for the State to conclude that, in most instances, the family will strive to give a lonely or even terrified minor advice that is both compassionate and mature." The Court thus disregarded both situations where this is not so and the difficulty such legislation would pose for many teenagers seeking abortions.

Finally, in *Rust v. Sullivan*, 500 U.S. 173, 111 S. Ct. 1759 (1991), the Supreme Court upheld regulations prohibiting doctors employed by recipients of Title X family planning funds from even mentioning abortion in the context of assisting pregnant (or non-pregnant) teenagers against both due process and First Amendment challenges. The Court demonstrated its hostility to abortion by applying its earlier decisions denying funding to the speech context. The regulations upheld make this clear:

> The regulations attach three principal conditions on the grant of federal funds for Title X projects. First, the regulations specify that a "Title X project may not provide counseling concerning the use of abortion as a method of family planning or provide referral for abortion as a method of family planning." . . .
> Second, the regulations broadly prohibit a Title X project from engaging in activities that "encourage, promote or advocate abortion as a method of family planning." . . .
> Third, the regulations require that Title X projects be organized so that they are "physically and financially separate" from prohibited abortion activities. . . .
> Id. *at* 1765–66.

Shortly after his inauguration, President Bill Clinton took action to rescind the "gag rule" challenged in *Rust v. Sullivan*. Finding it violative of the underlying statute, he instructed the new Secretary of the Department of Health and Human Services to issue new regulations governing the discussion and performance of abortions by providers receiving Title X monies, which were later enacted into law.

Particularly, given the extreme nature of the *Rust* holding, many doubted that *Roe* would survive when a Court containing a majority of Reagan and Bush appointees was asked once again to consider the abortion question. Nevertheless, it did survive challenge the following year—although in a more limited form. The decision in *Planned Parenthood of Southeastern Pennsylvania v. Casey* declined both to overrule the basic holding of *Roe* and to strike abortion restrictions previously stricken. In an unusual anonymous opinion, Justices O'Connor, Kennedy, and Souter explained their reasons for upholding *Roe* as well as all the restrictions except those requiring spousal notification. Chief Justice Rehnquist and Justices White, Scalia, and Thomas concurred in the judgment in part and dissented in part. Justices Blackmun and Stevens also filed separate opinions, indicating that they would uphold *Roe* but not the statute. The three-judge plurality is excerpted here. In reading it, consider what right is given constitutional protection, when it is protected by the Constitution, what justification the State must give for interfering with the right, and whose right it is. Consider also the ways the answers to these questions may have changed since the *Roe* decision was first issued.

PLANNED PARENTHOOD OF SOUTHEASTERN PENNSYLVANIA V. CASEY

U.S. Supreme Court, 1992.
505 U.S. 833, 112 S. Ct. 2791, 120 L.Ed.2d 674.

Justice O'CONNOR, Justice KENNEDY, and Justice SOUTER announced the judgment of the Court.

I

Liberty finds no refuge in a jurisprudence of doubt. Yet 19 years after our holding that the Constitution protects a woman's right to terminate her pregnancy in its early stages, *Roe v. Wade*, that definition of liberty is still questioned. Joining the respondents as amicus curiae, the United States, as it has done in five other cases in the last decade, again asks us to overrule *Roe*.

At issue in these cases are five provisions of the Pennsylvania Abortion Control Act of 1982 as amended in 1988 and 1989. . . . The Act requires that a woman seeking an abortion give her informed consent prior to the abortion procedure, and specifies that she be provided with certain information at least 24 hours before the abortion is performed. For a minor to obtain an abortion, the Act requires the informed consent of one of her parents, but provides for a judicial by-pass option if the minor does not wish to or cannot obtain a parent's consent. Another provision of the Act requires that, unless certain exceptions apply, a married woman

seeking an abortion must sign a statement indicating that she has notified her husband of her intended abortion. The Act exempts compliance with these three requirements in the event of a "medical emergency." . . . In addition to the above provisions regulating the performance of abortions, the Act imposes certain reporting requirements on facilities that provide abortion services.

Before any of these provisions took effect, the petitioners, who are five abortion clinics and one physician representing himself as well as a class of physicians who provide abortion services, brought this suit seeking declaratory and injunctive relief. . . . The District Court. . . . held all the provisions at issue here unconstitutional, entering a permanent injunction against Pennsylvania's enforcement of them. The Court of Appeals for the Third Circuit affirmed in part and reversed in part, upholding all of the regulations except for the husband notification requirement. . . .

After considering the fundamental constitutional questions resolved by *Roe*, principles of institutional integrity, and the rule of stare decisis, we are led to conclude this: the essential holding of *Roe v. Wade* should be retained and once again reaffirmed.

It must be stated at the outset and with clarity that *Roe's* essential holding, the holding we reaffirm, has three parts. First is a recognition of the right of the woman to choose to have an abortion before viability and to obtain it without undue interference from the State. Before viability, the State's interests are not strong enough to support a prohibition of abortion or the imposition of a substantial obstacle to the woman's effective right to elect the procedure. Second is a confirmation of the State's power to restrict abortions after fetal viability, if the law contains exceptions for pregnancies which endanger a woman's life or health. And third is the principle that the State has legitimate interests from the outset of the pregnancy in protecting the health of the woman and the life of the fetus that may become a child. These principles do not contradict one another, and we adhere to each.

II

. . . Men and women of good conscience can disagree, and we suppose some always shall disagree, about the profound moral and spiritual implications of terminating a pregnancy, even in its earliest stage. Some of us as individuals find abortion offensive to our most basic principles of morality, but that cannot control our decision. Our obligation is to define the liberty of all, not to mandate our own moral code. The underlying constitutional issue is whether the State can resolve these philosophic questions in such a definitive way that a woman lacks all choice in the matter, except perhaps in those rare circumstances in which the pregnancy is itself a danger to her own life or health, or is the result of rape or incest.

It is conventional constitutional doctrine that where reasonable people disagree the government can adopt one position or the other. That theorem, however, assumes a State of affairs in which the choice does not intrude upon a protected liberty. Thus, while some people might disagree about whether or not the flag should be saluted, or disagree about the proposition that it may not be defiled, we have ruled that a State may not compel or enforce one view or the other.

Our law affords constitutional protection to personal decisions relating to marriage, procreation, contraception, family relationships, child rearing, and education. Our cases recognize "the right of the individual, married or single, to be free from unwarranted governmental intrusion into matters so fundamentally affecting a person as the decision whether to bear or beget a child." Our precedents "have respected the private realm of family life which the State cannot enter." These matters, involving the most intimate and personal choices a person may make in a lifetime, choices central to personal dignity and autonomy, are central to the liberty protected by the Fourteenth Amendment. At the heart of liberty is the right to define one's own concept of existence, of meaning, of the universe, and of the mystery of human life. Beliefs about these matters could not define the attributes of personhood were they formed under compulsion of the State.

These considerations begin our analysis of the woman's interest in terminating her pregnancy but cannot end it, for this reason: though the abortion decision may originate within the zone of conscience and belief, it is more than a philosophic exercise. Abortion is a unique act. It is an act fraught with consequences for others: for the woman who must live with the implications of her decision, for the persons who perform and assist in the procedure; for the spouse, family, and society which must confront the knowledge that these procedures exist, procedures some deem nothing short of an act of violence against innocent human life; and, depending on one's beliefs, for the life or potential life that is aborted. Though abortion is conduct, it does not follow that the State is entitled to proscribe it in all instances. That is because the liberty of the woman is at stake in a sense unique to the human condition and so unique to the law. The mother who carries a child to full term is subject to anxieties, to physical constraints, to pain that only she must bear.

That these sacrifices have from the beginning of the human race been endured by woman with a pride that ennobles her in the eyes of others and gives to the infant a bond of love cannot alone be grounds for the State to insist she make the sacrifice. Her suffering is too intimate and personal for the State to insist, without more, upon its own vision of the woman's role, however dominant that vision has been in the course of our history and our culture. The destiny of the woman must be shaped to a large extent on her own conception of her spiritual imperatives and her place in society.

It should be recognized, moreover, that in some critical respects the abortion decision is of the same character as the decision to use contraception, to which *Griswold, Eisenstadt* and *Carey* afford constitutional protection. We have no doubt as to the correctness of those decisions. . . . *Roe* was, of course, an extension of those cases and, as the decision itself indicated, the separate States could act in some degree to further their own legitimate interests in protecting pre-natal life.

III

. . . We have seen how time has overtaken some of *Roe's* factual assumptions: advances in maternal health care allow for abortions safe to the mother later in pregnancy than was true in 1973 and advances in neonatal care have advanced viability to a point somewhat earlier. But these facts go only to the scheme of time limits on the realization of competing interests, and the divergences from the factual premises of 1973 have no bearing on the validity of *Roe's* central holding . . ., that viability marks the earliest point at which the State's interest in fetal life is constitutionally adequate to justify a legislative ban on nontherapeutic abortions. The soundness or unsoundness of that constitutional judgment in no sense turns on whether viability occurs at approximately 28 weeks, as was usual at the time of *Roe*, at 23 to 24 weeks, as it sometimes does today, or at some moment even slightly earlier in pregnancy, as it may if fetal respiratory capacity can somehow be enhanced in the future. Whenever it may occur, the attainment of viability may continue to serve as the critical fact, just as it has done since *Roe* was decided; which is to say that no change in *Roe's* factual underpinning has left its central holding obsolete, and none supports an argument for over-ruling it.

The sum of the precedential inquiry to this point shows *Roe's* underpinnings unweakened in any way affecting its central holding. While it has engendered disapproval, it has not been unworkable. An entire generation has come of age free to assume *Roe's* concept of liberty in defining the capacity of women to act in society, and to make reproductive decisions; no erosion of principle going to liberty or personal autonomy has left *Roe's* central holding a doctrinal remnant; *Roe* portends no developments at odds with other precedent for the analysis of personal liberty; and no changes of fact have rendered viability more or less appropriate as the point at which the balance of interests tips. Within the bounds of normal stare decisis analysis, then, and subject to the considerations on which it customarily turns, the stronger argument is for affirming *Roe's* central holding, with whatever degree of personal reluctance any of us may have, not for overruling it. . . .

IV

From what we have said so far it follows that it is a constitutional liberty of the woman to have some freedom to terminate her pregnancy. We conclude that the basic decision in *Roe* was based on a constitutional analysis which we cannot now repudiate. The woman's liberty is not so unlimited, however, that from the outset the State cannot show its concern for the life of the unborn, and at a later point in fetal development the State's interest in life has sufficient force so that the right of the woman to terminate the pregnancy can be restricted. . . .

Some guiding principles should emerge. What is at stake is the woman's right to make the ultimate decision, not a right to be insulated from all others in doing so.

Regulations which do no more than create a structural mechanism by which the State, or the parent or guardian of a minor, may express profound respect for the life of the unborn are permitted, if they are not a substantial obstacle to the woman's exercise of the right to choose. Unless it has that effect on her right of choice, a State measure designed to persuade her to choose childbirth over abortion will be upheld if reasonably related to that goal. Regulations designed to foster the health of a woman seeking an abortion are valid if they do not constitute an undue burden.

. . . We give this summary:

a.   To protect the central right recognized by *Roe v. Wade* while at the same time accommodating the State's profound interest in potential life, we will employ the undue burden analysis as explained in this opinion. An undue burden exists, and therefore a provision of law is invalid, if its purpose or effect is to place a substantial obstacle in the path of a woman seeking an abortion before the fetus attains viability.

b.   We reject the rigid trimester framework of *Roe v. Wade*. To promote the State's profound interest in potential life, throughout pregnancy the State may take measures to ensure that the woman's choice is informed, and measures designed to advance this interest will not be invalidated as long as their purpose is to persuade the woman to choose childbirth over abortion. These measures must not be an undue burden on the right.

c.   As with any medical procedure, the State may enact regulations to further the health or safety of a woman seeking an abortion. Unnecessary health regulations that have the purpose or effect of presenting a substantial obstacle to a woman seeking an abortion impose an undue burden on the right.

d.   Our adoption of the undue burden analysis does not disturb the central holding of *Roe v. Wade*, and we reaffirm that holding. Regardless of whether exceptions are made for particular circumstances, a State may not prohibit any woman from making the ultimate decision to terminate her pregnancy before viability.

e.   We also reaffirm *Roe's* holding that "subsequent to viability, the State in promoting its interest in the potentiality of human life may, if it chooses, regulate, and even proscribe, abortion except where it is necessary, in appropriate medical judgment, for the preservation of the life or health of the mother."

These principles control our assessment of the Pennsylvania statute, and we now turn to the issue of the validity of its challenged provisions.

V

. . . We now consider the separate statutory sections at issue.

[The three justices first determined that] the statute's definition of medical emergency [complied with *Roe's* bar on] interfering with a woman's choice to undergo an abortion procedure if continuing her pregnancy would constitute a threat to her health. . . .

We next consider the informed consent requirement. . . . [There, they concluded that] requiring that the woman be informed of the availability of information relating to fetal development and the assistance available should she decide to carry the pregnancy to full term is a reasonable measure to [e]nsure an informed choice, one which might cause the woman to choose childbirth over abortion. This requirement cannot be considered a substantial obstacle to obtaining an abortion, and, it follows, there is no undue burden. . . .

. . . The idea that important decisions will be more informed and deliberate if they follow some period of reflection does not strike us as unreasonable, particularly where the statute directs that important information become part of the background of the decision. . . . [A]s the District Court held, the waiting period has the effect of "increasing the cost and risk of delay of abortions," but the District Court did not conclude that the increased costs and potential delays amount to substantial obstacles. . . . Yet, as we have stated, under the undue burden standard a State is permitted to enact persuasive measures which favor childbirth over abortion, even if those measures do not further a health interest. And while the waiting period does limit a physician's discretion, that is not, standing alone, a reason to invalidate it. In light of the construction given the statute's definition of medical emergency by the Court of Appeals, and the District Court's findings, we cannot say that the waiting period imposes a real health risk. . . .

[Addressing the spousal notification provision, the Court observed that social science studies] and the District Court's findings reinforce what common sense would suggest. In well-functioning marriages, spouses discuss important intimate decisions such as whether to bear a child. But there are millions of women in this country who are the victims of regular physical and psychological abuse at the hands of their husbands. Should these women become pregnant, they may have very good reasons for not wishing to inform their husbands of their decision to obtain an abortion. Many may have justifiable fears of physical abuse, but may be no less fearful of the consequences of reporting prior abuse to the Commonwealth of Pennsylvania. Many may have a reasonable fear that notifying their husbands will provoke further instances of . . . abuse; these women are not exempt from [the] notification requirement. Many may fear devastating forms of psychological abuse from their husbands, including verbal harassment, threats of future violence, the destruction of possessions; physical confinement to the home, the withdrawal of financial support, or the disclosure of the abortion to family and friends. These methods of psychological abuse may act as even more of a deterrent to notification than the possibility of physical violence, but women who are the victims of the abuse are not exempt from [the] notification requirement. And many women who are pregnant as a result of sexual assaults by their husbands will be unable to avail

themselves of the exception for spousal sexual assault, because the exception requires that the woman have notified law enforcement authorities within 90 days of the assault, and her husband will be notified of her report once an investigation begins. If anything in this field is certain, it is that victims of spousal sexual assault are extremely reluctant to report the abuse to the government; hence, a great many spousal rape victims will not be exempt. . . .

. . . The unfortunate yet persisting conditions we document above will mean that in a large fraction of the cases in which [this provision] is relevant, it will operate as a substantial obstacle to a woman's choice to undergo an abortion. It is an undue burden, and therefore invalid. . . .

We next consider the parental consent provision. . . . Our cases establish, and we reaffirm today, that a State may require a minor seeking an abortion to obtain the consent of a parent or guardian, provided that there is an adequate judicial bypass procedure. Under these precedents, in our view, the one-parent consent requirement and judicial bypass procedure are constitutional. . . .

[Finally, the Court turned to] the recordkeeping and reporting requirements of the statute. . . . In *Danforth*, we held that recordkeeping and reporting provisions "that are reasonably directed to the preservation of maternal health and that properly respect a patient's confidentiality and privacy are permissible." We think that under this standard, all the provisions at issue here except that relating to spousal notice are constitutional. . . .

VI

Our Constitution is a covenant running from the first generation of Americans to us and then to future generations. It is a coherent succession. Each generation must learn anew that the Constitution's written terms embody ideas and aspirations that must survive more ages than one. We accept our responsibility not to retreat from interpreting the full meaning of the covenant in light of all of our

precedents. We invoke it once again to define the freedom guaranteed by the Constitution's own promise, the promise of liberty.

The Judgment Is Affirmed.

STUDY QUESTIONS

1. What interests did the plurality see at
play in abortion cases? Whose rights
are involved? To what extent do they

reflect equality as well as liberty concerns? To what extent does the Constitution protect them?
2. What is "the central holding of *Roe*"?
What aspects of the *Roe* decision are
rejected here? In what ways is the standard announced here different from the
one announced in *Roe*?
3. At what point does a regulatory measure become an "undue burden"?

In upholding *Roe v. Wade*, the joint opinion recognizes a right grounded in the liberty
aspect of the Due Process Clause, which includes bodily integrity and privacy interests,
to choose whether to continue her pregnancy. Requirements designed to further the woman's
health, such as informed consent provisions, are not necessarily inconsistent with this
right. Moreover, the decision as to what value to give the fetus must be an individual one.
The State cannot preclude all abortions in the name of protecting "unborn persons." The
authors of the joint opinion do make clear, however, that in their view, the State has an
interest in potential life from the moment of conception. At the point of viability, this
interest becomes strong enough to bar abortions that are not needed to protect the life and
health of the woman. But even before this point, the State may act to further its interest in
potential life. Thus, for example, a State may adopt provisions that seek to make sure the
woman considers the value of the potential life she is carrying.

Only when the stated regulations or restrictions place an "undue burden" on or pose
"substantial obstacles" for the woman would the three justices hold them unconstitutional.
Furthermore, as is evident from their opinion, findings as to impermissible burdens and obstacles must be very specific and fact based. In the course of discussing the provisions of the
Pennsylvania law in Section V of the decision, the three justices gave some indication of
what the Court means by "undue burden" and "substantial obstacles." Thus, the "informed
consent" provision that required giving particular information to the woman was upheld
because it was seen as enhancing, not interfering with, her decision. The spousal notification provision, however, was invalidated because it was seen as interfering with the rights
of women who feared physical or psychological abuse.

The period from 1993 to 1994 saw both the release of data revealing an enormous
drop in the abortion rate and three significant actions on the federal legal front helping
women seeking access to the procedure. The data, collected by the Alan Guttmacher
Institute, showed that in 1992, both the percentages of pregnancies ending in abortion
and the number of women between the ages of fifteen and forty-four obtaining abortions
were at their lowest levels since 1976. Explanations for the drop include the greater social acceptability of single motherhood, the higher proportion of women in their reproductive years who are less fertile, the wider and more effective use of contraceptives, and
increased difficulties in obtaining access to abortion facilities. The study also noted that
nationally, the number of facilities that perform abortions dropped 18 percent between
1982 and 1992.

Between 1994 and 1995, action concerning abortion rights took place on the State
and local, and national and international levels, reflecting judicial, legislative, and
diplomatic efforts. Despite a number of attempts to follow up on the suggestion in *Casey* that

unconstitutional burdens on the abortion right could be shown factually, essentially no court has so found. A series of cases have held that the failure of various States to provide Medicaid funding for abortions in cases of rape or incest violates the federal Medicaid law. Several federal courts entered decisions—and the Supreme Court has declined review—upholding the 1994 Freedom of Access to Clinic Entrances (FACE) statute, a law, imposing serious criminal and civil penalties on those who interfere with access to health clinics.

The developments on the legal front involve efforts to limit obstacles to abortion services. Early in 1994, the U.S. Supreme Court held that the National Organization for Women could proceed with its suit against a coalition of anti-abortion groups (the Pro-Live Action Network) and various individuals, alleging that they were members of a nationwide conspiracy to shut down abortion clinics through a pattern of racketeering activity including extortion. In *National Organization for Women, Inc. v. Scheidler*, 510 U.S. 249 (1994), a unanimous court held that such litigation is proper under the Racketeering Influenced and Corrupt Organization (RICO) chapter of the Organized Crime Control Act of 1970 even if the alleged racketeers did not act from an economic motive. In so ruling, the Court essentially allowed the National Organization of Women (NOW) to use the RICO statute to litigate claims similar to those rejected when brought as Section 1985 claims in *Bray v. Alexandria Women's Health Clinic*, 506 U.S. 263 (1993).

In its June 1994 decision, *Madsen v. Women's Health Center, Inc.*, 512 U.S. 753, the Supreme Court ruled that certain restrictions on anti-abortion demonstrations are constitutional. The case concerned a 1988 injunction entered by a Florida judge that, among other things, established buffer zones and noise restraints around a clinic and staff residences that had long been targets for demonstrators. The opinion, written by Chief Justice Rehnquist, upheld the 36-foot buffer zone around the clinic entrances and driveway as well as the noise restrictions on demonstrators outside the clinic. However, it struck down a 36-foot buffer zone around non-accessible areas of the clinic, a 300-foot no-approach zone intended to prevent demonstrators from coming in contact with patients and others without their consent, prohibitions on the display of "images observable to" patients inside the clinic, and 300-foot buffer zones around staff residences. The opinion made clear that the restraints upheld were necessitated by "clear abuse," and suggested that others might survive First Amendment challenge if more narrowly drawn. In Justice Rehnquist's words, "protecting a pregnant woman's freedom to seek lawful medical or counseling services, ensuring public safety and order, promoting free flow of traffic on public streets and sidewalks, protecting citizens' property rights and assuring residential privacy [are] quite sufficient to justify an appropriately tailored injunction." State courts have continued to enter stiff orders restricting picketing at clinics and residences. See, for example, *Murray v. Lawson*, 649 A.2d 1253 (N.J. 1994).

Congress also sought to address the problem of barriers to access by enacting, in May 1994, the FACE act. FACE imposes stiff civil and criminal penalties on persons who obstruct access to health clinics that provide reproductive services. The civil penalties range from $5,000 to $25,000, while the criminal penalties range from $100,000 to $250,000 plus imprisonment. Abortion foes have initiated lawsuits throughout the country in an effort to have FACE invalidated. The two district judges to rule so far, however, failed to credit their First Amendment claims.

It is fairly clear that the Supreme Court will ultimately decide the permissible range of FACE and other efforts to eliminate barriers to women's exercise of their right to procreative choice. Whether it will do so in a way that is satisfactory to feminists and others who wish to promote both reproductive freedom and free expression remains to be seen.

As we have seen, *Casey* changed the test to be used in evaluating restrictions on abortion from the "strict scrutiny" test used in cases involving fundamental rights to an "undue burden" test. In the years since that decision, both State and federal courts have grappled with the meaning of that test. Pro-choice advocates have, at times, succeeded in having restrictions invalidated using this new test. See, for example, *Women's Medical Professional Corporation v. Voinovich*, 911 F. Supp. 1051 (S.D. Ohio 1996) in which a criminal ban on the use of the D & X procedure and many late abortions was permanently enjoined, and *Janklow v. Planned Parenthood*, 63 F.2d 1452 (1995), cert. denied 116 S. Ct. 1582 (1996), in which the U.S. Supreme Court refused to disturb a lower federal court ruling that invalidated South Dakota's law requiring minors to notify one parent forty-eight hours in advance of seeking an abortion. These are, of course, extreme restrictions. Invalidation of others may be extremely difficult under *Casey*.

Apart from litigation under the *Casey* standard, pro-choice advocates have succeeded in obtaining limited funding for abortions for the medically indigent. Thus, a number of decisions have required States to comply with the Hyde Amendment's provision of Medicaid funding for abortions in cases of rape and incest as well as when the woman's life is in danger. See, for example, *Little Rock Family Planning Services v. Dallon*, 516 U.S. 474 (1996), in which the Supreme Court directed a Court of Appeals to enter an order enjoining Arkansas to comply with the reach of the Hyde Amendment.

One of the major reproductive debates of recent years involves legislation that bans a particular late-term abortion procedure known as dilation and extraction (D & X), also referred to by some as "partial birth abortion." Pro-choice advocates believe that banning a specific medical procedure is the first step toward banning all abortion procedures. Anti-abortion advocates have focused on this procedure because it can involve a viable fetus. It is not a commonly used procedure, and is usually used where the life and health of the mother is compromised from the pregnancy or in cases of severe birth defects that are discovered late term.

Congress twice passed legislation banning so-called partial birth abortions. Both times, the legislation was vetoed by President Clinton and Congress had insufficient support for a veto override. There have been several State statutes that have been enacted in recent years attempting to ban this particular procedure. In 2000, one such statute from the State of Nebraska reached the U.S. Supreme Court for review. In *Stenberg v. Carhart*, 530 U.S. 914 (2000), the Supreme Court found the Nebraska Statute banning D & X unconstitutional. The Court followed the precedent set down by the *Casey* court and found that the statute lacked the requisite exception for the "preservation of the health of the mother" and imposed an "undue burden" on a woman's ability to choose abortion. The undue burden resulted, in part, because the statute could be read to ban the more common procedure known as dilation and evacuation (D & E). In addition, banning the D & X procedure is legislating medical care, as the procedure is safer in certain cases than the D & E procedure. Anti-abortion advocates stepped up the pressure on Congress when President Clinton's term ended. In 2003, Congress again passed legislation banning so-called partial birth abortions.

On November 5, 2003, President Bush signed into law the Partial-Birth Abortion Ban Act of 2003. This Act made it a crime for a physician to knowingly perform a partial birth abortion. The penalty for the physician included up to two years in jail. Within one hour of this bill's signing, a federal court in Nebraska granted a temporary injunction on the bill. A federal court in New York followed with its own temporary injunction the very next day. The following are the decisions in both courts.

CARHART V. ASHCROFT
United States District Court, D. Nebraska.
Leroy CARHART, M.D., William G. Fitzhugh, M.D.,
William H. Knorr, M.D., and Jill L. Vibhakar, M.D., on behalf
of themselves and the patients they serve, Plaintiffs,

v.

John ASHCROFT, in his official capacity as Attorney General of the
United States, and his employees, agents and successors in office,
Defendant. No. 4:03 CV 3385. 287 F. Supp.2d 1015, Nov. 5, 2003.

MEMORANDUM AND ORDER

KOPF, Chief Judge.

Congress has passed the "Partial-Birth Abortion Ban Act of 2003." The President has signed it. After hearing the views of the parties, and considering the evidence offered by them, I now temporarily restrain enforcement of the Act.

The Supreme Court, citing the factual findings of eight different federal trial judges (appointed by four different Presidents) and the considered opinion of the American College of Obstetricians and Gynecologists, has found a very similar law unconstitutional because it banned "partial-birth abortions" without the requisite exception for the preservation of the health of the woman. *Stenberg v. Carhart*, 530 U.S. 914, 930–33, 120 S. Ct. 2597, 147 L.Ed.2d 743 (2000). The law challenged here appears to suffer from a similar vice. While it is also true that Congress found that a health exception is not needed, it is, at the very least, problematic whether I should defer to such a conclusion when the Supreme Court has found otherwise. *Id.* at 930–38, 120 S. Ct. 2597. Therefore, applying the familiar *Dataphase*[1] factors, and especially given the fact that the health of women may be harmed if I do otherwise,

IT IS ORDERED that:

1. The request for a temporary restraining order (a part of filing 3) is granted. That is, John Ashcroft, in his official capacity as Attorney General of the United States, and his employees, agents, and, successors in office, are temporarily restrained from enforcing the "Partial-Birth Abortion Ban Act of 2003," S.3., 108th Congress (not yet codified), against the plaintiffs and their officers, agents, servants, and employees, including those individuals and entities (both medical and non-medical) with whom plaintiffs work, teach, supervise, or refer. This temporary restraining order shall remain in effect until further order of the court.

2. Plaintiffs' counsel shall arrange and schedule a telephone conference call between counsel of record and the undersigned United States district judge to occur on Wednesday, November 12, 2003, to discuss scheduling of the preliminary injunction hearing, other progression-related issues, and whether the court should retain its own experts.

---

[1] *Dataphase Sys., Inc. v. C.L. Sys., Inc.*, 640 F.2d 109, 114 (8th Cir.1981) (en banc). (Court should consider four factors when deciding whether to grant injunctive relief: irreparable harm to the moving party, the balance of harms between the parties, the probability of success on the merits, and the public interest.)

NATIONAL ABORTION FEDERATION V. ASHCROFT

United States District Court, S.D. New York.
NATIONAL ABORTION FEDERATION, Mark I. Evans, M.D., Carolyn
Westhoff, M.D., M.Sc., Cassing Hammond, M.D., Marc Heller, M.D.,
Timothy R.B. Johnson, M.D., Stephen Chasen, M.D., Gerson
Weiss, M.D., on behalf of themselves and their patients, Plaintiffs,

v.

John ASHCROFT, in his capacity as Attorney General of the
United States, along with his officers, agents, servants, employees,
and successors in office, Defendant. No. 03 CIV.8695 (RCC).
287 F. Supp.2d 525, Nov. 6, 2003.

MEMORANDUM & ORDER

CASEY, District Judge.

Before the Court is Plaintiffs' Application for a Temporary Restraining Order, requesting that the Court enjoin the Attorney General of the United States from enforcing the Partial-Birth Abortion Ban Act of 2003 ("the Act"). The Act was signed on November 5, 2003, and took effect at 12:01 A.M. on November 6, 2003. Having considered the parties' written submissions and oral arguments, the Court hereby GRANTS Plaintiffs' Application.

To obtain a temporary restraining order, Plaintiffs must show irreparable harm and a likelihood of success on the merits. See *Jackson Dairy, Inc. v. H. P. Hood & Sons, Inc.*, 596 F.2d 70, 72 (2d Cir.1979); *Spencer Trask Software & Info. Servs. LLC v. RPost Int'l Ltd.*, 190 F. Supp.2d 577, 580 (S.D.N.Y.2002). Plaintiffs have met this standard.

First, Plaintiffs have made an adequate showing as to the requisite risk of harm. Second, Plaintiffs have shown a likelihood of success on the merits. Plaintiffs argue that the Act is unconstitutional because, among other things, it does not contain an exception to protect women's health. In *Stenberg v. Carhart*, 530 U.S. 914, 120 S. Ct. 2597, 147 L.Ed.2d 743 (2000), the Supreme Court declared unconstitutional a Nebraska statute banning partial-birth abortions based, in part, on the fact that the statute did not contain such an exception. *Id.* at 930, 120 S. Ct. 2597. In so holding, the *Stenberg* Court determined that a "division of medical opinion . . . at most means uncertainty, a factor that signals the presence of risk . . . [w]here a significant body of medical opinion believes a procedure may bring with it greater safety for some patients and explains the medical reasons supporting the view," then a health exception is constitutionally required. *Id.* at 937, 120 S. Ct. 2597. At oral argument, Defendant took the position that there remains a disagreement in the medical community as to whether the abortion procedures covered by the Act are ever necessary to protect a woman's health, and that Congress did not find a consensus on the matter. Given the Defendant's position, the Court is constrained, at this time, to conclude that it is substantially likely that Plaintiffs will succeed on the merits.

STUDY QUESTIONS

1. Why does the Court believe the underlying case has merit?
2. What did the Court mean when it referred to the makeup of the judges of the Supreme Court when *Stenberg* was decided? Do you think that is relevant?
3. Do you agree with the decision of the two federal courts? Why or why not?

In 2007, the U.S. Supreme Court had the opportunity to address the constitutionality of Partial-Birth Abortion Ban Act of 2003. A deeply divided Court found this statute to be constitutional, reversing the decisions of the Circuit Courts and upholding the ban on the D & X abortion procedure. As you read the excerpt of the majority opinion, look at how it distinguishes itself from the Supreme Court rulings in *Stenberg* and *Casey*.

Gonzalez v. Carhart

2007

U.S. Supreme Court

550 U.S. 124, 127 S.Ct. 1610

Justice KENNEDY delivered the opinion of the Court.

These cases require us to consider the validity of the Partial-Birth Abortion Ban Act of 2003 (Act), a federal statute regulating abortion procedures. In recitations preceding its operative provisions the Act refers to the Court's opinion in *133 Stenberg v. Carhart*, 530 U.S. 914, 120 S.Ct. 2597, 147 L.Ed.2d 743 (2000), which also addressed the subject of abortion procedures used in the later stages of pregnancy. Compared to the State statute at issue in Stenberg, the Act is more specific concerning the instances to which it applies and in this respect more precise in its coverage. We conclude the Act should be sustained against the objections lodged by the broad, facial attack brought against it.

. . . [W]e must determine whether the Act furthers the legitimate interest of the Government in protecting the life of the fetus that may become a child.

We assume the following principles for the purposes of this opinion. Before viability, a State "may not prohibit any woman from making the ultimate decision to terminate her pregnancy." It also may not impose upon this right an undue burden, which exists if a regulation's "purpose or effect is to place a substantial obstacle in the path of a woman seeking an abortion before the fetus attains viability." On the other hand, "[r]egulations which do no more than create a structural mechanism by which the State, or the parent or guardian of a minor, may express profound respect for the life of the unborn are permitted, if they are not a substantial obstacle to the woman's exercise of the right to choose." We now apply its standard to the cases at bar.

We begin with a determination of the Act's operation and effect. A straightforward reading of the Act's text demonstrates its purpose and the scope of its provisions: It regulates and proscribes, with exceptions or qualifications to be discussed, performing the intact D & E procedure.

We conclude that the Act is not void for vagueness, does not impose an undue burden from any overbreadth, and is not invalid on its face. The Act punishes "knowingly perform[ing]" a "partial-birth abortion." It defines the unlawful abortion in explicit terms.

The Act provides doctors "of ordinary intelligence a reasonable opportunity to know what is prohibited." Indeed, it sets forth "relatively clear guidelines as to prohibited conduct" and provides "objective criteria" to evaluate whether a doctor has performed a prohibited procedure. Unlike the statutory language in Stenberg that prohibited the delivery of a "substantial portion" of the fetus—where a doctor might question how much of the fetus is a substantial portion—the Act defines the line between potentially criminal conduct on the one hand and lawful abortion on the other. Doctors performing D & E will know that if they do not deliver a living fetus to an anatomical landmark they will not face criminal liability.

We next determine whether the Act imposes an undue burden, as a facial matter, because its restrictions on second-trimester abortions are too broad. A review of the statutory text discloses the limits of its reach. The Act prohibits intact D & E; and, notwithstanding respondents' arguments, it does not prohibit the D & E procedure in which the fetus is removed in parts.

Under the principles accepted as controlling here, the Act, as we have interpreted it, would be unconstitutional "if its purpose or effect is to place a substantial obstacle in the path of a woman seeking an abortion before the fetus attains viability." The abortions affected by the Act's regulations take place both previability and postviability; so the quoted language and the undue burden analysis it relies upon are applicable. The question is whether the Act, measured by its text in this facial attack, imposes a substantial obstacle to late-term, but previability, abortions. The Act does not on its face impose a substantial obstacle, and we reject this further facial challenge to its validity.

The Act's purposes are set forth in recitals preceding its operative provisions. A description of the prohibited abortion procedure demonstrates the rationale for the congressional enactment. The Act proscribes a method of abortion in which a fetus is killed just inches before completion of the birth process. Congress stated as follows: "Implicitly approving such a brutal and inhumane procedure by choosing not to prohibit it will further coarsen society to the humanity of not only newborns, but all vulnerable and innocent human life, making it increasingly difficult to protect such life". . . . The Act expresses respect for the dignity of human life.

The Act's furtherance of legitimate government interests bears upon, but does not resolve, the next question: whether the Act has the effect of imposing an unconstitutional burden on the abortion right because it does not allow use of the barred procedure where "necessary, in appropriate medical judgment, for [the] preservation of the . . .

health of the mother." The prohibition in the Act would be unconstitutional, under precedents we here assume to be controlling, if it "subject[ed] [women] to significant health risks." . . . [W]hether the Act creates significant health risks for women has been a contested factual question. The evidence presented in the trial courts and before Congress demonstrates both sides have medical support for their position.

There is documented medical disagreement whether the Act's prohibition would ever impose significant health risks on women. "[T]here continues to be a division of opinion among highly qualified experts regarding the necessity or safety of intact D & E." The question becomes whether the Act can stand when this medical uncertainty persists. The Court's precedents instruct that the Act can survive this facial attack. The Court has given State and federal legislatures wide discretion to pass legislation in areas where there is medical and scientific uncertainty.

Respondents have not demonstrated that the Act, as a facial matter, is void for vagueness, or that it imposes an undue burden on a woman's right to abortion based on its overbreadth or lack of a health exception. For these reasons the judgments of the Courts of Appeals for the Eighth and Ninth Circuits are reversed.

It Is So Ordered.

Justice THOMAS, with whom Justice SCALIA joins, concurring.

Justice Ginsburg in her dissenting opinion strongly disagrees with the reasoning in the Majority opinion concluding it is a marked departure from prior rulings of the Court, in particular in its failure to provide an exception for reasons involving the health of the mother. As excerpt of her dissent follows.

Justice GINSBURG, with whom Justice STEVENS, Justice SOUTER, and Justice BREYER join, dissenting.

In *Planned Parenthood of Southeastern Pa. v. Casey*, the Court declared that "[l]iberty finds no refuge in a jurisprudence of doubt."

There was, the Court said, an "imperative" need to dispel doubt as to "the meaning and reach" of the Court's 7-to-2 judgment, rendered nearly two decades earlier in *Roe v. Wade*. Responsive to that need, the Court endeavored to provide secure guidance to "[s]tate and federal courts as well as legislatures throughout the Union," by defining "the rights of the woman and the legitimate authority of the State respecting the termination of pregnancies by abortion procedures."

Taking care to speak plainly, the Casey Court restated and reaffirmed Roe's essential holding. First, the Court addressed the type of abortion regulation permissible prior to fetal viability. It recognized "the right of the woman to choose to have an abortion before viability and to obtain it without undue interference from the State." Second, the Court acknowledged "the State's power to restrict abortions after fetal viability, if the law contains exceptions for pregnancies which endanger the woman's life or health." Third, the Court confirmed that "the State has legitimate interests from the outset of the pregnancy in protecting the health of the woman and the life of the fetus that may become a child."

I dissent from the Court's disposition. Retreating from prior rulings that abortion restrictions cannot be imposed absent an exception safeguarding a woman's health, the Court upholds an Act that surely would not survive under the close scrutiny that previously attended State-decreed limitations on a woman's reproductive choices.

As Casey comprehended, at stake in cases challenging abortion restrictions is a woman's "control over her [own] destiny." "There was a time, not so long ago," when women were "regarded as the center of home and family life, with attendant special responsibilities that precluded full and independent legal status under the Constitution." Those views, this Court made clear in Casey, "are no longer consistent with our understanding of the family, the individual, or the Constitution." Women, it is now acknowledged, have the talent, capacity, and right "to participate equally in the economic and social life of the Nation." Their ability to realize their full potential, the Court recognized, is intimately connected to "their ability to control their reproductive lives." Thus, legal challenges to undue restrictions on abortion procedures do not seek to vindicate some generalized notion of privacy; rather, they center on a woman's autonomy to determine her life's course, and thus to enjoy equal citizenship stature.

The Court offers flimsy and transparent justifications for upholding a nationwide ban on intact D & E sans any exception to safeguard a women's health. Today's ruling, the Court declares, advances "a premise central to [Casey's] conclusion"—i.e., the Government's "legitimate and substantial interest in preserving and promoting fetal life." "[W]e must determine whether the Act furthers the legitimate interest of the Government in protecting the life of the fetus that may become a child." But the Act scarcely furthers that interest: The law saves not a single fetus from destruction, for it targets only a method of performing abortion. And surely the statute was not designed to protect the lives or health of pregnant women. In short, the Court upholds a law that, while doing nothing to "preserv[e] . . . fetal life," bars a woman from choosing intact D & E although her doctor "reasonably believes [that procedure] will best protect [her]."

In sum, the notion that the Partial-Birth Abortion Ban Act furthers any legitimate governmental interest is, quite simply, irrational. The Court's defense of the statute provides no saving explanation. In candor, the Act, and the Court's defense of it, cannot be understood as anything other than an effort to chip away at a right declared again and again by this Court—and with increasing comprehension of its centrality to women's lives. When "a statute burdens constitutional rights and all that can be said on its behalf is that it is the vehicle that legislators have chosen for expressing their hostility to those rights, the burden is undue. . . ."

STUDY QUESTIONS

1. How does the Supreme Court distinguish the holding in *Gonzalez* from its prior holding in *Casey* and *Stenberg*?

2. What is the basis for Justice Ginsburg's dissent? Why does she call the majority decision "irrational"?

3. Should the Court have provided an exception for the health of the mother? Why or why not?

The issue of abortion remains a hotly contested issue in today's society. Although the FACE act was signed into law by President Clinton in May 1994, incidents of clinic violence continue. New ways to address the violence have been sought out.

In 1998, anti-abortion groups were convicted of violating a 1970 federal law originally designed to prosecute mobsters. On April 21, 1998, a federal jury in Chicago awarded women's health clinics in Milwaukee, Wisconsin, and in Wilmington, Delaware, a total of $86,000 in damages. Plaintiffs in the suit alleged that three prominent organizers in the anti-abortion movement—Joseph Scheidler, Andrew Scholberg, and Timothy Murphy of the Chicago-based Pro-Life Action League—had directed activists involved in that group and in another anti-abortion organization, Operation Rescue, to use threats and acts of intimidation and extortion in their efforts to shut down clinics providing abortion services.

Concern over anti-abortion violence however continues. According to Kate Michelman, former president of NARAL Pro-Choice America, violence subsided after the 1990s due to increased security and the election of President George W. Bush, an abortion opponent. With the election of pro-choice President Barak Obama, concerns are renewed that anti-abortion violence will increase. In the wake of the June 2009 murder of Dr George Tiller, concern is mounting. Dr Tiller, a doctor known to perform late-term abortions, was gunned down in his Church in June of 2009. Michelman observed that "historically when those who oppose a woman's right to decide are frustrated politically they get more violent."

In the midst of the more restrictive movement against abortion, certain pro-choice strides have been made. The approval of RU 486, the so-called abortion pill, can be considered progress for abortion rights supporters.

In September 2000, the Food and Drug Administration approved the drug mifepristone, commonly referred to as RU 486, for use in pharmaceutical abortions. RU 486 prevents the fertilized egg from staying attached to the uterine wall, thereby inducing an abortion. The drug is administered in a doctor's office and does not require surgery. Many advocates believe that use of RU 486 will lower the number of surgical abortions and is a safer way to terminate a pregnancy. RU 486 has been widely used in Europe and other parts of the world.

In December 2003, the advisory committee to the Food and Drug Administration recommended approval of the "morning after pill" for sale over the counter. The morning after pill is different from RU 486. The medication, when taken within seventy-two hours after unprotected sex, prevents the egg from being fertilized. It is currently available from a physician and by prescription. Proponents of the drug believe that making it widely available to women will greatly reduce the number of unintended pregnancies and abortions.

One of the cornerstones of reproductive choice involves the freedom to make a choice to have a child or not. Much of the debate has revolved around access to contraception and abortion: the choice *not* to have children. There remains, however, continued debate regarding the choice to *have* children or reproduce in contravention of what the government believes is best. We previously discussed involuntary sterilization for people who were considered "feebleminded" and how that was abolished. Look now at the excerpt from a recent law review article and how the government has seen fit to, again, intervene in whether a woman should or should not have a child.

WHEN CRACK IS THE ONLY CHOICE
The Effect of a Negative Right of Privacy on Drug-Addicted Women
Dana Hirschenbaum

CRACK

"Prevent Child Abuse . . . $200 cash for drug addicts who participate in long-term birth control." This is one of the catch slogans used in advertisements by Children Requiring A Caring Kommunity (CRACK), a California-based organization whose stated goal is "to offer effective preventive measures to reduce the tragedy of numerous drug-affected pregnancies." The unorthodox solutions CRACK proposes for drug-addicted adults of childbearing age have drawn emotional responses from all sides. Essentially, the program offers drug-addicted women and men two hundred dollars cash if they agree to participate in sterilization or long-term birth control. For women, aside from sterilization via tubal ligation, long-term birth control options include Norplant, Depo-Provera and IUDs; for men, sterilization via vasectomy is the only option.

. . . The program inevitably raises the question of what would induce a woman to exchange her childbearing capabilities, even temporarily, for a mere two hundred dollars? . . . As this article will discuss, the answer likely lies in a combination of judicial opinions and legislative decisions that have provided low-income women with an incentive to participate due to a lack of other options.

THE RIGHT OF PRIVACY

. . . While the right of privacy with regard to childbearing decisions remains intact for those with access to private health care, it has been severely undercut for women dependent on the government for medical aid. To make matters worse, an additional set of burdens has been placed upon these women by criminal prosecutors hoping to make a dent in the increase in number of children born addicted to drugs.

CRIMINALIZATION OF PREGNANCY

In a series of State court cases across the country, prosecutors have attempted to find "creative" responses to the rise in drug use and the corresponding increase in the number of babies born affected by or addicted to drugs during the 1980s. The most well-known of these cases is *Johnson v. State*, in which Jennifer Johnson was tried and convicted of delivery of a controlled substance to minors. In its argument, the State relied on a Florida statute that made it a crime for an adult over eighteen years of age to "deliver" a controlled substance to a person under eighteen. Under this law, Johnson was accused of delivering cocaine to her children through the umbilical cord in the sixty to ninety seconds after birth and before the cord was cut. While the decision of

---

the lower court was eventually reversed by Florida's highest court, Johnson's prosecution was followed by a wave of others, all attempting to punish women for their behavior during pregnancy.

A popular tactic of many prosecutors has been to charge women with child abuse in the hope that courts will be willing to expand the definition of a "person" to include a fetus. In nearly all of the States where this has been attempted, however, courts have declined to make the required jump, relying mainly on the intent of the legislature in creating child protection laws. An exception to this general rule is South Carolina, which, in *Whitner v. State,* asserted that "South Carolina has long recognized that viable fetuses are persons holding certain legal rights and privileges." Ignoring the fact that this long history of recognition was concentrated in cases of tort law and criminal cases involving the actions of a third party against the fetus, the court relied on this construction of the law in order to hold Cornelia Whitner guilty of criminal child neglect for "causing her baby to be born with cocaine metabolites in its system by reason of [her] ingestion of crack cocaine during the third trimester of her pregnancy." In rendering its opinion, the court claimed to be concerned with child welfare. In reality, however, the court failed to recognize the fact that its overextension of the South Carolina child protection laws to fetuses would be likely to deter pregnant women from seeking any prenatal care at all, thereby leaving their future children potentially worse off than they had been under the original interpretation.

Finally, a handful of courts have attempted to remedy the situation by prohibiting women from becoming pregnant as a condition of probation. This approach was adopted by a California Superior Court judge in *People v. Pointer.* The defendant in Pointer was convicted of child endangerment for placing her children on a strict macrobiotic diet. As a result of the diet, one child "was seriously underdeveloped" and the other "suffered severe growth retardation and permanent neurological damage." After being found guilty by a jury and sentenced to five years of probation, the defendant was, among other things, instructed to "have no custody of any children, including her own, without prior court approval," and was restricted from "conceiv[ing] during the probationary period." Holding that the desired result of the trial court could be achieved in a less burdensome way, the appellate court rejected this requirement as "subversive of appellant's fundamental right to procreate" and, accordingly, struck it down.

This precedent, however, did not prevent a later California court from attempting to place the same restriction on a woman's right of privacy in making childbearing decisions. In *People v. Zaring,* the court sentenced the appellant, who had previously been found guilty of possession of heroin, to probation, ordering her "not to get pregnant during the term of [her] probation which is a term of five years." The judge then admonished the appellant, stating "[i]f you get pregnant, I'm going to send you to prison in large part because I want to protect the un-born child."

While this probation condition was overturned by the appellate court, it is likely that the damaging influence of its conditions, like that of other trial court convictions of pregnant and drug-addicted women discussed herein, had already been done. Average citizens are unlikely to follow legal decisions through the maze of appeals that the decisions must travel. Rather, citizens are likely to hear conversations and news stories discussing women being arrested for delivering drugs to or abusing their unborn children, and as a result, are then likely to avoid seeking out prenatal care or drug treatment. Not surprisingly, for those who remain willing to participate in drug treatment programs, the options are rather limited.

DRUG TREATMENT PROGRAMS

It is well documented that the demand for drug treatment programs surpasses its availability for pregnant women, women with young children, and Medicaid patients, all categories into which CRACK participants and women who have been prosecuted during pregnancy are likely to fall. According to a 1990 survey, "[t]he general shortage of treatment slots is aggravated by the unwillingness of many drug programs to include pregnant women."

CONCLUSION

Considering the lack of viable alternatives, it should come as no surprise that many indigent women are opting to eliminate even the possibility of becoming pregnant when presented with the impetus provided by CRACK. While the Supreme Court has clearly carved out a zone of privacy around decisions relating to family planning and childbearing into which the government may not intrude, the Court has failed to recognize that by ignoring external influences on this right, such as indigency, it has done little to extend protection to women without private resources. The Court may not deem this to be its responsibility, but it should realize that its failure to provide women with a full range of childbearing choices leaves them with few practical options.

The added pressure of the possibility of being criminally prosecuted for drug use during pregnancy and the inability to find available and effective drug treatment programs clearly creates further incentives for indigent women to participate in CRACK. While the creation of such incentives is neither illegal nor unconstitutional, it is also not in keeping with the principles which *Roe v. Wade* and its progeny intended to impart. While, technically, the government has not prevented women from obtaining abortions, securing prenatal care, or attending drug treatment, by failing to address that indigency is an impediment to receiving such services, the government has made it highly unlikely that poor women will pursue these options. Viewed in this light, it is difficult to maintain that the women who have participated in CRACK have made an illogical choice when faced with the option of having children they are physically, emotionally or financially unable to care for, or taking $200 to participate in long-term or permanent birth control. This, however, is a choice no woman should be forced to make when viable alternatives could easily be placed within her reach.

STUDY QUESTIONS

1. Do you agree with the Court's ruling that prevented a woman from conceiving other children?
2. Do you feel the same about the drug addict and the woman who fed her children a different diet?
3. Is there any difference between forced birth control or sterilization and removal of children from a home because of abuse or neglect?

II. APPLYING THE RIGHT TO REPRODUCTIVE CHOICE

Assisting Parenthood

Insemination by Donor

Artificial insemination was initially developed using the husband's sperm in an effort to address the fertility problems of married couples; eventually, the sperm of donors also came to be used. In the 1980s, as many as 20,000 women per year were reported artificially inseminated in the United States. Of these, 1,500 were unmarried. To ensure that the husband (in the case of a married couple) was officially regarded as the father in cases of donor insemination, laws originally designed for adultery situations were held to apply to artificial insemination. Thus, laws declaring the husband to be the father of any children born to the wife during marriage were interpreted to include children resulting from artificial insemination.

Recently, unmarried women—both lesbian and heterosexual—have sought insemination by donor as a way of procreating without being married or otherwise having the biological father involved. There are no laws in the United States prohibiting fertility clinics from providing services to single women, including lesbians. Access may, however, be restricted indirectly. For example, if a health plan does not cover infertility treatments, single women utilizing donor insemination must pay for the procedure themselves. For those women whose health insurance does cover infertility treatments, there is another hurdle; if their policies cover procedures for women who are "infertile"—defined as unable to conceive after a year or more of unprotected sexual intercourse—single women, including lesbians, are usually eliminated under that definition. Finally, although some States have enacted laws mandating that insurance companies afford some coverage for infertility treatment, insurance companies are allowed to require that the infertility treatment be medically necessary. A single woman's lack of a male partner is not usually viewed as such a medical necessity.

Insemination by donor continues to raise questions about whether the sperm-donor/biological father or the husband/social father should be officially recognized as the parent. However, as the following case illustrates, today's questions may take a slightly different form.

JHORDAN C. v. MARY K.

California Appellate Division, 1986.
179 Cal. App. 3d. 386, 224 Cal. Rptr. 530.

KING, Associate Justice.

. . . In late 1978 Mary decided to bear a child by artificial insemination and to raise the child jointly with Victoria, a close friend who lived in a nearby town. Mary sought a semen donor by talking to friends and acquaintances. This led to three or four potential donors with whom Mary spoke directly. She and Victoria ultimately chose Jhordan after he had one personal interview with Mary and one dinner at Mary's home.

The parties' testimony was in conflict as to what agreement they had concerning the role, if any, Jhordan would play in the child's life. According to Mary, she told Jhordan she did not want a donor who desired ongoing involvement with the child, but she did agree to let him see the child to satisfy his curiosity as to how the child would look. Jhordan, in contrast, asserts they agreed he and Mary would have an ongoing friendship, he would have ongoing contact with the child, and he would care for the child as much as two or three times per week.

None of the parties sought legal advice until long after the child's birth. They were completely unaware of the existence of Civil Code section 7005. They did not attempt to draft a written agreement concerning Jhordan's status.

Jhordan provided semen to Mary on a number of occasions during a six month period commencing in late January 1979. On each occasion he came to her home, spoke briefly with her, produced the semen, and then left. The record is unclear, but Mary, who is a nurse, apparently performed the insemination by herself or with Victoria.

. . . Mary gave birth to Devin on March 30, 1980. Victoria assisted in the delivery. Jhordan was listed as the father on Devin's birth certificate. Mary's roommate telephoned Jhordan that day to inform him of the birth. Jhordan visited Mary and Devin the next day and took photographs of the baby.

Five days later Jhordan telephoned Mary and said he wanted to visit Devin again. Mary initially resisted, but then allowed

Jhordan to visit, although she told him she was angry. During the visit Jhordan claimed a right to see Devin, and Mary agreed to monthly visits.

Through August 1980 Jhordan visited Devin approximately five times. Mary then terminated the monthly visits. Jhordan said he would consult an attorney if Mary did not let him see Devin. Mary asked Jhordan to sign a contract indicating he would not seek to be Devin's father, but Jhordan refused.

In December 1980 Jhordan filed an action against Mary to establish paternity and visitation rights. In June 1982, by stipulated judgment in a separate action by the County of Sonoma, he was ordered to reimburse the county for public assistance paid for Devin's support. . . . In November 1982 the court granted Jhordan weekly visitation with Devin at Victoria's home. . . .

After trial the court rendered judgment declaring Jhordan to be Devin's legal father. However, the court awarded sole legal and physical custody to Mary, and denied Jhordan any input into decisions regarding Devin's schooling, medical and dental care, and day-to-day maintenance. Jhordan received substantial visitation rights as recommended by a court-appointed psychologist. . . .

. . . Civil Code section 7005 . . . provides in pertinent part. "(a) If, under the supervision of a licensed physician and with the consent of her husband, a wife is inseminated artificially with semen donated by a man not her husband, the husband is treated in law as if he were the natural father of a child thereby conceived. . . . (b) The donor of semen provided to a licensed physician for use in artificial insemination of a woman other than the donor's wife is treated in law as if he were not the natural father of a child thereby conceived." . . .

[T]he California Legislature has afforded unmarried as well as married women a statutory vehicle for obtaining semen for artificial insemination without fear that the donor may claim paternity, and has likewise provided men with a statutory vehicle for donating semen to married and unmarried women alike without fear of liability for child support. Subdivision (b) States only one limitation on its application: the semen must be "provided to a licensed physician." Otherwise, whether impregnation occurs through artificial insemination or sexual intercourse, there can be a determination of paternity with the rights, duties and obligations such a determination entails. . . .

. . . . [T]here are at least two sound justifications upon which the statutory requirement of physician involvement might have been based. One relates to health: a physician can obtain a complete medical history of the donor (which may be of crucial importance to the child during his or her lifetime) and screen the donor for any hereditary or communicable diseases. . . .

Another justification for physician involvement is that the presence of a professional third party such as a physician can serve to create a formal, documented structure for the donor-recipient relationship, without which, as this case illustrates, misunderstandings between the parties regarding the nature of their relationship and the donor's relationship to the child would be more likely to occur.

It is true that nothing inherent in artificial insemination requires the involvement of a physician. Artificial insemination is, as demonstrated here, a simple procedure easily performed by a woman in her own home. Also, despite the reasons outlined above in favor of physician involvement, there are countervailing considerations against requiring it. A requirement of physician involvement, as Mary argues, might offend a woman's sense of privacy and reproductive autonomy, might result in burdensome costs to some women, and might interfere with a woman's desire to conduct the procedure in a comfortable environment such as her own home or to choose the donor herself. . . .

However, because of the way section 7005 is phrased, a woman (married or unmarried) can perform home artificial insemination or choose her donor and still obtain the benefits of the statute. . . . [A] woman who prefers home artificial insemination or who wishes to choose her donor can still obtain statutory protection from a donor's paternity claim through the relatively simple expedient of obtaining the semen, whether for home insemination or from a chosen donor (or both), through a licensed physician. . . .

Mary and Victoria next contend that even if section 7005, subdivision (b), by its terms does not apply where semen for artificial insemination has not been provided to a licensed physician, application of the statute to the present case is required by constitutional principles of equal protection and privacy. . . .

[T]he statutory provision at issue here— Civil Code section 7005, subdivision (b)—treats married and unmarried women equally. Both are denied application of the statute where semen has not been provided to a licensed physician. The true question presented is whether a completely different set of paternity statutes—affording protection to husband and wife from any claim of paternity by an outsider—denies equal protection by failing to provide similar protection to an unmarried woman. The simple answer is that, within the context of this question, a married woman and an unmarried woman are not similarly situated for purposes of equal protection analysis. In the case of a married woman, the marital relationship invokes a long-recognized social policy of preserving the integrity of the marriage. No such concerns arise where there is no marriage at all. Equal protection is not violated by providing that certain benefits or legal rights arise only out of the marital relationship. . . .

Mary and Victoria argue that the physician requirement . . . infringes a fundamental right to procreative choice, also encompassed by the constitutional right of privacy.

But the statute imposes no restriction on the right to bear a child. Unlike statutes in other jurisdictions proscribing artificial insemination other than by a physician, subdivision (b) of section 7005 does not forbid self-inseminations nor does the statute preclude personal selection of a donor or in any other way prevent women from artificially conceiving children under circumstances of their own choice. The statute simply addresses the perplexing question of the legal status of the semen donor, and provides a method of avoiding the legal consequences that might otherwise be dictated by traditional notions of paternity. . . .

We wish to stress that our opinion in this case is not intended to express any judicial preference toward traditional notions of family structure or toward providing a father where a single woman has chosen to bear a child. Public policy in these areas is best determined by the legislative branch of government, not the judicial. Our Legislature has already spoken and has afforded to unmarried women a statutory right to bear children by artificial insemination (as well as a right of men to donate semen) without fear of a paternity claim, through provision of the semen to a licensed physician. We simply hold that because Mary omitted to invoke Civil Code section 7005, subdivision (b), by obtaining Jhordan's semen through a licensed physician, and because the parties by all other conduct preserved Jhordan's status as a member of Devin's family, the trial court properly declared Jhordan to be Devin's legal father.

The Judgment Is Affirmed.

STUDY QUESTIONS

1. On what basis did the court determine that Jhordan C. should have rights as the child's father? Was that outcome inevitable?

2. Do you agree with the court's decision? Does such a decision have the effect of encouraging male responsibility for child rearing? Of discouraging women-determined family structures?

3. In light of *Jhordan C.*, how would you counsel an unmarried woman who wished to bear a child through donor insemination and preclude the biological father's obtaining parental rights?

California is not the only State that has determined that a known sperm donor should be granted parental rights where the parties disputed whether the donor would be considered a parent of the child. In Ohio, an appellate court found that Ohio's AID (alternative insemination by donor) statute, which stated that the donor for a non-spousal insemination would not be considered the legal or natural father of a resulting child, did not apply. In that case, the sperm donor was not anonymous and had asserted that he and the mother had an agreement that he would have a relationship with the child. *C. O. v. W. S.,* 64 Ohio Misc.2d 9, 639 N.E.2d 523 (1994). In a slightly different factual scenario, courts in New York and Minnesota have granted parental rights to a known sperm donor where the donor, the biological mother, and the mother's female partner had agreed the donor would not have any such rights in regard to the child. *Thomas S. v. Robin Y.,* 618 N.Y.S.2d 356 (N.Y. App. Div. 1994), *rev'g* 599 N.Y.S.2d 377 (Fam. Ct. 1993) (Although sperm donor had agreed he would not have parental rights, he was entitled to an order in his favor because he was the biological father; furthermore, estoppel principles did not apply because the child had known since she was three that the donor was her biological father and there had been some contact established.); and *LaChapelle v. Mitten,* 607 N.W.2d 151 (Minn. Ct. of App. 2000). (Despite written agreement that donor would have no rights or responsibility with respect to the child, and that the biological mother and her lesbian partner would have physical and legal custody of the child, upon severing of the donor's visitation and during suit involving both the donor and the now-estranged lesbian partner, the donor was adjudicated to be the biological father and joint legal custody was granted to the donor, the mother, and the estranged lesbian partner.) However, in Oregon, a court denied parental rights to the sperm donor who had established a strong relationship with the child, based upon the written agreement by the biological mother, her lesbian partner, and the donor stating that he would have no parental rights to the child. *Leckie v. Voorhies,* 875 P.2d 521 (Or. App. 1994). And, in Kansas, an unmarried woman who became the mother of twins with the use of sperm donated by an unmarried male friend was successful in having his action to determine paternity dismissed because Kansas law (K.S.A 38-1114(f)) States, in pertinent part: "The donor of semen provided to a licensed physician for use in artificial insemination of a woman other than the donor's wife is treated in law as if he were not the birth father of a child. . . ." *In re K.M.H.,* 285 Kan. 53, 169 P.3d 1025 (2007), *cert. denied* 555 U.S. 72 (2008). From these cases, it appears that women seeking to establish non-traditional family units excluding male parents would have better success preventing biological fathers from trying to "join the family" by using anonymous donors.

In Vitro Fertilization

In vitro fertilization (IVF) and related techniques involve the insertion of eggs obtained from a woman (or a donor) into the woman's body once they have been fertilized. First successfully used in the United States in the early 1980s, such techniques are both expensive and invasive. Although success rates have improved considerably in recent years, they come with other costs. For example, to maximize birth rates, doctors performing IVF often transfer multiple embryos, which increases the risk of multiple births. In addition, multiple birth babies are at a higher risk than single births to be premature or lower in birth weight. Nevertheless, IVF and other assisted reproduction technology services seem to be sought out increasingly to address female infertility problems often attributed to postponement of childbearing.

Here, too, questions may arise concerning the rights of the biological mother and the biological father.

DAVIS v. DAVIS

Supreme Court of Tennessee, 1992. 842 S.W.2d 588, *cert. den. sub. nom.*
Stowe v. Davis, 507 U.S. 911, 113 S. Ct. 1042 (1993).

DAUGHTREY, Justice.

This appeal presents a question of first impression, involving the disposition of the cryogenically-preserved product of *in vitro* fertilization (IVF), commonly referred to in the popular press and the legal journals as "frozen embryos." The case began as a divorce action, filed by the appellee, Junior Lewis Davis, against his then wife, appellant Mary Sue Davis. The parties were able to agree upon all terms of dissolution, except one: who was to have "custody" of the seven "frozen embryos" stored in a Knoxville fertility clinic that had attempted to assist the Davises in achieving a much-wanted pregnancy during a happier period in their relationship.

I. INTRODUCTION

Mary Sue Davis originally asked for control of the "frozen embryos" with the intent to have the[m] transferred to her own uterus, in a post-divorce effort to become pregnant. Junior Davis objected, saying that he preferred to leave the embryos in their frozen State until he decided whether or not he wanted to become a parent outside the bounds of marriage.

Based on its determination that the embryos were "human beings" from the moment of fertilization, the trial court awarded "custody" to Mary Sue Davis and directed that she "be permitted the opportunity to bring these children to term through implantation." The Court of Appeals reversed, finding that Junior Davis has a "constitutionally protected right not to beget a child where no pregnancy has taken place" and holding that "there is no compelling State interest to justify . . . ordering implantation against the will of either party." The Court of Appeals further held that "the parties share an interest in the seven fertilized ova" and remanded the case to the trial court for

entry of an order vesting them with "joint control . . . and equal voice over their disposition."

Mary Sue Davis then sought review in this Court, contesting the validity of the constitutional basis for the Court of Appeals decision. . . .

[The parties] both have remarried and Mary Sue Davis (now Mary Sue Stowe) has moved out of State. She no longer wishes to utilize the "frozen embryos" herself, but wants authority to donate them to a childless couple. Junior Davis is adamantly opposed to such donation and would prefer to see the "frozen embryos" discarded. The result is, once again, an impasse, but the parties' current legal position does have an effect on the probable outcome of the case, as discussed below.

At the outset, it is important to note the absence of two critical factors that might otherwise influence or control the result of this litigation. When the Davises signed up for the IVF program at the Knoxville clinic, they did not execute a written agreement specifying what disposition should be made of any unused embryos that might result from the cryopreservation process. Moreover, there was at that time no Tennessee statute governing such disposition, nor has one been enacted in the meantime. . . .

II. THE FACTS

Mary Sue Davis and Junior Lewis Davis met while they were both in the Army and stationed in Germany in the spring of 1979. After a period of courtship, they came home to the United States and were married on April 26, 1980. When their leave was up, they then returned to their posts in Germany as a married couple.

Within six months of returning to Germany, Mary Sue became pregnant but unfortunately suffered an extremely painful tubal pregnancy, as a result of which she had surgery to remove her right fallopian tube. This tubal pregnancy was followed by four others during the course of the marriage. After her fifth tubal pregnancy, Mary Sue chose to have her left fallopian tube ligated, thus leaving her without functional fallopian tubes by which to conceive naturally. The Davises attempted to adopt a child but, at the last minute, the child's birth-mother changed her mind about putting the child up for adoption. Other paths to adoption turned out to be prohibitively expensive. *In vitro* fertilization became essentially the only option for the Davises to pursue in their attempt to become parents.

As explained at trial, IVF involves the aspiration of ova from the follicles of a woman's ovaries, fertilization of these ova in a petri dish using the sperm provided by a man, and the transfer of the product of this procedure into the uterus of the woman from whom the ova were taken. Implantation may then occur, resulting in a pregnancy and, it is hoped, the birth of a child. . . .

IV. THE "PERSON" VS. "PROPERTY" DICHOTOMY

One of the fundamental issues the inquiry poses is whether the preembryos in this case should be considered "persons" or "property" in the contemplation of the law. The Court of Appeals held, correctly, that they cannot be considered "persons" under Tennessee law. The policy of the State on the subject matter before us may be gleaned from the State's treatment of fetuses in the womb. . . . The State's Wrongful Death Statute does not allow a wrongful death for a viable fetus that is not first born alive. Without live birth, the Supreme Court has said, a fetus is not a "person" within the meaning of the statute. Other enactments by the legislature demonstrate even more explicitly that viable fetuses in the womb are not entitled to the same protection as "persons." Tenn. Code Ann. § 39–15–201 incorporates the trimester approach to abortion outlined in *Roe v. Wade.* . . . This statutory scheme indicates that as embryos develop, they are accorded more respect than mere human cells because of their burgeoning potential for life. But, even after viability, they are not given legal status equivalent to that of a person already born. . . .

V. THE ENFORCEABILITY OF CONTRACT

. . . We believe, as a starting point, that an agreement regarding disposition of any untransferred preembryos in the event of contingencies (such as the death of one or more of the parties, divorce, financial reversals, or abandonment of the program) should be presumed valid and should be enforced as between the progenitors. This conclusion is in keeping with the proposition that the progenitors, having provided the gametic material giving rise to the preembryos, retain decision-making authority as to their disposition.

At the same time, we recognize that life is not static, and that human emotions run particularly high when a married couple is attempting to overcome infertility problems. It follows that the parties' initial "informed consent" to IVF procedures will often not be truly informed because of the near impossibility of anticipating, emotionally and psychologically, all the turns that events may take as the IVF process unfolds. Providing that the initial agreements may later be modified by agreement will, we think, protect the parties against some of the risks they face in this regard. But, in the absence of such agreed modification, we conclude that their prior agreements should be considered binding. . . .

VI. THE RIGHT OF PROCREATIONAL AUTONOMY

. . . For the purposes of this litigation it is sufficient to note that, whatever its ultimate constitutional boundaries, the right of procreational autonomy is composed of two rights of equal significance—the right to procreate and the right to avoid procreation. . . .

The equivalence of and inherent tension between these two interests are nowhere more evident than in the context of *in vitro* fertilization. None of the concerns about a woman's bodily integrity that have previously precluded men from controlling abortion decisions is applicable here. We are not unmindful of the fact that the trauma (including both emotional stress and physical discomfort) to which women are subjected in the IVF process is more severe than is the impact of the procedure on men. In this sense, it is fair to say that women contribute more to the IVF process than men. Their experience, however, must be viewed in light of the joys of parenthood that is desired or the relative anguish of a lifetime of unwanted parenthood. As they stand on the brink of potential parenthood, Mary Sue Davis and Junior Lewis Davis must be seen as entirely equivalent gamete-providers. . . .

. . . When weighed against the interests of the individuals and the burdens inherent in parenthood, the State's interest in the potential life of these preembryos is not sufficient to justify any infringement upon the freedom of these individuals to make their own decisions as to whether to allow a process to continue that may result in such a dramatic change in their lives as becoming parents.

. . . We conclude, moreover, that an interest in avoiding genetic parenthood can be significant enough to trigger the protections afforded to all other aspects of parenthood. The technological fact that someone unknown to these parties could gestate these preembryos does not alter the fact that these parties, the gamete-providers, would become parents in that event, at least in the genetic sense. The profound impact this would have on them supports their right to sole decisional authority as to whether the process of attempting to gestate these preembryos should continue. This brings us directly to the question of how to resolve the dispute that arises when one party wishes to continue the IVF process and the other does not. . . .

VII. BALANCING THE PARTIES' INTERESTS

Resolving disputes over conflicting interests of constitutional import is a task familiar to the courts. One way of resolving these disputes is to consider the positions of the parties, the significance of their interests, and the relative burdens that will be imposed by differing resolutions. In this case, the issue centers on the two aspects of procreational autonomy—the right to procreate and the right to avoid procreation. . . .

Junior Davis testified that he was the fifth youngest of six children. When he was five years old, his parents divorced, his mother had a nervous break-down, and he and three of his brothers went to live at a home for boys run by the Lutheran Church. . . .

In light of his boyhood experiences, Junior Davis is vehemently opposed to fathering a child that would not live with both parents. Regardless of whether he or Mary Sue had custody, he feels that the child's bond with the non-custodial parent would not be satisfactory. He testified very clearly that his concern was for the psychological obstacles a child in such a situation would face, as well as the burdens it would impose on him. Likewise, he is opposed to donation because the recipient couple might divorce, leaving the child (which he definitely would consider his own) in a single-parent setting.

Balanced against Junior Davis's interest in avoiding parenthood is Mary Sue Davis's interest in donating the preembryos to another couple for implantation. Refusal to permit donation of the preembryos would impose on her the burden of knowing that the lengthy IVF procedures she underwent were futile, and that the preembryos to which she contributed genetic material would never become children. While this is not an insubstantial emotional burden, we can only conclude that Mary Sue Davis's interest in donation is not as significant as the interest Junior Davis has in avoiding parenthood. If she were allowed to donate these preembryos, he would face a lifetime of either wondering about his parental status or knowing about his parental status but having no control over it. He testified quite clearly that if these preembryos were brought to term he would fight for custody of his child or children. Donation, if a child came of it, would rob him twice—his procreational autonomy would be defeated and his relationship with his offspring would be prohibited.

The case would be closer if Mary Sue Davis were seeking to use the preembryos herself, but only if she could not achieve parenthood by any other reasonable means. We recognize the trauma that Mary Sue has already experienced and the additional discomfort to which she would be subjected if she opts to attempt IVF again. Still, she would have a reasonable opportunity, through IVF, to try once again to achieve parenthood in all its aspects—genetic, gestational, bearing, and rearing.

Further, we note that if Mary Sue Davis were unable to undergo another round of IVF, or opted not to try, she could still achieve the child-rearing aspects of parenthood through adoption. The fact that she and Junior Davis pursued adoption indicates that, at least at one time, she was willing to forego genetic parenthood and would have been satisfied by the child-rearing aspects of parenthood alone.

VIII. Conclusion

In summary, we hold that disputes involving the disposition of preembryos produced by *in vitro* fertilization should be resolved, first, by looking to the preferences of the progenitors. If their wishes cannot be ascertained,

or if there is dispute, then their prior agreement concerning disposition should be carried out. If no prior agreement exists, then the relative interests of the parties in using or not using the preembryos must be weighed. Ordinarily, the party wishing to avoid procreation should prevail, assuming that the other party has a reasonable possibility of achieving parenthood by means other than use of the preembryos in question. If no other reasonable alternatives exist, then the argument in favor of using the preembryos to achieve pregnancy should be considered. However, if the party seeking control of the preembryos intends merely to donate them to another couple, the objecting party obviously has the greater interest and should prevail. . . .

For the Reasons Set Out Above, the Judgment of the Court of Appeals Is Affirmed. . . .

Study Questions

1. What did the court hold in this case? Would the result have been different if Mary Sue had sought to implant the embryo in her own body? What guidance did it give for future cases?
2. Do you agree that the desires of the woman and the man should be given equal weight? Why? Why not?

Since the Tennessee Supreme Court's decision in *Davis v. Davis*, other States have had to grapple with the issue of who "owns" a couple's frozen preembryos. In *Kass v. Kass*, the New York Court of Appeals agreed with the Tennessee Supreme Court's view on the enforceability of potential parents' signed agreements concerning the disposition of frozen preembryos. The New York Court of Appeals held that the divorcing couple's agreement reflected their decision to donate their preembryos to research in the event of a divorce. 91 N.Y.S.2d 554, 696 N.E.2d 179 (1998).

In 2000, the Massachusetts Supreme Judicial Court also considered the enforceability of preembryo disposition contracts. In that case, a divorcing couple had signed a total of seven disposition agreements; the couple filled out the first and, for the subsequent agreements, the husband signed in blank and the wife filled in the form. For each of the seven forms, under the section requesting disposition instructions if the couple separated, the wife filled in that the preembryos should be returned to her for implantation. The court held that the agreement should not be enforced and listed several reasons: the form was only intended to explain their relationship with the infertility clinic, not be a binding agreement between them regarding the disposition of their preembryos; the form did not contain a duration provision (and the wife was attempting to enforce it four years after they had signed, in significantly changed circumstances and over the husband's objection); the form referred to separation rather than divorce; and the form was not a separation agreement binding a couple in a divorce proceeding (no provision for custody, support, or maintenance in the event the wife conceives and gives birth to a child). In addition, the court stated that for public policy reasons, even if the couple's agreement was unambiguous, it would not enforce an agreement that compelled one donor to become a parent against his or her will. *A.Z. v. B.Z.*, 725 N.E.2d 1051 (Mass. 2000).

The following year, the New Jersey Supreme Court also held that the right of one person not to procreate should prevail over the other person's right to procreate. In this case, a divorced woman did not want her ex-husband to be able to either use their frozen preembryos or donate them to an infertile couple. The divorced couple had signed a consent agreement when the preembryos were created, but the New Jersey Supreme Court found that the form did not clearly manifest the parties' intent regarding the disposition of their preembryos in the event of the dissolution of their marriage. It also noted that the better rule concerning predisposition agreements is to enforce agreements entered into at the time the *in vitro* process is begun, subject to the right of either party to change his or her mind and notify the clinic in writing of that change, up to the point of use or destruction of any stored preembryos. *J.B. v. M.B.*, 170 N.J. 9, 783 A.2d 707 (2001).

In 2002, the Washington Supreme Court considered a case involving a divorcing couple's dispute over the disposition of donor eggs. Although the ex-wife had no biological connection to the preembryos, the court found that the egg donor contract granted her and her ex-husband equal rights to the eggs. The egg donor contract did not, however, relate to the resulting preembryos, but the cryopreservation contract did. It stated that if the couple could not reach a mutual decision regarding disposition of their preembryos, they must petition a court for instructions. The court, in turn, determined the couple's intent from their cryopreservation contract. In that contract, they designated that their preembryos would be preserved for five years and then thawed and not allowed to undergo further development unless they requested participation in the clinic's program for an additional time and the clinic agreed. The court found that more than five years had passed since the couple signed the consent form and that they had not sought an extension of the contract with the clinic; therefore, the decision of the lower court to award the frozen preembryos to the ex-husband was reversed. *Litowitz v. Litowitz*, 146 Wn.2d 514, 48 P.3d 261 (2002).

More recently, a Texas court had the opportunity to decide a case of first impression in that State: whether the award of frozen embryos to as part of a "just and right" division of community property was appropriate in light of the parties' prior written agreement to discard the embryos. In this case, the husband and wife had created the embryos with their eggs and sperm through IVF with the expectation that they would be implanted in the wife's uterus. As part of the clinic's process, they signed a number of documents including one entitled, "Informed consent for Cryopreservation of Embryos" ("embryo agreement"). Through that document, the couple authorized the clinic to store frozen embryos until the clinic determined appropriate conditions existed for transfer of the embryos to the wife's uterus and both spouses agreed to the transfer. According to the document, they chose to discard the embryos in case of divorce. The document also permitted them to withdraw their consent to the disposition of the embryos and discontinue their participation in the clinic's program. Ultimately, three embryos developed sufficiently to warrant cryopreservation. The night before the scheduled implantation, the husband expressed feelings to his wife that led him to withdraw his consent for the implantation. The day of the implantation they informed the doctor that the wife would not go through with implantation. A month later they signed an agreement to unfreeze the embryos for implantation. The agreement was contingent on the couple getting approval from a counselor, but the agreement never took effect because they did not go to counseling.

Ultimately the husband filed for divorce and the wife counterclaimed for divorce. The couple reached a final, binding agreement during mediation, except for the frozen embryos. At trial, the husband asked the court to uphold the couple's agreement and order the embryos discarded. The wife wanted to have the embryos implanted so she could have a biological child, but did not want her husband to have any parental rights or responsibilities if any children were born. The trial court awarded the embryos to the wife and the husband appealed to the Court of Appeals for the First District of Texas. The appellate court reviewed Texas' statute regarding children of assisted reproduction and determined that permitting a husband and wife to voluntarily enter into an agreement, before implantation, that would provide for an embryo's disposition in the event of a contingency, such as divorce, best serves the State's public policy and the interests of the parties. It also determined that, absent some ambiguity, a contract will be interpreted pursuant to its plain language. In this case, it was clear that if the parties divorced the frozen embryos were to be discarded; therefore, the trial court abused its discretion by not enforcing the couple's embryo agreement. The court reversed the decision of the trial court and remanded the case to the trial court to enter an order to discard the embryos and the U.S. Supreme Court denied certiorari. *Roman v. Roman*, 193 S.W.3d 40 (Tex. Civ. App. 2006), *cert. denied* 552 U.S. 6 (2008). Perhaps the Supreme Court's decision not to review this matter is a signal that this type of case implicates contract law rather than the fundamental right to procreate or not to procreate.

Contract Parenthood

Not all assisted parenthood involves biological ties for both parents. Some couples who are unwilling or unable to employ these techniques have turned to contract parenthood, whereby through artificial insemination with the husband's sperm, another woman bears a child whom she then relinquishes to the couple. The well-publicized case, *In re Matter of Baby* M, highlighted the problems that can occur when such a "surrogate" changes her mind.

IN THE MATTER OF BABY M
New Jersey Supreme Court, 1988.
573 A.2d. 1127.

WILENTZ, C. J.

In this matter the Court is asked to determine the validity of a contract that purports to provide a new way of bringing children into a family. For a fee of $10,000, a woman agrees to be artificially inseminated with the semen of another woman's husband; she is to conceive a child, carry it to term, and after its birth surrender it to the natural father and his wife. The intent of the contract is that the child's natural mother will thereafter be forever separated from her child. The wife is to adopt the child, and she and the natural father are to be regarded as its parents for all purposes. The contract providing for this is called a "surrogacy contract," the natural mother inappropriately called the "surrogate mother." . . .

I. FACTS

In February 1985, William Stern and Mary Beth Whitehead entered into a surrogacy contract. It recited that Stern's wife, Elizabeth, was infertile, that they wanted a child, and that Mrs. Whitehead was willing to provide that child as the mother with Mr. Stern as the father.

The contract provided that through artificial insemination using Mr. Stern's sperm, Mrs. Whitehead would become pregnant, carry the child to term, bear it, deliver it to the Sterns, and thereafter do whatever was necessary to terminate her maternal rights so that Mrs. Stern could thereafter adopt the child. Mrs. Whitehead's husband, Richard, was also a party to the contract; Mrs. Stern was not. Mr. Whitehead promised to do all acts necessary to rebut the presumption of paternity under the Parentage Act. N.J.S.A. 9:17-43a(1), -44a. Although Mrs. Stern was not a party to the surrogacy agreement, the contract gave her sole custody of the child in the event of Mr. Stern's death. Mrs. Stern's status as a nonparty to the surrogate parenting agreement presumably was to avoid the application of the baby-selling statute to this arrangement. N.J.S.A. 9:3-54.

Mr. Stern, on his part, agreed to attempt the artificial insemination and to pay Mrs. Whitehead $10,000 after the child's birth, on its delivery to him. In a separate contract, Mr. Stern agreed to pay $7,500 to the Infertility Center of New York ("ICNY"). The Center's advertising campaigns solicit surrogate mothers and encourage infertile couples to consider surrogacy. ICNY arranged for the surrogacy contract by bringing the parties together, explaining the process to them, furnishing the contractual form, and providing legal counsel.

The history of the parties' involvement in this arrangement suggests their good faith. William and Elizabeth Stern were married in July 1974, having met at the University of Michigan, where both were Ph.D. candidates. Due to financial considerations and Mrs. Stern's pursuit of a medical degree and residency, they decided to defer starting a family until 1981. Before then, however, Mrs. Stern learned that she might have multiple sclerosis and that the disease in some cases renders pregnancy a serious health risk. Her anxiety appears to have exceeded the actual risk, which current medical authorities assess as minimal. Nonetheless that anxiety was evidently quite real, Mrs. Stern fearing that pregnancy might precipitate blindness, paraplegia, or other forms of debilitation. Based on the perceived risk, the Sterns decided to forego having their own children. The decision had a special significance for Mr. Stern. Most of his family had been destroyed in the Holocaust. As the family's only survivor, he very much wanted to continue his bloodline.

Initially the Sterns considered adoption, but were discouraged by the substantial delay apparently involved and by the potential problem they saw arising from their age and their differing religious backgrounds. They were most eager for some other means to start a family.

The paths of Mrs. Whitehead and the Sterns to surrogacy were similar. Both responded to advertising by ICNY. The Sterns' response, following their inquiries into adoption, was the result of their long-standing decision to have a child. Mrs. Whitehead's response apparently resulted from her sympathy with family members and others who could have no children (she stated that she wanted to give another couple the "gift of life"); she also wanted the $10,000 to help her family. . . .

The two couples met to discuss the surrogacy arrangement and decided to go forward. On February 6, 1985, Mr. Stern and Mr. and Mrs. Whitehead executed the surrogate parenting agreement. After several artificial inseminations over a period of months, Mrs. Whitehead became pregnant. The pregnancy was uneventful and on March 27, 1986, Baby M was born. . . .

Mrs. Whitehead realized, almost from the moment of birth, that she could not part with this child. She had felt a bond with it even during pregnancy. . . .

Nonetheless, Mrs. Whitehead was, for the moment, true to her word. Despite powerful inclinations to the contrary, she turned her child over to the Sterns on March 30 at the Whiteheads' home. . . . The next day she went to the Sterns' home and told them how much she was suffering. . . .

The Sterns, concerned that Mrs. Whitehead might indeed commit suicide, not wanting under any circumstances to risk that, and in any event believing that Mrs. Whitehead would keep her word [and return the child], turned the child over to her. It was not until four months later, after a series of attempts to regain possession of the child, that Melissa was returned to the Sterns, having been forcibly removed from the home where she was then living with Mr. and Mrs. Whitehead, the home in Florida owned by Mary Beth Whitehead's parents. . . .

The Sterns' complaint, in addition to seeking possession and ultimately custody of the child, [seeks] enforcement of the surrogacy contract. Pursuant to the contract, it ask[s] that the child be permanently placed in their custody, that Mrs. Whitehead's parental rights be terminated, and that Mrs. Stern be allowed to adopt the child, i.e., that for all purposes, Melissa become the Sterns' child. . . .

II. Invalidity and Unenforceability of Surrogacy Contract

We have concluded that this surrogacy contract is invalid. Our conclusion has two bases: direct conflict with existing statutes and conflict with the public policies of this State, as expressed in its statutory and decisional law. . . .

A. Conflict with Statutory Provisions. The surrogacy contract conflicts with: (1) laws prohibiting the use of money in connection with adoptions; (2) laws requiring proof of parental unfitness or abandonment before termination of parental rights is ordered or an adoption is granted; and (3) laws that make surrender of custody and consent to adoption revocable in private placement adoptions.

(1) Our law prohibits paying or accepting money in connection with any placement of a child for adoption. *N.J.S.A.* 9:3-54a. Violation is a high misdemeanor. *N.J.S.A.* 9:3-54c. Excepted are fees of an approved agency (which must be a non-profit entity, *N.J.S.A.* 9:3-38a) and certain expenses in connection with childbirth. *N.J.S.A.* 9:3-54b. . . .

The payment of the $10,000 occurs only on surrender of custody of the child and "completion of the duties and obligations" of Mrs. Whitehead, including termination of her parental rights to facilitate adoption by Mrs. Stern. As for the contention that the Sterns are paying only for services and not for an adoption, we need note only that they would pay nothing in the event the child died before the fourth month of pregnancy, and only $1,000 if the child were stillborn, even though the "services" had been fully rendered. Additionally, one of Mrs. Whitehead's estimated costs, to be assumed by Mr. Stern, was an "Adoption Fee," presumably for Mrs. Whitehead's incidental costs in connection with the adoption. . . .

The evils inherent in baby bartering are loathsome for a myriad of reasons. The child is sold without regard for whether the purchasers will be suitable parents. . . . The natural mother does not receive the benefit of counseling and guidance to assist her in making a decision that may affect her for a lifetime. In fact, the monetary incentive to sell her child may, depending on her financial circumstances, make her decision less voluntary. Furthermore, the adoptive parents may not be fully informed of the natural parents' medical history. . . . The negative consequences of baby buying are potentially present in the surrogacy context, especially the potential for placing and adopting a child without regard to the interest of the child or the natural mother.

(2) The termination of Mrs. Whitehead's parental rights . . . fails to comply with the stringent requirements of New Jersey law. Our law, recognizing the finality of any termination of parental rights, provides for such termination only where there has been

a voluntary surrender of a child to an approved agency or to the Division of Youth and Family Services ("DYFS"), accompanied by a formal document acknowledging termination of parental rights . . . or where there has been a showing of parental abandonment or unfitness. A termination may ordinarily take one of three forms: an action by an approved agency, an action by DYFS, or an action in connection with a private placement adoption. The three are governed by separate statutes, but the standards for termination are substantially the same, except that whereas a written surrender is effective when made to an approved agency or to DYFS, there is no provision for it in the private placement context. . . .

Our statutes, and the cases interpreting them, leave no doubt that where there has been no written surrender to an approved agency or to DYFS, termination of parental rights will not be granted in this State absent a very strong showing of abandonment or neglect. That showing is required in every context in which termination of parental rights is sought, be it an action by an approved agency, an action by DYFS, or a private placement adoption proceeding, even where the petitioning adoptive parent is, as here, a stepparent. . . .

It is clear that a "best interests" determination is never sufficient to terminate parental rights; the statutory criteria must be proved.

In this case a termination of parental rights was obtained not by proving the statutory prerequisites but by claiming the benefit of contractual provisions. From all that has been stated above, it is clear that a contractual agreement to abandon one's parental rights, or not to contest a termination action, will not be enforced in our courts. The Legislature would not have so carefully, so consistently, and so substantially restricted termination of parental rights if it had intended to allow termination to be achieved by one short sentence in a contract.

Since the termination was invalid, it follows, as noted above, that adoption of Melissa by Mrs. Stern could not properly be granted. . . .

(3) Mrs. Whitehead, shortly after the child's birth, had attempted to revoke her consent and surrender by refusing, after the Sterns had allowed her to have the child "just for one week," to return Baby M to them. The trial court's award of specific performance therefore reflects its view that the consent to surrender the child was irrevocable. We accept the trial court's construction of the contract; indeed it appears quite clear that this was the parties' intent. Such a provision, however, making irrevocable the natural mother's consent to surrender custody of her child in a private placement adoption, clearly conflicts with New Jersey law. . . .

There is only one irrevocable consent, and that is the one explicitly provided for by statute: a consent to surrender of custody and a placement with an approved agency or with DYFS. The provision in the surrogacy contract, agreed to before conception, requiring the natural mother to surrender custody of the child without any right of revocation is one more indication of the essential nature of this transaction: the creation of a contractual system of termination and adoption designed to circumvent our statutes.

B. Public Policy Considerations. The surrogacy contract's invalidity, resulting from its direct conflict with the above statutory provisions, is further underlined when its goals and means are measured against New Jersey's public policy. The contract's basic premise, that the natural parents can decide in advance of birth which one is to have custody of the child, bears no relationship to the settled law that the child's best interests shall determine custody. . . .

The surrogacy contract guarantees permanent separation of the child from one of its natural parents. Our policy, however, has long been that to the extent possible, children should remain with and be brought up by both of their natural parents. . . .

The surrogacy contract violates the policy of this State that the rights of natural parents are equal concerning their child, the father's right no greater than the mother's. . . .

The policies expressed in our comprehensive laws governing consent to the surrender of a child . . . stand in stark contrast to the surrogacy contract and what it implies. Here there is no counseling, independent or otherwise, of the natural mother, no evaluation, no warning.

. . . Under the contract, the natural mother is irrevocably committed before she knows the strength of her bond with her child. She never makes a totally voluntary, informed decision, for quite clearly any decision prior to the baby's birth is, in the most important sense, uninformed, and any decision after that, compelled by a pre-existing contractual commitment, the threat of a lawsuit, and the inducement of a $10,000 payment, is less than totally voluntary. Her interests are of little concern to those who controlled this transaction.

Although the interest of the natural father and adoptive mother is certainly the predominant interest, realistically the *only* interest served, even they are left with less than what public policy requires. They know little about the natural mother, her genetic makeup, and her psychological and medical history. Moreover, not even a superficial attempt is made to determine their awareness of their responsibilities as parents.

Worst of all, however, is the contract's total disregard of the best interests of the child. There is not the slightest suggestion that any inquiry will be made at any time to determine the fitness of the Sterns as custodial parents, of Mrs. Stern as an adoptive parent, their superiority to Mrs. Whitehead, or the effect on the child of not living with her natural mother.

This is the sale of a child, or, at the very least, the sale of a mother's right to her child, the only mitigating factor being that one of the purchasers is the father. Almost every evil that prompted the prohibition of the payment of money in connection with adoptions exists here. . . .

The point is made that Mrs. Whitehead *agreed* to the surrogacy arrangement, supposedly fully understanding the consequences. Putting aside the issue of how compelling her need for money may have been, and

how significant her understanding of the consequences, we suggest that her consent is irrelevant. There are, in a civilized society, some things that money cannot buy. In America, we decided long ago that merely because conduct purchased by money was "voluntary" did not mean that it was good or beyond regulation and prohibition. . . .

Employers can no longer buy labor at the lowest price they can bargain for, even though that labor is "voluntary," or buy women's labor for less money than paid to men for the same job, or purchase the agreement of children to perform oppressive labor, or purchase the agreement of workers to subject themselves to unsafe or unhealthful working conditions. There are, in short, values that society deems more important than granting to wealth whatever it can buy, be it labor, love, or life. Whether this principle recommends prohibition of surrogacy, which presumably sometimes results in great satisfaction to all of the parties, is not for us to say. We note here only that, under existing law, the fact that Mrs. Whitehead "agreed" to the arrangement is not dispositive.

The long-term effects of surrogacy contracts are not known, but feared—the impact on the child who learns her life was bought, that she is the offspring of someone who gave birth to her only to obtain money; the impact on the natural mother as the full weight of her isolation is felt along with the full reality of the sale of her body and her child; the impact on the natural father and adoptive mother once they realize the consequences of their conduct. . . .

Beyond that is the potential degradation of some women that may result from this arrangement. In many cases, of course, surrogacy may bring satisfaction, not only to the infertile couple, but to the surrogate mother herself. The fact, however, that many women may not perceive surrogacy negatively but rather see it as an opportunity does not diminish its potential for devastation to other women.

In sum, the harmful consequences of this surrogacy arrangement appear to us all too palpable. In New Jersey the surrogate mother's agreement to sell her child is void. Its irrevocability infects the entire contract, as does the money that purports to buy it.

III. TERMINATION

Nothing in this record justifies a finding that would allow a court to terminate Mary Beth Whitehead's parental rights under the statutory standard. . . .

IV. CONSTITUTIONAL ISSUES

. . . The right to procreate very simply is the right to have natural children, whether through sexual intercourse or artificial insemination. It is no more than that. Mr. Stern has not been deprived of that right. Through artificial insemination of Mrs. Whitehead, Baby M is his child. The custody, care, companionship, and nurturing that follow birth are not parts of the right to procreation; they are rights that may also be constitutionally protected, but that involve many considerations other than the right of procreation. To assert that Mr. Stern's right of procreation gives him the right to the custody of Baby M would be to assert that Mrs. Whitehead's right of procreation does *not* give her the right to the custody of Baby M; it would be to assert that the constitutional right of procreation includes within it a constitutionally protected contractual right to destroy someone else's right of procreation. . . .

Mrs. Whitehead, on the other hand, asserts a claim that falls within the scope of a recognized fundamental interest protected by the Constitution. As a mother, she claims the right to the companionship of her child. This is a fundamental interest, constitutionally protected. Furthermore, it was taken away from her by the action of the court below. Whether that action under these circumstances would constitute a constitutional deprivation, however, we need not and do not decide. By virtue of our decision Mrs. Whitehead's constitutional complaint—that her parental rights have been unconstitutionally terminated—is moot. . . .

V. CUSTODY

Having decided that the surrogacy contract is illegal and unenforceable, we now must decide the custody question without regard to the provisions of the surrogacy contract that would give Mr. Stern sole and permanent custody. . . . The applicable rule given these circumstances is clear: the child's best interests determine custody. . . . The issue here is which life would be *better* for Baby M, one with primary custody in the Whiteheads or one with primary custody in the Sterns. . . .

There were eleven experts who testified concerning the child's best interests, either directly or in connection with matters related to that issue. Our reading of the record persuades us that the trial court's decision awarding custody to the Sterns (technically to Mr. Stern) should be affirmed. . . .

VI. VISITATION

The trial court's decision to terminate Mrs. Whitehead's parental rights precluded it from making any determination on visitation. 217 *N.J. Super.* at 399, 408. Our reversal of the trial court's order, however, requires delineation of Mrs. Whitehead's rights to visitation. It is apparent to us that this factually sensitive issue, which was never addressed below, should not be determined *de novo* by this Court. We therefore remand the visitation issue to the trial court for an abbreviated hearing and determination as set forth below. . . .

STUDY QUESTIONS

1. Why did the court reverse the trial court's order terminating parental rights? Do you agree that surrogacy contracts present the same dangers as payments for adoptions? Do you think the New Jersey Supreme Court would have refused to enforce the contract even in the absence of a State law prohibiting payments for adoptions?
2. Do you agree with the New Jersey Supreme Court that a woman agreeing to bear and relinquish a child under a

surrogacy agreement "never makes a to-tally voluntary, informed decision, for quite clearly any decision prior to the baby's birth is, in the most important sense, uninformed, and any decision after that, compelled by a pre-existing contractual commitment, the threat of a lawsuit, and the inducement of a [substantial] payment, is less than totally voluntary?" How does such a decision differ from the decision to enter into an agreement to perform difficult or dangerous work that a person may never have performed before?

3. In an omitted portion of the opinion, the court stated that "when father and mother are separated and disagree, at birth, on custody, only in an extreme,

truly rare, case should the child be taken from its mother . . . before the dispute is finally determined by the court on its merits." Do you agree? Does it make a difference whether the child is a product of a surrogacy arrangement or a more conventional relationship between the biological parents?

4. Mary Beth Whitehead was Baby M's mother in two senses: She both gave the egg and carried the pregnancy that produced Baby M. Is a woman who gestates a fetus produced by the egg and sperm of another couple also the mother of the resulting child in your view? What rights do you believe such a woman should have with respect to the child?

The *Baby* M case and the surrogacy issue generally caused a big controversy. State legislatures considered bills to permit, bills to regulate, and bills to ban parenthood contracts. A number of considerations shape the varying views. There is disagreement over whether a woman's "consent" to relinquish her child can ever be voluntary if it is given prior to birth. There is disagreement over whether commitments concerning children yet to be born are different than commitments concerning other future events. There is disagreement over the inevitability of exploitation resulting from class differences between the birth mother and the contracting couple. Finally, there is disagreement over whether it is possible to protect the birth mother, the child, and society in general from harmful aspects of the practice—and if so, how to do it.

As of 2005, approximately twenty-three States and the District of Columbia had enacted surrogacy laws or permitted surrogacy arrangements through case law, but their coverage varies widely. Some States prohibit paid surrogacy contracts, others prohibit unpaid surrogacy contracts, and still others prohibit both. Arizona, Indiana, Louisiana, Nebraska, New York, and North Dakota prohibit surrogate contracts. Michigan and D.C. not only prohibit surrogacy contracts, they also impose fines and jail time on anyone entering into such a contract. With respect to the States that allow surrogacy contracts, there is no uniformity. For example, Florida allows both traditional and gestational surrogacy contracts, but Louisiana, Illinois, and New Jersey permit only gestational surrogacy. Washington, Virginia, New Mexico, and Oregon permit uncompensated surrogacy contracts. Texas and Utah permit surrogacy contracts, but these agreements are heavily regulated and require that the intended parents be married. Tennessee, Virginia, Nevada, Florida, and New Hampshire also require that the intended parents be married and, in some instances, the married couple must be heterosexual. Some States ban payments to surrogates, but will allow payment of surrogates' expenses. Some State statutes create a presumption that the surrogate and her husband are the parents of the child, while others presume the biological father and wife are the parents. And, in some States, the contracting couple are presumed to be the parents, but the surrogate is given a period of time to change her mind.

The recent development of gestational surrogacy makes us ask to what extent is the situation different where there are two biological mothers—the genetic and the gestational. In gestational surrogacy, an egg taken from one woman is fertilized and placed in another woman who ultimately gives birth. Should the decision of such a woman not to relinquish the child she bears to its genetic parents be considered differently than Mary Beth White-head's decision not to relinquish Baby M to Bill Stern?

A recent California Supreme Court decision, *Johnson v. Calvert* 851, P.2d 776 (1993), concerned the unsuccessful claim of a gestational surrogate to parental rights. By contract, Anna Johnson was implanted with an embryo created by the egg and sperm of a wife and husband, Crispina Calvert and Mark Calvert. Johnson ultimately bore their genetic child.

The California Supreme Court made plain its view that a gestational surrogate does not have the rights of a biological mother. Thus, the Court held that a woman who, by agreement, has a zygote implanted in her and carries the resulting fetus to term provides a necessary and important service, but has no privacy, liberty, or other constitutional rights requiring recognition or protection of her status as "birth mother." The Court also refused to invalidate gestational surrogacy agreements on the grounds that they inevitably run afoul of constitutional prohibitions on involuntary servitude or tend to degrade and dehuman-ize women. This holding is particularly noteworthy in view of the fact that the gestational mother in *Johnson v. Calvert* was an African American, the genetic mother was Filipino, and the genetic father was Caucasian.

Two recent State court decisions suggest that gestational surrogacy may be more acceptable legally than "traditional" surrogacy. After *Johnson v. Calvert*, in which the California Su-preme Court awarded a child born by gestational surrogacy to the contracting couple, who were the biological parents, a middle-level California court held that a "traditional" surrogacy arrangement was unenforceable under the state adoption law. *Moschetta v. Moschetta*, 25 Cal. App. 4th 1218, 30 Cal. Rptr. 893 (1994). And, in *Soos v. Superior Court*, 897 P.2d 1356 (Ariz. App. Div. 1994), a middle-level Arizona court held that a statute intended to prohibit surrogacy was unconstitutional as applied to gestational surrogacy. The statute declared the surrogate or birth mother to be any resulting child's legal mother, and her husband (if she was married) was presumed to be the father. That presumption could be rebutted, however, by the biological father, who then became the legal father. Because there was no way for the genetic mother to replace the gestational mother as the legal mother, the statute was declared uncon-stitutional; it violated federal and State equal protection guarantees.

Concerns raised by the *Johnson* case, as well as the phenomenon of gestational surrogacy generally, involve its potential for class and race exploitation of surrogates by better-off contracting couples. Competing with these concerns, however, is the interest in allow-ing women to make contracts and the perceived need to designate both male and female "blood" parents as the parent.

Are donor insemination fertilization, *in vitro*, and other complex reproductive technolo-gies, or surrogacy arrangements the best way to combat fertility problems? One commentator suggests it would be better to address the causes of infertility, such as pelvic inflammatory dis-ease, medically prescribed drugs, devices, and operations and environmental and workplace hazards directly. She also argues for basic assistance to help infants survive their first year of life, as well as ways to integrate work and family so that childbearing will not be postponed beyond the point of fertility. Finally, she contends that it is important to address the social pain of infertility by expanding the ways adults may relate to children to include informal arrangements as well as adoption, step-parenthood, and foster care. *See* Nadine Taub, "Sur-rogacy: A Preferred Treatment for Infertility?" 16 *Law, Medicine and Health Care* 89 (1988).

Are there race and class overtones to emphasizing individual, high-tech approaches rather than aiming resources collectively at societal inequalities? Consider the following.

Race and the New Reproduction

Dorothy Roberts

Killing the Black Body: Race, Reproduction and the Meaning of Liberty,
New York: Pantheon, 1997. Excerpts from Chapter 6,
pp. 246–47, 250–53, 279–82, and 285.

A friend of mine recently questioned my interest in a custody battle covered on the evening news. A surrogate mother who had agreed to gestate a fetus for a fee decided she wanted to keep the baby. "Why are you always so fascinated by those stories?" he asked. "They have nothing to do with Black people." By "those stories" he meant the growing number of controversies occupying the headlines that involve children created by new methods of reproduction. More and more Americans are using a variety of technologies to facilitate conception, ranging from simple artificial insemination to expensive, advanced procedures such as *in vitro* fertilization (IVF) and egg donation. (footnote omitted)

In one sense my friend is right: the images that mark these controversies appear to have little to do with Black people and issues of race. Think about the snapshots that promote the new reproduction. They always show white people. And the baby produced often has blond hair and blue eyes—as if to emphasize her racial purity. The infertile suburban housewife's agonizing attempts to become pregnant via IVF; the rosy-cheeked baby held up to television cameras as the precious product of a surrogacy arrangement; the complaint that there are not enough babies for all the middle-class couples who desperately want to adopt; the fate of orphaned frozen embryos whose wealthy progenitors died in an airplane crash: all seem far removed from most Black people's lives. Yet it is precisely their racial subtext that gives these images much of their emotional appeal.

Ultimately my attraction to these stories stems from my interest in the devaluation of *Black* reproduction. As I have charted the proliferation of rhetoric and policies that degrade Black women's procreative decisions, I have also noticed that America is obsessed with creating and preserving genetic ties between white parents and their children. This chapter explores the reasons for the racial disparity that marks the new reproduction, as well as the impact of race on the right to recreate children by technological means. . . .

How Race Shapes the New Reproduction

While acknowledging that poor women of color are the most vulnerable to reproductive control, the feminist critique identifies male domination as the central source of the oppressive use of reproduction-assisting technologies. But these technologies reflect and reinforce a racist standard for procreation, as well. Similar to technologies that *prevent* births, the politics of technologies that *assist* births is shaped by race.

One of the most striking features of the new reproduction is that it is used almost exclusively by white people. Of course, the busiest fertility clinics can point to some Black middle-class patients; but they stand out as rare exceptions. Only about one-third of all couples experiencing infertility seek medical treatment at all; and only 10 to 15 percent of infertile couples seeking treatment use advanced techniques like IVF. (footnote omitted) Blacks make up a disproportionate number of infertile people *avoiding* reproductive technologies. White women seeking treatment for fertility problems are twice as likely to use high-tech treatments as Black women. (footnote omitted) Only 12.8 percent of Black women in the latest national survey used specialized infertility services such as fertility drugs, artificial insemination, tubal surgery, or IVF, compared with 27.2 percent of white women.

As my story that opened this chapter reflects, media images of the new reproduction mirror this racial disparity. Most of the news stories proclaiming the benefits of the technology involve infertile white couples. When the 1986 *Baby M* trial propelled the issue of surrogacy to national attention, major magazines and newspapers were plastered with photos of the parties (all white) battling for custody of Melissa.

Ten years later, in January 1996, the *New York Times* launched a prominent four-article series called "The Fertility Market." The front page displayed a photograph of the director of a fertility clinic surrounded by seven white children conceived there. The continuing page contained a picture of a set of beaming IVF triplets, also white. (footnote omitted)

The following June, *Newsweek* ran a cover story entitled "The Biology of Beauty" reporting scientific confirmation of human beings' inherent obsession with beauty. (footnote omitted) The article featured a striking full-page color spread of a woman with blond hair and blue eyes. The caption asked rhetorically: "Reproductive fitness: Would you want your children to carry this person's genes?" The answer, presumably, was supposed to be a resounding, universal "Yes!"

When we do read news accounts involving Black children created by these technologies, they are usually sensational stories intended to evoke revulsion precisely because of the children's race. Several years ago a white woman brought a highly publicized lawsuit against a fertility clinic she claimed had mistakenly inseminated her with a Black man's sperm, instead of her husband's, resulting in the birth of a Black child. (footnote omitted) The woman, who was the child's biological mother, demanded monetary damages for her injury, which she explained was due to the unbearable racial taunting her daughter suffered. Two reporters covering the story speculated that "[i]f the suit goes to trial, a jury could be faced with the difficult task of deciding damages involved in raising an interracial child." (footnote omitted) Although receiving the wrong sperm was an injury in itself, the fact that it came from someone of the wrong race added a unique dimension of harm to the error. This second harm to the mother was the fertility clinic's failure to deliver a crucial part of its service—a white child.

In a similar, but more bizarre, incident in The Netherlands in 1995, a woman who gave birth to twin boys as a result of IVF realized when the babies were two months old that one was white and one was Black. (footnote omitted) The Dutch fertility clinic mistakenly fertilized her eggs with sperm from both her husband and a Black man. A *Newsweek* article subtitled "A Fertility Clinic's Startling Error" reported that "while one boy was as blond as his parents, the other's skin was darkening and his brown hair was fuzzy." (footnote omitted) A large color photograph displayed the two infant twins, one white and one Black, sitting side by side—a racial intermingling that would not occur in nature. The image presented a new-age freak show, created by modern technology gone berserk.

The stories exhibiting blond-haired blue-eyed babies born to white parents portray the positive potential of the new reproduction. The stories involving the mixed-race children reveal its potential horror.

REASONS FOR THE DISPARITY

These images, along with the predominant use of fertility services by white couples, indisputably show that race affects the popularity of reproductive technologies in America. What are the reasons underlying this connection between race and the new reproduction?

First, it has nothing to do with rates of infertility. Blacks have an infertility rate one and one-half times *higher* than that of whites. (footnote omitted) (The racial disparity may actually be greater due to underreporting of infertility by married Black women.) While the overall infertility rate in America was declining, the infertility rate of young Black women tripled between 1965 and 1982. (footnote omitted) The reasons for the high incidence of infertility among Black women include untreated chlamydia and gonorrhea, STDs that can lead to pelvic inflammatory disease; nutritional deficiencies; complications of childbirth and abortion; and environmental and workplace hazards.

In fact, the profile of people most likely to use IVF is precisely the opposite of those most likely to be infertile. The people in the United States most likely to be infertile are poor, Black, and poorly educated. (footnote omitted) Most couples who use IVF and other high-tech procedures are white, highly educated, and affluent.

Besides, the new reproduction has far more to do with enabling people to have children who are genetically related to them than with helping infertile people to have children. (footnote omitted) *Baby* M and other well-known surrogacy cases involved fertile white men with an infertile wife who hired a surrogate so they could pass on their own genes to a child. Moreover, as many as half of the women who undergo IVF are themselves fertile, although their husbands are not. Both scenarios involve *fertile* people who use new reproductive technologies to create genetic offspring. In short, use of high-tech fertility treatment does not depend on the physical incapacity to produce a child.

Instead, the racial disparity appears to stem from a complex inter-play of financial barriers, cultural preferences, and more deliberate professional manipulation. . . .

THE BLACK GESTATIONAL SURROGATE

Gestational surrogacy separates the biological connection between mother and child into two parts—the gestational tie and the genetic tie. (footnote omitted) In gestational surrogacy, the hired gestator is implanted with an embryo produced by fertilizing the contracting mother's egg with the contracting father's sperm using IVF. The child therefore inherits the genes of both contracting parents and is genetically unrelated to her birth mother. This type of surrogate is treated even more like an "incubator" or "womb for rent" than paid gestators who contribute an egg to the deal. Gestational surrogacy disconnects the parents' valuable genes from the gestator's exploited reproductive capacity.

Gestational surrogacy allows a radical possibility that is at once very convenient and very dangerous: a Black woman can give birth to a white child. White men need no longer rely on white surrogates to produce their valuable white genetic inheritance. This possibility reverses the traditional presumptions about a mother's biological connection to her children. The law has always understood legal parentage to arise definitively from female, but not male, biology. (footnote omitted) The European-American tradition identifies a child's mother by the biological act of giving birth: at common law, a woman was the legal mother of the child she bore. But Black gestational surrogacy makes it imperative to legitimate the genetic tie between the (white) father and the child, rather than the biological, nongenetic tie between the (Black) birth mother and the child.

In *Johnson v. Calvert*, a gestational surrogacy dispute, the court legitimated the genetic relationship and denied the gestational one in order to reject a Black woman's bond with the child. (footnote omitted) The birth mother, Anna Johnson, was a former welfare recipient and a single mother of a three-year-old daughter. The genetic mother, Crispina Calvert, was Filipina, and the father, Mark Calvert, was white. The press, however, paid far more attention to Anna Johnson's race than to that of Crispina Calvert. It also portrayed the baby as white. During her pregnancy, Anna changed her mind about relinquishing the baby and both Anna and the Calverts filed lawsuits to gain parental rights to the child.

Judge Richard N. Parslow, Jr., framed the critical issue as determining the baby's "natural mother." Johnson's attorney relied on the historical presumption that the woman who gives birth to a child is the child's natural, and legal, mother. All States except Arkansas and Nevada apply an irrebuttable presumption of legal parenthood in favor of the birth mother. (footnote omitted) Yet Judge Parslow held that Johnson had no standing to sue for custody or visitation rights, and granted the Calverts sole custody of the baby. His reasoning centered on genetics. Judge Parslow described the Calverts as "desperate and longing for their own genetic product." (footnote omitted) He noted the need for genetically related children and compared gestation to a foster parents' temporary care for a child who is not genetically hers. (Robertson has similarly argued that the gestational surrogate is a "trustee" for the embryo and should be kept to "her promise to honor the genetic bond.") (footnote omitted)

Judge Parslow also equated a child's identity with her genetic composition: "We know more and more about traits now, how you walk, talk, and everything else, all sorts of things that develop out of your genes." (footnote omitted) On appeal, the California court of appeals also saw genetics as "a powerful factor in human relationships," writing, "The fact that another person is, literally, developed from a part of oneself can furnish the basis for a profound psychological bond. Heredity can provide a basis of connection between two individuals for the duration of their lives." (footnote omitted) The California Supreme Court affirmed this view, reducing the legal significance of gestation to mere evidence of the determinative *genetic* connection between mother and child.

The California courts reduced legal motherhood to the contribution of an egg to the procreative process. But the law need not place such primacy on genetic relatedness. There is little doubt, for example, that a court would not consider a woman who donated her eggs to an infertile couple to be the legal mother, despite her genetic connection to the child. By relying on the genetic tie to determine legal parenthood, the courts in the *Johnson* case ensured that a Black woman would not be the "natural mother" of a white child. . . .

Gestational surrogacy invokes the possibility that white middle-class couples will use Black women to gestate their babies. Since contracting couples need not be concerned about the gestator's genetic qualities (most important, her race), they may favor hiring the most economically vulnerable women in order to secure the lowest price for their services. Black gestators would be doubly disadvantaged in any custody dispute: besides being less able to afford a court battle, they are unlikely to win custody of the white child they bear, as the *Johnson* case demonstrates. Writer Katha Pollitt speculates that this legal advantage might have been the Calverts' motive for choosing a Black gestational surrogate in the first place. "Black women have, after all, always raised white children without acquiring any rights to them," Pollitt notes. "Now they can breed them, too." (footnote omitted)

Some writers had already predicted a caste of breeders, composed of women of color whose primary function would be to gestate the embryos of more valuable white women. (footnote omitted) These breeders, whose own genetic progeny would be considered worthless, might be sterilized. The vision of Black women's wombs in the service of white men conjures up images from slavery. Slave women were similarly compelled to breed children who would be owned by their masters and to breastfeed their masters' white infants, while neglecting their own children. In fact, Anna Johnson's lawyer likened the arrangement Johnson made with the Calverts to "a slave contract." (footnote omitted) . . .

WHAT SHOULD WE DO?

What does it mean that we live in a country in which white women disproportionately undergo expensive technologies to enable them to bear children, while Black women disproportionately undergo surgery that prevents them from being able to bear any? Surely this contradiction must play a critical part in current deliberations about the morality of these technologies. What exactly does race mean for our understanding of the new reproduction?

Let us consider three possible responses for social policy. First, we might acknowledge that race influences the use of reproductive technologies, but decide this does not justify interfering with individuals' liberty to use them. Second, we could work to ensure greater access to these technologies by providing public assistance or including them in insurance plans. Finally, we might determine that these technologies are harmful and that their use should therefore be discouraged.

STUDY QUESTIONS

1. How do modern reproductive techniques "reflect and reinforce a racist standard for procreation"? What is the connection between race and the use of these technologies? Do racial infertility rates correlate with the use of modern reproductive technology by race? Why or why not?

2. What types of scenarios involving black children created by modern reproductive technologies make it into the news? Do you agree or disagree with Roberts's assertion that stories about mixed-race children reveal the potential horrors of the new reproduction?

3. What effect does class status have on modern reproductive technology use? Who is most likely to act as a surrogate for an infertile couple?

4. What do you think of the judge's decision in *Johnson v. Calvert*? Does society view the birth of a white child to a black woman (surrogate) differently than the birth of a black child to a white (inseminated) woman? Should we?

Roberts references a prediction by some that the expanding use of assisted reproduction technologies will result in the creation of a ". . . caste of breeders, composed of women of color whose primary function would be to gestate the embryos of more valuable white women." But should this concern be directed only at surrogacy arrangements within the United States? Consider, for example, the developing business of international surrogacy. Couples who are unable to obtain the services of a surrogate in the United States because of restrictive regulation, high cost (medical, legal, and other allowable fees), or lack of women willing to be a surrogate, are seeking international options. In India, for example, where surrogacy is legal, the costs associated with the procedure are considerably lower than those in the United States. The more reasonable cost (even factoring in travel) makes surrogacy accessible to a wider class of individuals. It is not illegal to pay a surrogate in India, which makes it easier to attract candidates. And, given the economic status of the surrogates, it makes the fee attractive to both the surrogate and the couple. Is this akin to paying for babies? Is hiring the wombs of poor Indian women just another form of exploitation of disadvantaged, minority women? Does this practice create an ethical dilemma for American women? It will be interesting to see whether this growing "industry" stimulates the development of laws to keep it in check.

Birthing Arrangements

Our discussions of contraception, abortion, and sterilization have all centered on the question of procreative choice: the ability of individuals—particularly women—to determine if and when to have children. We now consider the conditions and arrangements under which their children will be born. As before, a key concern is the law's role in determining who may make such decisions, particularly in light of technological advances bearing on these conditions. Initially, we will consider decisions involving the choice of caregivers and the nature of the care given during pregnancy and childbirth.

Medical control of pregnancy and childbirth has historically been closely linked to the view that health care services for mothers and children, like other aspects of health care, are a private matter. In 1921, shortly after women received the vote, Congress enacted a program to reduce maternal and infant mortality, the country's first federally funded health care program. The Sheppard-Towner Act, which created a network of prenatal and well-baby centers, was an important victory for women reformers. They had fought to establish the principle that preventive health care was a public, not merely private, responsibility and to give women a primary role in community health and welfare. The centers were generally staffed by female physicians and public health nurses, leaving to male physicians in private practice the care of those who were already sick. Though very successful in providing the services mandated by the law, the program was dismantled by the end of the decade as a result of a highly effective campaign mounted by the medical profession under the leadership of the American Medical Association. With Sheppard-Towner's downfall, women lost their special role in the field of maternal and child health, and preventive health care shifted back to the male-dominated private sector.

Since that time, as of mid-1993, there has been no similar comprehensive program to combat infant and maternal mortality, despite some initiatives by the Clinton Administration. At present, some maternal and infant care services are available to the poor through Medicaid and other government programs. Although the United States has made great strides in reducing infant mortality, its infant mortality rates far exceed those of other industrialized nations. Moreover, black babies continue to die at nearly twice the rate of white babies. When race and class effects are combined, infant death rates are even higher. Among the problems low-income women face in seeking maternity care are the lack of community-based programs offering prenatal care, physicians' refusal to accept Medicaid patients, and hospital policies requiring large cash deposits as a condition for admitting uninsured patients.

The trend toward viewing childbirth as a medical rather than a natural event has had an important impact on the allocation of decision-making power as both a practical and a legal matter. This trend dates back at least to the nineteenth century, when the more "scientific" and predominately male medical profession sought to drive out "irregular," often female, health practitioners. By 1900, most middle- and upper-class women had accepted the idea that childbirth required a physician's intervention and supervision. However, 50 percent of babies—those of the rural poor and immigrant working classes in the cities—were still being delivered with the help of [stet] midwives. In the early twentieth century, despite evidence that midwives were actually safer than doctors, physicians succeeded in having the practice of midwifery narrowly restricted by a series of licensing requirements and other laws and regulations adopted at the State level.

Medical control has meant a change in the nature of care as well as a change in personnel. Doctors' care has been characterized by greater intervention, initially with forceps and later with hospitalization, anesthesia, and surgery. Increasing caesarean section rates, prenatal testing, and use of fetal monitors are modern manifestations of the treatment of pregnancy as a medical event. The women's health movement and other consumer drives of the late 1960s and 1970s have led women and men to question the benefits of this medical focus and prompted potential parents to seek greater control over childbearing. Some have sought to change their relations with physicians so as to participate more actively in the care. Others have expressed renewed interest in natural childbirth methods, midwifery, birthing centers, and home births.

Legal challenges to medical hegemony over pregnancy and childbirth have come about in a variety of ways. As middle- and upper-class consumers increasingly began to seek alternative forms of care, licensing boards and prosecutors cracked down on professional and lay midwives. In a well-publicized California case, for example, three unlicensed California midwives associated with the Santa Cruz Birth Center were prosecuted for practicing medicine without a license. In a unanimous opinion, the California Supreme Court held in *Bowland v. Municipal Court*, 556 P.2d. 1081 (1976), that attending normal childbirth did constitute practicing medicine and that only those midwives licensed before 1949, when the licensing provisions were abolished, could legally assist at births. This ruling was followed by new State legislation authorizing nurse-midwives to provide prenatal, intrapartum, and post-partum care, including family planning care, for the mother and immediate care for the infant, so long as they practiced under the general supervision of a physician. Midwives and consumers have fought similar battles in other jurisdictions to protect and extend the midwives' right to practice.

Other legal challenges to medical hegemony in the birthing context have involved providers' efforts to compel pregnant women to undergo caesarean sections rather than natural childbirth. A question clearly at stake in such cases is the weight to be accorded the interests of the fetus compared to those of the woman. In thinking about this area, consider whether you believe the woman or the medical profession is best able to determine the interests of the fetus.

IN RE A.C.
D.C. Court of Appeals, 1990.
573 A.2d 1234.

On hearing en banc TERRY, Associate Judge:

This case comes before the court for the second time. [In 1987, a three-judge court] denied a motion to stay an order of the trial court which had authorized a hospital to perform a caesarean section on a dying woman in an effort to save the life of her unborn child. The operation was performed, but both the mother and the child died. A few months later, the court ordered the case heard en banc and vacated the [earlier] opinion. . . .

We are confronted here with [a] profoundly difficult and complex [issue]. . . . [W]e must determine who has the right to decide the course of medical treatment for a patient who, although near death, is pregnant with a viable fetus. [The discussion of how that decision should be made if the patient cannot make it for herself is omitted.]

We hold that in virtually all cases the question of what is to be done is to be decided by the patient—the pregnant woman—on behalf of herself and the fetus. . . .

A.C. was first diagnosed as suffering from cancer at the age of thirteen. In the ensuing years she underwent major surgery several times, together with multiple radiation treatments and chemotherapy. A.C. married when she was twenty-seven, during a period of remission, and soon thereafter she became pregnant. She was excited about her pregnancy and very much wanted the child. Because of her medical history, she was referred in her fifteenth week of pregnancy to the high-risk pregnancy clinic at George Washington University Hospital.

On Tuesday, June 9, 1987, when A.C. was approximately twenty-five weeks pregnant, she went to the hospital for a scheduled check-up. Because she was experiencing pain in her back and shortness of breath, an x-ray was taken; revealing an apparently inoperable tumor which nearly filled her right lung. On Thursday, June 11, A.C. was admitted to the hospital as a patient. By Friday her condition had temporarily improved, and when asked if she really wanted to have her baby, she replied that she did.

Over the weekend A.C.'s condition worsened considerably. Accordingly, on Monday, June 15, members of the medical staff treating A.C. assembled, along with her family, in A.C.'s room. The doctors then informed her that her illness was terminal, and A.C. agreed to palliative treatment designed to extend her life until at least her twenty-eighth week of pregnancy. The "potential outcome [for] the fetus," according to the doctors, would be much better at twenty-eight weeks than at twenty-six weeks if it were necessary to "intervene." A.C. knew that the palliative treatment she had chosen presented some increased risk to the fetus, but she opted for this course both to prolong her life for at least another two weeks and to maintain her own comfort. When asked if she still wanted to have the baby, A.C. was somewhat equivocal, saying "something to the effect of 'I don't know, I think so.'" As the day moved toward evening, A.C.'s condition grew still worse, and at about 7:00 or 8:00 P.M. she consented to intubation to facilitate her breathing.

The next morning, June 16, the trial court convened a hearing at the hospital in response to the hospital's request for a declaratory judgment. The court appointed counsel for both A.C. and the fetus, and the District of Columbia was permitted to intervene for the fetus as parens patriae. The court heard testimony on the facts as we have summarized them, and further testimony that at twenty-six and a half weeks the fetus was viable, i.e., capable of sustained life outside of the mother, given artificial aid. A neonatologist, Dr. Maureen Edwards, testified that the chances of survival for a twenty-six week fetus delivered at the hospital might be as high as eighty percent, but that this particular fetus, because

of the mother's medical history, had only a fifty to sixty percent chance of survival. Dr. Edwards estimated that the risk of substantial impairment for the fetus, if it were delivered promptly, would be less than twenty percent. However, she noted that the fetus' condition was worsening appreciably at a rapid rate, and another doctor—Dr. Alan Weingold, an obstetrician who was one of A.C.'s treating physicians—stated that any delay in delivering the child by caesarean section lessened its chances of survival. . . .

There was no evidence before the court showing that A.C. consented to, or even contemplated, a caesarean section before her twenty-eighth week of pregnancy. There was, in fact, considerable dispute as to whether she would have consented to an immediate caesarean delivery at the time the hearing was held. . . .

. . . The operation took place, but the baby lived for only a few hours, and A.C. succumbed to cancer two days later.

. . . [O]ur analysis of this case begins with the tenet common to all medical treatment cases: that any person has the right to make an informed choice, if competent to do so, to accept or forego medical treatment. The doctrine of informed consent, based on this principle and rooted in the concept of bodily integrity, is ingrained in our common law. . . .

In the same vein, courts do not compel one person to permit a significant intrusion upon his or her bodily integrity for the benefit of another person's health. See, *McFall v. Shimp,* 10 Pa. D. & C.3d 90 (Allegheny County Ct. 1978) [refusing to order Shimp to donate bone marrow which was necessary to save the life of his cousin, McFall].

. . . It has been suggested that fetal cases are different because a woman who "has chosen to lend her body to bring [a] child into the world" has an enhanced duty to assure the welfare of the fetus, sufficient even to require her to undergo caesarean surgery. Robertson, Procreative Liberty, supra, 69 VA.L.REV. at 456. Surely, however, a fetus cannot have rights in this respect superior to those of a person who has already been born. . . .

In those rare cases in which a patient's right to decide her own course of treatment has been judicially overridden, courts have usually acted to vindicate the State's interest in protecting third parties, even if in fetal State. See *Jefferson v. Griffin Spalding County Hospital Authority*, 274 S.E.2d 457 (1981) (ordering that caesarean section be performed on a woman in her thirty-ninth week of pregnancy to save both the mother and the fetus); *Raleigh Fitkin-Paul Morgan Memorial Hospital v. Anderson*, 201 A.2d 537 (ordering blood transfusions over the objection of a Jehovah's Witness, in her thirty-second week of pregnancy, to save her life and that of the fetus), cert. denied, 377. U.S. 985 (1964). . . .

What we distill from the cases discussed in this section is that every person has the right, under the common law and the Constitution, to accept or refuse medical treatment. . . . Further, it matters not what the quality of a patient's life may be; the right of bodily integrity is not extinguished simply because someone is ill, or even at death's door. To protect that right against intrusion by others—family members, doctors, hospitals, or anyone else, however well-intentioned—we hold that a court must determine the patient's wishes by any means available, and must abide by those wishes unless there are truly extraordinary or compelling reasons to override them. . . .

. . . We hold . . . that without a competent refusal from A.C. to go forward with the surgery, and without a finding through substituted judgment that A.C. would not have consented to the surgery, it was error for the trial court to proceed to a balancing analysis, weighing the rights of A.C. against the interests of the State.

There are two additional arguments against overriding A.C.'s objections to caesarean surgery. First, as the American Public Health Association cogently States in its amicus curiae brief:

> Rather than protecting the health of women and children, court-ordered caesareans erode the element of trust that

permits a pregnant woman to communicate to her physician—without fear of reprisal—all information relevant to her proper diagnosis and treatment. An even more serious consequence of court-ordered intervention is that it drives women at high risk of complications during pregnancy and childbirth out of the health care system to avoid coerced treatment.

Second, and even more compellingly, any judicial proceeding in a case such as this will ordinarily take place—like the one before us here—under time constraints so pressing that it is difficult or impossible for the mother to communicate adequately with counsel, or for counsel to organize, an effective, factual and legal presentation in defense of her liberty and privacy interests and bodily integrity. Any intrusion implicating such basic values ought not to be lightly undertaken when the mother not only is precluded from conducting pre-trial discovery (to which she would be entitled as a matter of course in any controversy over even a modest amount of money) but also is in no position to prepare meaningfully for trial. . . .

. . . [I]n virtually all cases the decision of the patient, albeit discerned through the mechanism of substituted judgment, will control. We do not quite foreclose the possibility that a conflicting State interest may be so compelling that the patient's wishes must yield, but we anticipate that such cases will be extremely rare and truly exceptional. This is not such a case. . . .

Study Questions

1. Would the majority of the appellate court have required A.C. to submit to the cesarean section? Why not? Would it ever order such operations over the woman's wishes? Under what circumstances? Do you agree?

2. Are cases such as *Jefferson v. Griffin Spalding Cty. Hosp. Auth.*, 274 S.E.2d 457 (Ga. 1981), distinguishable from *In re A.C.* in that the medical procedure

used in the former was in the medical interests of both the woman and the fetus? Should the medical interest in attempting to preserve both their lives suffice to overcome religious objections on the part of the woman?

3. Was A.C. expressing her interests only or both her interests and her view of any future child's best interests? To what extent do you think the medical profession's views of the fetus's interests should replace the woman's? Does an American College of Obstetrics and Gynecology Ethics Committee finding that "[t]he welfare of the fetus is of the utmost importance to the majority of women: thus only rarely will a conflict arise" influence your views?

As the A.C. Court suggests, actual court decisions dealing with this situation are rare. Providers have, however, acted to supersede women's choices more often than the reported cases might suggest. Moreover, as in other areas, a race and class pattern is discernible in these actions. For example, as Janet Gallagher points out in "Fetus as Patient," in *Reproductive Laws for the 1990s* (S. Cohen and N. Taub, eds., Totowa, N.J.: Humana Press, 1989, p. 203), "[a] 1986 survey of doctors revealed that 81 percent of the pregnant women subjected to court-ordered interventions were black, Asian, or Hispanic; 44 percent were unmarried; 24 percent did not speak English as their primary language; and one [percent] were private patients." Furthermore, in an American College of Obstetricians and Gynecologists (ACOG) Committee on Ethics Opinion concerning ethical issues that arise in the care of pregnant women, the Committee stated that the vast majority of court-ordered cesarean deliveries were obtained against poor women of color, and that African-American women were ten times more likely to be reported for substance abuse during pregnancy to public health authorities than Caucasian women. *Maternal Decision Making, Ethics, and the Law*, ACOG Committee on Ethics Opinion No. 321, November 2005. Do these facts influence your views or suggest other alternatives to you?

ON-LINE RESOURCES

The National Organization of Women (NOW) Web site contains extensive information and resources on gender-related legal and public policy issues, including links to a timeline and past historical information on the issues of abortion and reproductive rights. www.now.org/index.html

Legal Momentum (formerly known as the NOW Legal Defense and Education Fund) is an invaluable resource for information on gender-related legal and public policy issues. www.legalmomentum.org

The Human Rights Campaign (HRC) has posted an article on surrogacy laws that includes a list of links to State surrogacy laws. This article may be accessed through HRC's Web site: www.hrc.org/issues/2486.htm

The Center for Disease Control (CDC) has a Web page that contains reproductive health highlights and links to interesting information, such as assisted reproductive technology reports: www.cdc.gov/reproductivehealth/

CHAPTER 8

SEXUALITY AND SEXUAL VIOLENCE

THE PREVIOUS CHAPTER dealt in large measure with laws that make it difficult to be sexually active without reproducing. By contrast, this chapter is concerned with law in relation to nonreproductive aspects of sexuality, including sexual violence. The chapter first explores the law's past and potential role in controlling women's sexual behavior and then turns to two problem areas: rape and pornography.

Earlier chapters have shown the close connection between notions of appropriate sexual behavior and limitations on women's opportunities. Historically, women who worked outside the home were often considered loose and immoral, and, as the *Dothard v. Rawlinson* case (see Chapter 3) shows, women have been foreclosed at times from employment to prevent sexual assaults. Expectations regarding sexual conduct have also had consequences in the family realm. For example, when women engage in sexual activity outside marriage, they risk losing custody of their children and their right to determine their household composition. Middle-class women receiving alimony and poor women receiving public assistance may also jeopardize their financial support by being sexually active.

Often embodied in religious or moral ideas, some of these constraints are gender-neutral; others are plainly gender based. Rethinking these constraints is a complex and controversial task. While there is general agreement that nonconsensual sexual violence is bad, there is little consensus otherwise about the desirability of different kinds of sexual activity or the possibilities for real consent in sexual matters. One reason it is so hard to agree on such matters is that we know so little about the origins and effects of sexual tastes and behavior. Evidence is increasing that sexual attraction is a natural, biological phenomenon, while we generally assume that it is a product of cultural factors that vary from time to time and place to place. Is it both? Does sexual activity—of particular kinds or in general—enhance or interfere with societal well-being?

Confusion about the spectre of sexual exploitation also makes it hard to agree about limits on sexual activity. Sexuality presents opportunities for gratification and fulfillment and, at the same time, makes people vulnerable to exploitation and abuse. Male sexual aggression has posed special problems for women. Some regard it as the most fundamental element in women's subordination, the one that drives women into dependence on other men for protection. Others see it as one of the many ways men dominate women. Given women's historic vulnerability, some protection seems in order. It is not clear, however, whether protections should explicitly recognize women's special vulnerability or take a gender-neutral form. As we have seen in the discussion of statutory rape laws in the *Michael M.* case (Chapter 2), protections against sexual aggression may also interfere with consensual gratification. Furthermore, it is difficult to determine in certain areas, such as prostitution, whether women are, in fact, victims of male oppression or autonomous agents who benefit from their activity. Thus, we are hard put to know whether or not to restrain the activity, let alone whether to pose the restraint in sex-based terms. These, then, are problems to ponder as we consider codes of sexual conduct.

I. CODES OF SEXUAL CONDUCT

Society has narrowly circumscribed the ways in which individuals may express themselves sexually. Both men and women are expected to express themselves sexually through heterosexual relationships. Though less so today than perhaps ten or fifteen years ago, the sexual double standard between men and women still exists. Many modern-day feminists would argue that women of the twenty-first century are freer to explore their own sexuality; however, the concept of "bad girl"/"good girl" still exists. Women who behave in a sexual manner are often regarded as "getting what they deserve" in situations involving violence or exploitation.

Feminist writings, appearing in a variety of contexts, have sought to expose the law's role in imposing these sex-based codes. One such passage appeared in a brief written by a feminist group formed to challenge a pornography ordinance discussed later in this chapter.

THE SEXUAL DOUBLE STANDARD IN THE LAW
Brief Amici Curiae of the Feminist Anti-Censorship Task Force, et al.
American Booksellers Assn., Inc. v. Hudnut
U.S. Court of Appeals, 7th Cir. No. 84–3147, pp. 4–8.

. . . The legal system has used many vehicles to enforce the sexual double standard which protected "good" women from both sexual activity and explicit speech about sex. For example, the common law of libel held that "an oral imputation of unchastity to a woman is actionable without proof of damage. . . . Such a rule never has been applied to a man, since the damage to his reputation is assumed not to be as great." W. Prosser. *Law of Torts.* pp. 759–60 (West, 1971).

The common law also reinforced the image of "good" women as asexual and vulnerable by providing husbands, but not wives, remedies for "interference" with his right to sole possession of his wife's body and services. The early writ of "ravishment" listed the wife with the husband's chattels. To this day, the action for criminal conversation allows the husband to maintain an action for trespass, not only when his wife is raped

"but also even though the wife had consented to it, or was herself the seducer and had invited and procured it, since it was considered that she was no more capable of giving a consent which would prejudice the husband's interests than was his horse . . . ."

W. Prosser, pp. 874–77.

Reprinted by permission of Nan D. Hunter, Esq., and Sylvia A. Law, Esq.

While denying the possibility that "good" women could be sexual, the common dealt harshly with the "bad" women who were. Prostitution laws often penalized only the woman, and not the man, and even facially neutral laws were and are enforced primarily against women.

Prostitution is defined as "the practice of a female offering her body to indiscriminate sexual intercourse with men," 63 AM.JUR. 2d *Prostitution*, Sec. 1 (1972), or submitting "to indiscriminate sexual intercourse which she invites or solicits." *Id.* A woman who has sexual relations with many men is a "common prostitute" and a criminal while a sexually active man is considered normal.

The sexual double standard is applied with particular force to young people. Statutory rape laws often punished men for consensual intercourse with a female under a certain age. Such laws reinforce the stereotype that in sex the man is the offender and the woman the victim, and that young men may legitimately engage in sex, at least with older people, while a young woman may not legally have sex with anyone.

The suppression of sexually explicit material most devastating to women was the restriction on dissemination of birth control information, common until 1971. In that year, the Supreme Court held that the constitutional right to privacy protects an unmarried person's right to access to birth control information. *Eisenstadt v. Baird*, 405 U.S. 438 (1971). To deny women access to contraception "prescribes pregnancy and the birth of an unwanted child as punishment for fornication." 405 U.S. at 448. For the previous century the federal Comstock law, passed in 1873, had prohibited mailing, transporting or importing of "obscene, lewd, or lascivious" items, specifically including all devices and information pertaining to "preventing contraception and producing abortion." Women were jailed for distributing educational materials regarding birth control to other women because the materials were deemed sexually explicit in that they

"contain[ed] pictures of certain organs of women" and because the materials were found to be "detrimental to public morals and welfare." *People v. Byrne*, 99 Misc. 1, 6 (N.Y. 1917).

The Mann Act also was premised on the notion that women require special protection from sexual activity. It forbids interstate transportation of women for purposes of "prostitution, debauchery, or any other immoral purposes," and was enacted to protect women from reportedly widespread abduction by bands of white slavers; coercing them into prostitution. As the legislative history reveals, the Act reflects the assumption that women have no will of their own and must be protected against themselves. Like the premises underlying this ordinance, the Mann Act assumed

> that women were naturally chaste and virtuous, and that no woman became a whore unless she had first been raped, drugged or deserted. [Its] image of the prostitute . . . was of a lonely and confused female . . . [Its proponents] maintained that prostitutes were the passive victims of social disequilibrium and the brutality of men . . . [Its] conception of female weakness and male domination left no room for the possibility that prostitutes might consciously choose their activities. Note, "The White Slave Traffic Act: The Historical Impact of a Criminal Law Policy of Women," 72 *Georgetown* L. J. 1111 (1984).

The Mann Act initially defined a "white slave" to include "only those women or girls who are literally slaves—those women who are owned and held as property and chattels . . . those women and girls who, if given a fair chance, would, in all human probability, have been good wives and mothers . . .," H.R. Rep. No.47, 61st Cong., 2d Sess. (1910) at 9–10. Over the years, the interpretation and use of the Act changed drastically to punish voluntary "immoral" acts even when no commercial intention or business profit was involved. See *Caminetti v. U.S.*, 242 U.S. 470 (1917); and *Cleveland v. U.S.*, 329 U.S. 14 (1946).

The term "other immoral acts" was held to apply to a variety of activities: the interstate transportation of a woman to work as a chorus girl in a theatre where the woman was exposed to smoking, drinking, and cursing; a dentist who met his young lover in a neighboring state and shared a hotel room to discuss her pregancy, two students at the University of Puerto Rico who had sexual intercouse on the way home from a date; and a man and woman who had lived together for four years and traveled around the country as man and wife while the man sold securities.

72 Georgetown L. J. at 1119.

Society's attempts to "protect" women's chastity through criminal and civil laws have resulted in restrictions on women's freedom to engage in sexual activity, to discuss it publicly and to protect themselves from the risk of pregnancy. These disabling restrictions reinforced the gender roles which have oppressed women for centuries. . . .

STUDY QUESTIONS

1. What is the sexual double standard to which the brief refers? How, according to the brief's authors, has the double standard limited the options open to women? Do you agree? Do you think the double standard has also limited the options open to men? In what ways?

2. What illustrations does the brief provide of ways in which the legal system has enforced the sexual double standard? What other examples have you encountered in this book? Have these legal vehicles always incorporated sex-based classifications? What are some examples that do not include sex-based classifications?

3. What stereotypes do the authors claim are reinforced by statutory rape laws? Are these similar to the assumptions the authors claim are reflected in the Mann Act? In your view, do such stereotypes and assumptions accurately depict the nature of social and sexual relations between women and men?

The Feminist Anti-Censorship Task Force brief points out that the legal system has, in the guise of protecting women, reflected and reinforced a double sexual standard that restricts women's freedom to engage in sexual activity. As we have seen in earlier chapters, sex-based classifications often depend on this double standard for their justification. Recall the Supreme Court decision in *Michael M.* (see Chapter 2), upholding a statutory rape law that punishes males but not females for engaging in sexual intercourse with a minor. Remember also the earlier case of *Goesaert* (see Chapter 1), indicating that women could constitutionally be denied jobs as bartenders in order to protect them from the tavern environment. Notions about proper sexual behavior for females have also led to the unequal application of facially neutral laws. Statutes defining juvenile delinquency in general terms, such as "incorrigibility" or "waywardness," have often been applied to punish girls, but not boys, for engaging in sexual acts.

Another way that the legal system embodies this sexual code relates to public nudity. In some jurisdictions, women, but not men, are subject to criminal prosecution if they appear unclothed to the waist in public. A recent decision by New York's highest court represents a successful challenge to this double standard.

People v. Santorelli

New York Court of Appeals, 1992. 600 N.E.2d 232.

The order of Monroe County Court should be reversed and the informations dismissed. . . .

Defendants were arrested for violating Penal Law § 245.01 (exposure of a person) when they bared "that portion of the breast which is below the top of the areola" in a Rochester public park. The statute, they urge, is discriminatory on its face since it defines "private or intimate parts" of a woman's but not a man's body as including a specific part of the breast. That assertion being made, it is settled that the People then have the burden of providing that there is an important government interest at stake and that the gender classification is substantially related to that interest (see, *Mississippi University for Women v. Hogan*). In this case, however, the People have made no attempt below and make none before us to demonstrate that the statute's discriminatory effect serves an important governmental interest or that the classification is based on a reasoned predicate. Moreover, the People do not dispute that New York is one of only two states which criminalizes the mere exposure by a woman in a public place of a specific part of her breast.

Despite the People's virtual default on the constitutional issue, we must construe a statute, which enjoys a presumption of constitutionality, to uphold its constitutionality if a rational basis can be found to do so. Penal Law § 245.01, when originally enacted, "was aimed at discouraging 'topless' waitresses and their promoters." Considering the statute's provenance, we held in [*People v.*] *Price* that a woman walking along a street wearing a fishnet, see-through pull-over blouse did not transgress the statute and that it "should not be applied to the noncommercial, perhaps accidental, and certainly not lewd, exposure alleged." Though the statute and the rationale for that decision are different, we believe that underlying principle of *People v. Price*

should be followed. We, therefore, conclude that Penal Law § 245.01 is not applicable to the conduct presented in these circumstances and that the City Court was correct in dismissing the informations.

TITONE, J. (concurring):

[After examining the legislative history of § 245.01, Justice Titone concluded that the] . . . Court's reliance on the "presumption of constitutionality" in these circumstances is thus nothing more than an artful means of avoiding a confrontation with an important constitutional problem. . . .

The equal protection analysis that the majority has attempted to avoid is certainly not a complex or difficult one. When a statute explicitly establishes a classification based on gender, as Penal Law § 245.01 unquestionably does, the State has the burden of showing that the classification is substantially related to the achievement of an important governmental objective (e.g., *Caban v. Mohammed; Craig v. Boren; People v. Liberta*). . . .

It is clear from the statute's legislative history, as well as our own case law and common sense, that the governmental objective to be served by Penal Law § 245.01 is to protect the sensibilities of those who wish to use the public beaches and parks in this State. And, since the statute prohibits the public exposure of female—but not male—breasts, it betrays an underlying legislative assumption that the sight of a female's uncovered breast in a public place is offensive to the average person in a way that the sight of a male's uncovered breast is not. It is this assumption that lies at the root of the statute's constitutional problem.

Although protecting public sensibilities is a generally legitimate goal for legislation, it is a tenuous basis for justifying a legislative classification that is based on gender, race or any other grouping that is associated with a history of social prejudice (see,

Hogan ["[c]are must be taken in ascertaining whether the statutory objective itself reflects archaic and stereotypic notions"]). Indeed, the concept of "public sensibility" itself, when used in these contexts, may be nothing more than a reflection of commonly held preconceptions and biases. One of the most important purposes to be served by the equal protection clause is to ensure that "public sensibilities" grounded in prejudice and unexamined stereotypes do not become enshrined as part of the official policy of government. Thus, where "public sensibilities" constitute the justification for a gender-based classification, the fundamental question is whether the particular "sensibility" to be protected is, in fact, a reflection of archaic prejudice or a manifestation of a legitimate government objective.

Viewed against these principles, the gender-based provisions of Penal Law § 245.01 cannot, on this record, withstand scrutiny. Defendants contend that apart from entrenched cultural expectations, there is really no objective reason why the exposure of female breasts should be considered any more offensive than the exposure of the male counterparts. They offered proof that, from an anatomical standpoint, the female breast is no more or less a sexual organ than is the male equivalent. They further contend that to the extent that many in our society may regard the uncovered female breast with a prurient interest that is not similarly aroused by the male equivalent, that perception cannot serve as a justification for differential treatment because it is itself a suspect cultural artifact rooted in centuries of prejudice and bias toward women. Indeed, there are many societies in other parts of the world—and even many locales within the United States—where the exposure of female breasts on beaches and in other recreational areas is commonplace and is generally regarded as unremarkable. It is notable that other jurisdictions have taken the position that breasts are not "private parts" and that breast exposure is not indecent behavior, and twenty-two states specifically confine their statutory public exposure prohibitions to uncovered genitalia.

The People in this case have not refuted this evidence or attempted to show the existence of evidence of their own to indicate that the non-lewd exposure of the female breast is in any way harmful to the public's health or well being. Nor have they offered any explanation as to why, the fundamental goal that Penal Law § 245.01 was enacted to advance—avoiding offense to citizens who use public beaches and parks—cannot be equally well served by other alternatives.

In summary, the People have offered nothing to justify a law that discriminates against women by prohibiting them from removing their tops and exposing their bare chests in public as men are routinely permitted to do. The mere fact that the statute's aim is the protection of "public sensibilities" is not sufficient to satisfy the state's burden of showing an "exceedingly persuasive justification" for a classification that expressly discriminates on the basis of sex. Accordingly, the gender-based classification established by Penal Law § 245.01 violates appellants' equal protection rights and, for that reason, I concur in the majority's result and vote to reverse the order below.

Order Reversed and Informations
Dismissed in a Memorandum.

STUDY QUESTIONS

1. Does the majority apply the Equal Protection Clause correctly in your opinion? According to the majority opinion, are there times when it is lawful to punish women for being stripped to the waist? Could the statute ever be applied to men?

2. What would the concurring justice do? Why?

Sexual conduct is also governed directly by a variety of laws concerning consensual sexual behavior. These laws generally proscribe sexual activity outside marriage and often limit the types of activity permitted within marriage. Rooted in ecclesiastical law, these statutes prohibit such conduct as fornication, adultery, and "crimes against nature," including oral and anal sex. As such, they have the effect of making heterosexuality the mandatory form of sexual expression and of reinforcing the importance of marriage and family. Laws of this type restrict the sexual freedom of both sexes by limiting the range of available opportunities for obtaining sexual gratification and fulfillment; but to the extent that marital and family obligations have been a source of difficulty for women, they harm women disproportionately.

The court sustained a number of decisions that failed to protect the private right of sexual activity between two consenting adults. Most notable was the Supreme Court's decision in *Bowers v. Hardwick*, 478 U.S. 186 (1986). There the Court explicitly refused to afford constitutional protection to homosexual conduct so as to invalidate a Georgia sodomy statute. As we saw in Chapter 6, it was not until June of 2003 that the Supreme Court reversed itself in the landmark decision *Lawrence v. Texas*, 539 U.S. 558 (2003), wherein the Supreme Court did invalidate a criminal prosecution of a homosexual couple for consensual sexual acts. In so doing, the Court rejected the moral argument and, instead, focused on the constitutional right to privacy and to be free from interference.

Also, as was discussed in Chapter 6, following the Supreme Court's decision in *Lawrence*, the Superior Court of Massachusetts opened another previously closed door: the right of gay couples to marry. It is too soon to understand the impact that these cases will have on the way in which we perceive sexual activity and what is considered acceptable behavior. The backlash response was almost immediate with the call for a federal constitutional amendment that would ban gay marriages. Couple these decisions with the relatively new and as yet unexplored technology of the Internet—Internet dating, chat rooms, and the like—and it is difficult to predict the changes that these decisions will bring in the future. They all form part of the emerging recognition that women are sexual beings and that their "right to be sexual" is as natural and acceptable as that of a man.

Even though the "right to be sexual" is unlikely to extend to coercive conduct, such as rape, the elimination of restraints on nominally consensual conduct might easily permit extremely destructive behavior that exploits and abuses the vulnerable, particularly women. In her article "Toward Recognition of a Right to Be Sexual," 7 *Women's Rights Law Reporter* 245 (1982), attorney Mary Dunlap captured this dilemma. As she pointed out:

> Once we have *rejected* the idea that "proper" sexual behavior in the female consists of nothing more, less or different than sexual intercourse within the bounds of legal marriage—aimed at pregnancy and resulting in childbirth and the fulfillment of the "noble and benign offices of wife and mother"—and once we have rejected all related notions of "impropriety" based on gender, we face a vast array of difficult questions.

The balance, and the controversy, revolves around how far that "right" extends. Is pornography an expression of a woman's sexuality? Can it be? Are these issues privacy issues, or do they fall into the realm of freedom of speech and association related to sex? Does tolerance of different approaches lead to coercive behaviors, exploitation, or violence? Is there a way to encourage tolerance for a diversity of behaviors?

There are no easy answers to these questions. The materials on rape and pornography that follow may assist you in formulating your own response. These materials explore the relation of law to what Dunlap calls "the realities of sexual violence, exploitation, and repressiveness of our society." Rape represents the epitome of sexual violence and the total negation of sexual autonomy for women. Pornography presents more complex situations, containing at once the potential for exploitation and repression. As you ponder the role of the law in these contexts, consider whether it is possible to formulate a right to be sexual that enhances the sexual freedom of both sexes and combats special behavior rules for women without, at the same time, making women vulnerable to further sexual abuse. Is it possible to experience sexual freedom, or is modern sexuality, however free, inevitably a socially constructed reflection of patriarchal values?

II. RAPE

The Law and Its Impact on Women

The forcible rape of women is now recognized as a crime against the person of the woman. This is a very recent development. Susan Brownmiller, one of the feminist writers who sensitized the public to the full dimensions of this crime, traced the historical origins of traditional rape law.

THE ORIGINS OF THE LAW OF RAPE
Susan Brownmiller
Against Our Will: Men, Women and Rape.
New York: Simon and Schuster, 1975, pp. 8–22.

A female definition of rape can be contained in a single sentence. If a woman chooses not to have intercourse with a specific man and the man chooses to proceed against her will, that is a criminal act of rape. Through no fault of woman, this is not and never has been the legal definition. . . . Rape entered the law through the back door, as it were, as a property crime of man against man. Woman, of course, was viewed as the property.

Ancient Babylonian and Mosaic law was codified on tablets centuries after the rise of formal tribal hierarchies and the permanent settlements known as city-states. Slavery, private property and the subjugation of women were facts of life, and the earliest written law that has come down to us reflects this stratified life. Written law in its origin was a solemn compact among men of property, designed to protect their own male interests by a civilized exchange of goods or silver *in place of force* wherever possible. The capture of females by force remained perfectly acceptable *outside* the tribe or city as one of the ready fruits of warfare, but clearly *within* the social order such a happenstance would lead to chaos. A payment of money to the father of the house was a much more civilized and less dangerous way of acquiring a wife. And so the bride price was codified, at fifty pieces of silver. By this circuitous route the first concept of criminal rape sneaked its tortuous way into man's definition of law. Criminal rape, as a patriarchal father saw it, was a violation of the new way of doing business. It was, in a phrase, the theft of virginity, an embezzlement of his daughter's fair price on the market. . . .

Concepts of rape and punishment in early English law are a wondrous maze of contradictory approaches reflecting a gradual humanization of jurisprudence in general, and in particular, man's eternal confusion, never quite resolved, as to whether the crime was a crime against a woman's body or a crime against his own estate. . . .

The comprehensive Statutes of Westminster put forward by Edward I at the close of the thirteenth century showed a gigantic advance in legal thinking as the Crown, and by "Crown" Americans should read "state," began to take an active interest in all kinds of rape prosecutions, not just those concerning violated virgins. Our modern principle of *statutory* rape—felonious carnal knowledge of a child in which her "consent" is altogether immaterial—dates from this time and these statutes.

Of critical significance, Westminster extended the king's jurisdiction to cover the forcible rape of married women as well as virgins, with no difference in punishment to offending males. To further erase the distinction between the rape of a virgin and the rape of a wife, the old, ignoble custom of redemption through marriage was permanently banned under suits by the king. In concession to the proprietary rights of husbands—for the Crown had ventured into an area it had never ventured into before—Westminster also saw fit to legislate a definition of lesser ravishment, a sort of misdemeanor, applicable in cases where it could be argued that a wife did not object strenuously enough to her own "defilement." The aggrieved party in these cases was the husband, and the wife was preemptorily stripped of her dower. *Within* a marriage, the theory went—and still goes—that there could be no such crime as rape by a husband since a wife's "consent" to her husband was a permanent part of the marriage vows and could not be withdrawn.

To give the new law teeth, Edward I decreed that if a raped woman or her kin failed to institute a private suit within forty days, the right to prosecute automatically passed to the Crown. This bold concept, applicable only to virgins in previous reigns, was a giant step for the law and for women. It meant that rape was no longer just a family misfortune and a threat to land and property, but an issue of public safety and state concern.

The First Statute of Westminster, enacted in 1275, set the Crown's penalty for rape at a paltry two years' imprisonment plus a fine at the king's pleasure, no doubt to ease the effect of a major transition, for what had occurred at the Parliament of Westminster was only tangentially and in retrospect a recognition of women's rights; its inexorable, historic purpose had been to consolidate political power in the hands of the king. But within a decade an emboldened Second Statute of Westminster amended the timorous First. By a new act of Parliament, any man who ravished "a married woman, dame or damsel" without her consent was guilty of a full-blown felony under the law of the Crown, and the penalty was death.

It read better on parchment than it worked in real life, but the concept of rape as a public wrong had been firmly established.

From the thirteenth to the twentieth century, little changed. The later giants of jurisprudence, Hale, Blackstone, Wigmore and the rest, continued to point a suspicious finger at the female victim and worry about her motivations and "good fame."

"If she be of evil fame and stand unsupported by others," Blackstone commented, "if she concealed the injury for any considerable time after she had the opportunity to complain, if the place where the act was alleged to be committed was where it was possible she might have been heard and she made no outcry, these and the like circumstances carry a strong but not conclusive presumption that her testimony is false or feigned."

STUDY QUESTIONS

1. Explain how rape was considered a crime against property. Does it retain any of this meaning in our society?

2. Why was the distinction between a virginal and nonvirginal victim given any significance in the Westminster statutes? Is a woman any less violated by forced intercourse after her first voluntary sexual relationship than before it?

3. Do you think that the death penalty is excessive for the crime of forcible rape?

Reforming the Law of Rape

Recognizing the tremendous psychological and physical toll taken by sexual violence, women organized in the 1970s to combat unwanted intercourse. Their initial efforts were directed at exposing the myth that women invite and enjoy rape and at providing support to victims through rape crisis centers and similar groups. They underscored the violent rather than the sexual aspect of rape and the restraints it has imposed on women's freedom of movement. They pointed out that the threat of violence has forced women to depend on men for protection and that the blame cast on rape victims has served to reinforce gender-based behavior codes.

Later efforts were addressed more directly to legal institutions. In particular, women sought to eliminate legal provisions that excused sexual violence, reinforced sex-based stereotypes, and allowed rape victims to be treated differently from victims of other crimes. Those efforts form the core of this section.

One of the special features of rape laws identified by Berger was their excessive penalty structure. As late as 1972, rape was a capital offense in sixteen states. Such provisions were declared unconstitutional in a 1977 case, *Coker v. Georgia*, 433 U.S. 584. The Supreme Court there reversed Georgia's imposition of the death penalty in a rape case on the ground that the death sentence for the rape of an adult woman was excessive in its severity and disproportionate to the gravity of the offense. This violated the Eighth Amendment's prohibition of cruel and unusual punishment. Women's rights groups supported this decision because such excessive penalties inhibited prosecutions of rape cases, reduced conviction rates, and reinforced sexist and racist attitudes.

Berger also pointed to three special rules that render rape charges more difficult to prosecute than other criminal cases: (1) the requirement that the victim's testimony be substantiated or corroborated by independent evidence; (2) the rule allowing evidence regarding the victim's reputation for chastity and/or prior sexual conduct; and (3) the rule authorizing cautionary jury instructions impugning the victim's credibility. Rules like these not only make convictions less likely in cases going to trial, but they also discourage victims from complaining and prosecutors from bringing rape charges to trial. The harsh operation of these rules, highlighted in the following cases, has led increasingly to their rejection by courts and legislatures.

Corroboration and evidentiary rules used in rape cases have traditionally allowed defendants to present testimony and question witnesses about the victim's sexual behavior and reputation. As a result, victims have often been subjected to extraordinarily intrusive and humiliating interrogations. The practical effect of such rules has been to put the victim on trial to determine whether, sexually speaking, she has been a "good girl." If she has not, the clear implication is her word is not worth accepting.

In the 1970s, a number of courts and legislatures reviewed and rejected rules of this type. For example, New York's corroboration requirement was repealed in 1974. Another example is the *McLean v. United States* case, set forth below. In reading it, you may find it helpful to know the meaning of some of the legal terminology appearing in the case: "Admissible" evidence is evidence that the judge should allow the jury to hear or see. Evidence that tends to prove a point in either side's case is regarded as "probative." "Prejudicial" evidence is evidence that is detrimental to a party's case, whether or not it bears on the issues before the court. "Credibility" refers to the believability of a witness. "Impeaching" the credibility of a witness refers to undercutting his testimony by showing the witness is untrustworthy or has a faulty memory.

McLean v. United States
Court of Appeals of the District of Columbia, 1977. 377 F.2d 74.

KERN, Associate Judge.

Appellant was tried by a jury and convicted of rape and sentenced to a term of fifteen years under the Federal Youth Corrections Act. On appeal, he urges that it was reversible error for the trial judge to exclude (a) testimony that the complaining witness had engaged in sexual relations *with others* on prior occasions, and (b) testimony that she had a reputation in the community for unchastity. Appellant offered this evidence to support his defense that the complaining witness consented to have intercourse with him.

The government's evidence disclosed that appellant and the complaining witness, who was seventeen at the time of the incident, were neighbors and had known each other for nine or ten years. On June 25, 1975 at about 9:30 P.M., complainant was at home with her friend, Diane Tyler, when appellant called and made arrangements with her to go to the movies. They left shortly thereafter in appellant's sister's car and drove to the vicinity of 14th and Sheridan Streets, N.W., where appellant told her that he had to speak to someone. Appellant went into an apartment house while complainant waited in the car. Several minutes later he returned and said that the stop-over would take longer than expected and invited her to accompany him inside. Moments after she entered the apartment three young men came into a room where she was sitting and with the assistance of appellant, forced her into an unlit bedroom. Complainant testified that she pleaded with appellant to make them stop, but instead he was helping them.

The four men disrobed her, held her down, and according to her testimony, made comments while appellant had intercourse with her. The other three in turn had intercourse with her and then left the room. . . .

Defense counsel requested a ruling at the beginning of trial whether he could offer witnesses who would testify that complainant had engaged in sexual intercourse with others in the past. The trial judge ruled that such evidence was not relevant to the issues at trial and therefore inadmissible. During trial appellant proffered two witnesses who testified in a hearing out of the presence of the jury that they had heard other members of the community comment on complainant's reputation for unchastity. The trial court refused to allow these witnesses to testify because they had not convinced the trial judge that there was an adequate basis for their knowledge of the prosecutrix's reputation.

Central to appellant's position in the instant case is his assertion that the probative value of proof of complainant's prior acts of sexual intercourse with others outweighs the prejudice to the complainant. The prejudice of such evidence is readily seen: it diverts the jury's attention to collateral matters and probes into the private life of the victim of a rape. . . . On the other hand, the probative value of the evidence is less easily recognized. Apparently, appellant views evidence of past sexual intercourse by a woman with others as admissible because it tends to establish her sexually promiscuous character which in turn tends to prove that on the particular occasion she consented to sexual intercourse with the accused rather than submitted against her will out of fear. We agree with the Supreme Court of Arizona in *Pope v. Superior Court*, 545 P.2d 946, 952 (1976), that "[t]he fact that a woman consented to sexual intercourse on one occasion is not substantial evidence that she consented on another, but in fact may indicate the contrary."

Generally, the law disfavors the admission of evidence of a person's character in order to prove conduct in conformity with that character. . . . There are exceptions to this general proposition, however, but none appear[s] to encompass the proffer here. . . .

We note that the recent trend in other jurisdictions is that specific acts of sexual intercourse on the part of the complaining witness are *not* admissible to prove that she consented to sexual intercourse with the accused.

We endorse the approach taken by these courts, *viz.*, the exclusion from evidence of prior acts of sexual intercourse with others besides the defendant because such evidence is not probative to the issue of the prosecutrix's consent.[5] . . .

We therefore conclude the trial court properly excluded evidence of the complainant's sexual relations with others than the accused.[6] . . .

. . . [T]he rationale for excluding evidence of specific acts of sexual intercourse applies *with equal force* to the exclusion of reputation testimony. The reputation of a woman for unchastity raises unnecessary collateral issues which are nearly impossible to rebut, it diverts the jury's attention from the principal issues at trial and it results in prejudice to the complaining witness which greatly outweighs its extremely limited probative value. Reputation testimony should not be admitted except in the most unusual cases where the probative value is precisely demonstrated and outweighs the prejudicial effect of the testimony.[9] . . .

Affirmed.

STUDY QUESTIONS

1. What is the difference between evidence regarding reputation for unchastity and evidence regarding prior sexual acts? What did the court identify as the possible relevance of each type of evidence? What assumptions about women's behavior underlie such reasoning?

2. Do you think that the fact that the victim had previously engaged in sexual intercourse with the defendant makes it more likely that she consented to intercourse on the occasion in question? Do you agree with the *McLean* court that the jury should be allowed to hear such evidence? Are there any circumstances in which the court would permit evidence regarding other prior sexual conduct and reputation to be introduced? Under what circumstances should courts permit such evidence to be introduced?

3. What might be the effect of the court's ruling in this case on rape victims' willingness to make criminal complaints? On prosecutors' willingness to bring charges? On the conviction rate in rape cases?

[5] We note that evidence of specific acts of sexual intercourse with the *defendant* himself should be admitted where either there may be an issue of identity at trial or to rebut the government's evidence that the prosecutrix did not consent to sexual intercourse on the particular occasion. . . .

[6] There can be *unusual circumstances* where the defense may inquire into specific sexual acts by the prosecutrix when the probative value of the evidence is clearly demonstrated *and* is shown to outweigh its prejudicial effect. As an example of such a situation, the Arizona Supreme Court in *Pope v. Superior Court* noted that evidence would be admissible "which directly refutes physical or scientific evidence, such as the victim's alleged loss of virginity, the origin of semen, disease or pregnancy". . . .

[9] The court in *Pope v. Superior Court*, supra at 953, would admit reputation testimony "[where] the defendant alleges the prosecutrix actually consented to an act of prostitution," or when the prosecution offered evidence of the complainant's chastity.

State courts considering statutes that limit evidence concerning the alleged rape victim's past sexual conduct have generally strained to uphold their constitutionality. The constitutionality of certain provisions became somewhat clearer when, with two dissents, the U.S. Supreme Court upheld one provision of the Michigan rape shield law.

MICHIGAN V. LUCAS

United States Supreme Court, 1991.
500 U.S. 145, 111 S.Ct. 1743, 114 L.Ed.2d 205.

Justice O'CONNOR delivered the opinion of the Court.

Because Nolan Lucas failed to give statutorily required notice of his intention to present evidence of an alleged rape victim's past sexual conduct, a Michigan trial court refused to let him present the evidence at trial. The Michigan Court of Appeals reversed, adopting a per se rule that preclusion of evidence of a rape victim's prior sexual relationship with a criminal defendant, violates the Sixth Amendment. We consider the propriety of this per se rule.

I

Like most States, Michigan has a "rape-shield" statute designed to protect victims of rape from being exposed at trial to harassing or irrelevant questions concerning their past sexual behavior. This statute prohibits a criminal defendant from introducing at trial evidence of an alleged rape victim's past sexual conduct, subject to two exceptions. One of the exceptions is relevant here. It permits a defendant to introduce evidence of his own past sexual conduct with the victim, provided that he follows certain procedures. Specifically, a defendant who plans to present such evidence must file a written motion and an offer of proof "within 10 days" after he is arraigned. The trial court may hold "an in camera hearing to determine whether the proposed evidence is admissible"—i.e., whether the evidence is material and not more prejudicial than probative.

Lucas was charged with two counts of criminal sexual conduct. The State maintained that Lucas had used a knife to force Wanda Brown, his ex-girlfriend, into his apartment, where he beat her and forced her to engage in several nonconsensual sex acts. At no time did Lucas file a written motion and offer of proof, as required by the statute. At the start of trial, however, Lucas' counsel asked the trial court to permit the defense to present evidence of a prior sexual relationship between Brown and Lucas, "even though I know it goes against the statute."

The trial court reviewed the statute then denied the motion, stating that "[n]one of the requirements set forth in [the statute] have been complied with." The court explained that Lucas' request was not made within the time required by Michigan law and that, as a result, no in camera hearing had been held to determine whether the past sexual conduct evidence was admissible. A bench trial then began, in which Lucas' defense was consent. The trial court did not credit his testimony. The court found Lucas guilty on two counts of criminal sexual assault and sentenced him to a prison term of 44 to 180 months. . . .

II

Michigan's rape-shield statute is silent as to the consequences of a defendant's failure to comply with the notice-and-hearing requirement. The trial court assumed, without explanation, that preclusion of the evidence was an authorized remedy. Assuming, arguendo, that the trial court was correct, the statute unquestionably implicates the Sixth

Amendment. To the extent that it operates to prevent a criminal defendant from presenting relevant evidence, the defendant's ability to confront adverse witnesses and present a defense is diminished. This does not necessarily render the statute unconstitutional. "[T]he right to present relevant testimony is not without limitation. The right 'may, in appropriate cases, bow to accommodate other legitimate interests in the criminal trial process.' " We have explained, for example, that "trial judges retain wide latitude" to limit reasonably a criminal defendant's right to cross-examine a witness "based on concerns about, among other things, harassment, prejudice, confusion of the issues, the witness's safety, or interrogation that is repetitive or only marginally relevant." Lucas does not deny that legitimate state interests support the notice-and-hearing requirement. The Michigan statute represents a valid legislative determination that rape victims deserve heightened protection against surprise, harassment, and unnecessary invasions of privacy. The statute also protects against surprise to the prosecution. . . .

The sole question presented for our review is whether the legitimate interests served by a notice requirement can ever justify precluding evidence of a prior sexual relationship between a rape victim and a criminal defendant. . . .

We have indicated that probative evidence may, in certain circumstances, be precluded when a criminal defendant fails to comply with a valid discovery rule. . . . [That precedent does not hold] that preclusion is permissible every time a discovery rule is violated. Rather, we acknowledged that alternative sanctions would be "adequate and appropriate in most cases." We stated explicitly, however, that there could be circumstances in which preclusion was justified because a less severe penalty "would perpetuate rather than limit the prejudice to the State and the harm to the adversary process.". . .

. . . [T]he Michigan Court of Appeals erred in adopting a per se rule that

Michigan's notice-and-hearing requirement violates the Sixth Amendment in all cases where it is used to preclude evidence of past sexual conduct between a rape victim and a defendant. The Sixth Amendment is not so rigid. The notice-and-hearing requirement serves legitimate state interests in protecting against surprise, harassment, and undue delay. Failure to comply with this requirement may in some cases justify even the severe sanction of preclusion. . . .

We express no opinion as to whether or not preclusion was justified in this case. The Michigan Court of Appeals, whose decision we review here, did not address whether the trial court abused its discretion on the facts before it. Rather, the Court of Appeals adopted a per se rule that preclusion is unconstitutional in all cases where the victim had a prior sexual relationship with the defendant. That judgment was error. We leave it to the Michigan courts to address in the first instance whether Michigan's rape-shield statute authorizes preclusion and whether, on the facts of this case, preclusion violated Lucas' rights under the Sixth Amendment.

The judgment of the Michigan Court of Appeals is vacated and remanded for further proceedings not inconsistent with this opinion.

It Is So Ordered.

STUDY QUESTIONS

1. Under the Michigan statute, what procedure is a rape defendant who seeks to introduce evidence as to the complainant's past sexual conduct with him required to follow? What consequences may flow from his failure to follow this procedure?
2. Would a trial court's ruling enforcing the statute's notice-and-hearing procedure always violate the Sixth Amendment's guarantee of the right to confront adverse witnesses? Why not?

Rape shield laws have met many of the concerns raised by feminists about the manner in which the courts handle rape cases. As a result of court decisions in the 1970s and 1980s, many of the special rules governing the trial of rape cases have been abolished. Lingering questions during that period were: what acts constituted rape, who could be raped, and by whom? Could an act between husband and wife legally be considered rape? The next case examines both issues of marital rape and whether rape can be based on the gender of the victim.

PEOPLE V. LIBERTA
Court of Appeals of New York, 1984. 64 N.Y.2d 152,
474 N.E.2d 567 485 N.Y.S.2d 207.

WACHTLER, Judge.

The defendant, while living apart from his wife pursuant to a Family Court order, forcibly raped and sodomized her in the presence of their 2 1/2 year old son. Under the New York Penal Law a married man ordinarily cannot be prosecuted for raping or sodomizing his wife. The defendant, however, though married at the time of the incident, is treated as an unmarried man under the Penal Law because of the Family Court order. On this appeal, he contends that because of the exemption for married men, the statutes for rape in the first degree (Penal Law, § 130.35) and sodomy in the first degree (Penal Law, § 130.50), violate the equal protection clause of the Federal Constitution (U.S. Const., 14th Amdt.). The defendant also contends that the rape statute violates equal protection because only men, and not women, can be prosecuted under it. . . .

A. THE MARITAL EXEMPTION

As noted above, under the Penal Law a married man ordinarily cannot be convicted of forcibly raping or sodomizing his wife. This is the so-called marital exemption for rape. . . . The assumption, even before the marital exemption was codified, that a man could not be guilty of raping his wife, is traceable to a statement made by the 17th century English jurist Lord Hale, who wrote: "[T]he husband cannot be guilty of a rape committed by himself upon his lawful wife, for by their mutual matrimonial consent and contract the wife hath given up herself in this kind unto her husband, which she cannot retract" (1 Hale, *History of Pleas of the Crown*, p. 629). Although Hale cited no authority for his statement it was relied on by State Legislatures which enacted rape statutes with a marital exemption and by courts which established a common-law exemption for husbands. . . .

We find that there is no rational basis for distinguishing between marital rape and nonmarital rape. The various rationales which have been asserted in defense of the exemption are either based upon archaic notions about the consent and property rights incident to marriage or are simply unable to withstand even the slightest scrutiny. We therefore declare the marital exemption for rape in the New York statute to be unconstitutional.

Lord Hale's notion of an irrevocable implied consent by a married woman to sexual intercourse has been cited most frequently in support of the marital exemption. . . . Any argument based on a supposed consent, however, is untenable. Rape is not simply a sexual act to which one party does not consent. Rather, it is a degrading, violent act which violates the bodily integrity of the victim and frequently causes severe, long-lasting physical and psychic harm. . . . To ever imply consent to such an act is irrational and absurd. Other than in the context of rape statutes, marriage has never been viewed as giving a husband the right to coerced intercourse on demand. . . . Certainly, then, a marriage license should not be viewed as a license for a husband to forcibly rape his wife with impunity. A married woman has the same right to control her own body as does an unmarried woman. . . . If a husband feels "aggrieved" by his wife's refusal to engage in sexual intercourse, he should seek relief in the courts governing domestic relations, not in "violent or forceful self-help." . . .

The other traditional justifications for the marital exemption were the common-law doctrines that a woman was the property of her husband and that the legal existence of the woman was "incorporated and consolidated into that of the husband" (Blackstone's Commentaries) . . . [The marital right of privacy is sometimes cited to justify the exemption.]

The marital exemption simply does not further marital privacy because this right of privacy protects consensual acts, not violent sexual assaults. . . . Just as a husband cannot invoke a right of marital privacy to escape liability for beating his wife, he cannot justifiably rape his wife under the guise of a right to privacy. . . .

Another rationale sometimes advanced in support of the marital exemption is that marital rape would be a difficult crime to prove. A related argument is that allowing such prosecutions could lead to fabricated complaints by "vindictive" wives. The difficulty of proof argument is based on the problem of showing lack of consent. Proving lack of consent, however, is often the most difficult part of any rape prosecution, particularly where the rapist and the victim had a prior relationship. . . . Similarly, the possibility that married women will fabricate complaints would seem to be no greater than the possibility of unmarried women doing so. . . . The criminal justice system with all of its built-in safeguards is presumed to be capable of handling any false complaints. Indeed, if the possibility of fabricated complaints were a basis for not criminalizing behavior which would otherwise be sanctioned, virtually all crimes other than homicides would go unpunished.

The final argument in defense of the marital exemption is that marital rape is not as serious an offense as other rape and is thus adequately dealt with by the possibility of prosecution under criminal statutes, such as assault statutes, which provide for less severe punishment. The fact that rape statutes exist, however, is a recognition that the harm caused by a forcible rape is different, and more severe, than the harm caused by an ordinary assault. . . .

Moreover, there is no evidence to support the argument that marital rape has less severe consequences than other rape. On the contrary, numerous studies have shown that marital rape is frequently quite violent and generally has *more* severe, traumatic effects on the victim than other rape. . . .

Among the recent decisions in this country addressing the marital exemption, only one court has concluded that there is a rational basis for it. We agree with the other courts which have analyzed the exemption, which have been unable to find any present justification for it. . . .

B. THE EXEMPTION FOR FEMALES

Under the Penal Law only males can be convicted of rape in the first degree. Insofar as the rape statute applies to acts of "sexual intercourse," which as defined in the Penal Law can only occur between a male and a female, it is true that a female cannot physically rape a female and that therefore there is no denial of equal protection when punishing only males for forcibly engaging in sexual intercourse with females. The equal protection issue, however, stems from the fact that the statute applies to males who forcibly rape females but does not apply to females who forcibly rape males.

Rape statutes historically applied only to conduct by males against females, largely because the purpose behind the proscriptions was to protect the chastity of women and thus their property value to their fathers or husbands. . . . New York's rape statute has always protected only females, and has thus applied only to males. . . . Presently New York is one of only 10 jurisdictions that does not have a gender-neutral statute for forcible rape. . . .

The People bear the burden of showing both the existence of an important objective and the substantial relationship between the discrimination in the statute and that objective. This burden is not met in the present case, and therefore the gender exemption also renders the statute unconstitutional.

The first argument advanced by the People in support of the exemption for females is that because only females can become pregnant the State may constitutionally differentiate between forcible rapes of females and forcible rapes of males. This court and the United States Supreme Court have upheld statutes which subject males to criminal liability for engaging in sexual intercourse with underage females without the converse being true (*People v. Whidden, Michael M. v. Sonoma County Superior Ct.*). The rationale behind these decisions was that the primary purpose of such "statutory rape" laws is to protect against the harm caused by teenage pregnancies, there being no need to provide the same protection to young males.

There is no evidence, however, that preventing pregnancies is a primary purpose of the statute prohibiting forcible rape, nor does such a purpose seem likely. Rather, the very fact that the statute proscribes "forcible compulsion" shows that its overriding purpose is to protect a woman from an unwanted, forcible, and often violent sexual intrusion into her body. Thus, due to the different purposes behind forcible rape laws and "statutory" (consensual) rape laws, the cases upholding the gender discrimination in the latter are not decisive with respect to the former, and the People cannot meet their burden here by simply stating that only females can become pregnant.

The People also claim that the discrimination is justified because a female rape victim "faces the probability of medical, sociological, and psychological problems unique to her gender." This same argument, when advanced in support of the discrimination in the statutory rape laws, was re-

jected by this court in *People v. Whidden* (51 N.Y.2d at p. 461), and it is no more convincing in the present case. "[A]n ' "archaic and overbroad" generalization' . . . which is evidently grounded in long-standing stereotypical notions of the differences between the sexes, simply cannot serve as a legitimate rationale for a penal provision that is addressed only to adult males."

Finally, the People suggest that a gender-neutral law for forcible rape is unnecessary, and that therefore the present law is constitutional because a woman either cannot actually rape a man or such attacks, if possible, are extremely rare. Although the "physiologically impossible" argument has been accepted by several courts, it is simply wrong. The argument is premised on the notion that a man cannot engage in sexual intercourse unless he is sexually aroused and if he is aroused then he is consenting to intercourse. "Sexual intercourse," however, "occurs upon any penetration, however slight"; this degree of contact can be achieved without a male being aroused and thus without his consent.

As to the "infrequency" argument, while forcible sexual assaults by females upon males are undoubtedly less common than those by males upon females, this numerical disparity cannot by itself make the gender discrimination constitutional. Women may well be responsible for a far lower number of all serious crimes than are men, but such a disparity would not make it permissible for the State to punish only men who commit, for example, robbery. . . . A gender-neutral law would indisputably better serve, even if only marginally, the objective of deterring and punishing forcible sexual assaults. The only persons "benefitted" by the gender exemption are females who forcibly rape males. As the Supreme Court has stated, "[a] gender-based classification which, as compared to a gender-neutral one, generates additional benefits only for those it has no reason to prefer cannot survive equal protection scrutiny" (*Orr v. Orr*).

Accordingly, we find that section 130.35 of the Penal Law violates equal protection.

Having found that the statutes for rape in the first degree and sodomy in the first degree are unconstitutionally underin-clusive, the remaining issue is the appropriate remedy for these equal protection violations. . . .

The question then is whether the Legislature would prefer to have statutes which cover forcible rape and sodomy, with no exemption for married men who rape or sodomize their wives and no exception made for females who rape males, or instead to have no statutes proscribing forcible rape and sodomy. In any case where a court must decide whether to sever an exemption or instead declare an entire statute a nullity it must look at the importance of the statute, the significance of the exemption within the over-all statutory scheme, and the effects of striking down the statute. . . . Statutes prohibiting such behavior are of the utmost importance, and to declare such statutes a nullity would have a disastrous effect on the public interest and safety. The inevitable conclusion is that the Legislature would prefer to eliminate the exemptions and thereby preserve the statutes. . . .

Though our decision does not "create a crime," it does, of course, enlarge the scope of two criminal statutes. We recognize that a court should be reluctant to expand criminal statutes, due to the danger of usurping the role of the Legislature, but in this case overriding policy concerns dictate our following such a course in light of the catastrophic effect that striking down the statutes and thus creating a hiatus would have. . . .

STUDY QUESTIONS

1. What possible justifications for the marital rape exemption did the court identify? Why did the court find these justifications inadequate?
2. Did the court consider the question of whether men can be rape victims? Do you believe men can be raped? By women or only by other men? Do men who are victims of homosexual rape or who are raped by women suffer the same sort of harm women rape victims suffer? Why? Why not?
3. How did the court distinguish the *Michael M.* case? Do you find the distinction convincing?
4. Some feminists see the traditional treatment of rape as distorting and overemphasizing women's sexuality. They advocate that rape be treated as a form of assault, rather than a separate crime. What arguments do you see for and against such a course?

In invalidating New York's marital rape exemption, the *Liberta* court rejected the notion that a woman expresses her consent to sexual relations with her husband whenever he wishes simply by marrying him. Imposing criminal liability on someone who justifies his unwanted sexual acts by such "consent" does not seem unfair since consent of this sort is obviously a fiction.

According to researchers at VAWnet (Violence Against Women Electronic Network), it is estimated that 10 percent to 14 percent of married women are raped by their husbands. It was not until 1993 that marital rape became a crime in all fifty states and the District of Columbia. In seventeen states and the District of Columbia, there are no exemptions from rape prosecution granted to husbands. In thirty-three states, however, there are still some exemptions from rape prosecution given to husbands, usually concerning the use of force. Research on this subject shows that marital rape has been linked most extensively with marital or intimate partner violence. This might be due to the fact that most of the gathering of information comes from women who seek assistance for physical abuse. Marital rape is categorized into three types. In *force-only rape,* the husband uses only the amount of force necessary to coerce his wife. In *battering rape,* husbands rape and batter their wives, the battering happening concurrently with or before or after the sexual assault. In *sadistic/obsessive rape,* husbands use torture or perverse sexual acts; pornography is often involved (Bergen, 1999).

Determining more generally when it is fair to impose a criminal liability for nonconsensual sexual relations, however, is not such an easy matter. Should a perpetrator be held criminally responsible for his sexual acts whenever the other party fails to express consent clearly? When the other party's words or conduct should have led the perpetrator to understand that there was no consent? Should liability be imposed only when the perpetrator actually knew that the acts were unwanted?

Traditional rape laws have avoided this problem by defining rape as sexual intercourse without consent, but then equating "without consent" with the use or threat of physical force. Many jurisdictions have continued this approach, though they have expanded the definition of force to include mental and economic coercion. A few jurisdictions have actually redefined lack of consent to mean the absence of words or conduct expressing freely given agreement. One effect of such provisions is to shift the focus at trial from the extent of the victim's resistance to the meaning to be accorded her conduct. Another may be to permit convictions where the other party made no verbal or physical response—whether positive or negative.

One possible challenge to a statute that redefines consent in this way is that it impermissibly criminalizes consensual sexual relations because consenting parties do not always show their consent through words or acts. The following case reveals one court's response to this argument.

STATE V. LEDERER
Court of Appeals of Wisconsin, 1980.
99 Wis.2d 430, 299 N.W.2d 457.

CANNON, Judge.

Defendant was convicted of third degree sexual assault contrary to sec. 940.225(3), Stats. Defendant challenges: the constitutionality of the consent definition as well as the sufficiency of evidence presented to establish that the victim had not consented . . . We find no error and affirm.

On July 11, 1978, defendant telephoned the prosecutrix at her residence. At the suggestion of the defendant, the prosecutrix agreed to inspect a residence for rental purposes. The prosecutrix met the defendant at a service station where she was dropped off by her roommate. Before leaving with the defendant, the prosecutrix took down the license number of defendant's van and gave it to her roommate. The prosecutrix got into defendant's van, and they drove to an unfurnished home in River Hills.

At the home, defendant began to disrobe the prosecutrix. The prosecutrix objected and pushed defendant's hand away. The defendant allegedly told her that it would be worse if she fought. She permitted the defendant to disrobe her. Defendant performed an act of sexual intercourse, despite the verbal protestations of the prosecutrix. Defendant fell asleep on top of the prosecutrix. When defendant awoke in the early hours of July 12, 1978, defendant performed a second act of sexual intercourse. Defendant again fell asleep with his arm and part of his body across the prosecutrix. A third act of intercourse was performed when defendant awoke, as well as an act of fellatio. Defendant then took several photographs of the prosecutrix in the nude. Acts of sexual intercourse and fellatio were again performed. Defendant then drove the prosecutrix home.

At trial, testimony was produced regarding the photographs of the prosecutrix in the nude found at the residence. Testimony was produced regarding the bedding found at the residence and the tests performed for saliva, blood and semen on the bedding. Testimony was also presented about a medical report prepared at Family Hospital. The trial court denied defendant's motion to dismiss at the close of the state's case. The defense rested without calling any witnesses. Judgment on the guilty verdict was entered October 12, 1979. . . .

. . . Defendant contends that application of the definition of consent contained in sec. 940.225(4) could subject an individual to punishment for engaging in consensual sexual activities where no testimony was produced regarding acts or words which evidenced freely given consent. We do not agree. . . .

The plain terms of sec. 940.225(3), Stats. define third degree sexual assault as sexual intercourse *without consent.* Consent is defined by sec. 940.225(4), as "words or overt actions by a person who is competent to give informed consent indicating a freely given agreement to have sexual intercourse or sexual contact." . . .

We reject defendant's contention that a defendant could be convicted under sec. 940.225(3), Stats., for engaging in consensual sexual relations. The plain terms of the statute require that the state must prove that the act of sexual intercourse must be without consent. In *Gates v. State* this court stated that for conviction for second degree sexual assault "[t]he State must introduce evidence that there was no consent, and this evidence must be sufficient to convince the jury beyond a reasonable doubt." Our supreme court has also determined that "[t]he plain wording of the statutory definition of consent demonstrates that failure to resist is not consent . . . ." *State v. Clark.* We hold that these definitions of consent apply equally well to third degree sexual assault. In so defining consent the legislature has relieved the state of the burden of proving that the victim resisted in order to establish that the act was nonconsensual.

Defendant contends that two parties may enter into consensual sexual relations without manifesting freely given consent through words or acts. We reject this contention as we know of no other means of communicating consent. . . .

. . . In reviewing a challenge to the sufficiency of the evidence "the question is whether the evidence, considered most favorably to the state, is 'so insufficient in probative value and force that it can be said as a matter of law that no trier of facts acting reasonably could be convinced to that degree of certitude which the law defines as beyond a reasonable doubt.'" *State v. Clark.*

The record discloses that the prosecutrix objected when the defendant initially disrobed her and continued to object throughout the night when defendant performed the various acts of sexual intercourse. The record further discloses that the prosecutrix testified that when asked to open her mouth prior to the performance of the act of fellatio she did not, but instead turned her head away and only complied when the defendant took her head in his hands. These actions on the part of the prosecutrix can hardly be said to be manifestations of consent, particularly when viewed together with the threat of the defendant that things would be worse if she did not comply. "No" means no, and precludes any finding that the prosecutrix consented to any of the sexual acts performed during the night. . . .

Affirmed

STUDY QUESTIONS

1. Under the applicable Wisconsin statute, what must the prosecution prove to obtain a valid conviction for sexual assault? Must it show resistance by the victim? Must it show that the victim expressed her lack of consent by words or conduct?

2. Do you think the defendant in this case actually understood that the prosecutrix had not consented to sexual intercourse and fellatio with him? Did the defendants in the other cases in this section?

3. Is there a risk under this law that men will be convicted of rape when they simply have not realized that the woman did not wish to have sexual intercourse? Does that strike you as unfair? As a practical matter, are prosecutors likely to proceed in such cases? Are women likely to complain about rape in these circumstances?

A recent New Jersey Supreme Court decision, *State of New Jersey in the Interest of M.T.S.*, 609 A.2d 1266 (1992), makes even clearer that sexual intercourse without affirmative consent is rape. The case involved two teenagers who were kissing and petting. When the young woman fell asleep, the young man penetrated her. She woke and asked him to stop, which he did. In ruling that no force is required, the Court spelled out the prosecutor's burden of proof.

> ... In short, in order to convict under the sexual assault statute in cases such as these, the State must prove beyond a reasonable doubt that there was sexual penetration and that it was accomplished without the affirmative and freely-given permission of the alleged victim. ... [S]uch proof can be based on evidence of conduct or words in light of surrounding circumstances and must demonstrate beyond a reasonable doubt that a reasonable person would not have believed that there was affirmative and freely-given permission. If there is evidence to suggest that the defendant reasonably believed that such permission had been given, the State must demonstrate either that defendant did not actually believe that affirmative permission had been freely given or that such a belief was unreasonable under all of the circumstances. Thus, the State bears the burden of proof throughout the case. Id. *at 1278*

While the M.T.S. case is part of an important new trend, its consequences may be mixed. On the one hand, the court's "no means no" approach seems to place a key limit on males' historical prerogatives. On the other hand, since the approach puts both the defendant's actual belief that the necessary affirmative permission was given under the circumstances and the reasonableness of any such belief in issue, the approach may once again make relevant evidence regarding the complainant's past sexual conduct.

In reaching the landmark M.T.S. decision, the court made plain it was well aware of today's concern over forced sexual intercourse between acquaintances. Although the concern is recent, the prevalence of nonstranger rapes has been known for some time. In the early 1980s, for example, more than half of all rapes were committed by male relatives, current or former husbands, boyfriends, or lovers.

Today, according to recent Department of Justice statistics, 85 percent of all rapes are committed by people known to the victims. Proof of consent, or lack thereof, is often key in the majority of date rape prosecutions. An example is the pending rape prosecution case of *People v. Kobe Bryant*, a basketball star accused of raping a woman fan. Two issues have emerged: consent and whether there is an exception to Colorado's rape shield laws to look at the victim's past behavior. The Trial Court in the *Kobe Bryant* case ultimately decided that although the rape shield laws were not unconstitutional the victim's sexually activity during the 72 hours before and after the alleged rape was admissible into evidence. That coupled with the fact that the victim's identity was disclosed may have impacted on her decision whether to testify or not. In the end, the victim refused to testify in the criminal case and in 2004 the criminal case was dismissed. A civil lawsuit brought by the victim was later settled. There are, however, some clear-cut times that consent cannot be given, even if it appears that both parties have consented. Most notable is when the victim is under the legal age of consent. As you can see from the next article regarding mandatory reporting of statutory rape cases, sometimes issues in addition to the criminality of certain behaviors drive policy makers to vigorously seek to enforce certain laws.

Treatment of statutory rape has been considered a constitutional question—to the extent that the laws treat women and men differently. Other concerns are now apparent.

CAUGHT BETWEEN TEEN AND THE LAW
Family Planning Programs and Statutory Rape Reporting
Patricia Donovan
The Guttmacher Report (June 1998), pp. 5–6.

Studies showing that at least half of babies born to mothers who are minors are fathered by adult men, and that the sexual partners of those women are often men 3–6 years older, prompted some policy makers in recent years to conclude that vigorous prosecution of statutory rape could significantly reduce high rates of adolescent pregnancy and child-bearing and lower welfare costs as well. Enthusiasm for this strategy has already begun to wane, however, in the face of evidence that it is not feasible for states to prosecute enough men to have an appreciable effect on teen pregnancy rates and birthrates.

But now, some conservative legislators have seized on enforcement of statutory rape—sexual intercourse in which one partner is deemed by law to be too young to consent—for another purpose. Announcing "a two-tier legislative assault on . . . Title X." Rep. Don Manzullo (R. IL) has introduced legislation to comply with state laws that mandate reporting child abuse, include statutory rape, and also to notify parents in writing before providing a prescription contraceptive to a minor. A second Manzullo bill contains only the reporting provision. . . .

. . . [T]here is a very broad range in what the states consider criminal activity. Under Kentucky law, for example, it is a first degree felony to have intercourse with a minor under age 12, a second degree offense if the minor is under 14 and the partner is 18 or older and a third degree felony if the minor is under 16 and the partner is at least 21. In California, on the other hand, sexual intercourse between two individuals who are not married is a crime if one is under 18, albeit a somewhat more serious offense if one partner is under 16 and the other over 21.

State reporting laws tend to be even more complicated, and adolescent service providers are often confused as to whether and under what circumstances statutory rape is a reportable offense. That is at least partly because statutory rape laws themselves do not have a reporting component. Instead, the obligation to report is governed by state child abuse statutes.

Every state requires cases of child abuse or neglect to be reported to either a child welfare agency or the police, and has designated certain individuals who have frequent contact with children—health care workers, school authorities and social workers, for example—to be mandatory reporters of known or suspected cases of abuse or neglect. In about half the states, the law appears to define child abuse to include at least some cases of statutory rape; in the remaining states, the definition of child abuse either does not encompass statutory rape or applies only to cases involving a family member or guardian.

TROUBLING QUESTIONS

Mandatory reporting of statutory rape raises a number of troubling questions. What is the purpose of mandatory reporting, and is the agency receiving the statutory rape reports equipped to handle them? Does a provider have an ethical obligation to inform its teenage clients in advance that certain information, if revealed, must be reported to authorities? If a provider does not inform minors in advance of its obligation to report, does it violate minors' expectation of confidentiality? Conversely, if the provider does inform minors of the potential consequences of revealing certain information, will young women refuse to discuss important health issues or other concerns? . . .

[According to Abigail English of the National Youth Law Center, the process that follows reporting] varies from state to state and

From *Caught Between Teens and the Law: Family Planning Programs and Statutory Rape Reporting*, by Donovan, P., The Guttmacher Report on Public Policy, 1(3): 5–7.

even from country to country, reflecting the broad discretion prosecutors have in deciding how to handle reports of statutory rape. Often, a statutory rape report is simply placed in a file without any action taken; in other cases, the prosecutor may conduct a preliminary investigation, contacting the minor's parents and her sexual partner in the process, but take no further action; and in some instances, the man will be charged with a crime.

Meanwhile, "the victim may go through hell when a case is reported," contends Michelle Oberman, a law professor at DePaul University who has studied the implications of enforcing statutory rape laws. "Her confidentiality is breached, and the most private aspects of her life become public record. And for what end? Are we really going to lock up all these men? She is victimized all over again."

Lack of action largely reflects the fact that child welfare agencies are overloaded and have to prioritize the cases they pursue, according to legal experts. Children, especially those who are very young and have been physically abused, are at the top of the list. Adolescents are a much lower priority, unless they are victims of intra familial sexual abuse.

"Mandatory reporting of child and youth maltreatment involves significant government intrusions into the lives of families," notes ABA's Davidson. "There is a significant risk that simply requiring professionals to report [statutory rape] to authorities, without proper training and necessary infrastructure, could do more harm than good," he warns, such as "deterring young people from getting medical care, and making it more difficult to identify fathers and collect child support payments.". . .

These are major concerns of adolescent service providers. Reproductive health care providers, for example, fear that pregnant and sexually active teenagers will not seek prenatal care, contraceptive services or STD screening, and that they will be unwilling to discuss personal problems if they think the provider will report their partners to authorities. . . .

[A consortium of social workers] warned that while "on the surface, enforcement of our state's statutory rape law seems good for the protection of adolescents, a closer examination of the implications reveals a multitude of unintended, negative consequences that could have disastrous effects on young families." It cited reports of teen mothers opting not to seek state services to which they were entitled for fear the welfare agency would take their child away. The young women were also reported to be afraid that their partner would be sent to jail, and some feared possible domestic violence if they cooperated with authorities. "This fear," the [consortium] pointed out, "pushes teens underground, away from their support services at a time when they may need them the most."

Mandatory reporting also poses another dilemma for service providers: Should they avoid asking questions that might trigger the reporting requirement, in order to protect minors' confidentiality, even if the answers to those questions may be crucial to providing high quality services, or should they ask the questions and make a report if required, even if in doing so they jeopardize their future relationship with young people?

Many providers feel they have an ethical responsibility to forewarn teenage clients that if they divulge the age of their sexual partner, the provider may have to report the man to the authorities. But, in warning a minor, experts say, the provider may deprive a young woman of a safe environment in which to discuss problems and concerns. Ultimately, concludes the ABA's Davidson, this may be a disservice to minors. "If you take actions that encourage a person not to talk, there is a strong risk they may not talk about more serious crimes as well.". . .

STUDY QUESTIONS

1. Do you believe that mandatory reporting requirements have a chilling effect on the disclosure of rape cases?
2. Is it "rape" if both participants are "underage"? Should it be?
3. What reasons did policy makers have to pursue statutory rape prosecution *besides* protecting an underage victim?

Cases involving the lack of consent also involve the physical or mental inability to give consent, such as when a person is highly intoxicated, unconscious, or incapacitated for other reasons. A more recent phenomenon is the use of date rape drugs. Drugs such as Rohypnal and Gamma Hydroxybutyrate or GHB produce loss of consciousness and the inability to recall events. Victims often do not know that they have been drugged or that they have been raped while under the influence of these drugs. Date rape drugs render the victim unable to defend herself, to call for help, and to recall any aspect of the events. Even in cases where the victim has awoken during the rape, she is usually so debilitated from the drug that she cannot in any way fight against the rape.

Prosecution of these cases is made equally difficult by the lack of memory associated with the attack and the lack of information on the part of law enforcement on how to gather evidence. Date rape drugs stay in the blood and urine for only a limited amount of time. If specimens are not obtained immediately after the attack, evidence of the drug disappears from the victim's system. Until recently, little was known about these drugs and how to prosecute drug-induced rape cases. In fact, possession and use of the drugs themselves was not necessarily punishable as a crime. Federal recognition of the importance of controlling these drugs culminated in legislation, signed by President Clinton in 1996, called the Drug-Induced Rape Prevention and Punishment Act. That act provided for harsh penalties for distribution and possession of one of these drugs. In 2000, the act was amended to add GHB as a prohibited drug.

The heightened awareness of sexual violence toward women in recent years and available funding through the Department of Justice have prompted a number of studies in an attempt to gain a better understanding of the issue and the effect on women. Studies have been conducted of college students; the prevalence of sexual violence toward women is nowhere more evident than on college campuses. A recent study by the Department of Justice looked at the level of violence and response to violence (Fisher, Cullen, & Turner, 2000).

THE SEXUAL VICTIMIZATION OF COLLEGE WOMEN
Bonnie S. Fisher, Francis T. Cullen, and Michael G. Turner
December 2000.

During the past decade, concern over the sexual victimization of female college students has escalated. In part, the interest in this problem has been spurred by increasing attention to the victimization of women in general; until the relatively recent past, female victims received very little attention. However, this is no longer true. Terms such as "date rape" and "domestic violence" have entered the public lexicon and signify the unprecedented, if still insufficient, notice given to women who have been victimized.

Attention to the sexual victimization of college women, however, also has been prompted by the rising fear that college campuses are not ivory towers but, instead, have become hot spots for criminal activity. Researchers have shown that college campuses and their students are not free from the risk of criminal victimization. It is noteworthy that large concentrations of young women come into contact with young men in a variety of public and private settings at various times on college campuses. Previous research suggests that these women are at greater risk for rape and other forms of sexual assault than women in the general population or in a comparable age group. College women might, therefore, be a group whose victimization warrants special attention.

Recognizing these risks, the U.S. Congress passed the Student Right-to-Know and Campus Security Act of 1990 (hereafter referred to as the act). This legislation mandates that colleges and universities participating in Federal student aid programs "prepare, publish, and distribute, through appropriate publications or mailings, to all current students and employees, and to any applicant for enrollment or employment upon request, an annual security report" containing campus security policies and campus crime statistics for that institution (see 20 U.S.C. 1092(f)(1)).[3] Congress has maintained an interest in campus crime issues, passing legislation that requires higher educational institutions to address the rights of victims of sexual victimization and to collect and publish additional crime statistics (e.g., murder and nonnegligent manslaughter, arson). For example, Congress amended the Act in 1992 to include the Campus Sexual Assault Victims' Bill of Rights, which requires colleges and universities (1) to

develop and publish as part of their annual security report their policies regarding the awareness and prevention of sexual assaults and (2) to afford basic rights to sexual assault victims.[4] The act was amended again in 1998 to include additional reporting obligations, extensive campus security-related provisions, and the requirement to keep a daily public crime log; some States already required a public log (Public Law 105-244). [5] The 1998 amendments also officially changed the name of the act to the Jeanne Clery Disclosure of Campus Security Policy and Campus Crime Statistics Act. In 1999, the U.S. Department of Justice awarded $8.1 million to 21 colleges and universities to combat sexual assault, domestic violence, and stalking.

STUDY QUESTIONS

1. What does the act require colleges to do?
2. Do you think that this demonstrates a changing view toward the sexual victimization of women? In what way?

What the study did show was that 2.8 percent of the sample had experienced either a completed rape (1.7 percent) or an attempted rape incident (1.1 percent). The victimization rate was 27.7 rapes per 1,000 female students. However, the *incidents* of rape were higher. For every 1,000 women attending institutions, there may well be 35 incidents of rape in a given academic year (based on a victimization rate of 35.3 per 1,000 college women). For a campus with 10,000 women, this would mean the number of rapes could exceed 350. Nearly 23 percent of women were multiple victims of rape or attempted rape.

The escalating violence toward women, and greater recognition of the harm that sexual and physical violence cause, not just to individual victims but to society as a whole, prompted the passage of the Violence Against Women Act (VAWA) of 1994. As we saw in Chapter 6, one of the landmark provisions of VAWA was the civil action for gender-motivated violence. That remedy was declared unconstitutional in *U.S. v. Morrison*. The Supreme Court in *Morrison* based its decision on the constitutional right of the federal government to intervene in what it believed were state or local issues. That left the door open for states and localities to create their local civil rights of action. Currently no state has created a civil action for gender-motivated violence, but some local legislatures in New York have, notably, New York City, Westchester County, and Rockland County. Some of the reasons for creating this private right of action are articulated best by Julie Goldscheid of the NOW Legal Defense and Education Fund testifying in support of local legislation.

TESTIMONY OF JULIE GOLDSCHEID, ACTING LEGAL DIRECTOR, NOW LEGAL DEFENSE AND EDUCATION FUND (CURRENTLY KNOWN AS LEGAL MOMENTUM)

Joint Hearing of the General Welfare and the Women's Issues
Committees on Intro 752-A
November 30, 2000.

In 1994, Congress enacted the Civil Rights Remedy ("Civil Rights Remedy") of the Violence Against Women Act ("VAWA"). [footnote omitted] That law enabled victims of gender-based crimes to recover damages from their perpetrators, provided that they could meet the statutory requirements. In passing this pioneering legislation after four years of legislative debate, Congress recognized that gender-based crimes constituted *bias* crimes that inflict harm on their victims and communities. [footnote omitted] Congress enacted the Civil Rights Remedy to give victims of these crimes the ability to recover damages for the particular harm that results from this violation of their civil rights.

Intro 752-A provides an essential remedy to victims of gender-motivated violence whose civil rights have been violated.

NOW Legal Defense strongly endorses Intro 752-A, which would provide victims of gender-motivated violence a private cause of action against their perpetrators—the same type of remedy provided by the VAWA Civil Rights Remedy before it was struck down. Civil rights recovery is important both because state tort laws are often inadequate and because gender-based violence implicates a different harm—a violation of the victim's civil rights.

II. GENDER-MOTIVATED VIOLENCE

Violence against women permeates criminal behavior in society. [footnote omitted] Some of this violence is gender motivated and violates the victim's civil rights. Yet, women are not afforded the same civil rights remedies as other protected classes. Federal law permits federal prosecution of bias crimes based on race, color, religion, or national origin, but not gender. [footnote omitted] Criminal and civil redress for gender-based crimes may be limited in other ways. Some states still prohibit or limit criminal prosecution of spousal rape or sexual violence between intimates. [footnote omitted] Other states still limit a spouse's ability to bring a tort action against her batterer. [footnote omitted] Neither New York City nor New York State law currently authorizes a damages cause of action for gender-based crimes. Only ten states and the District of Columbia currently have any provision recognizing gender-based crimes as a form of civil rights violation. [footnote omitted]

Nevertheless, like other bias-motivated violence, gender-based crimes inflict a different kind of harm that warrants a distinct form of recovery. [footnote omitted] The United States Supreme Court has acknowledged that bias-motivated conduct inflicts greater harm to individuals and society than other crimes because of the emotional impact on the victim, the potential for retaliatory crimes, and the possibility of provoking the broader community. [footnote omitted] Women live with the restriction that they cannot go places without the fear of being attacked. Often they cannot go home either because of the significant incidence of rapes and assaults by intimate partners. [footnote omitted] The result limits where women work, live, study, and travel. [footnote omitted]

Examples of the way gender-bias infuses crimes such as domestic violence, sexual assault and stalking abound. Perpetrators of crimes such as rape, domestic violence, and sexual assault commonly use misogynist epithets and language reflecting stereotypical views of women. In the *Morrison* case, for example, after allegedly raping Christy Brzonkala, the defendant used profanity and bragged to fellow college classmates about how he sexually exploited women. [footnote omitted] In domestic violence cases, it is extremely common for batterers to use misogynistic epithets while verbally abusing their partners. [footnote omitted] Batterers commonly attempt to coerce their partners' conformity to traditional gender roles by dictating the women's appearance, controlling with whom the women interact, and limiting where and when the women can socialize. [footnote omitted] Batterers also often interfere with their partners' employment, often the only avenue for economic independence, in an attempt to confine the women to a stereotypic role. [footnote omitted]

Gender motivation permeates crimes of violence against women committed in other contexts as well. One stark example occurred when a Florida college woman was raped at a fraternity house. [footnote omitted] The fraternity had videotaped the incident in which at least one man assaulted the woman while several others watched and commented about the rape, stating, for example, "[t]his is what you call . . . rape. Rape. Rape. Rape white trash," . . . "[i]t is rape-thirty in the morning." [footnote omitted] After viewing the video, local police arrested the woman for making a false report and claimed that the video demonstrated consent. And who can forget the horrific images of women being assaulted by gangs of cheering men displayed continuously on the news after the Puerto Rican Day Parade in this city? [footnote omitted]

III. *United States v. Morrison* and its Aftermath

The United States Supreme Court in *United States v. Morrison* ruled that the VAWA Civil Rights Remedy was an unconstitutional exercise of federal power. [footnote omitted] However, the Court hailed the authority of state and local governments to enact legislation to redress the crimes of domestic violence, sexual assault, and stalking that the Civil Rights Remedy was intended to cover. [footnote omitted] In cases advancing VAWA civil rights claims before the law was struck, court after court throughout the country recognized that domestic violence and sexual assault can violate the victim's civil rights. [footnote omitted] Even in the *Morrison* case, each court to address the facts at issue recognized that the violence may have been gender motivated. [footnote omitted] Now that the federal law is no longer in effect, it is all the more important for state and local governments to provide all appropriate remedies to prevent domestic violence, sexual assault and stalking, and to provide effective remedies when the crimes persist.

Intro 752-A represents just such a critical initiative. Similar legislation introduced in the Arizona, Illinois, and New York state legislatures would provide redress analogous to the VAWA civil rights remedy but none of these proposals have been enacted. [footnote omitted] New York City has the opportunity to be the first jurisdiction in the country to enact a civil rights remedy modeled after the historic VAWA federal law. To do so would mark an important advance in the City's commitment to civil rights and equality for all. Chief Justice Rehnquist recognized this in the *Morrison* opinion even while striking down the law, when he said that "no civilized system of justice could fail to provide [Christy Brzonkala] a remedy for the conduct of respondent Morrison." [footnote omitted]

Thank you.

Study Questions

1. Why does the proponent of this new law believe we need this sort of civil remedy?
2. What is the difference between gender-motivated violence and intimate partner violence?
3. Is the harm to the victim and to society different in these cases? How so?

In addition to the passage of the VAWA, Congress in 1994 also passed the Jacob Wetterling Act, and in 1996, an amendment known as "Megan's Law." These statutes, named after two children who were abducted and murdered by sexual predators, require states to establish registries for sex offenders and develop "community notification" programs or risk-losing federal funding. Though these sex offender registries are controversial on constitutional grounds and practical grounds, they have for the most part passed constitutional muster and are in place now in most localities.

Other critics suggest there may be limitations to current legal approaches, including the VAWA's civil rights approach. The conviction of world champion prizefighter Mike Tyson and the acquittal of William Kennedy Smith have brought to mind the history of discriminatory prosecutions and the continuing potential for racial discrimination. Focusing on the criminal context, attorney Jennifer Wriggins has pointed out that, "given existing disparities in punishments between Whites and Blacks an across-the-board increase would simply reproduce these inequalities." Such disparities, she suggests, implicitly indicate that men are being punished on racial grounds, not for committing rape. To press for use of the criminal law would both suggest that women accept a too male-oriented definition of sexual abuse and validate a criminal law system that has radical shortcomings in terms of treatments. See Jennifer Wriggins, "Rape, Racism and the Law," 6 *Harvard Women's Law Journal* 103 (1983). Law professor Kimberlé Crenshaw expresses related concerns.

VIOLENCE AGAINST WOMEN
Forging a Legal Response
Kimberlè Crenshaw

Address to the National Organization for Women Legal Defense and Education Fund Conference, New York, October 23, 1992.

Within the Black community, the relationship between sexual violence and racism is usually represented through images of Black men being falsely accused of the rape of white women. For example, the Scottsboro Boys, Emmett Till or other men in our community who have been unfairly and unjustly lynched serve to symbolize the subordinating interaction of racism and sexual violence. Yet the names and the experiences of Black women whose bodies also bore the signs of sexualized racial subordination are essentially lost to history. This marginalization of Black women's experiences of sexual violence has consequences even today. Consider the Clarence Thomas hearings; while Thomas was able to mobilize the Black community

by throwing down the lynching card, Anita Hill—had she wanted to play that game—could only draw on some hazy, vague images of Black women's sexual victimization.

The same tendency to center the Black male/white female dyad is apparent in the way sexual violence and race is currently read, not only within the Black community but with the society-at-large. For example, it is still the case, as studies have told us, that the disposition of defendants in rape trials is largely determined by the race of the defendant and the race of the victim. Black men who rape white women tend to receive longer sentences than any other racial dyad. This tends to be articulated in terms of discrimination against Black men, which, in fact, it is. Yet, the fact that Black men are punished disproportionately depending on the race of the victim—when the victim is white they're punished more, when the victim is Black they're punished less—is as much discrimination against Black female victims as it is discrimination against Black men. In a recent study in Dallas it was shown that the average sentence given to rapists of African American women was 2 years, while the average sentence given to rapists of white women was 10 years.

The reason that this disproportionality is seldom understood as racial discrimination against Black women is that racism is usually seen as relationships between different groups of men with respect to something else—property, resources or, in the case of sexual assault—women. It is racist, then, that Black men are punished more readily than white men when victims are white. Yet the fact that white women are more likely to see their rapists punished than Black women is not understood as racist, especially when the assailant is Black. So as long as racism is primarily seen as a male-male phenomenon, the racial stratification of women and the consequences for Black rape victims will not be understood as another moment of racism, either within society at large or within the Black community.

Some of these dynamics are apparent in the polarization over the Tyson/Washington rape trial. Many white feminists could not quite understand why there was so much support for Mike Tyson and so little support for Desiree Washington. One of the reasons why there was so little support for Desiree Washington was that the historical experience of lynching has created a ready response that is skeptical toward rape allegations and protective of Black defendants, particularly accomplished ones. The basic problem again is that as long as there are these statistics that suggest that race does play a role in rape adjudication, the reaction is going to be one that is going to be largely protective of those who are most readily recognized as racism's victims. In the case of sexual violence, it's Black men.

Now what kind of feminist reaction to this problem is appropriate? One factor that contributed to the polarization surrounding the Tyson case was the fact that many feminists rejoiced to a certain extent when Mike Tyson was convicted. There were op-ed pieces, for example, that characterized the conviction of Mike Tyson as vindication for what had happened to Patricia Bowman. This kind of uncritical celebration of something that was very painful for the Black community reinforces the tendency to see rape primarily as a white women's issue rather than an issue women across the board have to deal with. Of course I think that the use of race to deny the reality of rape in communities of color is an unfortunate, inaccurate, and emotionally damaging kind of political rhetoric. But I do believe that feminists need to take the concerns that fuel this rhetoric seriously in attempts to find ways to mobilize women of all races around this problem and to create a more cohesive movement.

The close connection between rape and lynching in this country reveals, then, that race exists just under the surface of rape. Historian Jacqueline Dowd Hall has written about how the history of lynching and the repression of Black male sexuality is closely linked to the repression of white female sexuality. Because contemporary events suggest that those links still exist, it behooves us to acknowledge and try to counter them.

Let me offer two recent examples; the cases of the Central Park jogger and Charles Stewart. We all know that what happened to the investment banker was a heinous crime, one that rightfully was condemned throughout society. Yet, I think many of us also have a hunch that part of the reaction to it, as exemplified by the full page ad taken out by Donald Trump calling for the death penalty for rapists, was as much a reaction to the particular race of the parties as to the actual rape itself. I think it would strain our imagination to think that Trump, or for that matter other men in his class, would have reacted in the same way had that investment banker been, let's say, a Black social service worker. We know this also for a fact: At least 28 other women were raped that week, and most of them women of color. One Black woman was gang raped and thrown down an elevator shaft and left to die in Brooklyn. Yet she received no outpouring of public concern. I urge you to also think about the Charles Stewart case. Consider how easy it was for Charles Stewart to divert attention from his own savagery by displacing the act onto those from whom savagery is expected, Black men.

Both of these events tell us how race still shapes the way violence is perceived in our society. It tells us first that certain victims count more than others and that certain assailants are feared more than others.

To the extent that prosecutors' choices are influenced by these very factors, not only Black women and Black men, but also the majority of white women, will be discriminated against in the distribution of resources in the criminal justice system. Prosecutors are political animals, and being rational actors that they are, they will no doubt make choices based on crimes that are easier to prosecute and which, depending on the likelihood of success, will reap most benefits. If attitudes remain that certain victims are truer victims because they've been abused by those who fit the stereotype of the threat, then the rest of us will be marginalized. An effective mobilization against violence, one that then does not reproduce racial cleavages and that empowers women across the board, cannot be silent on the question of racism, but must directly acknowledge and grapple with it. And by grappling with it, I don't mean simply repeating ad naseum that rape happens to all women, regardless of color. . . .

Let me give you an example of how our failure to actively name racism and address it can reproduce the marginalization of certain women. Many of you are familiar with the Violence Against Women Act. Much of the testimony supporting the VAW Act was based on the idea that violence is experienced across all races and across all classes, which is of course true. This testimony was meant to displace the stereotyped victim of domestic violence, which is usually imagined to be a poor woman or a woman of color. But the problem with stating that women of all races and classes confront domestic violence is that the reasons why domestic violence was not seen as an important problem as long as it was imagined to be a problem of the "other" never gets addressed. As a consequence then, the message heard by our white male senators is that we've got to do something about this problem now—it isn't just a "them" problem, it is an "us" problem. In fact, in the introductory comments to the VAW Act, many of the sponsors seemed to imply as much. In order to ensure that feminism reaches and incorporates the "other," that it reaches into communities where feminism is not yet taken seriously, we have to be willing to grapple with these questions of race.

Some feminists were also concerned about why, for example, many young African American women did not support Desiree Washington. There was an interesting newspaper article in the *Washington Post*. A woman was interviewing several Black women about their support or lack of support of Desiree Washington and they all repeated that Washington knew what she was getting into, that she shouldn't have gone up to his room. But as the reporter was interviewing these teenagers, they repeatedly told stories about the ways they had to confront threat of their own sexual abuse and the ways in which they were forced to look out for themselves. In fact, while the interview was going on, a couple of incidents actually happened where they had to negotiate their way around unwanted sexual aggression. One might ask how this contradiction can be. How can women, themselves threatened by sexual violence, fail to support a woman who was struggling to survive that very problem?

Unless women are given a way to step outside of the sexual system in which they are in, unless they are empowered to criticize and reject the gendered rules of conduct dictated by that system, they are going to be stuck trying to protect themselves by playing the game—no matter how subordinating—the best way they can. Indeed, the pressure to conform—and indeed, the threat of harm from not conforming—is so overwhelming that many women have yet to confront how their sexuality and freedom are forcefully constrained by the rules of the game. I believe that this is why many times women jurors are harder on rape victims than the men are. For some women, identifying too closely with a rape victim raises questions of their own vulnerability. Any way that that responsibility for what happened can be projected onto the rape victim is a way that they can protect themselves from the threat of sexual assault. You know this routine—if she hadn't been there, worn this or said that, the rape wouldn't have happened. Unless we can find ways of reaching out to women and showing them that it is the gender system that should be changed, not their behavior, then the only way in which women can imagine protecting themselves—both physically and emotionally—is to buy into the system, validating themselves as the good woman or the smart woman who is safe as opposed to the stupid woman or the sexually promiscuous woman who is raped.

As a last item, I think it's also important to recognize that when we try to reach across race and class issues to mobilize on questions of violence, it is important to recognize that gender bias is not the only violence that many women have to fear. There are any number of other kinds of violence that women have to deal with in their lives, and the singling out of gender as opposed to other sources of vulnerability strikes people who have to deal with other kinds of violence as once again the imposition of white middle-class concerns. We need a broader women's agenda, one that seeks to uncover the way violence shapes our lives across the board.

In conclusion, let me suggest a few approaches to develop boundary crossing strategies to address race. First, I think it's important to do more than to say all women experience violence. We have to be able to articulate the way different women experience violence in race and class terms. Second, I think it's important to propose and lobby for the equivalent of the Racial Justice Act. Some of you know that there was a proposal that was introduced in Congress to provide defendants who had been sentenced to death the ability to show that the penalty was distributed in a racially biased way. Where there were statistics to show that the penalty was distributed in a racially biased way, that sentence would be commuted to a life sentence. I think that if we are to politicize and to create a VAW Act, we should also try to find a way to make sure that the prosecutions will not be pursued in a racially biased way. Not only will it ensure that Black women and other women of color are equally protected, it will also make sure that white women who are not interracially raped will have the same access to resources as those rapes that fit the stereotype that the society seems to be most concerned about.

Thirdly, whenever a highly publicized interracial rape occurs, we should be sure to talk about the millions of interracial rapes that occur regularly. Moreover, we should show how women across the board are harmed by focusing on a particular kind of violent act rather than on all of the violent acts that occur on a day to day basis. Fourth, I think it's important to make sure that antiviolence resources are earmarked for communities of color, acknowledging that effective interventions will probably raise unique issues in different communities. And finally, we should remember that differences almost always matter, at some level, and consequently, we should always try to question and figure out how the differences are playing themselves out. I think that racial differences can strengthen a movement, but we have to be willing to accept and work with them. . . .

STUDY QUESTIONS

1. How does this country's racist history complicate discussions of today's sexual violence, according to Crenshaw?
2. What steps does Crenshaw suggest to take race into account and mobilize more effectively on questions of violence against women?

As technology and Internet usage increases, so does another means of victimization. "Cyber-stalking" is a term virtually unheard of in 1990, but today it is known as a means to terrorize and further violate. Cyber-stalking has earned the recognition of the Department of Justice and is the focus of several reports, both on its widespread use and methods to eliminate the abuse. Sexual predators who use the Internet to lure unsuspecting women and children into sexual situations are now being tracked and prosecuted by law enforcement.

All of this raises questions as to the continuing roles of sexuality between women and men, between what is consent and what is violation. Some believe more than simple legal reform is necessary to eliminate sexual coercion. Some still believe, as did Andrea Dworkin in a 1976 article, "The Rape Atrocity and the Boy Next Door," in *Our Blood: Prophecies and Discourses on Sexual Politics* (New York: Harper and Row, 1976, p. 22), that rape is a direct consequence of the polar definitions of men and women. She sees that men in our society are defined as aggressive, dominant, and powerful, while women are defined as passive, submissive, and powerless. Rape, then, is committed by exemplars of our social norms, not psychopaths or deviants. It occurs "when a man who is dominant by definition, takes a woman, who according to men and all organs of their culture was put on this earth for his use and gratification." *Id* at 45. It is the transformation of society and the change in the roles of women that has more to do with reform than the reform of the legal system itself.

The view presented by Dworkin raises other interesting questions, in particular, whether it is still relevant today. Does this theory mean that women "need protection" from men? Does this mean that women are not equal in their relations with men? These questions are worth considering as we continue to look at the interplay between the law and how it affects women.

III. PORNOGRAPHY

Historically, efforts to combat pornography have been associated with campaigns against prostitution and rape. As Judith Walkowitz has pointed out in her book, *Prostitution and Victorian Society, Women Class and the State* (Cambridge: Cambridge University Press, 1982), the late nineteenth-century feminist campaign against regulation of prostitution evolved into a broader social purity movement directed against prostitution, pornography, white slavery, and homosexuality. A key consequence of this movement in the United States was the Comstock Law enacted by Congress in 1873 (mentioned in Chapter 7). Like its twenty-two state counterparts, this law prohibited publication, possession, and dissemination of writings as well as drugs and articles associated with contraception and abortion.

In this century, the antipornography drive of the 1980s evolved from the antirape movement of the 1970s. Susan Brownmiller, for example, drew the connection this way in her book, *Against Our Will* (New York: Simon and Schuster, p. 394):

> The gut distaste that a majority of women feel when we look at pornography, a distaste that . . . comes, I think, from the gut knowledge that we and our bodies are being stripped, exposed and contorted for the purpose of ridicule to bolster that "masculine esteem" which gets its kick and sense of power from viewing females as anonymous, panting playthings, adult toys, dehumanized objects to be used, abused, broken and discarded.
>
> This, of course, is also the philosophy of rape. It is no accident (for, what else could be its purpose?) that females in the pornographic genre are depicted in two clearly delineated roles: as virgins who are caught and "banged" or as nymphomaniacs who are never sated. The most popular and prevalent pornographic fantasy combines the two: an innocent, untutored female is raped and "subjected to unnatural practices" that turn her into a raving, slobbering nymphomaniac, a dependent sexual slave who can never get enough of the big, male cock.

There can be no "equality" in porn, no female equivalent, no turning of the tables in the name of bawdy fun. Pornography, like rape, is a male invention, designed to dehumanize women, to reduce the female to an object of sexual access, not to free sensuality from moralistic or parental inhibition. The staple of porn will always be the naked female body, breasts and genitals exposed, because as man devised it, her naked body is the female's "shame," her private parts the private property of man, while his are the ancient, holy, universal, patriarchal instrument of his power, his rule by force over her.

Pornography is the undiluted essence of anti-female propaganda.

Copyright © 1975 by Susan Brownmiller. Reprinted by permission of SIMON & SCHUSTER, Inc.

There is, however, substantial controversy among today's feminists about the desirability of enacting antipornography legislation. Many, like Brownmiller, view such legislation as essential to combating sexual oppression. Others fear a repetition of repression associated with the social purity movements and subsequent censorship efforts. This section explores these twin concerns, first by reviewing traditional obscenity legislation and then by examining a new form of legislation that seeks to incorporate antipornography measures into existing civil rights laws.

The Traditional Approach

Sexual anatomy and sexual activities have long been the subjects of art. All major cultures have their collections of ancient erotic art and writings. Although this genre of expression has probably always had its opponents, organized resistance became apparent only around the time of the Reformation. Since that time, religious bodies have repeatedly objected to the explicit representation of sexual subjects on moral grounds. Central to their objections was the view that sexual activity and interests are permissible only in the context of procreation within marriage. Sexually explicit expression is thus objectionable for several reasons. It suggests that sexual activity is enjoyable and fulfilling in itself; it prompts impure thoughts, improper desires, and/or sinful motives in those who see it; at times, it represents activities that are intrinsically wrong because they occur outside the approved procreative context. These include masturbation, nonvaginal intercourse, and any sexual activity that occurs outside of marriage.

Censorship in the form of licensing was prevalent in England as early as the first half of the sixteenth century; however, pornographic publications were readily licensed while political works were more closely scrutinized. Obscenity legislation and prosecutions became more common in the second half of the nineteenth century with the advent of social purity movements in the United States and England. As we noted in Chapter 7, obscenity laws were used to prosecute birth control advocates for their speeches and publications prior to World War I.

In a series of decisions that came after World War I, the Supreme Court began to accord speech protection under the First Amendment. That protection does not extend to obscene speech, however. Thus, in considering speech that contains sexually explicit material, the Court has been forced to define obscenity. The Supreme Court has repeatedly struggled to articulate that definition. In its 1973 decision in *Miller v. California*, 413 U.S. 15, the Court set forth the definition that currently applies. The Court there held that a state may regulate a work of art that explicitly expresses sexual activity if: (1) the average person, applying contemporary community standards, would find that the work, taken as a whole, appeals to the prurient interest in sex; (2) the work depicts or describes, in a patently offensive way, sexual conduct specifically defined by the applicable state law; and (3) the work, taken as a whole, lacks serious literary, artistic, political, or scientific value. If any of these tests is not met, the material is protected by the First Amendment.

Although it had been argued that the "community standards" aspect of the *Miller* holding would increase the likelihood of conviction, surveys published during the late 1970s and early 1980s indicate that *Miller* did not lead to an increase in general prosecutions for obscenity.

In *Miller*, the Court held that unless the sexually expressive material can be shown to be obscene, it may not be regulated by the state. However, the Court permitted some departure from that principle in its 1976 decision in *Young v. American Mini Theatres*, 427 U.S. 50, which upheld several zoning ordinances that required the dispersal of "adult" movie theatres. Under the plurality opinion in *American Mini Theatres*, governments are permitted to restrict access to sexually explicit materials without reaching the question of whether the material is obscene. To reach this result, the Court endorsed the view that some types of expression are less deserving of First Amendment protection and may be regulated (although not completely suppressed) where they interfere with more important government interests, such as the improvement of the quality of life in an inner city. Where a certain type of expression is found to be of lesser importance, the burden of justification on the government is correspondingly lighter.

Several years after *American Mini Theatres*, the Court opened another avenue for government regulation of explicit sexual speech. In so doing, the Court focused on additional grounds for concern about such materials (i.e., the harm to children employed in the production of child pornography). A unanimous Court thus approved, in *New York v. Ferber*, 458. U.S. 747 (1982), an overt ban on one form of sexually explicit expression not because of its supposed corrupting influence on viewers but because of a legislative finding of tangible harm to the subject/model. Here, as in *American Mini Theatres*, the Court found it unnecessary to hold the materials obscene under *Miller* and again imposed only a minimal burden of justification on the government.

Two factors seem particularly important to the *Ferber* Court's decision to uphold a law imposing criminal sanctions on the production and distribution of nonobscene pornography: (1) the consensus on the dangers of child pornography manifested in the near universality of state efforts to outlaw it and (2) the strength of the social science data appearing to confirm the justices' intuitive sense that children who participate in the production of pornography suffer enduring psychological damage.

For many, the *Ferber* decision was evidence of an awakening on the part of the Supreme Court to the fact that the production of pornography often involves abuse and exploitation. Even though *Ferber* dealt only with child pornography, the decision encouraged some pornography opponents to believe that the Court might uphold state regulations directed at protecting women as a class from the psychological, emotional, and physical harm they saw caused by pornography. A new legal approach to the regulation of pornography was thus developed with the interests of women in mind.

The Civil Rights Approach

As we have seen, pornography foes have traditionally based their attacks on obscenity laws. Under current constitutional doctrine, the reach of these laws is limited by the *Miller* test. As opposition to pornography has hardened among a segment of the feminist community, some feminist strategists and legal theorists have devised a different approach. This approach seeks to restrict pornography because it subordinates women, thereby interfering with their civil rights. This civil rights approach has been the subject of considerable controversy.

The effort first surfaced in 1983, when proponents of the civil rights approach, law professor Catharine MacKinnon and author Andrea Dworkin, succeeded in convincing the Minneapolis City Council to consider their approach. Specifically, they persuaded the council to add pornography-based claims to the city's civil rights ordinance instead of enacting zoning legislation to curb the distribution of pornography in certain neighborhoods. More specifically, the proposed law allowed victims to file sex discrimination claims for damages on the ground that pornography promotes violence against women; keeps women subordinate; and inhibits access to equal employment, education, and other opportunities. The ordinance was approved by the council but immediately vetoed by the mayor, who believed it violated the First Amendment.

Next, in 1984, a revised version of that ordinance, introduced by a stop-ERA, anti-abortion, Eagle Forum city councilwoman, was enacted in Indianapolis. The revised law narrowed the definition to focus on violent pornography and created an exception for "soft-core" porn. Under the Indianapolis ordinance, pornography was defined as

> the graphic sexually explicit subordination of women, through pictures and/or words [and] one or more of the following:
>
> (i) women are presented dehumanized as sexual objects, things, or commodities; or
> (ii) women are presented as sexual objects who enjoy pain or humiliation; or
> (iii) women are presented as sexual objects who experience sexual pleasure in being raped; or
> (iv) women are presented as sexual objects tied up or cut up or mutilated or bruised or physically hurt; or
> (v) women are presented in postures or positions of sexual submission, servility, or display; or
> (vi) women's body parts—including but not limited to vaginas, breasts, or buttocks—are exhibited such that women are reduced to those parts; or
> (vii) women are presented as whores by nature; or
> (viii) women are presented being penetrated by objects or animals; or
> (ix) women are presented in scenarios of degradation, injury, torture, shown as filthy or inferior, bleeding, bruised, or hurt in a context that makes these conditions sexual.

Of the four causes of action in the ordinance, the most controversial was the trafficking clause, which covered the sale, distribution, or exhibition of pornography.

Although both experts and victims went on record in support of the approach, critics questioned the connection between pornography and harm. Members of the Feminist Anti-Censorship Taskforce, for example, pointed out that the ordinance did not mention nonviolent sexist images, such as those pervading advertisements. They also pointed out that the ordinance did nothing about violent images that were not sexist. Critics were particularly concerned that conservative judges would consider depictions of "loose women" or women who did not fit traditional role expectations to be pornographic.

Proponents of the ordinance, however, took the view that pornography is inevitably harmful to women; that it operates in a subliminal way; that it is extremely difficult, if not impossible, to correct with additional speech; and that pornography, together with the sexual violence that it engenders, keeps women from countering pornography with more speech. Thus, they argued that even pornography that does not fall within the definition of obscenity does not deserve constitutional protection and, in any event, the ordinance's restraints are justified by the compelling state interest in eliminating sex discrimination.

To date, few legislative bodies in this country have considered the civil rights approach to adult pornography, and only Indianapolis has enacted it into law. This is in part due to the strong disagreement within and without the feminist community regarding the benefits of the approach. As indicated, that disagreement turns in part on different evaluations of the available social science data on the consequences of exposure to adult pornography. Proponents of the civil rights approach claim experimental research demonstrates that pornography covered by the ordinance causes measurable harm to women. Their position gained some support from a 1986 report of the federal Attorney General's (Meese) Commission, which concluded that "available evidence strongly supports the hypothesis that substantial exposure to sexually violent materials . . . bears a crucial relationship to antisocial . . . and for some subgroups possibly unlawful acts of sexual violence." In her 1984 lecture, "Francis Biddle's Sister: Pornography, Civil Rights, and Speech" appearing in *Feminism Unmodified* (Cambridge: Harvard University Press, 1987, pp. 187–89), Catharine MacKinnon pointed to a number of studies showing a connection between pornography and violence. Some studies do show that under laboratory conditions, men exposed to expressly violent pornography are more willing to take aggressive action against women. Other studies show that exposure to certain pornography affects men's attitudes toward women, increasing their scores on such measures as hostility toward women, propensity to rape, condoning rape, and predicting that a person would rape or force sex on a woman if he knew that he would not get caught. MacKinnon also cited studies showing that long-term exposure to all pornography covered by the ordinance—whether or not it is expressly violent—makes men perceive a rape victim as more worthless and leaves them less able to see she was harmed. These studies, taken together with testimony by individual women, establish a causal connection between pornography and sexual aggression and sexual subordination in the view of those advocating the civil rights approach.

Opponents of antipornography legislation questioned the conclusions drawn from such studies on a number of grounds. As Barry Lynn, then an American Civil Liberties Union lawyer, pointed out in his article, " 'Civil Rights' Ordinances and the Attorney General's Commission: New Developments in Pornography Regulations," 21 *Harvard Civil Rights—Civil Liberties Law Review* 27 (1986), much of the research involved small numbers of college students exposed to violent pornography in a highly artificial laboratory setting without taking account of differences in past development and experience. Such studies, he argued, are of little value in predicting, real-world behavior based on repeated exposure to all types of pornography. Lynn and others questioned the relevance of rape-attitude studies for failing to distinguish between pornographic and nonpornographic stimuli and for failing to establish an adequate link between attitude and behavior. More generally, they questioned the claim made by ordinance proponents that pornography is central to the subordinate place of women in our society. How, they asked, can the effects of pornography be separated from the negative opinions about women and the subordination and dominance by violence that are promoted throughout the media?

The Indianapolis ordinance was challenged in federal court immediately after its enactment. Ordinance opponents pressed two traditional claims. First, they argued that the ordinance violated free speech guarantees inasmuch as its restraints were not limited to obscene materials and the city had demonstrated no compelling state interest to justify them. Second, they argued that the ordinance was unduly vague in its definition of pornography. Ruling in their favor on both grounds, the district court enjoined the ordinance.

On appeal, feminists who opposed the ordinance on less traditional grounds also made their views known. They did not dispute that pornography is extremely offensive; rather, they argued that the ordinance would be used to suppress sexually explicit material that responds to women's erotic tastes and needs and affirms their sexuality. They also saw the ordinance as constituting the type of protective legislation that reinforces sex-based stereotypes without effectively improving women's circumstances. The appellate court agreed with the district court that the ordinance was unconstitutional, but for other reasons.

AMERICAN BOOKSELLERS ASSOCIATION, INC. V. HUDNUT

United States Court of Appeals, Seventh Circuit, 1985.
771 F.2d 323, *aff'd,* 475 U.S. 1001 (1986).

EASTERBROOK, Circuit Judge. Indianapolis enacted an ordinance defining "pornography" as a practice that discriminates against women. "Pornography" is to be redressed through the administrative and judicial methods used for other discrimination. The City's definition of "pornography" is considerably different from "obscenity," which the Supreme Court has held is not protected by the First Amendment.

To be "obscene" under *Miller v. California,* "a publication must, taken as a whole, appeal to the prurient interest, must contain patently offensive depictions or descriptions of specified sexual conduct, and on the whole have no serious literary, artistic, political, or scientific value." Offensiveness must be assessed under the standards of the community. Both offensiveness and an appeal to something other than "normal, healthy sexual desires" are essential elements of "obscenity." . . .

The Indianapolis ordinance does not refer to the prurient interest, to offensiveness, or to the standards of the community. It demands attention to particular depictions, not to the work judged as a whole. It is irrelevant under the ordinance whether the work has literary, artistic, political, or scientific value. . . .

Civil rights groups and feminists have entered this case as amici on both sides. Those supporting the ordinance say that it will play an important role in reducing the tendency of men to view women as sexual objects, a tendency that leads to both unacceptable attitudes and discrimination in the workplace and violence away from it. Those opposing the ordinance point out that much radical feminist literature is explicit and depicts women in ways forbidden by the ordinance and that the ordinance would reopen old battles. It is unclear how Indianapolis would treat works from James Joyce's *Ulysses* to Homer's *Iliad;* both depict women as submissive objects for conquest and domination.

We do not try to balance the argument for and against an ordinance such as this. The ordinance discriminates on the ground of the content of the speech. Speech treating women in the approved way—in sexual encounters "premised on equality"—is lawful no matter how sexually explicit. Speech treating women in the disapproved way—as submissive in matters sexual or as enjoying humiliation—is unlawful no matter how significant the literary, artistic, or political qualities of the work taken as a whole. The state may not ordain preferred viewpoints in this way. The Constitution forbids the state to declare one perspective right and silence opponents. . . .

. . . Under the First Amendment the government must leave to the people the evaluation of ideas. Bald or subtle, an idea is as powerful as the audience allows it to be. A belief may be pernicious—the beliefs of Nazis led to the death of millions, those of the Klan to the repression of millions. A pernicious belief may prevail. Totalitarian governments today rule much of the planet, practicing suppression of billions and spreading dogma that may enslave others. One of the things that separates our society from theirs is our absolute right to propagate opinions that the government finds wrong or even hateful. . . .

Indianapolis justifies the ordinance on the ground that pornography affects thoughts. Men who see women depicted as subordinate are more likely to treat them so. Pornography is an aspect of dominance. It does not persuade people so much as change them. It works by socializing, by establishing the expected and the permissible. In this view pornography is not an idea; pornography is the injury.

There is much to this perspective. Beliefs are also facts. People often act in accordance with the images and patterns they find around them. People raised in a religion tend to accept the tenets of that religion, often without independent examination. People taught from birth that black people are fit only for slavery rarely rebelled against that creed; beliefs coupled with the self-interest of the masters established a social structure that inflicted great harm while enduring for centuries. Words and images act at the level of the subconscious before they persuade at the level of the conscious. Even the truth has little chance unless a statement fits within the framework of beliefs that may never have been subjected to rational study.

Therefore we accept the premises of this legislation. Depictions of subordination tend to perpetuate subordination. The subordinate status of women in turn leads to affront and lower pay at work, insult and injury at home, battery and rape on the streets. . . .

Yet this simply demonstrates the power of pornography as speech. . . .

Racial bigotry, anti-semitism, violence on television, reporters' biases—these and many more influence the culture and shape our socialization. None is directly answerable by more speech, unless that speech too finds its place in the popular culture. Yet all is protected as speech, however insidious. Any other answer leaves the government in control of all of the institutions of culture, the great censor and director of which thoughts are good for us. . . .

Much of Indianapolis's argument rests on the belief that when speech is "unanswerable," and the metaphor that there is a "marketplace of ideas," does not apply, the First Amendment does not apply either. . . .

The Supreme Court has rejected the position that speech must be "effectively answerable" to be protected by the Constitution. . . .

We come, finally, to the argument that pornography is "low value" speech, that it is enough like obscenity that Indianapolis may prohibit it. . . . True, pornography and obscenity have sex in common. But Indianapolis left out of its definition any reference to literary, artistic, political, or scientific value. The ordinance applies to graphic sexually explicit subordination in works great and small. . . .

. . . Free speech has been on balance an ally of those seeking change. Governments that want stasis start by restricting speech. Culture is a powerful force of continuity; Indianapolis paints pornography as part of the culture of power. Change in any complex system ultimately depends on the ability of outsiders to challenge accepted views and the reigning institutions. Without a strong guarantee of freedom of speech, there is no effective right to challenge what is. . . .

Affirmed.

STUDY QUESTIONS

1. Some pornography opponents distinguish pornography from other types of speech by pointing to its direct impact on women. As the court put it, "In this view, pornography is not an idea; pornography is the injury." To what extent did the court accept this view? Did it offer any remedy for the harm that pornography inflicts? Do you see any? Can you remedy the harm the same way you would remedy a vicious lie told about someone you care about?

2. The court made clear that the First Amendment protects hate messages of the Klan and the Nazi Party and concluded that pornography should be treated no differently. Do you think violent pornography is equivalent to such hate messages? If so, is there any reason to treat it differently?

3. Does the court accurately depict the views of feminists who support the ordinance? Of feminists who oppose it? Do you agree with the result? The reasoning? Why? Why not?

Following the court of appeals decision in *American Booksellers Association v. Hudnut,* the Supreme Court affirmed the decision without a hearing. However, this summary action is unlikely to resolve the controversy within the feminist community regarding the desirability of legal restrictions on pornography.

Despite their defeat in the *American Booksellers* case, antipornography forces continued their efforts, ultimately achieving success in Canada. There, the top court upheld a ban on the possession and sale of obscene material even though it acknowledged that the law violated the country's free speech guarantees. Thus, in *R. v. Butler and McCord,* 134 N.R. 81 (1992), the Canadian Supreme Court unanimously found the threat to equality resulting from the dissemination of obscene materials exploiting women and children sufficient to justify their criminalization.

Efforts of antipornography forces in this country have focused once again on legislation, pressing on the federal level for passage of the Pornography Victims Compensation Act. That law would punish distributors of pornography for the sexual assaults of others if the sexual assaults were "caused" by pornography distributed by the defendant. On the state level, they have pressed for legislation much like the Indianapolis ordinance at issue in the *American Booksellers* case.

Feminist controversy continues over these matters. The next selection highlights some of these concerns.

SIX QUESTIONS ABOUT PORNOGRAPHY
Women Against Pornography. New York, 1993.

Pornography has existed in other times and other cultures, but never has it been so readily available and so pernicious in content and effect. We are feminists who have fought for equal rights, civil liberties and social change.

The time has come for us to face the challenge of pornography and fight for its abolition.

Here are our replies to some common questions about pornography.

We ask you to think about them.

Isn't pornography a safety value? Doesn't it provide a harmless outlet for those men who might otherwise commit crimes of violence?

On the contrary, pornography contributes to the climate of violence around us. There is no evidence to support the claim that pornography reduces male violence and aggressive sexual behavior. We believe that there is a strong connection between the spread of pornography and the increase in rape, battering of women, and molesting of children. Violence on television and violence in society have been shown to imitate each other. Why should violence disguised as sexuality be an exception?

If you don't like pornography, who's forcing you to look at it?

We would like to look away, but we can't avoid seeing it. Images of brutality confront us everywhere, even in our own communities. Pictures of women in humiliating poses assault us from newsstands, billboards, movie marquees, record album covers, and even in the window displays of fashionable department stores.

Don't some women enjoy pornography?

Some women say so, but for centuries women have struggled to conform to male definitions of their sexuality. But those definitions change. Today pornography is said to be chic. The current dictate is "Enjoy pornography; it's good for both of us. If you don't, you're a prude." Name-calling is a powerful weapon. Pornography is protected in part by women's reluctance to speak out against it for fear of ridicule and rejection by men.

Okay, pornography is offensive, but don't we have to protect freedom of expression?

We affirm the First Amendment principle of free speech—however, we also believe that pornography constitutes a threat to our physical safety and emotional well-being. One concern must be balanced against another. Even the First Amendment "absolutists" among us agree that we must create a moral climate in which women's bodies cannot be exploited for profit. Others in our association, who also uphold the principle of free speech and the right of political dissent, maintain that the First Amendment was never intended to protect pornographic images: the rape, humiliation, torture and murder of women for erotic entertainment.

Where do you draw the line and who draws it?

We would draw the line wherever violence or hostility toward women is equated with sexual pleasure. We would draw the line wherever children are sexually exploited. We do not oppose sex education, erotic literature or erotic art. But the essence of pornography is the defamation of womanhood. That is why women must draw the line.

Isn't pornography really a trivial issue?

No, not when our most intimate relationships are affected by the way pornography teaches women and men to view themselves and each other. Not when pornography is a multi-million-dollar industry linked to organized crime, illicit drugs and prostitution. Nothing that has so powerful an impact on the mental and physical well-being of all of us can be dismissed as trivial.

STUDY QUESTIONS

1. Why does the Women Against Pornography believe it is important to work on its issue? Do you agree?
2. Doesn't censoring pornography violate the letter and the spirit of the First Amendment?
3. What other means do you see to combat pornography? What do you see as their strengths and weaknesses?

Some of the questions raised in the preceding article have arisen in the context of the debate about pornography and whether all feminists have the same view. These tensions flow from the different views that sexuality plays in today's society, how these roles relate to women, and how women are treated by society. To the extent there is a conflict amongst different feminist groups, the conflict may be more in the manner in which different groups approach these issues. The final chapter of this book will explore some emerging feminist issues and, in part, will look at this conflict in approach between the feminists of the 1960s and those of the twenty-first century, known as the Third Wave feminists.

ON-LINE RESOURCES

National Criminal Justice Reference Service
www.ncjrs.org/
Contains research and studies on many aspects of criminal justice issues such as victim services and immigration issues.

VAWnet Sexual Violence
www.vawnet.org/SexualViolence/
VAWnet is an electronic clearinghouse for information and materials on domestic violence, sexual assault, and related issues.

Violence Against Women Document Library, Sexual Assault
www.vaw.umn.edu/library/sexassault/
This site provides law, criminal justice, advocacy, and social service professionals with up-to-date information on interventions to stop violence against women.

CHAPTER 9

FEMINISM IN THE TWENTY-FIRST CENTURY

AS WE LOOK BACK through the preceding chapters we can see changes in the rights of women and a movement toward equality. In this century, women have the ability to measure where they are and set goals about where they want to be. Women may also have more power than they have ever had. Women have crashed through the glass ceiling in many areas and are beginning to crack it in others. Women are elected to hold office and are a recognized voting block that candidates need to contend with. Many of the issues that women struggled with in the 1960s and 1970s are no longer issues for the feminist movement of today.

Yet for all the strides that the women's movement has made, there is still much to do. While many of the early issues have been resolved, others remain. And as we will see in this chapter there are some issues such as the intersection between race and gender that feminists are reexamining. As we saw in Chapter 7, reproductive freedom has been in danger of erosion and although the 2009 elections of President Barak Obama and a fully democratic Congress bring hope to many pro-choice advocates, the U.S. Supreme Court continues to speak with a conservative voice and the debate for reproductive freedom continues. Throughout the prior administration, President George W. Bush often spoke of the sanctity of marriage, defined as marriage between a man and a woman and, during his administration, worked to try to pass a constitutional amendment banning same-sex marriage.

In the "have-it-all" world in which we live, we find that women sometimes have it all and *do it all*. Women are caretakers of their children and their parents. Women work at high-power jobs but earn less than their male counterparts. Women pay more for everyday expenses like haircuts and drycleaners. Sexual discrimination still exists; it simply has a different face than it did in the 1960s or the 1860s.

Issues of gender inequity not only persist in the United States but also remain prevalent in many parts of the world. Women are poorer than men—both in the United States and abroad. Stoning of women as punishment for sexual activity, trafficking of women and girls for sexual slavery, and genital mutilation are real issues that have been more in the forefront of the media and women's agendas. These international women's issues form part of the feminist movement and human rights movement in this country. The United States has attempted to address some issues, such as sex trafficking and genital mutilation, which have followed immigrant cultures into this country.

As we consider these remaining issues that are at the forefront of most agendas, we also need to consider where the feminist movement is today and where it is going. As the "second wave" feminists of the 1960s and 1970s begin to "age out," it is the younger generation of feminists who must pick up the mantle and continue to fight the "good fight." The feminist movement cannot escape the natural evolution that comes from the change in generations.

This final chapter will examine some remaining issues that affect women today, along with emerging international women's issues and the generational issues affecting the feminist movement.

I. WOMEN AND POVERTY

The *feminization of poverty* is a termed coined in 1976 by Diana Pearce, former director of the Women and Poverty Project of Wider Opportunities for Women. According to Pearce's observations, two-thirds of the poor in the United States were women over the age of 16 and women's economic status had declined from 1950 to the mid-1970s. The number of female heads of household was increasing, and divorce was contributing to poverty among women. She argued: "for many the price of that independence has been their pauperization and dependence on welfare."

The number of women in poverty has continued to steadily increase since the early 1990s. According to the latest Census Bureau Population Survey (2007 data) there are 37 million people living in poverty in the United States; over half are them are women. Poverty rates continue to be higher for women that men. In 2007, 13.8 percent of women were poor compared to 11.1 percent of men. And elderly women are more likely to be poor than men.

Women who do work earn less than their male counterparts. As you saw in Chapter 4, women continue to earn a disproportionately reduced income compared to men. The 2007 Census report indicates that women earn .78 cents for every dollar earned by a man in a similar employment. This actually is an increase from previous years, but it is still not equal. In 2007, the median income for women who worked full time was $33,370 compared to their male counterparts whose median income was $49,839. The majority of households that receive public benefits including food stamps or public assistance are female households. In addition to earning lower wages than men, women, for the most part, are still the primary caretakers of children and home. Feminist scholars and economists refer to the dual responsibility as wage earners and primary caretakers as "a woman's double burden."

Single women with children are the most vulnerable to economic constraints. In addition to facing the same obstacles as other women, they lack the second income necessary in these economic times. Women with children are sometimes forced to take part-time jobs with little or no benefits that rarely pay a living wage. Higher wage, full-time jobs can make demands on a single mother's time that she cannot meet. Moreover, finding safe and affordable child care is a persistent and widespread problem.

The feminization of poverty is based on the inequities women face in the workforce and on the domestic front. Many scholars believe that divorce reform was more harmful to women than beneficial and has resulted in women trading economic stability for custody, inadequate child support, and alimony awards that generally further impoverished women and children. In addition to economic conditions that result from family law issues, there are many who maintain that the Welfare Reform Act of 1996 resulted in further impoverishment of women and children.

Although a higher divorce rate has contributed to a significantly higher proportion of households headed by single women who are raising children on their own, divorce is not the sole explanation for the problem of women and poverty. This next selection explores the root causes of feminized poverty from a broader perspective and also looks at possible solutions.

THE FEMINIZATION OF POVERTY
YWCA 2007
By: Megan Thibos, Danielle Levine Loucks, Ph.D, Marcus Martin Ph.D

THE EMERGENCE OF A FEMINIZED POVERTY

Since the emergence of the term "feminization of poverty," scholars have noted that women are an enduring and consistently larger proportion of the poverty population than men. However, in her seminal essay introducing the concept, Diane Pearce pronounced that the feminization of poverty represented a fundamental paradox. Although the 1960s and 1970s were characterized by the women's liberation movement, fostering remarkable achievements in gender equality, affirmative action, and increased participation in the paid labor force, this era also represented a time during which poverty was identified as "a female problem." Despite all of the potential for the improvement of women's economic stability, women nonetheless accounted for a strikingly larger proportion of the poverty population....The advent and acceptability of divorce, and an increase in lifespan among women further promoted a gendered poverty, while social programs and income transfers intended to lift individuals out of poverty were less effective in achieving this goal for women than for men.

At present, research continues to confirm the presence of a gendered component to poverty, one that has become more evident and even more pronounced with the increase in female-headed households, and perhaps even more marked among the young and elderly female population. Not only are female heads of household more likely to be poor, but their poverty is more likely to be long term.... For women of color, especially Hispanic and African American women, the picture is bleaker still—so much so that Palmer introduced the concept of the "racial feminization of poverty" to describe their unique plight. Likewise, for immigrant women, who may be undocumented and unable to work legally in jobs that offer benefits, the barriers to financial stability are perhaps even more pronounced. Faced with economic hardship, language barriers, a lack of viable employment opportunities, and in some cases an uncertain legal status, the likelihood that women will be able to achieve a livable wage is minuscule. If we are to address these issues, the question we are inevitably left with is: What accounts for the enduring character of the feminization of poverty?

DEMOGRAPHIC SHIFTS & THE NATURE OF FAMILY

The majority of studies of the impoverishment of women point to two primary mechanisms that propel women into poverty at higher rates: demographic shifts and the economy. Since the "discovery" of the feminization of poverty, the character of social life has changed dramatically, as has the structure and nature of the family. A number of these demographic shifts have inevitably contributed to rising inequality for women and their children. The proportion of children born to unwed mothers has increased considerably since the 1950s.

Reprinted by permission of The Williams Institute Joint Policy Forum on the Feminization of Poverty.

Childbearing outside of marriage, coupled with a higher divorce rate, translate into a significantly higher proportion of households headed by single women who are raising children on their own. At the same time, the average life expectancy for both males and females has increased, yet women are consistently outliving their male counterparts. With a longer lifespan, women will require substantially more income to ensure their subsistence in their later years. Taken together, these changes in the constitution of family and general demographics have left women and mothers at a considerable disadvantage in terms of the financial resources available to care for themselves and their families.

Single parenthood appears to be the arena where the gendering of poverty is most apparent. However, it is not simply the lack of a dual income that contributes to the poverty of single mothers. If this were the case, we would expect to see equalization in poverty rates between single-father and single-mother households. And yet, the poverty rate among single-male heads of household was approximately 17.6%, while the rate for single-female heads of household was 36.9% in 2005. Clearly, the increase in the divorce rate has differentially impacted women, who disproportionately assume the role of primary caregiver when divorce occurs.

THE ECONOMY

Changing patterns of family structure are not the only mechanisms that contribute to the feminization of poverty. Most prominently, gender segregation in the labor market and other characteristics of the economy produce a set of circumstances that can also account for the observed concentration of poverty among women. Although Pearce and her contemporaries were writing at a time when labor market participation by women had just recently burgeoned, much of the same occupational sex segregation remains visible in current labor market dynamics. [(footnote omited)] Two perspectives dominate the literature on the economic forces that drive the feminization

of poverty: economic restructuring and the gender perspective.

The *economic restructuring* argument posits that shifts in the nation's economy essentially created a concentration of poverty and a lasting inequality in labor market participation and income for families, especially those headed by women....The second explanation, aptly named the *gender perspective*, is a body of research that also considers the unique employment experiences and characteristics of the labor market that impact women directly. [(footnote omitted)] For example, single heads of household face rising costs of childcare, in light of their dual role as primary wage earner and primary caregiver. Likewise, when entering the labor force, women find themselves facing discrimination in regard to issues of equity and sex segregation.

IMPLICATIONS OF THE FEMINIZATION OF POVERTY FOR PUBLIC POLICY

Implementing effective public policies at the national, state, and local levels will depend in part on what policymakers believe are the reasons for the feminization of poverty. As outlined earlier, there are generally two schools of thought:

■ The feminization of poverty exists because of significant changes in the family structure such that households headed by females are not only a larger proportion of households but also are disproportionately impacted by factors contributing to poverty compared with other types of households.

■ Structural changes in the economy have caused the displacement of many women into occupational sectors that are gender-specific, low-wage, and low-benefit employment opportunities—such as pink-collar jobs. Moreover, the shift into a knowledge-based economy has meant that those females with the least educational attainment and the least work skills will be least likely to experience work opportunities that can effectively and permanently move them and their families out of poverty.

Some research suggests that changes of family structure alone cannot account for the disproportionate number of female-headed households in poverty and that economic shifts at the national, state, and local levels significantly influence the trajectory of many of these women and their families. As a result, it is critical that the right public policies be in place that can assist female-headed households in moving out of a cycle of poverty and underemployment and into a life of self-sufficiency and empowerment. Our focus is on three broad public policy areas that can have a positive impact on moving female-headed households out of poverty and into the self-sufficiency that was the goal of the Welfare Reform Act of 1996 and other such measures. In addition, it is our belief that programmatic efforts, when aligned with the right public policies, can have a synergistic effect in reducing the feminization of poverty. A discussion on programmatic efforts will conclude this section.

EXPANDING EDUCATIONAL OPPORTUNITIES

Few people can argue against the increased benefits for additional years of schooling on income and wellbeing. The lifetime earning differences between a college graduate and a high school dropout is estimated to be more than $1.2 million. Although historically the earnings of males and females with equivalent educational attainment have not been the same, increased educational attainment nevertheless shrinks the wage gap and improves socioeconomic prospects for women. One study found that among impoverished women who were able to obtain a college degree, only 3% did not move out of the poverty threshold.

Public policy that promotes increased educational attainment among women in general, and particularly women who are heads of household, is crucial. Educational reforms at the high school level that strive to make students more college-ready can increase the likelihood that women go on to college before becoming mothers, while comprehensive educational assistance at the community college and university level for female heads of household looking to return to school can also be of benefit. In today's economy, all but the lowest-skill and lowest-paid jobs require some degree of technical training of the sort available at community colleges and vocational schools. While a university degree offers the greatest protection against poverty, an associate's degree in an applied field may offer the most accessible and viable way out of poverty for women already in the workforce and/or who have children. Efforts to reduce the feminization of poverty must also focus on the preventative benefits of greater educational support.

LIVABLE WAGES

Structural changes in the labor market have profoundly impacted the work opportunities and earnings potential for many women across the country. While women who have had the opportunity to obtain advanced levels of education have made significant gains with respect to occupational mobility and earnings potential, many women across the country who have not been able to further their education have found themselves unemployed, underemployed, and/or segregated into pink-collar occupations. As discussed earlier, pink-collar occupations frequently do not pay an adequate living wage. Some scholars also refer to the phenomenon as sub-employment. Not only have we shifted to a knowledge-based economy where low-skilled and unskilled workers are largely confined to low-wage service sector jobs, but additionally, income and wages have not kept pace with the cost of living. The result of this difficult work environment is that many women, particularly those with children, are finding it difficult to make ends meet and may experience long-term poverty. Perhaps the most important implication of the feminization of poverty is its impact on the children of women in poverty…. The solution to this situation must be comprehensive and intensive and include an effort to provide these women with gainful employment opportunities at a decent wage—one that can allow a single mother to support a family, pay for daycare, and afford decent housing.

Expanding governmental programs such as insurance assistance, housing assistance, and tax credits for women and their children are an important first step in addressing the feminization of poverty, but innovative public policies that provide women a chance to increase their skills conducive to employment in a knowledge-based economy is just as critical.

EQUITABLE WAGES & OCCUPATIONAL SEGREGATION

In 1970 an estimated 30 million women were in the labor force. This number increased to roughly 42 million in 1980 and roughly 53 million in 1990. Currently, an estimated 65 million are in the labor force—more than doubling the number of women in the labor force since the 1970s. Since 1959, the wage differential between men and women has improved from 60 cents on the dollar, but persists at 77 cents on the dollar in 2005, despite increased labor force participation, work experience, and educational attainment of women.

President Kennedy signed the Equal Pay Act in 1963. The Equal Pay Act made it illegal for a company to pay women at a lower rate than men employed in similar positions. At the time the act was signed, the ratio of average women's pay to men's pay was roughly 58%. Although the wage gap between men and women is a complex issue that scholars have examined for decades, work experience alone cannot entirely explain the wage gap. Hence, discrimination, occupational segregation, and other factors may contribute to continuing pay differentials between women and men.

As mentioned earlier, many occupations in this country have become gender specific, especially among low-skilled occupations. While blue-collar occupations, which are typically filled by men—such as construction and manufacturing—are declining in availability and desirability,

they still offer far better pay, benefits, and job security than pink-collar occupations, primarily filled by women. Pink-collar jobs are rarely unionized, typically pay an hourly rate, and usually offer no health insurance or other benefits. Moreover, the women working in pink-collar occupations often have very little chance of upward mobility. Public policy needs to address the issue of equitable wages and occupational segregation. Working women who not only contribute to the economy as members of the labor force but also bear the responsibility for the wellbeing and safety of their children deserve wages that will keep their families out of poverty. Equality in the workplace, equity in wages, and the end of barriers to entry into certain occupational sectors can be attained with the right public policy and the right national will. Not addressing these core issues driving the feminization of poverty could create a nation at risk. Women in America working full time deserve equitable access to the American Dream for themselves and their children.

Finally, a sufficient public policy response must also address the issue of part-time workers in America—most of whom are women. Taken together, occupational segregation and the prevalence of permanent part-time status can devalue women's role in the workplace, eroding the gains made by women over the past century.

CONCLUSION

Recently, politicians and academics have resurrected the idea of the "other America" or "two Americas" to describe the stark differences between the poor and the middle and upper classes. Harrington initially identified this "other America" in the early 1960s, and undoubtedly others noted its presence prior to this; yet despite social policy and public awareness, enduring inequality in our nation persists. However, the gendered character of poverty, or its feminization, is not confined to the United States or even to advanced industrial societies. Rather, it represents a global phenomenon. Around the world, with the exception of only a few nations, women experience the burden of poverty disproportionately. Although we have made strides in identifying and naming the problem, understanding the complex social and economic causes of the pauperization of women and the ways in which public policy can address the fundamental basis for such inequality proves much more challenging.

The implications of a feminized poverty go beyond the economic status of women. High rates of poverty among women also imply high rates of poverty among children, which threaten child wellbeing. Although many of the lifetime consequences of growing up and living in poverty are incalculable, research suggests that poverty is linked to poor nutrition, negative health outcomes, impaired cognitive development among children, lower levels of educational attainment, a shortened lifespan, and high levels of psychosocial stress. There is also strong evidence that suggests that children who grow up in poverty are more likely to be poor themselves as adults. The existence of an intergenerational component to the transmission of poverty suggests that

temporary income transfers and short-lived assistance programs alone will not solve the problem. Stories of female poverty survivors point to overwhelming failure—not of the individual spirit, but of social programs, welfare reform, and laws to protect women and their children. As Pearce noted nearly 30 years ago, "the poverty of men and the poverty of women are different problems, requiring different solutions." Until sustainable programs addressing the multi faceted causes and consequences of the feminization of poverty are developed, countless women and their children will continue to reside in the other America.

STUDY QUESTIONS

1. Describe the "feminization of poverty" what that phrase means. Do you believe this is a still valid issue today?
2. What are the causes of the feminized poverty?
3. What can be done to avert continued poverty of women? What public policy issues are implicated?

The issue of women and poverty is by no means an issue exclusive to the United States. The problem of poverty and its disparate affect on women is an issue of global proportions. Two-thirds of the world's poor are women, some earning less than a dollar per day. Many poor women face seemingly insurmountable challenges compared to men. They have less access to education, land, money and other resources. The United Nations has begun to take an active role in talking this issue with the creation of Women Watch dedicated to proving information and resources on gender equality and empowerment of women. (http://www.un.org/womenwatch/directory/gender_mainstreaming_10314.htm) and UNIFEM the United Nations Development fund dedicated to the same principle. http://www.unifem.org/ The United Nations interfaces with other agencies and groups to raise issues for awareness and mobilization. One such agency is the International Labor Organization (ILO).

The ILO issued a report in response to the 2009 economic crisis raising a concern that the "face of poverty" has gotten much younger. The report says the most recent global estimate indicated that more than 100 million girls are involved in child labor, and many are exposed to some of its worst forms. Girls face a number of particular problems that justify special attention, including:

■ Much work undertaken by girls is hidden from public view, which creates particular dangers. Girls make up the overwhelming number of children in domestic work in third-party households, and there are regular reports of the abuse of child domestic workers;

■ In their own homes, girls take on household chores to a much greater extent than boys. Combined with economic activity outside the household, this imposes a "double burden" that increases the risk of girls dropping out of school; and

■ In many societies, girls are in an inferior and vulnerable position and are more likely to lack basic education. This condition seriously restricts their future opportunities.

The report highlights the importance of investing in the education of girls as an effective way of tackling poverty. Educated girls are more likely to earn more as adults, marry later in life, have fewer and healthier children, and have decision-making power within the household. Educated mothers are also more likely to ensure that their own children are educated, thereby helping to avoid future child labor (http://www.ilo.org/global/lang--en/index.htm).

The global feminization of poverty is just one issue facing women outside the United States. The following section will look at other serious issues affecting international women.

II. INTERNATIONAL WOMEN'S ISSUES

One of the most serious international issues affecting women today is the trafficking of women and girls for the purpose of forced labor and sexual slavery. In 2000, Congress passed into law the Trafficking of Victims Protection Act of 2000. The Act contains outreach, educational, and punitive components. It provides for sanctions to governments that do not comply with minimum standards to prevent sexual trafficking and severe criminal penalties in the United States for those who violate the law. It also provides for continued reports to Congress on the status of trafficking of persons. Here is the June 2003 Report to Congress by the Department of State.

TRAFFICKING IN PERSONS REPORT
Released by the Office to Monitor and Combat Trafficking in Persons.
June 11, 2003.

The Secretary of State submits the annual "Victims of Trafficking and Violence Protection Act of 2000: Trafficking in Persons Report" to Congress. This report covers "severe forms of trafficking in persons" defined as:

> (a) sex trafficking in which a commercial sex act is induced by force, fraud, or coercion, or in which the person induced to perform such act has not attained 18 years of age; or (b) the recruitment, harboring, transportation, provision, or obtaining of a person for labor or services, through the use of force, fraud or coercion for the purpose of subjection to involuntary servitude, peonage, debt bondage, or slavery.

INTRODUCTION

As unimaginable as it seems, slavery and bondage still persist in the early twenty-first century. Millions of people around the world still suffer in silence in slave-like situations of forced labor and commercial sexual exploitation from which they cannot free themselves. Trafficking in persons is one of the greatest human rights challenges of our time. It is, as the International Labour Organization (ILO) points out, the "underside of globalization."

Human trafficking not only continues but appears to be on the rise worldwide.

Many nations are touched by it in some way, serving as source, transit, and destination countries where human beings are procured, transported, and enslaved through forced labor or forced sexual exploitation. Traffickers exploit the aspirations of those living in poverty and those seeking better lives. They use dramatic improvements in transportation and communications to sell men, women, and children into situations of forced labor and sexual slavery with virtually no risk of prosecution. The traffickers also exploit lack of political will by governments to tackle trafficking and its root causes. Corruption, weak inter-agency coordination, and low funding levels for ministries tasked with prosecuting traffickers, preventing trafficking, and protecting victims also enable traffickers to continue their operations. The transnational criminal nature of trafficking also overwhelms many countries' law enforcement agencies, which are not equipped to fight organized criminal networks that operate across national boundaries with impunity.

Who Is Being Trafficked?

Women, children and men are trafficked into the international sex trade and into forced labor situations throughout the world. Women are lured by promises of employment as shopkeepers, maids, seamstresses, nannies, or waitresses but then find themselves forced into prostitution upon arrival to their destination. Many victims are unaware that their travel documents will be seized, they will have to repay an enormous debt, or that they will be subject to brutal beatings if their earnings are unsatisfactory. These victims do not know how to escape the violence or where to go for help. The victims generally avoid authorities out of fear of being jailed or deported, especially if they have fraudulent documents. Traffickers often move victims from their home communities to other areas—within their country or to foreign countries—where the victim is often isolated, unable to speak the language and unfamiliar with the culture. Most importantly, the victims lose their support network of family and friends, thus making them more vulnerable to the traffickers' demands and threats.

Who Are the Traffickers and How Do They Recruit Individuals?

Traffickers use threats, intimidation and violence to force victims to engage in sex acts or to labor under conditions comparable to slavery for the traffickers' financial gain. Traffickers may be freelancers or members of organized criminal networks. They may recruit and find potential victims through advertisements in local newspapers offering good jobs at high pay in exciting cities or use fraudulent travel, modeling and matchmaking agencies to lure unsuspecting young men and women into trafficking schemes. A trafficker may be a family friend or someone well-known within the community who is able to convince the families that their children will be safer and better taken care of in a new place. Traffickers often mislead parents into believing that their children will be taught a useful skill or trade—but the children end up enslaved in small shops, on farms, or in domestic servitude. Traffickers also promise parents that they will marry their daughters—but the girls are forced into prostitution. Traffickers also kidnap and abduct victims.

What Is the Scope and Magnitude of the Problem?

No country is immune from trafficking. A recent U.S. Government estimate indicates that approximately 800,000–900,000 people annually are trafficked across international borders worldwide and between 18,000 and 20,000 of those victims are trafficked into the United States. This estimate includes men, women, and children trafficked into forced labor and sexual exploitation as defined in the Trafficking Victims Protection Act of 2000. This estimate does not include internal trafficking. The new figures were generated from a database that examined reports of specific trafficking incidents, counts of repatriated victims, estimates for victims worldwide, and victim demographics derived from analysis of information from press, governments, non-governmental and international organizations, and academic reports from 2000 to the present.

Why is Trafficking Flourishing?

Poverty and Desire for a Better Life

Traffickers exploit impoverished and vulnerable individuals seeking a better life. In countries with chronic unemployment, widespread poverty or a lack of economic opportunities, traffickers use promises of higher wages and good working conditions in foreign countries to lure individuals into their schemes. Many times the individuals have jobs or advanced degrees but believe the traffickers' promises because they want better lives.

Ignorance of Trafficking's Consequences

Most families and victims are unaware of the dangers of trafficking because of the "success stories," displays of wealth, or remittances back to villages from relatives working abroad or in urban areas that provide powerful incentives for others to migrate for work. The negative consequences of trafficking and horror stories do not often enough trickle back to rural areas or at-risk populations. Trafficking victims are often ashamed or afraid to return home if they have not made good money, have not fulfilled the terms of the working arrangements imposed by traffickers, have contracted a sexually transmitted disease or have lost social status.

Disruption of Societal Values

Greed and the widespread subjugation of women in much of the world facilitate trafficking. Poor countries have been flooded with images of wealth and prosperity beamed in through television or radio and lavish displays of wealth send powerful messages to impoverished citizens about the benefits of material acquisition. More often than not, an "ends justifies the means" rationale has taken root within communities to legitimize the source of the wealth, regardless of how acquired. The low status of women and girls in some societies contributes to the growing trafficking industry since female lives are not as highly valued as those of men and boys. Often, ethnic minorities or lower class groups are more vulnerable to trafficking. In some societies, the practice of entrusting poor children to more affluent relatives may lead to abusive and exploitative situations.

Political and Economic Instability

Areas of conflict and post-conflict as well as transitioning states are easy targets for those interested in plundering a country's resources, including exploitation of its people. Sudden political change, economic collapse, civil unrest, internal armed conflict, and natural disasters greatly increase the likelihood that a country will become a source of trafficking victims as displaced populations are highly vulnerable to exploitation, abuse, and trafficking. In these environments, the victims may be one of the few resources of marketable wealth. Hundreds of thousands of men, women, and children have been exploited in armed conflict zones, where government militaries and rebel commanders profit from the services of child soldiers, porters, and sex slaves, and in post-conflict and transitioning states where organized criminal groups often fill power vacuums created by war, political change, and economic upheaval.

Demand for Cheap Labor

Changes in formal and informal economies have increased the global demand for cheap and malleable labor in many areas of the world. In many countries, development patterns and imbalances between labor supply and the availability of legal work have created the demand for highly mobile workers to fulfill low-skill and service sector jobs. Lack of employment and educational opportunities in villages or poor urban areas create a ready pool of vulnerable workers.

High Profits

Modern-day slavery also thrives because of its profitability. United Nations estimates indicate that trafficking in persons generates 7 to 10 billion dollars annually for traffickers.

Human cargo can often be moved across borders and past immigration officials easier than narcotics or weapons caches, which are often seized when found. Trafficking victims, even if caught, can be re-trafficked. Traffickers can make additional money off victims by re-selling them to another employer after their often-inflated debt is paid. Traffickers may earn a few hundred to thousands of dollars for a trafficked child laborer and brothel owners may make a few thousand to tens of thousands of dollars for each woman forced into prostitution.

Low Risk

Traffickers often go unpunished for their crimes where there is little rule of law, lack of enforcement of existing anti-trafficking laws, and corruption of law enforcement institutions. Cases regularly fall apart due to a lack of protection for witnesses, family involvement in sending a son or daughter away, or fear of deportation. Victims of trafficking are afraid of retaliation from the traffickers, recrimination within their families and villages, and in cases of trafficking for sexual exploitation, the stigma of prostitution. Governments and rebels are rarely held responsible for the forcible recruitment of combatants and sex slavery involving countries formerly in conflict.

THE TOLL OF TRAFFICKING

Populations vulnerable to trafficking are growing with potentially disastrous effects on the entire world community. The number of orphans in many developing countries is rising dramatically, thanks to civil conflicts and HIV/AIDS. The rapid rise of child-headed households is creating fertile ground for traffickers.

Trafficking Is a Human Rights Violation and a Crime

Traffickers violate the universal rights of all persons to life, liberty, and freedom from slavery in all its forms. Trafficking undermines the basic need of a child to grow up in a protective environment and the human right of children to be free from sexual abuse and exploitation. Hundreds of men, women, and children die in transit or upon arrival at their destination. Thousands of victims are killed for refusing to submit to forced labor or sexual slavery, or for trying to escape. Others die from contracting diseases or suffering abuse during their enslavement.

Trafficking Increases Social Breakdown and Promotes Crime

The loss of family support networks makes the trafficking victim more vulnerable to the traffickers' demands and threats and contributes to the breakdown of societies. For families and communities, trafficking weakens parental authority, undermines extended family relationships, and eliminates the family's nurture and moral development of children. Trafficking interrupts the passage of knowledge and cultural values from parent to child and from generation to generation, weakening a core pillar of society. Victims who do return to their communities may be more likely to become involved in criminal activity.

Trafficking Deprives Countries of Human Capital

Trafficking has a negative impact on the labor market in countries, according to the ILO, contributing to an irretrievable loss of human resources for developing countries. Long-term effects of trafficking include depressed wages for all workers, a lower number of individuals left to care for an increasing number of elderly persons, social imbalances in the proportion of males to females, and an undereducated generation. Forcing children to work at an early age and subjecting them to 10 to 18 hours of work per day denies them access to the education necessary to break the cycle of poverty and illiteracy that makes conditions ripe for trafficking. At-risk individuals cannot acquire the skills necessary to compete in their country's labor market, leaving national labor forces ill-equipped to compete in the global economy, where success is based on skilled workers.

Trafficking Undermines Public Health

Trafficking brutalizes men, women, and children, exposing them to rape, torture, and to HIV/AIDS and other sexually transmitted and infectious diseases, violence, dangerous working conditions, poor nutrition, and drug and alcohol addiction. Increasing numbers of adults and children trafficked into prostitution as well as street children are contracting HIV/AIDS. Trafficked children are less likely to participate in immunization programs, defeating government efforts to eradicate early childhood diseases. Severe psychological trauma from separation, coercion, sexual abuse, and depression often leads to a life of crime, drug and alcohol addiction, and sexual violence.

Trafficking Subverts Government Authority

Many governments do not exercise control over the entire national territory. Trafficking operations thwart government attempts to exert that authority while undermining public safety, particularly the security of vulnerable populations. Some governments are unable to protect women and children, who have been kidnapped from their homes, schools, or refugee camps. Moreover, the bribes traffickers pay challenge a government's ability to combat corruption among law enforcement, immigration, and judicial officials.

Trafficking Funds Illicit Activities and Can Feed Organized Crime Activities

The profits from human trafficking may strengthen criminal groups by funding other illicit activities while weakening government attempts to establish rule of law. Organized criminal groups, gangs, document forgers, brothel owners, and corrupt police or immigration officials funnel trafficking profits into both legitimate and criminal activities. Human traffickers are often highly successful because of links with other transnational criminal groups, such as arms dealers, drug traffickers, and car theft rings, which provide them with safe and tested routes, access to cash, forged documents, and officials to bribe.

STUDY QUESTIONS

1. What is the magnitude of the problem?
2. What methods are used to force women and girls into the sex trade or forced labor?
3. What are some of the reasons that traffickers are so successful and what harm does this cause?
4. What is the U.S. government's interest in this issue?

Traffickers get their victims in a variety of ways: some are abducted, some are lured by offers of legitimate work that never materialize, and others are sold into slavery by impoverished families. Traffickers keep their victims close with threats of death to them or their families, physical force, and drugs.

The 2000 Act requires the Department of State to categorize countries by Tiers 1–3 based on their compliance with the minimum standards required by the Act.

MINIMUM STANDARDS

The "minimum standards for the elimination of trafficking" are summarized as follows. Governments should:

1. Prohibit trafficking and punish acts of trafficking.
2. Prescribe punishment commensurate with that for grave crimes, such as forcible sexual assault, for the knowing commission of trafficking in some of its most reprehensible forms (trafficking for sexual purposes, involving rape or kidnapping, or that causes a death).

3. Prescribe punishment that is sufficiently stringent to deter and that adequately reflects the offense's heinous nature for the knowing commission of any act of trafficking.

4. Make serious and sustained efforts to eliminate trafficking.

Countries that do not fully comply with the minimum standards and are not making significant efforts to do so are considered Tier 3 countries. Tier 3 countries could be subject to certain sanctions, notably withholding of nonhumanitarian, non-trade-related assistance. Countries that receive no such assistance would be subject to withholding of funding for participation in educational and cultural exchange programs. Consistent with the Act, such governments also would face U.S. opposition to assistance (except for humanitarian, trade-related, and certain development-related assistance) from international financial institutions, specifically the International Monetary Fund (IMF) and multilateral development banks such as the World Bank.

Another area of serious international concern is that of genital mutilation. This is a practice used in some thirty countries of Africa and the Middle East on young girls between the age of 4 and 12. It involves cutting off a young girl's clitoris and major and minor labia, sewing the area closed (sometimes with thorns), leaving only a small opening for urination and menstruation. This procedure is often carried out by force, using crude homemade instruments, without anesthetic or sterilization. The risk of physical and mental health complications are enormous, including excessive bleeding, HIV/AIDS from shared surgical equipment, infection, childbirth obstruction, damage to other organs, bladder damage, depression, shock, and hindered development. Young girls in the United States from immigrant groups that practice genital mutilation are in as much danger of this barbaric practice as young girls in one of the many countries abroad that continue the practice. To address this serious issue, the U.S. Congress passed the Immigrant Responsibility Act of 1996.

The next article examines female genital mutilation, why it is practiced, and concerns with the effectiveness of the 1996 legislation to control this practice.

FEMALE GENITAL MUTILATION
What Does the New Federal Law Really Mean?
Khadijah F. Sharif

INTRODUCTION

Wake up, girl, whispers Granny, as she shakes my shoulder gently. Jolted out of my dream, I dress myself quickly in a lappa skirt and blouse, then Granny and I join three other Fula girls and their relatives. We leave Freetown, Sierra Leone, by minibus and drive to a remote place in the bush. As the morning mist rises, I see a gathering of women and six or seven other girls. I am 10 years old, and though I do not yet know it, the events of this day will forever alter my life.

Bare-breasted dancers shuffling bell-laden feet and shaking maracas sing Temme, Susu and Mandingo songs. They dance around a blazing fire where several kettles boil water for the cooking of pepper soup, corn and rice. Abruptly the singing and dancing stop, and I stand with the other girls in a circle. The women make a ring around us, and the eldest woman enters our circle. "You are about to join Society," she says gravely, "and you must never reveal the ritual that is about to take place. Do you promise to keep these events secret forever?" Solemnly we nod our heads.

Next we are led to a round thatched hut, where we are blindfolded. I feel the women grab me, gag me and lay me down upon a matta. Be brave, they tell me. Crying is a disgrace. Suddenly I feel an excruciating pain. My clitoris is sliced off! I try to pull away, but the women hold me. I scream, but no sound comes [out]. Before my silent scream ends, a sharp blade has removed my labia majora and minora. As the women close my wounds with thorns and try to stanch the bleeding with scalding water, I faint from the pain.

*This is the story of Mariama L. Barrie, one of almost one hundred million victims of female genital mutilation in Africa alone. It illustrates the pain and horror inflicted on young girls and women in the name of cultural rights, religion and tradition. In recent years, the practice of female genital mutilation has received widespread attention throughout the world due to the increasingly high number of incidents involving the practice. The Centers for Disease Control and Prevention recently estimated that more than 150,000 women and girls of African origin and ancestry residing in the United States may be at risk of or have undergone female genital mutilation. The practice first gained United States media attention when Fauziya Kasinga won asylum to avoid persecution in her native land. Her case and significant anecdotal evidence of female genital mutilation led Congress to incorporate provisions prohibiting genital mutilation in the Illegal Immigration Reform and Immigrant Responsibility Act of 1996.

This Comment considers the growing number of immigrants who bring the traditional practice of female genital mutilation to the United States and examines the difficulty in protecting victims from the practice of female genital mutilation in insular communities. Part I outlines the three types of female genital mutilation, the cultural and religious reasons for the ritual, and

the existence of the practice in the United States. Part II examines the provisions of the Immigrant Responsibility Act of 1996. Part III recognizes that the passage of the Immigrant Responsibility Act of 1996 is timely, but argues that its implementation remains uncertain because victims and perpetrators are insulated within their communities. This Comment concludes that the legislation must provide specific provisions and funding to enable states and localities to (1) devote significant amounts of attention to educating communities about the dangers and horrors of the practice, (2) develop culturally sensitive outreach activities for victims of the ritual, and (3) involve governmental agencies and community-based organizations in the fight to abolish female genital mutilation.

I. FEMALE GENITAL MUTILATION: THE PRACTICE HERE AND ABROAD

A. The Female Genital Mutilation Procedure

Although the practice of female genital mutilation is performed on girls ranging from newborn babies to adolescents, the procedure is performed typically on girls at age seven. Women in more than forty countries have practiced female genital mutilation for over 2,500 years. In addition, estimates reveal that 100 million females of all ages in Africa alone have undergone some type of genital mutilation, and worldwide the practice affects well over 100 million women.

There are three types of female genital mutilation: the pharaonic type, the intermediate type and the sunna type. Pharaonic circumcision or infibulation is the oldest, the most prevalent, and the most brutal type of genital mutilation. It accounts for over eighty percent of the cases in the Sudan, one of the countries where female genital mutilation is prevalent. . . . There are two methods of infibulation: the classical

*This article was originally published as "Female Genital Mutilation: What Does the New Federal Law Really Mean?" 24 *Fordham Urban Law Journal* 409 (1997) and is reprinted with permission.

and the modernized. The former consists of removal of the clitoris, the labia minora, and the labia majora, with the two sides of the wound being brought together by different methods. In Eastern Sudan, adhesive substances such as sugar, egg, and cigarette papers are placed on the wound, left for three to fifteen days; and removed leaving a small opening. In Central and Northern Sudan, thorns wrapped in palm reed are used. In Western Sudan, adhesive substances, thorns, and strings are sometimes used. The girl's legs are bound together at the ankle, above the knees, and around the thighs for approximately fifteen to forty days to limit movement and to facilitate proper healing. To ensure tightness of the hole, a thorn is inserted into the vagina so that when the tissue heals, only this opening remains . . . .Excision, the intermediate type of female genital mutilation, consists of the removal of the clitoris, where the surface of the labia minora is roughened to allow stitching . . . .The sunna type is the mildest and least performed type of female genital mutilation. This procedure consists of removing only the tip of the prepuce of the clitoris. In some geographical areas, women apply a heated piece of stone or pearl to the prepuce of the clitoris to burn it away. In the other communities, only the tip or half of the clitoris is removed, the labia minora are intact, and there is no stitching.

B. Cultural and/or Religious Reasons for the Practice

In cultures that practice female genital mutilation, the ritual confers upon women full social acceptability, integration into the community, and serves as a rite of passage to womanhood. For many women in these cultures, the practice enables them to identify with their heritage and to enjoy recognition as full members of their ethnic group, enjoying social benefits and privileges.

Female genital mutilation is practiced predominantly in African and Middle Eastern countries among Muslim and non-Muslim tribal communities, among the Muslim populations in Malaysia and Indonesia, and within immigrant communities in the United States. Today, these communities continue to perform female genital mutilation because of the deep cultural and religious roots of the ritual in African society. Many practitioners believe that it is an Islamic custom encouraged by Prophet Muhammad but there is no textual authority for such belief. Others argue that because neither the Holy Qur'an nor the Islamic law mention the practice, female genital mutilation has no religious or legal authority under Islam. Non-practicing Muslims acknowledge that the procedure is primarily performed among Muslims, but, argue that the practice of female genital mutilation predates Islam. The idea that female genital mutilation is not a religious practice is supported by references to Islamic history. In addition, there is no evidence in Muslim history that the Prophet's wives were genitally mutilated.

Some scholars suggest that economics underlie the persistence of female genital mutilation. In many African and Middle Eastern countries, women are married off to eligible, wealthy males and, in exchange, their fathers receive substantial bride prices. The bride price depends on whether the woman is highly valued and found to be chaste. The bride must display her virginity as evidence of her virtue following the wedding. The anxieties surrounding this occasion and its general importance are highly intensified. The groom's family may examine the bride to ascertain her virginity, and only after they are satisfied that it is intact will the marriage be consummated.

Some commentators attribute the perpetuation of the practice to the notion of the sexual domination of women by men. Female genital mutilation inhibits the sexual desires of women, preserves virginity until marriage, and prevents women's outward enjoyment and sexual response. It hinders women from expressing sexual pleasure, protecting them from socially unacceptable behavior reserved only for men. Others believe that female genital mutilation developed as a means by which husbands could own and control women, rendering them silent, powerless and submissive.

C. Female Genital Mutilation in the United States

Immigrants from countries practicing female genital mutilation often retain their cultural traditions and religious beliefs. Based on the Census Bureau's findings that large numbers of immigrants from African countries reside in metropolitan areas, i.e., New York City, Newark, New Jersey, Washington, D.C., and Los Angeles, California, it is likely that many have undergone or are at risk of undergoing female genital mutilation. In addition, anecdotal stories of the ritual have been reported in these areas. Although governmental agencies continue to compile statistics on the number of women and girls at risk of genital mutilation, many immigrants fear disclosure because the subject of female genital mutilation is taboo. Female genital mutilation has received increased media exposure in the United States and internationally. The practice is decried by women's rights activists worldwide, and debated in the pages of widely accepted international human rights documents.

II. THE ILLEGAL IMMIGRATION REFORM AND IMMIGRANT RESPONSIBILITY ACT OF 1996

In September 1996, Congress passed the Immigrant Responsibility Act, sponsored by Representative Schroeder and Senator Reid, outlawing the rite of female genital mutilation in the United States. The passage of the federal law followed the enactment of various state laws against the practice. The Immigrant Responsibility Act identifies several goals including requiring doctors to report incidences of genital mutilation, prohibiting the performance of the ritual by unlicensed medical practitioners, guaranteeing persons who have undergone the ritual freedom from discrimination by medical practitioners, recommending the development of educational curricula for medical school students, and calling for the structure and implementation of outreach activities

that allow persons performing the ritual and persons trying to prevent the ritual to work collaboratively to stop the practice. The federal law also defines female genital mutilation as a criminal act. It provides that anyone who knowingly circumcises, excises, or infibulates the whole or any part of the labia majora, labia minora, or clitoris of another person who is under the age of 18 shall be fined or imprisoned for not more than 5 years or both. The bill also provides that no weight shall be given to the defense that the procedure was required as a matter of custom or ritual. The bill further provides that whoever denies medical care or services or otherwise discriminates against any person who has undergone female genital circumcision, excision, or infibulation or because that person has requested that female circumcision, excision, or infibulation be performed on any person, shall be fined or imprisoned not more than one year or both. The bill exempts the performance of medical procedures from prosecution. It provides that surgical operations are not violations of the bill where the procedure is necessary to an individual's health and if performed by a licensed medical practitioner in the place of its performance. The bill also allows the practitioners to perform genital surgery on a woman in labor or who has just given birth, for medical purposes connected with that labor or birth. The medical practitioner, midwife or person in training must be licensed to practice the procedure in the place where it is performed. Congress intended that the bill eradicate the practice of female genital mutilation in people's houses without the proper equipment and supervision. The bill allows students in the medical field to gain experience in treating these patients with unique medical circumstances.

In addition to providing penalties for violating the law, the bill contains an educational component. The Secretary of Health and Human Services must compile data on the number of women living in the United States who have been subjected to female genital mutilation (whether in the United States or in their countries of origin), including a specification of the number of girls under the age of 18 who have been subjected to such mutilation. The Secretary must also identify communities in the United States that practice female genital mutilation, and design and implement outreach activities to educate individuals about the physical and psychological health effects of the practice. The bill provides that the Secretary's outreach activities include collaboration with representatives of ethnic groups practicing female genital mutilation and with representatives of organizations with expertise in preventing the practice. Finally, the Secretary must develop recommendations for the education of medical and osteopathic medical school students regarding female genital mutilation and its medical complications. The bill does not mention how the law will be funded, monitored, or enforced.

III. PROBLEMS OF IMPLEMENTATION

The Immigrant Responsibility Act is a good first step towards eliminating the ritual. The law properly requires the compilation of the number of women and girls who have been affected by and are at risk of the practice here in the United States and the development of educational components to inform immigrant communities about the dangers of the practice. In addition, the law envisions persons performing the ritual and persons trying to stop the practice to work collaboratively to abolish female genital mutilation.

Although the law is important and timely, it is merely a skeleton of the law necessary to practically limit the occurrence of female genital mutilation in the United States. Although the bill identifies a myriad of goals, it has some significant flaws. The bill (a) lacks specificity in terms of how Health and Human Services will implement, administer and monitor the law, and does not mention how the bill will be funded, (b) is not culturally aware with regard to how Health and Human Services will infiltrate insular immigrant communities to obtain the information about the practice within those communities, and (c) places an unfair burden on medical personnel to report incidences of the ritual, disregarding the longstanding physician-patient confidentiality privilege. The lack of specificity in these areas leaves Health and Human Services with unbridled discretion to define the law's parameters and fails to provide detailed guidelines for the law's implementation.

STUDY QUESTIONS

1. What are female genital mutilations performed?
2. Do you believe that the 1996 Immigrant Responsibility Act adequately addresses this issue?
3. What more do you think should be done to address the issue?
4. Should this practice be protected under the U.S. Constitution? Explain.

As set out in the foregoing article, the effect of female genital mutilation is both physical and emotional. The procedure also results in continued effect on women throughout their lives. At marriage, the area must be torn, stretched, or cut open by the bridegroom, and then prevented from healing shut. This agonizingly painful procedure may take weeks or even months to complete. Giving birth becomes extremely dangerous for both the woman and her child, as the procedure prevents dilation beyond four of the ten centimeters required to pass the fetal head. The 1996 Act makes it a federal crime to perform genital mutilation on anyone under the age of 18 (i.e., under the age of consent). It is completely illegal in New York State, North Dakota, and Minnesota, and is banned in several countries including Canada, France, Sweden, and the United Kingdom.

The preceding are only two examples of violence against women abroad and their connection to the United States. There are other examples of violence against women in other countries. Most notably are acts of violence in Nigeria and the Sudan.

SLAVERY, VIOLENCE AGAINST WOMEN CONTINUE WORLDWIDE
Jessica Hanson and Anna Stanley

Despite extraordinary progress, women all over the world are still abused, enslaved, and violated on a daily basis. The new millennium does not greet all women with the freedom and hope they deserve as human beings.

Although poor and violent conditions for women span the entire globe, two countries have caught the attention of the international community.

YOUNG WOMEN FLOGGED IN NIGERIA

In Nigeria recently, two women were flogged for alleged fornication. The first caning transpired in late January, when 17-year-old Bariya Ibrahim Magazu was lashed 100 strokes after it was discovered that she had conceived a child out of wedlock. The girl, who gave birth and was breast-feeding at the time of her caning, had no representation at the trial where she said she was impregnated by one of three middle-aged men with whom her father pressured her to have intercourse.

Originally sentenced to 180 lashes, the 80 strokes imposed for "making unsubstantiated allegations" against the men (who denied having sex with her) were dropped. The punishment was reduced and postponed due to mounting international pressure, including from human rights groups in Nigeria and a rebuke from the Canadian High Commission in Nigeria. Lawyers on Magazu's behalf applied to the Sharia Court on Jan. 9 for a leave to appeal and a stay of execution. The punishment was reportedly suspended for 12 months, but despite this, Magazu was whipped 100 times on the morning of Jan.19.

The second young Nigerian woman is awaiting public flogging in November after being found guilty by a Sharia Court of engaging in pre-marital sex. Eighteen-year-old Attine Tanko was found guilty on Nov. 15 after the discovery that she was pregnant while unmarried. Tanko's 23-year-old boyfriend, who was also flogged 100 times and is currently sentenced to jail time, is the father. She has yet to give birth and is living with her family in wait. The court will allow the young woman to wean the baby for up to two years after she delivers, but she will receive the punishment of 100 lashes after that time.

WOMEN FORCED INTO SLAVERY NIGHTMARE IN SUDAN

Across the African continent in Sudan, abuses against women occur on a regular basis. Arab militias, under the command of the president of Sudan and armed by the government, raid Dinka villages and attack the local people. Old men and women are killed, and children and young women are taken for booty. The soldiers of this militia, known as Popular Defense Forces, systematically gang rape the enslaved African women and girls during and after these raids. Soldiers further torture the women with beatings, denial of food, and prolonged exposure to sun with their hands and feet tied together. Women slaves who are chosen as concubines by Arabs in northern Sudan are also genitally mutilated, a practice not normally followed by the people of this area.

STUDY QUESTIONS

1. Do you think that feminists in the United States have a role to play in the eradication of the mistreatment of women abroad?

2. Is the treatment of women abroad a feminist issue or best left to human rights organizations?

A case that made international headlines was that of Amina Lawal Kurami, who in March of 2002 was sentenced to death by stoning for bearing a child out of wedlock in Nigeria. The man she identified as the child's father denied the accusation and was acquitted for lack of evidence. In August of 2002, her appeal was denied. The judge said her sentence of death by stoning was to be carried out as soon as she weaned her daughter from breast-feeding.

In September of 2003, in what is considered a "victory for women's rights," the Nigerian Court of Appeals dismissed the case against Amina Lawal. Lawal's sentence of "death by stoning" was overturned. Of particular note was the unequal treatment she received compared to the man with whom she had sexual relations. Amina was sentenced to be stoned to death, while the man she was with was cleared when he brought three witnesses to testify on his behalf.

Violence against women, poverty and lack of adequate health care remains a global issue. According to Amnesty International, violence against women and girls represents a global health, economic development, and human rights problem. At least one out of every three women worldwide are beaten, coerced into sex, or otherwise abused in her lifetime, with rates reaching 70 percent in some countries.

The International Violence Against Women Act (I-VAWA) is an unprecedented effort by the United States to address violence against women globally. It directs the U.S. government to create a comprehensive, five-year strategy to reduce violence in ten to twenty diverse countries identified as having severe levels of violence against women.

The I-VAWA also makes the crisis of violence against women a top diplomatic priority. It creates an Office of Global Women's Initiatives in the State Department to coordinate all efforts, including aid, to combat violence. It also creates the Office of Global Women's Development at the Agency for International Development to integrate violence prevention into current foreign assistance activities.

More specifically, the I-VAWA would do the following:

- Increase Legal and Judicial Protection to Address Violence Against Women and Girls.
- Increase Health Sector Capacity to Address Violence Against Women and Girls.
- Change Social Norms to End Violence Against Women and Girls.
- Increase Women's Economic Opportunity and Education.
- Address Violence Against Women and Girls in Overseas Natural Disaster and Conflict-Related Humanitarian Situations.
- Increase U.S. Training of Overseas Foreign Security Forces on Violence Against Women and Girls.

(see Amnesty International Web site, http://www.amnestyusa.org/violence-against-women/page.do?id=1011012).

The U.S. House of Representatives recently voted to make the Office for Global Women's Issues permanent. It is still pending in the Senate.

III. Feminist Perspectives of the Twenty-First Century

Though women are closer to achieving equality in many areas, discrimination still exists which is often more hidden and subtle. An example can be seen in a 2002 survey conducted by the New York State Bar Association's Committee on Women in the Law. The survey examined the status of women in the law and the incidents of gender equity. Though women now comprise over 50 percent of law school admissions, many women attorneys still experience inequity based on their gender. Though blatant discrimination is much less prevalent, the survey found that more than 50 percent of the women attorneys and 25 percent of the men attorneys experienced or observed some form of gender discrimination against women either by spoken word or demeaning treatment. In a few cases surveyed, the discriminatory harassment included unwanted touching. The survey further found that in private law offices, even when age and length of service were factored in, only 41 percent of women attorneys earned over $100,000 compared to 71 percent of men attorneys. Most women perceived that they had to work harder and do a better job than men in order to get ahead. Though they advanced in firms, women were less likely to be part of the committees that made decisions regarding compensation and management.

By far, the number one issue affecting women attorneys was child care. Of the random sample, over 60 percent were women under 40, most with children under 6. Although parental leave was available to both men and women surveyed, it was disproportionately women attorneys who took parental leave. Having children greatly affected the women attorneys' ability to interact and advance in their work setting; having children did not impact a man's ability to do the same. New York State is not alone in these findings, as surveys conducted in other states and by the American Bar Association yielded similar results. Clearly, though women have advanced in the workplace, much if not most of the family responsibility falls on women, regardless of impact on their career.

Though this study looked at women attorneys in New York State, the surveyors compared its findings to studies in Kansas, North Carolina, Minnesota, and the American Bar Association. The results were similar in all of the studies. In 2003, a study conducted by the National Organization for Women, in the words of NOW President Kim Gandy, found "the ole boys club . . . alive and well in academia."

The following is an excerpt of that study.

A National Analysis of Diversity in Science and Engineering Faculties at Research Universities
Executive Summary

The first national and most comprehensive analysis to date of tenured and tenure track faculty in the "top 50" departments of science and engineering disciplines shows that females and minorities are significantly underrepresented.

- There are few tenured and tenure-track women faculty in these departments in research universities, even though a growing number of women are completing their PhDs. Qualified women are not going to science and engineering departments. In some engineering disciplines, there is a better match between the representation of females in PhD attainment versus the faculty, but these disciplines are the ones with very low percentages of females in PhD attainment.
- Underrepresented minority (URM) women faculty are almost nonexistent in science and engineering departments at research universities. In the "top 50" computer science departments, there are no Black, Hispanic, or Native American tenured or tenure track women faculty.
- The percentage of women in BS attainment in science and engineering continues to increase, but they are likely to find themselves without the female faculty needed for optimal role models.
- There are few female full professors in science and engineering; the percentage of women among full professors ranges from 3% to 15%. In all but one discipline surveyed, the highest percentage of female faculty is at the level of assistant professor.
- In most science disciplines studied, the percentage of women among recent PhD recipients is much higher than their percentage among assistant professors, the typical rank of recently hired faculty. Even in disciplines where women outnumber men earning PhDs, the percentage of assistant professors who are White male is greater than females. For example, in the biological sciences, 44.7% of the PhDs between 1993 and 2002 were women; while in 2002, they accounted for only 30.2% of the assistant professors.

In some disciplines, it is likely that a woman can get a bachelor of science without being taught by a female professor in that discipline; it is also possible for a woman to get a PhD in science or engineering without having access to a woman faculty member in her field.

The data demonstrate that while the representation of females in science and engineering PhD attainment has significantly increased in recent years, the corresponding faculties are still overwhelmingly dominated by White men.

There is a drastically disproportionate number of male professors as role models for male students. For example, in 2000, 48.2% of the students graduating with a BS in math were women, but in 2002, only 8.3% of the faculty was female.

A cycle is perpetuated. Women are less likely to enter and remain in science and engineering when they lack mentors and role models. In most science disciplines, the percentage of women among faculty recently hired is not comparable to that of recent women PhDs. This results in fewer female faculty to act as role models for female undergraduates and graduate students. Female students observe this in the course of sampling the environment. When female professors are not hired, treated fairly, and retained, female students perceive that they will be treated similarly. This dissuades them from persisting in that discipline.

This is not to say that only women can mentor women and girls. In the absence of female professors, male professors have been mentoring female students for decades. Because of the dearth of female professors and the impact this has on female student perceptions, the male faculty should (1) actively encourage female students to enter science and engineering and offer to become their mentors and (2) [e]nsure that the environment for the few female professors currently in science and engineering is one which female students will perceive as appealing. In the end, the presence, treatment, and fate of female professors will be most relevant to the lives, family responsibilities, and careers of typical female students and the choices and obstacles they will face.

Study Questions

1. How would you compare the study regarding women attorneys in New York to the study regarding women professors? Were the findings similar?

2. Do you think women professionals have gone as far as they can go?
3. What do you believe needs to change in order for women to achieve full equality—do you believe that is possible?

The studies discussed earlier are examples of the challenges still facing women of today. Consensus of what the key issues are and how to approach the challenges forms the backdrop for what can be viewed as a generational gap in feminism: the conflict between so-called second wave and third wave feminists. Though it is unlikely that second wave feminists would have agreed with the approach of the early suffragettes, there was no overlap between their era and the era of the feminists of the 1960s. That is not true today. Feminists of the 1960s and 1970s are still alive and well and their approach has clashed head-on with the feminism of the "generation Xers."

Many women of the 1960s and 1970s who consider themselves feminists lament that feminism is dead, that there are no feminists in the younger generations. Many women of the younger generation prickle at the notion that they are *not* feminists. They feel somewhat alienated from the feminists of the second wave and believe that the issues they face are different. Many believe that the approach of the second wave is outdated.

The following articles examine the views, issues, and approaches supported by third wave feminists. One such third wave feminist is Rebecca Walker, co-founder of the Third WAVE Direct Action Corporation, a national multicultural organization dedicated to facilitating and initiating young women's activism and empowerment. She has articulated much of what young feminists believe and how they compare themselves to second wave feminism.

She says:

> First of all, the whole idea of waves is erroneous in that there have been a million waves in women's activism, of course. But people seem to think about the first wave as being the suffragist movement, the second wave as being the activists of the late '60s or early '70s who did a lot of work around reproductive freedom and around separating sex from gender, helping us understand ways in which gender was totally constructed.
>
>   . . .we felt like a lot of the young women we talked to were alienated from the whole concept of feminism and were then stepping away from taking an active role in fighting for or even discussing issues of concern like sexual harassment or equal pay or discrimination in hiring. What we wanted to do was say this is a way for us to articulate a feminism that was not tied to any [of] perceptions of the second wave, which may have been alienating.

What's come out of that is a feminism that is decidedly not about taking on the big label of feminism, but is about taking a more active role in the fronts of many different issues, including not only women's issues, but issues of racial discrimination, sexual orientation, and gender. So the third wave is something that is multi-issue, multicultural, multisexual orientation, which means we can do projects ranging from voter registration to literacy to online activism to organizing gay pride marches (*Riding the Third Wave*, 1996, Amy Kay Nelson).

> . . .feminism of today's generation of young women need not be a mirror image of the feminism of our mothers.
>   To say this is not to criticize or disrespect Second Wavers, but simply to affirm and celebrate a new generation of feminist activism. She recognizes that, "the ever-shifting but ever-present ideals of feminism can't help but leave young women and men struggling with the reality of who we are. Constantly measuring up to some cohesive fully down-for-the-cause identity

without contradictions and messiness and lusts for power and luxury items is not a fun or easy task." As a result, today's young feminists are caught between the reality of our own generation and the pressure to be "good feminists" in paying homage to the legacies of our mothers' generation. (*Breathing Room, The Changing Face of Feminism,* Bronwen Blass, 2000)

The next article compares the issues of the second and third wave feminists.

DIFFERENT GENERATIONS, DIFFERENT ISSUES
Alana Wingfoot

One of the problems with communicating across any generation gap is that the two generations have different issues to deal with. What works for the older generation may not even apply to the younger; what is unthinkable to the older generation may be a necessity for the younger.

This applies, of course, to second- and third-wave feminism. Some second-wavers shake their heads over us and decry us for not being serious, for not being "real feminists"— more specifically, for not focusing on the same issues they focused on. Of COURSE we don't focus on the same issues—if you are a second-waver, how much time did you spend on getting the vote for women? (Not just for black women; for women in general?) Did you use the exact same methods that the first wave used? No, you didn't. And we face different issues and use different tools than you did, and the fourth wave will face yet another bundle of issues needing its own ways to handle them, and so forth.

Some of the differences between us:

SECOND WAVE	THIRD WAVE
Getting paid work, even if you're married or a mother	Getting *better* paid work, so we can support ourselves and our families.
Securing the right to an abortion.	Maintaining that right, and learning how to use it properly
Breaking the glass ceiling.	Leaving the building and climbing up to the roof.
Getting women into positions of political power	Getting women into positions of economic power
Getting day care	Changing our family and work structures so day care is less necessary.
Finding ways for women to have loving sexual relationships with other women	Finding ways for women to have loving-relationships with whatever gender they prefer, and yes, that includes the individuals with prominent external genitalia and obvious body hair
Breaking the silence about rape and sexual abuse.	Breaking the silence about consensual sex.
Giving women divorce and singlehood as options to het marriage	Making het marriage a better choice for the women who want it, while still keeping those other options
… Making it acceptable for women to delay or space their children with birth control	Making it possible to be a mother AND have a life. or even to not have children at all
Making it acceptable for mothers to work	Earning enough money so we can afford to become mothers.

We grew up in a different world. We run into different problems than you did. Is it any wonder that we work with different issues?

Another article discusses the differences between the generations.

ENGENDERING CHANGE
What's Up with Third Wave Feminism?
Krista Jacob

A new kind of activism is brewing among young women—"Third Wave Feminism." Many of us, inspired by larger theoretical discussions about race and sexuality, have started to place a greater emphasis on establishing multiracial alliances among women.

The movement seeks to broaden the parameters of feminism. Initially attracted to third wave feminism through the writings and activism of Rebecca Walker and Amy Richards, two well-known third wave feminists, I was impressed by a central tenet of third wave feminism:

> Include certain groups of women who have previously been excluded as a result of race, class, and sexual orientation prejudice.

Third wave feminism provides a forum for illuminating the multifaceted experiences of young women—a group that is consistently misrepresented by older generations, the mainstream media, and other avenues. Using young women's personal testimonies and autobiographical accounts, we reveal young women struggling to incorporate the lessons from the women's movement of the 60's and 70's (second wave feminism) into their own unique, lived experiences.

They show us that young women are celebrating their pluralities, embracing their personal and political contradictions (i.e., choosing to wear makeup while maintaining a critical stance toward the misogyny and racism inherent in the cosmetic industry), and refusing to follow a feminist party line.

The "feminist party line" refers to what many young feminists perceive to be constrictive and unfair expectations set up by certain mainstream definitions of feminism, such as you can't:

> wear makeup,
> shave your legs,
> wear dresses,
> have a traditional wedding, or
> celebrate your femininity

and still be considered a "feminist."

The underlying assumption is that these choices somehow compromise your feminist politics and are reflective of "selling out" to patriarchal values.

Though these expectations are by no means universal, many young women have expressed feelings of not "fitting in" with other feminists because of their refusal to live up to these standards.

As Rebecca Walker states in her book, *To Be Real: Telling the Truth and Changing the Face of Feminism*:

> For many of us it seems that to be a feminist in the way that we have seen or understood feminism is to conform to an identity and way of living that doesn't allow for individuality, complexity or less than perfect personal histories.

But this pluralism is not limited to third wave personal politics; it exists in the political realm as well. Witness the large numbers of young women who are working on a litany of issues such as:

> violence against women,
> sweatshop exploitation,
> reproductive freedom,
> affirmative action,
> race and class exploitation,
> death penalty,
> queer issues,
> sexuality,
> labor issues,
> welfare rights, and so on.

The existence of this new branch of feminism has sparked tensions between second

---

and third wave feminists. Though there is significant diversity of opinions among third and second wave feminists, and the tensions I speak of are certainly not universal, a generation gap exists that is worth exploring.

A criticism frequently leveled against third wave feminists is that they embrace their contradictions and so-called pluralities to such an extent that they compromise many important core feminist principles created by our feminist foremothers. For example, many young women's interest in exploring s/m sexuality is perceived by some to violate the feminist argument that the synthesis of sex and violence perpetuates violence and oppression of women.

Just as third wave feminists are more inclusive in their approach to race, class, and sexual orientation, they also attempt to be more inclusive of varying ideologies, even those that deviate somewhat from the traditional feminist party line.

Many second wave feminists charge that young women are ignorant about their history and are apathetic about their rights as women, whether it be their right to choose abortion, affirmative action, or women gaining the right to vote.

There certainly is some truth to this argument. Women's history continues to be neglected by most high school curricula, and issues important to women, people of color, and the gay/les/bi/trans community are consistently misrepresented by mainstream, conservative, corporate-controlled media.

However, in general, third wave feminists are not ignorant about women's issues. On the contrary, they simply believe that the current social and political climate is different than it was three decades ago and thus requires different political strategies.

For example, one point of contention for many older and younger feminists was the recent presidential election. Much to the chagrin of many second wave feminists, young women came out in droves to support Ralph Nader.

Though he had no chance of winning, many young women (and men) were frustrated with the behavior of the Clinton/Gore administration because the only issue they stood firm on was abortion. Their conservative stance on welfare, trade, labor issues, foreign policy, the death penalty, gays in the military, and same sex marriage compromised progressive agendas—driving the Democratic party farther to the center—and forcing feminists to choose between the "lesser of evils."

Frustration on the part of many second wave feminists is understandable considering their hard fought battles to elect pro-choice, pro-affirmative action, and pro-woman politicians, and to establish a unified feminist presence where there wasn't one before.

But second wave feminists have been criticized by lesbians, women of color and working class women for having a white middle class bias and for excluding the issues specific to them. Critics argue that the "unified feminist presence" was in fact a false sense of unity.

The many successes of the second wave feminist movement have afforded young women the privilege of employing more plural and comprehensive tactics. Unfortunately, this comprehensive approach to politics makes young women's activism look more fragmented, which can give the appearance of political inactivity or apathy.

These tensions should serve as a call to action for both older and younger feminists.

Older feminists should embrace and encourage young women's activism and find at least one young woman in their life to mentor and help navigate through the challenges of being young and feminist.

Younger feminists should actively seek out a feminist mentor, read about women's history—including the history of working class women, women of color, lesbian and bisexual women—and build on the knowledge gained through the second wave of feminism.

The future of feminism hinges on the success of these relationships.

An overview of issues facing third wave feminists can be found at a Web site called 3ʳᵈ WWWave. Here are excerpts about some of the issues facing women today and a third wave comparison with second wave feminists.

FEMINISM IS NOT DEAD
In Fact, It's on the Rise Again, But in a New Form
From 3ʳᵈ WWWave Web site,
http://www.3rdwwwave.com/

We are the 20- and 30-something women who have always known a world with feminism in it. We are putting a new face on feminism, taking it beyond the women's movement that our mothers participated in, bringing it back to the lives of *real women* who juggle jobs, kids, money, and personal freedom in a frenzied world. Women may have been granted grudging access to the job market, but we *still* bear much more of the burden than men: it costs more money to be a woman, we have to work harder just to be considered competent, we do all the emotional maintenance work in relationships, and all the old stereotypes that keep us from being respected unless we act like men remain firmly in place.

We've had enough!

- Enough with the guys who refuse to change their roles to match the changes women have made;
- Enough with the old notion that women are permanent victims who will never succeed against sexism;
- Enough with the women who think feminism is over because a few laws protect us and "we're all equal now";
- Enough with the male standard that puts women at a disadvantage in everyday life ("level playing field"—hah!)

. . . We've come a long way, even though we still have a long way to go, and we're more interested in finding solutions to the problems that confront us than concentrating only on the problems themselves. Women make less money than men for the same job—we know. But *what can we do about it*? Balancing a job and a family can be difficult for a woman. *How can we make it better*? We don't just want to sing the blues. We're in a better position now than we were even ten years ago, and we want to *use* our new power to help make the world a better place for ourselves and our kids, not just talk about what's gone wrong. How do we make it *right*?

This is not the second wave warmed over. We are building on what they accomplished and taking it in new directions appropriate for the 21st century. We've had enough—and we're doing something about it!

MONEY AND WOMEN

The Second Wave had a rather different relationship to money than women have now. Thirty five years ago women were, for the most part, unable to get independent credit. And it was much more difficult to buy a house or even a car without a man's name attached to the deal. The prevailing myth was that women weren't supposed to "sully themselves" with the dirty details of money. It was an easy myth to swallow: money *is* a nasty business—don't think for a minute that all those Wall Street traders, stockbrokers, and bankers are in this out of the goodness of their hearts!

The Second Wave wrapped itself in anticapitalist idealism, which was really just a variation on the prevailing myth about clean women and dirty money. They strove for independence (including financial independence) from men, but they wanted nothing to do with money.

The Third Wave has a different attitude. Money is power, and like all power, it can be used for good or ill or anything in between. As long as we exist in a lower tax bracket than the average man, we will have less political clout, less ability to help other women, and less financial freedom. There is nothing wrong with earning a lot of money! On these pages we explore how our attitudes about wealth and economics differ from those of the Second Wave, and we provide tips for earning and managing money.

WOMEN, MEN, AND FEMINISM

Second wave feminism focused rather exclusively on the needs of women, which was quite understandable considering the seriousness of sexism at that time. Reproductive choice, well-paying jobs, even merely getting independent credit were simply not possible for the majority of women. And so the second wave set about the demanding, exhausting task of securing these basic rights for women.

Now it's time to move beyond those basic rights to the next set of obstacles [that] separate women from completely fulfilling lives. It's time to acknowledge our connection to men—we are more similar than we are different. Most women do share their lives with men—as friends, coworkers, sisters, and wives—and rejecting men would mean denying an important part of their existence. Feminism has been painted as anti-man, but it is really pro-woman.

But we can't do the work for men, and we won't try. Social change requires efforts from *both* sides. We want to meet men in the middle, not do all the adjusting ourselves. We're here to encourage our brothers to do the hard work of examining themselves and their role, to pull themselves up by their bootstraps and start a genuine transformation of the male role— for our health and theirs.

RELATIONSHIPS

Second wave feminism made some amazing advances for women. When women of our generation think about the 60's and 70's feminists, it's important for us to realize that, before they dug in and started the hard work of changing things for us all, women:

- Couldn't get credit. No MasterCard, no Visa, no nothing. Gurl, you want those plane tickets, you'd better ask your hubby to get them for you. Oh, by the way, you *are* married, aren't you? You want those textbooks for college? Same thing.
- Could get fired by an employer because he wanted a man, and they wouldn't even try to hide it. "A man needs this job; he has to provide for his family." Well, maybe if the wife is going to work, it means they need the money, too.
- Fended off passes and gropes on the job without any legal recourse, whereas now we have some laws in place for us. "Oh, it's just flirting." Although this still has a lo-o-o-ong way to go.
- Were routinely laughed out of court if we tried to press charges of rape. "Were you wearing nice perfume?"
- Had much less chance of getting into college (did you know that nowadays, more four year degrees are awarded to women than men?). "We just don't like to accept girl applicants for law degrees. They just get pregnant and leave."

It wasn't the Ward and June paradise that some people think it was before the coming of feminism. It's important to remember that.

But the second wave also left behind some things that we have to deal with now. We don't want to buy into the old saying that, "A woman needs a man like a fish needs a bicycle." Sure, we don't need them—but they're nice to have around sometimes.

And that means that we have to start thinking about the problems that confront women with men—and not necessarily the more egregious problems of marital rape and wife beating, although those problems are crucial and must be solved. There has to be a feminist arena for talking not only about that, but about child care, sharing household duties, how to keep a marriage happy. There has to be a feminist way of talking about relationships between men and women without making it seem like rape and beatings are the whole subject.

DAILY LIVING

Daily life for women is different than it is for men. Although we work at similar jobs, and face the same challenge of getting enough sleep, food, work, and relaxation crammed into a 24-hour period, we still experience a different reality because of our gender.

It's not different in a fundamental sense—all people seek satisfying relationships, respect for their work, and a chance to grow and improve. But in a cultural sense, men and women still live worlds apart. Women are assumed to know nothing about cars, so we must be vigilant for auto mechanics who try to cheat us. We pay more for the basics of living, such as clothes and haircuts. We are expected to be "nice" and help others at the drop of a hat, so we must endure cries of "selfish bitch!" when we dare to work toward our *own* goals

or tell someone we just don't have time at the moment. We are criticized if we have too much money or power, or are too sexy.

Dealing with these little issues on a day-to-day basis isn't so bad, but over the years, they accumulate. Being an assertive, motivated, ambitious woman in this world is like enduring Chinese water torture. Drip, drip, drip—after a while, a huge fissure has worn away in your psyche. It is just plain *tiring* to spend day after day, year after year overcoming the small inequities, the petty comments, the seemingly harmless acts.

The third wave is about fixing these cultural inequities that women *still* encounter in daily life simply because we are women.

STUDY QUESTIONS

1. Are the issues between second and third wave feminists very different?
2. Do you agree with the perspective of the third wave feminists? How so?
3. What do you believe are the most important issues facing women today?
4. Do you believe that the conflict between second and third wave feminists negatively impacts on the ability to achieve equality?

As we have seen throughout this book, the ever-changing societal issues reflect the impact that feminists of their time made on the laws that govern our society. As our culture evolves, so too must our laws to meet these ever-changing issues. Whereas same sex marriage was not even contemplated by the early suffragettes, today it is contemplated and fought for by many feminists. Oftentimes laws that have a greater impact on our lives change more slowly than societal norms. It then becomes the role of those advocates for equality, women *and* men who aspire to be feminists, to push for changes in our laws that match the needs of all.

What have we learned about the intersection of gender and race? Is that an issue that mainstream feminists adequately address? Can they? This next section explores the concept of Intersectionality.

IV. INTERSECTIONALITY: RACE AND GENDER

Feminist jurisprudence is a philosophy of law based on the political, economic, and social equality of the sexes. As an area of the law it spans all issues that have gender aspects or implications. Although you have been presented with a variation on the aspect of feminism based on *generation*, there exist within the study of feminist jurisprudence different schools of thought and different approaches. The Legal Information Institute, an online resource sponsored by Cornell Law School, provides a good overview of the three schools of feminist philosophy.

The first is liberal feminism, in which the basic premise is that women are as rational as men and therefore should have equal opportunity to make their own choices. They seek to eradicate the differences based on gender and allow women to compete equally. The second philosophy refers to cultural feminists. This philosophy focuses on the differences between men and women and develops those differences. They believe that the domain men inhabit is characterized by rights and principles, and the one women inhabit is characterized by relationships, context, and reconciliation.

The third school of thought is that of the radical feminist. This approach focuses on inequality. Radical feminists believe that men have dominated women, creating inequality. It revolves around gender as power. Their approach is one where gender equality must be based on the differences between men and women, and not merely accommodate those differences.

What is missing from this analysis however is the discussion an aspect of feminist philosophy called intersectionality; the intersection of race and gender.

The intersection of the issues of race and gender reach back to the days of Susan B Anthony and Fredrick Douglass. There is a belief in feminist literature that Susan B Anthony and other members of the suffrage movement essentially "sold out" their Black counterparts in order to recruit Southern white women to the movement. That by addressing the issue of gender oppression but not racial oppression has done a grave disservice to minority women. Intersectionality is a social theory that holds that different issues of oppression do not act independent of each other. In other words the fact that a woman faces sexism is not enough to fully understand or describe her reality. It is also necessary to know her race, sexual orientation, or socioeconomic class in order to fully comprehend her challenges.

Intersectionality theory was developed in the 1960s and mid-1970s, some say, in response to the radical feminist movement of the 1960s. The term *intersectionality* was first coined by Kimberlé Williams Crenshaw, a law professor specializing in race and gender issues. The idea of intersectionality gained increased recognition in the 1990s through the work of sociologist Patricia Hill Collins. According to Collins, patterns of oppression are interrelated and are bound together by various systems such as race and gender in our society. Experiences of gender cannot be understood unless the influence of race is also considered. Many Feminists today believe one must understand intersectionality in order to achieve political and social equality.

Intersectionality began as a "re-visionist feminist theory" critical of the second wave feminism of the 1960s who believed that gender was the primary basis of oppression of women. Feminist women of color dispute this notion; that women were the same regardless of their racial or social circumstance. It was a recognition that that women were not homogenous and that the forms of oppression experienced by white middle-class women was very different from that experienced by black, poor, or disabled women. Intersectionality became a way for feminists to understand the ways in which gender, race, and class combined to "determine the female destiny."

Intersectionality, in addition to a way to understand the plight of all women, has practical applications in the manner in which we begin to address particular issues affecting women. One such application is in the field of social work. Social workers who do not take into account the intersection of various issues affecting women will not be as effective in addressing their problems. If the social worker does not understand the implication that other, seemingly unrelated issues have had on a person, that will not adequately provide the appropriate remedy. For example, telling a minority victim of domestic violence she "must call the police" is to ignore her culture's past history of racially motivated police oppression. A different approach must be developed in order to be a valid and affective approach for women of color.

Another example is in the labor market. When we look at issues of employment, wage parity, and poverty, we cannot look solely at the issue of gender. Within the issue of gender is another layer and that is of race. Differences of education, experience, and skill aside, women who fall into the bottom of the social hierarchy in terms of race or gender are more likely to be paid lower wages, subjected to stereotypes and discriminated against, or be hired for exploitive domestic positions. In order to fully understand and address the issue of labor market inequality, one must look not only at the issue of gender but also at the issue of race and social status.

To better help you to understand the concept of intersectionality, the following excerpt is an interview with prominent theorist Kimberlé Williams Crenshaw conducted by The American Bar Association in March of 2004.

INTERVIEW OF PROFESSOR KIMBERLE CRENSHAW

by Perspectives editorial board member Shelia Thomas,
on Intersectionality of Race and Gender

Kimberle Crenshaw was still in college when she realized that there were no class offerings addressing both race and gender issues. "In the Africana studies program at Cornell," she says, "the gender aspect of race was woefully underdeveloped. When women were discussed, it was not in political or economic contexts but rather those of literature and poetry. The serious political discourses were framed by men, and women came in at the periphery."

So Crenshaw delved into this intriguing area of thought. Now a professor of law at the UCLA School of Law and Columbia Law School, she earned a J.D. at Harvard Law School and an LL.M. at the University of Wisconsin Law School. She has published extensively in the areas of civil rights, black feminist legal theory, and race, racism, and the law.

Perspectives editorial board member Sheila Thomas spoke to Crenshaw in March.

INTERSECTIONALITY OF RACE AND GENDER

Perspectives: Tell me about the origins of your concept of intersectionality.

Crenshaw: It grew out of trying to conceptualize the way the law responded to issues where both race and gender discrimination were involved. What happened was like an accident, a collision. Intersectionality simply came from the idea that if you're standing in the path of multiple forms of exclusion, you are likely to get hit by both. These women are injured, but when the race ambulance and the gender ambulance arrive at the scene, they see these women of color lying in the intersection and they say, "Well, we can't figure out if this was just race or just sex discrimination. And unless they can show us which one it was, we can't help them."

Perspectives: And this is how the law treats the problem?

Crenshaw: It seemed to me to capture the initial reluctance of courts to credit the claims of women of color when they were seeking remedies for race and gender discrimination. If the injuries were simultaneously produced, the law, it seemed, was confounded.

Perspectives: Have there been times when you were personally discriminated against?

Crenshaw: I have a story I tell a lot. A member of our study group at Harvard was the first African-American member of a previously exclusive white club. He invited the rest of the group—me and another African-American man—to visit him at this club. When we knocked on the door, he opened it, stepped outside, and shut it quickly. He said that he was embarrassed because he had forgotten to tell us something about entering the building. My male friend immediately bristled, saying that if black people couldn't go through the front door, we weren't coming in at all. But our friend said, "No, no, no, that's not it—but women have to go through the back door." And my friend was totally okay with that.

Perspectives: How did that affect you?

Crenshaw: I understood that we can all stand together as long as we think that we are all equally affected by a particular discrimination, but the moment where a different barrier affects a subset of us, our solidarity often falls apart. I began to look at all the other ways that not only the race and civil rights agenda but the gender agenda are sometimes uninformed by and inattentive to the ways that subgroups experience discrimination.

There are institutional elisions as well. For example, at Harvard, when we were struggling to get the law school to interview and perhaps hire women and people of color, the school responded with two committees. One was a gender committee that studied women candidates; the other was a committee that studied candidates of color. Not too surprisingly, women of color seemed to fall through the cracks.

Perspectives: Would you call that discrimination?

Crenshaw: Traditional thinking might say, "Oh, well, they are intentionally discriminating against women of color." But the reality was that nobody really thought about women of color. In thinking about discrimination against women and people of color, women of color are frequently lost. Some of the very early cases where African-American women challenged employment policies of major industries were quite eye-opening because they showed that gender- and race-segregated industries had jobs that are deemed appropriate for blacks and jobs that are appropriate for women, but virtually none available for blacks who were women, or women who were black.

Perspectives: So where African-American men were on the line in the factory, there were no jobs for women because of gender discrimination, and where women were placed in the secretarial pool or front office, only white women were seen as appropriate as secretaries or personal assistants.

Crenshaw: Exactly. So African-American women said, "Hey, we are being discriminated against on the basis of both race and gender." They wanted to argue compound discrimination. Initially, though, it confounded the court. In *DeGraffenreid v. General Motors*, where black women's claims of race and gender discrimination in hiring were rejected, the court thought that if it gave these women leave to make this claim, they were going to be giving them a super remedy, something more than everybody else receives.

Look at this next perspective on the issue of intersectionality in a 2008 essay by Anna Carastathis, a student and teacher of feminist political theory at McGill and Concordia Montreal Canada.

INTERSECTIONALITY & FEMINISM
Submitted by Anna Carastathis 13 February, 2008

What do intersections have to do with feminism? Or with our lives as women and girls?

Quite a lot, it turns out.

Maybe you've heard this word thrown around in feminist classrooms or activist spaces. Maybe you haven't, but feel some frustration with the way generalizations about women and girls don't really describe your own experiences.

Maybe you've experienced being asked to focus on one aspect of who you are, and to ignore other aspects. Maybe you have been told that your identity is too complex for feminism, or you've seen that some versions of feminism pit your identity as a woman or girl against your other identities.

Maybe you've asked yourself, how do the parts of my identity relate to each other? What parts of my identity are relevant to feminism as a movement to end the oppression of women and girls? Why are some parts seen as relevant while others are dismissed or discounted in feminist organizing?

I'm going to talk to you about intersectionality as a language for identity forged through systematic social relations of oppression and privilege.

I opened this essay by naming a range of experiences that intersectionality tries to answer.

In what follows, I'm going to explain what "intersectionality" means, where it comes from, and how it is used to make feminism a movement that speaks for all of us, not just women with privilege who are able to hijack feminism for their own particular interests.

The word "intersectionality" comes out of a metaphor coined by the critical legal theorist Kimberlé Williams Crenshaw to explain how race oppression and gender oppression interact in Black women's lives.

In the 1980s, Crenshaw was trying to understand why US anti-discrimination law was failing to protect Black women in the workplace, and she discovered it was because the law distinguished between two kinds of discrimination: gendered discrimination and racialized discrimination.

That is, US law distinguished between discrimination against women (on the basis of their gender) and discrimination against Black, Latino, Asian, and Indigenous people (on the basis of their race).

But in her study of discrimination in workplaces, Crenshaw observed that Black women were discriminated against on both bases—their gender and their race—at once.

So, for example, Black women were the last group to be hired at a workplace she studied—after white women and Black men. When the boss decided to lay people off, Black women were fired because they were the least senior—the last to arrive. But that they were hired last was itself due to discrimination. This group of Black women took the company to court and the judge said, "there's no gender discrimination here because white women weren't fired. And there's no race discrimination here because Black men weren't fired."

So, Crenshaw concluded that discrimination against Black women in the workplace—as *Black women*—was invisible to legal concepts of discrimination that saw it in terms of "gender" only or in terms of "race" only. Black women's experiences of discrimination were rendered invisible by these ways of categorizing discriminatory practices.

Crenshaw argued that a similar thing happened in US feminist movements. Black women's issues—and the issues facing other women of colour, lesbians, and working class white women—became invisible as privileged white women defined "gender discrimination" and "gender oppression" in terms of their own particular experiences. They then overgeneralized those experiences and claimed they were shared by all women. But they weren't.

The problem was (and is) that although women of colour, lesbians, and working class women were always active in feminism in the US and Canada, feminism became dominated by white upper class women who retained identifications with men and white male power.

Despite the diversity of women in the feminist movement, and the increasing divergence between women's interests, privileged white feminists hijacked feminism for their own immediate interests. Let me give you three examples.

***

(1) FIRST EXAMPLE: REPRODUCTIVE RIGHTS

Privileged white feminists fought for reproductive rights like abortion and adequate contraception, under the banner of "choice," but ignored the widespread forced sterilization of Black and Indigenous women as well as of women with disabilities, in the US and Canada.

Worse than this, some women's rights campaigns for abortion actually advocated involuntary sterilization of poor women of colour. Birth control for wealthy white women was seen as going hand in hand with population control of poor communities of colour (primarily Indigenous, Black and poor white people).

For instance, Margaret Sanger, the founder of Planned Parenthood, forgot her working class origins and betrayed her early militant politics in advocating in the 1920s and 30s the "strategic" sterilization of "unfit" mothers (Angela Davis, 1981, p. 212–215).

(2) SECOND EXAMPLE: WORK

Privileged white feminists fought for increased access to professional jobs that were male dominated, ignoring the fact that women of colour, immigrant women, and working class white women were being overworked, often in places far away from their families, just to survive and support their children—sometimes in white feminists' homes, cleaning their floors and caring for their children.

For privileged white feminists, the problem became the "double shift": working during the day in a professional job, and coming home in the evening only to work more, caring for their husbands and children.

To lessen this workload, instead of demanding that their husbands pull their weight, or that the state provide an adequate accessible childcare, domestic work became offloaded to women of colour.

(3) THIRD EXAMPLE: THE STATE

Privileged white women fight for better political representation in the government and other state institutions—for instance, they fight to get more women members of parliament (MPs) in Canada, or more Supreme Court judges. In the current parliament, only about 21% of MPs are women. Fewer still, about 6%, are people of colour.

Even fewer 1.9% (or, six MPs) identify as Indigenous people.

But this kind of feminist fight for better political representation ignores the ways the Canadian state—as a colonial state of a nation of settlers built on stolen Indigenous land—systematically oppresses First Nations women, and exploits immigrant women's labour.

Getting more (white) women into parliament lends legitimacy to the Canadian government. That is, it makes it seem as if the government can do good things for women, if only the right people were to run it.

But Indigenous women whose ancestors were displaced from their territories and forced onto reserves, cut off from their spirituality, their languages, systems of governance, whose children were stolen and put into residential schools or white foster homes, know otherwise about the Canadian government, which did all these things.

They know this government isn't legitimate, and they knew more women MPs couldn't make it so. The problem was structural, not personal.

***

Intersectionality is a way of taking into consideration all of the factors that together make up our political identities: our gender, our race and ethnicity, our class and status in society, our sexuality, our physical abilities, our age, our national status, and so on.

As we have seen, privileged white feminists misrepresented a politics that defended their specific interests as a politics acting on behalf of all women.

Intersectionality tries to make visible the multiple factors that structure our experiences of oppression, and against which we have to struggle.

Some of these factors we share as women, others we do not.

But what intersectionality attempts to do is to show how our experiences as women are interconnected.

***

So, to sum up.

We all have intersectional identities that are shaped through systems of power relations, and through experiences of oppression.

If feminism is to be a truly liberatory politics seeking the freedom of all oppressed people, it has to recognize this important insight: that "I am not free while any woman is unfree, even when her shackles are very different from my own"—that I am not free as long as any oppressed person remains chained.

Privileged white feminists involved in the feminist movements in US and Canada failed to realize this, and instead continually overgeneralized their own specific experience as the experience of all women.

They fell prey to "divide and conquer" strategies that distracted them from realizing what is the real source of their oppression, and how the privileges they are granted in virtue of their race, class, heterosexuality and national status, are based on the oppression of other women.

Intersectionality helps us to understand how gender, class, race, and other factors in our experience fit together. It helps us come up with better feminist politics that seek the emancipation of all people—not just an élite minority of privileged women.

It helps us understand that some problems we share as women and girls, and others we don't share. But what we all share as oppressed people is a common enemy: a shared oppressor.

Intersectional approaches to feminist theorizing and activism can help us overcome the "Oppression Olympics" problem and the problem of having to focus on one aspect of one's identity at the expense of ignoring another.

Intersectionality can help us understand feminism as a much broader project than it has been construed by privileged white feminists in the US and Canada.

It can show us that as feminists we need to be antiracists, we need to oppose colonialism (starting with internal colonialism in Canada and the US of First Nations), imperialism and corporate globalization, and to defend the rights of workers to determine the conditions of their labour.

As feminists, we need to imagine alternatives to capitalism for organizing how we produce things to meet needs in our society. We need to recognize that war and violent domination are the flip side of "business as usual," and that we will never see true peace until we see justice enacted in our society.

Intersectionality can show us the connections between the imperialist wars on Iraq and Afghanistan, the war on Indigenous people struggling for self-determination by the Canadian and US states, the war on women, waged here and elsewhere through gendered and racialized violence, poverty, and exploitation.

And it can help us create feminist politics that embody our aspirations for a completely different world.

STUDY QUESTIONS

1. What is intersectionality, and how does it affect the way we view gender discrimination?
2. What are the practical implications of intersectionality?
3. How can intersectionality be integrated into modern feminist thinking and action?

Throughout this book, we have asked you to think of how you fit into the equation of equality. Do you perpetuate gender bias and gender-based discrimination? Are you a feminist, liberal, or radical? Have you thought of different approaches to these issues based on race? Do you believe that accommodations should be made on the basis of sex or that women should simply be treated equally? Do the laws adequately address societal issues of today?

Most feminists, both second and third wave, believe there is much work to do. With each advancement, a setback threatens. Reproductive freedom, the right to define for oneself what constitutes a relationship or makes up a family, the right to safe and affordable child care, the right to equal pay for equal work, and the right to an equal chance out of poverty with dignity are all issues that remain on the agenda as we approach the halfway mark of this decade.

Most believe there is still much work to be done. What do you think?

ON-LINE RESOURCES

Legal Information Institute
www.law.cornell.edu/
This is an excellent resource for legal research and information maintained by Cornell Law School.

Legal Momentum (formerly NOW Legal Defense and Education Fund)
www.legalmomentum.org/
Legal Momentum, formerly known as the NOW Legal Defense and Education Fund, is an invaluable resource for information on gender-related legal and public policy issues.

National Organization for Women
www.now.org/
This is the official site for NOW. It contains articles, reports, studies, and information pertaining to women's issues.

Office of International Women's Issues
www.state.gov/g/wi/
This is a U.S. Department of State site that contains several interesting articles and issue-oriented studies pertaining to international women's issues.

Third Wave Foundation
www.thirdwavefoundation.org/
This foundation Web site strives to bring equality to all. The Foundation provides for public information and philanthropy.

The 3rd WWWave
http://www.3rdwwwave.com/
This site reflects the unique view of women's issues and feminism in the generation of women who came of age in the 80s. It features information and discussion on issues related to politics, sexuality, daily life, sports, and hobbies.

ABBREVIATIONS

For additional assistance with legal abbreviations, see the latest edition of A *Uniform System of Citations* issued by the Harvard Law Review Association.

A.B.A.	American Bar Association		Idem.	The same
A.2d	Atlantic Reporter, 2d Series		i.e.	That is
ACLU	American Civil Liberties Union		Infra	Following
AFDC	Aid to Families with Dependent Children		L.Ed.2d	U.S. Supreme Court Reports, Lawyers' Edition, 2d Series
AFLA	Adolescent Family Life Act		Misc.2d	Miscellaneous Reports [of the New York courts], 2d Series
Am.Jur.2d	American Jurisprudence, 2d Edition			
ALI	American Law Institute		n.	Footnote number
Bl.Comm.	Blackstone's Commentaries		N.E.2d	North Eastern Reporter, 2d Series
BFOQ	Bona Fide Occupational Qualification		NOW	National Organization for Women
			N.W.2d	North Western Reporter, 2d Series
Cal.Rptr.	California Reporter		OFCCP	Office of Federal Contract Compliance Programs
C.F.R.	Code of Federal Regulations			
C.J.S.	Corpus Juris Secundum		P.2d	Pacific Reporter, Second Series
Cert.denied	Certiorari denied		PDA	Pregnancy Discrimination Act
Cir.	Cicuit, Circuit Court of Appeals		PPFA	Planned Parenthood Federation of America
EEOC	Equal Employment Opportunity Commission			
			Rev'd	Reversed
E.P.D.	Employment Practices Decisions		§,§§	Section, sections
ERA	Equal Rights Amendment		S.Ct.	Supreme Court Reporter
Et al.	And others		So.2d	Southern Reporter, 2d Series
Ex. Ord.	Executive Order		Sup.Ct.	Supreme Court
F.2d.	Federal Reporter, 2d Series		Supp.	Supplement
Fed.Reg.	Federal Register		Stat.	Statute, U.S. Statutes at Large
FEP	Fair Employment Practices		Supra	Above
F.R.D.	Federal Rules Decisions		UMPA	Uniform Marital Property Act
F.Supp.	Federal Supplement		U.S.	United States Reports
Ibid.	In the same place		U.S.C.	United States Code

APPENDIX A

SELECTED AMENDMENTS TO THE CONSTITUTION OF THE UNITED STATES (WITH YEAR OF RATIFICATION)

AMENDMENT XIII (1865)

Section 1. Neither slavery nor involuntary servitude, except as a punishment for crime whereof the party shall have been duly convicted, shall exist within the United States, or any place subject to their jurisdiction.

AMENDMENT XIV (1868)

Section 1. All persons born or naturalized in the United States and subject to the jurisdiction thereof, are citizens of the United States and of the State wherein they reside. No State shall make or enforce any law which shall abridge the privileges or immunities of citizens of the United States; nor shall any State deprive any person of life, liberty, or property, without due process of law; nor deny to any person within its jurisdiction the equal protection of the laws.

AMENDMENT XV (1870)

Section 1. The right of citizens of the United States to vote shall not be denied or abridged by the United States or by any State on account of race, color, or previous condition of servitude.

AMENDMENT XIX (1920)

The right of citizens of the United States to vote shall not be denied or abridged by the United States or by any State on account of sex.

APPENDIX B

COURT SYSTEMS

TRIAL AND APPELLATE COURTS

There are two parallel court systems in the United States: the federal courts and the state courts. Both systems have two principal types of courts: trial courts and appellate courts. Cases are usually initiated at the trial level: evidence is taken, and initial decisions are made. A trial court's decision becomes final if there is no attempt to have it reviewed by an appellate court within a specified time period. In reviewing a trial-level decision, an appellate court usually does not take additional evidence; it considers only whether the trial court properly disposed of the case as it was presented. An appellate court may affirm the decision below, or it may reverse and remand (send back) the case to the trial court with instructions on how to proceed. Less often, the appellate court reverses a decision and actually substitutes its own decision on the content of the case. Appellate courts in both the federal and state systems also review decisions made by administrative agencies, such as human services departments or civil rights divisions. Appellate decisions are usually made by several judges hearing the case together, while a single judge or a judge and a jury decide disputes at the trial level, and agency heads make decisions at the administrative level.

THE FEDERAL COURT SYSTEM

The structure of the federal court system is determined in part by provisions of the U.S. Constitution and in part by statutes passed by Congress under the power given to it by the Constitution. Federal courts are limited to hearing certain kinds of cases: cases involving federal law including federal constitutional questions; cases involving parties from different states where the amount in controversy exceeds ten thousand dollars; and cases involving actions by or against the federal government and its agencies. The principal trial courts in the federal system are organized along geographical lines and are called "district courts." A district may consist of a state, as in the District of New Jersey, or of a portion of a state, as in the Southern District of New York.

Prior to 1976, there was an exception known as the "three-judge district court." Under the past law, a special court consisting of one circuit judge and two district judges was convened to hear cases seeking to enjoin federal and state statutes on federal constitutional grounds. Appeals from injunctions issued by three-judge district courts went straight to the U.S. Supreme Court. As a result, some of the older cases in this book refer to three-judge districts and direct appeals rather than the tri-level, district-circuit-Supreme Court system now in effect in almost all cases.

Appeals are heard by courts of appeals, which are grouped into circuits. There are thirteen circuits. The First through the Eleventh Circuits are organized along geographical lines. The First Circuit, for example, hears appeals from the federal district courts in Maine, Massachusetts, New Hampshire, Puerto Rico, and Rhode Island. The Twelfth is the Court of Appeals for the District of Columbia Circuit, and the Thirteenth is the new Federal Circuit, which is a nationwide court hearing certain kinds of appeals, such as those involving patents, international trade, and tariffs. Federal appeals are usually heard by panels of three judges, although occasionally a case is decided by all the judges belonging to the circuit, who are then said to be sitting "en banc." This generally occurs in response to petitions for rehearing en banc filed by a losing party after a panel decision is issued.

The court of last resort in the federal system is the U.S. Supreme Court. Although suits brought by one state against another and a few other types of cases may begin in the Supreme Court, the overwhelming majority of cases heard by the Supreme Court begin in other courts. In theory, any case beginning in a federal district court may reach the Supreme Court. These cases, however, must first be considered at the circuit level, and they reach the Supreme Court only after the Court has given its permission (usually called "granting *certiorari*"). State court cases involving federal questions, such as the meaning of a federal statute or a constitutional provision, may also be reviewed by the U.S. Supreme Court once they are decided by the highest state court authorized to decide the particular case. Very few cases actually reach the Supreme Court, however.

STATE COURT SYSTEMS

State court systems vary from state to state. Usually determined by the state's constitution and state statutes, state court systems generally include intermediate appellate courts and a court of last resort. Names of the different levels also vary by state. For example, trial level courts are known as "superior courts" in California and New Jersey and as "supreme courts" in New York. The highest court is known as the "supreme court" in California and New Jersey and as the "court of appeals" in New York.

Unlike the federal system, state court systems include courts that may hear all kinds of cases without limits on subject matter or amount of money in controversy. Such courts are said to have "general jurisdiction." There are also special courts of limited jurisdiction in most states, such as municipal courts and domestic relations courts. These, too, vary from state to state.

COURT CITATIONS

References or citations to decisions indicate basic information about the cases and about how to find them. There are official and unofficial reports of the decisions from many court systems. They all follow a uniform format.

The citation for *Reed v. Reed*, the first case applying the equal protection clause to invalidate a state law discriminating on the basis of sex, is 404 U.S. 71, 92 S.Ct. 251, 30 L.Ed. 2d 225 (1971). "U.S." refers to *United States Reports*, the official reports of decisions by the United States Supreme Court; "S.Ct." refers to the *Supreme Court Reporter*, and "L.Ed. 2d" refers to the *U.S. Supreme Court Reports, Lawyers Edition, Second Series*, both unofficial reports of U.S. Supreme Court decisions. The first number in each case designates the volume of the particular report, and the second number designates the page. The date of the decision appears in parentheses. Thus, *Reed v. Reed*, decided by the U.S. Supreme Court in 1971, can be found in volume 404 of the *United States Reports*, beginning on page 71; in volume 92 of the *Supreme Court Reporter*, beginning on page 251; and in volume 30 of the *Lawyers Edition, Second Series*, beginning on page 225.

For further information, speak to a law librarian or consult a legal research reference, such as *The Legal Research Manual* by C. G. Wren and J. R. Wren (Madison, WI: A–R Editions, 1984).

APPENDIX C

MAP OF THE THIRTEEN FEDERAL CIRCUITS

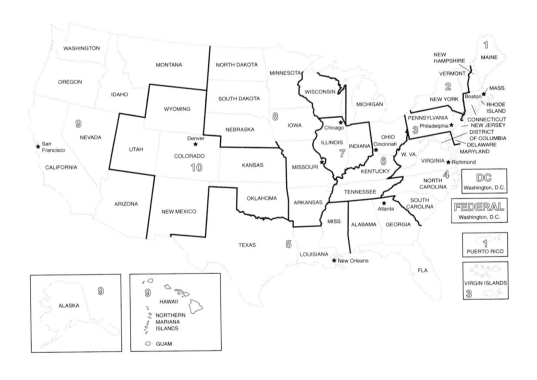

APPENDIX D

AN INTRODUCTION TO CASE BRIEFING

The word "brief" can refer to three different kinds of documents:

- an appellate brief
- a trial brief
- a case brief

An appellate brief is a party's formal written argument to a court of appeals on why a lower court's decision should be affirmed, modified, or reversed. A trial brief is an attorney's set of notes on how she proposes to conduct an upcoming trial. It is sometimes called a "trial manual" or "trial book." A case brief, our primary concern here, is an *analytical summary of an opinion.*

To "brief a case" means to identify the essential components of an opinion. This brief serves two functions:

a. to help you clarify your thinking on what the opinion "really" means
b. to provide you with a set of notes on the opinion to which you can refer later
   without having to reread the entire opinion every time you need to use it

There are many styles of briefing, and the same person may, in fact, employ several different styles of briefing for different purposes. The process, however, is the same regardless of the format used. The task of briefing consists of carefully reading and analyzing the opinion, of breaking down the information contained in the opinion into categories, and of organizing this data into a structured outline. [The following categories are often included in case briefs.]

1. The *Citation*
   Where the opinion can be found

2. The *Parties*
   Names, relationship, litigation status

3. The *Objectives* of the Parties
   What each side is seeking

4. The *Theory of the Litigation*
   The cause of action and the defense

5. The *Prior Proceedings*
   What happened below
6. The *Facts*
   Those facts that were key to the holdings
7. The *Issue(s)*
   The questions of law
8. The *Holding(s)*
   The answers to the issues
9. The *Reasoning*
   Why the court answered the issues the way it did
10. The *Disposition*
    What order was entered by the court as a result of its holdings
11. *Commentary* on opinion
    Concurring and dissenting opinions, personal views, counter brief (narrower or broader interpretations), history of the case, the case in sequence, case notes in law reviews. . . .*

The formats of case briefs vary depending on the needs of the reader. The following are examples of a long and a short version of case briefing formats.

LONG VERSION

Citation:

Muller v. Oregon, 208 U.S. 412 (1908)

Pages in Text:

23–25

Parties:

Muller is the plaintiff in error here and the defendant below.
   The state of Oregon is the defendant in error here and the prosecution below.

Objectives:

Muller wants his conviction overturned. The state of Oregon wants its law upheld and the conviction affirmed.

Cause of Action:

Muller violated an Oregon law that says employers cannot require women to work more than ten hours a day.

The preceding is from William P. Statsky and R. John Wernet, Jr., Case Analysis and Fundamentals of Legal Writing, 3d ed. (St. Paul: West, 1989), pp. 77–79.

Defense:

Muller: The law is unconstitutional because it violates liberty of contract guaranteed to by the Due Process Clause in the Fourteenth Amendment.

Prior Proceedings:

(1) Trial: conviction in state court. (2) Appeal: conviction upheld by the Oregon Supreme Court.

Present Proceedings:

U.S. Supreme Court review on writ of error.

Facts:

Muller employed a woman to work in his laundry for more hours than the legal limit.

Issue:

Does this statute setting maximum hours for women violate liberty of contract protected by the Due Process Clause of the Fourteenth Amendment?

Holding:

No

Reasoning:

1. This case differs from the maximum hour law for bakeries struck down in *Lochner v. New York* as an unreasonable interference with liberty of contract because the difference between the sexes justifies different rules.
2. Widely held beliefs, reflected in legislation and numerous reports and which the Court can note, indicate that women's physical structure and maternal functions place them at a disadvantage in the struggle for existence.
3. The state may limit individuals' liberty of contract where, as here, women's health and the "vigor of the race" justify such legislation.

Disposition:

Judgment affirmed.

Comments:

1. Then attorney, later Justice, Brandeis made empirical claims about women in arguing for the state of Oregon.
2. Arguments about women's right to contract equally with men were made by a male employer.

SHORT VERSION

Citation:

Muller v. Oregon, 208 U.S. 412 (1908)

Pages in Text:

23–25

Facts:

Ore. Sup. Ct. affirmed Muller's conviction for violating an Ore. statute prohibiting employment of women > 10 hrs/day. On writ of error, he challenged the statute, arguing state interference with liberty of contract in a way not justified by the health, welfare or safety of the community in viol'n of Due Process.

Disposition:

Affirmed.

Reasons:

1. *Lochner* distinguished. Difference between sexes justifies different rules.
2. Widely believed that physical structure and maternal functions of women place them at disadvantage in struggle for existence.
3. These factual beliefs are sufficient to justify legislation to protect women from the greed and passion of men, both for their own sake and for the good of the race [*sic*].

Comment:

The attorney Brandeis argued the case for the state using empirical claims to persuade the Court.

GLOSSARY

For additional assistance with legal terms and expressions, see *Black's Law Dictionary*, 6th ed., by Henry C. Black (St. Paul: West, 1991) or *Law Dictionary*, 5th ed, by Steven H. Gifis (New York: Barron's, 2003).

a priori   A form of reasoning that infers the truth of a proposition from other propositions assumed to be true.

ad litem   For the purposes of the suit.

administratrix   The person appointed to handle the affairs of someone who dies without leaving a will or without designating anyone to manage the will.

admissible   Evidence is admissible if, under applicable rules of evidence, it may be considered by the jury or other fact-finder at trials or formal hearings.

aegis   Protection or sponsorship.

affirm   To decide that the judgment of the court below is correct and should stand.

affirmative action   Any measure taken to ensure compliance with an existing obligation, generally used in context of efforts to desegregate.

alienage   The status of having been born in a foreign country.

alimony   The allowance that a court orders one to pay for the support of one's former spouse.

alimony pendente lite   The allowance one pays for the support of a spouse until one's suit for divorce has finally been decided.

allocatur   It is allowed.

amicus curiae   A friend of the court, generally used in connection with briefs submitted by nonparties expressing views on a pending case.

animus   Hostility.

appellant   The party who appeals a decision. The party who brings the proceeding to a court of review.

appellee   The party who argues before a reviewing court that the decision of the lower court should stand.

arguendo   For the sake of argument.

arrearage   The amount already due that has yet to be paid.

availability ratio   The proportion of women to men, of African Americans to whites, and so forth, in the pool of qualified persons in the relevant geographical area.

aver   Declare to be true.

back pay   A remedy available in employment and labor law cases. Courts frequently order employers found in violation of antidiscrimination statutes to pay plaintiffs the wages that they would have received but for the employer's unlawful practice.

bench trial   A trial in which the final decision is rendered by a judge without the participation of a jury.

benign classification   A legislative classification adopted for the purpose of advancing the welfare of members of a protected class.

bondsman   One who guarantees another's performance (i.e., who gives bond).

breach   Failure by a party to perform some contracted or agreed-upon act.

brief   A written statement, generally from the attorney of a party in a suit, that sets forth the legal argument that favors the decision desired by her client.

burden of persuasion   The duty of a party to convince the judge or jury of the truth of a claim. Failure to meet this duty results in a judgment against that party.

burden of production   The duty of a party to produce evidence on a particular issue.

burden of proof   The duty of a party to substantiate a claim. Includes both the burden of production and the burden of persuasion.

certiorari   Review of a decision by a court of review, usually initiated by a petition. The decision to grant or refuse this type of petition is discretionary.

chattels   Any tangible or movable thing; personal as opposed to real property, such as land.

citation   A reference to a legal authority, such as a case, a statute, or a regulation.

class action   A lawsuit brought by representative members of a large group of persons on behalf of all the members of the group.

common law   Legal rules or principles developed by the courts on a case-by-case basis, as opposed to statutory law, which is developed by the legislature, and regulatory law, which is developed by the executive branch.

common law property system   A system of allocating marital property according to which spouse has title.

community property system   A system of assigning ownership of property acquired during marriage to the spouses jointly.

comparable worth   A theory of pay equity that holds that wages paid to employees in various job categories should be proportionate to the value that the employer places on the tasks performed.

compensatory damages A money award granted by a court to a victim for the purpose of restoring the victim to his condition prior to the violation.

compensatory remedy Any sanction imposed by a court after finding of a violation that is aimed at restoring the injured party to the condition she would have enjoyed but for the violation. As distinguished from punitive and prophylactic remedies.

conciliation Any process short of trial by which a court or public official attempts to bring disputing parties into agreement.

consent decree A court order settling a lawsuit according to terms agreed by the parties.

consolidation The act or process of uniting several actions into one trial and judgment.

consortium The right of husband and wife to the company, cooperation, affection, and aid of the other. At common law, this right was vested only in the husband and referred mainly to the sexual services of his spouse.

constructive discharge If an employee involuntarily resigns to avoid intolerable and illegal requirements, courts regard the termination of employment as the equivalent of a discharge initiated by the employer.

contempt Courts may hold those appearing before them "in contempt" and impose punishment for disruptive and disobedient conduct.

corroboration Evidence that tends to confirm or substantiate a witness's testimony or other evidence.

coverture The legal condition of a married woman under common law.

credibility The believability of a witness.

cross-appeal A request by an appellee for review of one or more aspects of a lower court decision made after an appeal has already been initiated by the appellant.

custody Legal guardianship over a child granted to a parent in a divorce action; may include physical and/or decision-making custody.

damages Money given to a prevailing party in a lawsuit because of the unlawful conduct of the other party.

de minimus An issue, amount, or act that is not of sufficient importance to make a difference in the outcome of the case.

declaratory judgment A judgment of a court that establishes the rights of the parties or addresses a question of law without ordering that anything be done.

defendant In a civil suit, the party who is responding to a complaint. In a criminal suit, the party who is being prosecuted is also called "the accused."

demurrer A claim that, even if everything stated in the complaint were true, it would not be sufficient to find the violation that is alleged.

deposition A statement of a party or witness, given under oath, before trial begins. A deposition often takes a question-and-answer form.

directed verdict A verdict returned by a jury at the direction of the trial judge by whose instructions the jury is bound. In civil suits, either party may receive a directed verdict if the opposing party fails to present a prima facie case or a necessary defense. In criminal cases, there may be a directed verdict of acquittal but not of conviction.

discovery A pretrial procedure by which one party gains information that is held by the opposing party.

discretion The reasonable exercise of power by an official acting within the rights of his office.

disparate impact A method for analyzing claims that a policy or practice is discriminatory that focuses on the disproportionate effect the policy or practice has upon a particular group.

disparate treatment A method for analyzing claims that differences in treatment afforded individuals or groups are discriminatory.

dower That part of a husband's estate to which a wife is entitled upon his death.

en banc A hearing before all the members of a court.

enjoin To command or instruct someone to do or not to do something.

entirety The state of being whole and undivided.

entitlement A right to have something or to do something.

equitable distribution Allocation of marital property by the court without regard to title to achieve equity between the divorcing spouses.

equitable power The power of a court to act as fairness between the parties may require.

estate All that a person owns.

ex parte Refers to an application made by one party to a proceeding in the absence of the other.

feme-covert A married woman.

feme sole An unmarried woman.

grand jury A body of persons selected from the community for the purpose of investigating crimes and accusing persons of crimes.

gravaman The main point or essence of a complaint or argument.

guardian A person charged with the responsibility of taking care of a person or of managing the property of another.

hiring ratio The proportion of women to men, of African Americans to whites, and so forth, hired in a job category.

immunity An exemption from a duty or penalty.

impeach Testimony is impeached if doubt is cast upon its truthfulness. A person is impeached if she is removed from office.

imprimatur Mark of official approval or authorization.

indictment A formal accusation by a grand jury charging one or more persons with a crime.

indigent Anyone who is needy and poor.

information A written statement of a prosecutor accusing a person of a crime; an alternative to an indictment.

injunction A judicial order directing a party to perform or refrain from performing an act or activity.

inter alia Among other things.

intermediate scrutiny A standard used in equal protection cases that requires that the statutory classification be substantially related to the advancement of an important government interest.

intervening party A party permitted to participate in a suit after the plaintiff has initiated action against the defendant or defendants.

intestate Died without leaving directions for the disposition of one's property.

invidious Impermissible, sometimes including a tendency to arouse ill will or animosity.

jurisdiction The power to hear and decide a matter.

jurisprudence The theory behind law and legal systems.

jury instruction Direction given by the judge to the jury setting forth the law that is to guide the jury in its deliberations.

legal fiction Something known to be false but assumed in law to be true.

legislative history The record of legislative deliberations on a statute prior to its adoption.

liquidated damages An amount agreed upon by parties to a contract as a reasonable estimate of the damages owed to one party in the event that the contract is breached by the other.

litigation A lawsuit; a controversy in which legal rights are determined by a court.

magistrate A civil official with power to administer and enforce law.

mens rea The mental state accompanying a forbidden act.

model penal code A comprehensive code of statutes dealing with crime prepared as a model by the American Law Institute upon which a number of states have drawn in drafting their own penal codes.

moot A point is moot if it is debatable, arguable, or unresolved. A case is moot if the question to be determined does not rest on existing facts.

moral turpitude The state of being base, vile, or dishonest to a high degree. Indicative of depravity.

multiple regression analysis A method of statistical analysis that estimates the relative contribution of a number of independent variables to variations in a dependent variable.

municipal Pertaining to a local government unit, a city, or a town.

negligence Failure to act in the way that a reasonable person would in the circumstances.

overinclusive A statutory classification is overinclusive if not everyone designated as due similar treatment under the statute is similarly situated with respect to the advancement of the statutory objective.

overrule To supersede, annul, or make void by subsequent action or decision. A judicial decision is said to be overruled if a later decision by the same court or by a superior court in the same system expresses a contrary judgment on the same question of law.

parens patriae The state's power to protect and control the property and custody of minors and incompetent persons.

parish A district in Louisiana corresponding to a county.

parity An outcome that is the same as or equivalent to a result that would be generated by a fair procedure.

parole A conditional release of a person from serving the remainder of her criminal sentence in jail.

party A litigant; a person directly interested in the subject matter of the case and entitled to participate in its resolution.

per curiam An opinion "by the court" expressing the decision of the court but whose author is not identified.

petit jury An ordinary jury as opposed to a grand jury. Its function is to determine issues of fact and return verdicts.

petitioner One who presents a petition to a court.

plaintiff The party who initiates a civil lawsuit.

plurality decision A judgment of a reviewing court that is agreed to by a majority of the judges but that is not supported by any one opinion endorsed by a majority of the judges.

police power The power of governments at all levels to impose restrictions reasonably related to the promotion and maintenance of the health, safety, morals, and general welfare of the public.

poll tax A tax levied upon all persons within a specified class who live within a certain area. State requirements making payment of such taxes a prerequisite to registration and voting have been barred by the Twenty-Fourth Amendment to the U.S. Constitution.

preemption The doctrine that federal law takes priority over state and local legislation dealing with the same subject matter.

preferential treatment The award of positions to people on the basis of characteristics unrelated to qualifications for the positions. Often used in the context of debating efforts to eliminate discrimination.

prejudicial Causing unfair or preconceived judgments to come into play.

preponderance of the evidence The general standard of proof in civil cases. Evidence is said to meet this standard if it is more convincing than opposing evidence.

present value What something is worth now.

presumption An assumption, required by a rule of law, that certain factual claims are true. A presumption may be either "conclusive," in which case no contrary evidence will be considered, or "rebuttable," as is the presumption of innocence.

pretext An explanation that serves to disguise or obscure one's real purposes.

prima facie case A case sufficient on its face, that is, supported by sufficient evidence to shift the burden of persuasion to the defendant.

pro forma As a matter of established routine; for the sake of form.

probate The act or process of proving a will.

probative Tending to prove or establish a fact.

prophylactic remedy Any sanction imposed by a court that is aimed at preventing a recurrence of some violation.

proviso A condition or stipulation.

proxy A substitute; one person who is authorized to act for another.

punitive damages A money award granted by a court to a victim for the purpose of expressing its disapproval of the defendant's behavior and for the purpose of deterring others from similar conduct.

punitive remedy Any sanction imposed by a court after the finding of a violation that is aimed at expressing disapproval of the defendent's behavior.

quash To annul, make void, or overthrow a judicial decision.

quid pro quo An arrangement in which parties give one valuable thing in exchange for another; mutual consideration.

rational relation A standard used in equal protection cases that requires that the statutory classification be rationally related to the advancement of a legitimate government interest.

rebuttal The opportunity to introduce evidence that undermines confidence in the arguments made in support of a claim.

red circle A personnel practice used in connection with making major corrections to wage rates. Rates that are already at or higher than the target are held stable or "red circled" until the others catch up.

remand To send back for further deliberation or action.

remedy The means by which a right is enforced or an injury redressed.

respondeat superior The doctrine that holds a principal liable for the torts of his agent.

respondent The party who answers a petition.

reverse To overthrow, make void, annul, or set aside the judgment of a lower court.

sanction A coercive measure imposed for the purpose of enforcing legal rights after a finding of a violation.

show cause order An order directing one party to demonstrate why certain things should not be done. Usually used to bring an issue before a court or other tribunal on short notice.

sine qua non That without which a thing cannot be; a necessary condition.

special master A person appointed to assist a court in a particular case or type of case by hearing testimony, gathering evidence, and recommending a decision.

state action An act performed by, caused by, or otherwise attributable to a government or to an instrumentality of a government.

statutory classification Those characteristics used to identify people who will be treated similarly under the statute.

statutory objective The result that a statute promotes or the result that courts understand a statute to be aimed at promoting.

stipulation A term or condition in an agreement.

strict liability Liability that is not contingent upon a showing of mens rea or even of negligence.

strict scrutiny A standard used in equal protection cases that requires that a statutory classification be the least restrictive way of advancing a compelling government interest.

sua sponte On its own initiative.

sub judice Under judicial consideration.

sub silentio Without any notice being taken.

subpoena An order of a court compelling the appearance of a witness before a judicial proceeding.

sui juris Of his own right; not under any disability; possessing full rights and powers.

summary judgment A means by which a judge decides a suit without a full trial; this occurs when the facts of the situation are not in dispute and one party is entitled to the decision as a matter of law.

suspect classification A statutory classification that the courts suspect of being used to further discriminatory purposes against certain protected groups. Such classifications are subject to review under the strict scrutiny standard.

temporary restraining order A court order designed to maintain the status quo until the court has time to look fully into the matter.

testament The statement of a person's wishes concerning the disposition of his property after death.

tort Any civil wrong, independent of contract, resulting from the breach of a legal duty.

underinclusive A statutory classification is underinclusive if not everyone similarly situated in respect to the advancement of the statutory objective is designated as due similar treatment under the statute.

underutilization The condition of having fewer women and minorities in a particular job group than would reasonably be expected by their availability.

vacate To set aside or render void.

vel non Or not.

venire The panel of people from which a trial jury is chosen.

ward A person placed under the guardianship of another.

will A person's declaration of how her property is to be distributed after her death.

work force ratio The proportion of women to men, of African Americans to whites, and so forth, in any employment category.

workers' compensation A statutory system for covering employee expenses for injuries and sickness that arise out of and in the course of employment; funded by employer contributions.

writ One of a series of traditional court orders requiring that something be done or authorizing it to be done.

writ of error An early common law order that initiates an appeal of a lower court decision.

writ of habeas corpus An order initiating a proceeding whose function is to release an individual being held illegally by the state or by a private party.

wrongful death action A suit brought by the beneficiaries, alleging that decendent's death was caused by defendant's wrongful act and seeking to recover economic benefits lost as a result.

INDEX

THE LAW OF SEX DISCRIMINATION

FOURTH EDITION

J. Ralph Lindgren
Nadine Taub
Beth Anne Wolfson
Carla M. Palumbo

An honest and informative text on sex discrimination and the law, *The Law of Sex Discrimination* approaches the idea of using law to analyze sex discrimination from a variety of contexts: as an occasion for ideological disputes, as a reflection of contemporary policy debates over the future direction of society, and as part of the historical development of—and response to—feminism. Fully updated for 21st century, the text examines topics that range from reproductive rights to global trends in gender law, and includes appendices that deal with the court system, a brief discussion of how to outline cases, and a glossary of legal and technical terms.

This **Fourth Edition** contains current information on topics such as the "Mommy track," same-sex benefits and family-friendly policies, single-sex classrooms, same-sex marriage and same-sex adoption, the Family and Medical Leave Act, male reproduction, contraception, and abortion.

"Broad coverage of areas of law pertinent to gender discrimination [and] good choices of leading cases and debates, and of commentary."

-Patricia A. Boling, *Purdue University*

Debate. Participate. Advocate.

Our Mission: At **Wadsworth Political Science**, our goal is to publish current, relevant programs that help instructors create lively, engaging classrooms. We aim to further inspire those students who are passionate about the discipline, and to motivate beginning students by showing them that they can, indeed, make a difference.

Wadswo

Wadsworth, publishes tex of the course curriculum.

WADSWORTH
CENGAGE Learning

To learn more about Wadsworth, visit **www.cengage.com/wadsw**

Purchase any of our products at your local college store or at our preferred online store **www.ichapters.com**